The Selected Poetry & Prose of
Shelley

Introduction and Notes by
BRUCE WOODCOCK

Wordsworth Poetry Library

For my husband
ANTHONY JOHN RANSON
with love from your wife, the publisher.
Eternally grateful for your unconditional love.

Readers who are interested in other titles from
Wordsworth Editions are invited to visit our website at
www.wordsworth-editions.com

For our latest list and a full mail-order service, contact
Bibliophile Books, 5 Datapoint, South Crescent, London E16 4TL
TEL: +44 (0)20 7474 2474 FAX: +44 (0)20 7474 8589
ORDERS: orders@bibliophilebooks.com
WEBSITE: www.bibliophilebooks.com

First published in 1994 by Wordsworth Editions Limited
8B East Street, Ware, Hertfordshire SG12 9HJ
reset with Introduction and Notes 2002

ISBN 978 1 85326 408 5

Text © Wordsworth Editions Limited 2002
Introduction and Notes © Bruce Woodcock 2002

Wordsworth® is a registered trade mark of
Wordsworth Editions Limited

Wordsworth Editions
is the company founded in 1987 by
MICHAEL TRAYLER

Typeset in Great Britain by Antony Gray
Printed and bound by Clays Ltd, St Ives plc

Introduction

EARLY LIFE AND IDEAS

1792 *August 4* Percy Bysshe Shelley born at Field Place, Warnham, Sussex, son of Timothy Shelley MP and grandson of Bysshe Shelley, baronet and landowner.

1798 First lessons from Revd Mr Edwards.

1802 To school at Syon House Academy, Isleworth, near London.

1804 Enters Eton where he is bullied. Develops his scientific and literary knowledge.

1808 Begins writing to his cousin Harriet Grove; their friendship ends in 1810 due to religious objections by her family.

1810 *April* Gothic novel *Zastrozzi* published.

April 10 Matriculates at University College, Oxford.

September *Original Poetry by Victor and Cazire* (by Shelley and his sister Elizabeth) published and then withdrawn.

Michaelmas Begins residence at Oxford. Meets T. J. Hogg.

November *Posthumous Fragments of Margaret Nicholson* (written in conjunction with T. J. Hogg) published.

December Second Gothic novel *St Irvyne* published.

1811 *January* Meets Harriet Westbrook.

February *The Necessity of Atheism* (written with Hogg) issued.

March 25 Shelley expelled, with Hogg, from University College for refusing to answer questions about *The Necessity of Atheism*. Lives in London with Hogg.

July Cwm Elan, Radnorshire.

August 28 Elopes with Harriet Westbrook and marries her in Edinburgh. In York, where Hogg makes advances to Harriet. Keswick; meets the poet Robert Southey.

Shelley was born in 1792, the year in which the radical writer and activist Tom Paine and his works were outlawed and the French Revolution entered the phase of the Terror. His early life coincided with a period of repression, during which the English government did its best to stamp out radicalism, suppressing popular dissent and framing laws which left writers in fear of prosecution for treason. As a result, the first-generation Romantics, many of whom like Wordsworth and Coleridge had been supporters of the French Revolution, retreated into various forms of self-justifying idealism. They turned to mythology, nature, fantasy, the subjective life, asserting the visionary importance of the poet; and along with this escape from direct social engagement went a sense of guilt, betrayal and self-accusation. Many of Shelley's generation felt betrayed by the increasing conservatism of the great writers they admired, particularly Wordsworth. Both Byron and Shelley wrote savage satirical critiques of him, Byron in *The Vision of Judgement* and *Don Juan* and Shelley in his parody *Peter Bell the Third* (pp. 410–19).*

So the age in which Shelley grew up was one of significant contradictions and tensions with regard to the ardent optimism of earlier Romantic writing. Yet, from the outset, he himself was full of ardour, and had the spark of a progressive and revolutionary outlook. From a young age, he was fascinated by modern science, particularly physics and chemistry. At school he blew up his school-desk with explosives. At home he made fire balloons and experimented with electricity: one experiment took the form of tying a kite to the tail of a local tom-cat during a thunderstorm to discover the effects of lightning on a living body! When his parents finally, and with great relief, sent him off to Eton in 1804, as his carriage drew away, the chimney of their house exploded from a timing device young Percy had left as a farewell gesture. While at Eton he was renowned for blowing up an ancient oak tree and had his personal library of science books confiscated as a result. This obsession with experimental science remained throughout his life, and in her famous novel, his wife Mary partly based her portrait of the obsessive Victor Frankenstein on her husband. There was also a darker side to Shelley's excitable character: his enthusiasm for volcanoes was matched by his enjoyment of the mysterious and nightmarish; and he delighted in disturbing and frightening close friends, particularly women, with horrid speculations.

---

* All quotations from and references to Shelley's texts are to the present edition and are given as page numbers in brackets following the reference or quotation. Where the passage is not included in this edition, references are to the editions listed in the Bibliography. Wherever possible, the surname and page number follow in parentheses after the quotation.

Shelley's eccentric behaviour continued when he went to Oxford University in 1810. On one occasion, while deep in conversation with his first close friend T. J. Hogg about metempsychosis (the transmigration of souls), his obsession with philosophical enquiry led him to seize a passing baby from its mother's arms and earnestly question it about the nature of its Platonic pre-existence. The climax of Shelley's Oxford career came towards the end of his first year, in March 1811, when he published his pamphlet *The Necessity of Atheism*, a rationalistic exposé of organised religion in the radical tradition of Tom Paine's *The Age of Reason*, which went further than Paine in advocating outright atheism. College authorities were so outraged that they ordered the pamphlet to be burned; and Shelley himself was expelled from the university. He was nineteen years old.

His parents were not pleased. They were even less so when later that year he eloped with the sixteen-year-old Harriet Westbrook. They went off to Ireland 'to *forward as much as we can* the Catholic Emancipation' (Jones, Vol. 1, p. 231). Shelley seemed certain he could liberate the Irish from their colonial subjection to England single-handedly. He wrote his pamphlet *An Address to the Irish People*, and distributed four hundred copies around Dublin in three days, many by hand, throwing them to passers-by from the windows of his lodgings, stuffing them into passing carriages, while Harriet delighted in his passionate absurdities. The only real effect of this escapade was that when the Shelleys returned via Wales, disappointed at the lack of response, they were subjected to surveillance by British government spies. Whilst in Porthmadog, Shelley was convinced that one of them tried to assassinate him.

All this might seem rather madcap, but it does give a sense of Shelley's ardent concern for social improvement. He admits himself in his Preface to *Prometheus Unbound*: 'I have what a Scottish philosopher characteristically terms "a passion for reforming the world" ' (p. 228), and that comes through strongly in his writings. Some individual examples may serve as a brief guide to recurrent issues in the poems.

Tyranny One of Shelley's most well-known poems, 'Ozymandias' (1819), is an attack on tyranny and power, something he frequently returns to in other works like *Prometheus Unbound* (1819). Related political issues include attacks on aristocracy, law, militarism, poverty, labour and money. He had an extraordinarily acute sense of the inequalities promoted by a social system based on financial competition. Particularly relevant here are his Notes to the long poem *Queen Mab*. Published anonymously in 1812, this work was used throughout the nineteenth century by working-class educational organisa-tions like the Chartists, often without their being aware of its author's identity. The Notes form a series of explosively radical essays, in which, for example, he attacks wealth as 'a power usurped by the few, to compel the many to labour for their benefit' (p. 80). Shelley's awareness of the economic motor generating social injustice is a crucial part of his political analysis, as in his major political essay 'A Philosophical View of Reform' (1819) where he denounces merchants and bankers as 'a set of pelting wretches' (p. 613).

Gender and Sexuality   Shelley had a keen understanding that, like oppression, freedom is indivisible. Hence the cry of Cythna, the female revolutionary in *Laon and Cythna* (1817): 'Can man be free if woman be a slave?' (p. 150). The Notes to *Queen Mab* contain some remarkable material on women's oppression and free love (pp. 74–7). This last theme finds its most idealistic expression in 'Epipsychidion' (pp. 488–504). But the tensions involved in issues of sexuality also manifest themselves in his writing, and his own personal practice was far from unproblematic: his repeated attempts at living a utopian communal life frequently broke down in upset or disaster.

Religion   Two years after *The Necessity of Atheism*, Shelley completed another attack on religion called *A Refutation of Deism*, in which, while arguing about the virgin birth, he proclaims: 'It seems less credible that the God whose immensity is uncircumscribed by space, should have committed adultery with a carpenter's wife, than that some bold knaves or insane dupes had deceived the credulous' (Clark, p. 126). Unrestrained about his views in print, he also made a public display of his atheism. While travelling around Europe in 1816, he was so impressed by the awful power of the Swiss mountains that he signed in at local hotels as 'Shelley – Democrat, Philanthropist and Atheist' (in Greek) and his destination as 'L'Enfer' (Hell), a gesture which earned him lingering disapproval.

Imagination and Science   While scathingly critical of orthodox or established religions, Shelley nevertheless had a vivid sense of the living cosmos, and this was informed by his scientific interests. He has often been seen as the most ethereal of the Romantic poets, but in fact he is frequently the most elemental and material. His works are saturated with his enthusiasm for science, ancient and modern, a passion which was closely allied to his commitment to social change. A letter of 1813, expressing indignation at the prosecution of Leigh and John Hunt for libel and proposing a support fund, which he initiated with a £20 note he could ill afford, ended by requesting his recipient to send him information on 'whether or no the Position of the Earth on its poles is not yearly becoming less oblique? It is an astronomical affair' (Jones, Vol. 1, p. 353). A number of the Notes to *Queen Mab* are well-informed essays on astronomical affairs, while the poem itself contains vivid descriptions of a journey through the cosmos, sharply imagined in scientific terms. While in Pisa in 1820, his notebook juxtaposed drafts for poems alongside detailed notes on the science of agriculture, including observations on electrolysis, fertilisers and a list of all the known chemical elements. 'Mont Blanc' describes the mountain in language inspired by his reading of contemporary naturalists such as the Comte de Buffon (1707–88) or Horace Bénédict de Saussure (1740–99). Indeed, Shelley's view of social change is inseparable from his sense of geological evolution and upheaval. *Prometheus Unbound* expresses ideas of social revolution through Shelley's favourite imagery of volcanic eruption (Act 2, 4, 129–155, pp. 269–70), using precise descriptions of volcanic vents such as fumeroles (Act 2, 2, 53–4, p. 261). It also employs scientific notions of evolutionary development and fossils (Act 4, 296–314, pp. 299–300), accurately observed descriptions of moonlight through the atmosphere (Act 4, 206–35, pp. 297–8), speculations about electrical propulsion (Act 2, 4, 163–6, p. 270) and marvellous depictions of the interaction of the elements (Act 2, 3, 18–42, pp. 263–4). All this often adds intellectual precision to his imagery: even in his most lyrical poetry, his images embody ideas, demanding thought and interrogation.

Take this extract from his Gothic poem 'The Sensitive Plant', which describes the onset of sleep:

> . . . the beast, and the birds, and the insects were drowned
> In an ocean of dreams without a sound;
> Whose waves never mark, tho' they ever impress
> The light sand which paves it, consciousness.   [p. 426]

In this vivid psychological metaphor, Shelley presents the condition of sleep as being drowned in 'an ocean of dreams', the unconscious, which, unlike the real ocean, is without sound, as indeed sleep is. Where it meets the land, it is bordered by a light sandy beach, 'consciousness'; and the waves of the ocean break on to the beach, just as dreams and other elements of the unconscious impinge on consciousness; but they never mark it, because by definition, according to Freud, what is unconscious must necessarily remain hidden – only its effects are felt. This remarkable image makes us realise why Freud would later say that he wasn't the first to discover the unconscious, since poets had been there before.

Subsequent sections of this Introduction examine Shelley's major poems chronologically and offer some lines of thought about major works. More detailed information can be found in the Notes at the end of the volume.

POEMS FROM 1812–14

1812 *January*   Begins correspondence with William Godwin.

February   Dublin; writes *An Address to the Irish People* and *Proposals for an Association*. Begins active campaign for political reform. *A Declaration of Rights*. Addresses Catholic Committee and is reported to the Home Office by spies.

April   Nantgwillt, Wales.

June   Lynmouth. Under surveillance by Home Office spies.

July   *Letter to Lord Ellenborough; Queen Mab* begun (finished February 1813 and privately printed).

August 19   Arrest of Shelley's servant for pasting up *Declaration of Rights* at Barnstaple.

September   Tanyrallt, Tremadoc, Carnarvon. Involved in local development enterprise.

October   Visits London and meets Godwin.

November   Meets Thomas Love Peacock. Back in Wales.

1813 *February*   Flees Tremadoc after possibly politically motivated attack.

March   Back in Ireland.

April   Returns to London. Writes and publishes *A Vindication of Natural Diet*.

May   *Queen Mab* privately published.

June 28   Ianthe (daughter of Harriet and Shelley) born.

July   Moves to Bracknell, Berks.

October   Visits Lake District; Edinburgh; Windsor; *Refutation of Deism* written (published early 1814).

1814 *March 24*   Marries Harriet in Church of England ceremony.

May   Visits Godwin. Estrangement from Harriet; he goes to London.

July 28   Elopes with Mary Wollstonecraft Godwin and, together with her stepsister Jane (Claire) Clairmont, they go to France, then Switzerland.

September   Returns to London. Health and money problems.

November   Charles Bysshe (son of Harriet and Shelley) born.

Shelley's career is remarkable for its intensity and compression: he wrote his first notable work, *Queen Mab*, in 1812, and ten years later it was all over. In that period, he produced an astonishing range of work, while his life was characterised by restlessness, evident in the unsettled travelling he constantly undertook. At the same time, he was beset by money problems, ill health, failed schemes and fractured personal relationships, to which the fluctuating extremes of his own erratic temperament contributed, as he was well aware: 'I have been accustomed to consider myself as the most imprudent and unaccountable of mankind' (Jones, Vol. 1, p. 551). So, having married the sixteen-year-old Harriet Westbrook, Shelley then abandoned her and eloped again with the sixteen-year-old Mary Wollstonecraft Godwin, daughter of the feminist Mary Wollstonecraft and the radical William Godwin. Just for good measure, Mary's stepsister, the coincidentally sixteen-year-old Claire Clairmont, accompanied them. The full story of his life is vividly told in Richard Holmes's brilliant biography, *Shelley: The Pursuit* (see Bibliography).

Queen Mab

Queen Mab is an astonishing debut poem for a twenty-year-old poet, innovative in its formal variety, bravely radical in content. Its creaky fairy machinery thinly masks the forthright attacks on monarchy, religion, war and tyranny, and Shelley acknowledged it to be a product of his 'constitutional enthusiasm' (Jones, Vol. 1, p. 324). This aspect of his personality also inspired two sonnets in the same year, which commemorate his launching of balloons and bottles containing copies of his *Declaration of Rights*, aerial and oceanic propaganda exercises which were carefully observed by Home Office spies.

Shelley's campaign to promote radical thought is announced in the vehement opening epigram from Enlightenment rationalist Voltaire's onslaught on Christianity, 'Crush the infamous thing' (p. 3), a clarion call to action also adopted by the revolutionary French Jacobins of the 1790s, the Illuminists. This declaration is reinforced by the epigrams which follow, from Lucretius, who asserted he would 'free men's minds from the crippling bonds of superstition' (p. 3), and from Greek scientist Archimedes, who claimed he would be able to 'move the earth' (p. 3) given the right point of leverage. Like William Blake, Shelley saw injustice as linked in one poisonous system which must be uprooted: 'Let the axe / Strike at the root, the poison-tree will fall' (p. 27).

A testimony to the power of *Queen Mab* is the history of its readership. Shelley had the poem privately printed in 1813 in a fine production 'so as to catch the aristocrats: They will not read it, but their sons and daughters may' (Jones, Vol. 1, p. 361). He himself distributed about seventy of the two hundred and fifty copies. The remainder were purchased and published in 1821 under his own imprint by William Clark who, for his pains, was prosecuted by the Society for the Suppression of Vice. Later, radical bookseller Richard Carlile printed a new edition, from which point it became a founding work for the organic intellectuals of an emergent working-class educational and cultural movement linked to the developing trade unions and to Chartism. George Bernard Shaw, in his 1892 essay 'Shaming the Devil about Shelley', recalled the poem being described as 'the Chartists' Bible' (Holmes, p. 208). One reason for this impact was the remarkable series of Notes accompanying the poem, which distil Shelley's thinking at the time, deeply influenced as it was by the radical writing of Tom Paine, William Godwin and Mary Wollstonecraft among others. They deal with topics as varied as organised religion, the inequity of private property, marriage as a form of prostitution, astronomy, scientific speculations and vegetarianism.

The poem is worth outlining to indicate its major issues and some key passages. It opens with a sleeping woman, Ianthe, being woken into the spiritual dimension by the Fairy Queen, Mab, who promises her a vision. The fairy chariot's journey through the heavens (pp. 9–11) includes a marvellous example of Shelley's ability to create poetry inspired by the wonders of contemporary scientific discovery as he imagines the cosmos in action and writes two vivid Notes expounding his own astronomical knowledge. The arrival at Mab's 'etherial palace' (p. 12) leads to the core of the poem as Mab promises to teach Ianthe the 'secrets of the future' (p. 13) through a vision of the past and present. This visionary perspective echoes Shelley's view of the role of the poet as expressed in his essay 'A Defence of Poetry'. Like William Blake in the Introduction to *Songs of Experience*, he sees the poet as idealist (past), social critic (present) and prophetic visionary (future): the poet, he says, 'not only beholds intensely the present as it is, and discovers those laws according to which present things ought to be ordered, but he beholds the future in the present' (p. 637), a phrase which is anticipated in the poem (p. 21), and which the great Caribbean Marxist C. L. R. James took as the title of a volume of his own selected writings (1977).

Mab's vision begins with the past glories of tyrants and civilisations which have been swept away by the levelling effects of history, a theme recurring later in 'Ozymandias'. From this oppressive past of slavery and religious hypocrisy, Mab can 'glean/ A warning for the future' (p. 18). The view of the present starts with an assault on the power of monarchy which is blind to the oppressions it perpetrates. Yet we are also shown the wretched isolation and self-destructiveness of power, and the self-enslavement of the subject population which, manacled by acceptance and habit, never 'rears an arm / To dash him from his throne!' (p. 21). Against such social corruption, Mab sets reason and nature, occasioning one of Shelley's irrepressibly idealistic passages envisaging a future state of social virtue. Such visions are necessary to the dialectic of the poem, set as they are against powerful attacks on social corruption. Section 4 of the poem opens with a celebration of the beauties of

nature, which are then blotted out by a hellish portrayal of war as part of the
violent system of social injustice embodied in kingship. The crucial point
here is the assertion that human beings are not corrupt by nature:

> Nature? – no!
> Kings, priests, and statesmen, blast the human flower
> Even in its tender bud; their influence darts
> Like subtle poison through the bloodless veins
> Of desolate society.   [p. 27]

In this and the next section of the poem, Shelley presents an incisive account
of the interconnectedness of oppressions, social, personal, sexual and
psychological. Like Rousseau and Tom Paine, Shelley believes evil to be a
product of social inequality, the distortions brought about by an unjust
social hierarchy, rather than original sin:

> Let priest-led slaves cease to proclaim that man
> Inherits vice and misery, when force
> And falsehood hang even o'er the cradled babe,
> Stifling with rudest grasp all natural good.   [p. 28]

But the blame isn't all attributable to the social system. Like Blake, Shelley
sees a dialectical relationship between individual psychology and society.
Individualism and ignorant selfishness, 'at once / The cause and the effect of
tyranny' (p. 32), perpetuate the very conditions within which the individual
suffers. And here Shelley launches an attack on 'commerce', capitalism and
money, backed up by an extraordinary Note identifying human labour as the
source of all wealth (pp. 71–3), which has much in common with the
analysis offered later in the century by Karl Marx. As part of this critique,
Shelley includes an attack on prostitution, 'Even love is sold' (l. 189, p. 36),
prompting another remarkable accompanying Note in which he attacks
marriage as ownership, conjugal rights as slavery, and advocates free love
(pp. 74–7).

After another quick dose of optimism, in section 6 Mab presents Ianthe
with a vision of the horrors of institutional religion that pervert the natural
world into a system of ideological oppression, and against this she juxta-
poses the spirit of Nature or Necessity. Section 7 follows with a demolition of
all religions, but only as a preface to an all-out attack on Christianity,
through the figure of Ahasuerus who testifies how the malicious god Jehovah
perverted the world. This critique occasions a sequence of essay-length
Notes, aspects of which found their way into Shelley's pamphlet *A Refutation
of Deism* (1814). After this violent vision, Mab offers Ianthe comfort and

hope in a prophetic celebration of the natural world in which 'ambiguous man' (p. 56) can be socially renovated. But lest it seem too easy, Shelley intrudes a reminder of how alienated from natural liberty and equality human beings have been and continue to be, warning the reader that idealism should not be separated from a keen-eyed awareness of social injustice and of the obstacles to progress. What Mab doesn't describe is the means by which social renovation might take place, but presumably it would not simply be as a result of the vegetarianism which, in his final Note, Shelley advocates for counteracting criminal tendencies (see *A Vindication of Natural Diet*, pp. 571–83).

POEMS FROM 1815

January   Grandfather dies; comes to a settlement with his father.
February   Mary's first child born (dies after two weeks).
Summer   In Devon. Begins receiving annual income of £1000.
August   At Bishopsgate, Windsor Park. River trip along Thames with Mary and Peacock.
Autumn   Writes *Alastor*; Essays: 'On Love'; 'On Life'; 'Essay on Christianity'.

1815 sees Shelley writing poems critical of his past heroes, Wordsworth and Napoleon, for betraying progressive ideals. Other poems from this period are noticeably inward-looking and gloomy, perhaps a reflection of ill health and a sense of failure which had begun to afflict Shelley during the year. In addition, the death of Mary's first child was the first in a series of tragic family incidents, the suicide of the abandoned Harriet following in 1816. During his second marriage, Shelley was continually attracted to other women, and his relationship with Mary was increasingly dislocated by the early deaths of a number of their other children.

Alastor

At first sight, *Alastor* seems the stereotypical 'Romantic' poem, epitomising many conventional elements from writing of the time. Its central character is a solitary, the Poet, who has visionary ideals and communes with Nature. He becomes a Wanderer, undertaking a journey through suitably sublime and Gothic landscapes which mirror his own psychological state as he seeks his ideal love only to find death. But far from endorsing this portrait of self-obsession, Shelley's poem interrogates the clichés of the period and reveals their dangers. As in Keats's *The Fall of Hyperion*, the function of the poet himself is scrutinised. In his poem, Keats asks 'what benefit' the poet can be to the world, and asserts that poetry is 'not useless' and that the true poet is 'a sage;/A humanist, physician to all men', not a 'dreamer' (*The Fall of Hyperion* lines 167, 189–90, 199). In *Alastor*, Shelley also shows the dangers of being 'a dreamer' and of idealistic self-absorption, asserting the need for poetry and the poet to connect with the world. This element of 'instruction' in the poem is outlined in the Preface, where Shelley indicates that the Poet's 'self-centered seclusion was avenged by the furies of an irresistible passion' (p. 100). The Poet's problem is his over-intense idealism, awakened by the 'Power' of Nature. But as the Preface also indicates, those 'meaner spirits' who ignore such aspirations are in some senses worse, being 'morally dead' (p. 101). Both suffer from different forms of selfishness and anti-social individualism. The need for social connection is asserted as paramount since '[t]hose who love not their fellow-beings live unfruitful lives'. It is possible that this attack on the Poet has some connection with Shelley's critique of William Wordsworth for betraying his youthful commitments to social revolution by retiring into Nature and his own ego, as well as becoming politically conservative. The *Alastor* volume of 1815 contained an attack on Wordsworth for deserting truth and liberty (see 'To Wordsworth' [p. 120], which was probably composed in 1815), while later criticisms became more sarcastic (see *Peter Bell the Third*, pp. 410–19). More specifically, *Alastor* contains numerous echoes of Wordsworth's work, and the 'Preface' closes with a slightly inaccurate quotation from Wordsworth's 'My heart leaps up'. Shelley's fictional Poet is not meant to be taken as a portrait of Wordsworth, but more as an indictment of what his view of being a poet might mean. By implication *Alastor* argues that poets and poetry must be socially engaged if they are to be fruitful.

The poem opens with a Narrator who celebrates the powers of Nature, 'Mother of this unfathomable world' (p. 102), and who sees himself as a passive 'lyre' or wind harp, a Romantic image made famous by Coleridge's poem 'The Eolian Harp'. This 'wise passiveness', to quote Wordsworth's famous phrase from 'Expostulation and Reply', seems to be distinguished from the Poet's frantic pursuit of his visions; but the Narrator's acknowledgement of 'earth, ocean, air' as 'beloved brotherhood' suggests that he too might be suffering from the same self-absorbed condition as the poet, and indeed the very same image of the wind harp returns at the end to describe the dying Poet himself (pp. 117–18). His story begins from line 50 and his alienated solitude is stressed from the outset. Initially he seeks his 'solemn vision' (p. 103) in Nature as he wanders through exotic places. But his solipsism is revealed when, instead of responding to the ministrations of the Arab maiden who cares for him (pp. 104–5), he chooses to pursue a dream-maiden who becomes a vision of his desire. The passage describing the dream-consummation of this desire (p. 105) is overtly sexual, and its auto-eroticism indicates Shelley's view of the Poet as self-indulgent and self-obsessed in a manner which Freud would later describe as narcissistic. The post-coital aftermath of the Poet's dream disrupts his earlier communion with Nature and replaces it with a sense of the world as barren, this being implicitly the revenge of 'the spirit of sweet human love' who sent the Arab maiden who was 'spurned' (p. 106). But instead of turning to the actual Arab maiden for real love, the Poet chooses to seek the girl in the vision, the 'fair fiend' (p. 109) who epitomises the same kind of ambiguous idealisation of the female that Keats investigates in 'La Belle Dame Sans Merci'. Shelley's point here anticipates the psychoanalytical theories of Jacques Lacan who proposed that, as a result of psychological development in relation to the mother, male desire is founded upon loss or lack. As a result, men can 'lapse into a mystification of woman as the site of truth' (Mitchell and Rose, p. 137). Similarly, the Poet lapses into becoming the victim of his own egocentric delusions as he turns into a Gothic Wanderer and outcast in ways which anticipate aspects of Mary Shelley's *Frankenstein* (1818), an equally incisive exposé of the driven male ego. The descriptions of the Poet's journey begin now to mirror his psychological and emotional state even more explicitly. He finds a small boat (p. 109) in which he travels through a tumultuous ocean storm into a cavern (p. 110) with a whirlpool, which he avoids, and finally he enters the serene isolation of a sepulchral landscape, the intense description of which brings to mind the surreal sublimity of Shelley's German contemporary, the painter Caspar David Friedrich (pp. 115–17). The Spirit of the stream appears to him in his own reflection in the water (p. 113), epitomising his obsessive narcissism.

The ending of the poem is left to the Narrator, whose 'despair' (p. 120) we should perhaps question. Given the Narrator's problematic association with the Poet, we might see him as unreliable. After all, he is himself a poet lamenting the death of another poet's visionary pursuit, but not drawing any fruitful moral from the experience. He embodies the course of Wordsworth's career, which involved a loss of vision and a retreat into elegiac lament and the 'egotistical sublime', in Keats's famous phrase. It was precisely such 'gloom and misanthropy' (p. 134) that Shelley was to resist in his next poems.

POEMS FROM 1816

January   William, child of Mary and Shelley, born. *Alastor . . . and Other Poems* published.

May   To Geneva with Mary, his son William and Claire Clairmont; meets Byron.

June–July   Writes 'Mont Blanc', 'Hymn to Intellectual Beauty'.

September   Returns to England; Bath.

October   Suicide of Mary's half sister, Fanny.

November 9   Harriet commits suicide by drowning in Serpentine.

December   Meets Keats. Harriet's suicide discovered. Marries Mary.

'Mont Blanc'

'Mont Blanc' contains some of Shelley's characteristically powerful descriptions of extreme landscapes, informed by his enthusiasm for the developing contemporary science of geology as much as by the traditions of Romantic nature poetry. In terms of Romantic landscape poetry, the opening section recalls the connection of natural imagery with psychological exploration found in Coleridge's 'This Lime Tree Bower My Prison' (1797). Shelley similarly speculates on the relationship between the individual mind and external perceptions, overlapping images of the imagined view of the ravine of the Arve with an exploration of the mind itself as a channel for hidden 'influencings' (p. 126). This speculation anticipates the modern view of the mind as an irrational entity over which the individual has no control and as interconnected with surrounding environment in 'unremitting interchange' (p. 126).

The sublime awe of the shattered glacial landscape also embodies the Romantic dialectic of beauty and fear first marked out by Edmund Burke in his celebrated essay 'A Philosophical Enquiry into the Origin of our Ideas on the Sublime and the Beautiful' (1759), which proposed that the effects of terror and fear were more powerful, pleasurable and sublime than simple beauty. But Shelley develops this sense of the awesome grandeur of nature in his own individual direction. 'Mont Blanc' can be seen as his reply to Wordsworth's religion of Nature. As such, it expresses a radical scepticism, extending the explorations of atheism in the essays and invoking a disturbing sense of uncertainty about existence. That uncertainty can be detected in the frequently ambiguous expression and syntax of the poem. Instead of finding in nature 'Something far more deeply interfused', as Wordsworth does in 'Tintern Abbey', Shelley interrogates the grim and awful wilderness of glaciers and ice, senses their power, but feels no contact or reassurance, and receives no answer to his speculative questions. Wryly, he plays off the traditions of 'Poesy' (p. 126) and classical myth against the theories of contemporary geology:

> Is this the scene
> Where the old Earthquake-daemon taught her young
> Ruin? Were these their toys? Or did a sea
> Of fire envelop once this silent snow?
> None can reply – all seems eternal now.   [p. 127]

We should read that 'now' as a noun, rather than as an adverb modifying the phrase 'seems eternal'. The 'now' Shelley perceives is a kind of existential sense of being, whose meaning is only in the moment, not in any past explanations, and this perception leads him to confront Romantic pantheism head on:

> The wilderness has a mysterious tongue
> Which teaches awful doubt, or faith so mild,
> So solemn, so serene, that man may be,
> But for such faith, with nature reconciled.   [p. 127]

The phrase 'But for such faith' can be understood to mean 'by virtue of such faith'; indeed in his first version of the poem, Shelley sketched 'in such a faith' (Matthews and Everest, Vol. 1, p. 540), seeming uncertain of how to phrase this line. Whichever version one prefers, the ambiguous articulation represents Wordsworth's 'mild' faith as questionable, the force of '*may* be' taking precedence over any sense of reassurance and ironising such faith as somehow naïve or simplistic. The impact of this radical scepticism returns with the poem's final question, a feature characteristic of a number of classic second-generation Romantic poems, including Shelley's 'Ode to the West Wind' and Keats's 'Ode to a Nightingale'. In the final passage the expression again falters and struggles, deliberately, to capture the pressure of the questions being raised. The poem shifts to address Mont Blanc and the wilderness as part of the circumambient universe, inhabited by some undefined power. But on the evidence of the rest of the poem, this power has nothing in common with Wordsworth's mild faith: instead, it derives from Shelley's sense of the awe-inspiring 'sights' and 'sounds' of this extreme elemental landscape, contending unheard and unwatched by any human eye. The religious response seems almost irrelevant and meaningless in the face of this 'secret Strength of things', which suggests not so much belief as an existential 'thing-ness'. And Shelley closes by entertaining the awful possibility of the opposite, that there is merely no-thing-ness and no meaning at all, a 'vacancy' whose origins are in the human mind's inability to imagine any longer that any other power inhabits the universe. That incapacity would leave Mont Blanc unaffected as the 'everlasting universe of things' rolls on irregardless of humanity. On the basis of this disturbing scepticism, Shelley asserts that Nature and the mountain have a voice 'to repeal/Large codes of fraud and woe', since by realising their insignificance in the face of the larger forces of the natural universe, all human beings have is each other and the urgent necessity to treat one another fairly.

POEMS FROM 1817

March   Settles at Marlow near Peacock; writes and publishes *A Proposal for Putting Reform to the Vote*.

March 27   Denied custody of his children by Harriet, who are placed by Chancery Court (Lord Eldon, Lord Chancellor) under Guardianship.

Summer   Writes *Laon and Cythna; Prince Athanase*. Begins *Rosalind and Helen*.

September 2   Clara, his daughter by Mary, born.

Winter   *History of a Six Weeks' Tour* (written with Mary) published anonymously.

November   *Address . . . on the Death of the Princess Charlotte*.

December   *Laon and Cythna* published and withdrawn. Writes 'Ozymandias'.

Laon and Cythna *(extracts)*

Laon and Cythna, a tale of tyranny, revolutionary liberty and hope in twelve cantos, is Shelley's longest poem. It is particularly remarkable for its focus on sexual inequality: its heroine, Cythna, is one of a number of revolutionary female figures in Shelley's work, foregrounding the tyranny of male power and the potential for women to liberate themselves.

The poem is a cumbersome work in some ways, the outer shell of its spiritual vision sitting oddly with the much more down-to-earth central tale of human struggle; but, as so often, Shelley obviously wished to place this story of a defeated political revolution in the context of wider historical, geological and even cosmic processes. Despite this awkwardness, it has many powerful and inspiring passages. The extracts chosen for this volume represent some of the key aspects of the poem at its best and are accompanied by a summary of the action – line references are from the complete edition of the text for readers who wish to place these episodes in the context of the whole poem. While the story suffers from a lack of concrete historical placing, it nevertheless takes its initial impetus from what Shelley described as 'the master theme of the epoch in which we live – the French Revolution' (Jones, Vol. 1, p. 504). Shelley lived in the long shadow of this upheaval and his ardent attempts to explain what he saw as 'the failure of the French revolution to benefit mankind' (Jones, Vol. 1, p. 223) can be found in most of his great works, explicitly in *Prometheus Unbound*, *Laon and Cythna*, and implicitly in works such as *The Mask of Anarchy* and 'The Sensitive Plant'.

Often Shelley appears to be struggling to counteract his own temptations to give in to despair. *Laon and Cythna* opens:

> When the last hope of trampled France had failed
> Like a brief dream of unremaining glory,
> From visions of despair I rose [. . .]
>
> [Everest and Matthews, Vol. 2, p. 59]

and the rest of the poem presents a vision of revolutionary action both triumphant and defeated, ending with a paradisal vision of hope. One subject of the poem is the ebb and flow of revolutionary struggle within the currents of history. In the opening canto, the visionary depiction of a fight between the allegorical figures of an eagle and a serpent has been seen as epitomising cosmic conflicts between good and evil forces which are also at work in the individual psyche; but it can also be read as emblematic of the dialectic of history, a recurrent clash of contending forces whose outcome is never predictable. Like Antonio Gramsci, the Italian Marxist imprisoned by Mussolini, Shelley was keenly aware that political power is never assured: any hegemonic group needs to reinforce its dominance through a mixture of ideology and coercion if it is to remain in power. So in the main body of the poem, we see the rebels overthrow the tyrant Othman initially through the inspirational power of their ideas and words; idealistically, they then grant Othman his freedom, and he immediately organises a bloody counter-revolution. So on the one hand, the poem argues that revolutions must be enacted in accordance with the social vision that the revolutionaries aspire to if they are to avoid the bloody excesses which destroyed the French Revolution, and at the same time, Shelley interrogates the limits of such idealism. His desire to counteract the contemporary malaise of despair is matched by an intellectual commitment to analyse the problems of revolutionary aspirations, while maintaining a belief in the eventual triumph of liberty, freedom, equality and justice. This agenda proves difficult to sustain, which accounts to some extent for the forced or awkward qualities of the narrative.

The composition of the poem, over a period of about six months, was itself driven by the pressure of the times, historical and personal. Shelley's letters of 1817 capture the mood of intensifying crisis and potential confrontation over the issues of reform and social change in England at large; and while Shelley hoped for 'a most radical reform of the institutions of England', he was also anxious about 'such an utter overthrow as should leave us the prey of anarchy' (Jones, Vol. 1, p. 513). Personally, Shelley was motivated 'to leave some record of myself' (Jones, Vol. 1, p. 577) by his belief that he was seriously ill and possibly dying. Hence *Laon and Cythna* might constitute his only chance, as a poet and progressive thinker, to intervene directly into history and make some impact upon his time. In fact, the circumstances of its publication established a pattern which was to become frustratingly familiar over the next few years. Shelley was forced by his publisher to revise the work, with the new title *The Revolt of Islam*, in order to eliminate the incestuous relationship between brother and sister Laon and Cythna, and to subdue the poem's attack on organised religion as the apologist for tyranny. The insistence on revision was perhaps not surprising since the government was actively prosecuting works which expressed radical opinions. Shelley felt, however, that his revisions betrayed his original conception of the poem. The descriptions of sexual love between the two central characters and the attacks on established religious codes are integral parts of his challenge to custom and superstition as key elements in the ideology of oppression.

Preface The Preface offers a rationale for the poem and is particularly interesting for Shelley's views about the impact and aftermath of the French Revolution. He excuses the 'excesses' of the Revolution as being caused by the ingrained effects of a tyrannical society on those leading the movement for social change. With a double-edged irony, he describes the extremism as arising 'because a nation of men who had been dupes and slaves for centuries, were incapable of conducting themselves with the wisdom and tranquillity of freemen so soon as some of their fetters were partially loosened' (p. 133–4).

Shelley levels his criticism instead at the despair of those who had ideals for French liberty but who were 'morally ruined' by what 'appeared' to be the failure of their hopes (p. 134). Realising that the outcome of historical events cannot be judged by their immediate effects, he takes a wider perspective on the process of change as part of a historical dialectic, a crucial theme in the poem, and sees it as his mission to combat the self-indulgent 'gloom and misanthropy' resulting from the 'partial' views of his contemporaries. The rest of the Preface is in part a self-defence for a poem which was composed very quickly and in an unusual poetic form. He thereby ensures that readers should not see the poem as didactic, and towards the end he puts forward a spirited argument in favour of the freedom of the imagination.

Extract 1   Canto Second, verses 21–49. In the first Canto, the narrator rises from his vision of despair about France to witness an emblematic allegory of a struggle between an eagle and a serpent. This event is explained by a mysterious woman as she takes him on a journey in a boat to a temple where he is instructed to 'list and learn' (line 647; Everest and Matthews, Vol. 2, p. 92) from the spirit-form of Laon as he tells his story. At the opening of Canto Second, Laon describes life in a land dominated by tyrants while around him lie the ruins of previous civilisations based on 'less ungentle creeds' (line 760; Everest and Matthews, Vol. 2, p. 97). He is inspired by these visions to liberate the enslaved population. At the same time he describes his twelve-year-old sister Cythna. In this extract Cythna takes on the common Romantic role of the child of nature, uncorrupted by the effects of an unequal society, her natural liberty being a manifestation of the vision of freedom which Laon himself expresses. Laon himself learns from Cythna's example, discovering that nature reinforces his revolutionary ideas. In particular he realises that Cythna embodies the potential freedom of women from patriarchal constraint:

> Never will peace and human nature meet
> Till free and equal man and woman greet.
>
> [lines 994–5; p. 148]

In verse 43, with the resounding question, 'Can man be free if woman be a slave?' (line 1045; p. 150), Cythna proclaims the political legacy of Mary Wollstonecraft's work a generation earlier, the realisation that freedoms are indivisible and that gender inequality is a central chain in a linked series of oppressions. Her argument is as much an attack on the legal bonds of marriage and the male assertion of 'conjugal rights' as on the wider realities of male power.

Extract 2   Canto Fourth, verses 7–28. The second Canto ends with the two characters parting, and the third Canto portrays Laon's breakdown and madness. He experiences a nightmare of tyranny in which he is imprisoned and Cythna enslaved. His liberator is an old Hermit who rescues him at the end of Canto Third and cares for him. In this extract from Canto Fourth, the

Hermit describes how he was inspired by Laon's own visions of freedom to promote the message of revolution to his countrymen. The Hermit espouses the idealistic hope that 'blood need not flow' (line 1566; p. 155), believing that 'great is the strength/Of words' (1569–70; p. 155), and he instances a maiden (who is revealed later to be Cythna) whose message of freedom is so powerful as to make even her oppressors relinquish their power over her. This endorsement of passive resistance and rebellion is in part explained by the Hermit's belief that violent resistance merely involves replacing one kind of tyranny with another :

> If blood be shed, 'tis but a change and choice
>   Of bonds, – from slavery to cowardice
> A wretched fall!
>
> (lines 1657–9; p. 158)

He urges Laon to intervene in the momentarily-poised balance of forces between tyranny and resistance in order to bring about change through the power of his oratory.

Extract 3   Canto Fifth, verses 6–36. Laon goes to the Golden City to seek the maiden only to find war about to break out. In this extract he expresses his conviction that the cycles of violence must be broken through a doctrine of forgiveness, reconciliation and acceptance, since 'We are all brethren – even the slaves who kill/For hire, are men' (lines 1812–13; p. 160). The passage in verses 10–13 deals particularly with the futility of war, and was echoed by Wilfred Owen in his bitter vision of mutual forgiveness between enemies after death in 'Strange Meeting', that phrase appearing in line 1831. Even the tyrant Othman is included in this imaginary realisation of freedom through mutual acceptance. Laon finds Othman alone in his palace with only a child for company, a portrait of the sterile vacuity of power. Faced with the fallen tyrant, the people demand vengeance, but Laon persuades them that in their pursuit of true justice, they should forgive him (verses 33–4; p. 166). But the problems with this compassionate idealism are exposed by the 'smile which guile portended' on Othman's lips (line 2042; p. 167), which anticipates his treacherous betrayal of the concord agreed between the two sides. The Canto ends with Laon again meeting Cythna, who delivers a panegyric to freedom.

Extract 4   Canto Sixth, verses 2–41. The dangers of passive resistance are fully exposed as Othman initiates a counter-revolution. This extract depicts the ensuing battles with a vividness akin to Byron's anti-war passages in *Don*

Juan, in which he describes war as 'a brain-spattering, windpipe-slitting art' (*Don Juan*, Canto 9, verse 4). The defeat of the revolutionaries leads Laon and Cythna to retreat from their engagement with social change, turning instead to solitude, nature and each other. This passage describing 'the fearful overthrow/Of public hope' (lines 2597–8; p.175) echoes the Preface in its intent to combat the pernicious effects of despair brought about in the 'worshippers of public good' by the apparent reversals of French liberty (p. 134). As we saw with *Alastor* and 'To Wordsworth', Shelley had been critical of the retreat into self and nature by the first generation of Romantic writers, seeing it as a betrayal. This passage suggests the problematic, if unavoidable, dialectic between engagement and retreat, which has some bearing on the other major interest of this extract, the explicit expression of the sexual love between Laon and Cythna, made even more remarkable by their relationship as brother and sister (verses 33–40; pp. 176–8). Shelley links love with revolution, connecting change in the public sphere with the need for revolution in personal life, and after their love-making the two characters again turn their attention to how to re-sow the 'seeds of hope' (lines 2709; Everest and Matthews, Vol. 2, p. 174). Laon goes to the city in search of food only to meet a woman deranged by famine and the death of her children, enacting the apocalyptic effects of pestilence and war.

Extract 5   Canto Eighth, verse 3, to Canto Ninth, verse 25. In Canto Seventh, Cythna tells Laon of her sexual enslavement to the tyrant Othman, including a bizarre episode where she is imprisoned in an underwater cave and freed by an earthquake! Canto Eighth opens with her being saved by a boat. In this extract she delivers a speech to the mariners, attacking the human invention of God as a mechanism by which to oppress people, 'To scourge us into slaves'(line 3256; p. 180). She exhorts them to abandon their view of women as slaves, to throw off their own enslavement to money and to realise that human beings are in control of their own destiny. She offers the mariners such a vision of hope through the idea of self-forgiveness that they are moved to release the maidens who are kept enslaved on their boat.

The rest of this extract explores the fluctuating nature of power and revolutionary struggles. At the opening of Canto Ninth, Cythna arrives at the Golden City, but is dismayed to find the belief in liberty has evaporated. She nevertheless begins again, preaching 'Nature, and truth, and Liberty, and Love' (line 3524; p. 188). Her powerful appeals again shake the power of Othman the tyrant. Rather than being violent, his response is to shore up his position through ideological means, a kind of spin-doctoring which promotes the message that the status quo of slavery is at least safe and peaceful, as well as being the will of God. Ending her account of how she came to be in the City, Cythna turns to the imagery of autumn and spring which Shelley was again to use in 'Ode to the West Wind'. Here what is implicit in the ode is made explicit: the imagery of natural recurrence functions as an emblem for the undying hope of social regeneration. Tyranny is 'the winter of the world' (line 3685; p. 194), while the seeds 'sleeping in the soil' (line 3676; p. 193) are likened to captives buried in dungeons, whose imprisonment will be broken by new birth as 'Earth like an eagle springs' (line 3693; p. 194) from its chains.

The concluding cantos of the poem, however, show the necessity of bowing to the historical process. In Canto Tenth, Othman enlists help from other tyrants, lays his own kingdom waste in an attempt to eradicate revolt and uses a Christian priest to enforce an ideology of obedience to overcome the notions of revolt. The outcome in Canto Eleventh is that Laon, realising that hopes for change are over for the foreseeable future, goes to the city and gives himself up in a vain attempt to save Cythna's life. He also relinquishes the ideals of freedom and equality to America where he wishes Cythna to be conveyed. In the final canto, as Laon is being prepared for execution by fire, Cythna arrives to die with him as an inspiration to the future. The poem ends as it began with a visionary passage describing Laon and Cythna's after-death experience of a paradisal state where Cythna is reunited with her child.

'Ozymandias'

Along with 'Ode to the West Wind' and 'To a Skylark', this is a contender for the role of Shelley's most well-known poem, and as with them, its immediate descriptive appeal masks its deeper impact as a political poem. It is an attack on tyranny and power, an attack Shelley returns to in other works like *Prometheus Unbound* (1819) and his burlesque satiric drama *Oedipus Tyrannus, or Swellfoot the Tyrant* (1820). The sonnet is a satire on the pretensions of power, as characterised by the tyrant Ozymandias, whose personality is vividly hinted at in the 'sneer of cold command' which the hapless sculptor captured in his portrayal, presumably because he himself had suffered from Ozymandias's cruelty. The tyrant believes that he and his works will be more powerful than any foreseeable dynasty; but his message to the future becomes deeply ironic. He intended other despots, when looking at his achievements, to despair of being as powerful as he was; instead the wreck of his statue proclaims that no power endures in the face of the levelling effects of history. This vigorous poetry is all the more effective for the unspecific but vividly imagined description of the sands, captured with emphatic rhythms and wide empty vowels sounds.

POEMS FROM 1818

January   *The Revolt of Islam* (revised version of *Laon and Cythna*)
   issued.

March 12   Leaves England finally for Italy, with Mary, the two
   children, and Claire Clairmont.

May   Meets Maria and John Gisborne with Maria's son Henry.

Summer   Baths of Lucca; finishes *Rosalind and Helen*.

July   Translates Plato's *Symposium*; visits Venice, meets Byron, then
   to Este; 'Lines Written Among the Euganean Hills'.

September 24   His daughter Clara dies.

Autumn   Begins 'Julian and Maddalo'.

October   *Prometheus Unbound* begun.

November   Visits Rome, moves to Naples and visits volcanic areas;
   writes 'Stanzas Written in Dejection'.

1818 occasioned some of Shelley's most despairing writing, in 'Stanzas
Written in Dejection', as well as the beginnings of his most resilient,
Prometheus Unbound. The death of his one-year-old daughter Clara in
September, as a result of which Mary Shelley became deeply depressed, was
no doubt a major cause for his despair, while in addition his health was
precarious.

'Lines Written Among the Euganean Hills'

'Lines Written Among the Euganean Hills' begins as a meditation on
mortality but modulates into a reflection, at once scathing and moving, on
the temporary nature of power and tyranny. As so often, Shelley uses the
genre of the nature poem but transforms it into a vehicle for his most direct
social concerns. The opening imagines the turmoil of a shipwreck in a 'sea of
misery' (p. 195), in which a mariner drowns, and the vivid descriptions of
natural destruction and physical desolation are immediately linked to the
terrible injustices perpetrated by kings. Suddenly amid the darkness the sun
rises through the mist, as an explicit emblem of 'truth's rising day' (p. 199)
and 'thought-winged Liberty' (p. 200), dispelling the gloomy turmoil of the
opening storm and forming a diurnal framework for the poem's meditations.
But as this sun of freedom shines on Venice, Shelley recalls that the city is
doomed to sink beneath the waves, prompting the vivid images of underwa-
ter ruins which will reappear in 'Ode to the West Wind'. But as in that poem,
these images are a reminder of the transitory nature of power, and Shelley is
ready to sacrifice Venice to the waves should it be incapable of rising to
Freedom's call and throwing off the inglorious chains of oppression. There

follows a passage in which Shelley memorialises Venice as glorious only for sheltering 'a tempest cleaving Swan' (p. 199), Lord Byron. The 'universal light' (p. 200) of the sun-Liberty is shrouded in mist as Shelley contemplates Venice and Padua oppressed by the poison of lords like weeds, leading to a potentially apocalyptic vision of the reaction against oppression and a pessimistic lament that 'love or reason' (p. 201) cannot break the cycle of violence engendered by injustice. But as usual, Shelley resists the temptation to despair, and he imagines instead an aberrant unquenched spark from the flame of freedom kindling an inferno. As if exhausted by his reflections, he dissolves into the scene in a wonderful passage expressing his sense of the interconnectedness of all things in the universe (pp. 202–3). The opening image of the 'green isle', a haven of safety amid a 'sea of misery' (p. 195) which has echoed through the poem, returns once more. As autumnal evening falls, the final passage offers a vision of a utopian haven, a 'healing paradise' of 'brotherhood' which might regenerate 'the multitude', as a result of which the earth might 'grow young again' (p. 204). But this vision depends so categorically on the qualifications contained in the conditional tense, 'might', that it is impossible to shake off entirely the grim antitheses which the poem has juxtaposed against each other.

'Julian and Maddalo'

'Julian and Maddalo' is in part a celebration of place, the 'Paradise of exiles, Italy' (p. 207), and of the less obvious aspects of the Italian environment. It begins with an evocative description of a desolate seascape which recalls the atmosphere of George Crabbe's 'Peter Grimes', as it sets the scene for the rather Gothic tale which forms the main body of the work. The poem is a fictionalised conversation between Byron (Maddalo) and Shelley (Julian), but the fact that Shelley dramatises himself and his friend under the guise of two invented characters reminds us that we should not read the personal voices of any of Shelley's poems as a direct transcription. Even where the poems employ a first person, as here, we need to realise that the 'I' is an invention, a poetic strategy. In the case of 'Julian and Maddalo', Shelley discloses the fictionalising impulse of poetic creation in his Preface, where he describes the different and complementary characters of the two central figures, and there is undoubtedly a note of self-mockery at the end of his self-portrait when he reveals that 'Julian is rather serious' (p. 206).

The central conversation deals with Shelley's *bête noire*, organised religion and its attendant ills. Julian points out the natural innocence of Maddalo's daughter in a manner recalling Jean Jacques Rousseau's influential view of the child as a symbol of the true potential of human beings, unsullied by the mental manacles of religion or the inequalities of an unjust society. In response, Maddalo tells him, 'You talk Utopia' (p. 210), and offers an object-lesson in the dangers of such free-thinking, a visit to a man of similar opinions who has since gone mad. This solitary figure is another classic Romantic archetype, the wild hermit who is gifted with wisdom. His speech is addressed to the beloved who abandoned him and whom he forgives. Julian feels an empathy with the hermit and imagines that if he himself were 'an unconnected man' (p. 220) he might 'reclaim' him from his madness. Instead Julian leaves 'bright Venice' the next day, suggesting the flimsiness of his idealism, which is interrogated through the contrasts with Maddalo and the maniac. The poem's ending is peculiarly framed as a meeting many years later between Julian and Maddalo's now-grown daughter, who has become 'a wonder of this earth' (p. 221) and who, despite Julian calling her 'Child', assumes the dominant role in their conversation. In the strange refusal of the poem to tell us the full story of the hermit's fate and the controlling presence of this woman, there is a suggestive echo: Julian's self-association with the hermit and the framing of that story within his own, seem to imply an ambiguous, unspoken relationship between Julian and the 'Child'. It is part of the fictional self-interrogation which Shelley imposes on this self-portrait that his character might have been trapped in the same fatalistic cycle of experience he was so ready to challenge in theory. It reminds us that Shelley's own life at the time he wrote this poem was far from idyllic as a result of the deaths of his two children and his growing estrangement from his wife Mary. The bleakness of these circumstances produced one of his most despairing lyrics in 'Stanzas Written in Dejection, near Naples'.

POEMS FROM 1819

February   Visits Pompeii and Paestum.

Spring   Moves to Rome: *Prometheus* Acts 2 and 3. *Rosalind and Helen . . . with Other Poems* published.

May   Finishes 'Julian and Maddalo'; begins *The Cenci*.

June 7   His son William dies; Villa Valsovano, Leghorn.

September   Writes *The Mask of Anarchy* and other political poems.

October   Moves to Florence; writes 'Ode to the West Wind', *Peter Bell the Third*, 'A Philosophical View of Reform'.

November 12   Percy Florence, Mary's fourth child, born.

December   Completes *Prometheus*, Act 4.

During this productive year, Shelley wrote his most famous poem, 'Ode to the West Wind', completed what is classed by many as his major work,

Prometheus Unbound, along with his most powerful political poem *The Mask of Anarchy*, some great short poems, the underrated play *The Cenci*, and his satirical squib against Wordsworth, *Peter Bell the Third*, as well as beginning his major political essay 'A Philosophical View of Reform'. But then 1819 was a remarkable year in many ways, being a time of great ferment in Britain, a factor directly related to Shelley's output. So in order to understand the nature of the works he produced, we need to set them in a wider context.

1819 saw the production of two great odes about autumn. On 19 September, Keats, for whom this year was also miraculously productive, wrote 'To Autumn', with its famous celebration of this 'Season of mists and mellow fruitfulness'. On 20 October Shelley wrote his 'Ode to the West Wind', in which he hailed the wind as 'Thou breath of Autumn's being' (p. 401). Both poems are resonant with a sense of things ending, of decay, of impending destruction, death and dissolution. As we saw with the Preface to *Laon and Cythna,* Shelley himself was well aware that this sense of gloom and melancholy was not merely a personal one but an element of the age in which he lived. He saw that poem as an attempt to combat such hopelessness and 'infectious gloom' (p. 135). Yet by the autumn of 1819, Shelley too, it seems, had succumbed to the general atmosphere of hopelessness sufficiently to indulge his own form of melancholy in his 'Ode to the West Wind'. Keats's question in his ode 'To Autumn' sets the tone for this period and for the second generation of the Romantic writers more generally: 'Where are the songs of Spring? Aye, where are they? / Think not of them . . .' After the ardent certainties of Blake and early Wordsworth, what is noticeable about the second generation of Romantic writers is their scepticism. A number of significant poems, for example, end with questions rather than answers: Shelley's 'Ode to the West Wind' ('If Winter comes, can Spring be far behind?', p. 403); or Keats's 'Ode to a Nightingale' ('Gone is that music. Do I wake or sleep?'). How do we move in the space of thirty years from the spring songs of Blake's *Songs of Innocence* in 1789 to the autumnal songs of 1819? And how by 1819 did the ardently radical Shelley also come to express a sense of apparent disillusionment in his 'Ode to the West Wind'?

The answer lies in a combination of factors, literary and personal, historical and social. After all, 1819 seemed an opportune time for radicalism to re-emerge. While Shelley was in Italy, the volcano Etna erupted, a portent of fiery changes. Not only were Etna and Shelley erupting, but it seemed in Britain as if Shelley's prediction at the end of his sonnet 'England in 1819', that the 'glorious Phantom' of Liberty might burst forth again (p. 407), could come true. After the savage repression of the 1790s, the radical movement had effectively regrouped to incorporate the middle classes and Tories like William Cobbett, who were disaffected with repressive patriotism and the corrupt electoral system. By 1807 there was a new radical reform movement, sounding the need for change. Its main voices were William Cobbett, Orator Hunt and others who wished to divert any insurrectionary discontent into constitutional reform; some of its leaders, like Francis Place, were openly hostile to any popular agitation and saw middle-class reformers as the salvation of England. Shelley himself may have been more radical in temperament but he too contributed to this reform debate in 1817 with his pamphlet *A Proposal for Putting Reform to the Vote through the Kingdom*.

But it was equally evident that the government of Lord Liverpool would not listen to the reform movement and saw their proposals as potentially insurrectionary. Hence the extensive programme for building military barracks throughout England in areas of disaffection: London alone had a standing army of 138,000 men. In 1812, the reformist aristocrat MP for Westminster, Sir Francis Burdett, had complained that 'Ministers are intending to establish a military despotism in this country' (Foot, p. 36). Events quickly came to boiling-point. In 1817, the coach of the Prince Regent, notorious for his degenerate and profligate behaviour, was mobbed and stoned. The government response was to set up a House of Lords Committee, which reported that 'a traitorous conspiracy has been formed in the metropolis for the purpose of overthrowing, by means of a general insurrection, the established Government, laws, and Constitution' (Thompson, p. 700). As a result, savagely repressive measures were instigated, including the suspension of *Habeus Corpus* and the suppression of all reforming societies and clubs under an act against seditious meetings.

By 1819 England was virtually held down by force. Despite the moderation of the reformers' views, they were now as suppressed as the Jacobins had been in the 1790s. Some panicked: William Cobbett fled to America to escape any prosecution. Others decided to challenge the government's repressive measures openly: middle-class reformers hoped to channel any popular dissent into calls for constitutional change, but they were by no means strong enough to control a widespread popular movement. On the other hand the government ('Old Corruption' as it was called) believed that any concessions to reform would unleash the floodgates of revolution. This explosive confrontation led in 1819 to one of the most dramatic events of this period, an event which became known as Peterloo, in a mocking echo of the battle of Waterloo.

The reformers organised a mass meeting for 16 August on St Peter's Fields outside Manchester to claim the right of freedom for the press and for political organisations, and the vote for a limited franchise. It drew between 60,000 and 100,000 people, who were unarmed and were there to hear speeches from leading radicals. They were confronted by a cavalry of the Hussars and Yeomanry organised previously by Manchester magistrates. In the ensuing 'battle' the official figures were that 11 were killed and 421 injured, through sabre wounds or crushing by horses (more than a hundred of the injured were women and children) – and these were the official figures! As E. P. Thompson suggests, 'It really was a massacre' (Thompson, p. 752).

The effects of this event were volcanic. The government supported the Manchester magistrates, sending the congratulations of the prime minister, Lord Liverpool, and the thanks of the Prince Regent 'for their prompt, decisive, and efficient measures for the preservation of the public peace' (Thompson, p. 750). On the other side, the radicals and their supporters were galvanised with anger. And so was Shelley. He received the news in Italy by letter on 5 September. His response was immediate: 'The same day that your letter came, came news of the Manchester work, & the torrent of my indignation has not yet done boiling in my veins. I await anxiously to hear how the Country will express its sense of this bloody murderous oppression of its destroyers. "Something must be done . . . What yet I know not"' (Holmes, p. 529). And on 9 September he wrote to Peacock referring to the 'terrible and important news' from Manchester: 'These are, as it were, the distant thunders of the terrible storm which is approaching. The tyrants here, as in the French Revolution, have shed first blood. May their execrable lessons not be learnt with equal docility! I still think there will be no coming to close quarters until financial affairs decidedly bring the oppressors and the oppressed together. Pray let me have the *earliest* political news which you consider of importance at this crisis.' As Richard Holmes points out, Shelley's acute realisation that economic conditions would ignite the confrontation is notable (Holmes, pp. 531–2), and places him again in the ranks of radical political analysis leading to Karl Marx. Over the next twelve days Shelley wrote his most forceful political poem, the 91 stanzas of *The Mask of Anarchy* dealing directly with the Peterloo massacre, and the aftermath of this event reverberates through his later works.

The Mask of Anarchy *and other political poems*

The Mask of Anarchy is in colloquial ballad form with a simple four-stress metre similar to that found in the popular verses of broadsheets. Shelley designed it as a poem with popular appeal that might seize the moment of indignation, express it fervently and memorably, and become an instrument for shaping the decisive changes in which he himself could not take part directly.

The poem is in three main sections. The first part (stanzas 1–34; pp. 387–92) presents a vitriolic satire on the government of the day: in a brilliant reversal of the official view of events, the prime minister, Lord Liverpool, and his ministers are themselves commanded by Anarchy, an apocalyptic deity, and, in a medieval masque or dance of death, it is they who ride the horses that trampled the Peterloo crowd to death. But ironically, Anarchy also governs the people, who are 'adoring' (p. 388) of their own servitude, trapped by what William Blake called 'the mind-forg'd manacles' of oppression (Woodcock, p. 88). This section then introduces the figure of an unarmed mother, Hope, who in stanzas 22–5 (p. 390) is trampled under the horses' hooves as a sacrifice, only to be reborn in stanza 26, since Hope can never die.

In the second section of the poem (stanzas 34–63; pp. 392–6), Hope gives a long speech describing different kinds of freedom. In stanzas 39–51, she exposes the false freedom of a society that exploits the poor for the benefit of the rich; in stanzas 52–64, she presents a vision of true freedom, made up of equality, justice, wisdom and peace.

In the third part (stanzas 65–91; pp. 397–401), Hope calls for a series of massive demonstrations throughout England to claim political rights; and at this point it is important to realise that, effectively, the poem is set before the Peterloo massacre. For what Hope predicts is that one such demonstration of passive resistance will suffer the fate of the crowd at Peterloo. She insists that the crowds should face the bayonets and be massacred, because it will prove the iniquity of British law and justice: this itself will result in a violent reaction among the people, including the British soldiers, who will feel so ashamed of what has happened that they will turn instead to support those who desire freedom. The poem ends with a clarion call for armed resistance.

On 23 September, Shelley sent the poem to Leigh Hunt's radical journal *The Examiner*, expecting instant publication. Its popular form, inspirational call for action and vitriolic satire virtually guaranteed a wide audience, with the possibility of its being reprinted as a broadsheet popular edition. Meanwhile, during his impassioned composition of the poem, the government violently suppressed the radical movement, arresting all its main leaders. On 15 September, John Keats, who had been on London's streets among an estimated 300,000 people to watch the arrival in army custody of the famous radical Orator Hunt, wrote to his brother George: 'The whole distance from the Angel at Islington to the Crown and Anchor was lined with multitudes' (Thompson, p. 747). Two days later Keats wrote again about the arrest of another radical, the bookseller Carlile: 'He has been selling deistical pamphlets, republished Tom Paine, and many other works held in superstitious horror.' Using a very Shelleyan image, Keats continued with his views on the probable course of action by the government: 'After all, they are afraid to prosecute. They are afraid of his defence; it would be published in all the papers all over the empire. They shudder at this. The trials would light a flame they could not extinguish. Do you not think this of great import?' (Thompson, p. 798). Two days later, on 19 September, Keats sat down to write 'To Autumn', with its fatalistic acceptance of decay and corruption.

In this context, the publication of *The Mask of Anarchy* might have become the rallying call for radical action that Shelley desired; but it wasn't published. It didn't see the light of day until 1832, long after Shelley's death. Leigh Hunt feared prosecution, and decided to suppress the poem. His fears were far from groundless. By 1820, all the leading radicals were in prison. Sir Francis Burdett, the reforming aristocrat MP, wrote an open letter 'To the Electors of Westminster' as part of his protest about Peterloo, and as a result was prosecuted and convicted of seditious libel. At the trial, the judge, Mr Justice Best, directed the jury: 'If you find in [his writing] an appeal to the passions of the lower orders of the people, and not having a tendency to inform those who can correct abuses, it is a libel' (Holmes, p. 539). Undoubtedly *The Mask of Anarchy* fell into the former category, as did the other political poems Shelley wrote at this time, all of which he wished to collect in a 'little volume of *popular songs* wholly political, and destined to awaken and direct the imagination of the reformers' (Jones, Vol. 2, p. 191). They are among his most fiery denunciations of the corruptions of England. The sonnet 'England in 1819' (pp. 407) is a catalogue of oppressions. It opens by castigating George III and the corrupt court of the Prince Regent in a startlingly frank manner: the damning adjectives of the first line, 'An old, mad, blind, despised, and dying king', are enforced by the comma pauses, while the savage imagery (the aristocracy as 'the dregs of their dull race' and as 'leech-like') drives the angry tone. There is sharp irony and sarcasm in the description of the law as 'Golden and sanguine', while the image of the army as a 'two-edged sword' contains a veiled threat that the repressive force of the rulers may backfire against them. This is a society of living death, 'graves', but one which promises the rebirth of the 'glorious Phantom' of Liberty, yet this hope is severely qualified by that word 'Phantom' and by the phrasing of 'may / Burst'. The 'Song to the Men of England' (pp. 405–6) takes up the theme of exploitation which Shelley develops in his great political essay 'A Philosophical View of Reform' later this same year. Its popular ballad form and direct address leave one in no doubt as to its intent, but again it contains a sting in its tone by suggesting that the oppressed labourers are complicit in their own subjection.

'Ode to the West Wind'

For Shelley, the effects of the failure to publish *The Mask of Anarchy* and his book of popular songs were to be decisive, although he himself only began to register the full impact during the following year. By October 1819, Shelley was twenty-seven and beginning to notice threads of grey in his hair. On the 20th of that month he jotted down a verse describing the autumnal effects of dead leaves as like grey hairs. By the 25th, he had completed his 'Ode to the West Wind'. Along with 'To a Skylark', another of his most famous poems, this is so often read simply as a 'nature' poem; but it had its genesis in the intense contradictions being enacted and felt in the 'moment' of the Peterloo massacre. These include Shelley's dialectical awareness of the potential for reform and at the same time his realisation of the forces marshalled against change. As well as this historical insight, he also experienced personal feelings of impotence and hopelessness generated partly by his exile from England at this decisive time – 'asleep in Italy'(p. 387) as he saw himself at the beginning of *The Mask of Anarchy* – a feeling of failure to catch the tide of history in his role as a political poet and a sense of despair at the remorse-lessness of time and life. So, behind what appears to be simply a lyrical nature poem, we can see a whole network of factors – historical, social, personal – leading to its composition.

Despite Shelley's sense of defeat, his ode sees the decay and corruption of autumn not with the fatalism of Keats's 'To Autumn', but as a necessary part of the process leading to renewal. Shelley's west wind is the embodiment of transformation, connecting natural and social change. At the same time, the poem links these to the role of the poet as a breath of inspiration like the wind, a liberator challenging melancholy, a prophetic clarion heralding a new dawn with the 'incantation' (p. 403) of verse. The key images describing the wind are significantly paradoxical: it is 'destroyer and preserver' (p. 401), a 'spirit fierce' (p. 403) but also an 'enchanter' (p. 401). This dialectic is the key to the poem: simultaneously, Shelley sees the west wind as the spirit of revolutionary turmoil, embodying the contradictory forces of history, and as the spirit of poetic inspiration.

The poem is in five parts, each a sonnet in the *terza-rima* form of Dante's *The Divine Comedy* which Shelley was to use again in 'The Triumph of Life'. In the first section, Shelley presents his double vision of the west wind: it heralds winter, death and decay, but at the same time out of this destruction will come new life and growth. So the wind herds the diseased remnants of the old year: the leaves are described as 'pestilence-stricken multitudes' (p. 401), an image which invokes the oppressed and indoctrinated 'multitudes' adoring their own oppression in *The Mask of Anarchy* (p. 388); the seeds are like corpses, but they will undergo a revolutionary resurrection with the clarion call of the spring. The spring wind will be nurturing, 'Driving sweet buds like flocks to feed in air' (p. 401), a remarkable and lovely idea, as if the buds as they open on the trees were little woolly sheep, herded by the wind to graze in the air.

What is noticeable in this poem is how the images accumulate and transmute into each other organically. So from section 1 to 2, the imagery of the leaves carries over and is applied to the clouds which the wind shakes 'from the tangled boughs of Heaven and Ocean' (p. 402). But how can heaven and ocean be envisaged as having 'tangled boughs'? Again, this is an example of Shelley's almost scientific accuracy. The heavens and the ocean are separate, but they are intimately combined through natural processes: under the heat of the sun, water from the ocean evaporates up into the sky to form clouds. They are, then, in a sense, shaken 'from the tangled boughs of heaven and ocean', an almost meteorological image.

Equally marked is the increasingly apocalyptic note being sounded through this section, 'the approaching storm' (p. 402). A catastrophic upheaval is anticipated which Shelley again presents in terms of the cyclical upheavals of the natural world, embodying his sense of the impending social storm at home in Britain. To remind us of that connection, section 3 includes images of overthrown power, old palaces sunk below the Mediterranean, emblems of the transience of human aspiration like Ozymandias's statue. Even the 'Atlantic's level powers' (p. 402) have to give way before the superior force of the west wind, whose effects can even reach down to the depths of the ocean, making its 'foliage' fall like the leaves from the trees in section 1.

At the beginning of section 4, Shelley gathers together the main images of the poem – leaves, clouds, waves – and introduces a speaking voice, an 'I', a personal focus and source for the poem's address to the wind. So far the poem has addressed the wind with the repeated formula: 'thou . . hear, oh, hear', an insistent plea for attention, a prayer in fact to the wind to inspire and carry the poet with its destructive/creative power, to lift him up like the leaves, clouds and waves out of his present sense of personal and social decay, to free him from his present restrictions. It is a plea for liberation.

Shelley's lament at the end of this section comes close to self-pity, that voice of disenchantment and disillusion against which he had set his mind in the Preface to *Laon and Cythna*. But his aim here is uplift, not surrender, and he dissipates the self-pity with a marvellously throwaway gesture at the beginning of section 5:

> Make me thy lyre, even as the forest is:
> What if my leaves are falling like its own!   [p. 403]

These lines demand to be read with a kind of self-castigating wryness, a 'what-the-hell' tone of defiance; and from that point on, the verbal music of this remarkable finale carries us on to a climactic conclusion. The music and imagery of this prayer are literally willing into being the spirit embodied in the wind. The poem becomes its own subject: the dead leaves are suddenly the leaves of the page we are reading, scattered by the processes of history, and the words themselves are like sparks scattered from a dormant but unextinguished fire, capable of flaring into fiery life at any moment. And this was, in a real sense, true for Shelley's works: we have already noticed that *Queen Mab* was used throughout the nineteenth century by working-class educational organisations; and that his work was also read and quoted by Harriet Taylor, Karl Marx, Emily Pankhurst and Vera Britain to name but a few; while the final verses of *The Mask of Anarchy* appeared in the late 1970s on the record cover of the album *Sound Effects* by punk band The Jam. It is, then, as if the speaker of the poem is himself overtaken by his own words which contain the spirit of the wind and are carried on the wind, heralding like an apocalyptic trumpet the transformative powers of which the wind is the emblem.

And then, at the very climax of the poem, Shelley achieves a masterly balancing act: he ends not with an assertion, but with a question. It is a question capable of being read as an assertion of inevitable truth; 'can Spring be far behind?': it goes without saying, that it can't, which makes this a rhetorical question. But its phrasing allows for different degrees and tones of qualification which make its effects all the richer and more resonant: just notice the difference which occurs if the reader puts the stress on 'can', as opposed to 'far'. This qualification complicates the prophetic spirit of this poem in fruitful ways, leaving us poised on a cusp of a historical dialectic.

The Cenci

The Cenci, Shelley's only attempt at a true play as opposed to the poetic dramas *Prometheus Unbound* and *Hellas*, is an unfairly neglected work. Admittedly over-the-top in some aspects, it is more than a mere pastiche of Elizabethan or Jacobean tragedy. It might be difficult to claim great psychological conviction in its characterisation, but there is enough to make it a powerful and impressive dramatic début, and linguistically it has real impact.

Shelley describes the story behind the play in his Preface (pp. 310–14), where he asserts his purpose as being dramatic rather than didactic, and invokes Wordsworth's famous formula from the Preface to *Lyrical Ballads*, 'the real language of men', to describe the style. The dedicatory letter to Leigh Hunt identifies the links in the play between 'domestic and political tyranny' (p. 309). Shelley sees the connections between patriarchal oppressions in the home and those practised by such bastions of power as the Pope:

> He holds it of most dangerous example
> In aught to weaken the paternal power
> Being, as 'twere, the shadow of his own.
>
> [II, ii, 54–6; p. 334]

The incest Count Cenci imposes on his daughter Beatrice is merely the most extreme private form of his exploitations and manipulations. The portrayal of the count is savagely exaggerated, but this does not undermine the power of Shelley's exploration of utter amorality. Beatrice's stoicism moves through derangement into a strong portrait of an utterly resolute woman determined to have revenge. Even her momentary breakdown just before the end contributes to the sense of conviction about her as a character. Giacomo's erratic uncertainty and Orsino's Machiavellian scheming are persuasive enough to make the play work. Whereas other Romantic drama might seem theatrically unconvincing, *The Cenci* does work on stage, as a number of productions have testified. It was staged privately in 1886 to an audience of 2,400 people, including Robert Browning and Oscar Wilde, while during the twentieth century it had a number of productions, including Sybil Thorndike's in 1922, a broadcast on the BBC Third Programme in 1947, and performances by the Old Vic Company (1959 and 1985) and the Damned Poets' Theatre (1993). Notable European versions include a performance in Bolshevik Moscow in 1919–20, an Expressionist film by Mario Caserini which was shown in Dublin in 1909 by James Joyce, and an adaptation by Antonin Artaud in 1935 (Everest and Matthews, Vol. 2, pp. 719, 873).

Prometheus Unbound

The myth of Prometheus afforded Shelley the opportunity for his most complex treatment of the interrelationships between the various forms of injustice and oppression. In the Greek story as dramatised particularly by Aeschylus, Prometheus (meaning 'fore thinker' in Greek) was one of the old order of gods who were overthrown by a new order led by Zeus (Jupiter in Shelley's play). Prometheus helped Zeus achieve power only to see him become a tyrant. To make amends, Prometheus aided oppressed humanity by stealing fire from heaven and giving them wisdom. For his pains, Zeus chained him to a rock to have his entrails gnawed out daily by an eagle. In the lost Aeschylus sequel, Prometheus was to have been reconciled with Zeus, a situation Shelley rejects in his version of the story, as he explains in his Preface, since in his view there could be no reconciliation of 'the Champion with the Oppressor of mankind' (p. 225).

Prometheus Unbound is a visionary work, complementing the historically located poems such as *The Mask of Anarchy*. It functions simultaneously on psychological, social, historical and cosmic levels, achieving through poetic drama a complexity similar to that of Blake's mythology in his prophetic books. Prometheus's enchainment embodies the repression of the progressive elements in history (the drive towards freedom and equality), of human capacities (psychological and social), and the living potential of the universe as a whole. The play-poem dramatises the conflicts at work in Shelley's own age and the subsequent contradictions he felt within himself. In particular, as in *Laon and Cythna*, Shelley is still concerned to combat the collective gloom consequent upon the alleged failure of the French Revolution. He offers a release from the cyclical round of oppressive regimes through the role of Asia, representing love, as the balance to Prometheus, representing revolution, resistance and anti-authoritarianism. Shelley suggests that there is a need for an inner as well as an outer revolution, that revolution as a process should embody its own ideals through the manner in which it enacts itself, a theme which recalls the idealistic selflessness and compassion advocated in *Laon and Cythna*.

The Preface makes clear how simultaneously grounded and visionary Shelley wanted this work to be. He looks back to Milton, the republican poet, as his inspiration, hoping that the writers of his own age are similarly 'the companions and forerunners of some unimagined change in our social condition or the opinions which cement it. The cloud of mind is discharging its collected lightning' (p. 227). But he goes on to explain that he does not wish his poem to be seen as dedicated 'solely to the direct enforcement of reform [. . .] Didactic poetry is my abhorrence' (p. 228). *Prometheus Unbound* certainly has more in common with the glories of a lightning storm than a political tract.

Act 1 dramatises Prometheus chained to the rock suffering eternal torments; yet rather than curse his oppressor Jupiter, he pities him and wishes to rescind his earlier curse, since 'I wish no living thing to suffer pain' (Act 1, 305; p. 238). But while Prometheus has clearly been tempered by the effects of his beloved Asia (Love), the combined forces around him who aid in the overthrow of Jupiter suggest that forgiveness and resolve must go hand in hand. Equally important, the reiteration of Prometheus's curse leads to the realisation of his complicity in Jupiter's oppressive regime, since he gave Jupiter omnipotent power, and suggests that human beings are in control of their own fate if only they would realise it. Jupiter's Furies torment Prometheus with the recollection of the failure of historical attempts at liberty, and then he tortures himself in terms which recall the overthrow of the French Revolution by new forms of oppression:

> The nations thronged around, and cried aloud,
> As with one voice, Truth, liberty, and love!
> Sudden fierce confusion fell from heaven
> Among them: there was strife, deceit, and fear:
> Tyrants rushed in, and did divide the spoil.
>
> (Act 1, 650–54; p. 248)

His captivity embodies the post-revolutionary disenchantment and repression of Shelley's generation, in both social and psychological terms. But the whole dynamic of *Prometheus Unbound* is to confront and overcome this depressed state. As Mercury reveals, Prometheus himself holds the key to a secret which will overthrow Jupiter's tyranny; the problem is that Prometheus is not aware of what he knows. He is made aware through the offices of three sisters, Asia (Love), Ione (Memory) and Panthea (Hope), a female triumvirate embodying similar capacities to Blake's Bardic Present, Past and Future in the 'Introduction' to the *Songs of Experience* (Woodcock, pp. 58, 74). In Act 2, a dream of liberation leads Panthea and Ione to the cave of the monster Demogorgon who holds the answer to the riddle of how the imprisonment of Prometheus and humanity came about and how it might be overturned. In one of the most powerful scenes in the play, Asia interrogates Demogorgon, and rehearses Prometheus's fate and achievements as benefactor of mankind. Demogorgon can be seen as the force of historical necessity – Shelley's belief in the inevitable overthrow of tyranny by the forces of liberation – and the 'people monster' (Foot, p. 196), the embodiment of those forces. Shelley's conviction about the historical inevitability of oppression's downfall can be seen in his 'Fragment on Reform': 'The distribution of wealth no less than the spirit by which it is upheld and that by which it is assailed render the event inevitable. Call it reform or revolution, as you will, a change must take place, one of the consequences of which will be the wresting of political power from those who are at present the depositories of it' (Clark, p. 261). In response to Asia's insistence that she pierce the veil which hides the source of power and oppression, Demogorgon is forced to acknowledge that love is the only quality free of enslavement and he unveils the Spirit of the Hour in which Jupiter will be overthrown. Ironically, in Act 3 Demogorgon reveals himself to be the banished child of Jupiter, destined to overthrow him, the secret which Prometheus had known but had forgotten with his original curse. Locked together in the cyclical violence of tyrant against rebel, father against son, 'The conqueror and the conquered' (Act 3, 3, 78; p. 486), Jupiter and Demogorgon hurtle into the void. Act 3 then becomes a celebratory invocation of renewal for the earth and human-ity, ending with the Spirit of the Hour's panegyric to liberation, which envisages society and human psychology transformed:

> And behold, thrones were kingless, and men walked
> One with the other even as spirits do,
> None fawned, none trampled; hate, disdain, or fear,
> Self-love or self-contempt, on human brows
> No more inscribed.
>
> [Act 3, 4, 131–5; p. 287]

Shelley completed the first three acts of the play by April 1819, but returned to it later that year to add a fourth act which is a mystical song of the renewed cosmos, drawing out elements he had inserted into the original conception in order to broaden its implications. This act lacks the immedi-ate grounding in history and human psychology of the first three, replacing it with some intensely lyrical, yet scientifically inspired, speculations on the nature of the cosmos. A lot of the detailed imagery in Act 4 is enlivened and given substance for the reader by an awareness of such elements, all of them fully annotated in the Everest and Matthews edition. Nevertheless, it contains some remarkable writing, such as Panthea's vision of the over-throw of the accoutrements of powerful civilisations (lines 270–318; pp. 299–300), Earth's speech on the contradictions in humanity (lines 370–423; pp. 301–3), and the famous ending (quoted by Vaughan Williams in the last movement of his *Synfonia Antartica*), in which Demogorgon reminds the congregated celebrants how to reassert freedom should the forces of tyranny ever escape in the future. *Prometheus Unbound* is an extraordinarily varied work both in its subject-matter and in the profusion of verse forms which Shelley incorporates with such remarkable fluidity.

Peter Bell the Third (extracts)

Shelley described this satirical attack on Wordsworth as a 'party squib' (Jones, Vol. 2, p. 135), lamenting that 'perhaps no one will believe in anything in the shape of a joke from me' (Jones, Vol. 2, p. 164). Undoubtedly, despite his ironic self-description as 'rather serious' in the portrait of Julian in 'Julian and Maddalo' (p. 206), Shelley did have a lively sense of humour, expressed more directly in his life perhaps than his writing. *Peter Bell the Third* is hardly his best verse writing, being laboured at times, but it has a madcap wit that offsets the virulent satire of social hypocrisy and political corruption. Shelley saw Wordsworth, like Napoleon, as having betrayed his youthful radicalism (see the sonnets addressed to each of them, pp. 120, 124). In this poem he adopts the satirical manner of his friend Byron, whose own incendiary *The Vision of Judgement* (1821) attacked Southey and the Lake Poets with a comic brilliance Shelley hardly matches.

The occasion for Shelley's poem was the publication of Wordsworth's *Peter Bell* (1819) as well as a parody and savage review of it in Leigh Hunt's *The Examiner*. Shelley's Peter is a sarcastic composite sketch of Wordsworth and his associates, Coleridge and Southey, which speaks for itself. The later parts of the poem went on to attack Wordsworth for selling his poetic status for a state sinecure, writing poems which are 'the ghosts of what they were', with the result that the reviews which 'heaped abuse/On Peter, while he wrote for freedom', now praise him as he 'soothes Tyranny' (line 612–22). In the sections printed here, Peter has become the Devil's placeman inhabiting a London which is itself represented as a corrupt inferno.

POEMS FROM 1820

January   Moves to Pisa.

Spring   *The Cenci* published.

Summer   At Baths of San Giuliano, near Pisa; 'The Cloud'; 'The Sensitive Plant'; 'The Witch of Atlas'; 'To a Skylark'; 'Ode to Liberty'; *Oedipus Tyrannus, or Swellfoot the Tyrant.*

July   'Letter to Maria Gisborne'.

September   *Prometheus Unbound . . . with Other Poems* published.

Autumn   Pisa; meets Emilia Viviani.

December   *Oedipus Tyrannus, or Swellfoot the Tyrant* published and suppressed.

Shelley has a love of the fantastical, fantasy, even whimsy throughout his career, and perhaps in reaction to the political engagement and disappointment of 1819, the following year sees him produce two of his most whimsical poems, 'Letter to Maria Gisborne' and 'The Witch of Atlas'. It also finds him writing another of his most famous poems, 'To a Skylark'.

'To a Skylark'

This is one of a number of great poems from this period which use a bird as the vehicle for poetic exploration and as a correlative for the poetic process itself. Unlike Keats's brilliantly sluggish 'Ode to a Nightingale', Shelley's 'To a Skylark' is an urgent, active poem, in subject and effects. It transforms the reader's consciousness through its language, and demonstrates its message in the process, providing an enactment of the activity of the imagination. Like Keats with his nightingale, Shelley sees the skylark as elusive, to be sought for. But Keats's pursuit of the nightingale goes downwards into the half-light and eventually fails, that sense of lost vision being the subject of the poem, whereas the skylark is striven after upwards, with physical and intellectual energy. 'To a Skylark' is an uplifting poem, literally: it elevates the reader through its insistent imagining, in the energetic language of simile and metaphor, of the bird's flight – 'Higher still and higher', a line which itself contains a crafty linguistic paradox with the inclusion of 'still'.

In *A Defence of Poetry*, Shelley argues that the language of poetry is 'vitally metaphoric' (p. 635), and this poem demonstrates that linguistic vitality by making the abstract appear concrete. In the opening verses, Shelley addresses the noise of the skylark, since the bird itself is literally unseen and unseeable. Skylarks have a characteristic method of display and of distracting potential predators from their nests: they nest on the ground, so the small skylark flies strenuously high into the air warbling wildly as it goes in an unbroken melody which it produces through both in and out breaths, until it disappears, blending into the sky; and all that is left is the cascading notes of its song. So Shelley hails the bird not as a material being at all, but as a 'spirit', full of joy ('blithe'); in touch with heaven; and singing wildly with 'unpremeditated art' (p. 469), like an inspired poet.

Already, all the key elements of the symbolism are suggested: the bird embodies the spirit of inspiration, joy, idealism, aspiration, the human striving after something higher – art, vision, liberty, freedom. But as the next few verses suggest, these are qualities which seem out of reach, like the bird; they are no longer tangible in the material world – they seem to have disappeared, and if he is to make contact with them again, Shelley must make a strenuous effort to rise up like the bird. The images suggest both the insubstantiality of the bird and the felt, tangible presence of its influence through its song. And by analogy, all those things that the bird might embody – joy, inspiration, freedom – may seem to have vanished, but are nevertheless rediscoverable.

How? Through the imagination. As Shelley says at the opening of verse 7:

'What thou art we know not; / What is most like thee?' (p. 470). We no longer have a material sense of the bird and what it represents; so we have to use the imagination to invent similes and metaphors for what it is like. Hence, in the next section of the poem, Shelley develops some extraordinary figurative descriptions of this elusive bird-spirit, making its abstractness concrete. It is 'Like a Poet hidden / In the light of thought' (p. 470), an extraordinary notion. How can someone 'hide' in 'light'? And yet we talk of a 'blinding light', so powerful we cannot see. So 'thought' it seems is similarly blindingly powerful when inspired; and since we cannot *see* the bird but can *hear* its beautiful music, the analogy seems utterly appropriate – and illuminating!

For the rest of the poem, Shelley struggles after the bird through his urgent strenuous language, with its insistent similes – 'Like . . . like . . . like' – cascading images as the bird cascades its song: images of light (verses 7, 8, 10), music (verse 9), scent (verse 11), sound (verse 12). The language enacts the unpremeditated art of the bird: the words come seemingly unbidden and unstoppable, and overflow, until they themselves seem 'too much', like the scent of the rose in verse 11 (p. 470).

At this point, Shelley plays a masterly stroke. These increasingly frantic verbal equivalents reveal how his images cannot match up to the elusive truth he is trying to reach. Compared to the bird, hymns and chants, the arts of human beings, are 'an empty vaunt' (verse 14; p. 471). The human world itself is inadequate and cannot encompass the ideals embodied in the bird, just as the increasingly urgent language can't finally capture the bird, no matter how many 'likes' Shelley employs. As in Coleridge's *Kubla Khan*, the vision eludes the poet, and there is a sense of dislocation. In *Kubla Khan*, Coleridge has to resign his position as the 'I' of the poem, becoming one of the onlookers gazing in awe at 'him', the inspired and dangerous visionary. In his ending, Shelley achieves an equally remarkable turnaround: he surrenders the superiority of his art to that of the bird, and speaks as if the very poem we have just read were as yet non-existent:

> Teach me half the gladness
> That thy brain must know,
> Such harmonious madness
> From my lips would flow
> The world would listen then – as I am listening now.
>
> [p. 472]

Just as Shelley has been hypnotised by the bird's song, so we as readers or listeners have been hypnotised by the poet's. We are the future 'then' listening to his still-present 'now', despite the fact that he has been dust these one hundred and eighty years. It is a strange and powerful effect.

'Letter to Maria Gisborne'

This verse-letter was written while Shelley was staying at the home of the Gisbornes while they visited London to help find their son Henry a job as an engineer. While addressed to Maria, it is obviously written for the whole family to read. It declares its own inadequacies overtly at times, at one point giving up on a subject as 'Too vast a matter for so weak a rhyme' (p. 435). But this self-admission and the occasional nature of the poem lend it an endearing quality, whilst its whimsical wandering style makes it one of Shelley's most engagingly humane productions: we get close to the tangible and playful meanderings of his mind at work in the manner of Coleridge's conversation poems. That manner is established in the initial invocation which pictures Shelley as a spider weaving a web (the poem) which might catch the love and remembrance of his absent friends. The poem proper then begins as a inventory of the bizarre scientific clutter of Henry's study, whose strange contents astonish even Shelley, reminding him, among other things, of outlandish engines of torture. It then takes in reflections on the recent revolution in Spain, moves on to list the virtues of mutual friends, and ends with a catalogue of the delights Shelley will offer his friends next year in Italy, making the poem itself a kind of 'harmonious disarray' (p. 435) similar to that described on Henry's desk or the 'philosophic revel' (p. 441) Shelley envisages entertaining his guests with in the future.

'The Witch of Atlas'

Harold Bloom made a strong case for 'The Witch of Atlas' as 'Shelley's most inventive poem' (Bloom, p. xxxiii). Nevertheless, it is a poem difficult to analyse since in some ways it embodies the irrepressible transgressive whimsy of the imagination, perhaps a product of the sheer speed of writing since Shelley composed it in a mere two days. In addition to the activities described in the poem, the Witch plays 'pranks' (p. 463) which are so extraordinary that, having revealed as much, the poem refuses to divulge them and ends by saving the rest for another time:

> A tale more fit for the weird winter nights
> Than for these garish summer days, when we
> Scarcely believe much more than we can see.   [p. 463]

This ending is appropriately double-edged: it asserts that the broad light of reason allows no space for the imagination, and at the same time asserts that what we *do* see in the material world is in itself so amazing that we need no further wonders and have no use for illusion or fantasy. With characteristic brio, in her book *Sexual Personae*, Camille Paglia puts an intriguing spin on the hermaphrodite character as an emblem of 'sexual duality' (Paglia, p. 367). As the dedicatory poem reveals, Mary Shelley was less than impressed by her husband's latest visionary meanderings.

'The Sensitive Plant'

'The Sensitive Plant' is one of Shelley's strangest poems, a surreal nightmare in a ballad-like quatrain, which allows him to indulge his Gothic imagination to the full. It was written in the spring of 1820 in the aftermath of the extraordinary autumn of 1819 in which he attempted to intervene in contemporary politics with *The Mask of Anarchy* only to find his efforts thwarted. Not surprisingly then, this is a grim fable of defeated idealism and indeed of the dangers of idealism. The sensitive plant itself is an ambiguous emblem, 'companionless' (p. 423) in a paradisal garden, the description of which stresses the mutual and sensual interconnectedness of all the plants. It is also 'feeblest and yet the favourite' (p. 426) plant. Equally ambiguous is the attendant Lady to this Eden, who like the sensitive plant has 'no companion' (p. 427). Her over-idealistic mission of care leads her to cleanse the garden by banishing 'all killing insects and gnawing worms,/And things of obscene and unlovely forms' (p. 427); and having completed her task, she dies with the suddenness of Coleridge's albatross in his own surreal Gothic ballad *The Rime of the Ancient Mariner*. The third part sees the garden itself become 'cold and foul,/Like the corpse of her who had been its soul' (p. 429), Shelley's imagination delighting in the descriptions of loathsome decay as the creepy-crawlies come back with a vengeance and the garden corrupts into the most grotesque and horrible state. It is a remarkable tale, resonant with possible meanings. A contemporary view might see it as embodying the Freudian 'return of the repressed', in which the unconscious inevitably finds ways of erupting into our supposedly safe, sane normality. But equally Shelley makes plain in his conclusion to the poem that the paradisal garden was an emblem of perfection, an ideal which may have gone disastrously wrong but nevertheless remains – what has changed is us, not the ideals. Perhaps the Lady's strenuously idealistic attempt to purify the garden was itself a kind of tyranny, akin to Saint-Just's 'Republic of Virtue' (Marcus, p. 350), an attempt to enforce ideals and harmony. The shades of the French Revolution suggested here are reinforced by the image of winter's 'manacles' (p. 431).

POEMS FROM 1821

Early   Epipsychidion (published anonymously in May); meets Mr and Mrs Edward Williams ('Jane').

February–March   Writes *A Defence of Poetry*.

Apri   Lerici. Receives news of Keats's death.

Summer   Baths of San Giuliano.

May–June   Writes *Adonais* (published July); *Queen Mab* (pirated edition) published.

August   Travels to Ravenna; meets Byron. Writes *Hellas*.

Epipsychidion

Epipsychidion is an ardent love poem which paradoxically advocates free love (p. 493) and at the same time celebrates an exclusive and purely imaginary symbiotic union with one unattainable beloved. Its contradictoriness is probably partly a result of its origins. Shelley wrote the poem after meeting and, with Mary, taking some interest in the nineteen-year-old Emilia Viviani, the Emily of the poem. The daughter of the governor of Pisa, she was confined to a convent by her tyrannical father until her arranged marriage. Shelley instructed his publisher to print the poem anonymously with the peculiar prefatory advertisement, which describes the poem as the work of a non-existent deceased writer, a strategy which Shelley later described as 'no fiction' since the poem was 'a production of a portion of me already dead' (Jones, Vol. 2, pp. 262–3). He later described it as 'an idealised history of my life and feelings' (Jones, Vol. 2, p. 434). The poem depicts the male pursuit of an ideal woman, a fantasy-like figure like Thomas Hardy's 'Well-Beloved', a soul-mate who is an *alter ego*, the 'epi-psychidion' or 'soul of my soul' of the title. It indulges an excess of aspiration and desire while at the same time the very excess itself speaks of impossibility. The island paradise in the last section of the poem to which Shelley wishes Emily to sail with him is self-declaringly imaginary in its extremes of beauty – 'Beautiful as a wreck of Paradise', 'echoes of an antenatal dream' (pp. 500–1). It is an impossibly ideal utopia, like Andrew Marvell's ornately imaginary paradises in 'The Garden' or 'Bermudas', and Shelley transfers the desire for Emily on to the eroticised descriptions of this interweaving, intermixing, interpenetrating landscape:

> the isle's beauty, like a naked bride
> Glowing at once with love and loveliness
> Blushes and trembles at its own excess.   [p. 501]

This vision embodies an excess of self-consolation for the evident fact that, as the conclusion reveals, the desired love is impossible to consummate. As the poet's final address to his own creation reveals, all he really has is his imagination, his art, his words.

Adonais

Shelley had invited Keats to stay with him in Italy; but on his way, via Rome, Keats died in February 1821. When he found out two months later, Shelley began this poem. As with *Laon and Cythna*, the stanza form is modelled on Edmund Spenser's *The Faerie Queene*, and the effect of the longer last line is to create a mournful elegiac feeling absolutely fitting for this work in the tradition of pastoral elegy, looking back to the 'Elegy on the Death of Adonis' by the first-century-BC Greek poet Bion, which Shelley had translated in 1820. The almost obsessive quality of the lament and the intensive awareness of the processes of death in the first part of the poem culminate in the speech by Urania, from verses 25–9 (pp. 514–15), with its bleak view of the transitoriness of human life as being like that of ephemeral insects. This mood changes in the following stanzas, which recount various supportive responses to Keats and retaliations against the hostile reviews Shelley cites in his Preface as causing his death. Then from stanza 39 (p. 517), with 'He has outsoared the shadow of our night', the poem itself gradually soars to an antithetical mood of celebration, transforming the bleakness into a deeper sense of acceptance and continuing inspiration.

'Evening: Ponte Al Mare, Pisa'

Richard Holmes calls this beautifully simple piece a 'tone poem' enacting 'an interior landscape, an exact image of a human state of mind and spirit' (Holmes, p. 683). It is also an indication of an emerging capacity for starkness and spareness in Shelley's style, which was to achieve fuller expression in his final unfinished work 'The Triumph of Life' and perhaps hints at the direction in which his writing might have gone had he lived.

POEMS FROM 1822

1822 *January*   Meets Edward John Trelawny. Works on *Charles I*.
      Poems to Jane Williams begin.
      February   *Hellas* published.
      April   Moves to Bay of Spezia near Lerici.
      May–June   Writes 'The Triumph of Life'.
      July 1   Sails in his boat, *Don Juan*, with Williams to Livorno.
      July 8   Drowned with Williams on return voyage near Spezia.
      July 18   Body cast ashore near Viareggio.
      August 16   Body cremated.
      December 7   Burial of remains in Protestant Cemetery at Rome.
1824 *Posthumous Poems* published.
1832 *The Mask of Anarchy* published.
1847 First collected edition of works.

Lines: 'When the lamp is shattered'; 'To Jane: The Invitation'; 'To Jane: The Recollection'; 'With a Guitar, to Jane'; 'To Jane'; 'Lines Written in the Bay of Lerici'

These lyrics were written about Jane Williams at a point when Shelley's relationship with Mary was becoming more distanced and remote, a circumstance alluded to in the poems. They declare an idealised love which Shelley was safe from being able to enact since Jane was the devoted companion of Edward Williams, living as his wife and bearing his children. The poems express a complementary theme to the bleak 'The Triumph of Life': they celebrate momentary happiness in a way that epitomises the delusions the longer poem seeks to expose. As Shelley put it in a letter: 'Jane brings her guitar, and if the past and future could be obliterated, the present would content me so well that I could say with Faust to the present moment, "Remain, thou art so beautiful" ' (Jones, Vol. 2, p. 436). Whereas 'The Triumph of Life' shatters the illusion that such magic is possible, these endearing lyrics weave such vivid spells that the reader might at times almost believe it true.

'The Triumph of Life'

Shelley's final major poem was fittingly unfinished and breaks off abruptly as if its author had been snatched away in mid-sentence. That final incomplete line poses the question 'Then, what is Life?', followed by a few scraps and fragments, none of which hint at an answer. To the end Shelley was questing for knowledge with the sceptical intelligence he manifested throughout his career. 'The Triumph of Life' is a bleak visionary poem, written in a hard, uncompromising style stripped bare of all lyrical qualities. It takes its inspiration from Shelley's reading and translation of Dante. It uses the characteristic three-line stanza of the *terza rima* in a taut, sinewy manner suitable to the spare stark language. It also adopts a similar narrative structure to *The Divine Comedy*: there Dante as narrator is guided through his visions of hell by his mentor and master, the Latin poet Virgil; here, Shelley as narrator is led by the revolutionary Jean Jacques Rousseau. But it is indicative of the state of mind in which Shelley wrote this poem that, unlike Virgil in Dante's poem, Rousseau is not free from the hellish vision on which he provides commentary. He is revealed to be as much a victim of the macabre dance of life as the mad revelling crowd of deluded souls which flock self-destructively into the wake of Life's chariot as it drives in triumph through and over them, rather as Anarchy rides over the 'adoring multitude' in *The Mask of Anarchy* (p. 388). This 'triumph' is a cruel assertion of Life's dominance as a process over individual living beings which make it up, and it offers little consolation or cause for celebration. Caught in the mad frenzy of life in the present, the revelling but deluded maidens and youths seem ready to exult in their pleasure for ever, only to find themselves spewed out in the wake of Life's chariot as 'Old men and women foully disarrayed' (p. 543). It is a powerful expression of the relentlessness of the organic process of age, and of the contradictory sense of living in the moment as if in control of one's life, only to be catapulted through the years by the unstoppable whirlwind activity of time. Except for 'the sacred few' (p. 542) whose untameable spirits make them exempt from Life's triumph, the frenzy takes over all who come within its field of influence, catching up the great and insignificant alike, Napoleon, Voltaire, Frederick the Great, Catherine the Great – 'those spoilers spoiled' (p. 546), as Rousseau points out. He then reveals that he himself fell victim to the Bacchanalian carnival of Life, as an idealised female spirit offered him a drink which had the effect not of giving him an ideal transcendent vision but of turning his brain to 'sand' (p. 551) and sweeping him up into the multitude of doomed revellers. The true revelation seems to be not a celebration of the organic oneness of life but a stark realisation of the inescapability of that process, whatever ideals one might cherish.

The bleakness of Shelley's vision seems a distillation of all the bitter disappointments and tragedies that he and Mary suffered together and separately in their frenziedly brief seven years together, including, in the last months before his death, their increasing emotional separation and Mary's miscarriage (this being the fourth of their children to die), as well as the deaths of his sister-in-law's child by Lord Byron and of his own illegitimate child. What is remarkable is the 'cold eye' which he casts on this mad gaiety: it has something of the aloof tragedy verging on an absurdist awareness of life as inescapable mad farce which W. B. Yeats would bring to his work, but without Yeats's eventual comic acceptance. Its grim apocalyptic vision also has something in common with the bleak recognition of human futility in Wilfred Owen's 'Strange Meeting'.

PROSE

Shelley's prose is very varied and these samples represent some of the different aspects of his writings.

A Declaration of Rights

This pamphlet was written while in Dublin, which he visited with his first wife Harriet in 1812 intent on stimulating the Irish people into revolt against the yoke of British colonial occupation. Shelley composed the piece as a broadside to be posted on walls or distributed by hand. It summarises the main arguments of his longer pamphlet *An Address to the Irish People*.

A Letter to Lord Ellenborough

This is one of Shelley's most crisp assertions of the freedom of the press and speech as well as a rehearsal of the arguments on the illiberality and inconsistencies of Christianity and organised religion. It was occasioned by the arrest and trial of Daniel Eaton, a liberal London bookseller and publisher, on 6 March 1812 for publishing works by Tom Paine. Eaton was sentenced by Lord Ellenborough to the pillory and eighteen months imprisonment.

A Vindication of Natural Diet

Shelley became a vegetarian in 1812 and remained one for the rest of his life. Arguments for vegetarianism were current at the time, and Shelley refers to some of them and uses others. This essay also formed the substance for the last note to *Queen Mab*, where he adds a paragraph accepting that diet was not the only cause of mental and physical debilities. While Shelley makes no promise of 'Utopian advantages' (p. 575) for vegetarianism, his writings on diet have often provoked unjustly dismissive attitudes.

An Address to the People on the Death of the Princess Charlotte

Princess Charlotte, daughter of the despised Prince Regent, died on 6 November 1817 in childbirth, and this became the occasion for Shelley's most incisive political pamphlet. Charlotte was seen as more sympathetic towards reform than either her degenerate father or her mad grandfather, George III. Her death coincided with the judicial murder of three poor labourers, Jeremy Brandreth (a self-educated Baptist), Isaac Ludlam (a Methodist preacher) and William Turner (an independent stonemason), who had been tried for high treason because of their involvement in protests against rural poverty. But their insurrection had also been stimulated by a government spy, Oliver, while the jury for the trial was hand-picked by the authorities and the prisoners had been kept on remand with only bread and water. After conviction they were hung publicly and quartered. In some of his most powerful prose, Shelley uses the response to the deaths as a spring-board for arguing the urgency of political and economic reform.

A Philosophical View of Reform

Towards the end of 1819, in the aftermath of the Peterloo massacre and the contradictory poems of revolution and lament, Shelley began writing his greatest political essay, which was destined to languish unpublished until 1920. Unfinished as it is, 'A Philosophical View of Reform' is nevertheless the most impressive piece of political prose by any of the Romantic poets. Far from being of merely historical interest, its arguments still have relevance. Shelley gives his most extensive expression of radical principles and also displays a remarkable grasp of historical processes in the survey of social and political change past and present. More significantly, he explores how change might be achieved in England and offers a programme for it. As if that were not enough, he also gives us his subtle view of the relationships between literature and politics, something he returns to in his most famous essay, A Defence of Poetry, which adapted sections from this essay.

A Defence of Poetry

A Defence of Poetry was written in 1821, though not published until 1840. It began life as a light-hearted reply to Shelley's friend Thomas Love Peacock, who had written a humorous essay called 'The Four Ages of Poetry', in which he dismissed poetry's claims to importance. Shelley's reply soon outstripped its original jocular note and became an expression of his belief in the value and function of poetry.

One modern element in the essay is Shelley's keen sense of the inter-relationships between society and culture. He demonstrates the ways in which literature changes in relation to changing societies. But throughout he asserts a continuity of function for poetry and the poet. Poetry's function is to improve the human condition, but not through didacticism or tub-thumping proclamations. In his Preface to *Prometheus Unbound*, he had stated categorically that 'it is a mistake to suppose that I dedicate my poetical compositions solely to the direct enforcement of reform [. . .] Didactic poetry is my abhorrence' (p. 228). Of course, he does write about specific issues and events, and in this sense he does see the poet as critic of society's ills. But he also sees poetry as working through a process of consciousness-raising. Poems, he says in his Dedication to *The Cenci*, are 'visions which impersonate [. . .] the beautiful and the just' (p. 309); they are 'Eternity warning Time', as he puts it in 'A Philosophical View of Reform' (p. 632). Poems work by exhibiting ideal truths which might enlarge the individual's capacity for empathy, love and compassion.

In the Preface to *Prometheus Unbound*, he states this intent rather problematically: 'My purpose has hitherto been simply to familiarize the highly refined imagination of the more select classes of poetical readers with beautiful idealisms of moral excellence.' (p. 228) This formulation is problematic because of its élitism. In 'A Defence of Poetry' he is more subtle and extensive: 'to be a poet is to apprehend the true and the beautiful, in a word, the good' (p. 637). Poets, he argues, are 'those who imagine and express this indestructible order' of the beautiful and the good, the potential ideal perfection to which human beings aspire. They are, therefore, 'the institutors of laws, and the founders of civil society'. The poet combines and unites the role of prophet with that of legislator: 'For he not only beholds intensely the present as it is, and discovers those laws according to which present things ought to be ordered, but he beholds the future in the present' (p. 637). Similarly, in his Introduction to *Songs of Experience,* William Blake presents the Bard as the prophetic visionary who sees 'Present, Past and Future' (Woodcock, pp. 58, 74). For both writers, the poet has a transformative function: he sees the present 'as it is' and measures its deficiencies by comparison to an ideal, Blake's 'innocence' or Shelley's 'laws according to which present things ought to be ordered'. This dialectic between present and past, experience and innocence, simultaneously avoids cynicism and leads to a vision of future possibilities.

But how does this visionary function actually work? Not simply through argument or having a message, 'for [poetry] acts in a divine and un-apprehended manner, beyond and above consciousness' (pp. 640–1): gradually, '[i]t awakens and enlarges the mind itself by rendering it the receptacle of a thousand unapprehended combinations of thought. Poetry lifts the veil from the hidden beauty of the world, and makes familiar objects be as if they were not familiar' (p. 642). Poetry defamiliarises the world and expands the mind because its language is 'vitally metaphorical; that is, it marks the before unapprehended relations of things' (p. 637). Metaphor is the most energised element in poetic figurative language, more powerful than simile: instead of hypothesising 'this is *like* that', it states 'this *is* that'. So, in the example from 'The Sensitive Plant' (p. 423), Shelley doesn't say that dreams and the unconscious are like an ocean; he says they *are* an ocean; and the effect is more dynamic.

In other words, poetry makes life fresh by the use of the imagination. And, at this point, Shelley makes explicit how poetry can bring about social improvement:

> The great secret of morals is love; or a going out of our own nature, and an identification of ourselves with the beautiful which exists in thought, action, or person, not our own. A man, to be greatly good, must imagine intensely and comprehensively; he must put himself in the place of another and of many others [. . .] The great instrument of moral good is the imagination; and poetry administers to the effect by acting upon the cause. Poetry enlarges the circumference of the imagination [. . .] Poetry strengthens the faculty which is the organ of the moral nature of man, in the same manner as exercise strengthens a limb.   [p. 642]

Poetry cultivates the imagination, the faculty through which we achieve compassionate empathy with the rest of humanity. Here, Shelley reveals 'the connection of poetry and social good' (p. 646): it 'contains within itself the seeds [. . .] of social renovation' (p. 647).

This line of argument allows Shelley to end his essay with the magnificent claim that 'Poets are the unacknowledged legislators of the world' (p. 660): 'legislators' because they frame the ideal laws for human perfection and urge society towards them by the exercise of imagination and compassion; 'unacknowledged' because not only does society not recognise their true worth, neither do most poets! The idea of poets as prophets and legislators was familiar and can be found in George Puttenham's *The Arte of English Poesie* (1589), while Sir Philip Sidney pointed out in his *Defence of Poesie* (1595) that the Roman term for poet was *vates*, meaning 'a diviner, fore-seer or prophet'. Shelley's singular insight was to realise they are 'unacknowledged' both by their time and by themselves, that indeed writers can contribute to progressive history *despite* their own views or political tendencies. They speak 'words which express what they understand not' (p. 660): in other words poetry transcends the poet, and its progressive capacities are not to be measured by the limited views of the human being who created it. This allows for a very modern sense that there are often contradictions between the poem and the poet: a reactionary poet might well produce work which is capable of being read as progressive; while out of the many contradictions and tragedies of his own life, Shelley himself created 'visions which impersonate [. . .] the beautiful and the just' (p. 309).

BRUCE WOODCOCK
The University of Hull

BIBLIOGRAPHY

Editions

I am immensely indebted to the following in the preparation of this edition:

Harold Bloom (ed.), *Percy Bysshe Shelley: Selected Poetry*, Signet, New York 1966

David Lee Clark (ed.), *Shelley's Prose or The Trumpet of a Prophecy*, University of New Mexico, Albuquerque 1954

Kelvin Everest and Geoffrey Matthews (eds), *The Poems of Shelley, Volume 2 1817–1819*, Longman, London 2000

Paul Foot, *Shelley's Revolutionary Year*, Redwords, London 1990

A. S. B. Glover (ed.), *Shelley: Selected Poetry, Prose and Letters* Nonesuch, London 1951

F. L. Jones (ed.), *The Letters of Percy Bysshe Shelley*, 2 vols, Oxford University Press, Oxford 1964

Geoffrey Matthews and Kelvin Everest (eds), *The Poems of Shelley, Volume 1 1804–1817*, Longman, London 1989

Donald H. Reiman and Sharon B. Powers (eds), *Shelley's Poetry and Prose*, Norton, New York 1977

Secondary Reading

Paul Foot, *Red Shelley*, Sidgwick and Jackson, London 1980 – lively treatment of Shelley and politics

Richard Holmes, *Shelley: The Pursuit*, Quartet, London 1976 – brilliant and utterly engrossing biography, with excellent coverage of the poems – indispensable

Juliet Mitchell and Jacqueline Rose, *Feminine Sexuality: Jacques Lacan and the école freudienne*, Macmillan, London 1982

M. O'Neill (ed.), *Shelley*, Longman, London 1993 – collection of essays using more recent theoretical approaches

Camille Paglia, *Sexual Personae: Art and Decadence from Nefertiti to Emily Dickinson*, Penguin, Harmondsworth 1990

William St Clair, *The Godwins and the Shelleys: The Biography of a Family*, Faber, London 1989 – excellent examination of the relationships between them

R. B. Woodings (ed.), *Shelley: Modern Judgements*, Macmillan, London 1968 – collection of critical essays: see especially M. Wojcik, 'In Defence of Shelley', G. M. Matthews, 'A Volcano's Voice in Shelley' and K. N. Cameron, 'The Political Symbolism of *Prometheus Unbound*'

Background Reading

Marilyn Butler, *Romantics, Rebels and Reactionaries: English Literature and its Background 1760–1830*, Oxford University Press, Oxford 1981

Eric Hobsbawm, *The Age of Revolution: Europe 1789–1848*, Sphere, London 1977 – an excellent single-volume history

Greil Marcus, *Lipstick Traces: A Secret History of the Twentieth Century*, Secker and Warburg, London 1989

Simon Schama, *Citizens: A Chronicle of the French Revolution*, Viking, London 1989 –a remarkably vivid account

E. P. Thompson, *The Making of the English Working Class*, Penguin, Harmondsworth 1991 – classic historical recovery of this period

Bruce Woodcock and John Coates, *Combative Styles: Romantic Writing and Ideology*, University of Hull Press, Hull 1988 – contrasts the varied writings of Paine, Burke, Blake and De Quincey

Bruce Woodcock, *The Selected Poems of William Blake*, Wordsworth, Herts 2000 – uniform with this edition

Websites

Complete Poetry – ongoing annotated edition edited by Donald Reiman and Neil Freistat:
http://www.rc.umd.edu/editions/shelley/devil/CPPBS.html

Complete Poetical Works – old edition with no notes, but complete:
http://www.bartleby.com/139/

Shelley's Revolutionary Year – Paul Foot's essay from the above edition:
   http://www.fonseca.demon.co.uk/redwords/pages/shelleyintro.html

Shelley Resource Page:
   http://www.wam.umd.edu/~djb/shelley/home.html

The Shelley Chronology:
   http://www.rc.umd.edu/cstahmer/shelcron/

ACKNOWLEDGEMENTS

Immense thanks are due to Keith Carabine (series editor), Owen Knowles, John Hoyles and Les Garry for their invaluable corrections, suggestions and advice.

Contents

POEMS FROM 1818

POEMS FROM 1819

POEMS FROM 1820

POEMS FROM 1821

POEMS FROM 1822

PROSE

The Selected Poems & Prose of Shelley

POEMS FROM 1812–13

Queen Mab

A PHILOSOPHICAL POEM, WITH NOTES*

Ecrasez l'infame!   *Correspondance de Voltaire*

Avia Pieridum peragro loca, nullius ante
Trita solo; juvat integros accedere fonteis;
Atque haurire: juvatque novos decerpere flores.

* * *

Unde prius nulli velarint tempora musae
Primum quod magnis doceo de rebus; et arctis
Religionum animos nodis exsolvere pergo.

Lucretius, lib. iv

Δος που στω, και κοσμον κινησω.   *Archimedes*[1]

To Harriet — [2]

Whose is the love that, gleaming through the world,
Wards off the poisonous arrow of its scorn?
   Whose is the warm and partial praise,
   Virtue's most sweet reward?

Beneath whose looks did my reviving soul
Riper in truth and virtuous daring grow?
   Whose eyes have I gazed fondly on,
   And loved mankind the more?

Harriet! on thine: – thou wert my purer mind;
Thou wert the inspiration of my song;   10
   Thine are these early wilding flowers,
   Though garlanded by me.

Then press unto thy breast this pledge of love,
And know, though time may change and years may roll,
   Each flow'ret gathered in my heart
   It consecrates to thine.

* Lines on which Shelley comments in his Notes on pp. 66–97 are marked with an asterisk.

I

How wonderful is Death,
  Death and his brother Sleep!
One, pale as yonder waning moon
  With lips of lurid blue;
The other, rosy as the morn
  When throned on ocean's wave
  It blushes o'er the world:
Yet both so passing wonderful!

  Hath then the gloomy Power
Whose reign is in the tainted sepulchres   10
  Seized on her sinless soul?
  Must then that peerless form
Which love and admiration cannot view
Without a beating heart, those azure veins
Which steal like streams along a field of snow,
  That lovely outline, which is fair
    As breathing marble, perish?
    Must putrefaction's breath
  Leave nothing of this heavenly sight
    But loathsomeness and ruin?   20
  Spare nothing but a gloomy theme,
On which the lightest heart might moralise'?
  Or is it only a sweet slumber
    Stealing o'er sensation,
  Which the breath of roseate morning
    Chaseth into darkness?
    Will Ianthe wake again,
  And give that faithful bosom joy
  Whose sleepless spirit waits to catch
Light, life and rapture from her smile?   30

    Yes! she will wake again,
Although her glowing limbs are motionless,
    And silent those sweet lips,
    Once breathing eloquence
  That might have soothed a tiger's rage,

Or thawed the cold heart of a conqueror.
    Her dewy eyes are closed,
And on their lids, whose texture fine
Scarce hides the dark blue orbs beneath,   40
    The baby Sleep is pillowed:
    Her golden tresses shade
    The bosom's stainless pride,
    Curling like tendrils of the parasite
        Around a marble column.

    Hark! whence that rushing sound?
    'Tis like the wondrous strain
That round a lonely ruin swells,
Which, wandering on the echoing shore,
    The enthusiast hears at evening:
'Tis softer than the west wind's sigh;   50
'Tis wilder than the unmeasured notes
Of that strange lyre[3] whose strings
The genii of the breezes sweep:
    Those lines of rainbow light
Are like the moonbeams when they fall
Through some cathedral window, but the teints
    Are such as may not find
    Comparison on earth.

Behold the chariot of the Fairy Queen!
Celestial coursers paw the unyielding air;   60
Their filmy pennons at her word they furl,
And stop obedient to the reins of light:
    These the Queen of spells drew in,
    She spread a charm around the spot,
And leaning graceful from the ethereal car,
    Long did she gaze, and silently.
        Upon the slumbering maid.

Oh! not the visioned poet in his dreams,
When silvery clouds float through the wildered brain,
When every sight of lovely, wild and grand   70
    Astonishes, enraptures, elevates,
        When fancy at a glance combines

The wondrous and the beautiful, –
So bright, so fair, so wild a shape
   Hath ever yet beheld,
As that which reined the coursers of the air,
   And poured the magic of her gaze
     Upon the maiden's sleep.

   The broad and yellow moon
   Shone dimly through her form –   80
That form of faultless symmetry;
The pearly and pellucid car
   Moved not the moonlight's line:
   'Twas not an earthly pageant:
Those who had looked upon the sight,
   Passing all human glory,
   Saw not the yellow moon,
   Saw not the mortal scene,
   Heard not the night-wind's rush,
   Heard not an earthly sound,   90
   Saw but the fairy pageant,
   Heard but the heavenly strains
   That filled the lonely dwelling.

The Fairy's frame was slight, yon fibrous cloud,
That catches but the palest tinge of even,
And which the straining eye can hardly seize
When melting into eastern twilight's shadow,
Were scarce so thin, so slight; but the fair star
That gems the glittering coronet of morn
Sheds not a light so mild, so powerful,   100
As that which, bursting from the Fairy's form,
Spread a purpureal halo round the scene,
   Yet with an undulating motion,
   Swayed to her outline gracefully.

   From her celestial car
   The Fairy Queen descended,
   And thrice she waved her wand
Circled with wreaths of amaranth:
   Her thin and misty form

Moved with the moving air.   110
    And the clear silver tones,
        As thus she spoke, were such
As are unheard by all but gifted ear.

Fairy

    Stars! your balmiest influence shed!
    Elements! your wrath suspend!
    Sleep, Ocean, in the rocky bounds
        That circle thy domain!
    Let not a breath be seen to stir
    Around yon grass-grown ruin's height.
        Let even the restless gossamer   120
            Sleep on the moveless air!
            Soul of Ianthe! thou,
Judged alone worthy of the envied boon
That waits the good and the sincere; that waits
Those who have struggled, and with resolute will
Vanquished earth's pride and meanness, burst the chains,
The icy chains of custom, and have shone
The day-stars of their age; – Soul of Ianthe!
            Awake! arise!

            Sudden arose   130
        Ianthe's Soul; it stood
All beautiful in naked purity,
The perfect semblance of its bodily frame,
Instinct with inexpressible beauty and grace.
        Each stain of earthliness
    Had passed away, it reassumed
    Its native dignity, and stood
            Immortal amid ruin.

    Upon the couch the body lay,
        Wrapt in the depth of slumber: 140
    Its features were fixed and meaningless,
        Yet animal life was there,
    And every organ yet performed
    Its natural functions; 'twas a sight
Of wonder to behold the body and soul.

  The self-same lineaments, the same
  Marks of identity were there:
Yet, oh, how different! One aspires to Heaven,
Pants for its sempiternal heritage,
And ever changing, ever rising still,   150
  Wantons in endless being.
The other, for a time the unwilling sport
Of circumstance and passion, struggles on;
Fleets through its sad duration rapidly:
Then, like an useless and worn-out machine,
  Rots, perishes, and passes.

Fairy

  Spirit! who hast dived so deep;
  Spirit! who hast soared so high;
  Thou the fearless, thou the mild,
Accept the boon thy worth hath earned,   160
  Ascend the car with me.

Spirit

Do I dream? Is this new feeling
  But a visioned ghost of slumber?
  If indeed I am a soul,
A free, a disembodied soul.
  Speak again to me.

Fairy

I am the Fairy MAB: to me 'tis given
The wonders of the human world to keep:
The secrets of the immeasurable past,
In the unfailing consciences of men,   170
Those stern, unflattering chroniclers, I find:
The future, from the causes which arise
In each event, I gather: not the sting
Which retributive memory implants
In the hard bosom of the selfish man;
Nor that ecstatic and exulting throb
Which virtue's votary feels when he sums up
The thoughts and actions of a well-spent day,
Are unforeseen, unregistered by me:

And it is yet permitted me, to rend   180
The veil of mortal frailty, that the spirit,
Clothed in its changeless purity, may know
How soonest to accomplish the great end
For which it hath its being, and may taste
That peace, which in the end all life will share.
This is the meed of virtue; happy Soul,
    Ascend the car with me!

  The chains of earth's immurement
    Fell from Ianthe's spirit;
They shrank and brake like bandages of straw   190
  Beneath a wakened giant's strength.
    She knew her glorious change,
  And felt in apprehension uncontrolled
    New raptures opening round:
  Each day-dream of her mortal life,
  Each frenzied vision of the slumbers
    That closed each well-spent day,
    Seemed now to meet reality.

  The Fairy and the Soul proceeded;
    The silver clouds disparted;   200
And as the car of magic they ascended,
  Again the speechless music swelled,
  Again the coursers of the air
Unfurled their azure pennons, and the Queen,
    Shaking the beamy reins,
    Bade them pursue their way.

  The magic car moved on.
  The night was fair, and countless stars
  Studded heaven's dark blue vault, –
    Just o'er the eastern wave   210
  Peeped the first faint smile of morn: –
    The magic car moved on –
    From the celestial hoofs
  The atmosphere in flaming sparkles flew,
    And where the burning wheels
  Eddied above the mountain's loftiest peak,

Was traced a line of lightning.
Now it flew far above a rock,
   The utmost verge of earth,
The rival of the Andes, whose dark brow   220
   Lowered o'er the silver sea.

Far, far below the chariot's path,
   Calm as a slumbering babe,
   Tremendous Ocean lay.
The mirror of its stillness showed
   The pale and waning stars,
   The chariot's fiery track,
   And the grey light of morn
   Tinging those fleecy clouds
   That canopied the dawn.   230
  Seemed it, that the chariot's way
Lay through the midst of an immense concave,
Radiant with million constellations, tinged
   With shades of infinite colour,
   And semicircled with a belt[4]
   Flashing incessant meteors.

The magic car moved on.
   As they approached their goal
The coursers seemed to gather speed;
The sea no longer was distinguished; earth   240
   Appeared a vast and shadowy sphere;
   The sun's unclouded orb
   Rolled through the black concave;*
   Its rays of rapid light
Parted around the chariot's swifter course,
  And fell, like ocean's feathery spray
   Dashed from the boiling surge
   Before a vessel's prow.

The magic car moved on.
   Earth's distant orb appeared   250
The smallest light that twinkles in the heaven;
   Whilst round the chariot's way
   Innumerable systems rolled,*

And countless spheres diffused
    An ever-varying glory.
  It was a sight of wonder: some
  Were horned like the crescent moon;
  Some shed a mild and silver beam
  Like Hesperus[5] o'er the western sea;
  Some dash'd athwart with trains of flame,   260
  Like worlds to death and ruin driven;
Some shone like suns, and, as the chariot passed,
    Eclipsed all other light.

    Spirit of Nature! here!
In this interminable wilderness
Of worlds, at whose immensity
    Even soaring fancy staggers,
    Here is thy fitting temple.
      Yet not the lightest leaf
That quivers to the passing breeze   270
      Is less instinct with thee:
      Yet not the meanest worm
That lurks in graves and fattens on the dead
    Less shares thy eternal breath.
      Spirit of Nature! thou!
      Imperishable as this scene,
        Here is thy fitting temple.

II

If solitude hath ever led thy steps
    To the wild ocean's echoing shore,
      And thou hast lingered there,
      Until the sun's broad orb
    Seemed resting on the burnished wave,
      Thou must have marked the lines
    Of purple gold, that motionless
      Hung o'er the sinking sphere:
    Thou must have marked the billowy clouds
    Edged with intolerable radiancy   10
      Towering like rocks of jet
      Crowned with a diamond wreath.

And yet there is a moment,
   When the sun's highest point
Peeps like a star o'er ocean's western edge,
When those far clouds of feathery gold,
   Shaded with deepest purple, gleam
   Like islands on a dark blue sea;
Then has thy fancy soared above the earth,
    And furled its wearied wing   20
   Within the Fairy's fane.

   Yet not the golden islands
   Gleaming in yon flood of light,
    Nor the feathery curtains
   Stretching o'er the sun's bright couch,
   Nor the burnished ocean waves
    Paving that gorgeous dome,
  So fair, so wonderful a sight
As Mab's ethereal palace could afford.
Yet likest evening's vault, that faery Hall!   30
As Heaven, low resting on the wave, it spread
    Its floors of flashing light,
    Its vast and azure dome,
    Its fertile golden islands
    Floating on a silver sea;
Whilst suns their mingling beamings darted
Through clouds of circumambient darkness,
   And pearly battlements around
   Looked o'er the immense of Heaven.

   The magic car no longer moved.   40
    The Fairy and the Spirit
    Entered the Hall of Spells:
     Those golden clouds
   That rolled in glittering billows
   Beneath the azure canopy
With the ethereal footsteps, trembled not:
    The light and crimson mists,
Floating to strains of thrilling melody
   Through that unearthly dwelling,
Yielded to every movement of the will.   50

Upon their passive swell the Spirit leaned,
And, for the varied bliss that pressed around,
   Used not the glorious privilege
    Of virtue and of wisdom.

    Spirit! the Fairy said,
  And pointed to the gorgeous dome,
    This is a wondrous sight
  And mocks all human grandeur;
But, were it virtue's only meed, to dwell
In a celestial palace, all resigned   60
To pleasurable impulses, immured
Within the prison of itself, the will
Of changeless nature would be unfulfilled.
Learn to make others happy. Spirit, come!
This is thine high reward: – the past shall rise;
Thou shalt behold the present; I will teach
    The secrets of the future.

    The Fairy and the Spirit
Approached the overhanging battlement. –
    Below lay stretched the universe!   70
    There, far as the remotest line
    That bounds imagination's flight,
     Countless and unending orbs
   In mazy motion intermingled,
   Yet still fulfilled immutably
     Eternal nature's law.
     Above, below, around
     The circling systems formed
   A wilderness of harmony;
   Each with undeviating aim,   80
In eloquent silence, through the depths of space
    Pursued its wondrous way.

    There was a little light
That twinkled in the misty distance:
    None but a spirit's eye
    Might ken that rolling orb;
    None but a spirit's eye,

                   And in no other place
But that celestial dwelling, might behold
Each action of this earth's inhabitants.   90
              But matter, space and time
In those aerial mansions cease to act;
And all-prevailing wisdom, when it reaps
The harvest of its excellence, o'erbounds
Those obstacles, of which an earthly soul
              Fears to attempt the conquest.

   The Fairy pointed to the earth.
   The Spirit's intellectual eye
   Its kindred beings recognised.
The thronging thousands, to a passing view,   100
   Seemed like an anthill's citizens.
              How wonderful! that even
The passions, prejudices, interests
That sway the meanest being, the weak touch
              That moves the finest nerve,
              And in one human brain
Causes the faintest thought, becomes a link
              In the great chain of nature.

              Behold, the Fairy cried,
Palmyra's[6] ruined palaces! –   110
              Behold! where grandeur frowned;
              Behold! where pleasure smiled;
What now remains? – the memory
              Of senselessness and shame –
              What is immortal there?
              Nothing – it stands to tell
              A melancholy tale, to give
              An awful warning: soon
Oblivion will steal silently
              The remnant of its fame.   120
       Monarchs and conquerors there
Proud o'er prostrate millions trod –
The earthquakes of the human race;
Like them, forgotten when the ruin
              That marks their shock is past.

Beside the eternal Nile,
  The Pyramids have risen.
Nile shall pursue his changeless way:
  Those pyramids shall fall;
Yea! not a stone shall stand to tell   130
  The spot whereon they stood!
Their very site shall be forgotten,
  As is their builder's name!

Behold yon sterile spot;
Where now the wandering Arab's tent
  Flaps in the desert-blast.
There once old Salem's haughty fane[7]
Reared high to heaven its thousand golden domes,
  And in the blushing face of day
    Exposed its shameful glory.   140
Oh! many a widow, many an orphan cursed
The building of that fane; and many a father,
Worn out with toil and slavery, implored
The poor man's God to sweep it from the earth,
And spare his children the detested task
Of piling stone on stone, and poisoning
    The choicest days of life,
    To soothe a dotard's vanity.
There an inhuman and uncultured race
Howled hideous praises to their Demon-God;   150
They rushed to war, tore from the mother's womb
The unborn child, – old age and infancy
Promiscuous perished; their victorious arms
Left not a soul to breathe. Oh! they were fiends:
But what was he who taught them that the God
Of nature and benevolence hath given
A special sanction to the trade of blood?
His name and theirs are fading, and the tales
Of this barbarian nation, which imposture
Recites till terror credits, are pursuing   160
  Itself into forgetfulness.

Where Athens, Rome, and Sparta stood,
There is a moral desert now:

The mean and miserable huts,
The yet more wretched palaces,
Contrasted with those ancient fanes,
Now crumbling to oblivion;
The long and lonely colonnades,
Through which the ghost of Freedom stalks,
    Seem like a well-known tune,   170
Which in some dear scene we have loved to hear,
    Remembered now in sadness.
    But, oh! how much more changed,
    How gloomier is the contrast
    Of human nature there!
Where Socrates expired, a tyrant's slave,
A coward and a fool, spreads death around –
    Then, shuddering, meets his own.
Where Cicero and Antoninus[8] lived,
    A cowled and hypocritical monk   180
    Prays, curses and deceives.

    Spirit! ten thousand years
    Have scarcely past away,
Since, in the waste where now the savage drinks
His enemy's blood, and aping Europe's sons,
    Wakes the unholy song of war,
    Arose a stately city,
Metropolis of the western continent:
    There, now, the mossy column-stone,
Indented by time's unrelaxing grasp,   190
    Which once appeared to brave
    All, save its country's ruin;
    There the wide forest scene,
Rude in the uncultivated loveliness
    Of gardens long run wild,
Seems, to the unwilling sojourner, whose steps
    Chance in that desert has delayed,
Thus to have stood since earth was what it is.
    Yet once it was the busiest haunt,
Whither, as to a common centre, flocked   200
    Strangers, and ships, and merchandise:
    Once peace and freedom blest

The cultivated plain:
But wealth, that curse of man,
Blighted the bud of its prosperity:
Virtue and wisdom, truth and liberty,
Fled, to return not, until man shall know
  That they alone can give the bliss
    Worthy a soul that claims
Its kindred with eternity.   210

There's not one atom of yon earth
  But once was living man;
Nor the minutest drop of rain,
That hangeth in its thinnest cloud,
  But flowed in human veins:
  And from the burning plains
  Where Lybian monsters yell,
  From the most gloomy glens
  Of Greenland's sunless clime,
  To where the golden fields   220
  Of fertile England spread
  Their harvest to the day,
  Thou canst not find one spot
  Whereon no city stood.

  How strange is human pride!
I tell thee that those living things,
To whom the fragile blade of grass,
    That springeth in the morn
    And perisheth ere noon,
    Is an unbounded world;   230
I tell thee that those viewless beings,
Whose mansion is the smallest particle
  Of the impassive atmosphere,
    Think, feel and live like man;
That their affections and antipathies
    Like his, produce the laws
    Ruling their moral state;
    And the minutest throb
  That through their frame diffuses
    The slightest, faintest motion,   240

Is fixed and indispensable
As the majestic laws
That rule yon rolling orbs.

The Fairy paused. The Spirit,
In ecstacy of admiration, felt
All knowledge of the past revived; the events
          Of old and wondrous times,
Which dim tradition interruptedly
Teaches the credulous vulgar, were unfolded
     In just perspective to the view;   250
     Yet dim from their infinitude.
          The Spirit seemed to stand
High on an isolated pinnacle;
The flood of ages combating below,
The depth of the unbounded universe
          Above, and all around
Nature's unchanging harmony.

III

     Fairy! the Spirit said,
     And on the Queen of Spells
     Fixed her ethereal eyes,
     I thank thee. Thou hast given
A boon which I will not resign, and taught
A lesson not to be unlearned. I know
The past, and thence I will essay to glean
A warning for the future, so that man
May profit by his errors, and derive
     Experience from his folly: 10
For, when the power of imparting joy
Is equal to the will, the human soul
     Requires no other heaven.

Mab

Turn thee, surpassing Spirit!
Much yet remains unscanned.
Thou knowest how great is man,
Thou knowest his imbecility:

Yet learn thou what he is;
Yet learn the lofty destiny
Which restless time prepares   20
For every living soul.

Behold a gorgeous palace, that, amid
Yon populous city, rears its thousand towers
And seems itself a city. Gloomy troops
Of sentinals, in stern and silent ranks,
Encompass it around: the dweller there
Cannot be free and happy; hearest thou not
The curses of the fatherless, the groans
Of those who have no friend? He passes on:
The king, the wearer of a gilded chain   30
That binds his soul to abjectness, the fool
Whom courtiers nickname monarch, whilst a slave
Even to the basest appetites – that man
Heeds not the shriek of penury; he smiles
At the deep curses which the destitute
Mutter in secret, and a sullen joy
Pervades his bloodless heart when thousands groan
But for those morsels which his wantonness
Wastes in unjoyous revelry, to save
All that they love from famine: when he hears   40
The tale of horror, to some ready-made face
Of hypocritical assent he turns,
Smothering the glow of shame, that, spite of him,
Flushes his bloated cheek.
                                    Now to the meal
Of silence, grandeur, and excess, he drags
His palled unwilling appetite. If gold
Gleaming around, and numerous viands culled
From every clime, could force the loathing sense
To overcome satiety, – if wealth
The spring it draws from poisons not, – or vice,   50
Unfeeling, stubborn vice, converteth not
Its food to deadliest venom; then that king
Is happy; and the peasant who fulfils
His unforced task, when he returns at even,
And by the blazing faggot meets again

Her welcome for whom all his toil is sped,
Tastes not a sweeter meal.
                              Behold him now
Stretched on the gorgeous couch; his fevered brain
Reels dizzily awhile: but ah! too soon
The slumber of intemperance subsides,   60
And conscience, that undying serpent, calls
Her venomous brood to their nocturnal task.
Listen! he speaks! oh! mark that frenzied eye –
Oh! mark that deadly visage.

King
                              No cessation!
Oh! must this last for ever! Awful death,
I wish, yet fear to clasp thee! – Not one moment
Of dreamless sleep! O dear and blessed peace!
Why dost thou shroud thy vestal purity
In penury and dungeons? wherefore lurkest
With danger, death, and solitude; yet shun'st   70
The palace I have built thee? Sacred peace!
Oh visit me but once, but pitying shed
One drop of balm upon my withered soul.

The Fairy
Vain man! that palace is the virtuous heart,
And peace defileth not her snowy robes
In such a shed as thine. Hark! yet he mutters;
His slumbers are but varied agonies,
They prey like scorpions on the springs of life.
There needeth not the hell that bigots frame
To punish those who err: earth in itself   80
Contains at once the evil and the cure;
And all-sufficing nature can chastise
Those who transgress her law, – she only knows
How justly to proportion to the fault
The punishment it merits.
                              Is it strange
That this poor wretch should pride him in his woe?
Take pleasure in his abjectness, and hug
The scorpion that consumes him? Is it strange

That, placed on a conspicuous throne of thorns,
Grasping an iron sceptre, and immured   90
Within a splendid prison, whose stern bounds
Shut him from all that's good or dear on earth,
His soul asserts not its humanity?
That man's mild nature rises not in war
Against a king's employ? No – 'tis not strange.
He, like the vulgar, thinks, feels, acts and lives
Just as his father did; the unconquered powers
Of precedent and custom interpose
Between a *king* and virtue. Stranger yet,
To those who know not nature, nor deduce   100
The future from the present, it may seem,
That not one slave, who suffers from the crimes
Of this unnatural being; not one wretch,
Whose children famish, and whose nuptial bed
Is earth's unpitying bosom, rears an arm
To dash him from his throne!
                              Those gilded flies
That, basking in the sunshine of a court,
Fatten on its corruption! – what are they?
The drones of the community; they feed
On the mechanic's labour; the starved hind   110
For them compels the stubborn glebe to yield
Its unshared harvests; and yon squalid form,
Leaner than fleshless misery, that wastes
A sunless life in the unwholesome mine,
Drags out in labour a protracted death,
To glut their grandeur; many faint with toil
That few may know the cares and woe of sloth.

Whence, thinkest thou, kings and parasites arose?
Whence that unnatural line of drones, who heap
Toil and unvanquishable penury   120
On those who build their palaces, and bring
Their daily bread? – From vice, black loathsome vice;
From rapine, madness, treachery, and wrong;
From all that genders misery, and makes
Of earth this thorny wilderness; from lust,
Revenge, and murder . . . And when reason's voice,

Loud as the voice of nature, shall have waked
The nations; and mankind perceive that vice
Is discord, war, and misery; that virtue
Is peace, and happiness and harmony;   130
When man's maturer nature shall disdain
The playthings of its childhood; – kingly glare
Will lose its power to dazzle; its authority
Will silently pass by; the gorgeous throne
Shall stand unnoticed in the regal hall,
Fast falling to decay: whilst falsehood's trade
Shall be as hateful and unprofitable
As that of truth is now.
               Where is the fame
Which the vain-glorious mighty of the earth
Seek to eternise? Oh! the faintest sound   140
From time's light footfall, the minutest wave
That swells the flood of ages, whelms in nothing
The unsubstantial bubble. Aye! today
Stern is the tyrant's mandate, red the gaze
That flashes desolation, strong the arm
That scatters multitudes. Tomorrow comes!
That mandate is a thunder-peal that died
In ages past; that gaze, a transient flash
On which the midnight closed, and on that arm
The worm has made his meal.
               The virtuous man,   150
Who, great in his humility, as kings
Are little in their grandeur; he who leads
Invincibly a life of resolute good,
And stands amid the silent dungeon-depths
More free and fearless than the trembling judge,
Who, clothed in venal power, vainly strove
To bind the impassive spirit; – when he falls,
His mild eye beams benevolence no more:
Withered the hand outstretched but to relieve;
Sunk reason's simple eloquence, that rolled   160
But to appal the guilty. Yes! the grave
Hath quenched that eye, and death's relentless frost
Withered that arm: but the unfading fame
Which virtue hangs upon its votary's tomb;

The deathless memory of that man, whom kings
Call to their mind and tremble; the remembrance
With which the happy spirit contemplates
Its well-spent pilgrimage on earth,
Shall never pass away.

Nature rejects the monarch, not the man;   170
The subject, not the citizen: for kings
And subjects, mutual foes, forever play
A losing game into each other's hands,
Whose stakes are vice and misery. The man
Of virtuous soul commands not, nor obeys.
Power, like a desolating pestilence,
Pollutes what'er it touches; and obedience,
Bane of all genius, virtue, freedom, truth,
Makes slaves of men, and, of the human frame,
A mechanised automaton.
                              When Nero,   180
High over flaming Rome, with savage joy
Lowered like a fiend, drank with enraptured ear
The shrieks of agonising death, beheld
The frightful desolation spread, and felt
A new created sense within his soul
Thrill to the sight, and vibrate to the sound;
Thinkest thou his grandeur had not overcome
The force of human kindness? and, when Rome,
With one stern blow, hurled not the tyrant down,
Crushed not the arm red with her dearest blood,   190
Had not submissive abjectness destroyed
Nature's suggestions?
                        Look on yonder earth:
The golden harvests spring; the unfailing sun
Sheds light and life; the fruits, the flowers, the trees,
Arise in due succession; all things speak
Peace, harmony, and love. The universe,
In nature's silent eloquence, declares
That all fulfil the works of love and joy, –
All but the outcast man. He fabricates
The sword which stabs his peace; he cherisheth   200
The snakes that gnaw his heart; he raiseth up

The tyrant, whose delight is in his woe,
Whose sport is in his agony. Yon sun,
Lights it the great alone? Yon silver beams,
Sleep they less sweetly on the cottage thatch,
Than on the dome of kings? Is mother earth
A step-dame to her numerous sons, who earn
Her unshared gifts with unremitting toil;
A mother only to those puling babes
Who, nursed in ease and luxury, make men   210
The playthings of their babyhood, and mar,
In self-important childishness, that peace
Which men alone appreciate?

      Spirit of Nature! no,
The pure diffusion of thy essence throbs
  Alike in every human heart.
      Thou, aye, erectest there
  Thy throne of power unappealable:
  Thou art the judge beneath whose nod
  Man's brief and frail authority   220
      Is powerless as the wind
      That passeth idly by.
  Thine the tribunal which surpasseth
    The show of human justice,
      As God surpasses man.

      Spirit of Nature! thou
Life of interminable multitudes;
  Soul of those mighty spheres
Whose changeless paths thro' Heaven's deep silence lie;
    Soul of that smallest being,   230
      The dwelling of whose life
    Is one faint April sun-gleam; –
    Man, like these passive things,
Thy will unconsciously fulfilleth:
  Like theirs, his age of endless peace,
    Which time is fast maturing,
    Will swiftly, surely come;
And the unbounded frame, which thou pervadest,
    Will be without a flaw
  Marring its perfect symmetry.   240

IV

How beautiful this night! the balmiest sigh,
Which vernal zephyrs breathe in evening's ear,
Were discord to the speaking quietude
That wraps this moveless scene. Heaven's ebon vault,
Studded with stars unutterably bright,
Through which the moon's unclouded grandeur rolls,
Seems like a canopy which love had spread
To curtain her sleeping world. Yon gentle hills,
Robed in a garment of untrodden snow;
Yon darksome rocks, whence icicles depend,   10
So stainless, that their white and glittering spires
Tinge not the moon's pure beam; yon castled steep,
Whose banner hangeth o'er the time-worn tower
So idly, that rapt fancy deemeth it
A metaphor of peace; – all form a scene
Where musing solitude might love to lift
Her soul above this sphere of earthliness;
Where silence undisturbed might watch alone,
So cold! so bright, so still.
                              The orb of day,
In southern climes, o'er ocean's waveless field   20
Sinks sweetly smiling: not the faintest breath
Steals o'er the unruffled deep; the clouds of eve
Reflect unmoved the lingering beam of day;
And vesper's image on the western main
Is beautifully still. Tomorrow comes:
Cloud upon cloud, in dark and deepening mass,
Roll o'er the blackened waters; the deep roar
Of distant thunder mutters awfully;
Tempest unfolds its pinion o'er the gloom
That shrouds the boiling surge; the pitiless fiend,   30
With all his winds and lightnings, tracks his prey;
The torn deep yawns, – the vessel finds a grave
Beneath its jagged gulf.
                          Ah! whence yon glare
That fires the arch of heaven? – that dark red smoke
Blotting the silver moon? The stars are quenched

In darkness, and the pure and spangling snow
Gleams faintly through the gloom that gathers round!
Hark to that roar, whose swift and deaf'ning peals
In countless echoes through the mountains ring,
Startling pale midnight on her starry throne!   40
Now swells the intermingling din; the jar
Frequent and frightful of the bursting bomb;
The falling beam, the shriek, the groan, the shout,
The ceaseless clangor, and the rush of men
Inebriate with rage: – loud, and more loud
The discord grows; till pale death shuts the scene,
And o'er the conqueror and the conquered draws
His cold and bloody shroud. – Of all the men
Whom day's departing beam saw blooming there,
In proud and vigorous health; of all the hearts   50
That beat with anxious life at sunset there;
How few survive, how few are beating now!
All is deep silence, like the fearful calm
That slumbers in the storm's portentous pause;
Save when the frantic wail of widowed love
Comes shuddering on the blast, or the faint moan
With which some soul bursts from the frame of clay
Wrapt round its struggling powers.
                                    The grey morn
Dawns on the mournful scene; the sulphurous smoke
Before the icy wind slow rolls away,   60
And the bright beams of frosty morning dance
Along the spangling snow. There tracks of blood
Even to the forest's depth, and scattered arms,
And lifeless warriors, whose hard lineaments
Death's self could change not, mark the dreadful path
Of the outsallying victors: far behind,
Black ashes note where their proud city stood.
Within yon forest is a gloomy glen –
Each tree which guards its darkness from the day,
Waves o'er a warrior's tomb.
                                    I see thee shrink,   70
Surpassing Spirit! – wert thou human else?
I see a shade of doubt and horror fleet
Across thy stainless features: yet fear not;

This is no unconnected misery,
Nor stands uncaused, and irretrievable.
Man's evil nature, that apology
Which kings who rule, and cowards who crouch, set up
For their unnumbered crimes, sheds not the blood
Which desolates the discord-wasted land.
From kings, and priests, and statesmen, war arose,   80
Whose safety is man's deep unbettered woe,
Whose grandeur his debasement. Let the axe
Strike at the root, the poison-tree will fall;
And where its venomed exhalations spread
Ruin, and death, and woe, where millions lay
Quenching the serpent's famine, and their bones
Bleaching unburied in the putrid blast,
A garden shall arise, in loveliness
Surpassing fabled Eden.
                              Hath Nature's soul,
That formed this world so beautiful, that spread   90
Earth's lap with plenty, and life's smallest chord
Strung to unchanging unison, that gave
The happy birds their dwelling in the grove,
That yielded to the wanderers of the deep
The lovely silence of the unfathomed main,
And filled the meanest worm that crawls in dust
With spirit, thought, and love; on Man alone,
Partial in causeless malice, wantonly
Heaped ruin, vice, and slavery; his soul
Blasted with withering curses; placed afar   100
The meteor-happiness, that shuns his grasp,
But serving on the frightful gulf to glare,
Rent wide beneath his footsteps? Nature? – no!
Kings, priests, and statesmen, blast the human flower,
Even its tender bud: their influence darts
Like subtle poison through the bloodless veins
Of desolate society. The child,
Ere he can lisp his mother's sacred name,
Swells with the unnatural pride of crime, and lifts
His baby-sword even in a hero's mood.   110
This infant-arm becomes the bloodiest scourge
Of devastated earth: whilst specious names,

Learned in soft childhood's unsuspecting hour,
Serve as the sophisms with which manhood dims
Bright reason's ray, and sanctifies the sword
Upraised to shed a brother's innocent blood.
Let priest-led slaves cease to proclaim that man
Inherits vice and misery, when force
And falsehood hang even o'er the cradled babe,
Stifling with rudest grasp all natural good.   120
Ah! to the stranger-soul, when first it peeps
From its new tenement, and looks abroad
For happiness and sympathy, how stern
And desolate a tract is this wide world!
How withered all the buds of natural good!
No shade, no shelter from the sweeping storms
Of pitiless power! On its wretched frame,
Poisoned, perchance, by the disease and woe
Heaped on the wretched parent whence it sprung
By morals, law, and custom, the pure winds   130
Of heaven, that renovate the insect tribes,
May breathe not. The untainting light of day
May visit not its longings. It is bound
Ere it has life: yea, all the chains are forged
Long ere its being: all liberty and love
And peace is torn from its defencelessness;
Cursed from its birth, even from its cradle doomed
To abjectness and bondage!

Throughout this varied and eternal world
Soul is the only element, the block   140
That for uncounted ages has remained.
The moveless pillar of a mountain's weight
Is active, living spirit. Every grain
Is sentient both in unity and part,
And the minutest atom comprehends
A world of loves and hatreds: these beget
Evil and good: hence truth and falsehood spring;
Hence will and thought and action, all the germs
Of pain or pleasure, sympathy or hate,
That variegate the eternal universe.   150
Soul is not more polluted than the beams

Of heaven's pure orb, ere round their rapid lines
The taint of earth-born atmospheres arise.

Man is of soul and body, formed for deeds
Of high resolve, on fancy's boldest wing
To soar unwearied, fearlessly to turn
The keenest pangs to peacefulness, and taste
The joys which mingled sense and spirit yield.
Or he is formed for abjectness and woe,
To grovel on the dunghill of his fears,   160
To shrink at every sound, to quench the flame
Of natural love in sensualism, to know
That hour as blest when on his worthless days
The frozen hand of death shall set its seal,
Yet fear the cure, though hating the disease.
The one is man that shall hereafter be;
The other, man as vice has made him now.

War is the statesman's game, the priest's delight,
The lawyer's jest, the hired assassin's trade,
And, to those royal murderers, whose mean thrones   170
Are bought by crimes of treachery and gore,
The bread they eat, the staff on which they lean.
Guards, garbed in blood-red livery, surround
Their palaces, participate the crimes
That force defends, and from a nation's rage
Secure the crown, which all the curses reach
That famine, frenzy, woe and penury breathe.
These are the hired bravos who defend
The tyrant's throne* – the bullies of his fear:
These are the sinks and channels of worst vice,   180
The refuse of society, the dregs
Of all that is most vile: their cold hearts blend
Deceit with sternness, ignorance with pride,
All that is mean and villanous, with rage
Which hopelessness of good, and self-contempt,
Alone might kindle; they are decked in wealth,
Honour and power, then are sent abroad
To do their work. The pestilence that stalks
In gloomy triumph through some eastern land

Is less destroying. They cajole with gold,   190
And promises of fame, the thoughtless youth
Already crushed with servitude: he knows
His wretchedness too late, and cherishes
Repentance for his ruin, when his doom
Is sealed in gold and blood!
Those too the tyrant serve, who, skilled to snare
The feet of justice in the toils of law,
Stand, ready to oppress the weaker still;
And right or wrong will vindicate for gold,
Sneering at public virtue, which beneath   200
Their pitiless tread lies torn and trampled, where
Honour sits smiling at the sale of truth.

Then grave and hoary-headed hypocrites,
Without a hope, a passion, or a love,
Who, through a life of luxury and lies,
Have crept by flattery to the seats of power,
Support the system whence their honours flow . . .
They have three words: – well tyrants know their use,
Well pay them for the loan, with usury
Torn from a bleeding world! – God, Hell, and Heaven.   210
A vengeful, pitiless, and almighty fiend,
Whose mercy is a nickname for the rage
Of tameless tigers hungering for blood.
Hell, a red gulf of everlasting fire,
Where poisonous and undying worms prolong
Eternal misery to those hapless slaves
Whose life has been a penance for its crimes.
And Heaven, a meed for those who dare belie
Their human nature, quake, believe, and cringe
Before the mockeries of earthly power.   220

These tools the tyrant tempers to his work,
Wields in his wrath, and as he wills destroys,
Omnipotent in wickedness: the while
Youth springs, age moulders, manhood tamely does
His bidding, bribed by short-lived joys to lend
Force to the weakness of his trembling arm.

They rise, they fall; one generation comes

Yielding its harvest to destruction's scythe.
It fades, another blossoms: yet behold!
Red glows the tyrant's stamp-mark on its bloom,   230
Withering and cankering deep its passive prime.
He has invented lying words and modes,
Empty and vain as his own coreless heart;
Evasive meanings, nothings of much sound,
To lure the heedless victim to the toils
Spread round the valley of its paradise.

Look to thyself, priest, conqueror, or prince!
Whether thy trade is falsehood, and thy lusts
Deep wallow in the earnings of the poor,
With whom thy master was: – or thou delightst   240
In numbering o'er the myriads of thy slain,
All misery weighing nothing in the scale
Against thy short-lived fame: or thou dost load
With cowardice and crime the groaning land,
A pomp-fed king. Look to thy wretched self!
Aye, art thou not the veriest slave that e'er
Crawled on the loathing earth? Are not thy days
Days of unsatisfying listlessness?
Dost thou not cry, ere night's long rack is o'er,
When will the morning come? Is not thy youth   250
A vain and feverish dream of sensualism?
Thy manhood blighted with unripe disease?
Are not thy views of unregretted death
Drear, comfortless, and horrible? Thy mind,
Is it not morbid as thy nerveless frame,
Incapable of judgement, hope, or love?
And dost thou wish the errors to survive
That bar thee from all sympathies of good,
After the miserable interest
Thou holdst in their protraction?
                              When the grave   260
Has swallowed up thy memory and thyself,
Dost thou desire the bane that poisons earth
To twine its roots around thy coffined clay,
Spring from thy bones, and blossom on thy tomb,
That of its fruit thy babes may eat and die?

V

Thus do the generations of the earth
Go to the grave, and issue from the womb,
Surviving still the imperishable change
That renovates the world; even as the leaves
Which the keen frost-wind of the waning year
Has scattered on the forest soil, and heaped
For many seasons there, though long they choke,
Loading with loathsome rottenness the land,
All germs of promise. Yet when the tall trees
From which they fell, shorn of their lovely shapes,   10
Lie level with the earth to moulder there,
They fertilise the land they long deformed,
Till from the breathing lawn a forest springs
Of youth, integrity, and loveliness,
Like that which gave it life, to spring and die.
Thus suicidal selfishness, that blights
The fairest feelings of the opening heart,
Is destined to decay, whilst from the soil
Shall spring all virtue, all delight, all love,
And judgement cease to wage unnatural war   20
With passion's unsubduable array.
Twin-sister of religion, selfishness!
Rival in crime and falsehood, aping all
The wanton horrors of her bloody play;
Yet frozen, unimpassioned, spiritless,
Shunning the light, and owning not its name,
Compelled, by its deformity, to screen
With flimsy veil of justice and of right,
Its unattractive lineaments, that scare
All, save the brood of ignorance: at once   30
The cause and the effect of tyranny;
Unblushing, hardened, sensual, and vile;
Dead to all love but of its abjectness,
With heart impassive by more noble powers
Than unshared pleasure, sordid gain, or fame;
Despising its own miserable being,
Which still it longs, yet fears to disenthrall.

Hence commerce springs, the venal interchange
Of all that human art or nature yield;
Which wealth should purchase not, but want demand,   40
And natural kindness hasten to supply
From the full fountain of its boundless love,
For ever stifled, drained, and tainted now.
Commerce! beneath whose poison-breathing shade
No solitary virtue dares to spring,
But poverty and wealth with equal hand
Scatter their withering curses, and unfold
The doors of premature and violent death,
To pining famine and full-fed disease,
To all that shares the lot of human life,   50
Which poisoned body and soul, scarce drags the chain
That lengthens as it goes and clanks behind.

Commerce has set the mark of selfishness,
The signet of its all-enslaving power,
Upon a shining ore, and called it gold:
Before whose image bow the vulgar great,
The vainly rich, the miserable proud,
The mob of peasants, nobles, priests, and kings,
And with blind feelings reverence the power
That grinds them to the dust of misery.   60
But in the temple of their hireling hearts
Gold is a living god, and rules in scorn
All earthly things but virtue.

Since tyrants, by the sale of human life,
Heap luxuries to their sensualism, and fame
To their wide-wasting and insatiate pride,
Success has sanctioned to a credulous world
The ruin, the disgrace, the woe of war.
His hosts of blind and unresisting dupes
The despot numbers; from his cabinet   70
These puppets of his schemes he moves at will,
Even as the slaves by force or famine driven,
Beneath a vulgar master, to perform
A task of cold and brutal drudgery;
Hardened to hope, insensible to fear,

Scarce living pulleys of a dead machine,
Mere wheels of work and articles of trade,
That grace the proud and noisy pomp of wealth!

The harmony and happiness of man
Yields to the wealth of nations; that which lifts   80
His nature to the heaven of its pride,
Is bartered for the poison of his soul;
The weight that drags to earth his towering hopes,
Blighting all prospect but of selfish gain,
Withering all passion but of slavish fear,
Extinguishing all free and generous love
Of enterprise and daring, even the pulse
That fancy kindles in the beating heart
To mingle with sensation, it destroys, –
Leaves nothing but the sordid lust of self,   90
The grovelling hope of interest and gold,
Unqualified, unmingled, unredeemed
Even by hypocrisy.
                         And statesmen boast
Of wealth! The wordy eloquence that lives
After the ruin of their hearts, can gild
The bitter poison of a nation's woe,
Can turn the worship of the servile mob
To their corrupt and glaring idol fame,
From virtue, trampled by its iron tread,
Although its dazzling pedestal be raised   100
Amid the horrors of a limb-strewn field,
With desolated dwellings smoking round.
The man of ease, who, by his warm fireside,
To deeds of charitable intercourse,
And bare fulfilment of the common laws
Of decency and prejudice, confines
The struggling nature of his human heart,
Is duped by their cold sophistry; he sheds
A passing tear perchance upon the wreck
Of earthly peace, when near his dwelling's door   110
The frightful waves are driven, – when his son
Is murdered by the tyrant, or religion
Drives his wife raving mad. But the poor man,

Whose life is misery, and fear, and care;
Whom the morn wakens but to fruitless toil;
Who ever hears his famished offspring's scream,
Whom their pale mother's uncomplaining gaze
For ever meets, and the proud rich man's eye
Flashing command, and the heart-breaking scene
Of thousands like himself; he little heeds   120
The rhetoric of tyranny; his hate
Is quenchless as his wrongs; he laughs to scorn
The vain and bitter mockery of words,
Feeling the horror of the tyrant's deeds,
And unrestrained but by the arm of power,
That knows and dreads his enmity.

The iron rod of penury still compels
Her wretched slave to bow the knee to wealth,
And poison, with unprofitable toil,
A life too void of solace to confirm   130
The very chains that bind him to his doom.
Nature, impartial in munificence,
Has gifted man with all-subduing will.
Matter, with all its transitory shapes,
Lies subjected and plastic at his feet,
That, weak from bondage, tremble as they tread.
How many a rustic Milton has past by,
Stifling the speechless longings of his heart,
In unremitting drudgery and care!
How many a vulgar Cato has compelled   140
His energies, no longer tameless then,
To mould a pin, or fabricate a nail!
How many a Newton,[9] to whose passive ken
Those mighty spheres that gem infinity
Were only specks of tinsel, fixed in heaven
To light the midnights of his native town!

Yet every heart contains perfection's germ:
The wisest of the sages of the earth,
That ever from the stores of reason drew
Science and truth, and virtue's dreadless tone,   150
Were but a weak and inexperienced boy,

Proud, sensual, unimpassioned, unimbued
With pure desire and universal love,
Compared to that high being, of cloudless brain,
Untainted passion, elevated will,
Which death (who even would linger long in awe
Within his noble presence, and beneath
His changeless eyebeam) might alone subdue.
Him, every slave now dragging through the filth
Of some corrupted city his sad life,   160
Pining with famine, swoln with luxury,
Blunting the keenness of his spiritual sense
With narrow schemings and unworthy cares,
Or madly rushing through all violent crime,
To move the deep stagnation of his soul, –
Might imitate and equal.
                            But mean lust
Has bound its chains so tight around the earth,
That all within it but the virtuous man
Is venal: gold or fame will surely reach
The price prefixed by selfishness, to all   170
But him of resolute and unchanging will;
Whom, nor the plaudits of a servile crowd,
Nor the vile joys of tainting luxury,
Can bribe to yield his elevated soul
To tyranny or falsehood, though they wield
With blood-red hand the sceptre of the world.

All things are sold: the very light of heaven[10]
Is venal; earth's unsparing gifts of love,
The smallest and most despicable things
That lurk in the abysses of the deep,   180
All objects of our life, even life itself,
And the poor pittance which the laws allow
Of liberty, the fellowship of man,
Those duties which his heart of human love
Should urge him to perform instinctively,
Are bought and sold as in a public mart
Of undisguising selfishness, that sets
On each its price, the stamp-mark of her reign.
Even love is sold; the solace of all woe

Is turned to deadliest agony, old age   190
Shivers in selfish beauty's loathing arms,
And youth's corrupted impulses prepare
A life of horror from the blighting bane
Of commerce; whilst the pestilence that springs
From unenjoying sensualism, has filled
All human life with hydra-headed[11] woes.

Falsehood demands but gold to pay the pangs
Of outraged conscience; for the slavish priest
Sets no great value on his hireling faith:
A little passing pomp, some servile souls,   200
Whom cowardice itself might safely chain,
Or the spare mite of avarice could bribe
To deck the triumph of their languid zeal,
Can make him minister to tyranny.
More daring crime requires a loftier meed:
Without a shudder, the slave-soldier lends
His arm to murderous deeds, and steels his heart,
When the dread eloquence of dying men,
Low mingling on the lonely field of fame,
Assails that nature, whose applause he sells   210
For the gross blessings of a patriot mob,
For the vile gratitude of heartless kings,
And for a cold world's good word, – viler still!

There is a nobler glory, which survives
Until our being fades, and, solacing
All human care, accompanies its change;
Deserts not virtue in the dungeon's gloom.
And, in the precincts of the palace, guides
Its footsteps through that labyrinth of crime;
Imbues his lineaments with dauntlessness,   220
Even when, from power's avenging hand, he takes
Its sweetest, last and noblest title – death;
 – The consciousness of good, which neither gold,
Nor sordid fame, nor hope of heavenly bliss,
Can purchase; but a life of resolute good,
Unalterable will, quenchless desire
Of universal happiness, the heart

That beats with it in unison, the brain,
Whose ever wakeful wisdom toils to change
Reason's rich stores for its eternal weal.   230

This commerce of sincerest virtue needs
No mediative signs of selfishness,
No jealous intercourse of wretched gain,
No balancings of prudence, cold and long;
In just and equal measure all is weighed,
One scale contains the sum of human weal,
And one, the good man's heart.
                              How vainly seek
The selfish for that happiness denied
To aught but virtue! Blind and hardened, they,
Who hope for peace amid the storms of care,   240
Who covet power they know not how to use.
And sigh for pleasure they refuse to give, –
Madly they frustrate still their own designs;
And, where they hope that quiet to enjoy
Which virtue pictures, bitterness of soul,
Pining regrets, and vain repentances,
Disease, disgust, and lassitude, pervade
Their valueless and miserable lives.

But hoary-headed selfishness has felt
Its death-blow, and is tottering to the grave: 250
A brighter morn awaits the human day,
When every transfer of earth's natural gifts
Shall be a commerce of good words and works;
When poverty and wealth, the thirst of fame,
The fear of infamy, disease and woe,
War with its million horrors, and fierce hell
Shall live but in the memory of time,
Who, like a penitent libertine, shall start,
Look back, and shudder at his younger years.

VI

All touch, all eye, all ear,
The Spirit felt the Fairy's burning speech.
   O'er the thin texture of its frame,
The varying periods painted changing glows,
     As on a summer even,
When soul-enfolding music floats around,
   The stainless mirror of the lake
   Re-images the eastern gloom,
Mingling convulsively its purple hues
     With sunset's burnished gold.   10

     Then thus the Spirit spoke:
It is a wild and miserable world!
     Thorny, and full of care,
Which every fiend can make his prey at will.
   O Fairy! in the lapse of years,
     Is there no hope in store?
     Will yon vast suns roll on
   Interminably, still illuming
   The night of so many wretched souls,
     And see no hope for them?   20
Will not the universal Spirit e'er
Revivify this withered limb of Heaven?

     The Fairy calmly smiled
In comfort, and a kindling gleam of hope
   Suffused the Spirit's lineaments.
Oh! rest thee tranquil; chase those fearful doubts,
Which ne'er could rack an everlasting soul,
That sees the chains which bind it to its doom.
Yes! crime and misery are in yonder earth,
     Falsehood, mistake, and lust;   30
     But the eternal world
Contains at once the evil and the cure.
Some eminent in virtue shall start up,
     Even in perversest time:
The truths of their pure lips, that never die,

Shall bind the scorpion falsehood with a wreath
    Of ever-living flame,
Until the monster sting itself to death.

How sweet a scene will earth become!
Of purest spirits, a pure dwelling-place,   40
Symphonious with the planetary spheres;
When man, with changeless nature coalescing,
Will undertake regeneration's work,
When its ungenial poles no longer point
    To the red and baleful sun
    That faintly twinkles there.

    Spirit! on yonder earth,
  Falsehood now triumphs; deadly power
Has fixed its seal upon the lip of truth!
  Madness and misery are there!   50
The happiest is most wretched! Yet confide,
Until pure health-drops, from the cup of joy,
Fall like a dew of balm upon the world.
Now, to the scene I show, in silence turn,
And read the blood-stained charter of all woe,
Which nature soon, with recreating hand,
Will blot in mercy from the book of earth.
How bold the flight of passion's wandering wing,
How swift the step of reason's firmer tread,
How calm and sweet the victories of life,   60
How terrorless the triumph of the grave!
How powerless were the mightiest monarch's arm,
Vain his loud threat, and impotent his frown!
How ludicrous the priest's dogmatic roar!
The weight of his exterminating curse,
How light! and his affected charity,
To suit the pressure of the changing times,
What palpable deceit! – but for thy aid,
Religion! but for thee, prolific fiend,
Who peoplest earth with demons, hell with men,   70
And heaven with slaves!

Thou taintest all thou lookest upon! – the stars,

Which on thy cradle beamed so brightly sweet,
Were gods to the distempered playfulness
Of thy untutored infancy: the trees,
The grass, the clouds, the mountains, and the sea,
All living things that walk, swim, creep, or fly,
Were gods: the sun had homage, and the moon
Her worshipper. Then thou becamest a boy,
More daring in thy frenzies: every shape,   80
Monstrous or vast, or beautifully wild,
Which, from sensation's relics, fancy culls;
The spirits of the air, the shuddering ghost,
The genii of the elements, the powers
That give a shape to nature's varied works,
Had life and place in the corrupt belief
Of thy blind heart: yet still thy youthful hands
Were pure of human blood. Then manhood gave
Its strength and ardour to thy frenzied brain;
Thine eager gaze scanned the stupendous scene,   90
Whose wonders mocked the knowledge of thy pride:
Their everlasting and unchanging laws
Reproached thine ignorance. Awhile thou stoodst
Baffled and gloomy; then thou didst sum up
The elements of all that thou didst know;
The changing seasons, winter's leafless reign,
The budding of the heaven-breathing trees,
The eternal orbs that beautify the night,
The sunrise, and the setting of the moon,
Earthquakes and wars, and poisons and disease,   100
And all their causes, to an abstract point,
Converging, thou didst bend and called it God!
The self-sufficing, the omnipotent,
The merciful, and the avenging God!
Who, prototype of human misrule, sits
High in heaven's realm, upon a golden throne,
Even like an earthly king; and whose dread work,
Hell, gapes for ever for the unhappy slaves
Of fate, whom he created, in his sport,
To triumph in their torments when they fell!   110
Earth heard the name; earth trembled, as the smoke
Of his revenge ascended up to heaven,

Blotting the constellations; and the cries
Of millions, butchered in sweet confidence
And unsuspecting peace, even when the bonds
Of safety were confirmed by wordy oaths
Sworn in his dreadful name, rung through the land;
Whilst innocent babes writhed on thy stubborn spear,
And thou didst laugh to hear the mother's shriek
Of maniac gladness, as the sacred steel   120
Felt cold in her torn entrails!

Religion! thou wert then in manhood's prime:
But age crept on: one God would not suffice
For senile puerility; thou framedst
A tale to suit thy dotage, and to glut
Thy misery-thirsting soul, that the mad fiend
Thy wickedness had pictured, might afford
A plea for sating the unnatural thirst
For murder, rapine, violence, and crime,
That still consumed thy being, even when   130
Thou heardst the step of fate; – that flames might light
Thy funeral scene, and the shrill horrent shrieks
Of parents dying on the pile that burned
To light their children to thy paths, the roar
Of the encircling flames, the exulting cries
Of thine apostles, loud commingling there,
     Might sate thine hungry ear
     Even on the bed of death!

But now contempt is mocking thy grey hairs;
Thou art descending to the darksome grave,   140
Unhonoured and unpitied, but by those
Whose pride is passing by like thine, and sheds,
Like thine, a glare that fades before the sun
Of truth, and shines but in the dreadful night
That long has lowered above the ruined world.

Throughout these infinite orbs of mingling light,
Of which yon earth is one, is wide diffused
A spirit of activity and life,
That knows no term, cessation, or decay;

That fades not when the lamp of earthly life,   150
Extinguished in the dampness of the grave,
Awhile there slumbers, more than when the babe
In the dim newness of its being feels
The impulses of sublunary things,
And all is wonder to unpractised sense:
But, active, stedfast, and eternal, still
Guides the fierce whirlwind, in the tempest roars,
Cheers in the day, breathes in the balmy groves,
Strengthens in health, and poisons in disease;
And in the storm of change, that ceaselessly   160
Rolls round the eternal universe, and shakes
Its undecaying battlement, presides,
Apportioning with irresistible law
The place each spring of its machine shall fill;
So that when waves on waves tumultuous heap
Confusion to the clouds, and fiercely driven
Heaven's lightnings scorch the uprooted ocean-fords,
Whilst, to the eye of shipwrecked mariner,
Lone sitting on the bare and shuddering rock,
All seems unlinked contingency and chance: 170
No atom of this turbulence fulfils
A vague and unnecessitated task,
Or acts but as it must and ought to act.
Even the minutest molecule of light,
That in an April sunbeam's fleeting glow
Fulfils its destined, though invisible work,
The universal Spirit guides; nor less,
When merciless ambition, or mad zeal,
Has led two hosts of dupes to battlefield,
That, blind, they there may dig each other's graves,   180
And call the sad work glory, does it rule
All passions: not a thought, a will, an act,
No working of the tyrant's moody mind,
Nor one misgiving of the slaves who boast
Their servitude, to hide the shame they feel,
Nor the events enchaining every will,
That from the depths of unrecorded time
Have drawn all-influencing virtue, pass
Unrecognised, or unforeseen by thee,

Soul of the Universe! eternal spring   190
Of life and death, of happiness and woe,
Of all that chequers the phantasmal scene
That floats before our eyes in wavering light,
Which gleams but on the darkness of our prison,
    Whose chains and massy walls
    We feel, but cannot see.

Spirit of Nature! all-sufficing Power,
Necessity! thou mother of the world!
Unlike the God of human error, thou
Requirest no prayers or praises; the caprice   200
Of man's weak will belongs no more to thee
Than do the changeful passions of his breast
To thy unvarying harmony: the slave,
Whose horrible lusts spread misery o'er the world,
And the good man, who lifts, with virtuous pride,
His being, in the sight of happiness,
That springs from his own works; the poison-tree,
Beneath whose shade all life is withered up,
And the fair oak, whose leafy dome affords
A temple where the vows of happy love   210
Are registered, are equal in thy sight:
No love, no hate thou cherishest; revenge
And favouritism, and worst desire of fame,
Thou knowest not: all that the wide world contains
Are but thy passive instruments, and thou
Regardst them all with an impartial eye,
Whose joy or pain thy nature cannot feel,
    Because thou hast not human sense,
    Because thou art not human mind.

Yes! when the sweeping storm of time   220
Has sung its death-dirge o'er the ruined fanes
And broken altars of the almighty fiend,
Whose name usurps thy honours, and the blood
Through centuries clotted there, has floated down
The tainted flood of ages, shalt thou live
Unchangeable! A shrine is raised to thee,
    Which, nor the tempest-breath of time,

Nor the interminable flood,
  Over earth's slight pageant rolling,
    Availeth to destroy, –   230
The sensitive extension of the world.
  That wonderous and eternal fane,
Where pain and pleasure, good and evil join,
To do the will of strong necessity,
  And life, in multitudinous shapes,
Still pressing forward where no term can be,
  Like hungry and unresting flame
Curls round the eternal columns of its strength.

VII

Spirit

I was an infant when my mother went
To see an atheist burned. She took me there:
The dark-robed priests were met around the pile;
The multitude was gazing silently;
And as the culprit passed with dauntless mien,
Tempered disdain in his unaltering eye,
Mixed with a quiet smile, shone calmly forth:
The thirsty fire crept round his manly limbs;
His resolute eyes were scorched to blindness soon;
His death-pang rent my heart! the insensate mob   10
Uttered a cry of triumph, and I wept.
Weep not, child! cried my mother, for that man
Has said, There is no God.

Fairy

There is no God!
Nature confirms the faith his death-groan sealed:
Let heaven and earth, let man's revolving race,
His ceaseless generations tell their tale;
Let every part depending on the chain
That links it to the whole, point to the hand
That grasps its term! let every seed that falls
In silent eloquence unfold its store   20
Of argument: infinity within,

Infinity without, belie creation;
The exterminable spirit it contains
Is nature's only God; but human pride
Is skilful to invent most serious names
To hide its ignorance.
                    The name of God
Has fenced about all crime with holiness,
Himself the creature of his worshippers,
Whose names and attributes and passions change,
Seeva, Buddh, Foh, Jehovah,[12] God, or Lord,   30
Even with the human dupes who build his shrines,
Still serving o'er the war-polluted world
For desolation's watchword; whether hosts
Stain his death-blushing chariot-wheels, as on
Triumphantly they roll, whilst Brahmins[13] raise
A sacred hymn to mingle with the groans;
Or countless partners of his power divide
His tyranny to weakness; or the smoke
Of burning towns, the cries of female helplessness,
Unarmed old age, and youth, and infancy,   40
Horribly massacred, ascend to heaven
In honour of his name; or, last and worst,
Earth groans beneath religion's iron age,
And priests dare babble of a God of peace,
Even whilst their hands are red with guiltless blood,
Murdering the while, uprooting every germ
Of truth, exterminating, spoiling all,
Making the earth a slaughter-house!

        O Spirit! through the sense
By which thy inner nature was apprised   50
    Of outward shows, vague dreams have rolled,
    And varied reminiscences have waked
        Tablets that never fade;
    All things have been imprinted there,
    The stars, the sea, the earth, the sky,
    Even the unshapeliest lineaments
        Of wild and fleeting visions
            Have left a record there
            To testify of earth.

These are my empire, for to me is given   60
The wonders of the human world to keep,
And fancy's thin creations to endow
With manner, being, and reality;
Therefore a wondrous phantom, from the dreams
Of human error's dense and purblind faith,
I will evoke, to meet thy questioning.
       Ahasuerus,[14] rise!

    A strange and woe-worn wight
  Arose beside the battlement,
      And stood unmoving there.   70
His inessential figure cast no shade
    Upon the golden floor;
His port and mien bore mark of many years,
And chronicles of untold ancientness
Were legible within his beamless eye:
  Yet his cheek bore the mark of youth;
Freshness and vigour knit his manly frame;
The wisdom of old age was mingled there
  With youth's primaeval dauntlessness;
    And inexpressible woe,   80
Chastened by fearless resignation, gave
An awful grace to his all-speaking brow.

Spirit
Is there a God?

Ahasuerus
Is there a God! – aye, an almighty God,
And vengeful as almighty! Once his voice
Was heard on earth: earth shuddered at the sound;
The fiery-visaged firmament expressed
Abhorrence, and the grave of nature yawned
To swallow all the dauntless and the good
That dared to hurl defiance at his throne,   90
Girt as it was with power. None but slaves
Survived, – cold-blooded slaves, who did the work
Of tyrannous omnipotence; whose souls
No honest indignation ever urged

To elevated daring, to one deed
Which gross and sensual self did not pollute.
These slaves built temples for the omnipotent fiend,
Gorgeous and vast: the costly altars smoked
With human blood, and hideous paeans rung
Through all the long-drawn aisles. A murderer heard   100
His voice in Egypt, one whose gifts and arts
Had raised him to his eminence in power,
Accomplice of omnipotence in crime,
And confidant of the all-knowing one.
        These were Jehovah's words.

From an eternity of idleness
I, God, awoke; in seven days' toil made earth
From nothing; rested, and created man:
I placed him in a paradise, and there
Planted the tree of evil, so that he   110
Might eat and perish, and my soul procure
Wherewith to sate its malice, and to turn,
Even like a heartless conqueror of the earth,
All misery to my fame. The race of men
Chosen to my honour, with impunity
May sate the lusts I planted in their heart.
Here I command thee hence to lead them on,
Until, with hardened feet, their conquering troops
Wade on the promised soil through woman's blood,
And make my name be dreaded through the land.   120
Yet ever-burning flame and ceaseless woe
Shall be the doom of their eternal souls,
With every soul on this ungrateful earth,
Virtuous or vicious, weak or strong, – even all
Shall perish, to fulfil the blind revenge
(Which you, to men, call justice) of their God.
                                        The murderer's brow
Quivered with horror.
                        God omnipotent,
Is there no mercy? must our punishment
Be endless? will long ages roll away,   130
And see no term? Oh! wherefore hast thou made
In mockery and wrath this evil earth?

Mercy becomes the powerful – be but just:
O God! repent and save.
                              One way remains:
I will beget a Son, and he shall bear
The sins of all the world; he shall arise
In an unnoticed corner of the earth,
And there shall die upon a cross, and purge
The universal crime; so that the few
On whom my grace descends, those who are marked   140
As vessels to the honour of their God,
May credit this strange sacrifice, and save
Their souls alive: millions shall live and die,
Who ne'er shall call upon their Saviour's name,
But, unredeemed, go to the gaping grave.
Thousands shall deem it an old woman's tale,
Such as the nurses frighten babes withal:
These in a gulf of anguish and of flame
Shall curse their reprobation endlessly,
Yet tenfold pangs shall force them to avow,   150
Even on their beds of torment, where they howl,
My honour, and the justice of their doom.
What then avail their virtuous deeds, their thoughts
Of purity, with radiant genius bright,
Or lit with human reason's earthly ray?
Many are called, but few will I elect.
Do thou my bidding, Moses!

                              Even the murderer's cheek
Was blanched with horror, and his quivering lips
Scarce faintly uttered – O almighty one,
I tremble and obey!   160

O Spirit! centuries have set their seal
On this heart of many wounds, and loaded brain,
Since the Incarnate came: humbly he came,
Veiling his horrible Godhead in the shape
Of man, scorned by the world, his name unheard,
Save by the rabble of his native town,
Even as a parish demagogue. He led
The crowd; he taught them justice, truth, and peace,

In semblance; but he lit within their souls
The quenchless flames of zeal, and blest the sword   170
He brought on earth to satiate with the blood
Of truth and freedom his malignant soul.
At length his mortal frame was led to death.
I stood beside him: on the torturing cross
No pain assailed his unterrestrial sense;
And yet he groaned. Indignantly I summed
The massacres and miseries which his name
Had sanctioned in my country, and I cried,
Go! go! in mockery.
A smile of godlike malice reillumed   180
His fading lineaments. – I go, he cried.
But thou shalt wander o'er the unquiet earth
Eternally. – The dampness of the grave
Bathed my imperishable front. I fell,
And long lay tranced upon the charmed soil.
When I awoke hell burned within my brain,
Which staggered on its seat; for all around
The mouldering relics of my kindred lay,
Even as the Almighty's ire arrested them,
And in their various attitudes of death   190
My murdered children's mute and eyeless sculls
Glared ghastily upon me.
                              But my soul,
From sight and sense of the polluting woe
Of tyranny, had long learned to prefer
Hell's freedom to the servitude of heaven.
Therefore I rose, and dauntlessly began
My lonely and unending pilgrimage,
Resolved to wage unweariable war
With my almighty tyrant, and to hurl
Defiance at his impotence to harm   200
Beyond the curse I bore. The very hand
That barred my passage to the peaceful grave
Has crushed the earth to misery, and given
Its empire to the chosen of his slaves.
These have I seen, even from the earliest dawn
Of weak, unstable and precarious power;
Then preaching peace, as now they practise war,

So, when they turned but from the massacre
Of unoffending infidels, to quench
Their thirst for ruin in the very blood   210
That flowed in their own veins, and pitiless zeal
Froze every human feeling, as the wife
Sheathed in her husband's heart the sacred steel,
Even whilst its hopes were dreaming of her love;
And friends to friends, brothers to brothers stood
Opposed in bloodiest battlefield, and war,
Scarce satiable by fate's last death-draught waged,
Drunk from the winepress of the Almighty's wrath;
Whilst the red cross, in mockery of peace,
Pointed to victory! When the fray was done,   220
No remnant of the exterminated faith
Survived to tell its ruin, but the flesh,
With putrid smoke poisoning the atmosphere,
That rotted on the half-extinguished pile.

Yes! I have seen God's worshippers unsheathe
The sword of his revenge, when grace descended,
Confirming all unnatural impulses,
To sanctify their desolating deeds;
And frantic priests waved the ill-omened cross
O'er the unhappy earth: then shone the sun   230
On showers of gore from the upflashing steel
Of safe assassination, and all crime
Made stingless by the spirits of the Lord,
And blood-red rainbows canopied the land.

Spirit! no year of my eventful being
Has passed unstained by crime and misery,
Which flows from God's own faith. I've marked his slaves,
With tongues whose lies are venomous, beguile
The insensate mob, and, whilst one hand was red
With murder, feign to stretch the other out   240
For brotherhood and peace; and that they now
Babble of love and mercy, whilst their deeds
Are marked with all the narrowness and crime
That freedom's young arm dare not yet chastise,
Reason may claim our gratitude, who now

Establishing the imperishable throne
Of truth, and stubborn virtue, maketh vain
The unprevailing malice of my foe,
Whose bootless rage heaps torments for the brave,
Adds impotent eternities to pain,   250
Whilst keenest disappointment racks his breast
To see the smiles of peace around them play,
To frustrate or to sanctify their doom.

Thus have I stood, – through a wild waste of years
Struggling with whirlwinds of mad agony,
Yet peaceful, and serene, and self-enshrined,
Mocking my powerless tyrant's horrible curse
With stubborn and unalterable will,
Even as a giant oak, which heaven's fierce flame
Had scathed in the wilderness, to stand   260
A monument of fadeless ruin there;
Yet peacefully and movelessly it braves
The midnight conflict of the wintry storm,
    As in the sunlight's calm it spreads
    Its worn and withered arms on high
To meet the quiet of a summer's noon.

        The Fairy waved her wand:
        Ahasuerus fled
Fast as the shapes of mingled shade and mist,
That lurk in the glens of a twilight grove,   270
        Flee from the morning beam:
    The matter of which dreams are made
    Not more endowed with actual life
    Than this phantasmal portraiture
    Of wandering human thought.

VIII

The Fairy

The present and the past thou hast beheld:
It was a desolate sight. Now, Spirit, learn
   The secrets of the future. – Time!
Unfold the brooding pinion of thy gloom,
Render thou up thy half-devoured babes,
And from the cradles of eternity,
Where millions lie lulled to their portioned sleep
   By the deep murmuring stream of passing things,
Tear thou that gloomy shroud. – Spirit, behold
       Thy glorious destiny!   10

      Joy to the Spirit came.
Through the wide rent in Time's eternal veil,
Hope was seen beaming through the mists of fear:
     Earth was no longer hell;
     Love, freedom, health, had given
Their ripeness to the manhood of its prime,
     And all its pulses beat
Symphonious to the planetary spheres:
     Then dulcet music swelled
Concordant with the life-strings of the soul;   20
It throbbed in sweet and languid beatings there,
Catching new life from transitory death, –
Like the vague sighings of a wind at even,
That wakes the wavelets of the slumbering sea
And dies on the creation of its breath,
And sinks and rises, fails and swells by fits:
     Was the pure stream of feeling
     That sprung from these sweet notes,
And o'er the Spirit's human sympathies
With mild and gentle motion calmly flowed.   30

      Joy to the Spirit came, –
   Such joy as when a lover sees
The chosen of his soul in happiness,
     And witnesses her peace

Whose woe to him were bitterer than death,
    Sees her unfaded cheek
Glow mantling in first luxury of health,
    Thrills with her lovely eyes,
Which like two stars amid the heaving main
    Sparkle through liquid bliss.   40

Then in her triumph spoke the Fairy Queen:
I will not call the ghost of ages gone
To unfold the frightful secrets of its lore;
    The present now is past,
And those events that desolate the earth
Have faded from the memory of Time,
Who dares not give reality to that
Whose being I annul. To me is given
The wonders of the human world to keep,
Space, matter, time, and mind. Futurity   50
Exposes now its treasure; let the sight
Renew and strengthen all thy failing hope.
O human Spirit! spur thee to the goal
Where virtue fixes universal peace,
And midst the ebb and flow of human things,
Show somewhat stable, somewhat certain still,
A lighthouse o'er the wild of dreary waves.

The habitable earth is full of bliss;
Those wastes of frozen billows that were hurled
By everlasting snowstorms round the poles,   60
Where matter dared not vegetate or live,
But ceaseless frost round the vast solitude
Bound its broad zone of stillness, are unloosed;
And fragrant zephyrs there from spicy isles
Ruffle the placid ocean-deep, that rolls
Its broad, bright surges to the sloping sand,
Whose roar is wakened into echoings sweet
To murmur through the heaven-breathing groves
And melodise with man's blest nature there.

Those deserts of immeasurable sand,   70
Whose age-collected fervours scarce allowed

A bird to live, a blade of grass to spring,
Where the shrill chirp of the green lizard's love
Broke on the sultry silentness alone,
Now teem with countless rills and shady woods,
Cornfields and pastures and white cottages;
And where the startled wilderness beheld
A savage conqueror stained in kindred blood,
A tigress sating with the flesh of lambs,
The unnatural famine of her toothless cubs,   80
Whilst shouts and howlings through the desert rang,
Sloping and smooth the daisy-spangled lawn,
Offering sweet incense to the sunrise, smiles
To see a babe before his mother's door,
     Sharing his morning's meal
  With the green and golden basilisk
     That comes to lick his feet.

Those trackless deeps, where many a weary sail
Has seen above the illimitable plain,
Morning on night, and night on morning rise,   90
Whilst still no land to greet the wanderer spread
Its shadowy mountains on the sun-bright sea,
Where the loud roarings of the tempest-waves
So long have mingled with the gusty wind
In melancholy loneliness, and swept
The desert of those ocean solitudes,
But vocal to the sea-bird's harrowing shriek,
The bellowing monster, and the rushing storm,
Now to the sweet and many mingling sounds
Of kindliest human impulses respond.   100
Those lonely realms bright garden-isles begem,
With lightsome clouds and shining seas between,
And fertile valleys, resonant with bliss,
Whilst green woods overcanopy the wave,
Which like a toil-worn labourer leaps to shore,
To meet the kisses of the flow'rets there.

All things are recreated, and the flame
Of consentaneous love inspires all life:
The fertile bosom of the earth gives suck

To myriads, who still grow beneath her care,   110
Rewarding her with their pure perfectness:
The balmy breathings of the wind inhale
Her virtues, and diffuse them all abroad:
Health floats amid the gentle atmosphere,
Glows in the fruits, and mantles on the stream:
No storms deform the beaming brow of heaven,
Nor scatter in the freshness of its pride
The foliage of the ever-verdant trees;
But fruits are ever ripe, flowers ever fair,
And autumn proudly bears her matron grace,   120
Kindling a flush on the fair cheek of spring,
Whose virgin bloom beneath the ruddy fruit
Reflects its tint and blushes into love.

The lion now forgets to thirst for blood:
There might you see him sporting in the sun
Beside the dreadless kid; his claws are sheathed,
His teeth are harmless, custom's force has made
His nature as the nature of a lamb.
Like passion's fruit, the nightshade's tempting bane
Poisons no more the pleasure it bestows: 130
All bitterness is past; the cup of joy
Unmingled mantles to the goblet's brim,
And courts the thirsty lips it fled before.
But chief, ambiguous man, he that can know
More misery, and dream more joy than all;
Whose keen sensations thrill within his breast
To mingle with a loftier instinct there,
Lending their power to pleasure and to pain,
Yet raising, sharpening, and refining each;
Who stands amid the ever-varying world,   140
The burthen or the glory of the earth;
He chief perceives the change, his being notes
The gradual renovation, and defines
Each movement of its progress on his mind.

Man, where the gloom of the long polar night
Lowers o'er the snow-clad rocks and frozen soil,
Where scarce the hardiest herb that braves the frost

Basks in the moonlight's ineffectual glow,
Shrank with the plants, and darkened with the night;
His chilled and narrow energies, his heart,   150
Insensible to courage, truth, or love,
His stunted stature and imbecile frame,
Marked him for some abortion of the earth,
Fit compeer of the bears that roamed around,
Whose habits and enjoyments were his own:
His life a feverish dream of stagnant woe,
Whose meagre wants but scantily fulfilled,
Apprised him ever of the joyless length
Which his short being's wretchedness had reached;
His death a pang which famine, cold and toil,   160
Long on the mind, whilst yet the vital spark
Clung to the body stubbornly, had brought:
All was inflicted here that earth's revenge
Could wreak on the infringers of her law;
One curse alone was spared – the name of God.

Nor where the tropics bound the realms of day
With a broad belt of mingling cloud and flame,
Where blue mists through the unmoving atmosphere
Scattered the seeds of pestilence, and fed
Unnatural vegetation, where the land   170
Teemed with all earthquake, tempest and disease,
Was man a nobler being; slavery
Had crushed him to his country's bloodstained dust;
Or he was bartered for the fame of power,
Which all internal impulses destroying,
Makes human will an article of trade;
Or he was changed with Christians for their gold,
And dragged to distant isles, where to the sound
Of the flesh-mangling scourge, he does the work
Of all-polluting luxury and wealth,   180
Which doubly visits on the tyrants' heads
The long-protracted fullness of their woe;
Or he was led to legal butchery,
To turn to worms beneath that burning sun,
Where kings first leagued against the rights of men,
And priests first traded with the name of God.

Even where the milder zone afforded man
A seeming shelter, yet contagion there,
Blighting his being with unnumbered ills,
Spread like a quenchless fire; nor truth till late   190
Availed to arrest its progress, or create
That peace which first in bloodless victory waved
Her snowy standard o'er this favoured clime:
There man was long the train-bearer of slaves,
The mimic of surrounding misery,
The jackal of ambition's lion-rage,
The bloodhound of religion's hungry zeal.
Here now the human being stands adorning
This loveliest earth with taintless body and mind;
Blest from his birth with all bland impulses,   200
Which gently in his noble bosom wake
All kindly passions and all pure desires.
Him, still from hope to hope the bliss pursuing,
Which from the exhaustless lore of human weal
Dawns on the virtuous mind, the thoughts that rise
In time-destroying infiniteness, gift
With self-enshrined eternity, that mocks
The unprevailing hoariness of age,
And man, once fleeting o'er the transient scene
Swift as an unremembered vision, stands   210
Immortal upon earth: no longer now
He slays the lamb that looks him in the face,
And horribly devours his mangled flesh,
Which, still avenging nature's broken law,
Kindled all putrid humours in his frame,
All evil passions, and all vain belief,
Hatred, despair, and loathing in his mind,
The germs of misery, death, disease, and crime.
No longer now the winged habitants,
That in the woods their sweet lives sing away,   220
Flee from the form of man; but gather round,
And prune their sunny feathers on the hands
Which little children stretch in friendly sport
Towards these dreadless partners of their play.
All things are void of terror: man has lost
His terrible prerogative, and stands

An equal amidst equals: happiness
And science dawn though late upon the earth;
Peace cheers the mind, health renovates the frame;
Disease and pleasure cease to mingle here,   230
Reason and passion cease to combat there;
Whilst each unfettered o'er the earth extend
Their all-subduing energies, and wield
The sceptre of a vast dominion there;
Whilst every shape and mode of matter lends
Its force to the omnipotence of mind,
Which from its dark mine drags the gem of truth
To decorate its paradise of peace.

IX

O happy Earth! reality of Heaven!
To which those restless souls that ceaselessly
Throng through the human universe, aspire;
Thou consummation of all mortal hope!
Thou glorious prize of blindly-working will!
Whose rays, diffused throughout all space and time,
Verge to one point and blend for ever there:
Of purest spirits thou pure dwelling-place!
Where care and sorrow, impotence and crime,
Languor, disease, and ignorance dare not come: 10
O happy Earth, reality of Heaven!

Genius has seen thee in her passionate dreams,
And dim forebodings of thy loveliness
Haunting the human heart, have there entwined
Those rooted hopes of some sweet place of bliss
Where friends and lovers meet to part no more.
Thou art the end of all desire and will,
The product of all action; and the souls
That by the paths of an aspiring change
Have reached thy haven of perpetual peace,   20
There rest from the eternity of toil
That framed the fabric of thy perfectness.

Even Time, the conqueror, fled thee in his fear;
That hoary giant, who, in lonely pride,
So long had ruled the world, that nations fell
Beneath his silent footstep. Pyramids,
That for millenniums had withstood the tide
Of human things, his storm-breath drove in sand
Across that desert where their stones survived
The name of him whose pride had heaped them there.   30
Yon monarch, in his solitary pomp,
Was but the mushroom of a summer day,
That his light-winged footstep pressed to dust:
Time was the king of earth: all things gave way
Before him, but the fixed and virtuous will,
The sacred sympathies of soul and sense,
That mocked his fury and prepared his fall.

Yet slow and gradual dawned the morn of love;
Long lay the clouds of darkness o'er the scene,
Till from its native heaven they rolled away: 40
First, crime triumphant o'er all hope careered
Unblushing, undisguising, bold and strong;
Whilst falsehood, tricked in virtue's attributes,
Long sanctified all deeds of vice and woe,
Till done by her own venomous sting to death,
She left the moral world without a law,
No longer fettering passion's fearless wing,
Nor searing reason with the brand of God.
Then steadily the happy ferment worked;
Reason was free; and wild though passion went   50
Through tangled glens and wood-embosomed meads,
Gathering a garland of the strangest flowers,
Yet like the bee returning to her queen,
She bound the sweetest on her sister's brow,
Who meek and sober kissed the sportive child,
No longer trembling at the broken rod.

Mild was the slow necessity of death:
The tranquil Spirit failed beneath its grasp,
Without a groan, almost without a fear,
Calm as a voyager to some distant land,   60

And full of wonder, full of hope as he.
The deadly germs of languor and disease
Died in the human frame, and purity
Blest with all gifts her earthly worshippers.
How vigorous then the athletic form of age!
How clear its open and unwrinkled brow!
Where neither avarice, cunning, pride, or care,
Had stamped the seal of grey deformity
On all the mingling lineaments of time.
How lovely the intrepid front of youth!   70
Which meek-eyed courage decked with freshest grace;
Courage of soul, that dreaded not a name,
And elevated will, that journeyed on
Through life's phantasmal scene in fearlessness,
With virtue, love, and pleasure, hand in hand.

Then, that sweet bondage which is freedom's self,
And rivets with sensation's softest tie
The kindred sympathies of human souls,
Needed no fetters of tyrannic law:
Those delicate and timid impulses   80
In nature's primal modesty arose,
And with undoubting confidence disclosed
The growing longings of its dawning love,
Unchecked by dull and selfish chastity,
That virtue of the cheaply virtuous,
Who pride themselves in senselessness and frost.
No longer prostitution's venomed bane
Poisoned the springs of happiness and life;
Woman and man, in confidence and love,
Equal and free and pure together trod   90
The mountain-paths of virtue, which no more
Were stained with blood from many a pilgrim's feet.

Then, where, through distant ages, long in pride
The palace of the monarch-slave had mocked
Famine's faint groan, and penury's silent tear,
A heap of crumbling ruins stood, and threw
Year after year their stones upon the field,
Wakening a lonely echo; and the leaves

Of the old thorn, that on the topmost tower
Usurped the royal ensign's grandeur, shook 100
In the stern storm that swayed the topmost tower
And whispered strange tales in the whirlwind's ear.

Low through the lone cathedral's roofless aisles
The melancholy winds a death-dirge sung:
It were a sight of awfulness to see
The works of faith and slavery, so vast,
So sumptuous, yet so perishing withal!
Even as the corpse that rests beneath its wall.
A thousand mourners deck the pomp of death
Today, the breathing marble glows above 110
To decorate its memory, and tongues
Are busy of its life: tomorrow, worms
In silence and in darkness seize their prey.

Within the massy prison's mouldering courts,
Fearless and free the ruddy children played,
Weaving gay chaplets for their innocent brows
With the green ivy and the red wallflower,
That mock the dungeon's unavailing gloom;
The ponderous chains, and gratings of strong iron,
There rusted amid heaps of broken stone 120
That mingled slowly with their native earth:
There the broad beam of day, which feebly once
Lighted the cheek of lean captivity
With a pale and sickly glare, then freely shone
On the pure smiles of infant playfulness:
No more the shuddering voice of hoarse despair
Pealed through the echoing vaults, but soothing notes
Of ivy-fingered winds and gladsome birds
And merriment were resonant around.

These ruins soon left not a wreck behind: 130
Their elements, wide scattered o'er the globe,
To happier shapes were moulded, and became
Ministrant to all blissful impulses:
Thus human things were perfected, and earth,
Even as a child beneath its mother's love,

Was strengthened in all excellence, and grew
Fairer and nobler with each passing year.

Now Time his dusky pennons o'er the scene
Closes in stedfast darkness, and the past
Fades from our charmed sight. My task is done: 140
Thy lore is learned. Earth's wonders are thine own,
With all the fear and all the hope they bring.
My spells are past: the present now recurs.
Ah me! a pathless wilderness remains
Yet unsubdued by man's reclaiming hand.

Yet, human Spirit, bravely hold thy course,
Let virtue teach thee firmly to pursue
The gradual paths of an aspiring change:
For birth and life and death, and that strange state
Before the naked soul has found its home,   150
All tend to perfect happiness, and urge
The restless wheels of being on their way,
Whose flashing spokes, instinct with infinite life,
Bicker and burn to gain their destined goal:
For birth but wakes the spirit to the sense
Of outward shows, whose unexperienced shape
New modes of passion to its frame may lend;
Life is its state of action, and the store
Of all events is aggregated there
That variegate the eternal universe;   160
Death is a gate of dreariness and gloom,
That leads to azure isles and beaming skies
And happy regions of eternal hope.
Therefore, O Spirit! fearlessly bear on:
Though storms may break the primrose on its stalk,
Though frosts may blight the freshness of its bloom,
Yet Spring's awakening breath will woo the earth,
To feed with kindliest dews its favourite flower,
That blooms in mossy banks and darksome glens,
Lighting the greenwood with its sunny smile.   170

Fear not then, Spirit, death's disrobing hand,
So welcome when the tyrant is awake,

So welcome when the bigot's hell-torch burns;
'Tis but the voyage of a darksome hour,
The transient gulf-dream of a startling sleep.
Death is no foe to virtue: earth has seen
Love's brightest roses on the scaffold bloom,
Mingling with freedom's fadeless laurels there,
And presaging the truth of visioned bliss.
Are there not hopes within thee, which this scene   180
Of linked and gradual being has confirmed?
Whose stingings bade thy heart look further still,
When, to the moonlight walk by Henry led,
Sweetly and sadly thou didst talk of death?
And wilt thou rudely tear them from thy breast,
Listening supinely to a bigot's creed,
Or tamely crouching to the tyrant's rod,
Whose iron thongs are red with human gore?
Never: but bravely bearing on, thy will
Is destined an eternal war to wage   190
With tyranny and falsehood, and uproot
The germs of misery from the human heart.
Thine is the hand whose piety would soothe
The thorny pillow of unhappy crime,
Whose impotence an easy pardon gains,
Watching its wanderings as a friend's disease:
Thine is the brow whose mildness would defy
Its fiercest rage, and brave its sternest will,
When fenced by power and master of the world.
Thou art sincere and good; of resolute mind,   200
Free from heart-withering custom's cold control,
Of passion lofty, pure and unsubdued.
Earth's pride and meanness could not vanquish thee,
And therefore art thou worthy of the boon
Which thou hast now received: virtue shall keep
Thy footsteps in the path that thou hast trod,
And many days of beaming hope shall bless
Thy spotless life of sweet and sacred love.
Go, happy one, and give that bosom joy
    Whose sleepless spirit waits to catch   210
    Light, life and rapture from thy smile.

The Fairy waves her wand of charm.
Speechless with bliss the Spirit mounts the car,
That rolled beside the battlement,
Bending her beamy eyes in thankfulness.
  Again the enchanted steeds were yoked,
  Again the burning wheels inflame
The steep descent of heaven's untrodden way.
  Fast and far the chariot flew:
  The vast and fiery globes that rolled   220
  Around the Fairy's palace-gate
Lessened by slow degrees, and soon appeared
Such tiny twinklers as the planet orbs
That there attendant on the solar power
With borrowed light pursued their narrower way.
    Earth floated then below:
  The chariot paused a moment there;
    The Spirit then descended:
The restless coursers pawed the ungenial soil,
Snuffed the gross air, and then, their errand done,   230
Unfurled their pinions to the winds of heaven.

The Body and the Soul united then,
A gentle start convulsed Ianthe's frame:
Her veiny eyelids quietly unclosed;
Moveless awhile the dark blue orbs remained:
She looked around in wonder and beheld
Henry, who kneeled in silence by her couch,
Watching her sleep with looks of speechless love,
    And the bright beaming stars
    That through the casement shone.   240

Notes on Queen Mab

I, ll. 242–3 (p. 10)

The sun's unclouded orb
Rolled through the black concave

Beyond our atmosphere the sun would appear a rayless orb of fire in the
midst of a black concave. The equal diffusion of its light on earth is owing
to the refraction of the rays by the atmosphere, and their reflection from
other bodies. Light consists either of vibrations propagated through a
subtle medium, or of numerous minute particles repelled in all directions
from the luminous body. Its velocity greatly exceeds that of any substance
with which we are acquainted: observations on the eclipses of Jupiter's
satellites have demonstrated that light takes up no more than 8' 7" in
passing from the sun to the earth, a distance of 95,000,000 miles. – Some
idea may be gained of the immense distance of the fixed stars, when it is
computed that many years would elapse before light could reach this earth
from the nearest of them; yet in one year light travels 5,422,400,000,000
miles, which is a distance 5,707,600 times greater than that of the sun from
the earth.

I, ll. 252–3 (p. 10)

Whilst round the chariot's way
Innumerable systems rolled

The plurality of worlds – the indefinite immensity of the universe is a most
awful subject of contemplation. He who rightly feels its mystery and
grandeur, is in no danger of seduction from the falsehoods of religious
systems, or of deifying the principle of the universe. It is impossible to
believe that the Spirit that pervades this infinite machine, begat a son upon
the body of a Jewish woman; or is angered at the consequences of that
necessity, which is a synonym of itself. All that miserable tale of the Devil
and Eve, and an Intercessor, with the childish mummeries of the God of

the Jews, is irreconcilable with the knowledge of the stars. The works of his fingers have borne witness against him.

The nearest of the fixed stars is inconceivably distant from the earth, and they are probably proportionably distant from each other. By a calculation of the velocity of light, Sirius is supposed to be at least 54,224,000,000,000 miles from the earth.* That which appears only like a thin and silvery cloud streaking the heaven, is in effect composed of innumerable clusters of suns, each shining with its own light, and illuminating numbers of planets that revolve around them. Millions and millions of suns are ranged around us, all attended by innumerable worlds, yet calm, regular, and harmonious, all keeping the paths of immutable necessity.

Verse IV, ll. 178–9 (p. 29)

These are the hired bravos who defend
The tyrant's throne

To employ murder as a means of justice, is an idea which a man of an enlightened mind will not dwell upon with pleasure. To march forth in rank and file, and all the pomp of streamers and trumpets, for the purpose of shooting at our fellow-men as a mark; to inflict upon them all the variety of wound and anguish; to leave them weltering in their blood; to wander over the field of desolation, and count the number of the dying and the dead, – are employments which in thesis we may maintain to be necessary, but which no good man will contemplate with gratulation and delight. A battle we suppose is won: – thus truth is established, thus the cause of justice is confirmed! It surely requires no common sagacity to discern the connection between this immense heap of calamities and the assertion of truth or the maintenance of justice.

'Kings, and ministers of state, the real authors of the calamity, sit unmolested in their cabinet, while those against whom the fury of the storm is directed are, for the most part, persons who have been trepanned into the service, or who are dragged unwillingly from their peaceful homes into the field of battle. A soldier is a man whose business it is to kill those who never offended him, and who are the innocent martyrs of other men's

* See Nicholson's *Encyclopaedia*, art. Light.

iniquities. Whatever may become of the abstract question of the justifiableness of war, it seems impossible that the soldier should not be a depraved and unnatural being.

'To these more serious and momentous considerations it may be proper to add a recollection of the ridiculousness of the military character. Its first constituent is obedience: a soldier is, of all descriptions of men, the most completely a machine; yet his profession inevitably teaches him something of dogmatism, swaggering, and self-consequence: he is like the puppet of a showman, who, at the very time he is made to strut and swell and display the most farcical airs, we perfectly know cannot assume the most insignificant gesture, advance either to the right or the left, but as he is moved by his exhibitor.' Godwin's *Enquirer*,[15] Essay v.

I will here subjoin a little poem, so strongly expressive of my abhorrence of despotism and falsehood, that I fear lest it never again may be depictured so vividly. This opportunity is perhaps the only one that ever will occur of rescuing it from oblivion.

Falsehood and Vice[16]

A DIALOGUE

Whilst monarchs laughed upon their thrones
To hear a famished nation's groans,
And hugged the wealth wrung from the woe
That makes its eyes and veins o'erflow, –
Those thrones, high built upon the heaps
Of bones where frenzied famine sleeps,
Where slavery wields her scourge of iron,
Red with mankind's unheeded gore,
And war's mad fiends the scene environ,
Mingling with shrieks a drunken roar,   10
There Vice and Falsehood took their stand,
High raised above the unhappy land.

Falsehood

Brother! arise from the dainty fare,
Which thousands have toiled and bled to bestow;
A finer feast for thy hungry ear
Is the news that I bring of human woe.

Vice

And, secret one, what hast thou done,
To compare, in thy tumid pride, with me?
I, whose career, through the blasted year,
Has been tracked by despair and agony.   20

Falsehood

What have I done! – I have torn the robe
From baby truth's unsheltered form,
And round the desolated globe
Borne safely the bewildering charm:
My tyrant-slaves to a dungeon-floor
Have bound the fearless innocent,
And streams of fertilising gore
Flow from her bosom's hideous rent,
Which this unfailing dagger gave . . .
I dread that blood! – no more – this day   30
Is ours, though her eternal ray
Must shine upon our grave.
Yet know, proud Vice, had I not given
To thee the robe I stole from heaven,
Thy shape of ugliness and fear
Had never gained admission here.

Vice

And know, that had I disdained to toil,
But sate in my loathsome cave the while,
And ne'er to these hateful sons of heaven,
GOLD, MONARCHY, and MURDER, given;   40
Hadst thou with all thine art essayed
One of thy games then to have played,
With all thine overweening boast,
Falsehood! I tell thee thou hadst lost! –
Yet wherefore this dispute? – we tend,
Fraternal, to one common end;
In this cold grave beneath my feet,
Will our hopes, our fears, and our labours, meet.

Falsehood

I brought my daughter, RELIGION, on earth:
She smothered Reason's babes in their birth;   50

But dreaded their mother's eye severe, –
So the crocodile slunk off slily in fear,
And loosed her bloodhounds from the den . . .
They started from dreams of slaughtered men,
And, by the light of her poison eye,
Did her work o'er the wide earth frightfully:
The dreadful stench of her torches' flare,
Fed with human fat, polluted the air:
The curses, the shrieks, the ceaseless cries
Of the many-mingling miseries,   60
As on she trod, ascended high
And trumpeted my victory! –
Brother, tell what thou hast done.

Vice

I have extinguished the noonday sun,
In the carnage-smoke of battles won:
Famine, murder, hell and power
Were glutted in that glorious hour
Which searchless fate had stamped for me
With the seal of her security . . .
For the bloated wretch on yonder throne   70
Commanded the bloody fray to rise.
Like me he joyed at the stifled moan
Wrung from a nation's miseries;
While the snakes, whose slime even him *defiled*,
In ecstasies of malice smiled:
They thought 'twas theirs, – but mine the deed!
Theirs is the toil, but mine the meed –
Ten thousand victims madly bleed.
They dream that tyrants goad them there
With poisonous war to taint the air: 80
These tyrants, on their beds of thorn,
Swell with the thoughts of murderous fame,
And with their gains to lift my name
Restless they plan from night to morn:
I – I do all; without my aid
Thy daughter, that relentless maid,
Could never o'er a deathbed urge
The fury of her venomed scourge.

Falsehood

Brother, well: – the world is ours;
And whether thou or I have won,   90
The pestilence expectant lours
On all beneath yon blasted sun.
Our joys, our toils, our honours meet
In the milk-white and wormy winding-sheet:
A short-lived hope, unceasing care,
Some heartless scraps of godly prayer,
A moody curse, and a frenzied sleep
Ere gapes the grave's unclosing deep,
A tyrant's dream, a coward's start,
The ice that clings to a priestly heart,   100
A judge's frown, a courtier's smile,
Make the great whole for which we toil;
And, brother, whether thou or I
Have done the work of misery,
It little boots: thy toil and pain,
Without my aid, were more than vain;
And but for thee I ne'er had sate
The guardian of heaven's palace gate.

v, ll. 93–4 (p. 34)

And statesmen boast
Of wealth!

There is no real wealth but the labour of man. Were the mountains of gold
and the valleys of silver, the world would not be one grain of corn the
richer; no one comfort would be added to the human race. In consequence
of our consideration for the precious metals, one man is enabled to heap to
himself luxuries at the expense of the necessaries of his neighbour; a
system admirably fitted to produce all the varieties of disease and crime,
which never fail to characterise the two extremes of opulence and penury. A
speculator takes pride to himself as the promoter of his country's prosperity,
who employs a number of hands in the manufacture of articles avowedly
destitute of use, or subservient only to the unhallowed cravings of luxury

and ostentation. The nobleman, who employs the peasants of his neighbourhood in building his palaces, until *iam pauca aratro jugera, regiae moles relinquunt*,[17] flatters himself that he has gained the title of a patriot by yielding to the impulses of vanity. The show and pomp of courts adduce the same apology for its continuance; and many a fête has been given, many a woman has eclipsed her beauty by her dress, to benefit the labouring poor and to encourage trade. Who does not see that this is a remedy which aggravates, whilst it palliates, the countless diseases of society? The poor are set to labour – for what? Not the food for which they famish: not the blankets for want of which their babes are frozen by the cold of their miserable hovels: not those comforts of civilisation without which civilised man is far more miserable than the meanest savage; oppressed as he is by all its insidious evils, within the daily and taunting prospect of its innumerable benefits assiduously exhibited before him: – no; for the pride of power, for the miserable isolation of pride, for the false pleasures of the hundredth part of society. No greater evidence is afforded of the wide extended and radical mistakes of civilised man than this fact: those arts which are essential to his very being are held in the greatest contempt; employments are lucrative in an inverse ratio to their usefulness:* the jeweller, the toyman, the actor gains fame and wealth by the exercise of his useless and ridiculous art; whilst the cultivator of the earth, he without whom society must cease to subsist, struggles through contempt and penury, and perishes by that famine which, but for his unceasing exertions, would annihilate the rest of mankind.

I will not insult common sense by insisting on the doctrine of the natural equality of man. The question is not concerning its desirableness, but its practicability: so far as it is practicable, it is desirable. That state of human society which approaches nearer to an equal partition of its benefits and evils should, *caeteris paribus*,[18] be preferred: but so long as we conceive that a wanton expenditure of human labour, not for the necessities, not even for the luxuries of the mass of society, but for the egotism and ostentation of a few of its members, is defensible on the ground of public justice, so long we neglect to approximate to the redemption of the human race.

Labour is required for physical and leisure for moral improvement: from the former of these advantages the rich, and from the latter the poor, by the inevitable conditions of their respective situations, are precluded. A state which should combine the advantages of both, would be subjected to the

* See Rousseau, 'De l'Inégalité parmi les Hommes', note 7.

evils of neither. He that is deficient in firm health, or vigorous intellect, is but half a man: hence it follows that, to subject the labouring classes to unnecessary labour, is wantonly depriving them of any opportunities of intellectual improvement; and that the rich are heaping up for their own mischief the disease, lassitude, and ennui by which their existence is rendered an intolerable burthen.

English reformers exclaim against sinecures – but the true pension list is the rent-roll of the landed proprietors: wealth is a power usurped by the few to compel the many to labour for their benefit. The laws which support this system derive their force from the ignorance and credulity of its victims: they are the result of a conspiracy of the few against the many, who are themselves obliged to purchase this pre-eminence by the loss of all real comfort.

'The commodities that substantially contribute to the subsistence of the human species form a very short catalogue: they demand from us but a slender portion of industry. If these only were produced, and sufficiently produced, the species of man would be continued. If the labour necessarily required to produce them were equitably divided among the poor, and, still more, if it were equitably divided among all, each man's share of labour would be light, and his portion of leisure would be ample. There was a time when this leisure would have been of small comparative value: it is to be hoped that the time will come, when it will be applied to the most important purposes. Those hours which are not required for the production of the necessaries of life, may be devoted to the cultivation of the understanding, the enlarging our stock of knowledge, the refining our taste, and thus opening to us new and more exquisite sources of enjoyment.

*   *   *

'It was perhaps necessary that a period of monopoly and oppression should subsist, before a period of cultivated equality could subsist. Savages perhaps would never have been excited to the discovery of truth and the invention of art, but by the narrow motives which such a period affords. But surely, after the savage state has ceased, and men have set out in the glorious career of discovery and invention, monopoly and oppression cannot be necessary to prevent them from returning to a state of barbarism.' Godwin's *Enquirer*, Essay II. See also *Polit. Just.*, Book VIII, Ch. II.

It is a calculation of this admirable author, that all the conveniences of civilised life might be produced, if society would divide the labour equally among its members, by each individual being employed in labour two hours during the day.

v, ll. 112–13 (p. 34)

or religion
Drives his wife raving mad

I am acquainted with a lady of considerable accomplishments, and the mother of a numerous family, whom the Christian religion has goaded to incurable insanity. A parallel case is, I believe, within the experience of every physician.

> *Nam iam saepe homines patriam, carosque parentes*
> *Prodiderunt, vitare Acherusia templa petentes.*
>
> Lucretius[19]

v, l. 189 (p. 36)

Even love is sold

Not even the intercourse of the sexes is exempt from the despotism of positive institution. Law pretends even to govern the indisciplinable wanderings of passion, to put fetters on the clearest deductions of reason, and, by appeals to the will, to subdue the involuntary affections of our nature. Love is inevitably consequent upon the perception of loveliness. Love withers under constraint: its very essence is liberty: it is compatible neither with obedience, jealousy, nor fear: it is there most pure, perfect, and unlimited, where its votaries live in confidence, equality, and unreserve.

How long then ought the sexual connection to last? what law ought to specify the extent of the grievances which should limit its duration? A husband and wife ought to continue so long united as they love each other: any law which should bind them to cohabitation for one moment after the decay of their affection, would be a most intolerable tyranny, and the most unworthy of toleration. How odious an usurpation of the right of private judgement should that law be considered, which should make the ties of friendship indissoluble, in spite of the caprices, the inconstancy, the fallibility, and capacity for improvement of the human mind. And by so much would the fetters of love be heavier and more unendurable than those of friendship, as love is more vehement and capricious, more dependent on those delicate peculiarities of imagination, and less capable of reduction to the ostensible merits of the object.

The state of society in which we exist is a mixture of feudal savageness and imperfect civilisation. The narrow and unenlightened morality of the Christian religion is an aggravation of these evils. It is not even until lately that mankind have admitted that happiness is the sole end of the science of ethics, as of all other sciences; and that the fanatical idea of mortifying the flesh for the love of God has been discarded. I have heard, indeed, an ignorant collegian adduce, in favour of Christianity, its hostility to every worldly feeling!*

But if happiness be the object of morality, of all human unions and disunions; if the worthiness of every action is to be estimated by the quantity of pleasurable sensation it is calculated to produce, then the connection of the sexes is so long sacred as it contributes to the comfort of the parties, and is naturally dissolved when its evils are greater than its benefits. There is nothing immoral in this separation. Constancy has nothing virtuous in itself, independently of the pleasure it confers, and partakes of the temporising spirit of vice in proportion as it endures tamely moral defects of magnitude in the object of its indiscreet choice. Love is free: to promise for ever to love the same woman, is not less absurd than to promise to believe the same creed: such a vow in both cases, excludes us from all enquiry. The language of the votarist is this: The woman I now love may be infinitely inferior to many others: the creed I now profess may be a mass of errors and absurdities; but I exclude myself from all future information as to the amiability of the one and the truth of the other, resolving blindly, and in spite of conviction, to adhere to them. Is this the language of delicacy and reason? Is the love of such a frigid heart of more worth than its belief?

The present system of constraint does no more, in the majority of instances, than make hypocrites or open enemies. Persons of delicacy and virtue, unhappily united to one whom they find it impossible to love, spend the loveliest season of their life in unproductive efforts to appear otherwise than they are, for the sake of the feelings of their partner or the

---

* 'The first Christian emperor made a law by which seduction was punished with death: if the female pleaded her own consent, she also was punished with death; if the parents endeavoured to screen the criminals, they were banished and their estates were confiscated; the slaves who might be accessory were burned alive or forced to swallow melted lead. The very offspring of an illegal love were involved in the consequences of the sentence' – Gibbon's *Decline and Fall, &c.*, Vol. II, p. 210. See also, for the hatred of the primitive Christians to love and even marriage, p. 269.

welfare of their mutual offspring: those of less generosity and refinement openly avow their disappointment, and linger out the remnant of that union, which only death can dissolve, in a state of incurable bickering and hostility. The early education of their children takes its colour from the squabbles of the parents; they are nursed in a systematic school of ill humour, violence, and falsehood. Had they been suffered to part at the moment when indifference rendered their union irksome, they would have been spared many years of misery: they would have connected themselves more suitably, and would have found that happiness in the society of more congenial partners which is for ever denied them by the despotism of marriage. They would have been separately useful and happy members of society, who, whilst united, were miserable, and rendered misanthropical by misery. The conviction that wedlock is indissoluble holds out the strongest of all temptations to the perverse: they indulge without restraint in acrimony, and all the little tyrannies of domestic life, when they know that their victim is without appeal. If this connection were put on a rational basis, each would be assured that habitual ill temper would terminate in separation, and would check this vicious and dangerous propensity.

Prostitution is the legitimate offspring of marriage and its accompanying errors. Women, for no other crime than having followed the dictates of a natural appetite, are driven with fury from the comforts and sympathies of society. It is less venial than murder; and the punishment which is inflicted on her who destroys her child to escape reproach is lighter than the life of agony and disease to which the prostitute is irrecoverably doomed. Has a woman obeyed the impulse of unerring nature – society declares war against her, pitiless and eternal war: she must be the tame slave, she must make no reprisals; theirs is the right of persecution, hers the duty of endurance. She lives a life of infamy: the loud and bitter laugh of scorn scares her from all return. She dies of long and lingering disease: yet *she* is in fault, *she* is the criminal, *she* the froward and untameable child – and society, forsooth, the pure and virtuous matron, who casts her as an abortion from her undefiled bosom! Society avenges herself on the criminals of her own creation; she is employed in anathematising the vice today which yesterday she was the most zealous to teach. Thus is formed one tenth of the population of London: meanwhile the evil is twofold. Young men, excluded by the fanatical idea of chastity from the society of modest and accomplished women, associate with these vicious and miserable beings, destroying thereby all those exquisite and delicate sensibilities whose existence cold-hearted worldlings have denied; annihilating all genuine passion, and debasing that to a selfish feeling which is the excess of generosity and devotedness. Their body and mind alike crumble into a hideous wreck of humanity; idiocy and disease become perpetuated in their miserable offspring, and distant generations suffer for the bigoted morality of their forefathers. Chastity is a monkish and evangelical superstition, a greater foe to natural temperance even than unintellectual sensuality; it strikes at the root of all domestic happiness, and consigns more than half of the human race to misery, that some few may monopolise according to law. A system could not well have been devised more studiously hostile to human happiness than marriage.

I conceive that, from the abolition of marriage, the fit and natural arrangement of sexual connection would result. I by no means assert that the intercourse would be promiscuous: on the contrary; it appears, from the relation of parent to child, that this union is generally of long duration, and marked above all others with generosity and self-devotion. But this is a subject which it is perhaps premature to discuss. That which will result from the abolition of marriage, will be natural and right; because choice and change will be exempted from restraint.

In fact, religion and morality, as they now stand, compose a practical code of misery and servitude: the genius of human happiness must tear every leaf from the accursed book of God, ere man can read the inscription on his heart. How would morality, dressed up in stiff stays and finery, start from her own disgusting image, should she look in the mirror of nature!

vi, ll. 45–6 (p. 40)

To the red and baleful sun
That faintly twinkles there

The north polar star, to which the axis of the earth, in its present state of obliquity, points. It is exceedingly probable from many considerations, that this obliquity will gradually diminish, until the equator coincides with the ecliptic: the nights and days will then become equal on the earth throughout the year, and probably the seasons also. There is no great extravagance in presuming that the progress of the perpendicularity of the poles may be as rapid as the progress of intellect; or that there should be a perfect identity between the moral and physical improvement of the human species. It is certain that wisdom is not compatible with disease, and that, in the present state of the climates of the earth, health, in the true and comprehensive sense of the word, is out of the reach of civilised man. Astronomy teaches us that the earth is now in its progress, and that the poles are every year becoming more and more perpendicular to the ecliptic. The strong evidence afforded by the history of mythology, and geological researches, that some event of this nature has taken place already, affords a strong presumption that this progress is not merely an oscillation, as has been surmised by some late astronomers.* Bones of animals peculiar to the torrid zone have been found in the north of Siberia, and on the banks of the River Ohio. Plants have been found in the fossil state in the interior of Germany, which demand the present climate of Hindostan for their production.† The researches of M. Bailly§ establish the existence of a people who inhabited a tract in Tartary 49° north latitude, of greater antiquity than either the Indians, the Chinese, or the Chaldeans, from whom these nations derived their sciences and theology. We find, from the testimony of ancient writers, that Britain, Germany and France were much colder than at present, and that their great rivers were annually frozen over. Astronomy teaches us also that since this period the obliquity of the earth's position has been considerably diminished.

vi, l. 198 (p. 44)

Necessity! thou mother of the world!

He who asserts the doctrine of Necessity, means that, contemplating the events which compose the moral and material universe, he beholds only an immense and uninterrupted chain of causes and effects, no one of which could occupy any other place than it does occupy, or act in any other place than it does act. The idea of necessity is obtained by our experience of the connection between objects, the uniformity of the operations of nature, the constant conjunction of similar events, and the consequent inference of

* Laplace, *Système du Monde*
† Cabanis, *Rapports du Physique et du Moral de l'Homme*, Vol. II, p. 406
§ Bailly, *Lettres sur les Sciences, à Voltaire*

one from the other. Mankind are therefore agreed in the admission of necessity, if they admit that these two circumstances take place in voluntary action. Motive is, to voluntary action in the human mind, what cause is to effect in the material universe. The word liberty, as applied to mind, is analogous to the word chance as applied to matter: they spring from an ignorance of the certainty of the conjunction of antecedents and consequents.

Every human being is irresistibly impelled to act precisely as he does act: in the eternity which preceded his birth a chain of causes was generated, which, operating under the name of motives, make it impossible that any thought of his mind, or any action of his life, should be otherwise than it is. Were the doctrine of Necessity false, the human mind would no longer be a legitimate object of science, from like causes it would be in vain that we should expect like effects; the strongest motive would no longer be paramount over the conduct; all knowledge would be vague and undeterminate; we could not predict with any certainty that we might not meet as an enemy tomorrow him with whom we have parted in friendship tonight; the most probable inducements and the clearest reasonings would lose the invariable influence they possess. The contrary of this is demonstrably the fact. Similar circumstances produce the same unvariable effects. The precise character and motives of any man on any occasion being given, the moral philosopher could predict his actions with as much certainty as the natural philosopher could predict the effects of the mixture of any particular chemical substances. Why is the aged husbandman more experienced than the young beginner? Because there is a uniform, undeniable necessity in the operations of the material universe. Why is the old statesman more skilful than the raw politician? Because, relying on the necessary conjunction of motive and action, he proceeds to produce moral effects, by the application of those moral causes which experience has shown to be effectual. Some actions may be found to which we can attach no motives, but these are the effects of causes with which we are unacquainted. Hence the relation which motive bears to voluntary action is that of cause to effect; nor, placed in this point of view, is it, or ever has it been, the subject of popular or philosophical dispute. None but the few fanatics who are engaged in the herculean task of reconciling the justice of their God with the misery of man, will longer outrage common sense by the supposition of an event without a cause, a voluntary action without a motive. History, politics, morals, criticism, all grounds of reasonings, all principles of science, alike assume the truth of the doctrine of Necessity. No farmer carrying his corn to market doubts the sale of it at the market price. The master of a manufactory no more doubts that he can purchase the human labour necessary for his purposes, than that his machinery will act as they have been accustomed to act.

But, whilst none have scrupled to admit necessity as influencing matter, many have disputed its dominion over mind. Independently of its militating with the received ideas of the justice of God, it is by no means obvious to a superficial enquiry. When the mind observes its own operations, it feels no connection of motive and action: but as we know 'nothing more of causation than the constant conjunction of objects and the consequent inference of one from the other, as we find that these two circumstances are universally allowed to have place in voluntary action, we may be easily led to own that they are subjected to the necessity common to all causes'. The actions of the will have a regular conjunction with circumstances and characters; motive is, to voluntary action, what cause is to effect. But the only idea we can form of causation is a constant conjunction of similar objects, and the consequent inference of one from the other: wherever this is the case necessity is clearly established.

The idea of liberty, applied metaphorically to the will, has sprung from a misconception of the meaning of the word power. What is power? – *id quod potest*,[20] that which can produce any given effect. To deny power, is to say that nothing can or has the power to be or act. In the only true sense of the word power, it applies with equal force to the loadstone as to the human will. Do you think these motives, which I shall present, are powerful enough to rouse him? is a question just as common as, Do you think this lever has the power of raising this weight? The advocates of free-will assert that the will has the power of refusing to be determined by the strongest motive: but the strongest motive is that which, overcoming all others, ultimately prevails; this assertion therefore amounts to a denial of the will being ultimately determined by that motive which does determine it, which is absurd. But it is equally certain that a man cannot resist the strongest motive, as that he cannot overcome a physical impossibility.

The doctrine of Necessity tends to introduce a great change into the established notions of morality, and utterly to destroy religion. Reward and punishment must be considered, by the Necessarian, merely as motives which he would employ in order to procure the adoption or abandonment of any given line of conduct. Desert, in the present sense of the word, would no longer have any meaning; and he who should inflict pain upon another for no better reason than that he deserved it, would only gratify his revenge under pretence of satisfying Justice. It is not enough, says the advocate of free-will, that a criminal should be prevented from a repetition of his crime: he should feel pain, and his torments, when justly inflicted, ought precisely to be proportioned to his fault. But utility is morality; that which is incapable of producing happiness is useless, and though the crime of Damiens must be condemned, yet the frightful torments which revenge, under the name of justice, inflicted on this unhappy man, cannot be supposed to have augmented, even at the long run, the stock of pleasurable sensation in the world. At the same time, the doctrine of Necessity does not in the least diminish our disapprobation of vice. The conviction which all feel, that a viper is a poisonous animal, and that a tiger is constrained, by the inevitable condition of his existence, to devour men, does not induce us to avoid them less sedulously, or, even more, to hesitate in destroying them: but he would surely be of a hard heart, who, meeting with a serpent on a desert island, or in a situation where it was incapable of injury, should wantonly deprive it of existence. A Necessarian is inconsequent to his own principles if he indulges in hatred or contempt; the compassion which he feels for the criminal is unmixed with a desire of injuring him: he looks with an elevated and dreadless composure upon the links of the universal chain as they pass before his eyes; whilst cowardice, curiosity and inconsistency only assail him in proportion to the feebleness and indistinctness with which he has perceived and rejected the delusions of free-will.

Religion is the perception of the relation in which we stand to the principle of the universe. But if the principle of the universe be not an organic being, the model and prototype of man, the relation between it and human beings is absolutely none. Without some insight into its will respecting our actions religion is nugatory and vain. But will is only a mode of animal mind; moral qualities also are such as only a human being can possess; to attribute them to the principle of the universe is to annex to it properties incompatible with any possible definition of its nature. It is probable that the word God was originally only an expression denoting the unknown cause of the known events which men perceived in the universe. By the vulgar mistake of a metaphor for a real being, of a word for a thing, it became a man, endowed with human qualities and governing the universe as an earthly monarch governs his kingdom. Their addresses to this imaginary being, indeed, are much in the same style as those of subjects to a king. They acknowledge his benevolence, deprecate his anger, and supplicate his favour.

But the doctrine of Necessity teaches us that in no case could any event have happened otherwise than it did happen, and that, if God is the author of good, he is also the author of evil; that, if he is entitled to our gratitude for the one, he is entitled to our hatred for the other; that, admitting the existence of this hypothetic being, he is also subjected to the dominion of an immutable necessity. It is plain that the same arguments which prove that God is the author of food, light, and life, prove him also to be the author of poison, darkness, and death. The wide-wasting earthquake, the storm, the battle, and the tyranny, are attributable to this hypothetic being in the same degree as the fairest forms of nature, sunshine, liberty, and peace.

But we are taught, by the doctrine of Necessity, that there is neither good nor evil in the universe, otherwise than as the events to which we apply these epithets have relation to our own peculiar mode of being. Still less than with the hypothesis of a God will the doctrine of Necessity accord with the belief of a future state of punishment. God made man such as he is, and then damned him for being so: for to say that God was the author of all good, and man the author of all evil, is to say that one man made a straight line and a crooked one, and another man made the incongruity.

A Mahometan story, much to the present purpose, is recorded, wherein Adam and Moses are introduced disputing before God in the following manner. Thou, says Moses, art Adam, whom God created, and animated with the breath of life, and caused to be worshipped by the angels, and placed in Paradise, from whence mankind have been expelled for thy fault. Whereto Adam answered, Thou art Moses, whom God chose for his apostle, and entrusted with his word, by giving thee the tables of the law, and whom he vouchsafed to admit to discourse with himself. How many years dost thou find the law was written before I was created? Says Moses, Forty. And dost thou not find, replied Adam, these words therein, And Adam rebelled against his Lord and transgressed? Which Moses confessing, Dost thou therefore blame me, continued he, for doing that which God wrote of me that I should do, forty years before I was created, nay, for what was decreed concerning me fifty thousand years before the creation of heaven and earth? – Sale's *Preliminary Discourse to the Koran*,[21] p. 164.

VII, l. 13 (p. 45)

There is no God

This negation must be understood solely to affect a creative Deity. The hypothesis of a pervading Spirit, coeternal with the universe, remains unshaken.

A close examination of the validity of the proofs adduced to support any proposition is the only secure way of attaining truth, on the advantages of which it is unnecessary to descant: our knowledge of the existence of a Deity is a subject of such importance that it cannot be too minutely investigated; in consequence of this conviction we proceed briefly and impartially to examine the proofs which have been adduced. It is necessary first to consider the nature of belief.

When a proposition is offered to the mind, it perceives the agreement or disagreement of the ideas of which it is composed. A perception of their agreement is termed *belief*. Many obstacles frequently prevent this perception from being immediate; these the mind attempts to remove in order that the perception may be distinct. The mind is active in the investigation, in order to perfect the state of perception of the relation which the component ideas of the proposition bear to each, which is passive: the investigation being confused with the perception has induced many falsely to imagine that the mind is active in belief – that belief is an act of volition – in consequence of which it may be regulated by the mind. Pursuing, continuing this mistake, they have attached a degree of criminality to disbelief; of which, in its nature, it is incapable: it is equally incapable of merit.

Belief, then, is a passion, the strength of which, like every other passion, is in precise proportion to the degrees of excitement.

The degrees of excitement are three.

The senses are the sources of all knowledge to the mind; consequently their evidence claims the strongest assent.

The decision of the mind, founded upon our own experience, derived from these sources, claims the next degree.

The experience of others, which addresses itself to the former one, occupies the lowest degree.

(A graduated scale, on which should be marked the capabilities of propositions to approach to the test of the senses, would be a just barometer of the belief which ought to be attached to them.)

Consequently no testimony can be admitted which is contrary to reason; reason is founded on the evidence of our senses.

Every proof may be referred to one of these three divisions: it is to be considered what arguments we receive from each of them which should convince us of the existence of a Deity.

1st. The evidence of the senses. If the Deity should appear to us, if he should convince our senses of his existence, this revelation would necessarily command belief. Those to whom the Deity has thus appeared have the strongest possible conviction of his existence. But the God of Theologians is incapable of local visibility.

2d. Reason. It is urged that man knows that whatever is must either have had a beginning, or have existed from all eternity: he also knows, that whatever is not eternal must have had a cause. When this reasoning is applied to the universe, it is necessary to prove that it was created: until that is clearly demonstrated, we may reasonably suppose that it has endured from all eternity. We must prove design before we can infer a designer. The only idea which we can form of causation is derivable from the constant conjunction of objects, and the consequent inference of one from the other. In a case where two propositions are diametrically opposite, the mind believes that which is least incomprehensible; – it is easier to suppose that the universe has existed from all eternity than to conceive a being beyond its limits capable of creating it: if the mind sinks beneath the weight of one, is it an alleviation to increase the intolerability of the burthen?

The other argument, which is founded on a man's knowledge of his own existence, stands thus. A man knows not only that he now is, but that once he was not; consequently there must have been a cause. But our idea of causation is alone derivable from the constant conjunction of objects and the consequent inference of one from the other; and, reasoning experimentally, we can only infer from effects causes exactly adequate to those effects. But there certainly is a generative power which is effected by certain instruments: we cannot prove that it is inherent in these instruments; nor is the contrary hypothesis capable of demonstration: we admit that the generative power is incomprehensible; but to suppose that the same effect is produced by an eternal, omniscient, omnipotent being, leaves the cause in the same obscurity, but renders it more incomprehensible.

3d. Testimony. It is required that testimony should not be contrary to reason. The testimony that the Deity convinces the senses of men of his existence can only be admitted by us if our mind considers it less probable that these men should have been deceived than that the Deity should have appeared to them. Our reason can never admit the testimony of men who not only declare that they were eye witnesses of miracles but that the Deity was irrational: for he commanded that he should be believed, he proposed the highest rewards for faith, eternal punishments for disbelief. We can only command voluntary actions; belief is not an act of volition; the mind is even passive, or involuntarily active; from this it is evident that we have no sufficient testimony, or rather that testimony is insufficient to prove the being of a God. It has been before shown that it cannot be deduced from reason. They alone, then, who have been convinced by the evidence of the senses can believe it.

Hence it is evident that, having no proofs from either of the three sources of conviction, the mind *cannot* believe the existence of a creative God: it is also evident that, as belief is a passion of the mind, no degree of criminality is attachable to disbelief, and that they only are reprehensible who neglect to remove the false medium through which their mind views any subject of discussion. Every reflecting mind must acknowledge that there is no proof of the existence of a Deity.

God is an hypothesis, and, as such, stands in need of proof: the *onus probandi*[22] rests on the theist. Sir Isaac Newton says: *Hypotheses non fingo, quicquid enim ex phaenomenis non deducitur hypothesis vocanda est, et hypotheses vel metaphysicae, vel physicae, vel qualitatum occultarum, seu mechanicae, in philosophia locum non habent.*[23] To all proofs of the existence of a creative God apply this valuable rule. We see a variety of bodies possessing a variety of powers: we merely know their effects, we are in a state of ignorance with respect to their essences and causes. These Newton calls the phenomena of things, but the pride of philosophy is unwilling to admit its ignorance of their causes. From the phenomena, which are the objects of our senses, we attempt to infer a cause, which we call God, and gratuitously endow it with all negative and contradictory qualities. From this hypothesis we invent this general name, to conceal our ignorance of causes and essences. The being called God by no means answers with the conditions prescribed by Newton; it bears every mark of a veil woven by philosophical conceit, to hide the ignorance of philosophers even from themselves. They borrow the threads of its texture from the anthropomorphism of the vulgar. Words have been used by sophists for the same purposes, from the occult qualities of the peripatetics to the *effluvium* of Boyle and the *crinities* or *nebulae* of Herschel.[24] God is represented as infinite, eternal, incomprehensible; he is contained under every *predicate in non* that the logic of ignorance could fabricate. Even his worshippers allow that it is impossible to form any idea of him: they exclaim with the French poet,

Pour dire ce qu'il est, il faut être lui-même.[25]

Lord Bacon[26] says that 'atheism leaves to man reason, philosophy, natural piety, laws, reputation, and everything that can serve to conduct him to virtue, but superstition destroys all these, and erects itself into a tyranny over the understandings of men: hence atheism never disturbs the government, but renders man more clear-sighted, since he sees nothing beyond the boundaries of the present life.' Bacon's *Moral Essays*.

*   *   *

The enlightened and benevolent Pliny[27] thus publicly professes himself an atheist:

Quapropter effigiem Dei, formamque quaerere imbecillitatis humanae reor. Quisquis est Deus (si modo est alius) et quacunque in parte, totus est sensus, totus est visus, totus auditus, totus animae, totus animi, totus sui . . . Imperfectae vero in homine naturae praecipua solacia ne deum quidem posse omnia. Namque nec sibi potest mortem consciscere, si velit, quod homini dedit optimum in tantis vitae poenis: nec mortales aeternitate donare, aut revocare defunctos – nec facere ut qui vixit non vixerit, qui honores gessit non gesserit, nullumque habere in praeteritum ius, praeterquam oblivionis, atque (ut facetis quoque argumentis societas haec cum deo copuletur) ut bis dena viginti non sint, et multa similiter efficere non posse. Per quae declaratur haud dubie naturae potentia id quoque esse quod Deum vocamus.   [Pliny, *Nat. His. cap. de Deo*]

The consistent Newtonian is necessarily an atheist. See Sir W. Drummond's *Academical Questions*, Ch. III. Sir W. seems to consider the atheism to which it leads, as a sufficient presumption of the falsehood of the system of gravitation: but surely it is more consistent with the good faith of philosophy to admit a deduction from facts than an hypothesis incapable of proof, although it might militate with the obstinate preconceptions of the mob. Had this author, instead of inveighing against the guilt and absurdity of atheism, demonstrated its falsehood, his conduct would have been more suited to the modesty of the sceptic and the toleration of the philosopher.

Omnia enim per Dei potentiam facta sunt: immo quia naturae potentia nulla est nisi ipsa Dei potentia. Certum est nos eatenus Dei potentiam non intelligere, quatenus causas naturales ignoramus; adeoque stulte ad eandem Dei potentiam recurritur, quando rei alicuius, causam naturalem, sive est, ipsam Dei potentiam ignoramus.

[Spinoza,[28] *Tract. Theologico-Polit.*, Ch. I, p. 14]

VII, l. 67 (p. 47)

Ahasuerus, rise![29]

'Ahasuerus the Jew crept forth from the dark cave of Mount Carmel. Near two thousand years have elapsed since he was first goaded by never-ending restlessness to rove the globe from pole to pole. When our Lord was wearied with the burthen of his ponderous cross, and wanted to rest before the door of Ahasuerus, the unfeeling wretch drove him away with brutality. The Saviour of mankind staggered, sinking under the heavy load, but uttered no complaint. An angel of death appeared before Ahasuerus, and exclaimed indignantly, "Barbarian! thou hast denied rest to the Son of Man: be it denied thee also, until he comes to judge the world."

'A black demon, let loose from hell upon Ahasuerus, goads him now from country to country; he is denied the consolation which death affords, and precluded from the rest of the peaceful grave.

'Ahasuerus crept forth from the dark cave of Mount Carmel – he shook the dust from his beard – and taking up one of the skulls heaped there, hurled it down the eminence: it rebounded from the earth in shivered atoms. "This was my father!" roared Ahasuerus. Seven more sculls rolled down from rock to rock; while the infuriate Jew, following them with ghastly looks, exclaimed – "And these were my wives!" He still continued to hurl down skull after skull, roaring in dreadful accents – "And these, and these, and these were my children! They *could die*; but I! reprobate wretch, alas! I cannot die! Dreadful beyond conception is the judgement that hangs over me. Jerusalem fell – I crushed the sucking babe, and precipitated myself into the destructive flames. I cursed the Romans – but, alas! alas! the restless curse held me by the hair – and I could not die!

' "Rome the giantess fell – I placed myself before the falling statue – she fell, and did not crush me. Nations sprang up and disappeared before me; – but I remained and did not die. From cloud-encircled cliffs did I precipitate myself into the ocean but the foaming billows cast me upon the shore, and the burning arrow of existence pierced my cold heart again. I leaped into Etna's flaming abyss, and roared with the giants for ten long months, polluting with my groans the Mount's sulphurous mouth – ah! ten long months. The volcano fermented and in a fiery stream of lava cast me up. I lay torn by the torture-snakes of hell amid the glowing cinders, and yet continued to exist. – A forest was on fire: I darted on wings of fury and despair into the crackling wood. Fire dropped upon me from the trees, but the flames only singed my limbs; alas! it could not consume them. – I now mixed with the butchers of mankind, and plunged in the tempest of the raging battle. I roared defiance to the infuriate Gaul, defiance to the victorious German; but arrows and spears rebounded in shivers from my body. The Saracen's flaming sword broke upon my skull: balls in vain hissed upon me: the lightnings of battle glared harmless around my loins: in vain did the elephant trample on me, in vain the iron hoof of the wrathful steed! The mine, big with destructive power, burst upon me, and hurled me high in the air – I fell on heaps of smoking limbs, but was only singed. The giant's steel club rebounded from my body; the executioner's hand could not strangle me, the tiger's tooth could not pierce me, nor would the hungry lion in the circus devour me. I cohabited with poisonous snakes, and pinched the red crest of the dragon. The serpent stung, but could not destroy me. The dragon tormented, but dared not to devour me. – I now provoked the fury of tyrants: I said to Nero, 'Thou art a bloodhound!' I said to Christiern, 'Thou art a bloodhound!' I said to Muley Ismail, 'Thou art a bloodhound!' – The tyrants invented cruel torments, but did not kill me. Ha! not to be able to die – not to be able to die – not to be permitted to rest after the toils of life – to be doomed to be imprisoned for ever in the clay-formed dungeon – to be for ever clogged with this worthless body, its load of diseases and infirmities – to be condemned to [be]hold for millenniums that yawning monster Sameness, and Time, that hungry hyaena, ever bearing children, and ever devouring again her offspring! – Ha! not to be permitted to die! Awful avenger in heaven, hast thou in thine armoury of wrath a punishment more dreadful? then let it thunder upon me, command a hurricane to sweep me down to the foot of Carmel, that I there may lie extended; may pant, and writhe, and die!" '

This fragment is the translation of part of some German work, whose title I have vainly endeavoured to discover. I picked it up, dirty and torn, some years ago, in Lincoln's Inn Fields.

VII, ll. 135–6 (p. 49)

I will beget a Son, and he shall bear
The sins of all the world

A book is put into our hands when children, called the Bible, the purport of whose history is briefly this: That God made the earth in six days, and there planted a delightful garden, in which he placed the first pair of human beings. In the midst of the garden he planted a tree, whose fruit, although within their reach, they were forbidden to touch. That the Devil, in the shape of a snake, persuaded them to eat of this fruit; in consequence of which God condemned both them and their posterity yet unborn, to satisfy his justice by their eternal misery. That, four thousand years after these events (the human race in the meanwhile having gone unredeemed to perdition), God engendered with the betrothed wife of a carpenter in Judea (whose virginity was nevertheless uninjured) and begat a son, whose name was Jesus Christ; and who was crucified and died, in order that no more men might be devoted to hell-fire, he bearing the burthen of his father's displeasure by proxy. The book states, in addition, that the soul of whoever disbelieves this sacrifice will be burned with everlasting fire.

During many ages of misery and darkness this story gained implicit belief; but at length men arose who suspected that it was a fable and imposture, and that Jesus Christ, so far from being a God, was only a man like themselves. But a numerous set of men, who derived and still derive immense emoluments from this opinion, in the shape of a popular belief, told the vulgar that, if they did not believe in the Bible, they would be damned to all eternity; and burned, imprisoned, and poisoned all the unbiased and unconnected enquirers who occasionally arose. They still oppress them, so far as the people, now become more enlightened, will allow.

The belief in all that the Bible contains is called Christianity. A Roman governor of Judea, at the instance of a priest-led mob, crucified a man called Jesus eighteen centuries ago. He was a man of pure life, who desired to rescue his countrymen from the tyranny of their barbarous and degrading superstitions. The common fate of all who desire to benefit mankind awaited him. The rabble, at the instigation of the priests, demanded his death, although his very judge made public acknowledgement of his innocence. Jesus was sacrificed to the honour of that God with whom he was afterwards confounded. It is of importance, therefore, to distinguish between the pretended character of this being as the Son of God and the Saviour of the World, and his real character as a man, who, for a vain attempt to reform the world, paid the forfeit of his life to that overbearing tyranny which has since so long desolated the universe in his name. Whilst the one is a hypocritical demon, who announces himself as the God of compassion and peace, even whilst he stretches forth his blood-red hand with the sword of discord to waste the earth, having confessedly devised this scheme of desolation from eternity; the other stands in the foremost list of those true heroes who have died in the glorious martyrdom of liberty, and have braved torture, contempt, and poverty, in the cause of suffering humanity.*

The vulgar, ever in extremes, became persuaded that the crucifixion of Jesus was a supernatural event. Testimonies of miracles, so frequent in unenlightened ages, were not wanting to prove that he was something divine. This belief, rolling through the lapse of ages, met with the reveries of Plato and the reasonings of Aristotle, and acquired force and extent, until the divinity of Jesus became a dogma, which to dispute was death, which to doubt was infamy.

Christianity is now the established religion: he who attempts to impugn it must be contented to behold murderers and traitors take precedence of him in public opinion; though, if his genius be equal to his courage, and assisted by a peculiar coalition of circumstances, future ages may exalt him to a divinity, and persecute others in his name, as he was persecuted in the name of his predecessor in the homage of the world.

The same means that have supported every other popular belief have supported Christianity. War, imprisonment, assassination, and falsehood; deeds of unexampled and incomparable atrocity have made it what it is. The blood shed by the votaries of the God of mercy and peace, since the establishment of his religion, would probably suffice to drown all other sectaries now on the habitable globe. We derive from our ancestors a faith thus fostered and supported: we quarrel, persecute, and hate for its maintenance. Even under a government which, whilst it infringes the very right of thought and speech, boasts of permitting the liberty of the press, a man is pilloried and imprisoned because he is a deist, and no one raises his voice in the indignation of outraged humanity. But it is ever a proof that the falsehood of a proposition is felt by those who use coercion, not reasoning, to procure its admission; and a dispassionate observer would feel himself

---

* Since writing this note I have some reason to suspect that Jesus was an ambitious man who aspired to the throne of Judea.

more powerfully interested in favour of a man who, depending on the truth of his opinions, simply stated his reasons for entertaining them, than in that of his aggressor who, daringly avowing his unwillingness or incapacity to answer them by argument, proceeded to repress the energies and break the spirit of their promulgator by that torture and imprisonment whose infliction he could command.

Analogy seems to favour the opinion that as, like other systems, Christianity has arisen and augmented, so like them it will decay and perish; that as violence, darkness and deceit, not reasoning and persuasion, have procured its admission among mankind, so, when enthusiasm has subsided, and time, that infallible controverter of false opinions, has involved its pretended evidences in the darkness of antiquity, it will become obsolete; that Milton's poem alone will give permanency to the remembrance of its absurdities; and that men will laugh as heartily at grace, faith, redemption, and original sin, as they now do at the Metamorphosis of Jupiter, the miracles of Romish saints, the efficacy of witchcraft, and the appearance of departed spirits.

Had the Christian religion commenced and continued by the mere force of reasoning and persuasion, the preceding analogy would be inadmissible. We should never speculate on the future obsoleteness of a system perfectly conformable to nature and reason: it would endure so long as they endured; it would be a truth as indisputable as the light of the sun, the criminality of murder, and other facts, whose evidence, depending on our organisation and relative situations, must remain acknowledged as satisfactory so long as man is man. It is an incontrovertible fact, the consideration of which ought to repress the hasty conclusions of credulity, or moderate its obstinacy in maintaining them, that, had the Jews not been a fanatical race of men, had even the resolution of Pontius Pilate been equal to his candour, the Christian religion never could have prevailed, it could not even have existed: on so feeble a thread hangs the most cherished opinion of a sixth of the human race! When will the vulgar learn humility? When will the pride of ignorance blush at having believed before it could comprehend?

Either the Christian religion is true, or it is false: if true, it comes from God, and its authenticity can admit of doubt and dispute no further than its omnipotent author is willing to allow. Either the power or the goodness of God is called in question, if he leaves those doctrines most essential to the well being of man in doubt and dispute; the only ones which, since their promulgation, have been the subject of unceasing cavil, the cause of irreconcilable hatred. *If God has spoken, why is the Universe not convinced?*[30]

There is this passage in the Christian Scriptures: 'Those who obey not God, and believe not the Gospel of his Son, shall be punished with everlasting destruction.' This is the pivot upon which all religions turn: they all assume that it is in our power to believe or not to believe; whereas the mind can only believe that which it thinks true. A human being can only be supposed accountable for those actions which are influenced by his will. But belief is utterly distinct from and unconnected with volition: it is the apprehension of the agreement or disagreement of the ideas that compose any proposition. Belief is a passion, or involuntary operation of the mind, and, like other passions, its intensity is precisely proportionate to the degrees of excitement. Volition is essential to merit or demerit. But the Christian religion attaches the highest possible degrees of merit and demerit to that which is worthy of neither, and which is totally unconnected with the peculiar faculty of the mind, whose presence is essential to their being.

Christianity was intended to reform the world: had an all-wise Being planned it, nothing is more improbable than that it should have failed: omniscience would infallibly have foreseen the inutility of a scheme which experience demonstrates, to this age, to have been utterly unsuccessful.

Christianity inculcates the necessity of supplicating the Deity. Prayer may be considered under two points of view – as an endeavour to change the intentions of God, or as a formal testimony of our obedience. But the former case supposes that the caprices of a limited intelligence can occasionally instruct the Creator of the world how to regulate the universe; and the latter, a certain degree of servility analogous to the loyalty demanded by earthly tyrants. Obedience indeed is only the pitiful and cowardly egotism of him who thinks that he can do something better than reason.

Christianity, like all other religions, rests upon miracles, prophecies, and martyrdoms, No religion ever existed which had not its prophets, its attested miracles, and, above all, crowds of devotees who would bear patiently the most horrible tortures to prove its authenticity. It should appear that in no case can a discriminating mind subscribe to the genuineness of a miracle. A miracle is an infraction of nature's law, by a supernatural cause; by a cause acting beyond that eternal circle within which all things are included. God breaks through the law of nature, that he may convince mankind of the truth of that revelation which, in spite of his precautions, has been, since its introduction, the subject of unceasing schism and cavil.

Miracles resolve themselves into the following question* – Whether it is

* See Hume's *Essay*, Vol. II, p. 121.

more probable the laws of nature, hitherto so immutably harmonious, should have undergone violation, or that a man should have told a lie? Whether it is more probable that we are ignorant of the natural cause of an event, or that we know the supernatural one? That, in old times, when the powers of nature were less known than at present, a certain set of men were themselves deceived, or had some hidden motive for deceiving others; or that God begat a son, who, in his legislation, measuring merit by belief, evidenced himself to be totally ignorant of the powers of the human mind – of what is voluntary, and what is the contrary?

We have many instances of men telling lies – none of an infraction of nature's laws, those laws of whose government alone we have any knowledge or experience. The records of all nations afford innumerable instances of men deceiving others either from vanity or interest, or themselves being deceived by the limitedness of their views and their ignorance of natural causes: but where is the accredited case of God having come upon earth, to give the lie to his own creations? There would be something truly wonderful in the appearance of a ghost; but the assertion of a child that he saw one as he passed through the churchyard is universally admitted to be less miraculous.

But even supposing that a man should raise a dead body to life before our eyes, and on this fact rest his claim to being considered the son of God – the Humane Society restores drowned persons, and because it makes no mystery of the method it employs, its members are not mistaken for the sons of God. All that we have a right to infer from our ignorance of the cause of any event is that we do not know it: had the Mexicans attended to this simple rule when they heard the cannon of the Spaniards, they would not have considered them as gods: the experiments of modern chemistry would have defied the wisest philosophers of ancient Greece and Rome to have accounted for them on natural principles. An author of strong common sense has observed that 'a miracle is no miracle at second-hand'; he might have added, that a miracle is no miracle in any case; for until we are acquainted with all natural causes, we have no reason to imagine others.

There remains to be considered another proof of Christianity – Prophecy. A book is written before a certain event, in which this event is foretold; how could the prophet have foreknown it without inspiration; how could he have been inspired without God? The greatest stress is laid on the prophecies of Moses and Hosea on the dispersion of the Jews, and that of Isaiah concerning the coming of the Messiah. The prophecy of Moses is a collection of every possible cursing and blessing; and it is so far from being marvellous that the one of dispersion should have been fulfilled, that it would have been more surprising if, out of all these, none should have taken effect. In Deuteronomy, Ch. xxviii, verse 64, where Moses explicitly foretells the dispersion, he states that they shall there serve gods of wood and stone: 'And the Lord shall scatter thee among all people, from the one end of the earth even to the other, *and there thou shalt serve other gods, which neither thou nor thy fathers have known, even gods of wood and stone.*' The Jews are at this day remarkably tenacious of their religion. Moses also declares that they shall be subjected to these curses for disobedience to his ritual: 'And it shall come to pass if thou wilt not hearken unto the voice of the Lord thy God, to observe to do all the commandments and statutes which I command thee this day, that all these curses shall come upon thee, and overtake thee.' Is this the real reason? The third, fourth and fifth chapters of Hosea are a piece of immodest confession. The indelicate type might apply in a hundred senses to a hundred things. The fifty-third chapter of Isaiah is more explicit, yet it does not exceed in clearness the oracles of Delphos. The historical proof, that Moses, Isaiah and Hosea did write when they are said to have written, is far from being clear and circumstantial.

But prophecy requires proof in its character as a miracle; we have no right to suppose that a man foreknew future events from God, until it is demonstrated that he neither could know them by his own exertions, nor that the writings which contain the prediction could possibly have been fabricated after the event pretended to be foretold. It is more probable that writings, pretending to divine inspiration, should have been fabricated after the fulfilment of their pretended prediction than that they should have really been divinely inspired, when we consider that the latter supposition makes God at once the creator of the human mind and ignorant of its primary powers, particularly as we have numberless instances of false religions, and forged prophecies of things long past, and no accredited case of God having conversed with men directly or indirectly. It is also possible that the description of an event might have foregone its occurrence; but this is far from being a legitimate proof of a divine revelation, as many men, not pretending to the character of a prophet, have nevertheless, in this sense, prophesied.

Lord Chesterfield[31] was never yet taken for a prophet, even by a bishop, yet he uttered this remarkable prediction: 'The despotic government of France is screwed up to the highest pitch; a revolution is fast approaching; that revolution, I am convinced, will be radical and sanguinary.' This appeared in the letters of the prophet long before the accomplishment of this wonderful prediction. Now, have these particulars come to pass, or have they not? If they have how could the Earl have foreknown them without inspiration? If we admit the truth of the Christian religion on testimony such as this, we must admit, on the same strength of evidence, that God has affixed the highest rewards to belief, and the eternal tortures of the never-dying worm to disbelief; both of which have been demonstrated to be involuntary.

The last proof of the Christian religion depends on the influence of the Holy Ghost. Theologians divide the influence of the Holy Ghost into its ordinary and extraordinary modes of operation. The latter is supposed to be that which inspired the Prophets and Apostles; and the former to be the grace of God, which summarily makes known the truth of his revelation to those whose mind is fitted for its reception by a submissive perusal of his word. Persons convinced in this manner can do anything but account for their conviction, describe the time at which it happened, or the manner in which it came upon them. It is supposed to enter the mind by other channels than those of the senses, and therefore professes to be superior to reason founded on their experience.

Admitting, however, the usefulness or possibility of a divine revelation, unless we demolish the foundations of all human knowledge, it is requisite that our reason should previously demonstrate its genuineness; for, before we extinguish the steady ray of reason and common sense, it is fit that we should discover whether we cannot do without their assistance, whether or no there be any other which may suffice to guide us through the labyrinth of life:* for, if a man is to be inspired upon all occasions, if he is to be sure of a thing because he is sure, if the ordinary operations of the spirit are not to be considered very extraordinary modes of demonstration, if enthusiasm is to usurp the place of proof, and madness that of sanity, all reasoning is superfluous. The Mahometan dies fighting for his prophet, the Indian immolates himself at the chariot wheels of Brahma, the Hottentot worships an insect, the Negro a bunch of feathers, the Mexican sacrifices human victims! Their degree of conviction must certainly be very strong: it cannot arise from reasoning, it must from feelings, the reward of their prayers. If each of these should affirm, in opposition to the strongest possible arguments, that inspiration carried internal evidence, I fear their inspired brethren, the orthodox missionaries, would be so uncharitable as to pronounce them obstinate.

Miracles cannot be received as testimonies of a disputed fact, because all human testimony has ever been insufficient to establish the possibility of

* See Locke's *Essay on the Human Understanding*, Book IV, Ch. XIX, on Enthusiasm.

miracles. That which is incapable of proof itself is no proof of anything else. Prophecy has also been rejected by the test of reason. Those, then, who have been actually inspired, are the only true believers in the Christian religion.

> Mox numine viso
> Virginei tumuere sinus, innuptaque mater
> Arcano stupuit compleri viscera partu,
> Auctorem paritura suum. Mortalia corda
> Artificem texere poli, latuitque sub uno
> Pectore, qui totum late complectitur orbem.[32]

Claudian, *Carmen Paschale*

Does not so monstrous and disgusting an absurdity carry its own infamy and refutation with itself?

VIII, ll. 203–7 (p. 58)

> *Him, still from hope to hope the bliss pursuing,*
> *Which from the exhaustless lore of human weal*
> *Draws on the virtuous mind, the thoughts that rise*
> *In time-destroying infiniteness, gift*
> *With self-enshrined eternity, etc.*

Time is our consciousness of the succession of ideas in our mind. Vivid sensation, of either pain or pleasure, makes the time seem long, as the common phrase is, because it renders us more acutely conscious of our ideas. If a mind be conscious of an hundred ideas during one minute, by the clock, and of two hundred during another, the latter of these spaces would actually occupy so much greater extent in the mind as two exceed one in quantity. If, therefore, the human mind, by any future improvement of its sensibility, should become conscious of an infinite number of ideas in a minute, that minute would be eternity. I do not hence infer that the actual space between the birth and death of a man will ever be prolonged; but that his sensibility is perfectible, and that the number of ideas which his mind is capable of receiving is indefinite. One man is stretched on the rack during twelve hours; another sleeps soundly in his bed: the difference of time perceived by these two persons is immense; one hardly will believe that half an hour has elapsed, the other could credit that centuries had flown during his agony. Thus, the life of a man of virtue and talent, who should die in his thirtieth year, is, with regard to his own feelings, longer than that of a miserable priest-ridden slave, who dreams out a century of dullness. The one has perpetually cultivated his mental faculties, has rendered himself master of his thoughts, can abstract and generalise amid the lethargy of everyday business; the other can slumber over the brightest moments of his being, and is unable to remember the happiest hour of his life. Perhaps the perishing ephemeron enjoys a longer life than the tortoise.

> Dark flood of time!
> Roll as it listeth thee – I measure not
> By months or moments thy ambiguous course.
> Another may stand by me on the brink
> And watch the bubble whirled beyond his ken
> That pauses at my feet. The sense of love,
> The thirst for action, and the impassioned thought
> Prolong my being: if I wake no more,
> My life more actual living will contain
> Than some grey veteran's of the world's cold school,
> Whose listless hours unprofitably roll,
> By one enthusiast feeling unredeemed.[33]

See Godwin's *Polit. Just.*, Vol. I, p. 411; and Condorcet, *Esquisse d'un Tableau Historique des Progrès de l'Esprit Humain*, Epoque IX.

VIII, ll. 211–12 (p. 58)

No longer now
He slays the lamb that looks him in the face

[For this note, see 'A Vindication of Natural Diet', pp. 571–83.]

Sonnet: *On launching some Bottles filled with Knowledge into the Bristol Channel*

Vessels of heavenly medicine! may the breeze
    Auspicious waft your dark green forms to shore;
    Safe may ye stem the wide surrounding roar
Of the wild whirlwinds and the raging seas;
    And oh! if Liberty e'er deigned to stoop
From yonder lowly throne her crownless brow,
    Sure she will breathe around your emerald group
The fairest breezes of her West that blow.
    Yes! she will waft ye to some freeborn soul
Whose eye-beam, kindling as it meets your freight,   10
    Her heaven-born flame in suffering Earth will light,
Until its radiance gleams from pole to pole,
    And tyrant-hearts with powerless envy burst
    To see their night of ignorance dispersed.

Sonnet: *To a Balloon laden with Knowledge*

Bright ball of flame that through the gloom of even
    Silently takest thine ethereal way,
    And with surpassing glory dimm'st each ray
Twinkling amid the dark blue depths of Heaven, –
    Unlike the fire thou bearest, soon shalt thou
Fade like a meteor in surrounding gloom,
    Whilst that, unquenchable, is doomed to glow
A watch-light by the patriot's lonely tomb;
    A ray of courage to the oppressed and poor;
A spark, though gleaming on the hovel's hearth,   10
    Which through the tyrant's gilded domes shall roar;
A beacon in the darkness of the Earth;
    A sun which, o'er the renovated scene,
    Shall dart like Truth where Falsehood yet has been.

POEMS FROM 1814

Stanzas – April 1814

Away! the moor is dark beneath the moon,
   Rapid clouds have drank the last pale beam of even:
Away! the gathering winds will call the darkness soon,
   And profoundest midnight shroud the serene lights of heaven.
Pause not! The time is past! Every voice cries, Away!
   Tempt not with one last tear thy friend's ungentle mood:
Thy lover's eye, so glazed and cold, dares not entreat thy stay:
   Duty and dereliction guide thee back to solitude.

Away, away! to thy sad and silent home;
   Pour bitter tears on its desolated hearth;   10
Watch the dim shades as like ghosts they go and come,
   And complicate strange webs of melancholy mirth.
The leaves of wasted autumn woods shall float around thine head:
   The blooms of dewy spring shall gleam beneath thy feet:
But thy soul or this world must fade in the frost that binds the dead,
   Ere midnight's frown and morning's smile, ere thou and

                                  peace may meet.

The cloud shadows of midnight possess their own repose,
   For the weary winds are silent, or the moon is in the deep:
Some respite to its turbulence unresting ocean knows;
   Whatever moves, or toils, or grieves, hath its appointed sleep.   20
Thou in the grave shalt rest – yet till the phantoms flee
   Which that house and heath and garden made dear to thee erewhile,
Thy remembrance, and repentance, and deep musings are not free
   From the music of two voices and the light of one sweet smile.

POEMS FROM 1815

Alastor[34] *or The Spirit of Solitude*

PREFACE

The poem entitled *Alastor* may be considered as allegorical of one of the most interesting situations of the human mind. It represents a youth of uncorrupted feelings and adventurous genius led forth by an imagination, inflamed and purified through familiarity with all that is excellent and majestic, to the contemplation of the universe. He drinks deep of the fountains of knowledge, and is still insatiate. The magnificence and beauty of the external world sinks profoundly into the frame of his conceptions, and affords to their modifications a variety not to be exhausted. So long as it is possible for his desires to point towards objects thus infinite and unmeasured, he is joyous, and tranquil, and self-possessed. But the period arrives when these objects cease to suffice. His mind is at length suddenly awakened and thirsts for intercourse with an intelligence similar to itself. He images to himself the Being whom he loves. Conversant with speculations of the sublimest and most perfect natures, the vision in which he embodies his own imaginations unites all of wonderful, or wise, or beautiful, which the poet, the philosopher, or the lover could depicture. The intellectual faculties, the imagination, the functions of sense, have their respective requisitions on the sympathy of corresponding powers in other human beings. The Poet is represented as uniting these requisitions, and attaching them to a single image. He seeks in vain for a prototype of his conception. Blasted by his disappointment, he descends to an untimely grave.

The picture is not barren of instruction to actual men. The Poet's self-centred seclusion was avenged by the furies of an irresistible passion pursuing him to speedy ruin. But that Power which strikes the luminaries of the world with sudden darkness and extinction, by awakening them to too exquisite a perception of its influences, dooms to a slow and poisonous decay those meaner spirits that dare to abjure its dominion. Their destiny is more abject and inglorious as their delinquency is more contemptible and pernicious. They who, deluded by no generous error, instigated by no sacred thirst of doubtful knowledge, duped by no illustrious superstition, loving nothing on this earth, and cherishing no hopes beyond, yet keep aloof from sympathies with their kind, rejoicing neither in human joy nor mourning with human grief; these, and such as they, have their apportioned curse. They languish, because none feel with them their common nature. They are morally dead. They are neither friends, nor lovers, nor fathers, nor citizens of the world, nor benefactors of their country. Among those who attempt to exist without human sympathy, the pure and tender-hearted perish through the intensity and passion of their search after its communities, when the vacancy of their spirit suddenly makes itself felt. All else, selfish, blind, and torpid, are those unforeseeing multitudes who constitute, together with their own, the lasting misery and loneliness of the world. Those who love not their fellow-beings, live unfruitful lives, and prepare for their old age a miserable grave.

'The good die first,
And those whose hearts are dry as summer dust,
Burn to the socket!'[35]

14 December 1815

Nondum amabam, et amare amabam, quaerebam quid amarem, amans [a]mare.[36]

St Augustus,*Confessions*

Earth, ocean, air, beloved brotherhood!
If our great Mother has imbued my soul
With aught of natural piety to feel
Your love, and recompense the boon with mine;
If dewy morn, and odorous noon, and even,
With sunset and its gorgeous ministers,
And solemn midnight's tingling silentness;
If autumn's hollow sighs in the sere wood,
And winter robing with pure snow and crowns
Of starry ice the grey grass and bare boughs;   10
If spring's voluptuous pantings when she breathes
Her first sweet kisses, have been dear to me;
If no bright bird, insect, or gentle beast
I consciously have injured, but still loved
And cherished these my kindred; then forgive
This boast, beloved brethren, and withdraw
No portion of your wonted favour now!

Mother of this unfathomable world!
Favour my solemn song, for I have loved
Thee ever, and thee only; I have watched   20
Thy shadow, and the darkness of thy steps,
And my heart ever gazes on the depth
Of thy deep mysteries. I have made my bed
In charnels and on coffins, where black death
Keeps record of the trophies won from thee,
Hoping to still these obstinate questionings
Of thee and thine, by forcing some lone ghost
Thy messenger, to render up the tale
Of what we are. In lone and silent hours,
When night makes a weird sound of its own stillness,   30
Like an inspired and desperate alchemist
Staking his very life on some dark hope,
Have I mixed awful talk and asking looks
With my most innocent love, until strange tears
Uniting with those breathless kisses, made
Such magic as compels the charmed night
To render up thy charge: . . . and, though ne'er yet
Thou hast unveil'd thy inmost sanctuary,
Enough from incommunicable dream,
And twilight phantasms, and deep noonday thought,   40
Has shone within me, that serenely now
And moveless, as a long-forgotten lyre[37]
Suspended in the solitary dome
Of some mysterious and deserted fane,[38]
I wait thy breath, Great Parent, that my strain
May modulate with murmurs of the air,
And motions of the forests and the sea,
And voice of living beings, and woven hymns
Of night and day, and the deep heart of man.

There was a Poet whose untimely tomb   50
No human hands with pious reverence reared,
But the charmed eddies of autumnal winds
Built o'er his mouldering bones a pyramid
Of mouldering leaves in the waste wilderness: –
A lovely youth, – no mourning maiden decked
With weeping flowers, or votive cypress wreath,

The lone couch of his everlasting sleep: –
Gentle, and brave, and generous, – no lorn bard
Breathed o'er his dark fate one melodious sigh:
He lived, he died, he sung, in solitude.   60
Strangers have wept to hear his passionate notes,
And virgins, as unknown he past, have pined
And wasted for fond love of his wild eyes.
The fire of those soft orbs has ceased to burn,
And Silence, too enamoured of that voice,
Locks its mute music in her rugged cell.

  By solemn vision, and bright silver dream,
His infancy was nurtured. Every sight
And sound from the vast earth and ambient air,
Sent to his heart its choicest impulses.   70
The fountains of divine philosophy
Fled not his thirsting lips, and all of great,
Or good, or lovely, which the sacred past
In truth or fable consecrates, he felt
And knew. When early youth had past, he left
His cold fireside and alienated home
To seek strange truths in undiscovered lands.
Many a wide waste and tangled wilderness
Has lured his fearless steps; and he has bought
With his sweet voice and eyes, from savage men,   80
His rest and food. Nature's most secret steps
He like her shadow has pursued, where'er
The red volcano overcanopies
Its fields of snow and pinnacles of ice
With burning smoke, or where bitumen lakes
On black bare pointed islets ever beat
With sluggish surge, or where the secret caves
Rugged and dark, winding among the springs
Of fire and poison, inaccessible
To avarice or pride, their starry domes   90
Of diamond and of gold expand above
Numberless and immeasurable halls,
Frequent with crystal column, and clear shrines
Of pearl, and thrones radiant with chrysolite.
Nor had that scene of ampler majesty

Than gems or gold, the varying roof of heaven
And the green earth lost in his heart its claims
To love and wonder; he would linger long
In lonesome vales, making the wild his home,
Until the doves and squirrels would partake   100
From his innocuous hand his bloodless food,
Lured by the gentle meaning of his looks,
And the wild antelope, that starts whene'er
The dry leaf rustles in the brake, suspend
Her timid steps to gaze upon a form
More graceful than her own.
                              His wandering step[39]
Obedient to high thoughts, has visited
The awful ruins of the days of old:
Athens, and Tyre, and Balbec, and the waste
Where stood Jerusalem, the fallen towers   110
Of Babylon, the eternal pyramids,
Memphis and Thebes, and whatsoe'er of strange,
Sculptured on alabaster obelisk,
Or jasper tomb, or mutilated sphinx,
Dark Ethiopia in her desert hills
Conceals. Among the mined temples there,
Stupendous columns, and wild images
Of more than man, where marble demons watch
The Zodiac's brazen mystery, and dead men
Hang their mute thoughts on the mute walls around,   120
He lingered, poring on memorials
Of the world's youth, through the long burning day
Gazed on those speechless shapes, nor, when the moon
Filled the mysterious halls with floating shades,
Suspended he that task, but ever gazed
And gazed, till meaning on his vacant mind
Flashed like strong inspiration, and he saw
The thrilling secrets of the birth of time.

   Meanwhile an Arab maiden brought his food,
Her daily portion, from her father's tent,   130
And spread her matting for his couch, and stole
From duties and repose to tend his steps: –
Enamoured, yet not daring for deep awe

To speak her love: – and watched his nightly sleep,
Sleepless herself, to gaze upon his lips
Parted in slumber, whence the regular breath
Of innocent dreams arose: then, when red morn
Made paler the pale moon, to her cold home
Wildered, and wan, and panting, she returned.

The Poet wandering on,[40] through Arabie   140
And Persia, and the wild Carmanian waste,
And o'er the aerial mountains which pour down
Indus and Oxus from their icy caves,
In joy and exultation held his way;
Till in the vale of Cashmire, far within
Its loneliest dell, where odorous plants entwine
Beneath the hollow rocks a natural bower,
Beside a sparkling rivulet he stretched
His languid limbs. A vision on his sleep
There came, a dream of hopes that never yet   150
Had flushed his cheek. He dreamed a veiled maid
Sate near him, talking in low solemn tones.
Her voice was like the voice of his own soul
Heard in the calm of thought; its music long,
Like woven sounds of streams and breezes, held
His inmost sense suspended in its web
Of many-coloured woof and shifting hues.
Knowledge and truth and virtue were her theme,
And lofty hopes of divine liberty,
Thoughts the most dear to him, and poesy,   160
Herself a poet. Soon the solemn mood
Of her pure mind kindled through all her frame
A permeating fire: wild numbers then
She raised, with voice stifled in tremulous sobs
Subdued by its own pathos: her fair hands
Were bare alone, sweeping from some strange harp
Strange symphony, and in their branching veins
The eloquent blood told an ineffable tale.
The beating of her heart was heard to fill
The pauses of her music, and her breath   170
Tumultuously accorded with those fits
Of intermitted song. Sudden she rose,

As if her heart impatiently endured
Its bursting burthen: at the sound he turned,
And saw by the warm light of their own life
Her glowing limbs beneath the sinuous veil
Of woven wind, her outspread arms now bare,
Her dark locks floating in the breath of night,
Her beamy bending eyes, her parted lips
Outstretched, and pale, and quivering eagerly.   180
His strong heart sunk and sickened with excess
Of love. He reared his shuddering limbs and quelled
His gasping breath, and spread his arms to meet
Her panting bosom: . . . she drew back a while,
Then, yielding to the irresistible joy,
With frantic gesture and short breathless cry
Folded his frame in her dissolving arms.
Now blackness veiled his dizzy eyes, and night
Involved and swallowed up the vision; sleep,
Like a dark flood suspended in its course,   190
Rolled back its impulse on his vacant brain.

Roused by the shock he started from his trance –
The cold white light of morning, the blue moon
Low in the west, the clear and garish hills,
The distinct valley and the vacant woods,
Spread round him where he stood. Whither have fled
The hues of heaven that canopied his bower
Of yesternight? The sounds that soothed his sleep,
The mystery and the majesty of Earth,
The joy, the exultation? His wan eyes   200
Gaze on the empty scene as vacantly
As ocean's moon looks on the moon in heaven.
The spirit of sweet human love has sent
A vision to the sleep of him who spurned
Her choicest gifts. He eagerly pursues
Beyond the realms of dream that fleeting shade;
He overleaps the bounds. Alas! alas!
Were limbs, and breath, and being intertwined
Thus treacherously? Lost, lost, forever lost,
In the wide pathless desert of dim sleep,   210
That beautiful shape! Does the dark gate of death

Conduct to thy mysterious paradise,
O Sleep? Does the bright arch of rainbow clouds,
And pendent mountains seen in the calm lake,
Lead only to a black and watery depth,
While death's blue vault, with loathliest vapours hung,
Where every shade which the foul grave exhales
Hides its dead eye from the detested day,
Conduct, O Sleep, to thy delightful realms?
This doubt with sudden tide flowed on his heart,   220
The insatiate hope which it awakened, stung
His brain even like despair.
                                    While daylight held
The sky, the Poet kept mute conference
With his still soul. At night the passion came,
Like the fierce fiend of a distempered dream,
And shook him from his rest, and led him forth
Into the darkness. As an eagle grasped
In folds of the green serpent, feels her breast
Burn with the poison, and precipitates
Through night and day, tempest, and calm and cloud,   230
Frantic with dizzying anguish, her blind flight
O'er the wide aery wilderness: thus driven
By the bright shadow of that lovely dream,
Beneath the cold glare of the desolate night,
Through tangled swamps and deep precipitous dells,
Startling with careless step the moonlight snake,
He fled. Red morning dawned upon his flight,
Shedding the mockery of its vital hues
Upon his cheek of death. He wandered on[41]
Till vast Aornos seen from Petra's steep   240
Hung o'er the low horizon like a cloud;
Through Balk, and where the desolated tombs
Of Parthian kings scatter to every wind
Their wasting dust, wildly he wandered on,
Day after day, a weary waste of hours,
Bearing within his life the brooding care
That ever fed on its decaying flame.
And now his limbs were lean; his scattered hair
Sered by the autumn of strange suffering
Sung dirges in the wind; his listless hand   250

Hung like dead bone within its withered skin;
Life, and the lustre that consumed it, shone
As in a furnace burning secretly
From his dark eyes alone. The cottagers,
Who ministered with human charity
His human wants, beheld with wondering awe
Their fleeting visitant. The mountaineer,
Encountering on some dizzy precipice
That spectral form, deemed that the Spirit of wind
With lightning eyes, and eager breath, and feet   260
Disturbing not the drifted snow, had paused
In its career: the infant would conceal
His troubled visage in his mother's robe
In terror at the glare of those wild eyes,
To remember their strange light in many a dream
Of after-times; but youthful maidens, taught
By nature, would interpret half the woe
That wasted him, would call him with false names
Brother, and friend, would press his pallid hand
At parting, and watch, dim through tears, the path   270
Of his departure from their father's door.

        At length upon the lone Chorasmian shore
He paused, a wide and melancholy waste
Of putrid marshes. A strong impulse urged
His steps to the seashore. A swan was there,
Beside a sluggish stream among the reeds.
It rose as he approached, and with strong wings
Scaling the upward sky, bent its bright course
High over the immeasurable main.
His eyes pursued its flight. – 'Thou hast a home,   280
Beautiful bird; thou voyagest to thine home,
Where thy sweet mate will twine her downy neck
With thine, and welcome thy return with eyes
Bright in the lustre of their own fond joy.
And what am I that I should linger here,
With voice far sweeter than thy dying notes,
Spirit more vast than thine, frame more attuned
To beauty, wasting these surpassing powers
In the deaf air, to the blind earth, and heaven

That echoes not my thoughts?' A gloomy smile   290
Of desperate hope wrinkled his quivering lips.
For sleep, he knew, kept most relentlessly
Its precious charge, and silent death exposed,
Faithless perhaps as sleep, a shadowy lure,
With doubtful smile mocking its own strange charms.

   Startled by his own thoughts he looked around.
There was no fair fiend near him, not a sight
Or sound of awe but in his own deep mind.
A little shallop floating near the shore
Caught the impatient wandering of his gaze.   300
It had been long abandoned, for its sides
Gaped wide with many a rift, and its frail joints
Swayed with the undulations of the tide.
A restless impulse urged him to embark
And meet lone Death on the drear ocean's waste;
For well he knew that mighty Shadow loves
The slimy caverns of the populous deep.

   The day was fair and sunny, sea and sky
Drank its inspiring radiance, and the wind
Swept strongly from the shore, blackening the waves.   310
Following his eager soul, the wanderer
Leaped in the boat, he spread his cloak aloft
On the bare mast, and took his lonely seat,
And felt the boat speed o'er the tranquil sea
Like a torn cloud before the hurricane.

   As one that in a silver vision floats
Obedient to the sweep of odorous winds
Upon resplendent clouds, so rapidly
Along the dark and ruffled waters fled
The straining boat. – A whirlwind swept it on,   320
With fierce gusts and precipitating force,
Through the white ridges of the chafed sea.
The waves arose. Higher and higher still
Their fierce necks writhed beneath the tempest's scourge
Like serpents struggling in a vulture's grasp.
Calm and rejoicing in the fearful war

Of wave ruining on wave, and blast on blast
Descending, and black flood on whirlpool driven
With dark obliterating course, he sate:
As if their genii were the ministers   330
Appointed to conduct him to the light
Of those beloved eyes, the Poet sate
Holding the steady helm. Evening came on,
The beams of sunset hung their rainbow hues
High 'mid the shifting domes of sheeted spray
That canopied his path o'er the waste deep;
Twilight, ascending slowly from the east,
Entwin'd in duskier wreaths her braided locks
O'er the fair front and radiant eyes of day;
Night followed, clad with stars. On every side   340
More horribly the multitudinous streams
Of ocean's mountainous waste to mutual war
Rushed in dark tumult thundering, as to mock
The calm and spangled sky. The little boat
Still fled before the storm; still fled, like foam
Down the steep cataract of a wintry river;
Now pausing on the edge of the riven wave;
Now leaving far behind the bursting mass
That fell, convulsing ocean. Safely fled –
As if that frail and wasted human form,   350
Had been an elemental god.
                              At midnight
The moon arose: and lo! the ethereal cliffs
Of Caucasus, whose icy summits shone
Among the stars like sunlight, and around
Whose cavern'd base the whirlpools and the waves
Bursting and eddying irresistibly
Rage and resound for ever. – Who shall save? –
The boat fled on, – the boiling torrent drove, –
The crags closed round with black and jagged arms,
The shattered mountain overhung the sea,   360
And faster still, beyond all human speed,
Suspended on the sweep of the smooth wave,
The little boat was driven. A cavern there
Yawned, and amid its slant and winding depths
Ingulfed the rushing sea. The boat fled on

With unrelaxing speed. – 'Vision and Love!'
The Poet cried aloud, 'I have beheld
The path of thy departure. Sleep and death
Shall not divide us long!'

                The boat pursued
The windings of the cavern. Daylight shone   370
At length upon that gloomy river's flow;
Now, where the fiercest war among the waves
Is calm, on the unfathomable stream
The boat moved slowly. Where the mountain, riven,
Exposed those black depths to the azure sky,
Ere yet the flood's enormous volume fell
Even to the base of Caucasus, with sound
That shook the everlasting rocks, the mass
Filled with one whirlpool all that ample chasm;
Stair above stair the eddying waters rose,   380
Circling immeasurably fast, and laved
With alternating dash the knarled roots
Of mighty trees, that stretched their giant arms
In darkness over it. I' the midst was left,
Reflecting, yet distorting every cloud,
A pool of treacherous and tremendous calm.
Seized by the sway of the ascending stream,
With dizzy swiftness, round, and round, and round,
Ridge after ridge the straining boat arose,
Till on the verge of the extremest curve,   390
Where, through an opening of the rocky bank,
The waters overflow, and a smooth spot
Of glassy quiet mid those battling tides
Is left, the boat paused shuddering. – Shall it sink
Down the abyss? Shall the reverting stress
Of that resistless gulf embosom it?
Now shall it fall? – A wandering stream of wind,
Breathed from the west, has caught the expanded sail,
And, lo! with gentle motion, between banks
Of mossy slope, and on a placid stream,   400
Beneath a woven grove it sails, and, hark!
The ghastly torrent mingles its far roar,
With the breeze murmuring in the musical woods.

Where the embowering trees recede, and leave
A little space of green expanse, the cove
Is closed by meeting banks, whose yellow flowers[42]
For ever gaze on their own drooping eyes,
Reflected in the crystal calm. The wave
Of the boat's motion marred their pensive task,
Which nought but vagrant bird, or wanton wind,   410
Or falling spear-grass, or their own decay
Had e'er disturbed before. The Poet longed
To deck with their bright hues his withered hair,
But on his heart its solitude returned,
And he forbore. Not the strong impulse hid
In those flushed cheeks, bent eyes, and shadowy frame
Had yet performed its ministry: it hung
Upon his life, as lightning in a cloud
Gleams, hovering ere it vanish, ere the floods
Of night close over it.
     The noonday sun   420
Now shone upon the forest, one vast mass
Of mingling shade, whose brown magnificence
A narrow vale embosoms. There, huge caves,
Scooped in the dark base of their aery rocks
Mocking its moans, respond and roar for ever.
The meeting boughs and implicated leaves
Wove twilight o'er the Poet's path, as led
By love, or dream, or god, or mightier Death,
He sought in Nature's dearest haunt, some bank,
Her cradle, and his sepulchre. More dark   430
And dark the shades accumulate. The oak,
Expanding its immense and knotty arms,
Embraces the light beech. The pyramids
Of the tall cedar overarching, frame
Most solemn domes within, and far below,
Like clouds suspended in an emerald sky.
The ash and the acacia floating hang
Tremulous and pale. Like restless serpents, clothed
In rainbow and in fire, the parasites,
Starred with ten thousand blossoms, flow around   440
The grey trunks, and, as gamesome infants' eyes,
With gentle meanings, and most innocent wiles,

Fold their beams round the hearts of those that love,
These twine their tendrils with the wedded boughs
Uniting their close union; the woven leaves
Make net-work of the dark blue light of day,
And the night's noontide clearness, mutable
As shapes in the weird clouds. Soft mossy lawns
Beneath these canopies extend their swells,
Fragrant with perfumed herbs, and eyed with blooms   450
Minute yet beautiful. One darkest glen
Sends from its woods of musk-rose, twined with jasmine,
A soul-dissolving odour, to invite
To some more lovely mystery. Through the dell,
Silence and Twilight here, twin-sisters, keep
Their noonday watch, and sail among the shades,
Like vaporous shapes half seen; beyond, a well,
Dark, gleaming, and of most translucent wave,
Images all the woven boughs above,
And each depending leaf, and every speck   460
Of azure sky, darting between their chasms;
Nor aught else in the liquid mirror laves
Its portraiture, but some inconstant star
Between one foliaged lattice twinkling fair,
Or, painted bird, sleeping beneath the moon,
Or gorgeous insect floating motionless,
Unconscious of the day, ere yet his wings
Have spread their glories to the gaze of noon.

Hither the Poet came. His eyes beheld
Their own wan light through the reflected lines   470
Of his thin hair, distinct in the dark depth
Of that still fountain; as the human heart,
Gazing in dreams over the gloomy grave,
Sees its own treacherous likeness there. He heard
The motion of the leaves, the grass that sprung
Startled and glanced and trembled even to feel
An unaccustomed presence, and the sound
Of the sweet brook that from the secret springs
Of that dark fountain rose. A Spirit seemed
To stand beside him – clothed in no bright robes   480
Of shadowy silver or enshrining light,

Borrowed from aught the visible world affords
Of grace, or majesty, or mystery; –
But, undulating woods, and silent well,
And leaping rivulet, and evening gloom
Now deepening the dark shades, for speech assuming
Held commune with him, as if he and it
Were all that was, – only . . . when his regard
Was raised by intense pensiveness, . . . two eyes,
Two starry eyes, hung in the gloom of thought,   490
And seemed with their serene and azure smiles
To beckon him.

          Obedient to the light
That shone within his soul, he went, pursuing
The windings of the dell. – The rivulet
Wanton and wild, through many a green ravine
Beneath the forest flowed. Sometimes it fell
Among the moss with hollow harmony
Dark and profound. Now on the polished stones
It danced; like childhood laughing as it went:
Then, through the plain in tranquil wanderings crept,   500
Reflecting every herb and drooping bud
That overhung its quietness. – 'O stream!
Whose source is inaccessibly profound,
Whither do thy mysterious waters tend?
Thou imagest my life. Thy darksome stillness,
Thy dazzling waves, thy loud and hollow gulfs,
Thy searchless fountain, and invisible course
Have each their type in me: and the wide sky,
And measureless ocean may declare as soon
What oozy cavern or what wandering cloud   510
Contains thy waters, as the universe
Tell where these living thoughts reside, when stretched
Upon thy flowers my bloodless limbs shall waste
I' the passing wind!'

          Beside the grassy shore
Of the small stream he went; he did impress
On the green moss his tremulous step, that caught
Strong shuddering from his burning limbs. As one

Roused by some joyous madness from the couch
Of fever, he did move; yet, not like him,
Forgetful of the grave, where, when the flame   520
Of his frail exultation shall be spent,
He must descend. With rapid steps he went
Beneath the shade of trees, beside the flow
Of the wild babbling rivulet; and now
The forest's solemn canopies were changed
For the uniform and lightsome evening sky.
Grey rocks did peep from the spare moss, and stemmed
The struggling brook: tall spires of windlestrae[43]
Threw their thin shadows down the rugged slope,
And nought but knarled roots of ancient pines   530
Branchless and blasted, clenched with grasping roots
The unwilling soil. A gradual change was here,
Yet ghastly. For, as fast years flow away,
The smooth brow gathers, and the hair grows thin
And white, and where irradiate dewy eyes
Had shone, gleam stony orbs: – so from his steps
Bright flowers departed, and the beautiful shade
Of the green groves, with all their odorous winds
And musical motions. Calm, he still pursued
The stream, that with a larger volume now   540
Rolled through the labyrinthine dell; and there
Fretted a path through its descending curves
With its wintry speed. On every side now rose
Rocks, which, in unimaginable forms,
Lifted their black and barren pinnacles
In the light of evening, and its precipice
Obscuring the ravine, disclosed above,
'Mid toppling stones, black gulfs and yawning caves,
Whose windings gave ten thousand various tongues
To the loud stream. Lo! where the pass expands   550
Its stony jaws, the abrupt mountain breaks,
And seems, with its accumulated crags,
To overhang the world: for wide expand
Beneath the wan stars and descending moon
Islanded seas, blue mountains, mighty streams,
Dim tracts and vast, robed in the lustrous gloom
Of leaden-coloured even, and fiery hills

Mingling their flames with twilight, on the verge
Of the remote horizon. The near scene,
In naked and severe simplicity.   560
Made contrast with the universe. A pine,
Rock-rooted, stretched athwart the vacancy
Its swinging boughs, to each inconstant blast
Yielding one only response, at each pause
In most familiar cadence, with the howl
The thunder and the hiss of homeless streams
Mingling its solemn song, whilst the broad river,
Foaming and hurrying o'er its rugged path,
Fell into that immeasurable void
Scattering its waters to the passing winds.   570

Yet the grey precipice and solemn pine
And torrent, were not all; – one silent nook
Was there. Even on the edge of that vast mountain,
Upheld by knotty roots and fallen rocks,
It overlooked in its serenity
The dark earth, and the bending vault of stars.
It was a tranquil spot, that seemed to smile
Even in the lap of horror. Ivy clasped
The fissured stones with its entwining arms,
And did embower with leaves for ever green,   580
And berries dark, the smooth and even space
Of its inviolated floor, and here
The children of the autumnal whirlwind bore,
In wanton sport, those bright leaves, whose decay,
Red, yellow, or ethereally pale,
Rivals the pride of summer. 'Tis the haunt
Of every gentle wind, whose breath can teach
The wilds to love tranquillity. One step,
One human step alone, has ever broken
The stillness of its solitude: – one voice   590
Alone inspired its echoes; – even that voice
Which hither came, floating among the winds,
And led the loveliest among human forms
To make their wild haunts the depository
Of all the grace and beauty that endued
Its motions, render up its majesty,

Scatter its music on the unfeeling storm,
And to the damp leaves and blue cavern mould,
Nurses of rainbow flowers and branching moss,
Commit the colours of that varying cheek,   600
That snowy breast, those dark and drooping eyes.

    The dim and horned moon hung low, and poured
A sea of lustre on the horizon's verge
That overflowed its mountains. Yellow mist
Filled the unbounded atmosphere, and drank
Wan moonlight even to fullness: not a star
Shone, not a sound was heard; the very winds,
Danger's grim playmates, on that precipice
Slept, clasped in his embrace. – O, storm of death!
Whose sightless speed divides this sullen night: 610
And thou, colossal Skeleton, that, still
Guiding its irresistible career
In thy devastating omnipotence,
Art king of this frail world, from the red field
Of slaughter, from the reeking hospital,
The patriot's sacred couch, the snowy bed
Of innocence, the scaffold and the throne,
A mighty voice invokes thee. Ruin calls
His brother Death. A rare and regal prey
He hath prepared, prowling around the world;   620
Glutted with which thou mayst repose, and men
Go to their graves like flowers or creeping worms,
Nor ever more offer at thy dark shrine
The unheeded tribute of a broken heart.

    When on the threshold of the green recess
The wanderer's footsteps fell, he knew that death
Was on him. Yet a little, ere it fled,
Did he resign his high and holy soul
To images of the majestic past,
That paused within his passive being now,   630
Like winds that bear sweet music, when they breathe
Through some dim latticed chamber. He did place
His pale lean hand upon the rugged trunk
Of the old pine. Upon an ivied stone

Reclined his languid head, his limbs did rest,
Diffused and motionless, on the smooth brink
Of that obscurest chasm; – and thus he lay,
Surrendering to their final impulses
The hovering powers of life. Hope and despair,
The torturers, slept; no mortal pain or fear   640
Marred his repose, the influxes of sense,
And his own being unalloyed by pain,
Yet feebler and more feeble, calmly fed
The stream of thought, till he lay breathing there
At peace, and faintly smiling: – his last sight
Was the great moon, which o'er the western line
Of the wide world her mighty horn suspended,
With whose dun beams inwoven darkness seemed
To mingle. Now upon the jagged hills
It rests, and still as the divided frame   650
Of the vast meteor sunk, the Poet's blood,
That ever beat in mystic sympathy
With nature's ebb and flow, grew feebler still:
And when two lessening points of light alone
Gleamed through the darkness, the alternate gasp
Of his faint respiration scarce did stir
The stagnate night: – till the minutest ray
Was quenched, the pulse yet lingered in his heart.
It paused – it fluttered. But when heaven remained
Utterly black, the murky shades involved   660
An image, silent, cold, and motionless,
As their own voiceless earth and vacant air.
Even as a vapour fed with golden beams
That ministered on sunlight, ere the west
Eclipses it, was now that wonderous frame –
No sense, no motion, no divinity –
A fragile lute, on whose harmonious strings
The breath of heaven did wander – a bright stream
Once fed with many-voiced waves – a dream
Of youth, which night and time have quenched for ever, 670
Still, dark, and dry, and unremembered now.
    O, for Medea's[44] wondrous alchemy,
Which wheresoe'er it fell made the earth gleam
With bright flowers, and the wintry boughs exhale

From vernal blooms fresh fragrance! O, that God,
Profuse of poisons, would concede the chalice
Which but one living man has drained, who now,
Vessel of deathless wrath, a slave that feels
No proud exemption in the blighting curse
He bears, over the world wanders for ever,   680
Lone as incarnate death! O, that the dream
Of dark magician in his visioned cave,
Raking the cinders of a crucible
For life and power, even when his feeble hand
Shakes in its last decay, were the true law
Of this so lovely world! But thou art fled
Like some frail exhalation; which the dawn
Robes in its golden beams, – ah! thou hast fled!
The brave, the gentle, and the beautiful,
The child of grace and genius. Heartless things   690
Are done and said i' the world, and many worms
And beasts and men live on, and mighty Earth
From sea and mountain, city and wilderness,
In vesper low or joyous orison,
Lifts still its solemn voice: – but thou art fled –
Thou canst no longer know or love the shapes
Of this phantasmal scene, who have to thee
Been purest ministers, who are, alas!
Now thou art not. Upon those pallid lips
So sweet even in their silence, on those eyes   700
That image sleep in death, upon that form
Yet safe from the worm's outrage, let no tear
Be shed – not even in thought. Nor, when those hues
Are gone, and those divinest lineaments,
Worn by the senseless wind, shall live alone
In the frail pauses of this simple strain,
Let not high verse, mourning the memory
Of that which is no more, or painting's woe
Or sculpture, speak in feeble imagery
Their own cold powers. Art and eloquence,   710
And all the shows o' the world are frail and vain
To weep a loss that turns their lights to shade.
It is a woe too 'deep for tears',[45] when all
Is reft at once, when some surpassing Spirit,

Whose light adorned the world around it, leaves
Those who remain behind, not sobs or groans,
The passionate tumult of a clinging hope;
But pale despair and cold tranquillity,
Nature's vast frame, the web of human things,
Birth and the grave, that are not as they were.   720

To Wordsworth

Poet of Nature, thou hast wept to know
That things depart which never may return:
Childhood and youth, friendship and love's first glow,
Have fled like sweet dreams, leaving thee to mourn.
These common woes I feel. One loss is mine
Which thou too feel'st, yet I alone deplore.
Thou wert as a lone star, whose light did shine
On some frail bark in winter's midnight roar:
Thou hast like to a rock-built refuge stood
Above the blind and battling multitude: 10
In honoured poverty thy voice did weave
Songs consecrate to truth and liberty, –
Deserting these, thou leavest me to grieve,
Thus having been, that thou shouldst cease to be.

To —

Δακρυσι διοισω ποτμον 'αποτμον.[46]

O! there are spirits of the air,
    And genii of the evening breeze,
And gentle ghosts, with eyes as fair
    As star-beams among twilight trees: –
Such lovely ministers to meet
Oft hast thou turned from men thy lonely feet.

With mountain winds, and babbling springs,
    And moonlight seas, that are the voice
Of these inexplicable things,
    Thou didst hold commune, and rejoice   10
When they did answer thee; but they
Cast, like a worthless boon, thy love away.

And thou hast sought in starry eyes
    Beams that were never meant for thine –
Another's wealth: – tame sacrifice
    To a fond faith! still dost thou pine?
Still dost thou hope that greeting hands,
Voice, looks, or lips, may answer thy demands?

Ah! wherefore didst thou build thine hope
    On the false earth's inconstancy?   20
Did thine own mind afford no scope
    Of love, or moving thoughts to thee?
That natural scenes or human smiles
Could steal the power to wind thee in their wiles.

Yes, all the faithless smiles are fled
    Whose falsehood left thee broken-hearted;
The glory of the moon is dead;
    Night's ghosts and dreams have now departed;
Thine own soul still is true to thee,
But changed to a foul fiend through misery.   30

This fiend, whose ghastly presence ever
   Beside thee like thy shadow hangs,
Dream not to chase; – the mad endeavour
   Would scourge thee to severer pangs.
Be as thou art. Thy settled fate,
Dark as it is, all change would aggravate.

Mutability

We are as clouds that veil the midnight moon;
   How restlessly they speed, and gleam, and quiver,
Streaking the darkness radiantly! – yet soon
   Night closes round, and they are lost for ever:

Or like forgotten lyres,[47] whose dissonant strings
   Give various response to each varying blast,
To whose frail frame no second motion brings
   One mood or modulation like the last.

We rest. – A dream has power to poison sleep;
   We rise. – One wandering thought pollutes the day;   10
We feel, conceive or reason, laugh or weep;
   Embrace fond woe, or cast our cares away:

It is the same! – For, be it joy or sorrow,
   The path of its departure still is free:
Man's yesterday may ne'er be like his morrow;
   Nought may endure but Mutability.

A Summer-Evening Churchyard

LECHLADE, GLOUCESTERSHIRE

The wind has swept from the wide atmosphere
Each vapour that obscured the sunset's ray;
And pallid evening twines its beaming hair
In duskier braids around the languid eyes of day:
Silence and twilight, unbeloved of men,
Creep hand in hand from yon obscurest glen.

They breathe their spells towards the departing day,
Encompassing the earth, air, stars, and sea;
Light, sound, and motion own the potent sway,
Responding to the charm with its own mystery.   10
The winds are still, or the dry church-tower grass
Knows not their gentle motions as they pass.

Thou too, aerial Pile! whose pinnacles
Point from one shrine like pyramids of fire,
Obeyest in silence their sweet solemn spells,
Clothing in hues of heaven thy dim and distant spire,
Around whose lessening and invisible height
Gather among the stars the clouds of night.

The dead are sleeping in their sepulchres:
And, mouldering as they sleep, a thrilling sound,   20
Half sense, half thought, among the darkness stirs,
Breathed from their wormy beds all living things around,
And mingling with the still night and mute sky
Its awful hush is felt inaudibly.

Thus solemnised and softened, death is mild
And terrorless as this serenest night:
Here could I hope, like some enquiring child
Sporting on graves, that death did hide from human sight
Sweet secrets, or beside its breathless sleep
That loveliest dreams perpetual watch did keep.   30

Feelings of a Republican on the Fall of Bonaparte

I hated thee, fallen tyrant! I did groan
To think that a most unambitious slave,
Like thou, shouldst dance and revel on the grave
Of Liberty. Thou mightst have built thy throne
Where it had stood even now: thou didst prefer
A frail and bloody pomp which time has swept
In fragments towards oblivion. Massacre,
For this I prayed, would on thy sleep have crept,
Treason and Slavery, Rapine, Fear, and Lust,
And stifled thee, their minister. I know   10
Too late, since thou and France are in the dust,
That virtue owns a more eternal foe
Than force or fraud: old Custom, legal Crime,
And bloody Faith the foulest birth of time.

POEMS FROM 1816

Mont Blanc

LINES WRITTEN IN THE VALE OF CHAMOUNI

I

The everlasting universe of things
Flows through the mind, and rolls its rapid waves,
Now dark – now glittering – now reflecting gloom –
Now lending splendour, where from secret springs
The source of human thought its tribute brings
Of waters, – with a sound but half its own,
Such as a feeble brook will oft assume
In the wild woods, among the mountains lone,
Where waterfalls around it leap for ever,
Where woods and winds contend, and a vast river   10
Over its rocks ceaselessly bursts and raves.

II

Thus thou, Ravine of Arve – dark, deep Ravine –
Thou many-coloured, many-voiced vale,
Over whose pines, and crags, and caverns sail
Fast cloud shadows and sunbeams: awful scene,
Where Power in likeness of the Arve comes down
From the ice gulfs that gird his secret throne,
Bursting through these dark mountains like the flame
Of lightning thro' the tempest; – thou dost lie,
Thy giant brood of pines around thee clinging,   20
Children of elder time, in whose devotion
The chainless winds still come and ever came
To drink their odours, and their mighty swinging
To hear – an old and solemn harmony;
Thine earthly rainbows stretched across the sweep
Of the ethereal waterfall, whose veil
Robes some unsculptured image; the strange sleep
Which when the voices of the desert fail
Wraps all in its own deep eternity; –
Thy caverns echoing to the Arve's commotion,   30

A loud, lone sound no other sound can tame;
Thou art pervaded with that ceaseless motion,
Thou art the path of that unresting sound –
Dizzy Ravine! and when I gaze on thee
I seem as in a trance sublime and strange
To muse on my own separate phantasy,
My own, my human mind, which passively
Now renders and receives fast influencings,
Holding an unremitting interchange
With the clear universe of things around;   40
One legion of wild thoughts, whose wandering wings
Now float above thy darkness, and now rest
Where that or thou art no unbidden guest,
In the still cave of the witch Poesy,
Seeking among the shadows that pass by
Ghosts of all things that are, some shade of thee,
Some phantom, some faint image; till the breast
From which they fled recalls them, thou art there!

III

Some say that gleams of a remoter world
Visit the soul in sleep, – that death is slumber,   50
And that its shapes the busy thoughts outnumber
Of those who wake and live. – I look on high;
Has some unknown omnipotence unfurled
The veil of life and death? or do I lie
In dream, and does the mightier world of sleep
Spread far around and inaccessibly
Its circles? For the very spirit fails,
Driven like a homeless cloud from steep to steep
That vanishes among the viewless gales!
Far, far above, piercing the infinite sky,   60
Mont Blanc appears, – still, snowy, and serene –
Its subject mountains their unearthly forms
Pile around it, ice and rock; broad vales between
Of frozen floods, unfathomable deeps,
Blue as the overhanging heaven, that spread
And wind among the accumulated steeps;
A desert peopled by the storms alone,
Save when the eagle brings some hunter's bone,

And the wolf tracks her there – how hideously
Its shapes are heaped around! rude, bare, and high,   70
Ghastly, and scarred, and riven. – Is this the scene
Where the old Earthquake-demon taught her young
Ruin? Were these their toys? or did a sea
Of fire, envelope once this silent snow?
None can reply – all seems eternal now.
The wilderness has a mysterious tongue
Which teaches awful doubt, or faith so mild,
So solemn, so serene, that man may be
But for such faith with nature reconciled;
Thou hast a voice, great Mountain, to repeal   80
Large codes of fraud and woe; not understood
By all, but which the wise, and great, and good
Interpret, or make felt, or deeply feel.

IV

The fields, the lakes, the forests, and the streams,
Ocean, and all the living things that dwell
Within the daedal[48] earth; lightning, and rain,
Earthquake, and fiery flood, and hurricane,
The torpor of the year when feeble dreams
Visit the hidden buds, or dreamless sleep
Holds every future leaf and flower; – the bound   90
With which from that detested trance they leap;
The works and ways of man, their death and birth,
And that of him and all that his may be;
All things that move and breathe with toil and sound
Are born and die; revolve, subside and swell.
Power dwells apart in its tranquillity
Remote, serene, and inaccessible:
And *this*, the naked countenance of earth,
On which I gaze, even these primeval mountains
Teach the adverting mind. The glaciers creep   100
Like snakes that watch their prey, from their far fountains,
Slow rolling on; there, many a precipice,
Frost and the Sun in scorn of mortal power
Have piled: dome, pyramid, and pinnacle,
A city of death, distinct with many a tower
And wall impregnable of beaming ice.

Yet not a city, but a flood of ruin
Is there, that from the boundaries of the sky
Rolls its perpetual stream; vast pines are strewing
Its destined path, or in the mangled soil   110
Branchless and shattered stand; the rocks, drawn down
From yon remotest waste, have overthrown
The limits of the dead and living world,
Never to be reclaimed. The dwelling-place
Of insects, beasts, and birds, becomes its spoil;
Their food and their retreat for ever gone,
So much of life and joy is lost. The race
Of man, flies far in dread; his work and dwelling
Vanish, like smoke before the tempest's stream,
And their place is not known. Below, vast caves   120
Shine in the rushing torrent's restless gleam,
Which from those secret chasms in tumult welling
Meet in the vale, and one majestic River,
The breath and blood of distant lands, for ever
Rolls its loud waters to the ocean waves,
Breathes its swift vapours to the circling air.

V

Mont Blanc yet gleams on high: – the power is there,
The still and solemn power of many sights,
And many sounds, and much of life and death.
In the calm darkness of the moonless nights,   130
In the lone glare of day, the snows descend
Upon that Mountain; none beholds them there,
Nor when the flakes burn in the sinking sun,
Or the star-beams dart through them: – Winds contend
Silently there, and heap the snow with breath
Rapid and strong, but silently! Its home
The voiceless lightning in these solitudes
Keeps innocently, and like vapour broods
Over the snow. The secret strength of things
Which governs thought, and to the infinite dome   140
Of heaven is as a law, inhabits thee!
And what were thou, and earth, and stars, and sea,
If to the human mind's imaginings
Silence and solitude were vacancy?   *23 July 1816*

Hymn to Intellectual Beauty [49]

1

The awful shadow of some unseen Power
   Floats tho' unseen amongst us, – visiting
   This various world with as inconstant wing
As summer winds that creep from flower to flower, –
Like moonbeams that behind some piny mountain shower,
      It visits with inconstant glance
      Each human heart and countenance;
Like hues and harmonies of evening, –
      Like clouds in starlight widely spread, –
      Like memory of music fled, –   10
      Like aught that for its grace may be
Dear, and yet dearer for its mystery.

2

Spirit of Beauty, that dost consecrate
   With thine own hues all thou dost shine upon
   Of human thought or form, – where art thou gone?
Why dost thou pass away and leave our state.
This dim vast vale of tears, vacant and desolate?
      Ask why the sunlight not for ever
      Weaves rainbows o'er yon mountain river,
Why aught should fail and fade that once is shown,   20
      Why fear and dream and death and birth
      Cast on the daylight of this earth
      Such gloom, – why man has such a scope
For love and hate, despondency and hope?

3

No voice from some sublimer world hath ever
   To sage or poet these responses given –
   Therefore the names of Demon, Ghost, and Heaven
Remain the records of their vain endeavour,
Frail spells – whose uttered charm might not avail to sever,
      From all we hear and all we see,   30
      Doubt, chance, and mutability.

Thy light alone – like mist o'er mountains driven,
  Or music by the night wind sent,
  Thro' strings of some still instrument,
  Or moonlight on a midnight stream,
Gives grace and truth to life's unquiet dream.

4

Love, Hope, and Self-esteem, like clouds depart
 And come, for some uncertain moments lent.
 Man were immortal, and omnipotent,
Didst thou, unknown and awful as thou art,   40
Keep with thy glorious train firm state within his heart.
  Thou messenger of sympathies,
  That wax and wane in lover's eyes –
Thou – that to human thought art nourishment,
  Like darkness to a dying flame!
  Depart not as thy shadow came,
  Depart not – lest the grave should be,
Like life and fear, a dark reality.

5

While yet a boy I sought for ghosts, and sped
 Thro' many a listening chamber, cave and ruin,   50
 And starlight wood, with fearful steps pursuing
Hopes of high talk with the departed dead.
I called on poisonous names with which our youth is fed,
  I was not heard – I saw them not –
  When musing deeply on the lot
Of life, at that sweet time when winds are wooing
  All vital things that wake to bring
  News of birds and blossoming, –
  Sudden, thy shadow fell on me;
I shrieked, and clasped my hands in ecstacy!   60

6

I vowed that I would dedicate my powers
 To thee and thine – have I not kept the vow?
 With beating heart and streaming eyes, even now
I call the phantoms of a thousand hours
Each from his voiceless grave: they have in visioned bowers

     Of studious zeal or love's delight
     Outwatched with me the envious night –
They know that never joy illumed my brow
     Unlinked with hope that thou wouldst free
     This world from its dark slavery,   70
     That thou – O awful LOVELINESS,
Wouldst give whate'er these words cannot express.

7

The day becomes more solemn and serene
     When noon is past – there is a harmony
     In autumn, and a lustre in its sky,
Which thro' the summer is not heard or seen,
As if it could not be, as if it had not been!
     Thus let thy power, which like the truth
     Of nature on my passive youth
Descended, to my onward life supply   80
     Its calm – to one who worships thee,
     And every form containing thee,
     Whom, SPIRIT fair, thy spells did bind
To fear himself, and love all human kind.

POEMS FROM 1817

Laon and Cyntha or The Revolution of the Golden City

A VISION OF THE NINETEENTH CENTURY
IN THE STANZA OF SPENSER

Δος που στω και κοσμον κινησω – Archimedes

Ὅσαις δὲ βροτὸν ἔθνος ἀγλαΐαις ἁπτόμεσθα
   περαίνει πρὸς ἔσχατον
πλόον ναυσὶ δ' οὔτε πεζὸς ἰὼν ἂν εὕροις
ἐς Ὑπερβορέων ἀγῶνα θαυματὰν ὁδόν

Pindar, Πυθ, x[50]

PREFACE

The Poem which I now present to the world is an attempt from which I scarcely dare to expect success, and in which a writer of established fame might fail without disgrace. It is an experiment on the temper of the public mind, as to how far a thirst for a happier condition of moral and political society survives, among the enlightened and refined, the tempests which have shaken the age in which we live. I have sought to enlist the harmony of metrical language, the ethereal combinations of the fancy, the rapid and subtle transitions of human passion, all those elements which essentially compose a Poem, in the cause of a liberal and comprehensive morality, and in the view of kindling within the bosoms of my readers a virtuous enthusiasm for those doctrines of liberty and justice, that faith and hope in something good, which neither violence, nor misrepresentation, nor prejudice, can ever totally extinguish among mankind.

For this purpose I have chosen a story of human passion in its most universal character, diversified with moving and romantic adventures, and appealing, in contempt of all artificial opinions or institutions, to the common sympathies of every human breast. I have made no attempt to recommend the motives which I would substitute for those at present governing mankind by methodical and systematic argument. I would only awaken the feelings, so that the reader should see the beauty of true virtue, and be incited to those enquiries which have led to my moral and political creed, and that of some of the sublimest intellects in the world. The Poem therefore (with the exception of the first Canto, which is purely introductory) is narrative, not didactic. It is a succession of pictures illustrating the growth and progress of the individual mind aspiring after excellence, and devoted to the love of mankind; its influence in refining and making pure the most daring and uncommon impulses of the imagination, the understanding, and the senses; its impatience at 'all the oppressions which are done under the sun'; its tendency to awaken public hope and to enlighten and improve mankind; the rapid effects of the application of that tendency; the awakening of an immense nation from their slavery and degradation to a true sense of moral dignity and freedom; the bloodless dethronement of their oppressors, and the unveiling of the religious frauds by which they had been deluded into submission; the tranquillity of successful patriotism, and the universal toleration and benevolence of true philanthropy; the treachery and barbarity of hired soldiers; vice not the object of punishment and hatred, but kindness and pity; the faithlessness of tyrants; the confederacy of the Rulers of the World, and the restoration of the expelled Dynasty by foreign arms; the massacre and extermination of the Patriots, and the victory of established power; the consequences of legitimate despotism, civil war, famine, plague, superstition, and an utter extinction of the domestic affections; the judicial murder of the advocates of Liberty; the temporary triumph of oppression, that secure earnest of its final and inevitable fall; the transient nature of ignorance and error, and the eternity of genius and virtue. Such is the series of delineations of which the Poem consists. And if the lofty passions with which it has been my scope to distinguish this story, shall not excite in the reader a generous impulse, an ardent thirst for excellence, an interest profound and strong, such as belongs to no meaner desires – let not the failure be imputed to a natural unfitness for human sympathy in these sublime and animating themes. It is the business of the Poet to communicate to others the pleasure and the enthusiasm arising out of those images and feelings, in the vivid presence of which within his own mind consists at once his inspiration and his reward.

The panic which, like an epidemic transport, seized upon all classes of men during the excesses consequent upon the French Revolution is gradually giving place to sanity. It has ceased to be believed that whole generations of mankind ought to consign themselves to a hopeless inheritance of ignorance and misery, because a nation of men who had been dupes and slaves for centuries were incapable of conducting themselves with the wisdom and tranquillity of freemen so soon as some of their fetters were partially loosened. That their conduct could not have been marked by any other characters than ferocity and thoughtlessness is the historical fact from which liberty derives all its recommendations, and falsehood the worst features of its deformity. There is a reflux in the tide of human things which bears the shipwrecked hopes of men into a secure haven, after the storms are past. Methinks, those who now live have survived an age of despair.

The French Revolution may be considered as one of those manifestations of a general state of feeling among civilised mankind produced by a defect of correspondence between the knowledge existing in society and the improvement, or gradual abolition, of political institutions. The year 1788 may be assumed as the epoch of one of the most important crises produced by this feeling. The sympathies connected with that event extended to every bosom. The most generous and amiable natures were those which participated the most extensively in these sympathies. But such a degree of unmingled good was expected as it was impossible to realise. If the Revolution had been in every respect prosperous, then misrule and superstition would lose half their claims to our abhorrence, as fetters which the captive can unlock with the slightest motion of his fingers, and which do not eat with poisonous rust into the soul. The revulsion occasioned by the atrocities of the demagogues and the re-establishment of successive tyrannies in France was terrible, and felt in the remotest corner of the civilised world. Could they listen to the plea of reason who had groaned under the calamities of a social state, according to the provisions of which, one man riots in luxury whilst another famishes for want of bread? Can he who the day before was a trampled slave, suddenly become liberal-minded, forbearing, and independent? This is the consequence of the habits of a state of society to be produced by resolute perseverance and indefatigable hope, and long-suffering and long believing courage, and the systematic efforts of generations of men of intellect and virtue. Such is the lesson which experience teaches now. But, on the first reverses of hope in the progress of French liberty, the sanguine eagerness for good overleapt the solution of these questions, and for a time extinguished itself in the unexpectedness of their result. Thus many of the most ardent and tender-hearted of the worshippers of public good have been morally ruined by what a partial glimpse of the events they deplored appeared to show as the melancholy desolation of all their cherished hopes. Hence gloom and misanthropy have become the characteristics of the age in which we live, the solace of a disappointment that unconsciously finds relief only in the wilful exaggeration of its own despair. This influence has tainted the literature of the age with the hopelessness of the minds from which it flows.

Metaphysics,* and enquiries into moral and political science, have become little else than vain attempts to revive exploded superstitions, or sophisms like those† of Mr Malthus,[51] calculated to lull the oppressors of mankind into a security of everlasting triumph. Our works of fiction and poetry have been overshadowed by the same infectious gloom. But mankind appear to me to be emerging from their trance. I am aware, methinks, of a slow, gradual silent change. In that belief I have composed the following Poem.

I do not presume to enter into competition with our greatest contemporary Poets. Yet I am unwilling to tread in the footsteps of any who have preceded me. I have sought to avoid the imitation of any style of language or versification peculiar to the original minds of which it is the character, designing that even if what I have produced be worthless, it should still be properly my own. Nor have I permitted any system relating to mere words to divert the attention of the reader from whatever interest I may have succeeded in creating to my own ingenuity in contriving to disgust them according to the rules of criticism. I have simply clothed my thoughts in what appeared to me the most obvious and appropriate language. A person familiar with nature, and with the most celebrated productions of the human mind, can scarcely err in following the instinct, with respect to selection of language, produced by that familiarity.

There is an education peculiarly fitted for a Poet, without which genius and sensibility can hardly fill the circle of their capacities. No education indeed can entitle to this appellation a dull and unobservant mind, or one, though neither dull nor unobservant, in which the channels of communication between thought and expression have been obstructed or closed. How far it is my fortune to belong to either of the latter classes, I cannot know. I aspire to be something better. The circumstances of my accidental education have been favourable to this ambition. I have been familiar from boyhood with mountains and lakes, and the sea, and the solitude of forests: Danger, which sports upon the brink of precipices, has been my playmate. I have trodden the glaciers of the Alps, and lived under the eye of Mont Blanc. I have been a wanderer among distant fields. I have sailed down mighty rivers, and seen the sun rise and set, and the stars come

* I ought to except Sir W. Drummond's *Academical Questions*, a volume of very acute and powerful metaphysical criticism.

† It is remarkable, as a symptom of the revival of public hope, that Mr Malthus has assigned, in the later editions of his work, an indefinite dominion to moral restraint over the principle of population. This concession answers all the inferences from his doctrine unfavourable to human improvement, and reduces the 'Essay on Population' to a commentary illustrative of the unanswerableness of 'Political Justice'.

forth, whilst I have sailed night and day down a rapid stream among mountains. I have seen populous cities, and have watched the passions which rise and spread, and sink and change, amongst assembled multitudes of men. I have seen the theatre of the more visible ravages of tyranny and war, cities and villages reduced to scattered groups of black and roofless houses, and the naked inhabitants sitting famished upon their desolated thresholds. I have conversed with living men of genius. The poetry of ancient Greece and Rome, and modern Italy, and our own country, has been to me like external nature, a passion and an enjoyment. Such are the sources from which the materials for the imagery of my Poem have been drawn. I have considered Poetry in its most comprehensive sense, and have read the Poets and the Historians, and the Metaphysicians* whose writings have been accessible to me, and have looked upon the beautiful and majestic scenery of the earth as common sources of those elements which it is the province of the Poet to embody and combine. Yet the experience and the feelings to which I refer do not in themselves constitute men Poets, but only prepare them to be the auditors of those who are. How far I shall be found to possess that more essential attribute of Poetry, the power of awakening in others sensations like those which animate my own bosom, is that which, to speak sincerely, I know not; and which with an acquiescent and contented spirit, I expect to be taught by the effect which I shall produce upon those whom I now address.

I have avoided, as I have said before, the imitation of any contemporary style. But there must be a resemblance, which does not depend upon their own will, between all the writers of any particular age. They cannot escape from subjection to a common influence which arises out of an infinite combination of circumstances belonging to the times in which they live, though each is in a degree the author of the very influence by which his being is thus pervaded. Thus, the tragic poets of the age of Pericles;[52] the Italian revivers of ancient learning; those mighty intellects of our own country that succeeded the Reformation, the translators of the Bible, Shakespeare, Spenser, the dramatists of the reign of Elizabeth, and Lord Bacon;†[53] the colder spirits of the interval that succeeded; – all resemble each other, and differ from every other in their several classes. In this view of things, Ford[54] can no more be called the imitator of Shakespeare, than

---

* In this sense there may be such a thing as perfectibility in works of fiction, notwithstanding the concession often made by the advocates of human improvement that perfectibility is a term applicable only to science.

† Milton stands alone in the age which he illumined.

Shakespeare the imitator of Ford. There were perhaps few other points of resemblance between these two men than that which the universal and inevitable influence of their age produced. And this is an influence which neither the meanest scribbler nor the sublimest genius of any era can escape; and which I have not attempted to escape.

I have adopted the stanza of Spenser (a measure inexpressibly beautiful),[55] not because I consider it a finer model of poetical harmony than the blank verse of Shakespeare and Milton, but because in the latter there is no shelter for mediocrity: you must either succeed or fail. This perhaps an aspiring spirit should desire. But I was enticed also by the brilliancy and magnificence of sound which a mind that has been nourished upon musical thoughts can produce by a just and harmonious arrangement of the pauses of this measure. Yet there will be found some instances where I have completely failed in this attempt, and one, which I here request the reader to consider as an erratum, where there is left most inadvertently an alexandrine in the middle of a stanza.

But in this, as in every other respect, I have written fearlessly. It is the misfortune of this age that its Writers, too thoughtless of immortality, are exquisitely sensible to temporary praise or blame. They write with the fear of Reviews before their eyes. This system of criticism sprang up in that torpid interval when Poetry was not. Poetry, and the art which professes to regulate and limit its powers, cannot subsist together. Longinus could not have been the contemporary of Homer, nor Boileau of Horace.[56] Yet this species of criticism never presumed to assert an understanding of its own: it has always, unlike true science, followed not preceded the opinion of mankind, and would even now bribe with worthless adulation some of our greatest Poets to impose gratuitous fetters on their own imaginations and become unconscious accomplices in the daily murder of all genius either not so aspiring or not so fortunate as their own. I have sought therefore to write, as I believe that Homer, Shakespeare, and Milton wrote, with an utter disregard of anonymous censure. I am certain that calumny and misrepresentation, though it may move me to compassion, cannot disturb my peace. I shall understand the expressive silence of those sagacious enemies who dare not trust themselves to speak. I shall endeavour to extract from the midst of insult and contempt, and maledictions, those admonitions which may tend to correct whatever imperfections such censurers may discover in this my first serious appeal to the Public. If certain Critics were as clear-sighted as they are malignant, how great would be the benefit to be derived from their virulent writings! As it is, I fear I shall be malicious enough to be amused with their paltry tricks and lame invectives. Should the Public judge that my composition is worthless, I shall indeed bow before the tribunal from which Milton received his crown of immortality, and shall seek to gather, if I live, strength from that defeat, which may nerve me to some new enterprise of thought which may *not* be worthless. I cannot conceive that Lucretius,[57] when he meditated that poem whose doctrines are yet the basis of our metaphysical knowledge, and whose eloquence has been the wonder of mankind, wrote in awe of such censure as the hired sophists of the impure and superstitious noblemen of Rome might affix to what he should produce. It was at the period when Greece was led captive, and Asia made tributary to the Republic, fast verging itself to slavery and ruin, that a multitude of Syrian captives bigoted to the worship of their obscene Ashtaroth,[58] and the unworthy successors of Socrates and Zeno,[59] found there a precarious subsistence by administering, under the name of freedmen, to the vices and vanities of the great. These wretched men were skilled to plead, with a superficial but plausible set of sophisms, in favour of that contempt for virtue which is the portion of slaves, and that faith in portents, the most fatal substitute for benevolence in the imaginations of men, which arising from the enslaved communities of the East then first began to overwhelm the western nations in its stream. Were these the kind of men whose disapprobation the wise and lofty-minded Lucretius should have regarded with a salutary awe? The latest and perhaps the meanest of those who follow in his footsteps would disdain to hold life on such conditions.

The Poem now presented to the Public occupied little more than six months in the composition. That period has been devoted to the task with unremitting ardour and enthusiasm. I have exercised a watchful and earnest criticism on my work as it grew under my hands. I would willingly have sent it forth to the world with that perfection which long labour and revision is said to bestow. But I found that if I should gain something in exactness by this method, I might lose much of the newness and energy of imagery and language as it flowed fresh from my mind. And although the mere composition occupied no more than six months, the thoughts thus arranged were slowly gathered in as many years.

I trust that the reader will carefully distinguish between those opinions which have a dramatic propriety in reference to the characters which they are designed to elucidate and such as are properly my own. The erroneous and degrading idea which men have conceived of a Supreme Being, for instance, is spoken against, but not the Supreme Being itself. The belief which some superstitious persons whom I have brought upon the stage entertain of the Deity, as injurious to the character of his benevolence, is widely different from my own. In recommending also a great and important change in the spirit which animates the social institutions of mankind, I have avoided all flattery to those violent and malignant passions of our nature which are ever on the watch to mingle with and to alloy the most beneficial innovations. There is no quarter given to Revenge, or Envy, or Prejudice. Love is celebrated everywhere as the sole law which should govern the moral world.

In the personal conduct of my Hero and Heroine, there is one circumstance which was intended to startle the reader from the trance of ordinary life. It was my object to break through the crust of those outworn opinions on which established institutions depend. I have appealed therefore to the most universal of all feelings, and have endeavoured to strengthen the moral sense, by forbidding it to waste its energies in seeking to avoid actions which are only crimes of convention. It is because there is so great a multitude of artificial vices that there are so few real virtues. These feelings alone which are benevolent or malevolent are essentially good or bad. The circumstance of which I speak was introduced, however, merely to accustom men to that charity and toleration which the exhibition of a practice widely differing from their own has a tendency to promote.* Nothing indeed can be more mischievous than many actions, innocent in themselves, which might bring down upon individuals the bigoted contempt and rage of the multitude.

* The sentiments connected with and characteristic of this circumstance have no personal reference to the writer.

DEDICATION[60]

There is no danger to a man, that knows
What life and death is: there's not any law
Exceeds his knowledge; neither is it lawful
That he should stoop to any other law – CHAPMAN

TO MARY

1

So now my summer-task is ended, Mary,
    And I return to thee, mine own heart's home;
As to his Queen some victor Knight of Faery,
    Earning bright spoils for her inchanted dome;
    Nor thou disdain, that ere my fame become
A star among the stars of mortal night,
    If it indeed may cleave its natal gloom,
Its doubtful promise thus I would unite
With thy beloved name, thou Child of love and light.

2

The toil which stole from thee so many an hour,   10
    Is ended, – and the fruit is at thy feet!
No longer where the woods to frame a bower
    Which interlaced branches mix and meet,
    Or where with sound like many voices sweet,
Waterfalls leap among wild islands green,
    With framed for my lone boat a lone retreat
Of moss-grown trees and weeds, shall I be seen:
But beside thee, where still my heart has ever been.

3

Thoughts of great deeds were mine, dear Friend, when first
    The clouds which wrap this world from youth did pass.   20
I do remember well the hour which burst
    My spirits' sleep: a fresh May-dawn it was,
    When I walked forth upon the glittering grass,
And wept, I knew not why; until there rose
    From the near school-room, voices, that, alas!
Were but one echo from a world of woes –
The harsh and grating strife of tyrants and of foes.

4

And then I clasped my hands and looked around –
    – But none was near to mock my streaming eyes,
Which poured their warm drops on the sunny ground –   30
    So without shame, I spake: – 'I will be wise,
    And just, and free, and mild, if in me lies
Such power, for I grow weary to behold
    The selfish and the strong still tyrannise
Without reproach or check.' I then controlled
My tears, my heart grew calm, and I was meek and bold.

5

And from that hour did I with earnest thought
    Heap knowledge from forbidden mines of lore,
Yet nothing that my tyrants knew or taught
    I cared to learn, but from that secret store   40
    Wrought linked armour for my soul, before
It might walk forth to war among mankind;
    Thus power and hope were strengthened more and more
Within me, till there came upon my mind
A sense of loneliness, a thirst with which I pined.

6

Alas, that love should be a blight and snare
    To those who seek all sympathies in one! –
Such once I sought in vain; then black despair,
    The shadow of a starless night, was thrown
    Over the world in which I moved alone: –   50
Yet never found I one not false to me,
    Hard hearts, and cold, like weights of icy stone
Which crushed and withered mine, that could not be
Aught but a lifeless clod, until revived by thee.

7

Thou Friend, whose presence on my wintry heart
    Fell, like bright Spring upon some herbless plain;
How beautiful and calm and free thou wert
    In thy young wisdom, when the mortal chain
    Of Custom thou didst burst and rend in twain,

And walked as free as light the clouds among,   60
   Which many an envious slave then breathed in vain
From his dim dungeon, and my spirit sprung
To meet thee from the woes which had begirt it long.

8

No more alone through the world's wilderness,
   Although I trod the paths of high intent,
I journeyed now: no more companionless,
   Where solitude is like despair, I went. –
   There is the wisdom of a stern content
When Poverty can blight the just and good,
   When Infamy dares mock the innocent,   70
And cherished friends turn with the multitude
To trample: this was ours, and we unshaken stood!

9

Now has descended a serener hour,
   And with inconstant fortune, friends return;
Tho' suffering leaves the knowledge and the power
   Which says: – Let scorn be not repaid with scorn.
   And from thy side two gentle babes are born
To fill our home with smiles, and thus are we
   Most fortunate beneath life's beaming morn;
And these delights, and thou, have been to me   80
The parents of the Song I consecrate to thee.

10

Is it, that now my inexperienced fingers
   But strike the prelude of a loftier strain?
Or, must the lyre on which my spirit lingers
   Soon pause in silence, ne'er to sound again,
   Tho' it might shake the Anarch Custom's reign,
And charm the minds of men to Truth's own sway,
   Holier than was Amphion's? I would fain
Reply in hope – but I am worn away,
And Death and Love are yet contending for their prey.   90

11

And what art thou? I know, but dare not speak:
    Time may interpret to his silent years.
Yet in the paleness of thy thoughtful cheek,
    And in the light thine ample forehead wears,
    And in thy sweetest smiles, and in thy tears,
And in thy gentle speech, a prophecy
    Is whispered, to subdue my fondest fears:
And thro' thine eyes, even in thy soul I see
A lamp of vestal fire burning internally.

12

They say that thou wert lovely from thy birth,   100
    Of glorious parents, thou aspiring Child.
I wonder not – for One then left this earth
    Whose life was like a setting planet mild,
    Which clothed thee in the radiance undefiled
Of its departing glory; still her fame
    Shines on thee, thro' the tempests dark and wild
Which shake these latter days; and thou canst claim
The shelter, from thy Sire, of an immortal name.

13

One voice came forth from many a mighty spirit,
    Which was the echo of three thousand years;   110
And the tumultuous world stood mute to hear it,
    As some lone man who in a desert hears
    The music of his home: – unwonted fears
Fell on the pale oppressors of our race,
    And Faith, and Custom, and low-thoughted cares,
Like thunder-stricken dragons, for a space
Left the torn human heart, their food and dwelling-place.

14

Truth's deathless voice pauses among mankind!
    If there must be no response to my cry –
If men must rise and stamp with fury blind   120
    On his pure name who loves them, – thou and I,
    Sweet friend! can look from our tranquillity

Like lamps into the world's tempestuous night, –
    Two tranquil stars, while clouds are passing by
Which wrap them from the foundering seaman's sight,
That burn from year to year with unextinguished light.

from CANTO SECOND

XXI

I had a little sister, whose fair eyes
    Were loadstars of delight, which drew me home
When I might wander forth; nor did I prize
    Aught human thing beneath Heaven's mighty dome   850
    Beyond this child: so when sad hours were come,
And baffled hope like ice still clung to me,
    Since kin were cold, and friends had now become
Heartless and false, I turned from all, to be,
Cythna, the only source of tears and smiles to thee.

XXII

What wert thou then? A child most infantine,
    Yet wandering far beyond that innocent age
In all but its sweet looks and mien divine;
    Even then, methought, with the world's tyrant rage
    A patient warfare thy young heart did wage,   860
When those soft eyes of scarcely conscious thought,
    Some tale, or thine own fancies, would engage
To overflow with tears, or converse fraught
With passion, o'er their depths its fleeting light had wrought.

XXIII

She moved upon this earth a shape of brightness,
    A power, that from its objects scarcely drew
One impulse of her being – in her lightness
    Most like some radiant cloud of morning dew,
    Which wanders thro' the waste air's pathless blue,
To nourish some far desert: she did seem   870
    Beside me, gathering beauty as she grew,
Like the bright shade of some immortal dream
Which walks, when tempest sleeps, the wave of life's dark stream.

XXIV

As mine own shadow was this child to me,
    A second self, far dearer and more fair;
Which clothed in undissolving radiancy,
    All those steep paths which languor and despair
    Of human things, had made so dark and bare,
But which I trod alone – nor, till bereft
    Of friends, and overcome by lonely care,   880
Knew I what solace for that loss was left,
Though by a bitter wound my trusting heart was cleft.

XXV

Once she was dear, now she was all I had
    To love in human life, this sister sweet,
This child of twelve years old – so she was made
    My sole associate, and her willing feet
    Wandered with mine where earth and ocean meet,
Beyond the aerial mountains whose vast cells
    The unreposing billows ever beat,
Thro' forests wide and old, and lawny dells,   890
Where boughs of incense droop over the emerald wells.

XXVI

And warm and light I felt her clasping hand
    When twined in mine: she followed where I went,
Thro' the lone paths of our immortal land.
    It had no waste, but some memorial lent
    Which strung me to my toil – some monument
Vital with mind: then, Cythna by my side,
    Until the bright and beaming day were spent,
    Would rest, with looks entreating to abide,
Too earnest and too sweet ever to be denied.   900

XXVII

And soon I could not have refused her – thus
    For ever, day and night, we two were ne'er
Parted, but when brief sleep divided us:
    And when the pauses of the lulling air
    Of noon beside the sea, had made a lair

For her soothed senses, in my arms she slept,
　　And I kept watch over her slumbers there,
　　While, as the shifting visions o'er her swept,
Amid her innocent rest by turns she smil'd and wept.

XXVIII

And, in the murmur of her dreams was heard   910
　　Sometimes the name of Laon: – suddenly
She would arise, and like the secret bird
　　Whom sunset wakens, fill the shore and sky
　　With her sweet accents – a wild melody!
Hymns which my soul had woven to Freedom, strong
　　The source of passion, whence they rose, to be;
Triumphant strains, which, like a spirit's tongue,
To the inchanted waves that child of glory sung.

XXIX

Her white arms lifted thro' the shadowy stream
　　Of her loose hair – oh, excellently great   920
Seemed to me then my purpose, the vast theme
　　Of those impassioned songs, when Cythna sate
　　Amid the calm which rapture doth create
After its tumult, her heart vibrating,
　　Her spirit o'er the ocean's floating state
From her deep eyes far wandering, on the wing
Of visions that were mine, beyond its utmost spring.

XXX

For, before Cythna loved it, had my song
　　Peopled with thoughts the boundless universe,
A mighty congregation, which were strong   930
　　Where'er they trod the darkness to disperse
　　The cloud of that unutterable curse
Which clings upon mankind: – all things became
　　Slaves to my holy and heroic verse,
Earth, sea and sky, the planets, life and fame
And fate, or whate'er else binds the world's wondrous frame.

XXXI

And this beloved child thus felt the sway
   Of my conceptions, gathering like a cloud
The very wind on which it rolls away:
     Her's too were all my thoughts, ere yet endowed   940
     With music and with light, their fountains flowed
In poesy; and her still and earnest face,
     Pallid with feelings which intensely glowed
Within, was turned on mine with speechless grace,
Watching the hopes which there her heart had learned to trace.

XXXII

In me, communion with this purest being
   Kindled intenser zeal, and made me wise
In knowledge, which in her's mine own mind seeing,
     Left in the human world few mysteries:
     How without fear of evil or disguise   950
Was Cythna! – what a spirit strong and mild,
     Which death, or pain or peril could despise,
Yet melt in tenderness! what genius wild,
Yet mighty, was inclosed within one simple child!

XXXIII

New lore was this – old age with its grey hair,
   And wrinkled legends of unworthy things,
And icy sneers, is nought: it cannot dare
     To burst the chains which life for ever flings
     On the entangled soul's aspiring wings.
So is it cold and cruel, and is made   960
     The careless slave of that dark power which brings
Evil, like blight, on man, who, still betrayed,
Laughs o'er the grave in which his living hopes are laid.

XXXIV

Nor are the strong and the severe to keep
   The empire of the world: thus Cythna taught
Even in the visions of her eloquent sleep,
     Unconscious of the power thro' which she wrought
     The woof of such intelligible thought,

As from the tranquil strength which cradled lay
   In her smile-peopled rest, my spirit sought   970
Why the deceiver and the slave has sway
O'er heralds so divine of truth's arising day.

XXXV

Within that fairest form, the female mind
   Untainted by the poison clouds which rest
On the dark world, a sacred home did find:
   But else, from the wide earth's maternal breast,
   Victorious Evil, which had dispossest
All native power, had those fair children torn,
   And made them slaves to soothe his vile unrest,
And minister to lust its joys forlorn,   980
Till they had learned to breathe the atmosphere of scorn.

XXXVI

This misery was but coldly felt, 'till she
   Became my only friend, who had indued
My purpose with a wider sympathy;
   Thus, Cythna mourned with me the servitude
   In which the half of humankind were mewed
Victims of lust and hate, the slaves of slaves,
   She mourned that grace and power were thrown as food
   To the hyena lust, who, among graves,
Over his loathed meal, laughing in agony, raves.   990

XXXVII

And I, still gazing on that glorious child.
   Even as these thoughts flushed o'er her. – 'Cythna sweet,
Well with the world art thou unreconciled;
   Never will peace and human nature meet
   Till free and equal man and woman greet
Domestic peace; and ere this power can make
   In human hearts its calm and holy seat;
   This slavery must be broken' – as I spake,
From Cythna's eyes a light of exultation brake.

XXXVIII

She replied earnestly: – 'It shall be mine,   1000
   This task, mine, Laon! – thou hast much to gain;
Nor wilt thou at poor Cythna's pride repine,
   If she should lead a happy female train
   To meet thee over the rejoicing plain,
When myriads at thy call shall throng around
   The golden City.' – Then the child did strain
My arm upon her tremulous heart, and wound
Her own about my neck, till some reply she found.

XXXIX

I smiled, and spake not – 'wherefore dost thou smile
   At what I say? Laon, I am not weak,   1010
And though my cheek might become pale the while,
   With thee, if thou desirest, will I seek
   Through their array of banded slaves to wreak
Ruin upon the tyrants. I had thought
   It was more hard to turn my unpractised cheek
To scorn and shame, and this beloved spot
And thee, O dearest friend, to leave and murmur not.

XL

'Whence came I what I am? Thou, Laon, knowest
   How a young child should thus undaunted be;
Methinks, it is a power which thou bestowest,   1020
   Through which I seek, by most resembling thee,
   So to become most good, and great and free,
Yet far beyond this Ocean's utmost roar
   In towers and huts are many like to me,
Who, could they see thine eyes, or feel such lore
As I have learnt from them, like me would fear no more.

XLI

'Think'st thou that I shall speak unskilfully,
   And none will heed me? I remember now,
How once, a slave in tortures doomed to die,
   Was saved, because in accents sweet and low   1030
   He sung a song his Judge loved long ago,

As he was led to death. – All shall relent
     Who hear me – tears as mine have flowed, shall flow,
Hearts beat as mine now beats, with such intent
As renovates the world; a will omnipotent!

XLII

'Yes, I will tread Pride's golden palaces,
     Thro' Penury's roofless huts and squalid cells
Will I descend, where'er in abjectness
     Woman with some vile slave her tyrant dwells,
     There with the music of thine own sweet spells   1040
Will disenchant the captives, and will pour
     For the despairing, from the crystal wells
Of thy deep spirit, reason's mighty lore,
And power shall then abound, and hope arise once more.

XLIII

'Can man be free if woman be a slave?
     Chain one who lives, and breathes this boundless air,
To the corruption of a closed grave!
     Can they whose mates are beasts, condemned to bear
     Scorn, heavier far than toil or anguish, dare
To trample their oppressors? in their home   1050
     Among their babes, thou knowest a curse would wear
The shape of woman – hoary crime would come
Behind, and fraud rebuild religion's tottering dome.

XLIV

'I am a child: – I would not yet depart.
     When I go forth alone, bearing the lamp
Aloft which thou hast kindled in my heart,
     Millions of slaves from many a dungeon damp
     Shall leap in joy, as the benumbing cramp
Of ages leaves their limbs – no ill may harm
     Thy Cythna ever – truth its radiant stamp   1060
Has fixed, as an invulnerable charm,
Upon her children's brow, dark falsehood to disarm.

XLV

'Wait yet awhile for the appointed day –
    Thou wilt depart, and I with tears shall stand
Watching thy dim sail skirt the ocean grey;
    Amid the dwellers of this lonely land
    I shall remain alone – and thy command
Shall then dissolve the world's unquiet trance,
    And, multitudinous as the desert sand
Borne on the storm, its millions shall advance,   1070
Thronging round thee, the light of their deliverance.

XLVI

'Then, like the forests of some pathless mountain,
    Which from remotest glens two warring winds
Involve in fire, which not the loosened fountain
    Of broadest floods might quench, shall all the kinds
    Of evil, catch from our uniting minds
The spark which must consume them; – Cythna then
    Will have cast off the impotence that binds
Her childhood now, and thro' the paths of men   1079
Will pass, as the charmed bird that haunts the serpent's den.

XLVII

'We part! – O Laon, I must dare, nor tremble,
    To meet those looks no more! – Oh, heavy stroke,
Sweet brother of my soul! can I dissemble
    The agony of this thought?' – As thus she spoke
    The gathered sobs her quivering accents broke,
And in my arms she hid her beating breast.
    I remained still for tears – sudden she woke
As one awakes from sleep, and wildly prest
My bosom, her whole frame impetuously possest.

XLVIII

'We part to meet again – but yon blue waste,   1090
    Yon desert wide and deep holds no recess,
Within whose happy silence, thus embraced
    We might survive all ills in one caress:
    Nor doth the grave – I fear 'tis passionless –

Nor yon cold vacant Heaven: – we meet again
   Within the minds of men, whose lips shall bless
Our memory, and whose hopes its light retain
When these dissevered bones are trodden in the plain.'

XLIX

I could not speak, tho' she had ceased, for now
   The fountains of her feeling, swift and deep,   1100
Seemed to suspend the tumult of their flow;
   So we arose, and by the starlight steep
   Went homeward – neither did we speak nor weep,
But pale, were calm with passion – thus subdued
   Like evening shades that o'er the mountains creep,
We moved towards our home; where, in this mood,
Each from the other sought refuge in solitude.

from CANTO FOURTH

VII

Thus slowly from my brain the darkness rolled,
   My thoughts their due array did re-assume
Thro' the enchantments of that Hermit old;   1470
   Then I bethought me of the glorious doom
   Of those who sternly struggle to relume
The lamp of Hope o'er man's bewildered lot,
   And, sitting by the waters, in the gloom
Of eve, to that friend's heart I told my thought –
That heart which had grown old, but had corrupted not.

VIII

That hoary man had spent his livelong age
   In converse with the dead, who leave the stamp
Of ever-burning thoughts on many a page,
   When they are gone into the senseless damp   1480
   Of graves; – his spirit thus became a lamp
Of splendour, like to those on which it fed.
   Through peopled haunts, the City and the Camp,
Deep thirst for knowledge had his footsteps led,
And all the ways of men among mankind he read.

IX

But custom maketh blind and obdurate
　　The loftiest hearts: – he had beheld the woe
In which mankind was bound, but deemed that fate
　　Which made them abject, would preserve them so;
　　And in such faith, some steadfast joy to know,　　　　　1490
He sought this cell: but when fame went abroad,
　　That one in Argolis did undergo
Torture for liberty, and that the crowd
High truths from gifted lips had heard and understood;

X

And that the multitude was gathering wide;
　　His spirit leaped within his aged frame,
In lonely peace he could no more abide,
　　But to the land on which the victor's flame
　　Had fed, my native land, the Hermit came:
Each heart was there a shield, and every tongue　　　　　1500
　　Was as a sword of truth – young Laon's name
Rallied their secret hopes, tho' tyrants sung
Hymns of triumphant joy our scattered tribes among.

XI

He came to the lone column on the rock,
　　And with his sweet and mighty eloquence
The hearts of those who watched it did unlock,
　　And made them melt in tears of penitence.
　　They gave him entrance free to bear me thence.
'Since this,' the old man said, 'seven years are spent,
　　While slowly truth on thy benighted sense　　　　　1510
Has crept; the hope which wildered it has lent
Meanwhile, to me the power of a sublime intent.

XII

'Yes, from the records of my youthful state,
　　And from the lore of bards and sages old,
From whatsoe'er my wakened thoughts create
　　Out of the hopes of thine aspirings bold,
　　Have I collected language to unfold

Truth to my countrymen; from shore to shore
   Doctrines of human power my words have told,
They have been heard, and men aspire to more   1520
Than they have ever gained or ever lost of yore.

XIII

'In secret chambers parents read, and weep,
   My writings to their babes, no longer blind;
And young men gather when their tyrants sleep,
   And vows of faith each to the other bind;
   And marriageable maidens, who have pined
With love, till life seemed melting thro' their look,
   A warmer zeal, a nobler hope now find;
And every bosom thus is rapt and shook,   1529
Like autumn's myriad leaves in one swoln mountain-brook.

XIV

'The tyrants of the Golden City tremble
   At voices which are heard about the streets,
The ministers of fraud can scarce dissemble
   The lies of their own heart; but when one meets
   Another at the shrine, he inly weets,
Tho' he says nothing, that the truth is known;
   Murderers are pale upon the judgement seats,
And gold grows vile even to the wealthy crone,
And laughter fills the Fane, and curses shake the Throne.

XV

'Kind thoughts, and mighty hopes, and gentle deeds   1540
   Abound, for fearless love, and the pure law
Of mild equality and peace, succeeds
   To faiths which long have held the world in awe,
   Bloody, and false, and cold: – as whirlpools draw
All wrecks of Ocean to their chasm, the sway
   Of thy strong genius, Laon, which foresaw
This hope, compels all spirits to obey,
Which round thy secret strength now throng in wide array.

XVI

'For I have been thy passive instrument' –
  (As thus the old man spake, his countenance   1550
Gleamed on me like a spirit's) – 'thou hast lent
  To me, to all, the power to advance
  Towards this unforeseen deliverance
From our ancestral chains – aye, thou didst rear
  That lamp of hope on high, which time, nor chance,
Nor change may not extinguish, and my share
Of good was o'er the world its gathered beams to bear.

XVII

'But I, alas! am both unknown and old,
  And though the woof of wisdom I know well
To dye in hues of language, I am cold   1560
  In seeming, and the hopes which inly dwell,
  My manners note that I did long repel;
But Laon's name to the tumultuous throng
  Were like the star whose beams the waves compel
And tempests, and his soul-subduing tongue
Were as a lance to quell the mailed crest of wrong.

XVIII

'Perchance blood need not flow, if thou at length
  Wouldst rise, perchance the very slaves would spare
Their brethren and themselves; great is the strength
  Of words – for lately did a maiden fair,   1570
  Who from her childhood has been taught to bear
The tyrant's heaviest yoke, arise, and make
  Her sex the law of truth and freedom hear,
And with these quiet words – "for thine own sake
I prithee spare me" – did with ruth so take

XIX

'All hearts, that even the torturer who had bound
  Her meek calm frame, ere it was yet impaled,
Loosened her, weeping then; nor could be found
  One human hand to harm her – unassailed
  Therefore she walks thro' the great City, veiled   1580

In virtue's adamantine eloquence,
   'Gainst scorn, and death and pain thus trebly mailed.
And blending in the smiles of that defence,
The Serpent and the Dove, Wisdom and Innocence.

XX

'The wild-eyed women throng around her path:
   From their luxurious dungeons, from the dust
Of meaner thralls, from the oppressor's wrath.
   Or the caresses of his sated lust
   They congregate: – in her they put their trust;
The tyrants send their armed slaves to quell   1590
   Her power; – they, even like a thunder gust
Caught by some forest, bend beneath the spell
Of that young maiden's speech, and to their chiefs rebel.

XXI

'Thus she doth equal laws and justice teach
   To woman, outraged and polluted long;
Gathering the sweetest fruit in human reach
   For those fair hands now free, while armed wrong
   Trembles before her look, tho' it be strong;
Thousands thus dwell beside her, virgins bright,
   And matrons with their babes, a stately throng!   1600
Lovers renew the vows which they did plight
In early faith, and hearts long parted now unite,

XXII

'And homeless orphans find a home near her,
   And those poor victims of the proud, no less,
Fair wrecks, on whom the smiling world with stir
   Thrusts the redemption of its wickedness: –
   In squalid huts, and in its palaces
Sits Lust alone, while o'er the land is borne
   Her voice, whose awful sweetness doth repress
All evil, and her foes relenting turn,   1610
And cast the vote of love in hope's abandoned urn.

XXIII

'So in the populous City, a young maiden
　　Has baffled Havoc of the prey which he
Marks as his own, whene'er with chains o'erladen
　　Men make them arms to hurl down tyranny,
　　False arbiter between the bound and free;
And o'er the land, in hamlets and in towns
　　The multitudes collect tumultuously,
And throng in arms; but tyranny disowns   1619
Their claim, and gathers strength around its trembling thrones.

XXIV

'Blood soon, altho' unwillingly to shed,
　　The free cannot forbear – the Queen of Slaves,
The hoodwinked Angel of the blind and dead,
　　Custom, with iron mace points to the graves
　　Where her own standard desolately waves
Over the dust of Prophets and of Kings.
　　Many yet stand in her array – "she paves
Her path with human hearts", and o'er it flings
The wildering gloom of her immeasurable wings.

XXV

'There is a plain beneath the City's wall,   1630
　　Bounded by misty mountains, wide and vast,
Millions there lift at Freedom's thrilling call
　　Ten thousand standards wide, they load the blast
　　Which bears one sound of many voices past,
And startles on his throne their sceptered foe:
　　He sits amid his idle pomp aghast,
And that his power hath past away, doth know –
Why pause the victor swords to seal his overthrow?

XXVI

'The tyrant's guards resistance yet maintain:
　　Fearless, and fierce, and hard as beasts of blood;   1640
They stand a speck amid the peopled plain;
　　Carnage and ruin have been made their food
　　From infancy – ill has become their good,

And for its hateful sake their will has wove
    The chains which eat their hearts – the multitude
Surrounding them, with words of human love,
Seek from their own decay their stubborn minds to move.

XXVII

'Over the land is felt a sudden pause,
    As night and day those ruthless bands around
The watch of love is kept: – a trance which awes   1650
    The thoughts of men with hope – as when the sound
    Of whirlwind, whose fierce blasts the waves and
                    clouds confound,
Dies suddenly, the mariner in fear
    Feels silence sink upon his heart – thus bound,
The conquerors pause, and oh! may freemen ne'er
Clasp the relentless knees of Dread the murderer!

XXVIII

'If blood be shed, 'tis but a change and choice
    Of bonds, – from slavery to cowardice
A wretched fall! – Uplift thy charmed voice,
    Pour on those evil men the love that lies   1660
    Hovering within those spirit-soothing eyes –
Arise, my friend, farewell!' – As thus he spake,
    From the green earth lightly I did arise,
As one out of dim dreams that doth awake,
And looked upon the depth of that reposing lake.

from CANTO FIFTH

VI

Thus, while with rapid lips and earnest eyes
    We talked, a sound of sweeping conflict spread,
As from the earth did suddenly arise;
    From every tent roused by that clamour dread,
    Our bands outsprung and seized their arms – we sped
Towards the sound: our tribes were gathering far.   1770
    Those sanguine slaves amid ten thousand dead
Stabbed in their sleep, trampled in treacherous war,
The gentle hearts whose power their lives had sought to spare.

VII

Like rabid snakes, that sting some gentle child
    Who brings them food, when winter false and fair
Allures them forth with its cold smiles, so wild
    They rage among the camp; – they overbear
    The patriot host – confusion, then despair
Descends like night – when 'Laon!' one did cry:
    Like a bright ghost from Heaven, that shout did scare   1780
The slaves, and widening thro' the vaulted sky,
Seemed sent from Earth to Heaven in sign of victory.

VIII

In sudden panic those false murderers fled,
    Like insect tribes before the northern gale:
But swifter still, our hosts encompassed
    Their shattered ranks, and in a craggy vale,
    Where even their fierce despair might nought avail,
Hemmed them around! – and then revenge and fear
    Made the high virtue of the patriots fail:
One pointed on his foe the mortal spear –   1790
I rushed before its point, and cried, 'Forbear, forbear!'

IX

The spear transfixed my arm that was uplifted
    In swift expostulation, and the blood
Gushed round its point: I smiled, and – 'Oh! thou gifted
    With eloquence which shall not be withstood,
    Flow thus!' – I cried in joy, 'thou vital flood,
Until my heart be dry, ere thus the cause
    For which thou wert aught worthy be subdued –
Ah, ye are pale, – ye weep, – your passions pause, –
'Tis well! ye feel the truth of love's benignant laws.   1800

X

'Soldiers, our brethren and our friends are slain.
    Ye murdered them, I think, as they did sleep!
Alas, what have ye done? the slightest pain
    Which ye might suffer, there were eyes to weep;
    But ye have quenched them – there were smiles to steep

Your hearts in balm, but they are lost in woe;
 And those whom love did set his watch to keep
Around your tents truth's freedom to bestow,
Ye stabbed as they did sleep – but they forgive ye now.

XI

'O wherefore should ill ever flow from ill,   1810
 And pain still keener pain forever breed?
We all are brethren – even the slaves who kill
 For hire, are men; and to avenge misdeed
 On the misdoer, doth but Misery feed
With her own broken heart! O Earth, O Heaven!
 And thou, dread Nature, which to every deed
And all that lives, or is, to be hath given,
Even as to thee have these done ill, and are forgiven.

XII

'Join then your hands and hearts, and let the past
 Be as a grave which gives not up its dead   1820
To evil thoughts' – a film then overcast
 My sense with dimness, for the wound, which bled
 Freshly, swift shadows o'er mine eyes had shed.
When I awoke, I lay 'mid friends and foes,
 And earnest countenances on me shed
The light of questioning looks, whilst one did close
My wound with balmiest herbs, and soothed me to repose;

XIII

And one whose spear had pierced me, leaned beside
 With quivering lips and humid eyes; – and all
Seemed like some brothers on a journey wide 1830
 Gone forth, whom now strange meeting did befall
 In a strange land, round one whom they might call
Their friend, their chief, their father, for assay
 Of peril, which had saved them from the thrall
Of death, now suffering. Thus the vast array
Of those fraternal bands were reconciled that day.

XIV

Lifting the thunder of their acclamation,
   Towards the City then the multitude,
And I among them, went in joy – a nation
   Made free by love; – a mighty brotherhood   1840
   Linked by a jealous interchange of good;
A glorious pageant, more magnificent
   Than kingly slaves arrayed in gold and blood,
When they return from carnage, and are sent
In triumph bright beneath the populous battlement.

XV

Afar, the city walls were thronged on high,
   And myriads on each giddy turret clung,
And to each spire far lessening in the sky,
   Bright pennons on the idle winds were hung;
   As we approached a shout of joyance sprung   1850
At once from all the crowd, as if the vast
   And peopled Earth its boundless skies among
The sudden clamour of delight had cast,
When from before its face some general wreck had past.

XVI

Our armies thro' the City's hundred gates
   Were poured, like brooks which to the rocky lair
Of some deep lake, whose silence them awaits,
   Throng from the mountains when the storms are there:
   And as we passed thro' the calm sunny air
A thousand flower-inwoven crowns were shed,   1860
   The token flowers of truth and freedom fair,
And fairest hands bound them on many a head,
Those angels of love's heaven, that over all was spread.

XVII

I trod as one tranced in some rapturous vision:
   Those bloody bands so lately reconciled,
Were, ever as they went, by the contrition
   Of anger turned to love from ill beguiled,
   And every one on them more gently smiled,

Because they had done evil: – the sweet awe
 Of such mild looks made their own hearts grow mild, 1870
And did with soft attraction ever draw
Their spirits to the love of freedom's equal law.

XVIII

And they, and all, in one loud symphony
 My name with Liberty commingling, lifted,
'The friend and the preserver of the free!
 The parent of this joy! ' and fair eyes gifted
 With feelings, caught from one who had uplifted
The light of a great spirit, round me shone;
 And all the shapes of this grand scenery shifted
Like restless clouds before the steadfast sun, – 1880
Where was that Maid? I asked, but it was known of none.

XIX

Laone was the name her love had chosen,
 For she was nameless, and her birth none knew:
Where was Laone now? The words were frozen
 Within my lips with fear; but to subdue
 Such dreadful hope, to my great task was due,
And when at length one brought reply, that she
 Tomorrow would appear, I then withdrew
To judge what need for that great throng might be,
For now the stars came thick over the twilight sea. 1890

XX

Yet need was none for rest or food to care,
 Even tho' that multitude was passing great,
Since each one for the other did prepare
 All kindly succour. – Therefore to the gate
 Of the Imperial House, now desolate,
I past, and there was found aghast, alone,
 The fallen Tyrant! – silently he sate
Upon the footstool of his golden throne,
Which starred with sunny gems, in its own lustre shone.

XXI

Alone, but for one child, who led before him   1900
    A graceful dance: the only living thing
Of all the crowd, which thither to adore him
    Flocked yesterday, who solace sought to bring
    In his abandonment! – she knew the King
Had praised her dance of yore, and now she wove
    Its circles, aye weeping and murmuring
'Mid her sad task of unregarded love,
That to no smiles it might his speechless sadness move.

XXII

She fled to him, and wildly clasped his feet   1909
    When human steps were heard: – he moved nor spoke,
Nor changed his hue, nor raised his looks to meet
    The gaze of strangers – our loud entrance woke
    The echoes of the hall, which circling broke
The calm of its recesses, – like a tomb
    Its sculptured walls vacantly to the stroke
Of footfalls answered, and the twilight's gloom,
Lay like a charnel's mist within the radiant dome.

XXIII

The little child stood up when we came nigh;
    Her lips and cheeks seemed very pale and wan,
But on her forehead, and within her eye   1920
    Lay beauty, which makes hearts that feed thereon
    Sick with excess of sweetness; on the throne
She leaned; – the King with gathered brow, and lips
    Wreathed by long scorn, did inly sneer and frown
With hue like that when some great painter dips
His pencil in the gloom of earthquake and eclipse.

XXIV

She stood beside him like a rainbow braided
    Within some storm, when scarce its shadows vast
From the blue paths of the swift sun have faded;
    A sweet and solemn smile, like Cythna's, cast   1930
    One moment's light, which made my heart beat fast,

O'er that child's parted lips – a gleam of bliss,
 A shade of vanished days, – as the tears past
Which wrapt it, even as with a father's kiss
I pressed those softest eyes in trembling tenderness.

XXV

The sceptred wretch then from that solitude
 I drew, and, of his change compassionate,
With words of sadness soothed his rugged mood.
  But he, while pride and fear held deep debate,
  With sullen guile of ill-dissembled hate   1940
Glared on me as a toothless snake might glare:
  Pity, not scorn, I felt, tho' desolate
 The desolator now, and unaware
The curses which he mocked had caught him by the hair.

XXVI

I led him forth from that which now might seem
 A gorgeous grave; thro' portals sculptured deep
With imagery beautiful as dream
  We went, and left the shades which tend on sleep
  Over its unregarded gold to keep
Their silent watch. – The child trod faintingly,   1950
  And as she went, the tears which she did weep
 Glanced in the starlight; wildered seemed she,
And when I spake, for sobs she could not answer me.

XXVII

At last the tyrant cried, 'She hungers, slave,
 Stab her, or give her bread!' – It was a tone
Such as sick fancies in a new made grave
  Might hear. I trembled, for the truth was known,
  He with this child had thus been left alone,
And neither had gone forth for food, – but he
  In mingled pride and awe cowered near his throne, 1960
 And she a nursling of captivity
Knew nought beyond those walls, nor what such
            change might be.

XXVIII

And he was troubled at a charm withdrawn
    Thus suddenly; that scepters ruled no more –
That even from gold the dreadful strength was gone,
    Which once made all things subject to its power –
    Such wonder seized him, as if hour by hour
The past had come again; and the swift fall
    Of one so great and terrible of yore,
To desolateness, in the hearts of all   1970
Like wonder stirred, who saw such awful change befall.

XXIX

A mighty crowd, such as the wide land pours
    Once in a thousand years, now gathered round
The fallen tyrant; – like the rush of showers
    Of hail in spring, pattering along the ground,
    Their many footsteps fell, else came no sound
From the wide multitude: that lonely man
    Then knew the burthen of his change, and found,
Concealing in the dust his visage wan,
Refuge from the keen looks which thro' his bosom ran.   1980

XXX

And he was faint withal: I sate beside him
    Upon the earth, and took that child so fair
From his weak arms, that ill might none betide him
    Or her; – when food was brought to them, her share
    To his averted lips the child did bear,
But when she saw he had enough, she ate
    And wept the while; – the lonely man's despair
Hunger then overcame, and of his state
Forgetful, on the dust as in a trance he sate.

XXXI

Slowly the silence of the multitudes   1990
    Past, as when far is heard in some lone dell
The gathering of a wind among the woods –
    And he is fallen! they cry, he who did dwell
    Like famine or the plague, or aught more fell

Among our homes, is fallen! the murderer
   Who slaked his thirsting soul as from a well
Of blood and tears with ruin! he is here!
Sunk in a gulf of scorn from which none may him rear!

XXXII

Then was heard – He who judged let him be brought
   To judgement! blood for blood cries from the soil   2000
On which his crimes have deep pollution wrought!
   Shall Othman only unavenged despoil?
   Shall they who by the stress of grinding toil
Wrest from the unwilling earth his luxuries,
   Perish for crime, while his foul blood may boil,
Or creep within his veins at will? – Arise!
And to high justice make her chosen sacrifice.

XXXIII

'What do ye seek? what fear ye?' then I cried,
   Suddenly starting forth, 'that ye should shed
The blood of Othman – if your hearts are tried   2010
   In the true love of freedom, cease to dread
   This one poor lonely man – beneath Heaven spread
In purest light above us all, thro' earth
   Maternal earth, who doth her sweet smiles shed
For all, let him go free; until the worth
Of human nature win from these a second birth.

XXXIV

'What call ye *justice*? is there one who ne'er
   In secret thought has wished another's ill? –
Are ye all pure? let those stand forth who hear,
   And tremble not. Shall they insult and kill,   2020
   If such they be? their mild eyes can they fill
With the false anger of the hypocrite?
   Alas, such were not pure – the chastened will
Of virtue sees that justice is the light
Of love, and not revenge, and terror and despite.'

XXXV

The murmur of the people slowly dying,
    Paused as I spake, then those who near me were,
Cast gentle looks where the lone man was lying
    Shrouding his head, which now that infant fair
    Clasped on her lap in silence; – thro' the air   2030
Sobs were then heard, and many kissed my feet
    In pity's madness, and to the despair
Of him whom late they cursed, a solace sweet
His very victims brought – soft looks and speeches meet.

XXXVI

Then to a home for his repose assigned,
    Accompanied by the still throng he went
In silence, where to soothe his rankling mind,
    Some likeness of his ancient state was lent;
    And if his heart could have been innocent
As those who pardoned him, he might have ended   2040
    His days in peace; but his straight lips were bent,
Men said, into a smile which guile portended,
A sight with which that child like hope with fear was blended.

from CANTO SIXTH

II

And till we came even to the City's wall
    And the great gate, then, none knew whence or why,
Disquiet on the multitudes did fall:
    And first, one pale and breathless past us by,
    And stared and spoke not; – then with piercing cry
A troop of wild-eyed women, by the shrieks
    Of their own terror driven, – tumultuously   2350
Hither and thither hurrying with pale cheeks,
Each one from fear unknown a sudden refuge seeks –

III

Then, rallying cries of treason and of danger
     Resounded: and – 'They come! to arms! to arms!
The Tyrant is amongst us, and the stranger
     Comes to enslave us in his name! to arms!'
     In vain: for Panic, the pale fiend who charms
Strength to forswear her right, those millions swept
     Like waves before the tempest – these alarms
Came to me, as to know their cause I leapt   2360
On the gate's turret, and in rage and grief and scorn I wept!

IV

For to the North I saw the town on fire,
     And its red light made morning pallid now,
Which burst over wide Asia; – louder, higher,
     The yells of victory and the screams of woe
     I heard approach, and saw the throng below
Stream through the gates like foam-wrought waterfalls
     Fed from a thousand storms – the fearful glow
Of bombs flares overhead – at intervals
The red artillery's bolt mangling among them falls.   2370

V

And now the horsemen come – and all was done
     Swifter than I have spoken – I beheld
Their red swords flash in the unrisen sun.
     I rushed among the rout, to have repelled
     That miserable flight – one moment quelled
By voice and looks and eloquent despair,
     As if reproach from their own hearts withheld
Their steps, they stood; but soon came pouring there
New multitudes, and did those rallied bands o'erbear.

VI

I strove, as drifted on some cataract   2380
     By irresistible streams, some wretch might strive
Who hears its fatal roar: – the files compact
     Whelmed me, and from the gate availed to drive
     With quickening impulse, as each bolt did rive

Their ranks with bloodier chasm: – into the plain
    Disgorged at length the dead and the alive
In one dread mass, were parted, and the stain
Of blood from mortal steel fell o'er the fields like rain.

VII

For now the despot's bloodhounds with their prey,
    Unarmed and unaware, were gorging deep   2390
Their gluttony of death; the loose array
    Of horsemen o'er the wide fields murdering sweep,
    And with loud laughter for their tyrant reap
A harvest sown with other hopes; the while,
    Far overhead, ships from Propontis[61] keep
A killing rain of fire: – when the waves smile
As sudden earthquakes light many a volcano isle.

VIII

Thus sudden, unexpected feast was spread
    For the carrion fowls of Heaven. – I saw the sight –
I moved – I lived – as o'er the heaps of dead,   2400
    Whose stony eyes glared in the morning light
    I trod; – to me there came no thought of flight,
But with loud cries of scorn which whoso heard
    That dreaded death, felt in his veins the might
Of virtuous shame return, the crowd I stirred,
And desperation's hope in many hearts recurred.

IX

A band of brothers gathering round me, made,
    Although unarmed, a steadfast front, and still
Retreating, with stern looks beneath the shade
    Of gathered eyebrows, did the victors fill   2410
    With doubt even in success; deliberate will
Inspired our growing troop; not overthrown
    It gained the shelter of a grassy hill,
And ever still our comrades were hewn down,
And their defenceless limbs beneath our footsteps strown.

X

Immovably we stood – in joy I found,
  Beside me then, firm as a giant pine
Among the mountain vapours driven around,
  The old man whom I loved – his eyes divine
  With a mild look of courage answered mine,   2420
And my young friend was near, and ardently
  His hand grasped mine a moment – now the line
Of war extended, to our rallying cry,
As myriads flocked in love and brotherhood to die.

XI

For ever while the sun was climbing Heaven
  The horseman hewed our unarmed myriads down
Safely, tho' when by thirst of carnage driven
  Too near, those slaves were swiftly overthrown
  By hundreds leaping on them: – flesh and bone
Soon made our ghastly ramparts; then the shaft   2430
  Of the artillery from the sea was thrown
More fast and fiery, and the conquerors laugh'd
In pride to hear the wind our screams of torment waft.

XII

For on one side alone the hill gave shelter,
  So vast that phalanx of unconquered men,
And there the living in the blood did welter
  Of the dead and dying, which, in that green glen,
  Like stifled torrents, made a plashy fen
Under the feet – thus was the butchery waged   2449
  While the sun clomb Heaven's eastern steep – but when
It 'gan to sink – a fiercer combat raged,
For in more doubtful strife the armies were engaged.

XIII

Within a cave upon the hill were found
  A bundle of rude pikes, the instrument
Of those who war but on their native ground
  For natural rights: a shout of joyance sent
  Even from our hearts the wide air pierced and rent,

As those few arms the bravest and the best
   Seized, and each sixth, thus armed, did now present
A line which covered and sustained the rest,   2450
A confident phalanx, which the foes on every side invest.

XIV

That onset turned the foes to flight almost,
   But soon they saw their present strength, and knew
That coming night would to our resolute host
   Bring victory; so dismounting close they drew
   Their glittering files, and then the combat grew
Unequal but most horrible; – and ever
   Our myriads, whom the swift bolt overthrew,
Or the red sword, failed like a mountain river
Which rushes forth in foam to sink in sands for ever.   2460

XV

Sorrow and shame, to see with their own kind
   Our human brethren mix, like beasts of blood
To mutual ruin armed by one behind
   Who sits and scoffs! – That friend so mild and good,
   Who like its shadow near my youth had stood,
Was stabbed! – my old preserver's hoary hair
   With the flesh clinging to its roots, was strewed
Under my feet! – I lost all sense or care,
And like the rest I grew desperate and unaware.

XVI

The battle became ghastlier – in the midst   2470
   I paused, and saw, how ugly and how fell,
O Hate! thou art, even when thy life thou shed'st
   For love. The ground in many a little dell
   Was broken, up and down whose steeps befell
Alternate victory and defeat, and there
   The combatants with rage most horrible
Strove, and their eyes started with cracking stare,
And impotent their tongues they lolled into the air,

XVII

Flaccid and foamy, like a mad dog's hanging;
    Want, and moon-madness, and the pest's swift bane   2480
When its shafts smite – while yet its bow is twanging –
    Have each their mark and sign – some ghastly stain;
    And this was thine, O War! of hate and pain,
Thou loathed slave. I saw all shapes of death,
    And ministered to many o'er the plain,
While carnage in the sunbeam's warmth did seethe,
Till twilight o'er the east wove her serenest wreath.

XVIII

The few who yet survived, resolute and firm
    Around me fought. At the decline of day
Winding above the mountain's snowy term   2490
    New banners shone: they quivered in the ray
    Of the sun's unseen orb – ere night the array
Of fresh troops hemmed us in – of those brave bands
    I soon survived alone – and now I lay
Vanquished and faint, the grasp of bloody hands
I felt, and saw on high the glare of falling brands:

XIX

When on my foes a sudden terror came,
    And they fled, scattering – lo! with reinless speed
A black Tartarian horse of giant frame
    Comes trampling over the dead, the living bleed   2500
    Beneath the hoofs of that tremendous steed,
On which, like to an Angel, robed in white,
    Sate one waving a sword; the hosts recede
And fly, as thro' their ranks with awful might,
Sweeps in the shadow of eve that Phantom swift and bright;

XX

And its path made a solitude. – I rose
    And marked its coming; it relaxed its course
As it approached me, and the wind that flows
    Thro' night, bore accents to mine ear whose force
    Might create smiles in death. – The Tartar horse   2510

Paused, and I saw the shape its might which swayed,
    And heard her musical pants, like the sweet source
Of waters in the desert, as she said,
'Mount with me, Laon, now' – I rapidly obeyed.

XXI

Then: 'Away! away!' she cried, and stretched her sword
    As 'twere a scourge over the courser's head,
And lightly shook the reins: – We spake no word
    But like the vapour of the tempest fled
    Over the plain; her dark hair was dispread
Like the pine's locks upon the lingering blast;   2520
    Over mine eyes its shadowy strings it spread
Fitfully, and the hills and streams fled fast,
As o'er their glimmering forms the steed's broad shadow past.

XXII

And his hoofs ground the rocks to fire and dust,
    His strong sides made the torrents rise in spray,
And turbulence as of a whirlwind's gust
    Surrounded us; – and still away! away!
    Thro' the desert night we sped, while she alway
Gazed on a mountain which we neared, whose crest,
    Crowned with a marble ruin, in the ray   2530
Of the obscure stars gleamed; – its rugged breast
The steed strained up, and then his impulse did arrest.

XXIII

A rocky hill which overhung the Ocean: –
    From that lone ruin, when the steed that panted
Paused, might be heard the murmur of the motion
    Of waters, as in spots forever haunted
    By the choicest winds of Heaven, which are enchanted
To music by the wand of Solitude,
    That wizard wild, and the far tents, implanted
Upon the plain, be seen by those who stood   2540
Thence marking the dark shore of Ocean's curved flood.

XXIV

One moment these were heard and seen – another
. Past; and the two who stood beneath that night,
Each only heard, or saw, or felt the other;
  As from the lofty steed she did alight,
  Cythna (for, from the eyes whose deepest light
Of love and sadness made my lips feel pale
  With influence strange of mournfullest delight,
My own sweet sister looked), with joy did quail,
And felt her strength in tears of human weakness fail.   2550

XXV

And, for a space in my embrace she rested,
  Her head on my unquiet heart reposing,
While my faint arms her languid frame invested:
  At length she looked on me, and half unclosing
  Her tremulous lips, said: 'Friend, thy bands were losing
The battle, as I stood before the King
  In bonds. – I burst them then, and swiftly choosing
The time, did seize a Tartar's sword, and spring
Upon his horse, and swift as on the whirlwind's wing,

XXVI

'Have thou and I been borne beyond pursuer,   2560
  And we are here.' – Then turning to the steed,
She pressed the white moon on his front with pure
  And rose-like lips, and many a fragrant weed
  From the green ruin plucked, that he might feed; –
But I to a stone seat that Maiden led,
  And kissing her fair eyes, said, 'Thou hast need
Of rest,' and I heaped up the courser's bed
In a green mossy nook, with mountain flowers dispread.

XXVII

Within that ruin, where a shattered portal
  Looks to the eastern stars, abandoned now   2570
By man, to be the home of things immortal,
  Memories, like awful ghosts which come and go,
  And must inherit all he builds below,

When he is gone, a hall stood; o'er whose roof
   Fair clinging weeds with ivy pale did grow,
Clasping its grey rents with a verdurous woof,
A hanging dome of leaves, a canopy moon-proof.

XXIII

The autumnal winds, as if spellbound, had made
   A natural couch of leaves in that recess,
Which seasons none disturbed, but in the shade   2580
   Of flowering parasites, did spring love to dress
   With their sweet blooms the wintry loneliness
Of those dead leaves, shedding their stars, whene'er
   The wandering wind her nurslings might caress;
Whose intertwining fingers ever there,
Made music wild and soft that filled the listening air.

XXIX

We know not where we go, or what sweet dream
   May pilot us thro' caverns strange and fair
Of far and pathless passion, while the stream
   Of life, our bark doth on its whirlpools bear,   2590
   Spreading swift wings as sails to the dim air;
Nor should we seek to know, so the devotion
   Of love and gentle thoughts be heard still there
Louder and louder from the utmost Ocean
Of universal life, attuning its commotion.

XXX

To the pure all things are pure! Oblivion wrapt
   Our spirits, and the fearful overthrow
Of public hope was from our being snapt,
   Tho' linked years had bound it there; for now
   A power, a thirst, a knowledge, which below   2600
All thoughts, like light beyond the atmosphere,
   Clothing its clouds with grace, doth ever flow,
Came on us, as we sate in silence there,
Beneath the golden stars of the clear azure air.

XXXI

In silence which doth follow talk that causes
   The baffled heart to speak with sighs and tears,
When wildering passion swalloweth up the pauses
   Of inexpressive speech: – the youthful years
   Which we together past, their hopes and fears,
The common blood which ran within our frames,   2610
   That likeness of the features which endears
The thoughts expressed by them, our very names,
And all the winged hours which speechless memory claims,

XXXII

Had found a voice, – and ere that voice did pass,
   The night grew damp and dim, and thro' a rent
Of the ruin where we sate, from the morass,
   A wandering Meteor, by some wild wind sent,
   Hung high in the green dome, to which it lent
A faint and pallid lustre; while the song
   Of blasts, in which its blue hair quivering bent,   2620
Strewed strangest sounds the moving leaves among;
A wondrous light, the sound as of a spirit's tongue.

XXXIII

The Meteor showed the leaves on which we sate,
   And Cythna's glowing arms, and the thick ties
Of her soft hair which bent with gathered weight
   My neck near hers, her dark and deepening eyes,
   Which, as twin phantoms of one star that lies
O'er a dim well, move, though the star reposes,
   Swam in our mute and liquid ecstacies,
Her marble brow, and eager lips, like roses,   2630
With their own fragrance pale, which spring but half uncloses.

XXXIV

The Meteor to its far morass returned:
   The beating of our veins one interval
Made still; and then I felt the blood that burned
   Within her frame, mingle with mine, and fall
   Around my heart like fire; and over all

A mist was spread, the sickness of a deep
    And speechless swoon of joy, as might befall
Two disunited spirits when they leap
In union from this earth's obscure and fading sleep.   2640

XXXV

Was it one moment that confounded thus
    All thought, all sense, all feeling, into one
Unutterable power, which shielded us
    Even from our own cold looks, when we had gone
    Into a wide and wild oblivion
Of tumult and of tenderness? or now
    Had ages, such as make the moon and sun,
The seasons and mankind their changes know,
Left fear and time unfelt by us alone below?

XXXVI

I know not. What are kisses whose fire clasps   2650
    The failing heart in languishment, or limb
Twined within limb? or the quick dying gasps
    Of the life meeting, when the faint eyes swim
    Thro' tears of a wide mist, boundless and dim,
In one caress? What is the strong control
    Which leads the heart that dizzy steep to climb,
Where far over the world those vapours roll,
Which blend two restless frames in one reposing soul?

XXXVII

It is the shadow which doth float unseen,
    But not unfelt, o'er blind mortality,   2660
Whose divine darkness fled not from that green
    And lone recess, where lapt in peace did lie
    Our linked frames, till, from the changing sky,
That night and still another day had fled;
    And then I saw and felt. The moon was high,
And clouds, as of a coming storm, were spread
Under its orb, – loud winds were gathering overhead.

XXXVIII

Cythna's sweet lips seemed lurid in the moon,
  Her fairest limbs with the night wind were chill,
And her dark tresses were all loosely strewn   2670
    O'er her pale bosom: – all within was still,
    And the sweet peace of joy did almost fill
The depth of her unfathomable look; –
    And we sate calmly, though that rocky hill,
The waves contending in its caverns strook,
For they foreknew the storm, and the grey ruin shook.

XXXIX

There we unheeding sate, in the communion
  Of interchanged vows, which, with a rite
Of faith most sweet and sacred, stamped our union. –
    Few were the living hearts which could unite   2680
    Like ours, or celebrate a bridal night
With such close sympathies, for to each other
    Had high and solemn hopes, the gentle might
Of earliest love, and all the thoughts which smother
Cold Evil's power, now linked a sister and a brother.

XL

And such is Nature's modesty, that those
  Who grow together cannot choose but love,
If faith or custom do not interpose,
    Or common slavery mar what else might move
    All gentlest thoughts; as in the sacred grove   2690
Which shades the springs of Ethiopian Nile,
    That living tree, which, if the arrowy dove
Strike with her shadow, shrinks in fear awhile.
But its own kindred leaves clasps while the sunbeams smile;

XLI

And clings to them, when darkness may dissever
  The close caresses of all duller plants
Which bloom on the wide earth – thus we for ever
    Were linked, for love had nurst us in the haunts
    Where knowledge, from its secret source enchants

Young hearts with the fresh music of its springing,   2700
　　Ere yet its gathered flood feeds human wants,
As the great Nile feeds Egypt, ever flinging
Light on the woven boughs which o'er its waves are swinging.

from CANTO EIGHTH

III

'We past the islets, borne by wind and stream,
　　And as we sailed, the Mariners came near
And thronged around to listen; – in the gleam
　　Of the pale moon I stood, as one whom fear   3220
　　May not attaint, and my calm voice did rear:
"Ye all are human – yon broad moon gives light
　　To millions who the selfsame likeness wear,
Even while I speak – beneath this very night,
Their thoughts flow on like ours, in sadness or delight.

IV

' "What dream ye? Your own hands have built a home,
　　Even for yourselves on a beloved shore:
For some, fond eyes are pining till they come,
　　How they will greet him when his toils are o'er,
　　And laughing babes rush from the well-known door!   3230
Is this your care? ye toil for your own good –
　　Ye feel and think – has some immortal power
Such purposes? or in a human mood,
Dream ye that God thus builds for man in solitude?

V

' "What then is God? ye mock yourselves and give
　　A human heart to what ye cannot know:
As if the cause of life could think and live!
　　'Twere as if man's own works should feel, and show
　　The hopes, and fears, and thoughts from which they flow.
And he be like to them. Lo! Plague is free   3240
　　To waste, Blight, Poison, Earthquake, Hail, and Snow,
Disease, and Want, and worse Necessity
Of hate and ill, and Pride, and Fear, and Tyranny.

VI

' "What then is God? Some moon-struck sophist stood
    Watching the shade from his own soul upthrown
Fill Heaven and darken Earth, and in such mood
    The Form he saw and worshipped was his own,
    His likeness in the world's vast mirror shown;
And 'twere an innocent dream, but that a faith
    Nursed by fear's dew of poison, grows thereon,   3250
And that men say, God has appointed Death
On all who scorn his will to wreak immortal wrath.

VII

' "Men say they have seen God, and heard from God,
    Or known from others who have known such things,
And that his will is all our law, a rod
    To scourge us into slaves – that Priests and Kings,
    Custom, domestic sway, aye, all that brings
Man's free-born soul beneath the oppressor's heel,
    Are his strong ministers, and that the stings
Of death will make the wise his vengeance feel,   3260
Tho' truth and virtue arm their hearts with tenfold steel.

VIII

' "And it is said, that God will punish wrong;
    Yes, add despair to crime, and pain to pain!
And his red hell's undying snakes among
    Will bind the wretch on whom he fixed a stain,
    Which, like a plague, a burthen, and a bane,
Clung to him while he lived; – for, love and hate,
    Virtue and vice, they say, are difference vain –
The will of strength is right – this human state
Tyrants, that they may rule, with lies thus desolate.   3270

IX

' "Alas, what strength? opinion is more frail
    Than yon dim cloud now fading on the moon
Even while we gaze, tho' it awhile avail
    To hide the orb of truth – and every throne
    Of Earth or Heaven, tho' shadow, rests thereon,

One shape of many names: – for this ye plough
  The barren waves of ocean, hence each one
Is slave or tyrant, all betray and bow,
Command, or kill, or fear, or wreak, or suffer woe.

X

' "Its names are each a sign which maketh holy   3280
  All power – aye, the ghost, the dream, the shade
Of power, – lust, falsehood, hate, and pride, and folly;
  The pattern whence all fraud and wrong is made,
  A law to which mankind has been betrayed;
And human love is as the name well known
  Of a dear mother, whom the murderer laid
In bloody grave, and, into darkness thrown,
Gathered her wildered babes around him as his own.

XI

' "O Love! who to the hearts of wandering men
  Art as the calm to Ocean's weary waves!   3290
Justice, or truth, or joy! those only can
  From slavery and religion's labyrinth caves
  Guide us, as one clear star the seaman saves.
To give to all an equal share of good,
  To track the steps of freedom tho' thro' graves
She pass, to suffer all in patient mood,
To weep for crime tho' stained with thy friend's dearest blood.

XII

' "To feel the peace of self-contentment's lot,
  To own all sympathies, and outrage none,
And in the inmost bowers of sense and thought,   3300
  Until life's sunny day is quite gone down,
  To sit and smile with Joy, or, not alone,
To kiss salt tears from the worn cheek of Woe;
  To live, as if to love and live were one, –
This is not faith or law, nor those who bow
To thrones on Heaven or Earth, such destiny may know.

XIII

' "But children near their parents tremble now,
 Because they must obey – one rules another,
For it is said God rules both high and low,
 And man is made the captive of his brother;   3310
 And Hate is throned on high with Fear his mother,
Above the Highest – and those fountain-cells,
 Whence love yet flowed when faith had choked all other,
Are darkened – Woman, as the bond-slave, dwells
Of man a slave; and life is poisoned in its wells.

XIV

' "Man seeks for gold in mines, that he may weave
 A lasting chain for his own slavery; –
In fear and restless care that he may live
 He toils for others, who must ever be
 The joyless thralls of like captivity;   3320
He murders, for his chiefs delight in ruin;
 He builds the altar, that its idol's fee
May be his very blood; he is pursuing
O, blind and willing wretch! his own obscure undoing.

XV

' "Woman! – she is his slave, she has become
 A thing I weep to speak – the child of scorn,
The outcast of a desolated home,
 Falsehood, and fear, and toil, like waves have worn
 Channels upon her cheek, which smiles adorn,
As calm decks the false Ocean: – well ye know   3330
 What Woman is, for none of Woman born
Can choose but drain the bitter dregs of woe
Which ever from the oppressed to the oppressors flow.

XVI

' "This need not be; ye might arise, and will
 That gold should lose its power, and thrones their glory;
That love, which none may bind, be free to fill
 The world, like light; and evil faith, grown hoary
 With crime, be quenched and die. – Yon promontory

Even now eclipses the descending moon! –
   Dungeons and palaces are transitory –   3340
High temples fade like vapour – Man alone
Remains, whose will has power when all beside is gone.

XVII

' "Let all be free and equal! – from your hearts
   I feel an echo; thro' my inmost frame
Like sweetest sound, seeking its mate, it darts –
   Whence come ye, friends? alas, I cannot name
   All that I read of sorrow, toil, and shame
On your worn faces; as in legends old
   Which make immortal the disastrous fame
Of conquerors and impostors false and bold,   3350
The discord of your hearts, I in your looks behold.

XVIII

' "Whence come ye, friends? from pouring human blood
   Forth on the earth? or bring ye steel and gold,
That Kings may dupe and slay the multitude?
   Or from the famished poor, pale, weak, and cold,
   Bear ye the earnings of their toil? unfold!
Speak! are your hands in slaughter's sanguine hue
   Stained freshly? have your hearts in guile grown old?
Know yourselves thus! ye shall be pure as dew,
And I will be a friend and sister unto you.   3360

XIX

' "Disguise it not – we have one human heart –
   All mortal thoughts confess a common home:
Blush not for what may to thyself impart
   Stains of inevitable crime: the doom
   Is this, which has, or may, or must become
Thine, and all humankind's. Ye are the spoil
   Which Time thus marks for the devouring tomb,
Thou and thy thoughts and they, and all the toil
Wherewith ye twine the rings of life's perpetual coil.

XX

‘ "Disguise it not – ye blush for what ye hate,   3370
    And Enmity is sister unto Shame;
Look on your mind – it is the book of fate –
    Ah! it is dark with many a blazoned name
    Of misery – all are mirrors of the same;
But the dark fiend who with his iron pen,
    Dipped in scorn's fiery poison, makes his fame
Enduring there, would o'er the heads of men
Pass harmless, if they scorned to make their hearts his den.

XXI

‘ "Yes, it is Hate – that shapeless friendly thing
    Of many names, all evil, some divine,   3380
Whom self-contempt arms with a mortal sting;
    Which, when the heart its snaky folds entwine,
    Is wasted quite, and when it doth repine
To gorge such bitter prey, on all beside
    It turns with ninefold rage, as with its twine
When Amphisbaena[62] some fair bird has tied,
Soon o'er the putrid mass he threats on every side.

XXII

‘ "Reproach not thine own soul, but know thyself,
    Nor hate another's crime, nor loathe thine own.
It is the dark idolatry of self,   3390
    Which, when our thoughts and actions once are gone,
    Demands that man should weep, and bleed, and groan;
O vacant expiation! be at rest. –
    The past is Death's, the future is thine own;
And love and joy can make the foulest breast
A paradise of flowers, where peace might build her nest.

XXIII

‘ "Speak thou! whence come ye?" – A Youth made reply,
    " Wearily, wearily o'er the boundless deep
We sail; – thou readest well the misery
    Told in these faded eyes, but much doth sleep   3400
    Within, which there the poor heart loves to keep,

Or dare not write on the dishonoured brow;
　　Even from our childhood have we learned to steep
The bread of slavery in the tears of woe,
And never dreamed of hope or refuge until now.

XXIV

' "Yes – I must speak – my secret should have perished
　　Even with the heart it wasted, as a brand
Fades in the dying flame whose life it cherished,
　　But that no human bosom can withstand
　　Thee, wondrous Lady, and the mild command   3410
Of thy keen eyes: – yes, we are wretched slaves,
　　Who from their wonted loves and native land
Are reft, and bear o'er the dividing waves
The unregarded prey of calm and happy graves.

XXV

' "We drag afar from pastoral vales the fairest
　　Among the daughters of those mountains lone,
We drag them there, where all things best and rarest
　　Are stained and trampled: – years have come and gone
　　Since, like the ship which bears me, I have known
No thought; – but now the eyes of one dear Maid   3420
　　On mine with light of mutual love have shone –
She is my life, – I am but as the shade
Of her, – a smoke sent up from ashes, soon to fade.

XXVI

' "For she must perish in the tyrant's hall –
　　Alas, alas!" – He ceased, and by the sail
　　Sate cowering – but his sobs were heard by all,
And still before the ocean and the gale
　　The ship fled fast 'till the stars 'gan to fail,
And round me gathered with mute countenance,
　　The Seamen gazed, the Pilot, worn and pale   3430
　　With toil, the Captain with grey locks, whose glance
Met mine in restless awe– they stood as in a trance.

XXVII

' "Recede not! pause not now! thou art grown old,
    But Hope will make thee young, for Hope and Youth
Are children of one mother, even Love – behold!
    The eternal stars gaze on us! – is the truth
    Within your soul? care for your own, or ruth
For other's sufferings? do ye thirst to bear
    A heart which not the serpent custom's tooth
May violate? – be free! and even here,   3440
Swear to be firm till death!" they cried, "We swear! we swear!"

XXVIII

'The very darkness shook, as with a blast
    Of subterranean thunder, at the cry;
The hollow shore its thousand echoes cast
    Into the night, as if the sea, and sky,
    And earth rejoiced with new-born liberty.
For in that name they swore! Bolts were undrawn,
    And on the deck, with unaccustomed eye,
The captives gazing stood, and every one   3449
Shrank as the inconstant torch upon her countenance shone.

XXIX

'They were earth's purest children, young and fair,
    With eyes the shrines of unawakened thought,
And brows as bright as spring or morning, ere
    Dark time had there its evil legend wrought
    In characters of cloud which wither not. –
The change was like a dream to them; but soon
    They knew the glory of their altered lot,
In the bright wisdom of youth's breathless noon,
Sweet talk, and smiles, and sighs, all bosoms did attune.

XXX

'But one was mute, her cheeks and lips most fair,   3460
    Changing their hue like lilies newly blown,
Beneath a bright acacia's shadowy hair,
    Waved by the wind amid the sunny noon,
    Showed that her soul was quivering; and full soon

That Youth arose, and breathlessly did look
    On her and me, as for some speechless boon:
I smiled, and both their hands in mine I took,
And felt a soft delight from what their spirits shook.

from CANTO NINTH

I

'That night we anchored in a woody bay,
    And sleep no more around us dared to hover   3470
Than, when all doubt and fear has passed away,
    It shades the couch of some unresting lover,
    Whose heart is now at rest: thus night passed over
In mutual joy: – around, a forest grew
    Of poplars and dark oaks, whose shade did cover
The waning stars prankt in the waters blue,
And trembled in the wind which from the morning flew.

II

'The joyous mariners, and each free maiden,
    Now brought from the deep forest many a bough,
With woodland spoil most innocently laden;   3480
    Soon wreaths of budding foliage seemed to flow
    Over the mast and sails, the stern and prow
Were canopied with blooming boughs, – the while
    On the slant sun's path o'er the waves we go
Rejoicing, like the dwellers of an isle
Doomed to pursue those waves that cannot cease to smile.

III

'The many ships spotting the dark blue deep
    With snowy sails, fled fast as ours came nigh,
In fear and wonder; and on every steep
    Thousands did gaze, they heard the startling cry,   3490
    Like earth's own voice lifted unconquerably
To all her children, the unbounded mirth,
    The glorious joy of thy name – Liberty!
They heard! – As o'er the mountains of the earth
From peak to peak leap on the beams of morning's birth:

IV

'So from that cry over the boundless hills,
    Sudden was caught one universal sound,
Like a volcano's voice, whose thunder fills
    Remotest skies, – such glorious madness found
    A path thro' human hearts with stream which drowned
Its struggling fears and cares, dark custom's brood,   3501
    They knew not whence it came, but felt around
A wide contagion poured – they called aloud
On Liberty – that name lived on the sunny flood.

V

'We reached the port – alas! from many spirits
    The wisdom which had waked that cry, was fled,
Like the brief glory which dark Heaven inherits
    From the false dawn, which fades ere it is spread,
    Upon the night's devouring darkness shed:
Yet soon bright day will burst – even like a chasm
    Of fire, to burn the shrouds outworn and dead,   3510
    Which wrap the world; a wide enthusiasm,
To cleanse the fevered world as with an earthquake's spasm!

VI

'I walked thro' the great City then, but free
    From shame or fear; those toil-worn Mariners
And happy Maidens did encompass me;
    And like a subterranean wind that stirs
    Some forest among caves, the hopes and fears
From every human soul, a murmur strange
    Made as I passed; and many wept, with tears
Of joy and awe, and winged thoughts did range,   3520
And half-extinguished words, which prophesied of change.

VII

'For with strong speech I tore the veil that hid
    Nature, and Truth, and Liberty, and Love, –
As one who from some mountain's pyramid,
    Points to the unrisen sun! – the shades approve
    His truth, and flee from every stream and grove.

Thus, gentle thoughts did many a bosom fill, –
    Wisdom, the mail of tried affections wove
For many a heart, and tameless scorn of ill,   3530
Thrice steeped in molten steel the unconquerable will.

VIII

'Some said I was a maniac wild and lost;
    Some, that I scarce had risen from the grave
The Prophet's virgin bride, a heavenly ghost; –
    Some said, I was a fiend from my weird cave,
    Who had stolen human shape, and o'er the wave,
The forest and the mountain came; – some said
    I was the child of God, sent down to save
Women from bonds and death, and on my head
The burden of their sins would frightfully be laid.   3540

IX

'But soon my human words found sympathy
    In human hearts: the purest and the best,
As friend with friend, made common cause with me,
    And they were few, but resolute; – the rest,
    Ere yet success the enterprise had blest,
Leagued with me in their hearts; – their meals, their slumber,
    Their hourly occupations were possest
By hopes which I had arm'd to overnumber
Those hosts of meaner cares, which life's strong
                                        wings encumber.

X

'But chiefly women, whom my voice did waken   3550
    From their cold, careless, willing slavery,
Sought me: one truth their dreary prison has shaken, –
    They looked around, and lo! they became free!
    Their many tyrants, sitting desolately
In slave-deserted halls, could none restrain;
    For wrath's red fire had withered in the eye,
Whose lightning once was death, – nor fear, nor gain
Could tempt one captive now to lock another's chain.

XI

'Those who were sent to bind me, wept, and felt
   Their minds outsoar the bonds which clasped them round,
Even as a waxen shape may waste and melt   3561
   In the white furnace; and a visioned swound,
   A pause of hope and awe the City bound,
Which, like the silence of a tempest's birth,
   When in its awful shadow it has wound
The sun, the wind, the ocean, and the earth,
Hung terrible, ere yet the lightnings have leaped forth.

XII

'Like clouds inwoven in the silent sky,
   By winds from distant regions meeting there,
In the high name of truth and liberty,   3570
   Around the City millions gathered were,
   By hopes which sprang from many a hidden lair;
Words, which the lore of truth in hues of grace
   Arrayed, thine own wild songs which in the air
Like homeless odours floated, and the name
Of thee, and many a tongue which thou hadst dipped in flame.

XIII

'The Tyrant knew his power was gone, but Fear,
   The nurse of Vengeance, bade him wait the event –
That perfidy and custom, gold and prayer,
   And whatsoe'er, when force is impotent,   3580
   To fraud the sceptre of the world has lent,
Might, as he judged, confirm his failing sway.
   Therefore, throughout the streets, the Priests he sent
To curse the rebels. To their God did they
For Earthquake, Plague, and Want, kneel in the public way.

XIV

'And grave and hoary men were bribed to tell
   From seats where law is made the slave of wrong,
How glorious Athens in her splendour fell,
   Because her sons were free, – and that among
   Mankind, the many to the few belong,   3590

By God, and Nature, and Necessity.
    They said, that age was truth, and that the young
Marred with wild hopes the peace of slavery,
With which old times and men had quelled the vain and free.

XV

'And with the falsehood of their poisonous lips
    They breathed on the enduring memory
Of sages and of bards a brief eclipse;
    There was one teacher, and must ever be,
    They said, even God, whom the necessity
Of rule and wrong had armed against Mankind,
His slave and his avenger there to be;   3600
    That we were weak and sinful, frail and blind,
And that the will of one was peace, and we
Should seek for nought on earth but toil and misery.

XVI

' "For thus we might avoid the hell hereafter."
    So spake the hypocrites, who cursed and lied;
Alas, their sway was past, and tears and laughter
    Clung to their hoary hair, withering the pride
    Which in their hollow hearts dared still abide;
And yet obscener slaves with smoother brow,
    And sneers on their strait lips, thin, blue and wide,   3610
    Said, that the rule of men was over now,
And hence, the subject world to woman's will must bow.

XVII

'And gold was scattered thro' the streets, and wine
    Flowed at a hundred feasts within the wall.
In vain! the steady towers in Heaven did shine
    As they were wont, nor at the priestly call
    Left plague her banquet in the Ethiop's hall,
Nor Famine from the rich man's portal came,
    Where at her ease she ever preys on all
Who throng to kneel for food: nor fear, nor shame,   3620
Nor faith, nor discord, dimmed hope's newly kindled flame.

XVIII

'For gold was as a god whose faith began
    To fade, so that its worshippers were few,
And Hell and Awe, which in the heart of man
    Is God itself; the Priests its downfall knew,
    As day by day their altars lonelier grew,
Till they were left alone within the fane;
    The shafts of falsehood unpolluting flew,
And the cold sneers of calumny were vain
The union of the free with discord's brand to stain.   3630

XIX

'The rest thou knowest – Lo! we two are here –
    We have survived a ruin wide and deep –
Strange thoughts are mine – I cannot grieve or fear,
    Sitting with thee upon this lonely steep
    I smile, though human love should make me weep.
We have survived a joy that knows no sorrow,
    And I do feel a mighty calmness creep
Over my heart, which can no longer borrow
Its hues from chance or change, dark children of tomorrow.

XX

'We know not what will come – yet, Laon, dearest,   3640
    Cythna shall be the prophetess of love,
Her lips shall rob thee of the grace thou wearest,
    To hide thy heart, and clothe the shapes which rove
    Within the homeless future's wintry grove;
For I now, sitting thus beside thee, seem
    Even with thy breath and blood to live and move,
And violence and wrong are as a dream
Which rolls from steadfast truth an unreturning stream.

XXI

'The blasts of autumn drive the winged seeds
    Over the earth, – next come the snows, and rain,   3650
And frosts, and storms, which dreary winter leads
    Out of his Scythian cave, a savage train;
    Behold! Spring sweeps over the world again,

Shedding soft dews from her ethereal wings;
   Flowers on the mountains, fruits over the plain,
And music on the waves and woods she flings,
And love on all that lives, and calm on lifeless things.

XXII

'O Spring, of hope, and love, and youth, and gladness
   Wind-winged emblem! brightest, best and fairest!
Whence comest thou, when, with dark winter's sadness   3660
   The tears that fade in sunny smiles thou sharest;
   Sister of joy, thou art the child who wearest
Thy mother's dying smile, tender and sweet;
   Thy mother Autumn, for whose grave thou bearest
Fresh flowers, and beams like flowers, with gentle feet,
Disturbing not the leaves which are her winding-sheet.

XXIII

'Virtue, and Hope, and Love, like light and Heaven,
   Surround the world. – We are their chosen slaves.
Has not the whirlwind of our spirit driven
   Truth's deathless germs to thought's remotest caves?   3670
   Lo, Winter comes! – the grief of many graves,
The frost of death, the tempest of the sword,
   The flood of tyranny, whose sanguine waves
Stagnate like ice at Faith, the enchanter's word,
And bind all human hearts in its repose abhorred.

XXIV

'The seeds are sleeping in the soil: meanwhile
   The tyrant peoples dungeons with his prey,
Pale victims on the guarded scaffold smile
   Because they cannot speak; and, day by day,
   The moon of wasting Science wanes away   3680
Among her stars, and in that darkness vast
   The sons of earth to their foul idols pray,
And grey Priests triumph, and like blight or blast
A shade of selfish care o'er human looks is cast.

XXV

'This is the Winter of the world; – and here
   We die, even as the winds of Autumn fade,
Expiring in the frore and foggy air. –
   Behold! Spring comes, tho' we must pass, who made
   The promise of its birth, – even as the shade
Which from our death, as from a mountain, flings   3690
   The future, a broad sunrise; thus arrayed
As with the plumes of overshadowing wings,
From its dark gulf of chains, Earth like an eagle springs.'

Ozymandias [63]

I met a traveller from an antique land
Who said: Two vast and trunkless legs of stone
Stand in the desert. Near them, on the sand,
Half sunk, a shattered visage lies, whose frown,
And wrinkled lip, and sneer of cold command,
Tell that its sculptor well those passions read
Which yet survive, stamped on these lifeless things,
The hand that mocked them, and the heart that fed;
And on the pedestal these words appear:
'My name is Ozymandias, king of kings: 10
Look on my works, ye Mighty, and despair!'
Nothing beside remains. Round the decay
Of that colossal wreck, boundless and bare
The lone and level sands stretch far away.

POEMS FROM 1818

Lines written among the Euganean Hills [64]

OCTOBER 1818

Many a green isle needs must be
In the deep wide sea of misery,
Or the mariner, worn and wan,
Never thus could voyage on
Day and night, and night and day,
Drifting on his dreary way,
With the solid darkness black
Closing round his vessel's track;
Whilst above the sunless sky,
Big with clouds, hangs heavily,   10
And behind the tempest fleet
Hurries on with lightning feet,
Riving sail, and cord, and plank,
Till the ship has almost drank
Death from the o'er-brimming deep;
And sinks down, down, like that sleep
When the dreamer seems to be
Weltering through eternity;
And the dim low line before
Of a dark and distant shore   20
Still recedes, as ever still
Longing with divided will,
But no power to seek or shun,
He is ever drifted on
O'er the unreposing wave
To the haven of the grave.
What, if there no friends will greet;
What, if there no heart will meet
His with love's impatient beat;
Wander wheresoe'er he may,   30
Can he dream before that day
To find refuge from distress

In friendship's smile, in love's caress?
Then 'twill wreak him little woe
Whether such there be or no:
Senseless is the breast, and cold,
Which relenting love would fold;
Bloodless are the veins and chill
Which the pulse of pain did fill;
Every little living nerve   40
That from bitter words did swerve
Round the tortured lips and brow,
Are like sapless leaflets now
Frozen upon December's bough.

On the beach of a northern sea
Which tempests shake eternally,
As once the wretch there lay to sleep,
Lies a solitary heap,
One white skull and seven dry bones,
On the margin of the stones,   50
Where a few grey rushes stand,
Boundaries of the sea and land:
Nor is heard one voice of wail
But the sea-mews, as they sail
O'er the billows of the gale;
Or the whirlwind up and down
Howling, like a slaughtered town,
When a king in glory rides
Through the pomp of fratricides:
Those unburied bones around   60
There is many a mournful sound;
There is no lament for him,
Like a sunless vapour, dim,
Who once clothed with life and thought
What now moves nor murmurs not.

Aye, many flowering islands lie
In the waters of wide Agony:
To such a one this morn was led
My bark, by soft winds piloted:
'Mid the mountains Euganean   70

I stood listening to the paean
With which the legioned rooks did hail
The sun's uprise majestical;
Gathering round with wings all hoar,
Thro' the dewy mist they soar
Like grey shades, till th' eastern heaven
Bursts, and then, as clouds of even,
Flecked with fire and azure, lie
In the unfathomable sky,
So their plumes of purple grain,   80
Starred with drops of golden rain,
Gleam above the sunlight woods,
As in silent multitudes
On the morning's fitful gale
Thro' the broken mist they sail,
And the vapours cloven and gleaming
Follow down the dark steep streaming,
Till all is bright, and clear, and still,
Round the solitary hill.

Beneath is spread like a green sea   90
The waveless plain of Lombardy,
Bounded by the vaporous air,
Islanded by cities fair;
Underneath day's azure eyes
Ocean's nursling, Venice lies,
A peopled labyrinth of walls,
Amphitrite's[65] destined halls,
Which her hoary sire now paves
With his blue and beaming waves.
Lo! the sun upsprings behind,   100
Broad, red, radiant, half reclined
On the level quivering line
Of the waters chrystalline;
And before that chasm of light,
As within a furnace bright,
Column, tower, and dome, and spire,
Shine like obelisks of fire,
Pointing with inconstant motion
From the altar of dark ocean

To the sapphire-tinted skies;   110
As the flames of sacrifice
From the marble shrines did rise,
As to pierce the dome of gold
Where Apollo spoke of old.

Sun-girt City, thou hast been
Ocean's child, and then his queen;
Now is come a darker day,
And thou soon must be his prey,
If the power that raised thee here
Hallow so thy watery bier.   120
A less drear ruin then than now,
With thy conquest-branded brow [66]
Stooping to the slave of slaves
From thy throne, among the waves
Wilt thou be, when the sea-mew
Flies, as once before it flew,
O'er thine isles depopulate,
And all is in its ancient state,
Save where many a palace gate
With green sea-flowers overgrown   130
Like a rock of ocean's own,
Topples o'er the abandoned sea
As the tides change sullenly.
The fisher on his watery way,
Wandering at the close of day,
Will spread his sail and seize his oar
Till he pass the gloomy shore,
Lest thy dead should, from their sleep
Bursting o'er the starlight deep,
Lead a rapid masque of death   140
O'er the waters of his path.

Those who alone thy towers behold
Quivering through aerial gold,
As I now behold them here,
Would imagine not they were
Sepulchres, where human forms,
Like pollution-nourished worms,

To the corpse of greatness cling,
Murdered, and now mouldering:
But if Freedom should awake   150
In her omnipotence, and shake
From the Celtic Anarch's hold
All the keys of dungeons cold,
Where a hundred cities lie
Chained like thee, ingloriously,
Thou and all thy sister band
Might adorn this sunny land,
Twining memories of old time
With new virtues more sublime;
If not, perish thou and they,   160
Clouds which stain truth's rising day
By her sun consumed away,
Earth can spare ye: while like flowers,
In the waste of years and hours,
From your dust new nations spring
With more kindly blossoming.

Perish – let there only be
Floating o'er thy hearthless sea,
As the garment of thy sky
Clothes the world immortally,   170
One remembrance, more sublime
Than the tattered pall of time,
Which scarce hides thy visage wan: –
That a tempest-cleaving Swan[67]
Of the songs of Albion,[68]
Driven from his ancestral streams
By the might of evil dreams,
Found a nest in thee; and Ocean
Welcomed him with such emotion
That its joy grew his, and sprung   180
From his lips like music flung
O'er a mighty thunder-fit,
Chastening terror: – what though yet
Poesy's unfailing River,
Which thro' Albion winds for ever,
Lashing with melodious wave

Many a sacred poet's grave,
Mourn its latest nursling fled!
What though thou with all thy dead
Scarce can for this fame repay   190
Aught thine own, – oh, rather say
Though thy sins and slaveries foul
Overcloud a sunlike soul!
As the ghost of Homer clings
Round Scamander's[69] wasting springs;
As divinest Shakespeare's might
Fills Avon and the world with light,
Like omniscient power which he
Imaged 'mid mortality;
As the love from Petrarch's urn,[70]   200
Yet amid yon hills doth burn,
A quenchless lamp by which the heart
Sees things unearthly; – so thou art,
Mighty spirit – so shall be
The city that did refuge thee.

Lo, the sun floats up the sky
Like thought-winged Liberty,
Till the universal light
Seems to level plain and height;
From the sea a mist has spread,   210
And the beams of morn lie dead
On the towers of Venice now,
Like its glory long ago.
By the skirts of that grey cloud
Many-domed Padua proud
Stands, a peopled solitude,
'Mid the harvest shining plain,
Where the peasant heaps his grain
In the garner of his foe,
And the milk-white oxen slow   220
With the purple vintage strain,
Heaped upon the creaking wain,
That the brutal Celt may swill
Drunken sleep with savage will;
And the sickle to the sword

Lies unchanged, though many a lord,
Like a weed whose shade is poison,
Overgrows this region's foison,
Sheaves of whom are ripe to come
To destruction's harvest home: 230
Men must reap the things they sow,
Force from force must ever flow,
Or worse; but 'tis a bitter woe
That love or reason cannot change
The despot's rage, the slave's revenge.

Padua, thou within whose walls
Those mute guests at festivals,
Son and Mother, Death and Sin,
Played at dice for Ezzelin,[71]
Till Death cried, 'I win, I win!'   240
And Sin cursed to lose the wager,
But Death promised to assuage her.
That he would petition for
Her to be made Vice-Emperor,
When the destined years were o'er
Over all between the Po
And the eastern Alpine snow,
Under the mighty Austrian.
Sin smiled so as Sin only can,
And since that time, aye, long before   250
Both have ruled from shore to shore,
That incestuous pair, who follow
Tyrants as the sun the swallow.
As Repentance follows Crime,
And as changes follow Time.

In thine halls the lamp of learning,[72]
Padua, now no more is burning;
Like a meteor, whose wild way
Is lost over the grave of day,
It gleams betrayed and to betray: 260
Once remotest nations came
To adore that sacred flame,

When it lit not many a hearth
On this cold and gloomy earth:
Now new fires from antique light
Spring beneath the wide world's might;
But their spark lies dead in thee,
Trampled out by tyranny.
As the Norway woodman quells,
In the depth of piny dells,   270
One light flame among the brakes,
While the boundless forest shakes,
And its mighty trunks are torn
By the fire thus lowly born:
The spark beneath his feet is dead,
He starts to see the flames it fed
Howling through the darkened sky
With a myriad tongues victoriously,
And sinks down in fear: so thou,
O tyranny, beholdest now   280
Light around thee, and thou hearest
The loud flames ascend, and fearest:
Grovel on the earth; aye, hide
In the dust thy purple pride!

Noon descends around me now:
'Tis the noon of autumn's glow,
When a soft and purple mist
Like a vaporous amethyst,
Or an air-dissolved star
Mingling light and fragrance, far   290
From the curved horizon's bound
To the point of heaven's profound,
Fills the overflowing sky;
And the plains that silent lie
Underneath; the leaves unsodden
Where the infant frost has trodden
With his morning-winged feet,
Whose bright print is gleaming yet;
And the red and golden vines,
Piercing with their trellised lines   300
The rough, dark-skirted wilderness;

The dun and bladed grass no less,
Pointing from this hoary tower
In the windless air; the flower
Glimmering at my feet; the line
Of the olive-sandalled Apennine
In the south dimly islanded;
And the Alps, whose snows are spread
High between the clouds and sun;
And of living things each one;   310
And my spirit which so long
Darkened this swift stream of song,
Interpenetrated lie
By the glory of the sky;
Be it love, light, harmony,
Odour, or the soul of all
Which from heaven like dew doth fall,
Or the mind which feeds this verse
Peopling the lone universe.

Noon descends, and after noon   320
Autumn's evening meets me soon,
Leading the infantine moon,
And that one star, which to her
Almost seems to minister
Half the crimson light she brings
From the sunset's radiant springs;
And the soft dreams of the morn
(Which like winged winds had borne
To that silent isle, which lies
'Mid remembered agonies,   330
The frail bark of this lone being)
Pass, to other sufferers fleeing,
And its ancient pilot, Pain,
Sits beside the helm again.

Other flowering isles must be
In the sea of life and agony:
Other spirits float and flee
O'er that gulf: even now, perhaps,
On some rock the wild wave wraps,

With folded wings they waiting sit   340
For my bark, to pilot it
To some calm and blooming cove,
Where for me, and those I love,
May a windless bower be built,
Far from passion, pain, and guilt,
In a dell 'mid lawny hills,
Which the wild sea-murmur fills,
And soft sunshine, and the sound
Of old forests echoing round,
And the light and smell divine   350
Of all flowers that breathe and shine:
We may live so happy there,
That the spirits of the air,
Envying us, may even entice
To our healing paradise
The polluting multitude;
But their rage would be subdued
By that clime divine and calm,
And the winds whose wings rain balm
On the uplifted soul, and leaves   360
Under which the bright sea heaves;
While each breathless interval
In their whisperings musical
The inspired soul supplies
With its own deep melodies;
And the love which heals all strife
Circling, like the breath of life,
All things in that sweet abode
With its own mild brotherhood:
They, not it would change; and soon   370
Every sprite beneath the moon
Would repent its envy vain,
And the earth grow young again.

Julian and Maddalo

A CONVERSATION

PREFACE

The meadows with fresh streams, the bees with thyme,
The goats with the green leaves of budding Spring,
Are saturated not – nor Love with tears.

VIRGIL's *Gallus*

Count Maddalo is a Venetian nobleman of ancient family and of great fortune, who, without mixing much in the society of his countrymen, resides chiefly at his magnificent palace in that city. He is a person of the most consummate genius, and capable, if he would direct his energies to such an end, of becoming the redeemer of his degraded country. But it is his weakness to be proud: he derives, from a comparison of his own extraordinary mind with the dwarfish intellects that surround him, an intense apprehension of the nothingness of human life. His passions and his powers are incomparably greater than those of other men and, instead of the latter having been employed in curbing the former, they have mutually lent each other strength. His ambition preys upon itself, for want of objects which it can consider worthy of exertion. I say that Maddalo is proud, because I can find no other word to express the concentred and impatient feelings which consume him; but it is on his own hopes and affections only that he seems to trample, for in social life no human being can be more gentle, patient, and unassuming than Maddalo. He is cheerful, frank, and witty. His more serious conversation is a sort of intoxication; men are held by it as by a spell. He has travelled much; and there is an inexpressible charm in his relation of his adventures in different countries.

Julian is an Englishman of good family, passionately attached to those philosophical notions which assert the power of man over his own mind, and the immense improvements of which, by the extinction of certain moral superstitions, human society may be yet susceptible. Without concealing the evil in the world, he is for ever speculating how good may be made superior. He is a complete infidel, and a scoffer at all things reputed holy; and Maddalo takes a wicked pleasure in drawing out his taunts against religion. What Maddalo thinks on these matters is not exactly known. Julian, in spite of his heterodox opinions, is conjectured by his friends to possess some good qualities. How far this is possible, the pious reader will determine. Julian is rather serious.

Of the Maniac I can give no information. He seems, by his own account, to have been disappointed in love. He was evidently a very cultivated and amiable person when in his right senses. His story, told at length, might be like many other stories of the same kind: the unconnected exclamations of his agony will perhaps be found a sufficient comment for the text of every heart.

I rode one evening with Count Maddalo
Upon the bank of land which breaks the flow
Of Adria towards Venice: a bare strand
Of hillocks, heaped from ever-shifting sand,
Matted with thistles and amphibious weeds,
Such as from earth's embrace the salt ooze breeds,
Is this; an uninhabited seaside,
Which the lone fisher, when his nets are dried,
Abandons; and no other object breaks
The waste, but one dwarf tree and some few stakes   10
Broken and unrepaired, and the tide makes
A narrow space of level sand thereon,
Where 'twas our wont to ride while day went down.
This ride was my delight. I love all waste
And solitary places; where we taste
The pleasure of believing what we see
Is boundless, as we wish our souls to be:
And such was this wide ocean, and this shore
More barren than its billows; and yet more
Than all, with a remembered friend I love   20
To ride as then I rode; – for the winds drove
The living spray along the sunny air
Into our faces; the blue heavens were bare,
Stripped to their depths by the awakening north;
And, from the waves, sound like delight broke forth
Harmonising with solitude, and sent
Into our hearts aerial merriment.

So, as we rode, we talked; and the swift thought,
Winging itself with laughter, lingered not,

But flew from brain to brain, – such glee was ours,   30
Charged with light memories of remembered hours,
None slow enough for sadness: till we came
Homeward, which always makes the spirit tame.
This day had been cheerful but cold, and now
The sun was sinking, and the wind also.
Our talk grew somewhat serious, as may be
Talk interrupted with such raillery
As mocks itself, because it cannot scorn
The thoughts it would extinguish: – 'twas forlorn,
Yet pleasing, such as once, so poets tell,   40
The devils held within the dales of Hell
Concerning God, freewill and destiny:
Of all that earth has been or yet may be,
All that vain men imagine or believe,
Or hope can paint or suffering may achieve,
We descanted, and I (for ever still
Is it not wise to make the best of ill?)
Argued against despondency, but pride
Made my companion take the darker side.
The sense that he was greater than his kind   50
Had struck, methinks, his eagle spirit blind
By gazing on its own exceeding light.
Meanwhile the sun paused ere it should alight,
Over the horizon of the mountains; – Oh
How beautiful is sunset, when the glow
Of Heaven descends upon a land like thee,
Thou paradise of exiles, Italy!
Thy mountains, seas and vineyards and the towers
Of cities they encircle! – it was ours
To stand on thee, beholding it; and then,   60
Just where we had dismounted, the Count's men
Were waiting for us with the gondola. –
As those who pause on some delightful way
Tho' bent on pleasant pilgrimage, we stood
Looking upon the evening, and the flood
Which lay between the city and the shore
Paved with the image of the sky . . . the hoar
And aery Alps towards the north appeared
Thro' mist, a heaven-sustaining bulwark reared

Between the east and west; and half the sky   70
Was roofed with clouds of rich emblazonry,
Dark purple at the zenith, which still grew
Down the steep west into a wondrous hue
Brighter than burning gold, even to the rent
Where the swift sun yet paused in his descent
Among the many folded hills: they were
Those famous Euganean hills, which bear,
As seen from Lido thro' the harbour piles
The likeness of a clump of peaked isles –
And then, as if the earth and sea had been   80
Dissolved into one lake of fire, were seen
Those mountains towering as from waves of flame
Around the vaporous sun, from which there came
The inmost purple spirit of light, and made
Their very peaks transparent. 'Ere it fade,'
Said my companion, 'I will show you soon
A better station' – so, o'er the lagune
We glided, and from that funereal bark
I leaned, and saw the city, and could mark
How from their many isles, in evening's gleam,   90
Its temples and its palaces did seem
Like fabrics of enchantment piled to Heaven.
I was about to speak, when – 'We are even
'Now at the point I meant,' said Maddalo,
And bade the gondolieri cease to row.
'Look, Julian, on the west, and listen well
If you hear not a deep and heavy bell.'
I looked, and saw between us and the sun
A building on an island; such a one
As age to age might add, for uses vile,   100
A windowless, deformed and dreary pile;
And on the top an open tower, where hung
A bell, which in the radiance swayed and swung:
We could just hear its hoarse and iron tongue:
The broad sun sank behind it, and it tolled
In strong and black relief. – 'What we behold
Shall be the madhouse and its belfry tower,'
Said Maddalo, 'and ever at this hour,
Those who may cross the water hear that bell,

Which calls the maniacs, each one from his cell,   110
To vespers.' – 'As much skill as need to pray,
In thanks or hope for their dark lot, have they
To their stern maker,' I replied. 'Oh, ho!
You talk as in years past,' said Maddalo.
' 'Tis strange men change not. You were ever still
Among Christ's flock a perilous infidel,
A wolf for the meek lambs – if you can't swim,
Beware of Providence.' I looked on him,
But the gay smile had faded in his eye,
'And such,' – he cried, 'is our mortality,   120
And this must be the emblem and the sign
Of what should be eternal and divine! –
And like that black and dreary bell, the soul,
Hung in a heaven-illumined tower, must toll
Our thoughts and our desires to meet below
Round the rent heart and pray – as madmen do;
For what? they know not, till the night of death,
As sunset that strange vision, severeth
Our memory from itself, and us from all
We sought and yet were baffled.' I recall   130
The sense of what he said, altho' I mar
The force of his expressions. The broad star
Of day meanwhile had sunk behind the hill,
And the black bell became invisible,
And the red tower looked grey, and all between,
The churches, ships and palaces, were seen
Huddled in gloom; – into the purple sea
The orange hues of heaven sank silently.
We hardly spoke, and soon the gondola
Conveyed me to my lodgings by the way.   140

     The following morn was rainy, cold and dim:
Ere Maddalo arose, I called on him,
And whilst I waited with his child I played;
A lovelier toy sweet Nature never made:
A serious, subtle, wild, yet gentle being,
Graceful without design and unforeseeing,
With eyes – Oh! speak not of her eyes! – which seem
Twin mirrors of Italian Heaven, yet gleam

With such deep meaning as we never see
But in the human countenance. With me   150
She was a special favourite: I had nursed
Her fine and feeble limbs when she came first
To this bleak world; and she yet seemed to know
On second sight her ancient playfellow,
Less changed than she was by six months or so;
For after her first shyness was worn out
We sate there, rolling billiard balls about,
When the Count entered. Salutations past,
'The words you spoke last night might well have cast
A darkness on my spirit – if man be   160
The passive thing you say, I should not see
Much harm in the religions and old saws
(Tho' I may never own such leaden laws)
Which break a teachless nature to the yoke:
Mine is another faith;' – thus much I spoke
And, noting he replied not, added: 'See
This lovely child, blithe, innocent and free,
She spends a happy time with little care,
While we to such sick thoughts subjected are
As came on you last night. It is our will   170
That thus enchains us to permitted ill –
We might be otherwise – we might be all
We dream of, happy, high, majestical.
Where is the love, beauty and truth we seek
But in our mind? and if we were not weak,
Should we be less in deed than in desire?'
'Aye, if we were not weak – and we aspire
How vainly to be strong!' said Maddalo:
'You talk Utopia.' 'It remains to know,'
I then rejoined, 'and those who try may find   180
How strong the chains are which our spirit bind;
Brittle perchance as straw . . . We are assured
Much may be conquered, much may be endured
Of what degrades and crushes us. We know
That we have power over ourselves to do
And suffer – what, we know not till we try;
But something nobler than to live and die –
So taught those kings of old philosophy,

Who reigned before religion made men blind;
And those who suffer with their suffering kind   190
Yet feel this faith, religion.' 'My dear friend,'
Said Maddalo, 'my judgement will not bend
To your opinion, tho' I think you might
Make such a system refutation-tight,
As far as words go. I knew one like you,
Who to this city came some months ago,
With whom I argued in this sort, and he
Is now gone mad, – and so he answered me,
Poor fellow! But if you would like to go,
We'll visit him, and his wild talk will show   200
How vain are such aspiring theories.'
'I hope to prove the induction otherwise,
And that a want of that true theory still,
Which seeks a "soul of goodness" in things ill
Or in himself or others, has thus bowed
His being: – there are some by nature proud,
Who patient in all else demand but this:
To love and be beloved with gentleness;
And being scorned, what wonder if they die
Some living death? This is not destiny   210
But man's own wilful ill.'
                    As thus I spoke
Servants announced the gondola, and we
Through the fast-falling rain and high-wrought sea
Sailed to the island where the madhouse stands.
We disembarked. The clap of tortured hands,
Fierce yells and howlings and lamentings keen,
And laughter where complaint had merrier been,
Moans, shrieks, and curses, and blaspheming prayers
Accosted us. We climbed the oozy stairs
Into an old courtyard. I heard on high,   220
Then, fragments of most touching melody,
But looking up saw not the singer there –
Through the black bars in the tempestuous air
I saw, like weeds on a wrecked palace growing,
Long tangled locks flung wildly forth and flowing,
Of those who on a sudden were beguiled
Into strange silence, and looked forth and smiled,

Hearing sweet sounds. – Then I: 'Methinks there were
A cure of these with patience and kind care,
If music can thus move . . . But what is he   230
Whom we seek here?' 'Of his sad history
I know but this,' said Maddalo: 'he came
To Venice a dejected man, and fame
Said he was wealthy, or he had been so;
Some thought the loss of fortune wrought him woe;
But he was ever talking in such sort
As you do – but more sadly; – he seemed hurt,
Even as a man with his peculiar wrong,
To hear but of the oppression of the strong,
Or those absurd deceits (I think with you   240
In some respects, you know) which carry through
The excellent impostors of this earth
When they outface detection. He had worth,
Poor fellow! but a humorist in his way.'
'Alas, what drove him mad?' 'I cannot say;
A lady came with him from France, and when
She left him and returned, he wandered then
About yon lonely isles of desert sand
Till he grew wild – he had no cash or land
Remaining – the police had brought him here –   250
Some fancy took him and he would not bear
Removal; so I fitted up for him
Those rooms beside the sea, to please his whim;
And sent him busts, and books, and urns for flowers,
Which had adorned his life in happier hours,
And instruments of music. You may guess
A stranger could do little more or less
For one so gentle and unfortunate.
And those are his sweet strains which charm the weight
From madmen's chains, and make this hell appear   260
A heaven of sacred silence, hushed to hear.'
'Nay, this was kind of you – he had no claim,
As the world says.' 'None but the very same
Which I on all mankind, were I as he
Fallen to such deep reverse; – his melody
Is interrupted – now we hear the din
Of madmen, shriek on shriek, again begin;

Let us now visit him; after this strain,
He ever communes with himself again,
And sees nor hears not any.' Having said   270
These words we called the keeper, and he led
To an apartment opening on the sea –
There the poor wretch was sitting mournfully
Near a piano, his pale fingers twined
One with the other, and the ooze and wind
Rushed thro' an open casement, and did sway
His hair, and starred it with the brackish spray;
His head was leaning on a music book,
And he was muttering, and his lean limbs shook;
His lips were pressed against a folded leaf,   280
In hue too beautiful for health, and grief
Smiled in their motions as they lay apart –
As one who wrought from his own fervid heart
The eloquence of passion; soon he raised
His sad meek face and eyes lustrous and glazed
And spoke – sometimes as one who wrote and thought
His words might move some heart that heeded not
If sent to distant lands: and then as one
Reproaching deeds never to be undone,
With wondering self-compassion; then his speech   290
Was lost in grief, and then his words came each
Unmodulated, cold, expressionless;
But that from one jarred accent you might guess
It was despair made them so uniform:
And all the while the loud and gusty storm
Hissed thro' the window, and we stood behind,
Stealing his accents from the envious wind
Unseen. I yet remember what he said
Distinctly, such impression his words made.

'Month after month,' he cried, 'to bear this load,   300
And as a jade urged by the whip and goad
To drag life on, which like a heavy chain
Lengthens behind with many a link of pain! –
And not to speak my grief – O, not to dare
To give a human voice to my despair,
But live and move and, wretched thing! smile on,

As if I never went aside to groan,
And wear this mask of falsehood even to those
Who are most dear – not for my own repose.
Alas! no scorn or pain or hate could be   310
So heavy as that falsehood is to me –
But that I cannot bear more altered faces
Than needs must be, more changed and cold embraces,
More misery, disappointment and mistrust
To own me for their father . . . Would the dust
Were covered in upon my body now!
That the life ceased to toil within my brow!
And then these thoughts would at the least be fled;
Let us not fear such pain can vex the dead.

    'What Power delights to torture us? I know   320
That to myself I do not wholly owe
What now I suffer, tho' in part I may.
Alas none strewed sweet flowers upon the way
Where, wandering heedlessly, I met pale Pain,
My shadow, which will leave me not again.
If I have erred, there was no joy in error,
But pain and insult and unrest and terror;
I have not, as some do, bought penitence
With pleasure, and a dark yet sweet offence;
For then, – if love and tenderness and truth   330
Had overlived hope's momentary youth,
My creed should have redeemed me from repenting.
But loathed scorn and outrage unrelenting
Met love excited by far other seeming
Until the end was gained . . . as one from dreaming
Of sweetest peace, I woke, and found my state
Such as it is. –
           'O thou, my spirit's mate –
Who, for thou art compassionate and wise,
Wouldst pity me from thy most gentle eyes
If this sad writing thou shouldst ever see –   340
My secret groans must be unheard by thee;
Thou wouldst weep tears bitter as blood to know
Thy lost friend's incommunicable woe.

'Ye few by whom my nature has been weighed
In friendship, let me not that name degrade
By placing on your hearts the secret load
Which crushes mine to dust. There is one road
To peace and that is truth, which follow ye!
Love sometimes leads astray to misery.
Yet think not tho' subdued – and I may well   350
Say that I am subdued – that the full hell
Within me would infect the untainted breast
Of sacred nature with its own unrest;
As some perverted beings think to find
In scorn or hate a medicine for the mind
Which scorn or hate have wounded – O, how vain!
The dagger heals not but may rend again . . .
Believe that I am ever still the same
In creed as in resolve, and what may tame
My heart, must leave the understanding free,   360
Or all would sink in this keen agony –
Nor dream that I will join the vulgar cry,
Or with my silence sanction tyranny,
Or seek a moment's shelter from my pain
In any madness which the world calls gain;
Ambition or revenge or thoughts as stern
As those which make me what I am, or turn
To avarice or misanthropy or lust . . .
Heap on me soon, O grave, thy welcome dust!
Till then the dungeon may demand its prey,   370
And poverty and shame may meet and say –
Halting beside me on the public way –
"That love-devoted youth is ours – let's sit
Beside him – he may live some six months yet."
Or the red scaffold, as our country bends,
May ask some willing victim, or ye friends
May fall under some sorrow which this heart
Or hand may share or vanquish or avert;
I am prepared, in truth with no proud joy,
To do or suffer aught, as when a boy   380
I did devote to justice and to love
My nature, worthless now! . . .
                              'I must remove

A veil from my pent mind. 'Tis torn aside!
O, pallid as death's dedicated bride,
Thou mockery which art sitting by my side,
Am I not wan like thee? at the grave's call
I haste, invited to thy wedding-ball,
To greet the ghastly paramour for whom
Thou hast deserted me . . . and made the tomb
Thy bridal bed . . . but I beside your feet   390
Will lie and watch ye from my winding sheet –
Thus . . . wide awake tho' dead . . . Yet stay, O stay,
Go not so soon – I know not what I say –
Hear but my reasons . . I am mad, I fear,
My fancy is o'erwrought . . . thou art not here . . .
Pale art thou, 'tis most true. . . but thou art gone,
Thy work is finished . . . I am left alone! –

    * * *

 'Nay, was it I who wooed thee to this breast
Which, like a serpent, thou envenomest
As in repayment of the warmth it lent?   400
Didst thou not seek me for thine own content?
Did not thy love awaken mine? I thought
That thou wert she who said, "You kiss me not
Ever; I fear you do not love me now," –
In truth I loved even to my overthrow
Her who would fain forget these words: but they
Cling to her mind, and cannot pass away.

    * * *

 'You say that I am proud – that when I speak
My lip is tortured with the wrongs which break
The spirit it expresses . . . Never one   410
Humbled himself before, as I have done!
Even the instinctive worm on which we tread
Turns, tho' it wound not – then with prostrate head
Sinks in the dust and writhes like me – and dies?
No: wears a living death of agonies!
As the slow shadows of the pointed grass
Mark the eternal periods, his pangs pass,
Slow, ever-moving – making moments be
As mine seem – each an immortality!

    * * *

'That you had never seen me – never heard   420
My voice, and more than all had ne'er endured
The deep pollution of my loathed embrace –
That your eyes ne'er had lied love in my face –
That, like some maniac monk, I had torn out
The nerves of manhood by their bleeding root
With mine own quivering fingers, so that ne'er
Our hearts had for a moment mingled there
To disunite in horror! These were not
With thee like some suppressed and hideous thought,
Which flits athwart our musings, but can find   430
No rest within a pure and gentle mind . . .
Thou sealedst them with many a bare broad word,
And ceredst my memory o'er them, – for I heard
And can forget not . . . they were ministered,
One after one, those curses. Mix them up
Like self-destroying poisons in one cup,
And they will make one blessing which thou ne'er
Didst imprecate for, on me, – death!

                    *   *   *

                                        'It were
A cruel punishment for one most cruel,
If such can love, to make that love the fuel   440
Of the mind's hell; hate, scorn, remorse, despair:
But *me* – whose heart a stranger's tear might wear
As water-drops the sandy fountain-stone,
Who loved and pitied all things, and could moan
For woes which others hear not, and could see
The absent with the glance of phantasy,
And with the poor and trampled sit and weep,
Following the captive to his dungeon deep;
Me – who am as a nerve o'er which do creep
The else-unfelt oppressions of this earth,   450
And was to thee the flame upon thy hearth,
When all beside was cold; – that thou on me
Shouldst rain these plagues of blistering agony –
Such curses are from lips once eloquent
With love's too partial praise! Let none relent
Who intend deeds too dreadful for a name
Henceforth, if an example for the same

They seek . . . for thou on me lookedst so, and so –
And didst speak thus . . and thus . . . I live to show
How much men bear and die not!

     *   *   *

                        'Thou wilt tell   460
With the grimace of hate how horrible
It was to meet my love when thine grew less;
Thou wilt admire how I could e'er address
Such features to love's work . . . this taunt, tho' true
(For indeed Nature nor in form nor hue
Bestowed on me her choicest workmanship),
Shall not be thy defence . . . for since thy lip
Met mine first, years long past, since thine eye kindled
With soft fire under mine, I have not dwindled
Nor changed in mind or body, or in aught   470
But as love changes what it loveth not
After long years and many trials.
                           'How vain
Are words! I thought never to speak again,
Not even in secret, – not to my own heart –
But from my lips the unwilling accents start
And from my pen the words flow as I write,
Dazzling my eyes with scalding tears . . . my sight
Is dim to see that charactered in vain
On this unfeeling leaf which burns the brain
And eats into it . . . blotting all things fair   480
And wise and good which time had written there.

   'Those who inflict must suffer, for they see
The work of their own hearts, and this must be
Our chastisement or recompense – O child!
I would that thine were like to be more mild
For both our wretched sakes . . . for thine the most
Who feelest already all that thou hast lost,
Without the power to wish it thine again;
And as slow years pass, a funereal train,
Each with the ghost of some lost hope or friend   490
Following it like its shadow, wilt thou bend
No thought on my dead memory?

     *   *   *

                        'Alas, love,
Fear me not . . . against thee I would not move
A finger in despite. Do I not live
That thou mayst have less bitter cause to grieve?
I give thee tears for scorn and love for hate;
And that thy lot may be less desolate
Than his on whom thou tramplest, I refrain
From that sweet sleep which medicines all pain.
Then, when thou speakest of me, never say   500
He could forgive not. Here I cast away
All human passions, all revenge, all pride;
I think, speak, act no ill; I do but hide
Under these words, like embers, every spark
Of that which has consumed me – Quick and dark
The grave is yawning . . . as its roof shall cover
My limbs with dust and worms, under and over,
So let oblivion hide this grief . . . the air
Closes upon my accents, as despair
Upon my heart – let death upon despair!'   510

     He ceased and, overcome, leant back awhile;
Then rising, with a melancholy smile
Went to a sofa, and lay down, and slept
A heavy sleep, and in his dreams he wept
And muttered some familiar name, and we
Wept without shame in his society.
I think I never was impressed so much;
The man who was not must have lacked a touch
Of human nature . . . Then we lingered not,
Although our argument was quite forgot,   520
But, calling the attendants, went to dine
At Maddalo's; yet neither cheer nor wine
Could give us spirits, for we talked of him,
And nothing else, till daylight made stars dim;
And we agreed his was some dreadful ill
Wrought on him boldly, yet unspeakable,
By a dear friend; some deadly change in love
Of one vowed deeply which he dreamed not of;
For whose sake he, it seemed, had fixed a blot
Of falsehood on his mind which flourished not   530

But in the light of all-beholding truth;
And having stamped this canker on his youth
She had abandoned him – and how much more
Might be his woe, we guessed not – he had store
Of friends and fortune once, as we could guess
From his nice habits and his gentleness;
These were now lost . . . it were a grief indeed
If he had changed one unsustaining reed
For all that such a man might else adorn.
The colours of his mind seemed yet unworn;   540
For the wild language of his grief was high
Such as in measure were called poetry;
And I remember one remark which then
Maddalo made. He said: 'Most wretched men
Are cradled into poetry by wrong:
They learn in suffering what they teach in song.'

    If I had been an unconnected man,
I, from this moment, should have formed some plan
Never to leave sweet Venice, – for to me
It was delight to ride by the lone sea;   550
And then, the town is silent – one may write
Or read in gondolas by day or night,
Having the little brazen lamp alight,
Unseen, uninterrupted; books are there,
Pictures, and casts from all those statues fair
Which were twin-born with poetry, and all
We seek in towns, with little to recall
Regrets for the green country. I might sit
In Maddalo's great palace, and his wit
And subtle talk would cheer the winter night   560
And make me know myself, and the firelight
Would flash upon our faces, till the day
Might dawn and make me wonder at my stay:
But I had friends in London too: the chief
Attraction here was that I sought relief
From the deep tenderness that maniac wrought
Within me – 'twas perhaps an idle thought,
But I imagined that if day by day
I watched him, and but seldom went away,

And studied all the beatings of his heart   570
With zeal, as men study some stubborn art
For their own good, and could by patience find
An entrance to the caverns of his mind,
I might reclaim him from his dark estate:
In friendships I had been most fortunate –
Yet never saw I one whom I would call
More willingly my friend; and this was all
Accomplished not; such dreams of baseless good
Oft come and go in crowds and solitude   580
And leave no trace – but what I now designed
Made for long years impression on my mind.
The following morning, urged by my affairs
I left bright Venice.
                    After many years
And many changes I returned; the name
Of Venice, and its aspect, was the same;
But Maddalo was travelling far away
Among the mountains of Armenia.
His dog was dead. His child had now become
A woman; such as it has been my doom
To meet with few, a wonder of this earth   590
Where there is little of transcendent worth,
Like one of Shakespeare's women: kindly she
And with a manner beyond courtesy
Received her father's friend; and when I asked
Of the lorn maniac, she her memory tasked,
And told, as she had heard, the mournful tale:
'That the poor sufferer's health began to fail
Two years from my departure, but that then
The lady who had left him came again.
Her mien had been imperious, but she now   600
Looked meek – perhaps remorse had brought her low.
Her coming made him better, and they stayed
Together at my father's – for I played
As I remember with the lady's shawl –
I might be six years old. But after all
She left him' . . . 'Why! her heart must have been tough:
How did it end?' 'And was not this enough?
They met they parted.' – 'Child, is there no more?'

'Something within that interval which bore
The stamp of *why* they parted, *how* they met,   610
Yet if thine aged eyes disdain to wet
Those wrinkled cheeks with youth's remembered tears
Ask me no more, but let the silent years
Be closed and cered over their memory
As yon mute marble where their corpses lie.'
I urged and questioned still: she told me how
All happened – but the cold world shall not know.

Stanzas Written in Dejection, near Naples

1

The sun is warm, the sky is clear,
    The waves are dancing fast and bright,
Blue isles and snowy mountains wear
    The purple noon's transparent might,
    The breath of the moist earth is light,
Around its unexpanded buds;
    Like many a voice of one delight,
The winds, the birds, the ocean floods,
The City's voice itself is soft like Solitude's.

2

I see the Deep's untrampled floor   10
    With green and purple seaweeds strown;
I see the waves upon the shore,
    Like light dissolved in star-showers, thrown:
    I sit upon the sands alone,
The lightning of the noontide ocean
    Is flashing round me, and a tone
Arises from its measured motion,
How sweet! did any heart now share in my emotion.

3

Alas! I have nor hope nor health,
   Nor peace within nor calm around,   20
Nor that content surpassing wealth
   The sage in meditation found,
     And walked with inward glory crowned –
Nor fame, nor power, nor love, nor leisure.
   Others I see whom these surround –
   Smiling they live and call life pleasure; –
To me that cup has been dealt in another measure.

4

Yet now despair itself is mild,
   Even as the winds and waters are:
I could lie down like a tired child,   30
   And weep away the life of care
     Which I have borne and yet must bear,
Till death like sleep might steal on me,
   And I might feel in the warm air
   My cheek grow cold, and hear the sea
Breathe o'er my dying brain its last monotony.

5

Some might lament that I were cold,
   As I, when this sweet day is gone,
Which my lost heart, too soon grown old,
   Insults with this untimely moan;   40
     They might lament – for I am one
Whom men love not, – and yet regret,
   Unlike this day, which, when the sun
   Shall on its stainless glory set,
Will linger, though enjoyed, like joy in memory yet.

Sonnet

Lift not the painted veil which those who live
Call Life: though unreal shapes be pictured there,
And it but mimic all we would believe
With colours idly spread, – behind, lurk Fear
And Hope, twin destinies; who ever weave
The shadows, which the world calls substance, there.
I knew one who had lifted it – he sought,
For his lost heart was tender, things to love,
But found them not, alas! nor was there aught
The world contains, the which he could approve.   10
Through the unheeding many he did move,
A splendour among shadows, a bright blot
Upon this gloomy scene, a Spirit that strove
For truth, and like the Preacher[73] found it not.

POEMS FROM 1819

Prometheus Unbound

A LYRICAL DRAMA IN FOUR ACTS

'Audisne haec, Amphiarae, sub terram abdite?'[74]

PREFACE

The Greek tragic writers, in selecting as their subject any portion of their national history or mythology, employed in their treatment of it a certain arbitrary discretion. They by no means conceived themselves bound to adhere to the common interpretation or to imitate in story as in title their rivals and predecessors. Such a system would have amounted to resignation of those claims to preference over their competitors which incited the composition. The Agamemnonian[75] story was exhibited on the Athenian theatre with as many variations as dramas.

I have presumed to employ a similar licence. The 'Prometheus Unbound' of Aeschylus supposed the reconciliation of Jupiter with his victim as the price of the disclosure of the danger threatened to his empire by the consummation of his marriage with Thetis. Thetis, according to this view of the subject, was given in marriage to Peleus, and Prometheus, by the permission of Jupiter,[76] delivered from his captivity by Hercules. Had I framed my story on this model, I should have done no more than have attempted to restore the lost drama of Aeschylus; an ambition which, if my preference to this mode of treating the subject had incited me to cherish, the recollection of the high comparison such an attempt would challenge might well abate. But, in truth, I was averse from a catastrophe so feeble as that of reconciling the Champion with the Oppressor of mankind. The moral interest of the fable, which is so powerfully sustained by the sufferings and endurance of Prometheus, would be annihilated if we could conceive of him as unsaying his high language and quailing before his successful and perfidious adversary. The only imaginary being resembling in any degree Prometheus, is Satan; and Prometheus is, in my judgement, a more poetical character than Satan, because, in addition to courage, and majesty, and firm and patient opposition to omnipotent force, he is susceptible of being described as exempt from the taints of ambition, envy, revenge, and a desire for personal aggrandisement, which, in the Hero of Paradise Lost, interfere with the interest. The character of Satan engenders in the mind a pernicious casuistry which leads us to weigh his faults with his wrongs, and to excuse the former because the latter exceed all measure. In the minds of those who consider that magnificent fiction with a religious feeling it engenders something worse. But Prometheus is, as it were, the type of the highest perfection of moral and intellectual nature, impelled by the purest and the truest motives to the best and noblest ends.

This Poem was chiefly written upon the mountainous ruins of the Baths of Caracalla, among the flowery glades, and thickets of odoriferous blossoming trees, which are extended in ever winding labyrinths upon its immense platforms and dizzy arches suspended in the air. The bright blue sky of Rome, and the effect of the vigorous awakening spring in that divinest climate, and the new life with which it drenches the spirits even to intoxication, were the inspiration of this drama. The imagery which I have employed will be found, in many instances, to have been drawn from the operations of the human mind, or from those external actions by which they are expressed. This is unusual in modern poetry, although Dante and Shakespeare are full of instances of the same kind: Dante indeed more than any other poet, and with greater success. But the Greek poets, as writers to whom no resource of awakening the sympathy of their contemporaries was unknown, were in the habitual use of this power; and it is the study of their works (since a higher merit would probably be denied me) to which I am willing that my readers should impute this singularity.

One word is due in candour to the degree in which the study of contemporary writings may have tinged my composition, for such has been a topic of censure with regard to poems far more popular, and indeed more deservedly popular, than mine. It is impossible that anyone who inhabits the same age with such writers as those who stand in the foremost ranks of our own can conscientiously assure himself that his language and tone of thought may not have been modified by the study of the productions of those extraordinary intellects. It is true that not the spirit of their genius but the forms in which it has manifested itself are due less to the peculiarities of their own minds than to the peculiarity of the moral and intellectual condition of the minds among which they have been produced. Thus a number of writers possess the form whilst they want the spirit of those whom, it is alleged, they imitate; because the former is the endowment of the age in which they live, and the latter must be the uncommunicative lightning of their own mind.

The peculiar style of intense and comprehensive imagery which distinguishes the modern literature of England has not been, as a general power, the product of the imitation of any particular writer. The mass of capabilities remains at every period materially the same; the circumstances which awaken it to action perpetually change. If England were divided into forty republics, each equal in population and extent to Athens, there is no reason to suppose but that, under institutions not more perfect than those of Athens, each would produce philosophers and poets equal to those who (if we except Shakespeare) have never been surpassed. We owe the great writers of the golden age of our literature to that fervid awakening of the public mind which shook to dust the oldest and most oppressive form of the Christian religion. We owe Milton to the progress and development of the same spirit: the sacred Milton was, let it ever be remembered, a republican, and a bold enquirer into morals and religion. The great writers of our own age are, we have reason to suppose, the companions and forerunners of some unimagined change in our social condition or the opinions which cement it. The cloud of mind is discharging its collected lightning, and the equilibrium between institutions and opinions is now restoring, or is about to be restored.

As to imitation, poetry is a mimetic art. It creates, but it creates by combination and representation. Poetical abstractions are beautiful and new, not because the portions of which they are composed had no previous existence in the mind of man or in nature, but because the whole produced by their combination has some intelligible and beautiful analogy with those sources of emotion and thought, and with the contemporary condition of them: one great poet is a masterpiece of nature which another not only ought to study but must study. He might as wisely and as easily determine that his mind should no longer be the mirror of all that is lovely in the visible universe, as exclude from his contemplation the beautiful which exists in the writings of a great contemporary. The pretence of doing it would be a presumption in any but the greatest; the effect, even in him, would be strained, unnatural, and ineffectual. A poet is the combined product of such internal powers as modify the nature of others; and of such external influences as excite and sustain these powers; he is not one, but both. Every man's mind is, in this respect, modified by all the objects of nature and art; by every word and every suggestion which he ever admitted to act upon his consciousness; it is the mirror upon which all forms are reflected, and in which they compose one form. Poets, not otherwise than philosophers, painters, sculptors, and musicians, are, in one sense, the creators, and, in another, the creations, of their age. From this subjection the loftiest do not escape. There is a similarity between Homer and Hesiod, between Aeschylus and Euripides, between Virgil and Horace, between Dante and Petrarch, between Shakespeare and Fletcher, between Dryden and Pope; each has a generic resemblance under which their specific distinctions are arranged. If this similarity be the result of imitation, I am willing to confess that I have imitated.

Let this opportunity be conceded to me of acknowledging that I have what a Scotch philosopher characteristically terms, 'a passion for reforming the world': what passion incited him to write and publish his book, he omits to explain. For my part I had rather be damned with Plato and Lord Bacon, than go to Heaven with Paley and Malthus.[77] But it is a mistake to suppose that I dedicate my poetical compositions solely to the direct enforcement of reform, or that I consider them in any degree as containing a reasoned system on the theory of human life. Didactic poetry is my abhorrence; nothing can be equally well expressed in prose that is not tedious and supererogatory in verse. My purpose has hitherto been simply to familiarise the highly refined imagination of the more select classes of poetical readers with beautiful idealisms of moral excellence; aware that until the mind can love, and admire, and trust, and hope, and endure, reasoned principles of moral conduct are seeds cast upon the highway of life which the unconscious passenger tramples into dust, although they would bear the harvest of his happiness. Should I live to accomplish what I purpose, that is, produce a systematical history of what appear to me to be the genuine elements of human society, let not the advocates of injustice and superstition flatter themselves that I should take Aeschylus rather than Plato as my model.

The having spoken of myself with unaffected freedom will need little apology with the candid; and let the uncandid consider that they injure me less than their own hearts and minds by misrepresentation. Whatever talents a person may possess to amuse and instruct others, be they ever so inconsiderable, he is yet bound to exert them: if his attempt be ineffectual, let the punishment of an unaccomplished purpose have been sufficient; let none trouble themselves to heap the dust of oblivion upon his efforts; the pile they raise will betray his grave which might otherwise have been unknown.

DRAMATIS PERSONAE

PROMETHEUS
APOLLO
DEMOGORGON
MERCURY
HERCULES
JUPITER
THE EARTH
OCEAN
ASIA ⎫
PANTHEA ⎬ *Oceanides*
IONE ⎭
THE PHANTASM OF JUPITER
THE SPIRIT OF EARTH
THE SPIRIT OF THE MOON
SPIRITS OF THE HOURS
SPIRITS, ECHOES, FAUNS, FURIES

ACT I

SCENE: *A ravine of icy rocks in the Indian Caucasus.* PROMETHEUS *is discovered bound to the precipice.* PANTHEA *and* IONE *are seated at his feet. Time: night. During the scene, morning slowly breaks.*

Prometheus Monarch of Gods and Demons, and all Spirits
     But One, who throng those bright and rolling worlds
     Which Thou and I alone of living things
     Behold with sleepless eyes! regard this Earth
     Made multitudinous with thy slaves, whom thou
     Requitest for knee-worship, prayer, and praise,
     And toil, and hecatombs of broken hearts,
     With fear and self-contempt and barren hope.
     Whilst me, who am thy foe, eyeless in hate,
     Hast thou made reign and triumph, to thy scorn,   10
     O'er mine own misery and thy vain revenge.
     Three thousand years of sleep-unsheltered hours,
     And moments aye divided by keen pangs

Till they seemed years, torture and solitude,
Scorn and despair, – these are mine empire.
More glorious far than that which thou surveyest
From thine unenvied throne, O Mighty God!
Almighty, had I deigned to share the shame
Of thine ill tyranny, and hung not here
Nailed to this wall of eagle-baffling mountain,   20
Black, wintry, dead, unmeasured; without herb,
Insect, or beast, or shape or sound of life.
Ah me! alas, pain, pain ever, for ever!

No change, no pause, no hope! Yet I endure.
I ask the Earth, have not the mountains felt?
I ask yon Heaven, the all-beholding Sun,
Has it not seen? The Sea, in storm or calm,
Heaven's ever-changing Shadow, spread below,
Have its deaf waves not heard my agony?
Ah me! alas, pain, pain ever, for ever!   30

The crawling glaciers pierce me with the spears
Of their moon-freezing chrystals, the bright chains
Eat with their burning cold into my bones.
Heaven's winged hound, polluting from thy lips
His beak in poison not his own, tears up
My heart; and shapeless sights come wandering by,
The ghastly people of the realm of dream,
Mocking me: and the Earthquake-fiends are charged
To wrench the rivets from my quivering wounds
When the rocks split and close again behind: 40
While from their loud abysses howling throng
The genii of the storm, urging the rage
Of whirlwind, and afflict me with keen hail.
And yet to me welcome is day and night,
Whether one breaks the hoar frost of the morn,
Or starry, dim, and slow, the other climbs
The leaden-coloured east; for then they lead
The wingless, crawling hours, one among whom
– As some dark Priest hales the reluctant victim –
Shall drag thee, cruel King, to kiss the blood   50
From these pale feet, which then might trample thee

If they disdained not such a prostrate slave.
Disdain! Ah no! I pity thee. What ruin
Will hunt thee undefended thro' wide Heaven!
How will thy soul, cloven to its depth with terror,
Gape like a hell within! I speak in grief,
Not exultation, for I hate no more,
As then ere misery made me wise. The curse
Once breathed on thee I would recall. Ye Mountains,
Whose many-voiced Echoes, through the mist   60
Of cataracts, flung the thunder of that spell!
Ye icy Springs, stagnant with wrinkling frost,
Which vibrated to hear me, and then crept
Shuddering thro' India! Thou serenest Air,[78]
Thro' which the Sun walks burning without beams!
And ye swift Whirlwinds, who on poised wings
Hung mute and moveless o'er yon hushed abyss,
As thunder, louder than your own, made rock
The orbed world! If then my words had power,
Though I am changed so that aught evil wish   70
Is dead within; although no memory be
Of what is hate, let them not lose it now!
What was that curse? for ye all heard me speak.

First Voice from the mountains

Thrice three hundred thousand years
    O'er the Earthquake's couch we stood:
Oft, as men convulsed with fears,
    We trembled in our multitude.

Second Voice from the springs

Thunderbolts had parched our water,
    We had been stained with bitter blood,
And had run mute, 'mid shrieks of slaughter,   80
    Thro' a city and a solitude.

Third Voice from the air

I had clothed, since Earth uprose,
    Its wastes in colours not their own,
And oft had my serene repose
    Been cloven by many a rending groan.

Fourth Voice from the whirlwinds

We had soared beneath these mountains
   Unresting ages; nor had thunder,
Nor yon volcano's flaming fountains,
   Nor any power above or under,
   Ever made us mute with wonder.   90

First Voice

But never bowed our snowy crest
As at the voice of thine unrest.

Second Voice

Never such a sound before
To the Indian waves we bore.
A pilot asleep on the howling sea
Leaped up from the deck in agony,
And heard, and cried, 'Ah, woe is me!'
And died as mad as the wild waves be.

Third Voice

By such dread words from Earth to Heaven
My still realm was never riven: 100
When its wound was closed, there stood
Darkness o'er the day like blood.

Fourth Voice

And we shrank back: for dreams of ruin
To frozen caves our flight pursuing
Made us keep silence – thus – and thus –
Though silence is as hell to us.

The Earth   The tongueless Caverns of the craggy hills
Cried, 'Misery!' then; the hollow Heaven replied,
'Misery!' And the Ocean's purple waves,
Climbing the land, howled to the lashing winds,   110
And the pale nations heard it, 'Misery!'

Prometheus   I heard a sound of voices: not the voice
Which I gave forth. Mother, thy sons and thou
Scorn him, without whose all-enduring will
Beneath the fierce omnipotence of Jove,

Both they and thou had vanished, like thin mist
Unrolled on the morning wind. Know ye not me,
The Titan? He who made his agony
The barrier to your else all-conquering foe?
Oh, rock-embosomed lawns, and snow-fed streams,   120
Now seen athwart frore vapours, deep below,
Through whose o'ershadowing woods I wandered once
With Asia, drinking life from her loved eyes;
Why scorns the spirit which informs ye, now
To commune with me? me alone, who check'd,
As one who checks a fiend-drawn charioteer,
The falsehood and the force of him who reigns
Supreme, and with the groans of pining slaves
Fills your dim glens and liquid wildernesses:
Why answer ye not, still? Brethren!

The Earth   They dare not.   130
Prometheus   Who dares? for I would hear that curse again.
Ha, what an awful whisper rises up!
'Tis scarce like sound: it tingles thro' the frame
As lightning tingles, hovering ere it strike.
Speak, Spirit! from thine inorganic voice
I only know that thou art moving near
And love. How cursed I him?

The Earth   How canst thou hear
Who knowest not the language of the dead?
Prometheus   Thou art a living spirit; speak as they.
The Earth   I dare not speak like life, lest Heaven's fell King   140
Should hear, and link me to some wheel of pain
More torturing than the one whereon I roll.
Subtle thou art and good, and tho' the Gods
Hear not this voice, yet thou art more than God
Being wise and kind: earnestly hearken now.
Prometheus   Obscurely thro' my brain, like shadows dim,
Sweep awful thoughts, rapid and thick. I feel
Faint, like one mingled in entwining love;
Yet 'tis not pleasure.

The Earth   No, thou canst not hear:
Thou art immortal, and this tongue is known   150
Only to those who die.

Prometheus   And what art thou,

O melancholy Voice?

The Earth   I am the Earth,
Thy mother; she within whose stony veins,
To the last fibre of the loftiest tree
Whose thin leaves trembled in the frozen air,
Joy ran, as blood within a living frame,
When thou didst from her bosom, like a cloud
Of glory, arise, a spirit of keen joy!
And at thy voice her pining sons uplifted
Their prostrate brows from the polluting dust,   160
And our almighty Tyrant with fierce dread
Grew pale, until his thunder chained thee here.
Then, see those million worlds which burn and roll
Around us: their inhabitants beheld
My sphered light wane in wide Heaven; the sea
Was lifted by strange tempest, and new fire
From earthquake-rifted mountains of bright snow
Shook its portentous hair beneath Heaven's frown;
Lightning and Inundation vexed the plains;
Blue thistles bloomed in cities; foodless toads   170
Within voluptuous chambers panting crawled:
When Plague had fallen on man, and beast, and worm,
And Famine; and black blight on herb and tree;
And in the corn, and vines, and meadow-grass,
Teemed ineradicable poisonous weeds
Draining their growth, for my wan breast was dry
With grief; and the thin air, my breath, was stained
With the contagion of a mother's hate
Breathed on her child's destroyer; aye, I heard
Thy curse, the which, if thou rememberest not,   180
Yet my innumerable seas and streams,
Mountains, and caves, and winds, and yon wide air,
And the inarticulate people of the dead,
Preserve, a treasured spell. We meditate
In secret joy and hope those dreadful words
But dare not speak them.

Prometheus   Venerable mother!
All else who live and suffer take from thee
Some comfort; flowers, and fruits, and happy sounds,
And love, though fleeting; these may not be mine.

	But mine own words, I pray, deny me not.	190
The Earth	They shall be told. Ere Babylon was dust,	

The Earth But mine own words, I pray, deny me not.   190
They shall be told. Ere Babylon was dust,
The Magus Zoroaster,[79] my dead child,
Met his own image walking in the garden.
That apparition, sole of men, he saw.
For know there are two worlds of life and death:
One that which thou beholdest; but the other
Is underneath the grave, where do inhabit
The shadows of all forms that think and live
Till death unite them and they part no more;
Dreams and the light imaginings of men,   200
And all that faith creates or love desires,
Terrible, strange, sublime and beauteous shapes.
There thou art, and dost hang, a writhing shade,
'Mid whirlwind-peopled mountains; all the gods
Are there, and all the powers of nameless worlds,
Vast, sceptred phantoms; heroes, men, and beasts;
And Demogorgon, a tremendous gloom;
And he, the supreme Tyrant, on his throne
Of burning gold. Son, one of these shall utter
The curse which all remember. Call at will   210
Thine own ghost, or the ghost of Jupiter,
Hades or Typhon,[80] or what mightier Gods
From all-prolific Evil, since thy ruin,
Have sprung and trampled on my prostrate sons.
Ask, and they must reply: so the revenge
Of the Supreme may sweep thro' vacant shades,
As rainy wind thro' the abandoned gate
Of a fallen palace.

Prometheus   Mother, let not aught
Of that which may be evil, pass again
My lips, or those of aught resembling me.   220
Phantasm of Jupiter, arise, appear!

Ione

My wings are folded o'er mine ears:
    My wings are crossed o'er mine eyes:
Yet thro' their silver shade appears,
    And thro' their lulling plumes arise,
A Shape, a throng of sounds;

> May it be no ill to thee,
>   O thou of many wounds!
> Near whom, for our sweet sister's sake,
> Ever thus we watch and wake.   230

Panthea

> The sound is of whirlwind underground,
>   Earthquake, and fire, and mountains cloven;
> The shape is awful like the sound,
>   Clothed in dark purple, star-inwoven.
> A sceptre of pale gold
>   To stay steps proud, o'er the slow cloud
> His veined hand doth hold.
> Cruel he looks, but calm and strong,
> Like one who does, not suffers wrong.

Phantasm of Jupiter	Why have the secret powers of this strange world 240 Driven me, a frail and empty phantom, hither On direst storms? What unaccustomed sounds Are hovering on my lips, unlike the voice With which our pallid race hold ghastly talk In darkness? And, proud sufferer, who art thou?
Prometheus	Tremendous Image, as thou art must be He whom thou shadowest forth. I am his foe, The Titan. Speak the words which I would hear, Although no thought inform thine empty voice.
The Earth	Listen! And tho' your echoes must be mute, 250 Grey mountains, and old woods, and haunted springs, Prophetic caves, and isle-surrounding streams, Rejoice to hear what yet ye cannot speak.
Phantasm	A spirit seizes me and speaks within: It tears me as fire tears a thundercloud.
Panthea	See, how he lifts his mighty looks, the Heaven Darkens above.
Ione	He speaks! O shelter me!
Prometheus	I see the curse on gestures proud and cold, And looks of firm defiance, and calm hate, And such despair as mocks itself with smiles, 260 Written as on a scroll: yet speak: Oh, speak!

Phantasm

Fiend, I defy thee! with a calm, fixed mind,
　　All that thou canst inflict I bid thee do;
Foul Tyrant both of Gods and Humankind,
　　One only being shalt thou not subdue.
Rain then thy plagues upon me here,
Ghastly disease, and frenzying fear;
And let alternate frost and fire
Eat into me, and be thine ire
Lightning, and cutting hail, and legioned forms   270
Of furies, driving by upon the wounding storms.

Aye, do thy worst. Thou art omnipotent.
　　O'er all things but thyself I gave thee power,
And my own will. Be thy swift mischiefs sent
　　To blast mankind, from yon ethereal tower.
Let thy malignant spirit move
In darkness over those I love:
On me and mine I imprecate
The utmost torture of thy hate;
And thus devote to sleepless agony,   280
This undeclining head while thou must reign on high.

But thou, who art the God and Lord: O thou,
　　Who fillest with thy soul this world of woe,
To whom all things of Earth and Heaven do bow
　　In fear and worship: all-prevailing foe!
I curse thee! let a sufferer's curse
Clasp thee, his torturer, like remorse;
Till thine Infinity shall be
A robe of envenomed agony;
And thine Omnipotence a crown of pain,   290
To cling like burning gold round thy dissolving brain.

Heap on thy soul, by virtue of this Curse,
　　Ill deeds, then be thou damned, beholding good;
Both infinite as is the universe,
　　And thou, and thy self-torturing solitude.
An awful image of calm power
Though now thou sittest, let the hour

     Come, when thou must appear to be
     That which thou art internally.
     And after many a false and fruitless crime   300
     Scorn track thy lagging fall thro' boundless space and time.

Prometheus   Were these my words, O Parent?
The Earth   They were thine.
Prometheus   It doth repent me: words are quick and vain;
     Grief for awhile is blind and so was mine.
     I wish no living thing to suffer pain.

The Earth

     Misery, Oh misery to me,
     That Jove at length should vanquish thee.
     Wail, howl aloud, Land and Sea,
     The Earth's rent heart shall answer ye.
     Howl, Spirits of the living and the dead,   310
     Your refuge, your defence lies fallen and vanquished.

First Echo

     Lies fallen and vanquished!

Second Echo

     Fallen and vanquished!

Ione

     Fear not: 'tis but some passing spasm,
       The Titan is unvanquished still.
     But see, where thro' the azure chasm
       Of yon forked and snowy hill
     Trampling the slant winds on high
       With golden-sandalled feet, that glow
     Under plumes of purple dye,   320
     Like rose-ensanguined ivory,
       A Shape comes now,
     Stretching on high from his right hand
     A serpent-cinctured wand.

Panthea   'Tis Jove's world-wandering herald, Mercury.

Ione

And who are those with hydra tresses
   And iron wings that climb the wind,
Whom the frowning God represses
   Like vapours steaming up behind,
Clanging loud, an endless crowd –   330

Panthea

   These are Jove's tempest-walking hounds,
Whom he gluts with groans and blood,
   When charioted on sulphurous cloud
     He bursts Heaven's bounds.

Ione

Are they now led, from the thin dead
On new pangs to be fed?

Panthea	The Titan looks as ever, firm, not proud.
First Fury	Ha! I scent life!
Second Fury	Let me but look into his eyes!
Third Fury	The hope of torturing him smells like a heap

Of corpses, to a death-bird after battle.   340

First Fury   Darest thou delay, O Herald! take cheer, Hounds
Of Hell: what if the Son of Maia[81] soon
Should make us food and sport – who can please long
The Omnipotent?

Mercury   Back to your towers of iron,
And gnash, beside the streams of fire and wail,[82]
Your foodless teeth. Geryon, arise! and Gorgon,
Chimaera, and thou Sphinx,[83] subtlest of fiends
Who ministered to Thebes Heaven's poisoned wine,
Unnatural love, and more unnatural hate:
These shall perform your task.

First Fury   Oh, mercy! mercy!   350
We die with our desire: drive us not back!

Mercury   Crouch then in silence.
                Awful Sufferer!
To thee unwilling, most unwillingly
I come, by the great Father's will driven down,

To execute a doom of new revenge.
Alas! I pity thee, and hate myself
That I can do no more: aye from thy sight
Returning, for a season, heaven seems hell,
So thy worn form pursues me night and day,
Smiling reproach. Wise art thou, firm and good,   360
But vainly wouldst stand forth alone in strife
Against the Omnipotent; as yon clear lamps
That measure and divide the weary years
From which there is no refuge, long have taught
And long must teach. Even now thy Torturer arms
With the strange might of unimagined pains
The powers who scheme slow agonies in Hell,
And my commission is to lead them here,
Or what more subtle, foul, or savage fiends
People the abyss, and leave them to their task.   370
Be it not so! there is a secret known
To thee, and to none else of living things,
Which may transfer the sceptre of wide Heaven,
The fear of which perplexes the Supreme:
Clothe it in words, and bid it clasp his throne
In intercession; bend thy soul in prayer,
And like a suppliant in some gorgeous fane,
Let the will kneel within thy haughty heart:
For benefits and meek submission tame
The fiercest and the mightiest.

Prometheus   Evil minds   380
Change good to their own nature. I gave all
He has; and in return he chains me here
Years, ages, night and day: whether the Sun
Split my parched skin, or in the moony night
The chrystal-winged snow cling round my hair:
Whilst my beloved race is trampled down
By his thought-executing ministers.
Such is the tyrants' recompense: 'tis just:
He who is evil can receive no good;
And for a world bestowed, or a friend lost,   390
He can feel hate, fear, shame; not gratitude:
He but requites me for his own misdeed.
Kindness to such is keen reproach, which breaks

With bitter stings the light sleep of Revenge.
Submission, thou dost know I cannot try:
For what submission but that fatal word,
The death-seal of mankind's captivity,
Like the Sicilian's[84] hair-suspended sword,
Which trembles o'er his crown, would he accept,
Or could I yield? Which yet I will not yield.   400
Let others flatter Crime, where it sits throned
In brief Omnipotence: secure are they:
For Justice, when triumphant, will weep down
Pity, not punishment, on her own wrongs,
Too much avenged by those who err. I wait,
Enduring thus, the retributive hour
Which since we spake is even nearer now.
But hark, the hell-hounds clamour: fear delay:
Behold! Heaven lowers under thy Father's frown.

Mercury   Oh, that we might be spared: I to inflict   410
And thou to suffer! Once more answer me:
Thou knowest not the period of Jove's power?

Prometheus   I know but this, that it must come.

Mercury   Alas!
Thou canst not count thy years to come of pain?

Prometheus   They last while Jove must reign: nor more, nor less
Do I desire or fear.

Mercury   Yet pause, and plunge
Into Eternity, where recorded time,
Even all that we imagine, age on age,
Seems but a point, and the reluctant mind
Flags wearily in its unending flight,   420
Till it sink, dizzy, blind, lost, shelterless;
Perchance it has not numbered the slow years
Which thou must spend in torture, unreprieved?

Prometheus   Perchance no thought can count them, yet they pass.

Mercury   If thou might'st dwell among the Gods the while,
Lapped in voluptuous joy?

Prometheus   I would not quit
This bleak ravine, these unrepentant pains.

Mercury   Alas! I wonder at, yet pity thee.

Prometheus   Pity the self-despising slaves of Heaven,
Not me, within whose mind sits peace serene,   430

	As light in the sun, throned: how vain is talk!
	Call up the fiends.
Ione	O sister, look! White fire
	Has cloven to the roots yon huge snow-loaded cedar;
	How fearfully God's thunder howls behind!
Mercury	I must obey his words and thine: alas!
	Most heavily remorse hangs at my heart!
Panthea	See where the child of Heaven, with winged feet,
	Runs down the slanted sunlight of the dawn.
Ione	Dear sister, close thy plumes over thine eyes
	Lest thou behold and die: they come: they come
	Blackening the birth of day with countless wings,
	And hollow underneath, like death.
First Fury	Prometheus!
Second Fury	Immortal Titan!
Third Fury	Champion of Heaven's slaves'
Prometheus	He whom some dreadful voice invokes is here,
	Prometheus, the chained Titan. Horrible forms,
	What and who are ye? Never yet there came
	Phantasms so foul thro' monster-teeming Hell
	From the all-miscreative brain of Jove;
	Whilst I behold such execrable shapes,
	Methinks I grow like what I contemplate,
	And laugh and stare in loathsome sympathy.
First Fury	We are the ministers of pain, and fear,
	And disappointment, and mistrust, and hate,
	And clinging crime; and as lean dogs pursue
	Thro' wood and lake some struck and sobbing fawn,
	We track all things that weep, and bleed, and live,
	When the great King betrays them to our will.
Prometheus	Oh! many fearful natures in one name.
	I know ye; and these lakes and echoes know
	The darkness and the clangour of your wings.
	But why more hideous than your loathed selves
	Gather ye up in legions from the deep?
Second Fury	We knew not that: Sisters, rejoice, rejoice!
Prometheus	Can aught exult in its deformity?
Second Fury	The beauty of delight makes lovers glad,
	Gazing on one another: so are we.
	As from the rose which the pale priestess kneels

440

450

460

	To gather for her festal crown of flowers	
	The aerial crimson falls, flushing her cheek,	
	So from our victim's destined agony	470
	The shade which is our form invests us round,	
	Else we are shapeless as our mother Night.	

Prometheus   I laugh your power, and his who sent you here,
To lowest scorn. Pour forth the cup of pain.

First Fury   Thou thinkest we will rend thee bone from bone,
And nerve from nerve, working like fire within?

Prometheus   Pain is my element, as hate is thine;
Ye rend me now: I care not.

Second Fury   Dost imagine
We will but laugh into thy lidless eyes?

Prometheus   I weigh not what ye do, but what ye suffer, 480
Being evil. Cruel was the power which called
You, or aught else so wretched, into light.

Third Fury   Thou think'st we will live thro' thee, one by one,
Like animal life, and tho' we can obscure not
The soul which burns within, that we will dwell
Beside it, like a vain loud multitude
Vexing the self-content of wisest men:
That we will be dread thought beneath thy brain,
And foul desire round thine astonished heart,
And blood within thy labyrinthine veins 490
Crawling like agony.

Prometheus   Why, ye are thus now;
Yet am I king over myself, and rule
The torturing and conflicting throngs within,
As Jove rules you when Hell grows mutinous.

Chorus of Furies

From the ends of the earth, from the ends of the earth,
Where the night has its grave and the morning its birth,
                    Come, come, come!
O ye who shake hills with the scream of your mirth,
When cities sink howling in ruin; and ye
Who with wingless footsteps trample the sea, 500
And close upon Shipwreck and Famine's track,
Sit chattering with joy on the foodless wreck;
                    Come, come, come!

Leave the bed, low, cold, and red,
Strewed beneath a nation dead;
Leave the hatred, as in ashes
   Fire is left for future burning:
It will burst in bloodier flashes
   When ye stir it, soon returning:
Leave the self-contempt implanted   510
In young spirits, sense-enchanted,
   Misery's yet unkindled fuel:
Leave Hell's secrets half unchanted
   To the maniac dreamer; cruel
More than ye can be with hate
   Is he with fear.
      Come! come, come!
We are steaming up from Hell's wide gate
   And we burthen the blasts of the atmosphere,
   But vainly we toil till ye come here.   520

Ione   Sister, I hear the thunder of new wings.
Panthea These solid mountains quiver with the sound
Even as the tremulous air: their shadows make
The space within my plumes more black than night.

First Fury

Your call was as a winged car
Driven on whirlwinds fast and far;
It rapt us from red gulfs of war.

Second Fury

From wide cities, famine-wasted;

Third Fury

Groans half heard, and blood untasted;

Fourth Fury

Kingly conclaves stern and cold,   530
Where blood with gold is bought and sold;

Fifth Fury

From the furnace, white and hot,
In which —

A Fury

Speak not: whisper not:
I know all that ye would tell,
But to speak might break the spell
Which must bend the Invincible,
 The stern of thought;
He yet defies the deepest power of Hell.

A Fury

Tear the veil!

Another Fury

It is torn.

Chorus

    The pale stars of the morn
Shine on a misery, dire to be borne.   540
Dost thou faint, mighty Titan? We laugh thee to scorn.
Dost thou boast the clear knowledge thou waken'dst for man?
Then was kindled within him a thirst which outran
Those perishing waters; a thirst of fierce fever,
Hope, love, doubt, desire, which consume him for ever.
  One came forth of gentle worth
  Smiling on the sanguine earth;
  His words outlived him, like swift poison
   Withering up truth, peace, and pity.
  Look! where round the wide horizon   550
   Many a million-peopled city
   Vomits smoke in the bright air.
  Hark that outcry of despair!
  'Tis his mild and gentle ghost
   Wailing for the faith he kindled:
  Look again, the flames almost
   To a glow-worms lamp have dwindled:
The survivors round the embers
  Gather in dread.
       Joy, joy, joy!   560
Past ages crowd on thee, but each one remembers.
And the future is dark, and the present is spread
Like a pillow of thorns for thy slumberless head.

Semichorus 1

Drops of bloody agony flow
From his white and quivering brow.
Grant a little respite now:
See a disenchanted nation
Springs like day from desolation;
To truth its state is dedicate,
And Freedom leads it forth, her mate;   570
A legioned band of linked brothers
Whom Love calls children –

Semichorus II

'Tis another's:
See how kindred murder kin:
'Tis the vintage-time for death and sin:
Blood, like new wine, bubbles within:
'Till Despair smothers
The struggling world, which slaves and tyrants win.

[*All the* FURIES *vanish, except one.*

Ione   Hark, sister! what a low yet dreadful groan
           Quite unsuppressed is tearing up the heart
           Of the good Titan, as storms tear the deep,   580
           And beasts hear the sea moan in inland caves.
           Darest thou observe how the fiends torture him?

Panthea   Alas! I looked forth twice, but will no more.

Ione   What didst thou see?

Panthea   A woeful sight: a youth
           With patient looks nailed to a crucifix.

Ione   What next?

Panthea   The heaven around, the earth below
           Was peopled with thick shapes of human death,
           All horrible, and wrought by human hands,
           And some appeared the work of human hearts,
           For men were slowly killed by frowns and smiles: 590
           And other sights too foul to speak and live
           Were wandering by. Let us not tempt worse fear
           By looking forth: those groans are grief enough.

Fury   Behold an emblem: those who do endure
           Deep wrongs for man, and scorn, and chains, but heap
           Thousandfold torment on themselves and him.

Prometheus	Remit the anguish of that lighted stare;
	Close those wan lips; let that thorn-wounded brow
	Stream not with blood; it mingles with thy tears!
	Fix, fix those tortured orbs in peace and death, 600
	So thy sick throes shake not that crucifix,
	So those pale fingers play not with thy gore.
	O, horrible! Thy name I will not speak,
	It hath become a curse. I see, I see
	The wise, the mild, the lofty, and the just,
	Whom thy slaves hate for being like to thee,
	Some hunted by foul lies from their heart's homes,
	An early-chosen, late-lamented home;
	As hooded ounces cling to the driven hind;
	Some linked to corpses in unwholesome cells: 610
	Some – Hear I not the multitude laugh loud? –
	Impaled in lingering fire: and mighty realms
	Float by my feet, like sea-uprooted isles,
	Whose sons are kneaded down in common blood
	By the red light of their own burning homes.
Fury	Blood thou canst see, and fire; and canst heal groans;
	Worse things, unheard, unseen, remain behind.
Prometheus	Worse?
Fury	In each human heart terror survives
	The ravin it has gorged: the loftiest fear
	All that they would disdain to think were true: 620
	Hypocrisy and custom make their minds
	The fanes of many a worship, now outworn.
	They dare not devise good for man's estate,
	And yet they know not that they do not dare.
	The good want power, but to weep barren tears.
	The powerful goodness want: worse need for them.
	The wise want love; and those who love want wisdom;
	And all best things are thus confused to ill.
	Many are strong and rich, and would be just,
	But live among their suffering fellow-men 630
	As if none felt: they know not what they do.
Prometheus	Thy words are like a cloud of winged snakes;
	And yet I pity those they torture not.
Fury	Thou pitiest them? I speak no more! [*Vanishes.*
Prometheus	Ah woe!

Ah woe! Alas! pain, pain ever, for ever!
I close my tearless eyes, but see more clear
Thy works within my woe-illumed mind,
Thou subtle tyrant! Peace is in the grave.
The grave hides all things beautiful and good:
I am a God and cannot find it there,   640
Nor would I seek it: for, though dread revenge,
This is defeat, fierce king, not victory.
The sights with which thou torturest gird my soul
With new endurance, till the hour arrives
When they shall be no types of things which are.

Panthea   Alas! what sawest thou more?

Prometheus   There are two woes;
To speak, and to behold; thou spare me one.
Names are there, Nature's sacred watchwords, they
Were borne aloft in bright emblazonry;
The nations thronged around, and cried aloud,   650
As with one voice, Truth, liberty, and love!
Suddenly fierce confusion fell from heaven
Among them: there was strife, deceit, and fear:
Tyrants rushed in, and did divide the spoil.
This was the shadow of the truth I saw.

The Earth   I felt thy torture, son, with such mixed joy
As pain and virtue give. To cheer thy state
I bid ascend those subtle and fair spirits,
Whose homes are the dim caves of human thought,
And who inhabit, as birds wing the wind,   660
Its world-surrounding ether: they behold
Beyond that twilight realm, as in a glass,
The future: may they speak comfort to thee!

Panthea   Look, sister, where a troop of spirits gather,
Like flocks of clouds in spring's delightful weather,
Thronging in the blue air!

Ione   And see! more come,
Like fountain-vapours when the winds are dumb,
That climb up the ravine in scattered lines.
And, hark! is it the music of the pines?
Is it the lake? Is it the waterfall?   670

Panthea   'Tis something sadder, sweeter far than all.

Chorus of Spirits

From unremembered ages we
Gentle guides and guardians be
Of heaven-oppressed mortality;
And we breathe, and sicken not,
The atmosphere of human thought:
Be it dim, and dank, and grey,
Like a storm-extinguished day,
Travelled o'er by dying gleams;
  Be it bright as all between   680
Cloudless skies and windless streams,
  Silent, liquid, and serene;
As the birds within the wind,
  As the fish within the wave,
As the thoughts of man's own mind
  Float thro' all above the grave;
We make there our liquid lair,
Voyaging cloudlike and unpent
Thro' the boundless element:
Thence we bear the prophecy   690
Which begins and ends in thee!

Ione   More yet come, one by one: the air around them
Looks radiant as the air around a star.

First Spirit

On a battle-trumpet's blast
I fled hither, fast, fast, fast,
'Mid the darkness upward cast.
From the dust of creeds outworn,
From the tyrant's banner torn,
Gathering 'round me, onward borne.
There was mingled many a cry –   700
Freedom! Hope! Death! Victory!
Till they faded thro' the sky;
And one sound, above, around,
One sound beneath, around, above,
Was moving; 'twas the soul of love:
'Twas the hope, the prophecy,
Which begins and ends in thee.

Second Spirit

A rainbow's arch stood on the sea,
Which rocked beneath, immovably;
And the triumphant storm did flee,   710
Like a conqueror, swift and proud,
Between with many a captive cloud
A shapeless, dark and rapid crowd,
Each by lightning riven in half:
I heard the thunder hoarsely laugh:
Mighty fleets were strewn like chaff
And spread beneath a hell of death
O'er the white waters. I alit
On a great ship lightning-split,
And speeded hither on the sigh   720
Of one who gave an enemy
His plank, then plunged aside to die.

Third Spirit

I sate beside a sage's bed,
And the lamp was burning red
Near the book where he had fed,
When a Dream with plumes of flame
To his pillow hovering came,
And I knew it was the same
Which had kindled long ago
Pity, eloquence, and woe;   730
And the world awhile below
Wore the shade its lustre made.
It has borne me here as fleet
As Desire's lightning feet:
I must ride it back ere morrow,
Or the sage will wake in sorrow.

Fourth Spirit

On a poet's lips I slept
Dreaming like a love-adept
In the sound his breathing kept;
Nor seeks nor finds he mortal blisses,   740
But feeds on the aerial kisses
Of shapes that haunt thought's wildernesses.

He will watch from dawn to gloom
The lake-reflected sun illume
The yellow bees in the ivy-bloom,
Nor heed, nor see, what things they be;
But from these create he can
Forms more real than living man,
Nurslings of immortality!
One of these awakened me,   750
And I sped to succour thee.

Ione

Behold'st thou not two shapes from the east and west
Come, as two doves to one beloved nest,
Twin nurslings of the all-sustaining air
On swift still wings glide down the atmosphere?
And hark! their sweet, sad voices! 'tis despair
Mingled with love and then dissolved in sound.

Panthea   Canst thou speak, sister? all my words are drowned.
Ione   Their beauty gives me voice. See how they float
            On their sustaining wings of skiey grain,   760
            Orange and azure deepening into gold:
            Their soft smiles light the air like a star's fire.

Chorus of Spirits

Hast thou beheld the form of Love?

Fifth Spirit

                        As over wide dominions
I sped, like some swift cloud that wings the wide
                                    air's wildernesses,
That planet-crested shape swept by on lightning-braided
                                    pinions,
    Scattering the liquid joy of life from his ambrosial tresses:
His footsteps paved the world with light; but as I past
                                    'twas fading,
    And hollow Ruin yawned behind: great sages bound
                                    in madness,
And headless patriots, and pale youths who perished,
                                    unupbraiding,

Gleamed in the night. I wandered o'er, till thou,
                              O King of sadness,   770
Turned by thy smile the worst I saw to recollected
                                        gladness.

Sixth Spirit

Ah, sister! Desolation is a delicate thing:
   It walks not on the earth, it floats not on the air,
But treads with lulling footstep, and fans with silent wing
   The tender hopes which in their hearts the best
                              and gentlest bear;
Who, soothed to false repose by the fanning plumes above
   And the music-stirring motion of its soft and busy feet,
Dream visions of aerial joy, and call the monster, Love,
   And wake, and find the shadow Pain, as he whom
                              now we greet.

Chorus

Tho' Ruin now Love's shadow be,   780
Following him, destroyingly,
   On Death's white and winged steed,
Which the fleetest cannot flee,
   Trampling down both flower and weed,
Man and beast, and foul and fair,
Like a tempest thro' the air;
Thou shalt quell this horseman grim,
Woundless though in heart or limb.

Prometheus   Spirits! how know ye this shall be?

Chorus

In the atmosphere we breathe,   790
As buds grow red when the snowstorms flee,
   From spring gathering up beneath,
Whose mild winds shake the elder brake,
And the wandering herdsmen know
That the white-thorn soon will blow:
      Wisdom, Justice, Love, and Peace,
      When they struggle to increase,
         Are to us as soft winds be

    To shepherd boys, the prophecy
    Which begins and ends in thee.   800

Ione   Where are the Spirits fled?
Panthea   Only a sense
    Remains of them, like the omnipotence
    Of music, when the inspired voice and lute
    Languish, ere yet the responses are mute,
    Which thro' the deep and labyrinthine soul,
    Like echoes thro' long caverns, wind and roll.
Prometheus How fair these air-born shapes! and yet I feel
    Most vain all hope but love; and thou art far,
    Asia! who, when my being overflowed,
    Wert like a golden chalice to bright wine   810
    Which else had sunk into the thirsty dust.
    All things are still: alas! how heavily
    This quiet morning weighs upon my heart;
    Tho' I should dream I could even sleep with grief
    If slumber were denied not. I would fain
    Be what it is my destiny to be,
    The saviour and the strength of suffering man,
    Or sink into the original gulf of things:
    There is no agony, and no solace left;
    Earth can console, Heaven can torment no more. 820
Panthea Hast thou forgotten one who watches thee
    The cold dark night, and never sleeps but when
    The shadow of thy spirit falls on her?
Prometheus I said all hope was vain but love: thou lovest.
Panthea Deeply in truth; but the eastern star looks white,
    And Asia waits in that far Indian vale
    The scene of her sad exile; rugged once
    And desolate and frozen, like this ravine;
    But now invested with fair flowers and herbs,
    And haunted by sweet airs and sounds, which flow 830
    Among the woods and waters, from the ether
    Of her transforming presence, which would fade
    If it were mingled not with thine. Farewell!

END OF THE FIRST ACT

ACT 2, SCENE 1

Morning. A lovely vale in the Indian Caucasus. ASIA *alone.*

Asia   From all the blasts of heaven thou hast descended:
              Yes, like a spirit, like a thought, which makes
              Unwonted tears throng to the horny eyes,
              And beatings haunt the desolated heart,
              Which should have learnt repose: thou hast descended
              Cradled in tempests; thou dost wake, O Spring!
              O child of many winds! As suddenly
              Thou comest as the memory of a dream,
              Which now is sad because it hath been sweet;
              Like genius, or like joy which riseth up   10
              As from the earth, clothing with golden clouds
              The desert of our life.
              This is the season, this the day, the hour;
              At sunrise thou shouldst come, sweet sister mine,
              Too long desired, too long delaying, come!
              How like death-worms the wingless moments crawl!
              The point of one white star is quivering still
              Deep in the orange light of widening morn
              Beyond the purple mountains: thro' a chasm
              Of wind-divided mist the darker lake   20
              Reflects it: now it wanes: it gleams again
              As the waves fade, and as the burning threads
              Of woven cloud unravel in pale air:
              'Tis lost! and thro' yon peaks of cloudlike snow
              The roseate sunlight quivers: hear I not
              The Aeolian music of her sea-green plumes
              Winnowing the crimson dawn?   [PANTHEA *enters*
                                        I feel, I see
              Those eyes which burn thro' smiles that fade in tears,
              Like stars half quenched in mists of silver dew.
              Beloved and most beautiful, who wearest   30
              The shadow of that soul by which I live,
              How late thou art! the sphered sun had climbed
              The sea; my heart was sick with hope, before
              The printless air felt thy belated plumes.

Panthea	Pardon, great Sister! but my wings were faint
	With the delight of a remembered dream,
	As are the noontide plumes of summer winds
	Satiate with sweet flowers. I was wont to sleep
	Peacefully, and awake refreshed and calm
	Before the sacred Titan's fall, and thy

40

Unhappy love, had made, thro' use and pity,
Both love and woe familiar to my heart
As they had grown to thine: erewhile I slept
Under the glaucous caverns of old Ocean
Within dim bowers of green and purple moss,
Our young Ione's soft and milky arms
Locked then, as now, behind my dark, moist hair,
While my shut eyes and cheek were pressed within
The folded depth of her life-breathing bosom:
But not as now, since I am made the wind

50

Which fails beneath the music that I bear
Of thy most wordless converse; since dissolved
Into the sense with which love talks, my rest
Was troubled and yet sweet; my waking hours
Too full of care and pain.

Asia   Lift up thine eyes,
And let me read thy dream.

Panthea   As I have said
With our sea-sister at his feet I slept.
The mountain mists, condensing at our voice
Under the moon, had spread their snowy flakes,
From the keen ice shielding our linked sleep.

60

Then two dreams came. One, I remember not.
But in the other his pale wound-worn limbs
Fell from Prometheus, and the azure night
Grew radiant with the glory of that form
Which lives unchanged within, and his voice fell
Like music which makes giddy the dim brain,
Faint with intoxication of keen joy:
'Sister of her whose footsteps pave the world
With loveliness – more fair than aught but her,
Whose shadow thou art – lift thine eyes on me.'

70

I lifted them: the overpowering light
Of that immortal shape was shadowed o'er

By love; which, from his soft and flowing limbs,
And passion-parted lips, and keen, faint eyes,
Steamed forth like vaporous fire; an atmosphere
Which wrapt me in its all-dissolving power,
As the warm ether of the morning sun
Wraps ere it drinks some cloud of wandering dew.
I saw not, heard not, moved not, only felt
His presence flow and mingle thro' my blood   80
Till it became his life, and his grew mine,
And I was thus absorb'd, until it past,
And like the vapours when the sun sinks down,
Gathering again in drops upon the pines,
And tremulous as they, in the deep night
My being was condensed; and as the rays
Of thought were slowly gathered, I could hear
His voice, whose accents lingered ere they died
Like footsteps of weak melody: thy name
Among the many sounds alone I heard   90
Of what might be articulate; tho' still
I listened thro' the night when sound was none.
Ione wakened then, and said to me:
'Canst thou divine what troubles me tonight?
I always knew what I desired before,
Nor ever found delight to wish in vain,
But now I cannot tell thee what I seek;
I know not; something sweet, since it is sweet
Even to desire; it is thy sport, false sister;
Thou hast discovered some enchantment old,   100
Whose spells have stolen my spirit as I slept
And mingled it with thine: for when just now
We kissed, I felt within thy parted lips
The sweet air that sustained me, and the warmth
Of the life-blood, for loss of which I faint,
Quivered between our intertwining arms.'
I answered not, for the Eastern star grew pale,
But fled to thee.

Asia   Thou speakest, but thy words
Are as the air: I feel them not: Oh, lift
Thine eyes, that I may read his written soul!   110

Panthea   I lift them tho' they droop beneath the load

	Of that they would express: what canst thou see
	But thine own fairest shadow imaged there?
Asia	Thine eyes are like the deep, blue, boundless heaven
	Contracted to two circles underneath
	Their long, fine lashes; dark, far, measureless,
	Orb within orb, and line thro' line inwoven.
Panthea	Why lookest thou as if a spirit past?
Asia	There is a change: beyond their inmost depth

Asia
Thine eyes are like the deep, blue, boundless heaven
Contracted to two circles underneath
Their long, fine lashes; dark, far, measureless,
Orb within orb, and line thro' line inwoven.

Panthea
Why lookest thou as if a spirit past?

Asia
There is a change: beyond their inmost depth
I see a shade, a shape: 'tis He, arrayed   120
In the soft light of his own smiles, which spread
Like radiance from the cloud-surrounded moon.
Prometheus, it is thine! depart not yet!
Say not those smiles that we shall meet again
Within that bright pavilion which their beams
Shall build o'er the waste world? The dream is told.
What shape is that between us? Its rude hair
Roughens the wind that lifts it, its regard
Is wild and quick, yet 'tis a thing of air
For thro' its grey robe gleams the golden dew   130
Whose stars the noon has quench'd not.

Dream   Follow! Follow!

Panthea   It is mine other dream.

Asia   It disappears.

Panthea   It passes now into my mind. Methought
As we sate here, the flower-enfolding buds
Burst on yon lightning-blasted almond tree,
When swift from the white Scythian wilderness
A wind swept forth wrinkling the Earth with frost:
I looked, and all the blossoms were blown down;
But on each leaf was stamped, as the blue bells
Of Hyacinth[85] tell Apollo's written grief,   140
O, FOLLOW, FOLLOW!

Asia   As you speak, your words
Fill, pause by pause, my own forgotten sleep
With shapes. Methought among these lawns together
We wandered, underneath the young grey dawn,
And multitudes of dense white fleecy clouds
Were wandering in thick flocks along the mountains
Shepherded by the slow, unwilling wind;
And the white dew on the new bladed grass,

Just piercing the dark earth, hung silently;
And there was more which I remember not: 150
But on the shadows of the moving clouds,
Athwart the purple mountain slope, was written
FOLLOW, O, FOLLOW! As they vanished by,
And on each herb, from which Heaven's dew had fallen,
The like was stamped, as with a withering fire,
A wind arose among the pines; it shook
The clinging music from their boughs, and then
Low, sweet, faint sounds, like the farewell of ghosts,
Were heard: O, FOLLOW, FOLLOW, FOLLOW ME!
And then I said: 'Panthea, look on me.'   160
But in the depth of those beloved eyes
Still I saw, FOLLOW, FOLLOW!

Echo   Follow, follow!
Panthea   The crags, this clear spring morning, mock our voices
              As they were spirit-tongued.

Asia   It is some being
              Around the crags. What fine clear sounds! O, list!

Echoes (unseen)

Echoes we: listen!
    We cannot stay:
As dew-stars glisten
    Then fade away –
        Child of Ocean!   170

Asia   Hark! Spirits speak. The liquid responses
              Of their aerial tongues yet sound.

Panthea   I hear.

Echoes

O, follow, follow,
    As our voice recedeth
Thro' the caverns hollow,
    Where the forest spreadeth;

(more distant)

O, follow, follow!
Thro' the caverns hollow,
As the song floats thou pursue,

   Where the wild bee never flew,   180
   Thro' the noontide darkness deep,
   By the odour-breathing sleep
   Of faint night flowers, and the waves
   At the fountain-lighted caves,
   While our music, wild and sweet,
   Mocks thy gently falling feet,
     Child of Ocean!

Asia Shall we pursue the sound? It grows more faint
  And distant.

Panthea   List! the strain floats nearer now.

     Echoes

   In the world unknown   190
    Sleeps a voice unspoken;
   By thy step alone
    Can its rest be broken;
    Child of Ocean!

Asia How the notes sink upon the ebbing wind!

     Echoes

   O, follow, follow!
   Thro' the caverns hollow,
   As the song floats thou pursue,
   By the woodland noontide dew;
   By the forests, lakes, and fountains 200
   Thro' the many-folded mountains;
   To the rents, and gulfs, and chasms,
   Where the Earth reposed from spasms,
   On the day when He and thou
   Parted, to commingle now;
    Child of Ocean!

Asia Come, sweet Panthea, link thy hand in mine,
  And follow, ere the voices fade away.

SCENE 2

A forest, intermingled with rocks and caverns. ASIA *and* PANTHEA
pass into it. The two young fauns are sitting on a rock listening.

Semichorus of Spirits I

The path thro' which that lovely twain
   Have past, by cedar, pine, and yew,
   And each dark tree that ever grew,
   Is curtained out from Heaven's wide blue;
Nor sun, nor moon, nor wind, nor rain,
      Can pierce its interwoven bowers,
   Nor aught, save where some cloud of dew,
Drifted along the earth-creeping breeze,
Between the trunks of the hoar trees,
      Hangs each a pearl in the pale flowers   10
   Of the green laurel, blown anew;
And bends, and then fades silently,
One frail and fair anemone:
Or when some star of many a one
That climbs and wanders thro' steep night,
Has found the cleft thro' which alone
Beams fall from high those depths upon
Ere it is borne away, away,
By the swift Heavens that cannot stay,
It scatters drops of golden light,   20
Like lines of rain that ne'er unite:
And the gloom divine is all around;
And underneath is the mossy ground.

Semichorus II

There the voluptuous nightingales,
   Are awake thro' all the broad noonday.
When one with bliss or sadness fails,
      And thro' the windless ivy-boughs,
   Sick with sweet love, droops dying away
On its mate's music-panting bosom;
Another from the swinging blossom,   30

Watching to catch the languid close
Of the last strain, then lifts on high
The wings of the weak melody,
Till some new strain of feeling bear
The song, and all the woods are mute;
When there is heard thro' the dim air
The rush of wings, and rising there
Like many a lake-surrounded flute,
Sounds overflow the listener's brain
So sweet, that joy is almost pain.   40

Semichorus 1

There those enchanted eddies play
Of echoes, music-tongued, which draw,
By Demogorgon's mighty law,
With melting rapture, or sweet awe,
All spirits on that secret way;
As inland boats are driven to Ocean
Down streams made strong with mountain-thaw:
And first there comes a gentle sound
To those in talk or slumber bound,
And wakes the destined – Soft emotion   50
Attracts, impels them: those who saw
Say from the breathing earth behind
There steams a plume-uplifting wind
Which drives them on their path, while they
Believe their own swift wings and feet
The sweet desires within obey:
And so they float upon their way,
Until, still sweet, but loud and strong,
The storm of sound is driven along,
Sucked up and hurrying: as they fleet   60
Behind, its gathering billows meet
And to the fatal mountain bear
Like clouds amid the yielding air.

First Faun   Canst thou imagine where those spirits live
Which make such delicate music in the woods?
We haunt within the least frequented caves
And closest coverts, and we know these wilds,

Yet never meet them, tho' we hear them oft:
Where may they hide themselves?

Second Faun   'Tis hard to tell:

I have heard[86] those more skilled in spirits say,   70
The bubbles, which the enchantment of the sun
Sucks from the pale faint water-flowers that pave
The oozy bottom of clear lakes and pools,
Are the pavilions where such dwell, and float
Under the green and golden atmosphere
Which noontide kindles thro' the woven leaves;
And when these burst, and the thin fiery air,
The which they breathed within those lucent domes,
Ascends to flow like meteors thro' the night,
They ride on them, and rein their headlong speed,   80
And bow their burning crests, and glide in fire
Under the waters of the earth again.

First Faun   If such live thus, have others other lives,
Under pink blossoms, or within the bells
Of meadow flowers, or folded violets deep,
Or on their dying odours, when they die,
Or in the sunlight of the sphered dew?

Second Faun   Aye, many more which we may well divine.
But, should we stay to speak, noontide would come,
And thwart Silenus[87] find his goats undrawn,   90
And grudge to sing those wise and lovely songs
Of fate, and chance, and God, and Chaos old,
And Love, and the chained Titan's woful doom,
And how he shall be loosed, and make the earth
One brotherhood: delightful strains which cheer
Our solitary twilights, and which charm
To silence the unenvying nightingales.

SCENE 3

A pinnacle of rock among mountains. ASIA *and* PANTHEA.

Panthea   Hither the sound has borne us – to the realm
Of Demogorgon, and the mighty portal,
Like a volcano's meteor-breathing chasm,
Whence the oracular vapour is hurled up
Which lonely men drink wandering in their youth,
And call truth, virtue, love, genius, or joy,
That maddening wine of life, whose dregs they drain
To deep intoxication; and uplift,
Like Maenads[88] who cry loud, Evoe! Evoe!
The voice which is contagion to the world.   10

Asia   Fit throne for such a Power! Magnificent!
How glorious art thou, Earth! And if thou be
The shadow of some spirit lovelier still,
Though evil stain its work, and it should be
Like its creation, weak yet beautiful,
I could fall down and worship that and thee.
Even now my heart adoreth: Wonderful!
Look, sister, ere the vapour dim thy brain:
Beneath is a wide plain of billowy mist,
As a lake, paving in the morning sky,   20
With azure waves which burst in silver light,
Some Indian vale. Behold it, rolling on
Under the curdling winds, and islanding
The peak whereon we stand, midway, around,
Encinctured by the dark and blooming forests,
Dim twilight-lawns, and stream-illumed caves,
And wind-enchanted shapes of wandering mist;
And far on high the keen sky-cleaving mountains
From icy spires of sunlike radiance fling
The dawn, as lifted Ocean's dazzling spray,   30
From some Atlantic islet scattered up,
Spangles the wind with lamp-like water-drops.
The vale is girdled with their walls, a howl
Of cataracts from their thaw-cloven ravines
Satiates the listening wind, continuous, vast,

Awful as silence. Hark! the rushing snow!
The sun-awakened avalanche! whose mass,
Thrice sifted by the storm, had gathered there
Flake after flake, in heaven-defying minds
As thought by thought is piled, till some great truth   40
Is loosened, and the nations echo round,
Shaken to their roots, as do the mountains now.

Panthea   Look how the gusty sea of mist is breaking
In crimson foam, even at our feet! it rises
As Ocean at the enchantment of the moon
Round foodless men wrecked on some oozy isle.

Asia   The fragments of the cloud are scattered up;
The wind that lifts them disentwines my hair;
Its billows now sweep o'er mine eyes; my brain
Grows dizzy; see'st thou shapes within the mist?   50

Panthea   A countenance with beckoning smiles: there burns
An azure fire within its golden locks!
Another and another: hark! they speak!

Song of Spirits

To the deep, to the deep,
  Down, down!
Through the shade of sleep,
Through the cloudy strife
Of Death and of Life;
Through the veil and the bar
Of things which seem and are   60
Even to the steps of the remotest throne,
  Down, down!

While the sound whirls around,
  Down, down!
As the fawn draws the hound,
As the lightning the vapour,
As a weak moth the taper;
Death, despair; love, sorrow;
Time both; today, tomorrow;
As steel obeys the spirit of the stone,   70
  Down, down.

Through the grey, void abysm,
       Down, down!
Where the air is no prism,
And the moon and stars are not,
And the cavern-crags wear not
The radiance of Heaven,
Nor the gloom to Earth given,
Where there is one pervading, one alone.
       Down, down!   80

In the depth of the deep,
       Down, down!
Like veiled lightning asleep,
Like the spark nursed in embers,
The last look Love remembers,
Like a diamond, which shines
On the dark wealth of mines,
A spell is treasur'd but for thee alone.
       Down, down!

We have bound thee, we guide thee;   90
       Down, down!
With the bright form beside thee;
Resist not the weakness
Such strength is in meekness
That the Eternal, the Immortal,
Must unloose through life's portal
The snake-like Doom coiled underneath his throne
       By that alone.

SCENE 4

The cave of DEMOGORGON. ASIA *and* PANTHEA.

Panthea	What veiled form sits on that ebon throne?
Asia	The veil has fallen.
Panthea	I see a mighty darkness
	Filling the seat of power, and rays of gloom
	Dart round, as light from the meridian sun,
	Ungazed upon and shapeless; neither limb,
	Nor form, nor outline; yet we feel it is
	A living Spirit.
Demogorgon	Ask what thou wouldst know.
Asia	What canst thou tell?
Demogorgon	All things thou dar'st demand.
Asia	Who made the living world?
Demogorgon	God.
Asia	Who made all
	That it contains? thought, passion, reason, will,
	Imagination?
Demogorgon	God: Almighty God.
Asia	Who made that sense which, when the winds of spring
	In rarest visitation, or the voice
	Of one beloved heard in youth alone,
	Fills the faint eyes with falling tears which dim
	The radiant looks of unbewailing flowers,
	And leaves this peopled earth a solitude
	When it returns no more?
Demogorgon	Merciful God.
Asia	And who made terror, madness, crime, remorse,
	Which from the links of the great chain of things,
	To every thought within the mind of man
	Sway and drag heavily, and each one reels
	Under the load towards the pit of death;
	Abandoned hope, and love that turns to hate;
	And self-contempt, bitterer to drink than blood;
	Pain, whose unheeded and familiar speech
	Is howling, and keen shrieks, day after day;

10

20

	And Hell, or the sharp fear of Hell?
Demogorgon	He reigns.
Asia	Utter his name: a world pining in pain
	Asks but his name: curses shall drag him down.
Demogorgon	He reigns.
Asia	I feel, I know it: who?
Demogorgon	He reigns.
Asia	Who reigns? There was the Heaven and Earth at first,

        And Light and Love; then Saturn, from whose throne
Time fell, an envious shadow: such the state
Of the earth's primal spirits beneath his sway,
As the calm joy of flowers and living leaves
Before the wind or sun has withered them
And semivital worms; but he refused
The birthright of their being, knowledge, power,
The skill which wields the elements, the thought
Which pierces this dim universe like light,
Self-empire, and the majesty of love;
For thirst of which they fainted. Then Prometheus
Gave wisdom, which is strength, to Jupiter,
And with this law alone, 'Let man be free,'
Clothed him with the dominion of wide Heaven.
To know nor faith, nor love, nor law; to be
Omnipotent but friendless is to reign;
And Jove now reigned; for on the race of man
First famine, and then toil, and then disease,
Strife, wounds, and ghastly death unseen before,
Fell; and the unseasonable seasons drove
With alternating shafts of frost and fire,
Their shelterless, pale tribes to mountain caves:
And in their desert hearts fierce wants he sent,
And mad disquietudes, and shadows idle
Of unreal good, which levied mutual war,
So ruining the lair wherein they raged.
Prometheus saw, and waked the legioned hopes
Which sleep within folded Elysian flowers,
Nepenthe, Moly, Amaranth,[89] fadeless blooms,
That they might hide with thin and rainbow wings
The shape of Death; and Love he sent to bind
The disunited tendrils of that vine

Which bears the wine of life, the human heart;
And he tamed fire which, like some beast of prey,
Most terrible, but lovely, played beneath
The frown of man; and tortured to his will
Iron and gold, the slaves and signs of power,
And gems and poisons, and all subtlest forms   70
Hidden beneath the mountains and the waves.
He gave man speech, and speech created thought,
Which is the measure of the universe;
And Science struck the thrones of earth and heaven,
Which shook, but fell not; and the harmonious mind
Poured itself forth in all-prophetic song;
And music lifted up the listening spirit
Until it walked, exempt from mortal care,
Godlike, o'er the clear billows of sweet sound;
And human hands first mimicked and then mocked,   80
With moulded limbs more lovely than its own,
The human form, till marble grew divine;
And mothers, gazing, drank the love men see
Reflected in their race, behold, and perish.
He told the hidden power of herbs and springs,
And Disease drank and slept. Death grew like sleep.
He taught the implicated orbits woven
Of the wide-wandering stars; and how the sun
Changes his lair, and by what secret spell
The pale moon is transformed, when her broad eye   90
Gazes not on the interlunar sea:
He taught to rule, as life directs the limbs,
The tempest-winged chariots of the Ocean,
And the Celt knew the Indian. Cities then
Were built, and through their snow-like columns flowed
The warm winds, and the azure ether shone,
And the blue sea and shadowy hills were seen.
Such, the alleviations of his state,
Prometheus gave to man, for which he hangs
Withering in destined pain: but who rains down   100
Evil, the immedicable plague, which, while
Man looks on his creation like a God
And sees that it is glorious, drives him on
The wreck of his own will, the scorn of earth,

The outcast, the abandoned, the alone?
Not Jove: while yet his frown shook Heaven, aye when
His adversary from adamantine chains
Cursed him, he trembled like a slave. Declare
Who is his master? Is he too a slave?

Demogorgon All spirits are enslaved which serve things evil: 110
Thou knowest if Jupiter be such or no.

Asia Whom called'st thou God?

Demogorgon   I spoke but as ye speak,
For Jove is the supreme of living things.

Asia Who is the master of the slave?

Demogorgon   If the abysm
Could vomit forth its secrets. But a voice
Is wanting, the deep truth is imageless;
For what would it avail to bid thee gaze
On the revolving world? What to bid speak
Fate, Time, Occasion, Chance and Change? To these
All things are subject but eternal Love.   120

Asia So much I asked before, and my heart gave
The response thou hast given; and of such truths
Each to itself must be the oracle.
One more demand; and do thou answer me
As my own soul would answer, did it know
That which I ask. Prometheus shall arise
Henceforth the sun of this rejoicing world:
When shall the destined hour arrive?

Demogorgon   Behold!

Asia The rocks are cloven, and through the purple night
I see cars drawn by rainbow-winged steeds   130
Which trample the dim winds: in each there stands
A wild-eyed charioteer urging their flight.
Some look behind, as fiends pursued them there,
And yet I see no shapes but the keen stars:
Others, with burning eyes, lean forth, and drink
With eager lips the wind of their own speed,
As if the thing they loved fled on before,
And now, even now, they clasped it. Their bright locks
Stream like a comet's flashing hair: they all
Sweep onward.

Demogorgon   These are the immortal Hours,   140

	Of whom thou didst demand. One waits for thee.
Asia	A spirit with a dreadful countenance
	Checks its dark chariot by the craggy gulf.
	Unlike thy brethren, ghastly charioteer,
	Who art thou? Whither wouldst thou bear me? Speak!
Spirit	I am the shadow of a destiny
	More dread than is my aspect: ere yon planet
	Has set, the darkness which ascends with me
	Shall wrap in lasting night heaven's kingless throne.
Asia	What meanest thou?
Panthea	That terrible shadow floats

150

Up from its throne, as may the lurid smoke
Of earthquake-ruined cities o'er the sea.
Lo! it ascends the car; the coursers fly
Terrified: watch its path among the stars
Blackening the night!

Asia   Thus I am answered: strange!
Panthea   See, near the verge, another chariot stays;
An ivory shell inlaid with crimson fire,
Which comes and goes within its sculptured rim
Of delicate strange tracery; the young spirit
That guides it has the dove-like eyes of hope;   160
How its soft smiles attract the soul! as light
Lures winged insects thro' the lampless air.

Spirit

My coursers[90] are fed with the lightning,
    They drink of the whirlwind's stream,
And when the red morning is bright'ning
    They bathe in the fresh sunbeam;
    They have strength for their swiftness I deem,
Then ascend with me, daughter of Ocean.

I desire: and their speed makes night kindle;
    I fear: they outstrip the Typhoon;   170
Ere the cloud piled on Atlas can dwindle
    We encircle the earth and the moon:
    We shall rest from long labours at noon:
Then ascend with me, daughter of Ocean.

SCENE 5

The car pauses within a cloud on the top of a snowy mountain.
ASIA, PANTHEA, *and the* SPIRIT OF THE HOUR.

Spirit

	On the brink of the night and the morning	
	My coursers are wont to respire;	
	But the Earth has just whispered a warning	
	That their flight must be swifter than fire:	
	They shall drink the hot speed of desire!	
Asia	Thou breathest on their nostrils, but my breath	
	Would give them swifter speed.	
Spirit	Alas! it could not.	
Panthea	Oh Spirit! pause, and tell whence is the light	
	Which fills this cloud? the sun is yet unrisen.	
Spirit	The sun will rise not until noon. Apollo	10
	Is held in heaven by wonder; and the light	
	Which fills this vapour, as the aerial hue	
	Of fountain-gazing roses fills the water,	
	Flows from thy mighty sister.	
Panthea	Yes, I feel –	
Asia	What is it with thee, sister? Thou art pale.	
Panthea	How thou art changed! I dare not look on thee;	
	I feel but see thee not. I scarce endure	
	The radiance of thy beauty. Some good change	
	Is working in the elements, which suffer	
	Thy presence thus unveiled. The Nereids[91] tell	20
	That on the day when the clear hyaline	
	Was cloven at thine uprise, and thou didst stand	
	Within a veined shell, which floated on	
	Over the calm floor of the crystal sea,	
	Among the Aegean isles, and by the shores	
	Which bear thy name: love, like the atmosphere	
	Of the sun's fire filling the living world,	
	Burst from thee, and illumined earth and heaven	
	And the deep ocean and the sunless caves	
	And all that dwells within them; till grief cast	30
	Eclipse upon the soul from which it came:	

Such art thou now; nor is it I alone,
Thy sister, thy companion, thine own chosen one,
But the whole world which seeks thy sympathy.
Hearest thou not sounds i' the air which speak the love
Of all articulate beings? Feelest thou not
The inanimate winds enamoured of thee? List!   [*Music*

Asia   Thy words are sweeter than aught else but his
Whose echoes they are: yet all love is sweet,
Given or returned. Common as light is love,   40
And its familiar voice wearies not ever.
Like the wide heaven, the all-sustaining air,
It makes the reptile equal to the God:
They who inspire it most are fortunate,
As I am now; but those who feel it most
Are happier still, after long sufferings,
As I shall soon become.

Panthea   List! Spirits speak.

                    Voice in the air, singing.

Life of Life! thy lips enkindle
    With their love the breath between them;
And thy smiles before they dwindle   50
    Make the cold air fire; then screen them
In those looks, where whoso gazes
Faints, entangled in their mazes.

Child of Light! thy limbs are burning
    Thro' the vest which seems to hide them;
As the radiant lines of morning
    Thro' the clouds ere they divide them;
And this atmosphere divinest
Shrouds thee wheresoe'er thou shinest.

Fair are others; none beholds thee,   60
    But thy voice sounds low and tender
Like the fairest, for it folds thee
    From the sight, that liquid splendour,
And all feel, yet see thee never,
As I feel now, lost for ever!

Lamp of Earth! where'er thou movest
  Its dim shapes are clad with brightness
And the souls of whom thou lovest
  Walk upon the winds with lightness,
Till they fail, as I am failing,   70
Dizzy, lost, yet unbewailing!

Asia

My soul is an enchanted boat,
  Which, like a sleeping swan, doth float
Upon the silver waves of thy sweet singing;
  And thine doth like an angel sit
  Beside the helm conducting it,
Whilst all the winds with melody are ringing.
  It seems to float ever, for ever,
  Upon that many-winding river,
  Between mountains, woods, abysses,   80
  A paradise of wildernesses!
Till, like one in slumber bound,
Borne to the ocean, I float down, around,
Into a sea profound, of ever-spreading sound:

  Meanwhile thy spirit lifts its pinions
  In music's most serene dominions;
Catching the winds that fan that happy heaven.
  And we sail on, away, afar.
  Without a course, without a star,
But, by the instinct of sweet music driven;   90
  Till through Elysian garden islets
By thee, most beautiful of pilots,
  Where never mortal pinnace glided,
  The boat of my desire is guided:
Realms where the air we breathe is love,
Which in the winds and on the waves doth move,
Harmonising this earth with what we feel above.

  We have pass'd Age's icy caves,
  And Manhood's dark and tossing waves,
And Youth's smooth ocean, smiling to betray: 100
  Beyond the glassy gulfs we flee

Of shadow-peopled Infancy,
Through Death and Birth, to a diviner day:
A paradise of vaulted bowers,
Lit by downward-gazing flowers,
And watery paths that wind between
Wildernesses calm and green,
Peopled by shapes too bright to see,
And rest, having beheld; somewhat like thee;
Which walk upon the sea, and chaunt melodiously!   110

END OF THE SECOND ACT

ACT 3, SCENE 1

Heaven. JUPITER *on his throne;* THETIS *and the other deities assembled.*

Jupiter	Ye congregated powers of heaven, who share
	The glory and the strength of him ye serve,
	Rejoice! henceforth I am omnipotent.
	All else had been subdued to me; alone
	The soul of man, like unextinguished fire,
	Yet burns towards heaven with fierce reproach, and doubt,
	And lamentation, and reluctant prayer,
	Hurling up insurrection, which might make
	Our antique empire insecure, though built
	On eldest faith, and hell's coeval, fear;

Ye congregated powers of heaven, who share
The glory and the strength of him ye serve,
Rejoice! henceforth I am omnipotent.
All else had been subdued to me; alone
The soul of man, like unextinguished fire,
Yet burns towards heaven with fierce reproach, and doubt,
And lamentation, and reluctant prayer,
Hurling up insurrection, which might make
Our antique empire insecure, though built
On eldest faith, and hell's coeval, fear;   10
And tho' my curses thro' the pendulous air,
Like snow on herbless peaks, fall flake by flake,
And cling to it; tho' under my wrath's night
It climb the crags of life, step after step,
Which wound it, as ice wounds unsandalled feet.
It yet remains supreme o'er misery,
Aspiring, unrepressed, yet soon to fall:
Even now have I begotten a strange wonder,
That fatal child, the terror of the earth,
Who waits but till the destined hour arrive,   20
Bearing from Demogorgon's vacant throne
The dreadful might of ever-living limbs
Which clothed that awful spirit unbeheld,
To redescend, and trample out the spark.
Pour forth heaven's wine, Idaean Ganymede,[92]
And let it fill the Daedal[93] cups like fire,
And from the flower-inwoven soil divine
Ye all-triumphant harmonies arise,
As dew from earth under the twilight stars:
Drink! be the nectar circling thro' your veins   30
The soul of joy, ye ever-living Gods,
Till exultation burst in one wide voice
Like music from Elysian winds.
                                        And thou
Ascend beside me, veiled in the light

Of the desire which makes thee one with me,
Thetis,[94] bright image of eternity!
When thou didst cry, 'Insufferable might!
God! Spare me! I sustain not the quick flames,
The penetrating presence; all my being,
Like him whom the Numidian seps[95] did thaw   40
Into a dew with poison, is dissolved,
Sinking thro' its foundations:' even then
Two mighty spirits, mingling, made a third
Mightier than either, which, unbodied now,
Between us floats, felt, although unbeheld,
Waiting the incarnation, which ascends
(Hear ye the thunder of the fiery wheels
Griding the winds?) from Demogorgon's throne.
Victory! victory! Feel'st thou not, O world,
The earthquake of his chariot thundering up   50
Olympus?
            [*The car of the* SPIRIT OF THE HOUR *arrives.* DEMOGORGON
                descends and moves towards the throne of JUPITER.
            Awful shape, what art thou? Speak!

Demogorgon   Eternity. Demand no direr name.
Descend, and follow me down the abyss.
I am thy child, as thou wert Saturn's child;
Mightier than thee: and we must dwell together
Henceforth in darkness. Lift thy lightnings not.
The tyranny of heaven none may retain,
Or reassume, or hold, succeeding thee:
Yet if thou wilt, as 'tis the destiny
Of trodden worms to writhe till they are dead,   60
Put forth thy might.

Jupiter   Detested prodigy!
Even thus beneath the deep Titanian prisons
I trample thee! thou lingerest?
                            Mercy! mercy!
No pity, no release, no respite! Oh,
That thou wouldst make mine enemy my judge,
Even where he hangs, seared by my long revenge,
On Caucasus! he would not doom me thus.
Gentle, and just, and dreadless, is he not
The monarch of the world? What then art thou?

No refuge! no appeal!
                              Sink with me then,   70
We two will sink on the wide waves of ruin,
Even as a vulture and a snake outspent
Drop, twisted in inextricable fight,
Into a shoreless sea. Let hell unlock
Its mounded oceans of tempestuous fire,
And whelm on them into the bottomless void
This desolated world, and thee, and me,
The conqueror and the conquered, and the wreck
Of that for which they combated.
                                        Ai! Ai!
The elements obey me not. I sink   80
Dizzily down, ever, for ever, down.
And, like a cloud, mine enemy above
Darkens my fall with victory! Ai, Ai!

SCENE 2

The mouth of a great river in the island Atlantis. OCEAN *is discovered*
reclining near the shore; APOLLO *stands beside him.*

Ocean	He fell, thou sayest, beneath his conqueror's frown?
Apollo	Aye, when the strife was ended which made dim
	The orb I rule, and shook the solid stars,
	The terrors of his eye illumined heaven
	With sanguine light, through the thick ragged skirts
	Of the victorious darkness, as he fell:
	Like the last glare of day's red agony,
	Which, from a rent among the fiery clouds,
	Burns far along the tempest-wrinkled deep.
Ocean	He sank to the abyss? To the dark void? 10
Apollo	An eagle so caught in some bursting cloud
	On Caucasus, his thunder-baffled wings
	Entangled in the whirlwind, and his eyes
	Which gazed on the undazzling sun, now blinded
	By the white lightning, while the ponderous hail
	Beats on his struggling form, which sinks at length

	Prone, and the aerial ice clings over it.

Ocean   Henceforth the fields of Heaven-reflecting sea
           Which are my realm, will heave, unstain'd with blood,
           Beneath the uplifting winds, like plains of corn   20
           Swayed by the summer air; my streams will flow
           Round many-peopled continents, and round
           Fortunate isles; and from their glassy thrones
           Blue Proteus and his humid nymphs shall mark
           The shadow of fair ships, as mortals see
           The floating bark of the light-laden moon
           With that white star, its sightless pilot's crest,
           Borne down the rapid sunset's ebbing sea:
           Tracking their path no more by blood and groans,
           And desolation, and the mingled voice   30
           Of slavery and command; but by the light
           Of wave-reflected flowers, and floating odours,
           And music soft, and mild, free, gentle voices,
           That sweetest music, such as spirits love.

Apollo   And I shall gaze not on the deeds which make
           My mind obscure with sorrow, as eclipse
           Darkens the sphere I guide; but list, I hear
           The small, clear, silver lute of the young Spirit
           That sits i' the morning star.

Ocean   Thou must away;
           Thy steeds will pause at even, till when farewell: 40
           The loud deep calls me home even now to feed it
           With azure calm out of the emerald urns
           Which stand for ever full beside my throne.
           Behold the Nereids under the green sea,
           Their wavering limbs borne on the wind-like stream,
           Their white arms lifted o'er their streaming hair
           With garlands pied and starry sea-flower crowns,
           Hastening to grace their mighty sister's joy.
                                   [*A sound of waves is heard.*
           It is the unpastured sea hungering for calm.
           Peace, monster; I come now. Farewell.

Apollo   Farewell.

SCENE 3

Caucasus. PROMETHEUS, HERCULES, IONE, *the* EARTH, SPIRITS,
ASIA, *and* PANTHEA, *borne in the car with the* SPIRIT OF THE
HOUR. HERCULES *unbinds* PROMETHEUS *who descends.*

Hercules	Most glorious among spirits, thus doth strength
	To wisdom, courage, and long-suffering love,
	And thee, who art the form they animate,
	Minister like a slave.
Prometheus	Thy gentle words

Are sweeter even than freedom long desired
And long delayed.
                Asia, thou light of life,
Shadow of beauty unbeheld: and ye,
Fair sister nymphs, who made long years of pain
Sweet to remember, thro' your love and care;
Henceforth we will not part. There is a cave,   10
All overgrown with trailing odorous plants,
Which curtain out the day with leaves and flowers,
And paved with veined emerald, and a fountain
Leaps in the midst with an awakening sound.
From its curved roof the mountain's frozen tears
Like snow, or silver, or long diamond spires,
Hang downward, raining forth a doubtful light:
And there is heard the ever-moving air,
Whispering without from tree to tree, and birds,
And bees; and all around are mossy seats,   20
And the rough walls are clothed with long soft grass;
A simple dwelling, which shall be our own;
Where we will sit and talk of time and change,
As the world ebbs and flows, ourselves unchanged.
What can hide mar from mutability?
And if ye sigh, then I will smile; and thou,
Ione, shalt chaunt fragments of sea-music,
Until I weep, when ye shall smile away
The tears she brought, which yet were sweet to shed.
We will entangle buds and flowers and beams   30
Which twinkle on the fountain's brim, and make

Strange combinations out of common things,
Like human babes in their brief innocence;
And we will search, with looks and words of love,
For hidden thoughts, each lovelier than the last,
Our unexhausted spirits; and like lutes
Touched by the skill of the enamoured wind,
Weave harmonies divine, yet ever new,
From difference sweet where discord cannot be;
And hither come, sped on the charmed winds,   40
Which meet from all the points of heaven, as bees
From every flower aerial Enna[96] feeds,
At their known island-homes in Himera,
The echoes of the human world, which tell
Of the low voice of love, almost unheard,
And dove-eyed pity's murmured pain, and music,
Itself the echo of the heart, and all
That tempers or improves man's life now free;
And lovely apparitions, dim at first,
Then radiant, as the mind, arising bright   50
From the embrace of beauty, whence the forms
Of which these are the phantoms, casts on them
The gathered rays which are reality
Shall visit us, the progeny immortal
Of Painting, Sculpture, and rapt Poesy,
And arts, tho' unimagined, yet to be.
The wandering voices and the shadows these
Of all that man becomes, the mediators
Of that best worship love, by him and us
Given and returned; swift shapes and sounds, which grow
More fair and soft as man grows wise and kind,   61
And, veil by veil, evil and error fall:
Such virtue has the cave and place around.
                                    [*turning to the* SPIRIT OF THE HOUR
For thee, fair Spirit, one toil remains. Ione,
Give her that curved shell, which Proteus[97] old
Made Asia's nuptial boon, breathing within it
A voice to be accomplished, and which thou
Didst hide in grass under the hollow rock.

Ione   Thou most desired Hour, more loved and lovely
Than all thy sisters, this is the mystic shell;   70

See the pale azure fading into silver
Lining it with a soft yet glowing light:
Looks it not like lulled music sleeping there?

Spirit It seems in truth the fairest shell of Ocean:
Its sound must be at once both sweet and strange.

Prometheus Go, borne over the cities of mankind
On whirlwind-footed coursers: once again
Outspeed the sun around the orbed world;
And as thy chariot cleaves the kindling air,
Thou breathe into the many-folded shell, 80
Loosening its mighty music; it shall be
As thunder mingled with clear echoes: then
Return; and thou shalt dwell beside our cave.

And thou, O Mother Earth! –

The Earth   I hear, I feel;
Thy lips are on me, and their touch runs down
Even to the adamantine central gloom
Along these marble nerves; 'tis life, 'tis joy,
And thro' my withered, old, and icy frame
The warmth of an immortal youth shoots down
Circling. Henceforth the many children fair 90
Folded in my sustaining arms; all plants,
And creeping forms, and insects rainbow-winged,
And birds, and beasts, and fish, and human shapes,
Which drew disease and pain from my wan bosom,
Draining the poison of despair, shall take
And interchange sweet nutriment; to me
Shall they become like sister-antelopes
By one fair dam, snow-white and swift as wind
Nursed among lilies near a brimming stream.
The dew-mists of my sunless sleep shall float 100
Under the stars like balm: night-folded flowers
Shall suck unwithering hues in their repose:
And men and beasts in happy dreams shall gather
Strength for the coming day, and all its joy:
And death shall be the last embrace of her
Who takes the life she gave, even as a mother
Folding her child, says, 'Leave me not again.'

Asia Oh, mother! wherefore speak the name of death?

Cease they to love, and move, and breathe, and speak,
Who die?

The Earth   It would avail not to reply: 110
Thou art immortal, and this tongue is known
But to the uncommunicating dead.
Death is the veil which those who live call life:
They sleep, and it is lifted: and meanwhile
In mild variety the seasons mild
With rainbow-skirted showers, and odorous winds,
And long blue meteors cleansing the dull night,
And the life-kindling shafts of the keen sun's
All-piercing bow, and the dew-mingled rain
Of the calm moonbeams, a soft influence mild,   120
Shall clothe the forests and the fields, aye, even
The crag-built deserts of the barren deep,
With ever-living leaves, and fruits, and flowers.
And thou! There is a cavern where my spirit
Was panted forth in anguish whilst thy pain
Made my heart mad, and those who did inhale it
Became mad too, and built a temple there,
And spoke, and were oracular, and lured
The erring nations round to mutual war,
And faithless faith, such as Jove kept with thee;   130
Which breath now rises, as amongst tall weeds
A violet's exhalation, and it fills
With a serener light and crimson air
Intense, yet soft, the rocks and woods around;
It feeds the quick growth of the serpent vine,
And the dark linked ivy tangling wild,
And budding, blown, or odour-faded blooms
Which star the winds with points of coloured light,
As they rain thro' them, and bright golden globes
Of fruit, suspended in their own green heaven,   140
And thro' their veined leaves and amber stems
The flowers whose purple and translucid bowls
Stand ever mantling with aerial dew,
The drink of spirits: and it circles round,
Like the soft waving wings of noonday dreams,
Inspiring calm and happy thoughts, like mine,
Now thou art thus restored. This cave is thine.

Arise! Appear!
                    [*A* SPIRIT *rises in the likeness of a winged child.*
                    This is my torch-bearer;
Who let his lamp out in old time with gazing
On eyes from which he kindled it anew   150
With love, which is as fire, sweet daughter mine,
For such is that within thine own. Run, wayward,
And guide this company beyond the peak
Of Bacchic Nysa,[98] Maenad-haunted mountain,
And beyond Indus and its tribute rivers,
Trampling the torrent streams and glassy lakes
With feet unwet, unwearied, undelaying,
And up the green ravine, across the vale,
Beside the windless and crystalline pool,
Where ever lies, on unerasing waves,   160
The image of a temple, built above,
Distinct with column, arch, and architrave,
And palm-like capital, and over-wrought,
And populous with most living imagery,
Praxitelean[99] shapes, whose marble smiles
Fill the hushed air with everlasting love.
It is deserted now, but once it bore
Thy name, Prometheus; there the emulous youths
Bore to thy honour through the divine gloom
The lamp which was thine emblem; even as those   170
Who bear the untransmitted torch of hope
Into the grave, across the night of life,
As thou hast borne it most triumphantly
To this far goal of Time. Depart, farewell.
Beside that temple is the destined cave.

SCENE 4

A forest. In the background a cave. PROMETHEUS, ASIA,
PANTHEA, IONE, *and the* SPIRIT OF THE EARTH.

Ione   Sister, it is not earthly: how it glides
                Under the leaves! how on its head there burns
                A light, like a green star, whose emerald beams
                Are twined with its fair hair! how, as it moves,
                The splendour drops in flakes upon the grass!
                Knowest thou it?

Panthea   It is the delicate spirit
                That guides the earth thro' heaven. From afar
                The populous constellations call that light
                The loveliest of the planets; and sometimes
                It floats along the spray of the salt sea,   10
                Or makes its chariot of a foggy cloud,
                Or walks thro' fields or cities while men sleep,
                Or o'er the mountain tops, or down the rivers,
                Or thro' the green waste wilderness, as now,
                Wondering at all it sees. Before Jove reigned
                It loved our sister Asia, and it came
                Each leisure hour to drink the liquid light
                Out of her eyes, for which it said it thirsted
                As one bit by a dipsas,[100] and with her
                It made its childish confidence, and told her   20
                All it had known or seen, for it saw much,
                Yet idly reasoned what it saw; and called her,
                For whence it sprung it knew not, nor do I,
                Mother, dear mother.

The Spirit of the Earth [*running to Asia*]
                                  Mother, dearest mother;
                May I then talk with thee as I was wont?
                May I then hide my eyes in thy soft arms,
                After thy looks have made them tired of joy?
                May I then play beside thee the long noons,
                When work is none in the bright silent air?

Asia   I love thee, gentlest being, and henceforth   30
                Can cherish thee unenvied: speak, I pray:

Thy simple talk once solaced, now delights.

Spirit of the Earth   Mother, I am grown wiser, though a child
Cannot be wise like thee, within this day;
And happier too; happier and wiser both.
Thou knowest that toads, and snakes, and loathly worms,
And venomous and malicious beasts, and boughs
That bore ill berries in the woods, were ever
An hindrance to my walks o'er the green world:
And that, among the haunts of humankind,   40
Hard-featured men, or with proud, angry looks,
Or cold, staid gait, or false and hollow smiles,
Or the dull sneer of self-loved ignorance,
Or other such foul masks, with which ill thoughts
Hide that fair being whom we spirits call man:
And women too, ugliest of all things evil
(Tho' fair, even in a world where thou art fair,
When good and kind, free and sincere like thee),
When false or frowning made me sick at heart
To pass them, tho' they slept, and I unseen.   50
Well, my path lately lay thro' a great city
Into the woody hills surrounding it:
A sentinel was sleeping at the gate:
When there was heard a sound, so loud, it shook
The towers amid the moonlight, yet more sweet
Than any voice but thine, sweetest of all;
A long, long sound, as it would never end:
And all the inhabitants leapt suddenly
Out of their rest, and gathered in the streets,
Looking in wonder up to Heaven, while yet   60
The music pealed along. I hid myself
Within a fountain in the public square,
Where I lay like the reflex of the moon
Seen in a wave under green leaves; and soon
Those ugly human shapes and visages
Of which I spoke as having wrought me pain,
Past floating thro' the air, and fading still
Into the winds that scattered them; and those
From whom they past seemed mild and lovely forms
After some foul disguise had fallen, and all   70
Were somewhat changed, and after brief surprise

And greetings of delighted wonder, all
Went to their sleep again: and when the dawn
Came, would'st thou think that toads, and snakes, and efts,
Could e'er be beautiful? yet so they were,
And that with little change of shape or hue:
All things had put their evil nature off:
I cannot tell my joy, when o'er a lake
Upon a drooping bough with night-shade twined,
I saw two azure halcyons clinging downward   80
And thinning one bright bunch of amber berries,
With quick long beaks, and in the deep there lay
Those lovely forms imaged as in a sky;
So, with my thoughts full of these happy changes,
We meet again, the happiest change of all.

Asia   And never will we part, till thy chaste sister,
Who guides the frozen and inconstant moon,
Will look on thy more warm and equal light
Till her heart thaw like flakes of April snow,
And love thee.

Spirit of the Earth   What; as Asia loves Prometheus?   90
Asia   Peace, wanton, thou art yet not old enough.
Think ye by gazing on each other's eyes
To multiply your lovely selves, and fill
With sphered fires the interlunar air?

Spirit of the Earth   Nay, mother, while my sister trims her lamp
'Tis hard I should go darkling.

Asia   Listen; look!
                    [*The* SPIRIT OF THE HOUR *enters.*

Prometheus   We feel what thou hast heard and seen: yet speak.
Spirit of the Hour   Soon as the sound had ceased whose thunder filled
The abysses of the sky and the wide earth,
There was a change: the impalpable thin air   100
And the all-circling sunlight were transformed,
As if the sense of love dissolved in them
Had folded itself round the sphered world.
My vision then grew clear, and I could see
Into the mysteries of the universe:
Dizzy as with delight I floated down,
Winnowing the lightsome air with languid plumes,
My coursers sought their birthplace in the sun,

Where they henceforth will live exempt from toil
Pasturing flowers of vegetable fire.   110
And where my moonlike car will stand within
A temple, gazed upon by Phidian forms
Of thee, and Asia, and the Earth, and me,
And you fair nymphs, looking the love we feel;
In memory of the tidings it has borne;
Beneath a dome fretted with graven flowers,
Poised on twelve columns of resplendent stone,
And open to the bright and liquid sky,
Yoked to it by an amphisbaenic snake.[101]
The likeness of those winged steeds will mock   120
The flight from which they find repose. Alas,
Whither has wandered now my partial tongue
When all remains untold which ye would hear?
As I have said I floated to the earth:
It was, as it is still, the pain of bliss
To move, to breathe, to be: I wandering went
Among the haunts and dwellings of mankind,
And first was disappointed not to see
Such mighty change as I had felt within
Expressed in outward things; but soon I looked,   130
And behold, thrones were kingless, and men walked
One with the other even as spirits do,
None fawned, none trampled; hate, disdain, or fear,
Self-love or self-contempt, on human brows
No more inscribed, as o'er the gate of hell,
'All hope abandon ye who enter here;'
None frowned, none trembled, none with eager fear
Gazed on another's eye of cold command,
Until the subject of a tyrant's will
Became, worse fate, the abject of his own,   140
Which spurred him, like an outspent horse, to death.
None wrought his lips in truth-entangling lines
Which smiled the lie his tongue disdained to speak;
None, with firm sneer, trod out in his own heart
The sparks of love and hope till there remained
Those bitter ashes, a soul self-consumed,
And the wretch crept a vampire among men,
Infecting all with his own hideous ill;

None talked that common, false, cold, hollow talk
Which makes the heart deny the *yes* it breathes,   150
Yet question that unmeant hypocrisy
With such a self-mistrust as has no name.
And women, too, frank, beautiful, and kind
As the free heaven which rains fresh light and dew
On the wide earth, passed gentle radiant forms,
From custom's evil taint exempt and pure;
Speaking the wisdom once they could not think,
Looking emotions once they feared to feel,
And changed to all which once they dared not be,
Yet being now, made earth like heaven: nor pride,   160
Nor jealousy, nor envy, nor ill shame,
The bitterest of those drops of treasured gall,
Spoilt the sweet taste of the nepenthe,[102] love.

Thrones, altars, judgement-seats, and prisons; wherein,
And beside which, by wretched men were borne
Sceptres, tiaras, swords, and chains, and tomes
Of reasoned wrong, glozed on by ignorance,
Were like those monstrous and barbaric shapes,
The ghosts of a no more remembered fame,
Which, from their unworn obelisks, look forth   170
In triumph o'er the palaces and tombs
Of those who were their conquerors, mouldering round.
These imaged, to the pride of kings and priests,
A dark yet mighty faith, a power as wide
As is the world it wasted, and are now
But an astonishment; even so the tools
And emblems of its last captivity,
Amid the dwellings of the peopled earth,
Stand, not o'erthrown, but unregarded now.
And those foul shapes, abhorred by god and man,   180
Which, under many a name and many a form
Strange, savage, ghastly, dark and execrable,
Were Jupiter, the tyrant of the world;
And which the nations, panic-stricken, served
With blood, and hearts broken by long hope, and love
Dragged to his altars soiled and garlandless,
And slain amid men's unreclaiming tears,

Flattering the thing they feared, which fear was hate,
Frown, mouldering fast, o'er their abandoned shrines:
The painted veil, by those who were, called life,   190
Which mimicked, as with colours idly spread,
All men believed or hoped, is torn aside;
The loathsome mask has fallen, the man remains
Sceptreless, free, uncircumscribed, but man
Equal, unclassed, tribeless, and nationless,
Exempt from awe, worship, degree, the king
Over himself; just, gentle, wise: but man
Passionless; no, yet free from guilt or pain,
Which were, for his will made or suffered them,
Nor yet exempt, tho' ruling them like slaves,   200
From chance, and death, and mutability,
The clogs of that which else might oversoar
The loftiest star of unascended heaven,
Pinnacled dim in the intense inane.

END OF THE THIRD ACT

ACT 4

SCENE. *A part of the forest near the cave of* PROMETHEUS.
PANTHEA *and* IONE *are sleeping: they awaken gradually during
the first song.*

Voice of unseen Spirits

The pale stars are gone!
For the sun, their swift shepherd,
To their folds them compelling,
In the depths of the dawn,
Hastes, in meteor-eclipsing array, and they flee
Beyond his blue dwelling,
As fawns flee the leopard.
But where are ye?

A train of dark forms and shadows passes by confusedly singing.

Here, oh, here:
We bear the bier   10
Of the Father of many a cancelled year!
Spectres we
Of the dead Hours be,
We bear Time to his tomb in eternity.

Strew, oh, strew
Hair, not yew!
Wet the dusty pall with tears, not dew!
Be the faded flowers
Of Death's bare bowers
Spread on the corpse of the King of Hours!   20

Haste, oh, haste!
As shades are chased,
Trembling, by day, from heaven's blue waste
We melt away,
Like dissolving spray,
From the children of a diviner day,
With the lullaby

> Of winds that die
> On the bosom of their own harmony!

Ione

> What dark forms were they?   30

Panthea

> The past Hours weak and grey,
> With the spoil which their toil
>   Raked together
> From the conquest but One could foil.

Ione

> Have they past?

Panthea

>   They have past;
> They outspeeded the blast,
> While 'tis said, they are fled:

Ione

> Whither, oh, whither?

Panthea

> To the dark, to the past, to the dead.

Voice of unseen Spirits

> Bright clouds float in heaven,   40
> Dew-stars gleam on earth,
> Waves assemble on ocean,
> They are gathered and driven
> By the storm of delight, by the panic of glee!
> They shake with emotion,
> They dance in their mirth.
>   But where are ye?

> The pine boughs are singing
> Old songs with new gladness,
> The billows and fountains   50
> Fresh music are flinging,
> Like the notes of a spirit from land and from sea;

The storms mock the mountains
With the thunder of gladness.
But where are ye?

Ione   What charioteers are these?
Panthea   Where are their chariots?

Semichorus of Hours

The voice of the Spirits of Air and of Earth
    Have drawn back the figured curtain of sleep
Which covered our being and darkened our birth
    In the deep.

A Voice

In the deep?

Semichorus II

                    Oh, below the deep.   60

Semichorus I

An hundred ages we had been kept
    Cradled in visions of hate and care,
And each one who waked as his brother slept,
    Found the truth –

Semichorus II

                    Worse than his visions were!

Semichorus I

We have heard the lute of Hope in sleep;
    We have known the voice of Love in dreams,
We have felt the wand of Power, and leap –

Semichorus II

As the billows leap in the morning beams!

Chorus

Weave the dance on the floor of the breeze,
    Pierce with song heaven's silent light,   70
Enchant the day that too swiftly flees,
    To check its flight ere the cave of night.

Once the hungry Hours were hounds
   Which chased the day like a bleeding deer,
And it limped and stumbled with many wounds
   Through the nightly dells of the desert year.

But now, oh weave the mystic measure
   Of music, and dance, and shapes of light,
Let the Hours, and the spirits of might and pleasure,
   Like the clouds and sunbeams, unite.

A Voice

                            Unite!   80

Panthea   See, where the Spirits of the human mind
Wrapt in sweet sounds, as in bright veils, approach.

Chorus of Spirits

We join the throng
   Of the dance and the song,
By the whirlwind of gladness borne along;
   As the flying-fish leap
   From the Indian deep,
And mix with the sea-birds half asleep.

Chorus of Hours

Whence come ye, so wild and so fleet,
For sandals of lightning are on your feet,   90
And your wings are soft and swift as thought,
And your eyes are as love which is veiled not?

Chorus of Spirits

We come from the mind
   Of human kind
Which was late so dusk, and obscene, and blind,
   Now 'tis an ocean
   Of clear emotion,
A heaven of serene and mighty motion.

From that deep abyss
   Of wonder and bliss,   100
Whose caverns are crystal palaces;

From those skiey towers
Where Thought's crowned powers
Sit watching your dance, ye happy Hours!

From the dim recesses
Of woven caresses,
Where lovers catch ye by your loose tresses;
From the azure isles,
Where sweet Wisdom smiles,
Delaying your ships with her siren wiles.   110

From the temples high
Of Man's ear and eye,
Roofed over Sculpture and Poesy;
From the murmurings
Of the unsealed springs
Where Science bedews her Daedal wings.

Years after years,
Through blood, and tears,
And a thick hell of hatreds, and hopes, and fears;
We waded and flew,   120
And the islets were few
Where the bud-blighted flowers of happiness grew.

Our feet now, every palm,
Are sandalled with calm,
And the dew of our wings is a rain of balm;
And, beyond our eyes,
The human love lies
Which makes all it gazes on Paradise.

Chorus of Spirits and Hours

Then weave the web of the mystic measure;
From the depths of the sky and the ends of the earth,
Come, swift Spirits of might and of pleasure,   131
Fill the dance and the music of mirth,
As the waves of a thousand streams rush by
To an ocean of splendour and harmony!

Chorus of Spirits

Our spoil is won,[103]
Our task is done,
We are free to dive, or soar, or run;
Beyond and around,
Or within the bound
Which clips the world with darkness round.   140

We'll pass the eyes
Of the starry skies
Into the hoar deep to colonise:
Death, Chaos, and Night,
From the sound of our flight,
Shall flee, like mist from a tempest's might.

And Earth, Air, and Light,
And the Spirit of Might,
Which drives round the stars in their fiery flight;
And Love, Thought, and Breath,   150
The powers that quell Death,
Wherever we soar shall assemble beneath.

And our singing shall build
In the void's loose field
A world for the Spirit of Wisdom to wield;
We will take our plan
From the new world of man,
And our work shall be called the Promethean.

Chorus of Hours

Break the dance, and scatter the song;
Let some depart, and some remain.   160

Semichorus I

We, beyond heaven, are driven along:

Semichorus II

Us the enchantments of earth retain:

Semichorus I

Ceaseless, and rapid, and fierce, and free,
With the Spirits which build a new earth and sea,
And a heaven where yet heaven could never be;

Semichorus II

Solemn, and slow, and serene, and bright,
Leading the Day and outspeeding the Night,
With the powers of a world of perfect light;

Semichorus I

We whirl, singing loud, round the gathering sphere,
Till the trees, and the beasts, and the clouds appear   170
From its chaos made calm by love, not fear.

Semichorus II

We encircle the ocean and mountains of earth,
And the happy forms of its death and birth
Change to the music of our sweet mirth.

Chorus of Hours and Spirits

Break the dance, and scatter the song,
    Let some depart, and some remain,
Wherever we fly we lead along
In leashes, like starbeams, soft yet strong,
    The clouds that are heavy with love's sweet rain.

Panthea   Ha! they are gone!
Ione   Yet feel you no delight   180
From the past sweetness?
Panthea   As the bare green hill
When some soft cloud vanishes into rain,
Laughs with a thousand drops of sunny water
To the unpavilioned sky!
Ione   Even whilst we speak
New notes arise. What is that awful sound?
Panthea   'Tis the deep music of the rolling world
Kindling within the strings of the waved air
Aeolian modulations.
Ione   Listen too,
How every pause is filled with under-notes,

         Clear, silver, icy, keen awakening tones, 190
         Which pierce the sense, and live within the soul,
         As the sharp stars pierce winter's crystal air
         And gaze upon themselves within the sea.

Panthea   But see where through two openings in the forest
         Which hanging branches overcanopy,
         And where two runnels of a rivulet,
         Between the close moss violet-inwoven,
         Have made their path of melody, like sisters
         Who part with sighs that they may meet in smiles,
         Turning their dear disunion to an isle 200
         Of lovely grief, a wood of sweet sad thoughts;
         Two visions of strange radiance float upon
         The ocean-like enchantment of strong sound,
         Which flows intenser, keener, deeper yet
         Under the ground and through the windless air.

Ione   I see a chariot like that thinnest boat,
         In which the mother of the months is borne
         By ebbing light into her western cave,
         When she upsprings from interlunar dreams,
         O'er which is curved an orb-like canopy 210
         Of gentle darkness, and the hills and woods
         Distinctly seen through that dusk aery veil,
         Regard like shapes in an enchanter's glass;
         Its wheels are solid clouds, azure and gold,
         Such as the genii of the thunderstorm,
         Pile on the floor of the illumined sea
         When the sun rushes under it; they roll
         And move and grow as with an inward wind;
         Within it sits a winged infant, white
         Its countenance, Iike the whiteness of bright snow, 220
         Its plumes are as feathers of sunny frost,
         Its limbs gleam white, through the wind-flowing folds
         Of its white robe, woof of ethereal pearl.
         Its hair is white, the brightness of white light
         Scattered in strings; yet its two eyes are heavens
         Of liquid darkness, which the Deity
         Within seems pouring, as a storm is poured
         From jagged clouds, out of their arrowy lashes,
         Tempering the cold and radiant air around,

With fire that is not brightness; in its hand   230
It sways a quivering moonbeam, from whose point
A guiding power directs the chariot's prow
Over its wheeled clouds, which as they roll
Over the grass, and flowers, and waves, wake sounds,
Sweet as a singing rain of silver dew.

Panthea   And from the other opening in the wood
Rushes, with loud and whirlwind harmony,
A sphere, which is as many thousand spheres,
Solid as chrystal, yet through all its mass
Flow, as through empty space, music and light: 240
Ten thousand orbs involving and involved,
Purple and azure, white, and green, and golden,
Sphere within sphere; and every space between
Peopled with unimaginable shapes,
Such as ghosts dream dwell in the lampless deep,
Yet each inter-transpicuous, and they whirl
Over each other with a thousand motions,
Upon a thousand sightless axles spinning,
And with the force of self-destroying swiftness,
Intensely, slowly, solemnly roll on,   250
Kindling with mingled sounds, and many tones,
Intelligible words and music wild.
With mighty whirl the multitudinous orb
Grinds the bright brook into an azure mist
Of elemental subtlety, Iike light;
And the wild odour of the forest flowers,
The music of the living grass and air,
The emerald light of leaf-entangled beams
Round its intense yet self-conflicting speed,
Seem kneaded into one aerial mass   260
Which drowns the sense. Within the orb itself,
Pillowed upon its alabaster arms,
Like to a child o'erwearied with sweet toil,
On its own folded wings, and wavy hair,
The Spirit of the Earth is laid asleep,
And you can see its little lips are moving,
Amid the changing light of their own smiles,
Like one who talks of what he loves in dream.

Ione   'Tis only mocking the orb's harmony.

Panthea   And from a star upon its forehead, shoot,   270
Like swords of azure fire, or golden spears
With tyrant-quelling myrtle overtwined,
Embleming heaven and earth united now,
Vast beams like spokes of some invisible wheel
Which whirl as the orb whirls, swifter than thought,
Filling the abyss with sun-like lightnings,
And perpendicular now, and now transverse,
Pierce the dark soil, and as they pierce and pass,
Make bare the secrets of the earth's deep heart;
Infinite mines of adamant and gold,   280
Valueless stones, and unimagined gems,
And caverns on crystalline columns poised
With vegetable silver overspread;
Wells of unfathomed fire, and water springs
Whence the great sea, even as a child is fed,
Whose vapours clothe earth's monarch mountain-tops
With kingly, ermine snow. The beams flash on
And make appear the melancholy ruins
Of cancelled cycles; anchors, beaks of ships;
Planks turned to marble; quivers, helms, and spears,   290
And gorgon-headed targes, and the wheels
Of scythed chariots, and the emblazonry
Of trophies, standards, and armorial beasts,
Round which death laughed, sepulchred emblems
Of dead destruction, ruin within ruin!
The wrecks beside of many a city vast,
Whose population which the earth grew over
Was mortal, but not human; see, they lie
Their monstrous works, and uncouth skeletons,
Their statues, homes and fanes; prodigious shapes   300
Huddled in grey annihilation, split,
Jammed in the hard, black deep; and over these,
The anatomies of unknown winged things,
And fishes which were isles of living scale,
And serpents, bony chains, twisted around
The iron crags, or within heaps of dust
To which the tortuous strength of their last pangs
Had crushed the iron crags; and over these
The jagged alligator, and the might

Of earth-convulsing behemoth, which once   310
Were monarch beasts, and on the slimy shores,
And weed-overgrown continents of earth,
Increased and multiplied like summer worms
On an abandoned corpse, till the blue globe
Wrapped deluge round it like a cloak, and they
Yelled, gasped, and were abolished; or some God
Whose throne was in a comet, past, and cried,
Be not! And like my words they were no more.

The Earth

The joy, the triumph, the delight, the madness!
  The boundless, overflowing, bursting gladness,   320
The vaporous exultation not to be confined!
  Ha! ha! the animation of delight
  Which wraps me, like an atmosphere of light,
And bears me as a cloud is borne by its own wind.

The Moon

Brother mine, calm wanderer,
  Happy globe of land and air,
Some Spirit is darted like a beam from thee,
  Which penetrates my frozen frame,
  And passes with the warmth of flame,
With love, and odour, and deep melody   330
  Through me, through me!

The Earth

Ha! ha! the caverns of my hollow mountains,
  My cloven fire-crags, sound-exulting fountains
Laugh with a vast and inextinguishable laughter.
  The oceans, and the deserts, and the abysses
  Of the deep air's unmeasured wildernesses,
Answer from all their clouds and billows, echoing after.

They cry aloud as I do. Sceptred curse,
  Who all our green and azure universe
Threatenedst to muffle round with black destruction, sending
  A solid cloud to rain hot thunder-stones,   341
  And splinter and knead down my children's bones
All I bring forth, to one void mass battering and blending.

Until each crag-like tower, and storeyed column,
Palace, and obelisk, and temple solemn,
My imperial mountains crowned with cloud, and snow,
and fire;
My sea-like forests, every blade and blossom
Which finds a grave or cradle in my bosom,
Were stamped by thy strong hate into a lifeless mire.

How art thou sunk, withdrawn, covered, drunk up   350
By thirsty nothing, as the brackish cup
Drained by a desert-troop, a little drop for all;
And from beneath, around, within, above,
Filling thy void annihilation, love
Bursts in like light on caves cloven by the thunder-ball.

The Moon

The snow upon my lifeless mountains
Is loosened into living fountains,
My solid oceans flow, and sing, and shine:
A spirit from my heart bursts forth,
It clothes with unexpected birth   360
My cold bare bosom: Oh! it must be thine
On mine, on mine!

Gazing on thee I feel, I know
Green stalks burst forth, and bright flowers grow,
And living shapes upon my bosom move:
Music is in the sea and air,
Winged clouds soar here and there,
Dark with the rain new buds are dreaming of:
'Tis love, all love!

The Earth

It interpenetrates my granite mass,   370
Through tangled roots and trodden clay doth pass,
Into the utmost leaves and delicatest flowers;
Upon the winds, among the clouds 'tis spread,
It wakes a life in the forgotten dead,
They breathe a spirit up from their obscurest bowers.

And like a storm bursting its cloudy prison
With thunder, and with whirlwind, has arisen
Out of the lampless caves of unimagined being:
With earthquake shock and swiftness making shiver
Thought's stagnant chaos, unremoved for ever,   380
Till hate, and fear, and pain, light-vanquished shadows, fleeing,

Leave Man, who was a many-sided mirror,
Which could distort to many a shape of error,
This true fair world of things, a sea reflecting love;
Which over all his kind as the sun's heaven
Gliding o'er ocean, smooth, serene, and even,
Darting from starry depths radiance and life, doth move.

Leave man, even as a leprous child is left,
Who follows a sick beast to some warm cleft
Of rocks, through which the might of healing springs
                                        is poured;
Then when it wanders home with rosy smile,   391
Unconscious, and its mother fears awhile
It is a spirit, then, weeps on her child restored.

Man, oh, not men! a chain of linked thought,
Of love and might to be devoted not,
Compelling the elements with adamantine stress;
As the sun rules, even with a tyrant's gaze,
The unquiet republic of the maze
Of planets, struggling fierce towards heaven's free wilderness.

Man, one harmonious soul of many a soul,   400
Whose nature is its own divine control,
Where all things flow to all, as rivers to the sea;
Familiar acts are beautiful through love;
Labour, and pain, and grief, in life's green grove
Sport like tame beasts, none knew how gentle they could be!

His will, with all mean passions, bad delights,
And selfish cares, its trembling satellites,
A spirit ill to guide, but mighty to obey,
Is as a tempest-winged ship, whose helm
Love rules, through waves which dare not overwhelm,   410
Forcing life's wildest shores to own its sovereign sway.

All things confess his strength. Through the cold mass
  Of marble and of colour his dreams pass;
Bright threads whence mothers weave the robes their
                                       children wear;
  Language is a perpetual orphic song,
  Which rules with Daedal harmony a throng
Of thoughts and forms, which else senseless and shapeless were.

  The lightning is his slave; heaven's utmost deep
  Gives up her stars, and like a flock of sheep
They pass before his eye, are numbered, and roll on!   420
  The tempest is his steed, he strides the air;
  And the abyss shouts from her depth laid bare,
Heaven, hast thou secrets? Man unveils me; I have none.

The Moon

  The shadow of white death has past
  From my path in heaven at last,
A clinging shroud of solid frost and sleep;
  And through my newly-woven bowers,
  Wander happy paramours,
Less mighty, but as mild as those who keep
    Thy vales more deep.   430

The Earth

  As the dissolving warmth of dawn may fold
  A half unfrozen dew-globe, green, and gold,
And crystalline, till it becomes a winged mist,
  And wanders up the vault of the blue day,
  Outlives the noon, and on the sun's last ray
Hangs o'er the sea, a fleece of fire and amethyst.

The Moon

  Thou art folded, thou art lying
  In the light which is undying
Of thine own joy, and heaven's smile divine;
  All suns and constellations shower   440
  On thee a light, a life, a power
Which doth array thy sphere; thou pourest thine
    On mine, on mine!

The Earth

I spin beneath my pyramid of night,
  Which points into the heavens dreaming delight,
Murmuring victorious joy in my enchanted sleep;
  As a youth lulled in love-dreams faintly sighing,
  Under the shadow of his beauty lying,
Which round his rest a watch of light and warmth
                                    doth keep.

The Moon

As in the soft and sweet eclipse,   450
  When soul meets soul on lovers' lips,
High hearts are calm, and brightest eyes are dull;
  So when thy shadow falls on me,
  Then am I mute and still, by thee
Covered; of thy love, Orb most beautiful,
      Full, oh, too full!

Thou art speeding round the sun
Brightest world of many a one; –
Green and azure sphere which shinest
With a light which is divinest   460
Among all the lamps of Heaven
To whom life and light is given;
I, thy crystal paramour
Borne beside thee by a power
Like the polar Paradise,
Magnet-like of lovers' eyes;
I, a most enamoured maiden
Whose weak brain is overladen
With the pleasure of her love,
Maniac-like around thee move   470
Gazing, an insatiate bride,
On thy form from every side
Like a Maenad, round the cup
Which Agave lifted up
In the weird Cadmaean forest.
Brother, wheresoe'er thou soarest
I must hurry, whirl and follow
Through the heavens wide and hollow,

Sheltered by the warm embrace
Of thy soul from hungry space,   480
Drinking from thy sense and sight
Beauty, majesty, and might,
As a lover or a cameleon
Grows like what it looks upon,
As a violet's gentle eye
Gazes on the azure sky
Until its hue grows like what it beholds,
As a grey and watery mist
Glows like solid amethyst
Athwart the western mountain it enfolds,   490
When the sunset sleeps
Upon its snow.

The Earth

And the weak day weeps
That it should be so.
Oh, gentle Moon, the voice of thy delight
Falls on me like thy clear and tender light
Soothing the seaman, borne the summer night,
Through isles for ever calm;
Oh, gentle Moon, thy crystal accents pierce
The caverns of my pride's deep universe,   500
Charming the tiger joy, whose tramplings fierce
Made wounds which need thy balm.

Panthea   I rise as from a bath of sparkling water,
A bath of azure light, among dark rocks,
Out of the stream of sound.

Ione   Ah me! sweet sister,
The stream of sound has ebbed away from us,
And you pretend to rise out of its wave,
Because your words fall like the clear, soft dew
Shaken from a bathing wood-nymph's limbs and hair.

Panthea   Peace! peace! A mighty Power, which is as darkness,   510
Is rising out of Earth, and from the sky
Is showered like night, and from within the air
Bursts, like eclipse which had been gathered up
Into the pores of sunlight: the bright visions,

Wherein the singing spirits rode and shone,
Gleam like pale meteors through a watery night.
Ione There is a sense of words upon mine ear.
Panthea An universal sound like words: Oh, list!

Demogorgon

Thou, Earth, calm empire of a happy soul,
   Sphere of divinest shapes and harmonies,   520
Beautiful orb! gathering as thou dost roll
   The love which paves thy path along the skies:

The Earth

I hear: I am as a drop of dew that dies.

Demogorgon

Thou, Moon, which gazest on the nightly Earth
   With wonder, as it gazes upon thee;
Whilst each to men, and beasts, and the swift birth
   Of birds, is beauty, love, calm, harmony:

The Moon

I hear: I am a leaf shaken by thee!

Demogorgon

Ye kings of suns and stars, Daemons and Gods,
   Ethereal Dominations, who possess   530
Elysian, windless, fortunate abodes
   Beyond Heaven's constellated wilderness:

A Voice from above

Our great Republic hears, we are blest, and bless.

Demogorgon

Ye happy dead, whom beams of brightest verse
   Are clouds to hide, not colours to portray,
Whether your nature is that universe
   Which once ye saw and suffered –

A Voice from beneath

               Or as they
Whom we have left, we change and pass away.

Demogorgon

Ye elemental Genii, who have homes
    From man's high mind even to the central stone   540
Of sullen lead; from Heaven's star-fretted domes
    To the dull weed some sea-worm battens on:

A confused Voice

We hear: thy words waken Oblivion.

Demogorgon

Spirits, whose homes are flesh: ye beasts and birds,
    Ye worms, and fish; ye living leaves and buds;
Lightning and wind; and ye untameable herds,
    Meteors and mists, which feed air's solitudes:

A Voice

Thy voice to us is wind among still woods.

Demogorgon

Man, who wert once a despot and a slave;
    A dupe and a deceiver; a decay;   550
A traveller from the cradle to the grave
    Through the dim night of this immortal day:

All

Speak: thy strong words may never pass away.

Demogorgon

This is the day, which down the void abysm
At the Earth-born's spell yawns for Heaven's despotism,
    And Conquest is dragged captive through the deep:
Love, from its awful throne of patient power
In the wise heart, from the last giddy hour
    Of dread endurance, from the slippery, steep,
And narrow verge of crag-like agony, springs   560
And folds over the world its healing wings.

Gentleness, Virtue, Wisdom, and Endurance,
These are the seals of that most firm assurance
    Which bars the pit over Destruction's strength;

And if, with infirm hand, Eternity,
Mother of many acts and hours, should free
    The serpent that would clasp her with his length;
These are the spells by which to reassume
An empire o'er the disentangled doom.

To suffer woes which Hope thinks infinite;   570
To forgive wrongs darker than death or night;
    To defy Power, which seems omnipotent;
To love, and bear; to hope till Hope creates
From its own wreck the thing it contemplates;
    Neither to change, nor falter, nor repent;
This, like thy glory, Titan, is to be
Good, great and joyous, beautiful and free;
This is alone Life, Joy, Empire, and Victory.

The Cenci

A TRAGEDY IN FIVE ACTS

DEDICATION TO LEIGH HUNT, ESQ.[104]

My dear Friend, I inscribe with your name, from a distant country, and after an absence whose months have seemed years, this the latest of my literary efforts.

Those writings which I have hitherto published, have been little else than visions which impersonate my own apprehensions of the beautiful and the just. I can also perceive in them the literary defects incidental to youth and impatience; they are dreams of what ought to be, or may be. The drama which I now present to you is a sad reality. I lay aside the presumptuous attitude of an instructor, and am content to paint, with such colours as my own heart furnishes, that which has been. Had I known a person more highly endowed than yourself with all that it becomes a man to possess, I had solicited for this work the ornament of his name. One more gentle, honourable innocent and brave; one of more exalted toleration for all who do and think evil, and yet himself more free from evil; one who knows better how to receive, and how to confer a benefit, though he must ever confer far more than he can receive; one of simpler, and, in the highest sense of the word, of purer life and manners I never knew: and I had already been fortunate in friendships when your name was added to the list.

In that patient and irreconcilable enmity with domestic and political tyranny and imposture which the tenor of your life has illustrated, and which, had I health and talents, should illustrate mine, let us, comforting each other in our task, live and die.

All happiness attend you!

Your affectionate friend,

PERCY B. SHELLEY
Rome, 29 May 1819

PREFACE

A manuscript was communicated to me during my travels in Italy, which was copied from the archives of the Cenci Palace at Rome, and contains a detailed account of the horrors which ended in the extinction of one of the noblest and richest families of that city during the Pontificate of Clement VIII, in the year 1599. The story is that an old man, having spent his life in debauchery and wickedness, conceived at length an implacable hatred towards his children; which showed itself towards one daughter under the form of an incestuous passion, aggravated by every circumstance of cruelty and violence. This daughter, after long and vain attempts to escape from what she considered a perpetual contamination both of body and mind, at length plotted with her mother-in-law and brother to murder their common tyrant. The young maiden, who was urged to this tremendous deed by an impulse which overpowered its horror, was evidently a most gentle and amiable being, a creature formed to adorn and be admired, and thus violently thwarted from her nature by the necessity of circumstance and opinion. The deed was quickly discovered, and, in spite of the most earnest prayers made to the Pope by the highest persons in Rome, the criminals were put to death. The old man had during his life repeatedly bought his pardon from the Pope, for capital crimes of the most enormous and unspeakable kind, at the price of a hundred thousand crowns; the death therefore of his victims can scarcely be accounted for by the love of justice. The Pope, among other motives for severity, probably felt that whoever killed the Count Cenci deprived his treasury of a certain and copious source of revenue.* Such a story, if told so as to present to the reader all the feelings of those who once acted it, their hopes and fears, their confidences and misgivings, their various interests, passions and opinions, acting upon and with each other, yet all conspiring to one tremendous end, would be as a light to make apparent some of the most dark and secret caverns of the human heart.

On my arrival at Rome I found that the story of the Cenci was a subject not to be mentioned in Italian society without awakening a deep and breathless interest; and that the feelings of the company never failed to

---

* The Papal Government formerly took the most extraordinary precautions against the publicity of facts which offer so tragical a demonstration of its own wickedness and weakness; so that the communication of the manuscript had become, until very lately, a matter of some difficulty.

incline to a romantic pity for the wrongs, and a passionate exculpation of the horrible deed to which they urged her, who has been mingled two centuries with the common dust. All ranks of people knew the outlines of this history, and participated in the overwhelming interest which it seems to have the magic of exciting in the human heart. I had a copy of Guido's picture of Beatrice which is preserved in the Colonna Palace, and my servant instantly recognised it as the portrait of *La Cenci*.

This national and universal interest which the story produces and has produced for two centuries and among all ranks of people in a great city, where the imagination is kept for ever active and awake, first suggested to me the conception of its fitness for a dramatic purpose. In fact, it is a tragedy which has already received, from its capacity of awakening and sustaining the sympathy of men, approbation and success. Nothing remained, as I imagined, but to clothe it to the apprehensions of my countrymen in such language and action as would bring it home to their hearts. The deepest and the sublimest tragic compositions, *King Lear* and the two plays in which the tale of Oedipus is told, were stories which already existed in tradition, as matters of popular belief and interest, before Shakespeare and Sophocles made them familiar to the sympathy of all succeeding generations of mankind.

This story of the Cenci is indeed eminently fearful and monstrous: anything like a dry exhibition of it on the stage would be insupportable. The person who would treat such a subject must increase the ideal, and diminish the actual horror of the events, so that the pleasure which arises from the poetry which exists in these tempestuous sufferings and crimes may mitigate the pain of the contemplation of the moral deformity from which they spring. There must also be nothing attempted to make the exhibition subservient to what is vulgarly termed a moral purpose. The highest moral purpose aimed at in the highest species of the drama is the teaching the human heart, through its sympathies and antipathies, the knowledge of itself; in proportion to the possession of which knowledge, every human being is wise, just, sincere, tolerant and kind. If dogmas can do more, it is well: but a drama is no fit place for the enforcement of them. Undoubtedly, no person can be truly dishonoured by the act of another; and the fit return to make to the most enormous injuries is kindness and forbearance, and a resolution to convert the injurer from his dark passions by peace and love. Revenge, retaliation, atonement, are pernicious mistakes. If Beatrice had thought in this manner, she would have been wiser and better; but she would never have been a tragic character: the few whom such an exhibition would have interested, could never have been sufficiently interested for a dramatic purpose, from the want of finding sympathy in their interest among the mass who surround them. It is in the restless and anatomising casuistry with which men seek the justification of Beatrice, yet feel that she has done what needs justification; it is in the superstitious horror with which they contemplate alike her wrongs and their revenge; that the dramatic character of what she did and suffered consists.

I have endeavoured as nearly as possible to represent the characters as they probably were, and have sought to avoid the error of making them actuated by my own conceptions of right or wrong, false or true: thus under a thin veil converting names and actions of the sixteenth century into cold impersonations of my own mind. They are represented as Catholics, and as Catholics deeply tinged with religion. To a Protestant apprehension there will appear something unnatural in the earnest and perpetual sentiment of the relations between God and men which pervade the tragedy of the Cenci. It will especially be startled at the combination of an undoubting persuasion of the truth of the popular religion with a cool and determined perseverance in enormous guilt. But religion in Italy is not, as in Protestant countries, a cloak to be worn on particular days; or a passport which those who do not wish to be railed at carry with them to exhibit; or a gloomy passion for penetrating the impenetrable mysteries of our beings which terrifies its possessor at the darkness of the abyss to the brink of which it has conducted him. Religion coexists, as it were, in the mind of an Italian Catholic, with a faith in that of which all men have the most certain knowledge. It is interwoven with the whole fabric of life. It is adoration, faith, submission, penitence, blind admiration; not a rule for moral conduct. It has no necessary connection with any one virtue. The most atrocious villain may be rigidly devout, and without any shock to established faith, confess himself to be so. Religion pervades intensely the whole frame of society, and is according to the temper of the mind which it inhabits, a passion, a persuasion, an excuse, a refuge; never a check. Cenci himself built a chapel in the court of his Palace, and dedicated it to St Thomas the Apostle, and established masses for the peace of his soul. Thus, in the first scene of the fourth act, Lucretia's design in exposing herself to the consequences of an expostulation with Cenci, after having administered the opiate, was to induce him by a feigned tale to confess himself before death; this being esteemed by Catholics as essential to salvation; and she only relinquishes her purpose when she perceives that her perseverance would expose Beatrice to new outrages.

I have avoided with great care in writing this play the introduction of what is commonly called mere poetry, and I imagine there will scarcely be found a detached simile or a single isolated description, unless Beatrice's description of the chasm appointed for her father's murder should be judged to be of that nature.*

In a dramatic composition the imagery and the passion should interpenetrate one another, the former being reserved simply for the full development and illustration of the latter. Imagination is as the immortal God which should assume flesh for the redemption of mortal passion. It is thus that the most remote and the most familiar imagery may alike be fit for dramatic purposes when employed in the illustration of strong feeling, which raises what is low, and levels to the apprehension that which is lofty, casting over all the shadow of its own greatness. In other respects I have written more carelessly; that is, without an over-fastidious and learned choice of words. In this respect I entirely agree with those modern critics who assert that in order to move men to true sympathy we must use the familiar language of men, and that our great ancestors, the ancient English poets, are the writers a study of whom might incite us to do that for our own age which they have done for theirs. But it must be the real language of men in general and not that of any particular class to whose society the writer happens to belong. So much for what I have attempted; I need not be assured that success is a very different matter: particularly for one whose attention has but newly been awakened to the study of dramatic literature.

I endeavoured whilst at Rome to observe such monuments of this story as might be accessible to a stranger. The portrait of Beatrice at the Colonna Palace is most admirable as a work of art: it was taken by Guido during her confinement in prison. But it is most interesting as a just representation of one of the loveliest specimens of the workmanship of Nature. There is a fixed and pale composure upon the features: she seems sad and stricken down in spirit, yet the despair thus expressed is lightened by the patience of gentleness. Her head is bound with folds of white drapery from which the yellow strings of her golden hair escape, and fall about her neck. The moulding of her face is exquisitely delicate; the eyebrows are distinct and arched; the lips have that permanent meaning of imagination and sensibility which suffering has not repressed and which it seems as if death scarcely could extinguish. Her forehead is large and clear; her eyes which we are told were remarkable for their vivacity, are swollen with weeping and lustreless, but beautifully tender and serene. In the whole mien there is a

* An idea in this speech was suggested by a most sublime passage in *El Purgatorio de San Patricio* of Calderon: the only plagiarism which I have intentionally committed in the whole piece.

simplicity and dignity which, united with her exquisite loveliness and deep sorrow, are inexpressibly pathetic. Beatrice Cenci appears to have been one of those rare persons in whom energy and gentleness dwell together without destroying one another: her nature was simple and profound. The crimes and miseries in which she was an actor and a sufferer are as the mask and the mantle in which circumstances clothed her for her impersonation on the scene of the world.

The Cenci Palace is of great extent; and, though in part modernised, there yet remains a vast and gloomy pile of feudal architecture in the same state as during the dreadful scenes which are the subject of this tragedy. The palace is situated in an obscure corner of Rome, near the quarter of the Jews, and from the upper windows you see the immense ruins of Mount Palatine, half hidden under their profuse overgrowth of trees. There is a court in one part of the palace (perhaps that in which Cenci built the chapel to St Thomas), supported by granite columns and adorned with antique friezes of fine workmanship, and built up, according to the ancient Italian fashion, with balcony over balcony of open-work. One of the gates of the palace, formed of immense stones and leading through a passage, dark and lofty and opening into gloomy subterranean chambers, struck me particularly.

Of the Castle of Petrella, I could obtain no further information than that which is to be found in the manuscript.

DRAMATIS PERSONAE

COUNT FRANCESCO CENCI

GIACOMO }
BERNARDO } *his sons*

BEATRICE *his daughter*

LUCRETIA *wife of Cenci and stepmother of his children*

CARDINAL CAMILLO

ORSINO *a prelate*

SAVELLA *the Pope's legate*

OLIMPIO }
MARZIO } *assassins*

ANDREA *servant to Cenci*

Nobles, Judges, Guards, Servants

The SCENE *lies principally in Rome, but changes during the Fourth Act to Petrella, a castle among the Apulian Apennines.* TIME: *During the pontificate of Clement VIII.*

ACT I, SCENE 1

An apartment in the Cenci Palace. Enter COUNT CENCI *and* CARDINAL CAMILLO.

Camillo	That matter of the murder is hushed up
	If you consent to yield his Holiness
	Your fief[105] that lies beyond the Pincian gate. –
	It needed all my interest in the conclave
	To bend him to this point: he said that you
	Bought perilous impunity with your gold;
	That crimes like yours if once or twice compounded
	Enriched the Church, and respited from hell
	An erring soul which might repent and live: –
	But that the glory and the interest
	Of the high throne he fills, little consist
	With making it a daily mart of guilt
	As manifold and hideous as the deeds
	Which you scarce hide from men's revolted eyes.
Cenci	The third of my possessions – let it go!
	Aye, I once heard the nephew of the Pope

10

Had sent his architect to view the ground,
Meaning to build a villa on my vines
The next time I compounded with his uncle:
I little thought he should outwit me so!   20
Henceforth no witness – not the lamp – shall see
That which the vassal threatened to divulge
Whose throat is choked with dust for his reward.
The deed he saw could not have rated higher
Than his most worthless life: – it angers me!
Respited me from Hell! – So may the Devil
Respite their souls from Heaven. No doubt Pope Clement,
And his most charitable nephews, pray
That the Apostle Peter and the Saints
Will grant for their sake that I long enjoy   30
Strength, wealth, and pride, and lust, and length of days
Wherein to act the deeds which are the stewards
Of their revenue. – But much yet remains
To which they show no title.

Camillo   Oh, Count Cenci!
So much that thou mightst honourably live
And reconcile thyself with thine own heart
And with thy God, and with the offended world.
How hideously look deeds of lust and blood
Thro' those snow-white and venerable hairs! –
Your children should be sitting round you now,   40
But that you fear to read upon their looks
The shame and misery you have written there.
Where is your wife? Where is your gentle daughter?
Methinks her sweet looks, which make all things else
Beauteous and glad, might kill the fiend within you.
Why is she barred from all society
But her own strange and uncomplaining wrongs?
Talk with me, Count, – you know I mean you well.
I stood beside your dark and fiery youth
Watching its bold and bad career, as men   50
Watch meteors, but it vanished not – I marked
Your desperate and remorseless manhood; now
Do I behold you in dishonoured age
Charged with a thousand unrepented crimes.
Yet I have ever hoped you would amend,

	And in that hope have saved your life three times.	
Cenci	For which Aldobrandino[106] owes you now	

       And in that hope have saved your life three times.

Cenci   For which Aldobrandino[106] owes you now
       My fief beyond the Pincian. – Cardinal,
       One thing, I pray you, recollect henceforth,
       And so we shall converse with less restraint.   60
       A man you knew spoke of my wife and daughter –
       He was accustomed to frequent my house;
       So the next day *his* wife and daughter came
       And asked if I had seen him; and I smiled:
       I think they never saw him any more.

Camillo Thou execrable man, beware! –

Cenci   Of thee?
       Nay, this is idle: – We should know each other.
       As to my character for what men call crime,
       Seeing I please my senses as I list,
       And vindicate that right with force or guile,   70
       It is a public matter, and I care not
       If I discuss it with you. I may speak
       Alike to you and my own conscious heart –
       For you give out that you have half reformed me,
       Therefore strong vanity will keep you silent
       If fear should not; both will, I do not doubt.
       All men delight in sensual luxury,
       All men enjoy revenge; and most exult
       Over the tortures they can never feel –
       Flattering their secret peace with others' pain.   80
       But I delight in nothing else. I love
       The sight of agony, and the sense of joy,
       When this shall be another's, and not mine.
       And I have no remorse and little fear,
       Which are, I think, the checks of other men.
       This mood has grown upon me, until now
       Any design my captious fancy makes
       The picture of its wish, and it forms none
       But such as men like you would start to know,
       Is as my natural food and rest debarred   90
       Until it be accomplished.

Camillo   Art thou not
       Most miserable?

Cenci   Why, miserable? –

No. – I am what your theologians call
Hardened; – which they must be in impudence,
So to revile a man's peculiar taste.
True, I was happier than I am, while yet
Manhood remained to act the thing I thought;
While lust was sweeter than revenge; and now
Invention palls: – Aye, we must all grow old –
And but that there yet remains a deed to act   100
Whose horror might make sharp an appetite
Duller than mine – I'd do, – I know not what.
When I was young I thought of nothing else
But pleasure; and I fed on honey sweets:
Men, by St Thomas! cannot live like bees,
And I grew tired: – yet, till I killed a foe,
And heard his groans, and heard his children's groans,
Knew I not what delight was else on earth,
Which now delights me little. I the rather
Look on such pangs as terror ill conceals,   110
The dry fixed eyeball; the pale quivering lip,
Which tell me that the spirit weeps within
Tears bitterer than the bloody sweat of Christ.
I rarely kill the body, which preserves,
Like a strong prison, the soul within my power,
Wherein I feed it with the breath of fear
For hourly pain.

Camillo   Hell's most abandoned fiend
Did never, in the drunkenness of guilt,
Speak to his heart as now you speak to me;
I thank my God that I believe you not.   120

                    Enter ANDREA

Andrea   My Lord, a gentleman from Salamanca
Would speak with you.

Cenci   Bid him attend me in
The grand saloon.   [*Exit* ANDREA

Camillo   Farewell; and I will pray
Almighty God that thy false, impious words
Tempt not his spirit to abandon thee.   [*Exit* CAMILLO

Cenci   The third of my possessions! I must use
Close husbandry, or gold, the old man's sword,
Falls from my withered hand. But yesterday

There came an order from the Pope to make
Fourfold provision for my cursed sons;   130
Whom I had sent from Rome to Salamanca,
Hoping some accident might cut them off;
And meaning if I could to starve them there.
I pray thee, God, send some quick death upon them!
Bernardo and my wife could not be worse
If dead and damned: – then, as to Beatrice –
[*looking around him suspiciously*]
I think they cannot hear me at that door;
What if they should? And yet I need not speak
Though the heart triumphs with itself in words.
O thou most silent air, that shalt not hear   140
What now I think! Thou, pavement, which I tread
Towards her chamber, – let your echoes talk
Of my imperious step scorning surprise,
But not of my intent! – Andrea!

Enter ANDREA

Andrea	My lord?
Cenci	Bid Beatrice attend me in her chamber
	This evening: – no, at midnight and alone.

[*Exeunt*

SCENE II

A garden of the Cenci Palace. Enter BEATRICE *and* ORSINO, *as in
conversation.*

Beatrice	Pervert not truth,
	Orsino. You remember where we held
	That conversation; – nay, we see the spot
	Even from this cypress; – two long years are past
	Since, on an April midnight, underneath
	The moonlight ruins of mount Palatine,
	I did confess to you my secret mind.
Orsino	You said you loved me then.
Beatrice	You are a Priest,
	Speak to me not of love.
Orsino	I may obtain

	The dispensation of the Pope to marry.	10
	Because I am a Priest do you believe	
	Your image, as the hunter some struck deer,	
	Follows me not whether I wake or sleep?	
Beatrice	As I have said, speak to me not of love;	
	Had you a dispensation I have not;	
	Nor will I leave this home of misery	
	Whilst my poor Bernard, and that gentle lady	
	To whom I owe life, and these virtuous thoughts,	
	Must suffer what I still have strength to share.	
	Alas, Orsino! all the love that once	20
	I felt for you, is turned to bitter pain.	
	Ours was a youthful contract, which you first	
	Broke, by assuming vows no Pope will loose.	
	And thus I love you still, but holily,	
	Even as a sister or a spirit might;	
	And so I swear a cold fidelity.	
	And it is well perhaps we shall not marry.	
	You have a sly, equivocating vein	
	That suits me not. – Ah, wretched that I am!	
	Where shall I turn? Even now you look on me	30
	As you were not my friend, and as if you	
	Discovered that I thought so, with false smiles	
	Making my true suspicion seem your wrong.	
	Ah! No, forgive me; sorrow makes me seem	
	Sterner than else my nature might have been;	
	I have a weight of melancholy thoughts,	
	And they forbode, – but what can they forbode	
	Worse than I now endure?	
Orsino	All will be well.	
	Is the petition yet prepared? You know	
	My zeal for all you wish, sweet Beatrice;	40
	Doubt not but I will use my utmost skill	
	So that the Pope attend to your complaint.	
Beatrice	Your zeal for all I wish; – Ah me, you are cold!	
	Your utmost skill . . . speak but one word . . . [Aside] Alas!	
	Weak and deserted creature that I am,	
	Here I stand bickering with my only friend! [To ORSINO	
	[To Orsino] This night my father gives a sumptuous feast,	
	Orsino; he has heard some happy news	

From Salamanca, from my brothers there,
And with this outward show of love he mocks   50
His inward hate. 'Tis bold hypocrisy,
For he would gladlier celebrate their deaths,
Which I have heard him pray for on his knees:
Great God! that such a father should be mine!
But there is mighty preparation made,
And all our kin, the Cenci, will be there,
And all the chief nobility of Rome.
And he has bidden me and my pale Mother
Attire ourselves in festival array.
Poor lady! She expects some happy change   60
In his dark spirit from this act; I none.
At supper I will give you the petition:
Till when – farewell.

Orsino   Farewell.   [*Exit* BEATRICE
                         I know the Pope
Will ne'er absolve me from my priestly vow
But by absolving me from the revenue
Of many a wealthy see; and, Beatrice,
I think to win thee at an easier rate.
Nor shall he read her eloquent petition:
He might bestow her on some poor relation
Of his sixth cousin, as he did her sister,   70
And I should be debarred from all access.
Then as to what she suffers from her father,
In all this there is much exaggeration: –
Old men are testy and will have their way;
A man may stab his enemy, or his vassal,
And live a free life as to wine or women,
And with a peevish temper may return
To a dull home, and rate his wife and children;
Daughters and wives call this foul tyranny.
I shall be well content if on my conscience   80
There rest no heavier sin than what they suffer
From the devices of my love – a net
From which she shall escape not. Yet I fear
Her subtle mind, her awe-inspiring gaze,
Whose beams anatomise me nerve by nerve
And lay me bare, and make me blush to see

My hidden thoughts. – Ah, no! A friendless girl
Who clings to me, as to her only hope: –
I were a fool, not less than if a panther
Were panic-stricken by the antelope's eye,   90
If she escape me.

[*Exit*

SCENE III

A magnificent hall in the Cenci Palace. A banquet. Enter CENCI,
LUCRETIA, BEATRICE, ORSINO, CAMILLO, NOBLES.

Cenci	Welcome, my friends and kinsmen; welcome ye,
	Princes and Cardinals, pillars of the church,
	Whose presence honours our festivity.
	I have too long lived like an anchorite,
	And in my absence from your merry meetings
	An evil word is gone abroad of me;
	But I do hope that you, my noble friends,
	When you have shared the entertainment here,
	And heard the pious cause for which 'tis given

And we have pledged a health or two together,   10
Will think me flesh and blood as well as you;
Sinful indeed, for Adam made all so,
But tender-hearted, meek and pitiful.

First Guest   In truth, my Lord, you seem too light of heart,
Too sprightly and companionable a man,
To act the deeds that rumour pins on you.
[*To his companion*] I never saw such blithe and open cheer
In any eye!

Second Guest   Some most desired event,
In which we all demand a common joy,
Has brought us hither; let us hear it, Count.   20

Cenci   It is indeed a most desired event.
If when a parent from a parent's heart
Lifts from this earth to the great father of all
A prayer, both when he lays him down to sleep,
And when he rises up from dreaming it;
One supplication, one desire, one hope,
That he would grant a wish for his two sons,

	Even all that he demands in their regard –
	And suddenly beyond his dearest hope,
	It is accomplished, he should then rejoice, 30
	And call his friends and kinsmen to a feast,
	And task their love to grace his merriment,
	Then honour me thus far – for I am he.
Beatrice	[to Lucretia] Great God! How horrible! Some dreadful ill
	Must have befallen my brothers.
Lucretia	Fear not, Child,
	He speaks too frankly.
Beatrice	Ah! My blood runs cold.
	I fear that wicked laughter round his eye,
	Which wrinkles up the skin even to the hair.
Cenci	Here are the letters brought from Salamanca;
	Beatrice, read them to your mother. God! 40
	I thank thee! In one night didst thou perform,
	By ways inscrutable, the thing I sought.
	My disobedient and rebellious sons
	Are dead! – Why dead! – What means this change of cheer?
	You hear me not, I tell you they are dead;
	And they will need no food or raiment more:
	The tapers that did light them the dark way
	Are their last cost. The Pope, I think, will not
	Expect I should maintain them in their coffins.
	Rejoice with me – my heart is wondrous glad. 50
Beatrice	[Lucretia sinks, half fainting; Beatrice supports her]
	It is not true! – Dear lady, pray look up.
	Had it been true, there is a God in Heaven,
	He would not live to boast of such a boon.
	Unnatural man, thou knowest that it is false.
Cenci	Aye, as the word of God; whom here I call
	To witness that I speak the sober truth; –
	And whose most favouring Providence was shown
	Even in the manner of their deaths. For Rocco
	Was kneeling at the mass, with sixteen others,
	When the church fell and crushed him to a mummy, 60
	The rest escaped unhurt. Cristofano
	Was stabbed in error by a jealous man,
	Whilst she he loved was sleeping with his rival;
	All in the self-same hour of the same night;

Which shows that Heaven has special care of me.
I beg those friends who love me, that they mark
The day a feast upon their calendars.
It was the twenty-seventh of December:
Aye, read the letters if you doubt my oath.
[*The assembly appears confused; several of the guests rise*]

First Guest   Oh, horrible! I will depart –

Second Guest   And I. –

Third Guest   No, stay!   70

I do believe it is some jest; tho' faith!
'Tis mocking us somewhat too solemnly.
I think his son has married the Infanta,
Or found a mine of gold in El Dorado;
'Tis but to season some such news; stay, stay!
I see 'tis only raillery by his smile.

Cenci   [*filling a bowl of wine, and lifting it up*]
O thou bright wine, whose purple splendour leaps
And bubbles gaily in this golden bowl
Under the lamplight, as my spirits do,
To hear the death of my accursed sons!   80
Could I believe thou wert their mingled blood,
Then would I taste thee like a sacrament,
And pledge with thee the mighty Devil in Hell,
Who, if a father's curses, as men say,
Climb with swift wings after their children's souls,
And drag them from the very throne of Heaven,
Now triumphs in my triumph! – But thou art
Superfluous; I have drunken deep of joy,
And I will taste no other wine tonight.
Here, Andrea! Bear the bowl around.

A Guest   [*rising*]   Thou wretch!   90
Will none among this noble company
Check the abandoned villain?

Camillo   For God's sake
Let me dismiss the guests! You are insane,
Some ill will come of this.

Second Guest   Seize, silence him!

First Guest   I will!

Third Guest   And I!

Cenci   [*addressing those who rise with a threatening gesture*]

Who moves? Who speaks?
[*Turning to the company*]   'tis nothing,
Enjoy yourselves. – Beware! For my revenge
Is as the sealed commission of a king
That kills, and none dare name the murderer.
[*The banquet is broken up; several of the guests are departing*]

Beatrice

I do entreat you, go not, noble guests;
What, although tyranny and impious hate   100
Stand sheltered by a father's hoary hair?
What, if 'tis he who clothed us in these limbs
Who tortures them, and triumphs? What, if we,
The desolate and the dead, were his own flesh,
His children and his wife, whom he is bound
To love and shelter? Shall we therefore find
No refuge in this merciless wide world?
Oh, think what deep wrongs must have blotted out
First love, then reverence in a child's prone mind,
Till it thus vanquish shame and fear! O, think!   110
I have borne much, and kissed the sacred hand
Which crushed us to the earth, and thought its stroke
Was perhaps some paternal chastisement!
Have excused much, doubted; and when no doubt
Remained, have sought by patience, love and tears
To soften him, and when this could not be
I have knelt down through the long sleepless nights
And lifted up to God, the father of all,
Passionate prayers: and when these were not heard
I have still borne, – until I meet you here,   120
Princes and kinsmen at this hideous feast
Given at my brothers' deaths. Two yet remain,
His wife remains and I, whom if ye save not,
Ye may soon share such merriment again
As fathers make over their children's graves.
Oh! Prince Colonna, thou art our near kinsman,
Cardinal, thou art the Pope's chamberlain,
Camillo, thou art chief justiciary,
Take us away!

Cenci

[*He has been conversing with* CAMILLO *during the first part of*
BEATRICE's *speech; he hears the conclusion, and now advances*]
                    I hope my good friends here

	Will think of their own daughters – or perhaps	130
	Of their own throats – before they lend an ear	
	To this wild girl.	

Beatrice   [*Not noticing the words of Cenci*] Dare no one look on me?
None answer? Can one tyrant overbear
The sense of many best and wisest men?
Or is it that I sue not in some form
Of scrupulous law, that ye deny my suit?
Oh, God! That I were buried with my brothers!
And that the flowers of this departed spring
Were fading on my grave! And that my father
Were celebrating now one feast for all!   140

Camillo   A bitter wish for one so young and gentle;
Can we do nothing? –

Colonna   Nothing that I see.
Count Cenci were a dangerous enemy:
Yet I would second anyone.

A Cardinal   And I.

Cenci   Retire to your chamber, insolent girl!

Beatrice   Retire thou, impious man! Aye, hide thyself
Where never eye can look upon thee more!
Wouldst thou have honour and obedience
Who art a torturer? Father, never dream,
Though thou mayst overbear this company,   150
But ill must come of ill. – Frown not on me!
Haste, hide thyself, lest with avenging looks
My brothers' ghosts should hunt thee from thy seat!
Cover thy face from every living eye,
And start if thou but hear a human step:
Seek out some dark and silent corner, there,
Bow thy white head before offended God,
And we will kneel around, and fervently
Pray that he pity both ourselves and thee.

Cenci   My friends, I do lament this insane girl   160
Has spoilt the mirth of our festivity.
Good-night, farewell; I will not make you longer
Spectators of our dull domestic quarrels.
Another time. –   [*Exeunt all but* CENCI *and* BEATRICE
My brain is swimming round;
Give me a bowl of wine! Thou painted viper!

Beast that thou art! Fair and yet terrible!
I know a charm shall make thee meek and tame,
Now get thee from my sight!   [*Exit* BEATRICE
                         Here, Andrea,
Fill up this goblet with Greek wine. I said
I would not drink this evening; but I must;   170
For, strange to say, I feel my spirits fail
With thinking what I have decreed to do. –
[*Drinking the wine*]
Be thou the resolution of quick youth
Within my veins, and manhood's purpose stern,
And age's firm, cold, subtle villainy;
As if thou wert indeed my children's blood
Which I did thirst to drink! The charm works well;
It must be done; it shall be done, I swear!
                                                   [*Exit*

END OF THE FIRST ACT

ACT II, SCENE I

An apartment in the Cenci Palace. Enter LUCRETIA *and* BERNARDO.

Lucretia	Weep not, my gentle boy; he struck but me
	Who have borne deeper wrongs. In truth, if he
	Had killed me, he had done a kinder deed.
	O God Almighty, do thou look upon us,
	We have no other friend but only thee!
	Yet weep not; though I love you as my own,
	I am not your true mother.
Bernardo	Oh more, more,
	Than ever mother was to any child,
	That have you been to me! Had he not been
	My father, do you think that I should weep?
Lucretia	Alas! Poor boy, what else couldst thou have done?

Enter BEATRICE

Beatrice	[*in a hurried voice*] Did he pass this way? Have
	you seen him, brother?
	Ah! no, that is his step upon the stairs;
	'Tis nearer now; his hand is on the door;
	Mother, if I to thee have ever been
	A duteous child, now save me! Thou, great God,
	Whose image upon earth a father is,
	Dost thou indeed abandon me? He comes;
	The door is opening now; I see his face;
	He frowns on others, but he smiles on me,
	Even as he did after the feast last night.

Enter a servant

	Almighty God, how merciful thou art!
	'Tis but Orsino's servant. – Well, what news?
Servant	My master bids me say, the Holy Father
	Has sent back your petition thus unopened. [*giving a paper*]
	And he demands at what hour 'twere secure
	To visit you again?
Lucretia	At the Ave Mary. [*Exit servant*
	So, daughter, our last hope has failed; Ah me!
	How pale you look: you tremble, and you stand
	Wrapped in some fixed and fearful meditation,

Line numbers: 10, 20, 30

As if one thought were over strong for you:
Your eyes have a chill glare; O dearest child!
Are you gone mad? If not, pray speak to me.

Beatrice   You see I am not mad: I speak to you.

Lucretia   You talked of something that your father did
After that dreadful feast? Could it be worse
Than when he smiled, and cried, My sons are dead!
And everyone looked in his neighbour's face
To see if others were as white as he?
At the first word he spoke I felt the blood   40
Rush to my heart, and fell into a trance;
And when it past I sat all weak and wild;
Whilst you alone stood up, and with strong words
Checked his unnatural pride; and I could see
The devil was rebuked that lives in him.
Until this hour thus you have ever stood
Between us and your father's moody wrath
Like a protecting presence: your firm mind
Has been our only refuge and defence:
What can have thus subdued it? What can now   50
Have given you that cold melancholy look,
Succeeding to your unaccustomed fear?

Beatrice   What is it that you say? I was just thinking
'Twere better not to struggle any more.
Men like my father have been dark and bloody,
Yet never – O! Before worse comes of it
'Twere wise to die: it ends in that at last.

Lucretia   Oh, talk not so, dear child! Tell me at once
What did your father do or say to you?
He stayed not after that accursed feast   60
One moment in your chamber. – Speak to me.

Bernardo   Oh, sister, sister, prithee, speak to us!

Beatrice   [*speaking very slowly with a forced calmness*]
It was one word, Mother, one little word;
One look, one smile. [*wildly*] Oh! He has trampled me
Under his feet, and made the blood stream down
My pallid cheeks. And he has given us all
Ditch-water, and the fever-stricken flesh
Of buffaloes, and bade us eat or starve,
And we have eaten. – He has made me look

On my beloved Bernardo, when the rust   70
Of heavy chains has gangrened his sweet limbs,
And I have never yet despaired – but now!
What could I say? [*recovering herself*]
                  Ah! no, 'tis nothing new.
The sufferings we all share have made me wild:
He only struck and cursed me as he passed;
He said, he looked, he did; – nothing at all
Beyond his wont, yet it disordered me.
Alas! I am forgetful of my duty,
I should preserve my senses for your sake.

Lucretia   Nay, Beatrice; have courage my sweet girl.   80
If anyone despairs it should be I
Who loved him once, and now must live with him
Till God in pity call for him or me.
For you may, like your sister, find some husband,
And smile, years hence, with children round your knees;
Whilst I, then dead, and all this hideous coil
Shall be remembered only as a dream.

Beatrice   Talk not to me, dear lady, of a husband.
Did you not nurse me when my mother died?
Did you not shield me and that dearest boy?   90
And had we any other friend but you
In infancy, with gentle words and looks,
To win our father not to murder us?
And shall I now desert you? May the ghost
Of my dead Mother plead against my soul
If I abandon her who filled the place
She left, with more, even, than a mother's love!

Bernardo   And I am of my sister's mind. Indeed
I would not leave you in this wretchedness,
Even though the Pope should make me free to live   100
In some blithe place, like others of my age,
With sports, and delicate food, and the fresh air.
Oh, never think that I will leave you, Mother!

Lucretia   My dear, dear children!
                Enter CENCI, *suddenly*
Cenci   What! Beatrice here!
Come hither! [*She shrinks back, and covers her face*]
              Nay, hide not your face, 'tis fair;

Look up! Why, yesternight you dared to look
With disobedient insolence upon me,
Bending a stern and an enquiring brow
On what I meant; whilst I then sought to hide
That which I came to tell you – but in vain.   110

Beatrice   [*wildly, staggering towards the door*]
Oh, that the earth would gape! Hide me, oh God!

Cenci   Then it was I whose inarticulate words
Fell from my lips, and who with tottering steps
Fled from your presence, as you now from mine.
Stay, I command you – from this day and hour
Never again, I think, with fearless eye,
And brow superior, and unaltered cheek,
And that lip made for tenderness or scorn,
Shalt thou strike dumb the meanest of mankind;
Me least of all. Now get thee to thy chamber!   120
Thou too, loathed image of thy cursed mother,
[*to Bernardo*] Thy milky, meek face makes me sick with hate!
                    [*Exeunt* BEATRICE *and* BERNARDO

[*Aside*] So much has past between us as must make
Me bold, her fearful. – 'Tis an awful thing
To touch such mischief as I now conceive:
So men sit shivering on the dewy bank,
And try the chill stream with their feet; once in . . .
How the delighted spirit pants for joy!

Lucretia   [*advancing timidly towards him*] Oh, husband! Pray
                                        forgive poor Beatrice,
She meant not any ill.

Cenci   Nor you perhaps?   130
Nor that young imp, whom you have taught by rote
Parricide with his alphabet? Nor Giacomo?
Nor those two most unnatural sons, who stirred
Enmity up against me with the Pope?
Whom in one night merciful God cut off:
Innocent lambs! They thought not any ill.
You were not here conspiring? You said nothing
Of how I might be dungeoned as a madman;
Or be condemned to death for some offence,
And you would be the witnesses? – This failing,   140
How just it were to hire assassins, or

Put sudden poison in my evening drink?
Or smother me when overcome by wine?
Seeing we had no other judge but God,
And he had sentenced me, and there were none
But you to be the executioners
Of his decree enregistered in heaven?
Oh, no! You said not this?

Lucretia   So help me God,
I never thought the things you charge me with!

Cenci   If you dare speak that wicked lie again   150
I'll kill you. What! It was not by your counsel
That Beatrice disturbed the feast last night?
You did not hope to stir some enemies
Against me, and escape, and laugh to scorn
What every nerve of you now trembles at?
You judged that men were bolder than they are;
Few dare to stand between their grave and me.

Lucretia   Look not so dreadfully! By my salvation
I knew not aught that Beatrice designed;
Nor do I think she designed anything   160
Until she heard you talk of her dead brothers.

Cenci   Blaspheming liar! You are damned for this!
But I will take you where you may persuade
The stones you tread on to deliver you:
For men shall there be none but those who dare
All things – not question that which I command.
On Wednesday next I shall set out: you know
That savage rock, the Castle of Petrella:
'Tis safely walled, and moated round about:
Its dungeons underground, and its thick towers   170
Never told tales; though they have heard and seen
What might make dumb things speak. – Why do you linger?
Make speediest preparation for the journey!   [*Exit* LUCRETIA
The all-beholding sun yet shines: I hear
A busy stir of men about the streets;
I see the bright sky through the window panes:
It is a garish, broad, and peering day;
Loud, light, suspicious, full of eyes and ears,
And every little corner, nook and hole
Is penetrated with the insolent light.   180

Come darkness! Yet, what is the day to me?
And wherefore should I wish for night, who do
A deed which shall confound both night and day?
'Tis she shall grope through a bewildering mist
Of horror: if there be a sun in heaven
She shall not dare to look upon its beams;
Nor feel its warmth. Let her then wish for night;
The act I think shall soon extinguish all
For me: I bear a darker, deadlier gloom
Than the earth's shade, or interlunar air,   190
Or constellations quenched in murkiest cloud,
In which I walk secure and unbeheld
Towards my purpose. – Would that it were done!

[*Exit*

SCENE II

A chamber in the Vatican.
Enter CAMILLO *and* GIACOMO, *in conversation.*

Camillo	There is an obsolete and doubtful law
	By which you might obtain a bare provision
	Of food and clothing –
Giacomo	Nothing more? Alas!
	Bare must be the provision which strict law
	Awards, and aged, sullen avarice pays.
	Why did my father not apprentice me
	To some mechanic trade? I should have then
	Been trained in no highborn necessities
	Which I could meet not by my daily toil.
	The eldest son of a rich nobleman
	Is heir to all his incapacities;
	He has wide wants, and narrow powers. If you,
	Cardinal Camillo, were reduced at once
	From thrice-driven beds of down, and delicate food,
	A hundred servants, and six palaces,
	To that which nature doth indeed require – ?
Camillo	Nay, there is reason in your plea; 'twere hard.
Giacomo	'Tis hard for a firm man to bear: but I

10

Have a dear wife, a lady of high birth,
Whose dowry in ill hour I lent my father   20
Without a bond or witness to the deed:
And children, who inherit her fine senses,
The fairest creatures in this breathing world;
And she and they reproach me not. Cardinal,
Do you not think the Pope would interpose
And stretch authority beyond the law?

Camillo   Though your peculiar case is hard, I know
The Pope will not divert the course of law.
After that impious feast the other night
I spoke with him, and urged him then to check   30
Your father's cruel hand; he frowned and said,
'Children are disobedient, and they sting
Their fathers' hearts to madness and despair,
Requiting years of care with contumely.
I pity the Count Cenci from my heart;
His outraged love perhaps awakened hate,
And thus he is exasperated to ill.
In the great war between the old and young,
I, who have white hairs and a tottering body,
Will keep at least blameless neutrality.'   40
Enter ORSINO
You, my good Lord Orsino, heard those words.

Orsino   What words?

Giacomo   Alas, repeat them not again!
There then is no redress for me, at least
None but that which I may achieve myself,
Since I am driven to the brink. – But, say,
My innocent sister and my only brother
Are dying underneath my father's eye.
The memorable torturers of this land,
Galeaz Visconti, Borgia, Ezzelin,[107]
Never inflicted on their meanest slave   50
What these endure; shall they have no protection?

Camillo   Why, if they would petition to the Pope
I see not how he could refuse it – yet
He holds it of most dangerous example
In aught to weaken the paternal power,
Being, as 'twere, the shadow of his own.

	I pray you now excuse me. I have business
	That will not bear delay. [*Exit* CAMILLO
Giacomo	But you, Orsino,
	Have the petition: wherefore not present it?
Orsino	I have presented it, and backed it with

I have presented it, and backed it with   60
My earnest prayers, and urgent interest;
It was returned unanswered. I doubt not
But that the strange and execrable deeds
Alleged in it – in truth they might well baffle
Any belief – have turned the Pope's displeasure
Upon the accusers from the criminal:
So I should guess from what Camillo said.

Giacomo My friend, that palace-walking devil Gold
Has whispered silence to his Holiness:
And we are left, as scorpions ringed with fire.   70
What should we do but strike ourselves to death?
For he who is our murderous persecutor
Is shielded by a father's holy name,
Or I would – [*stops abruptly*]

Orsino   What? Fear not to speak your thought.
Words are but holy as the deeds they cover:
A priest who has forsworn the God he serves;
A judge who makes truth weep at his decree;
A friend who should weave counsel, as I now,
But as the mantle of some selfish guile;
A father who is all a tyrant seems,   80
Were the profaner for his sacred name.

Giacomo Ask me not what I think; the unwilling brain
Feigns often what it would not; and we trust
Imagination with such phantasies
As the tongue dares not fashion into words,
Which have no words, their horror makes them dim
To the mind's eye. – My heart denies itself
To think what you demand.

Orsino   But a friend's bosom
Is as the inmost cave of our own mind
Where we sit shut from the wide gaze of day,   90
And from the all-communicating air.
You look what I suspected –

Giacomo   Spare me now!

I am as one lost in a midnight wood,
Who dares not ask some harmless passenger
The path across the wilderness, lest he,
As my thoughts are, should be – a murderer.
I know you are my friend, and all I dare
Speak to my soul that will I trust with thee.
But now my heart is heavy, and would take
Lone counsel from a night of sleepless care.   100
Pardon me, that I say farewell – farewell!
I would that to my own suspected self
I could address a word so full of peace.

Orsino   Farewell! – Be your thoughts better or more bold.

                                          [*Exit* GIACOMO

I had disposed the Cardinal Camillo
To feed his hope with cold encouragement:
It fortunately serves my close designs
That 'tis a trick of this same family
To analyse their own and other minds.
Such self-anatomy shall teach the will   110
Dangerous secrets: for it tempts our powers,
Knowing what must be thought, and may be done,
Into the depth of darkest purposes:
So Cenci fell into the pit; even I,
Since Beatrice unveiled me to myself,
And made me shrink from what I cannot shun,
Show a poor figure to my own esteem,
To which I grow half reconciled. I'll do
As little mischief as I can; that thought
Shall fee the accuser conscience.
                 [*After a pause*] Now what harm   120
If Cenci should be murdered? – Yet, if murdered,
Wherefore by me? And what if I could take
The profit, yet omit the sin and peril
In such an action? Of all earthly things
I fear a man whose blows outspeed his words;
And such is Cenci: and while Cenci lives
His daughter's dowry were a secret grave
If a priest wins her. – Oh, fair Beatrice!
Would that I loved thee not, or loving thee
Could but despise danger and gold and all   130

That frowns between my wish and its effect,
Or smiles beyond it! There is no escape . . .
Her bright form kneels beside me at the altar,
And follows me to the resort of men,
And fills my slumber with tumultuous dreams,
So when I wake my blood seems liquid fire;
And if I strike my damp and dizzy head
My hot palm scorches it: her very name,
But spoken by a stranger, makes my heart
Sicken and pant; and thus unprofitably   140
I clasp the phantom of unfelt delights
Till weak imagination half possesses
The self-created shadow. Yet much longer
Will I not nurse this life of feverous hours:
From the unravelled hopes of Giacomo
I must work out my own dear purposes.
I see, as from a tower, the end of all:
Her father dead; her brother bound to me
By a dark secret, surer than the grave;
Her mother scared and unexpostulating   150
From the dread manner of her wish achieved:
And she! – Once more take courage my faint heart;
What dares a friendless maiden matched with thee?
I have such foresight as assures success:
Some unbeheld divinity doth ever,
When dread events are near, stir up men's minds
To black suggestions; and he prospers best,
Not who becomes the instrument of ill,
But who can flatter the dark spirit, that makes
Its empire and its prey of other hearts,   160
Till it become his slave . . . as I will do.   [*Exit*

END OF THE SECOND ACT

ACT III, SCENE I

An apartment in the Cenci Palace. LUCRETIA, *to her enter* BEATRICE.

Beatrice   [*she enters staggering, and speaks wildly*]
                Reach me that handkerchief! – My brain is hurt;
                My eyes are full of blood; just wipe them for me . . .
                I see but indistinctly . . .
Lucretia   My sweet child,
                You have no wound; 'tis only a cold dew
                That starts from your dear brow . . . Alas! Alas!
                What has befallen?
Beatrice   How comes this hair undone?
                Its wandering strings must be what blind me so,
                And yet I tied it fast. – O, horrible!
                The pavement sinks under my feet! The walls
                Spin round! I see a woman weeping there,   10
                And standing calm and motionless, whilst I
                Slide giddily as the world reels . . . My God!
                The beautiful blue heaven is flecked with blood!
                The sunshine on the floor is black! The air
                Is changed to vapours such as the dead breathe
                In charnel pits! Pah! I am choked! There creeps
                A clinging, black, contaminating mist
                About me . . . 'tis substantial, heavy, thick,
                I cannot pluck it from me, for it glues
                My fingers and my limbs to one another,   20
                And eats into my sinews, and dissolves
                My flesh to a pollution, poisoning
                The subtle, pure, and inmost spirit of life!
                My God! I never knew what the mad felt
                Before; for I am mad beyond all doubt!
                [*More wildly*] No, I am dead! These putrefying limbs
                Shut round and sepulchre the panting soul
                Which would burst forth into the wandering air! [*A pause*]
                What hideous thought was that I had even now?
                'Tis gone; and yet its burthen remains here   30
                O'er these dull eyes . . . upon this weary heart!
                O world! O life! O day! O misery!

Lucretia	What ails thee, my poor child? She answers not: Her spirit apprehends the sense of pain, But not its cause; suffering has dried away The source from which it sprung . . .
Beatrice	[*franticly*] Like Parricide . . . Misery has killed its father: yet its father Never like mine . . . O God! What thing am I?
Lucretia	My dearest child, what has your father done?

Beatrice	[*doubtfully*] Who art thou, questioner? I have no father. 40
	[*aside*] She is the madhouse nurse who tends on me,
	It is a piteous office. [*To Lucretia, in a slow, subdued voice*]
	                         Do you know
	I thought I was that wretched Beatrice
	Men speak of, whom her father sometimes hales
	From hall to hall by the entangled hair;
	At others, pens up naked in damp cells
	Where scaly reptiles crawl, and starves her there,
	Till she will eat strange flesh. This woeful story
	So did I overact in my sick dreams,
	That I imagined . . . no, it cannot be! 50
	Horrible things have been in this wild world,
	Prodigious mixtures, and confusions strange
	Of good and ill; and worse have been conceived
	Than ever there was found a heart to do.
	But never fancy imaged such a deed
	As . . . [*pauses, suddenly recollecting herself*]
	                Who art thou? Swear to me, ere I die
	With fearful expectation, that indeed
	Thou art not what thou seemest . . . Mother!

Lucretia	Oh! My sweet child, know you . . .
Beatrice	Yet speak it not: For then if this be truth, that other too 60 Must be a truth, a firm enduring truth, Linked with each lasting circumstance of life, Never to change, never to pass away. Why so it is. This is the Cenci Palace; Thou art Lucretia; I am Beatrice. I have talked some wild words, but will no more. Mother, come near me: from this point of time,

I am . . . [*her voice dies away faintly*]

Lucretia   Alas! What has befallen thee, child?
What has thy father done?

Beatrice   What have I done?
Am I not innocent? Is it my crime   70
That one with white hair, and imperious brow,
Who tortured me from my forgotten years,
As parents only dare, should call himself
My father, yet should be – ! Oh, what am I?
What name, what place, what memory shall be mine?
What retrospects, outliving even despair?

Lucretia   He is a violent tyrant, surely, child:
We know that death alone can make us free;
His death or ours. But what can he have done
Of deadlier outrage or worse injury?   80
Thou art unlike thyself; thine eyes shoot forth
A wandering and strange spirit. Speak to me,
Unlock those pallid hands whose fingers twine
With one another.

Beatrice   'Tis the restless life
Tortured within them. If I try to speak
I shall go mad. Aye, something must be done;
What, yet I know not . . . something which shall make
The thing that I have suffered but a shadow
In the dread lightning which avenges it;
Brief, rapid, irreversible, destroying   90
The consequence of what it cannot cure.
Some such thing is to be endured or done:
When I know what, I shall be still and calm,
And never anything will move me more.
But now! – O blood, which art my father's blood,
Circling thro' these contaminated veins,
If thou, poured forth on the polluted earth,
Could wash away the crime, and punishment
By which I suffer . . . no, that cannot be!
Many might doubt there were a God above   100
Who sees and permits evil, and so die:
That faith no agony shall obscure in me.

Lucretia   It must indeed have been some bitter wrong:
Yet what, I dare not guess. Oh, my lost child,

Hide not in proud impenetrable grief
Thy sufferings from my fear.

Beatrice   I hide them not.
What are the words which you would have me speak?
I, who can feign no image in my mind
Of that which has transformed me: I, whose thought
Is like a ghost shrouded and folded up   110
In its own formless horror. Of all words,
That minister to mortal intercourse,
Which wouldst thou hear? For there is none to tell
My misery: if another ever knew
Aught like to it, she died as I will die,
And left it, as I must, without a name.
Death! Death! Our law and our religion call thee
A punishment and a reward . . . Oh, which
Have I deserved?

Lucretia   The peace of innocence;
Till in your season you be called to heaven.   120
Whate'er you may have suffered, you have done
No evil. Death must be the punishment
Of crime, or the reward of trampling down
The thorns which God has strewed upon the path
Which leads to immortality.

Beatrice   Aye, death . . .
The punishment of crime. I pray thee, God,
Let me not be bewildered while I judge.
If I must live day after day, and keep
These limbs, the unworthy temple of thy spirit,
As a foul den from which what thou abhorrest   130
May mock thee, unavenged . . . it shall not be!
Self-murder . . . no, that might be no escape,
For thy decree yawns like a Hell between
Our will and it: – O! In this mortal world
There is no vindication and no law
Which can adjudge and execute the doom
Of that through which I suffer.

                      Enter ORSINO

[*She approaches him solemnly*]   Welcome, Friend!
I have to tell you that, since last we met,
I have endured a wrong so great and strange,

	That neither life nor death can give me rest.	140
	Ask me not what it is, for there are deeds
	Which have no form, sufferings which have no tongue.
Orsino	And what is he who has thus injured you?
Beatrice	The man they call my father: a dread name.
Orsino	It cannot be . . .
Beatrice	What it can be, or not,
	Forbear to think. It is, and it has been;
	Advise me how it shall not be again.
	I thought to die; but a religious awe
	Restrains me, and the dread lest death itself
	Might be no refuge from the consciousness	150
	Of what is yet unexpiated. Oh, speak!
Orsino	Accuse him of the deed, and let the law
	Avenge thee.
Beatrice	Oh, ice-hearted counsellor!
	If I could find a word that might make known
	The crime of my destroyer; and that done,
	My tongue should like a knife tear out the secret
	Which cankers my heart's core; aye, lay all bare
	So that my unpolluted fame should be
	With vilest gossips a stale-mouthed story;
	A mock, a bye-word, an astonishment: –	160
	If this were done, which never shall be done,
	Think of the offender's gold, his dreaded hate,
	And the strange horror of the accuser's tale,
	Baffling belief, and overpowering speech;
	Scarce whispered, unimaginable, wrapt
	In hideous hints . . . Oh, most assured redress!
Orsino	You will endure it then?
Beatrice	Endure? – Orsino,
	It seems your counsel is small profit.
	[*Turns from him and speaks half to herself*] Aye,
	All must be suddenly resolved and done.
	What is this undistinguishable mist	170
	Of thoughts, which rise, like shadow after shadow,
	Darkening each other?
Orsino	Should the offender live?
	Triumph in his misdeed? and make, by use,
	His crime, whate'er it is, dreadful no doubt,

	Thine element; until thou mayest become	
	Utterly lost; subdued even to the hue	
	Of that which thou permittest?	
Beatrice	[*to herself*] Mighty death!	
	Thou double-visaged shadow! Only judge!	
	Rightfullest arbiter! [*She retires absorbed in thought*]	
Lucretia	If the lightning	
	Of God has e'er descended to avenge . . .	180
Orsino	Blaspheme not! His high Providence commits	
	Its glory on this earth, and their own wrongs	
	Into the hands of men; if they neglect	
	To punish crime . . .	
Lucretia	But if one, like this wretch,	
	Should mock with gold, opinion, law and power?	
	If there be no appeal to that which makes	
	The guiltiest tremble? If because our wrongs,	
	For that they are unnatural, strange and monstrous,	
	Exceed all measure of belief? Oh, God!	
	If, for the very reasons which should make	190
	Redress most swift and sure, our injurer triumphs?	
	And we, the victims, bear worse punishment	
	Than that appointed for their torturer?	
Orsino	Think not	
	But that there is redress where there is wrong,	
	So we be bold enough to seize it.	
Lucretia	How?	
	If there were any way to make all sure,	
	I know not . . . but I think it might be good	
	To . . .	
Orsino	Why, his late outrage to Beatrice;	
	For it is such, as I but faintly guess,	
	As makes remorse dishonour, and leaves her	200
	Only one duty, how she may avenge:	
	You, but one refuge from ills ill endured;	
	Me, but one counsel . . .	
Lucretia	For we cannot hope	
	That aid, or retribution, or resource	
	Will arise thence, where every other one	
	Might find them with less need. [*Beatrice advances*]	
Orsino	Then . . .	

Beatrice	Peace, Orsino!
	And, honoured Lady, while I speak I pray
	That you put off, as garments overworn,
	Forbearance and respect, remorse and fear,
	And all the fit restraints of daily life, 210
	Which have been borne from childhood, but which now
	Would be a mockery to my holier plea.
	As I have said, I have endured a wrong
	Which, though it be expressionless, is such
	As asks atonement; both for what is past,
	And lest I be reserved, day after day,
	To load with crimes an overburthened soul,
	And be . . . what ye can dream not. I have prayed
	To God, and I have talked with my own heart,
	And have unravelled my entangled will, 220
	And have at length determined what is right.
	Art thou my friend, Orsino? False or true?
	Pledge thy salvation ere I speak.
Orsino	I swear
	To dedicate my cunning, and my strength,
	My silence, and whatever else is mine,
	To thy commands.
Lucretia	You think we should devise
	His death?
Beatrice	And execute what is devised,
	And suddenly. We must be brief and bold.
Orsino	And yet most cautious.
Lucretia	For the jealous laws
	Would punish us with death and infamy 230
	For that which it became themselves to do.
Beatrice	Be cautious as ye may, but prompt. Orsino,
	What are the means?
Orsino	I know two dull, fierce outlaws,
	Who think man's spirit as a worm's, and they
	Would trample out, for any slight caprice,
	The meanest or the noblest life. This mood
	Is marketable here in Rome. They sell
	What we now want.
Lucretia	Tomorrow before dawn,
	Cenci will take us to that lonely rock,

Petrella, in the Apulian Apennines.[108]   240
If he arrive there . . .

Beatrice   He must not arrive.
Orsino   Will it be dark before you reach the tower?
Lucretia   The sun will scarce be set.
Beatrice   But I remember
Two miles on this side of the fort, the road
Crosses a deep ravine; 'tis rough and narrow,
And winds with short turns down the precipice;
And in its depth there is a mighty rock,
Which has, from unimaginable years,
Sustained itself with terror and with toil
Over a gulf, and with the agony   250
With which it clings seems slowly coming down;
Even as a wretched soul, hour after hour,
Clings to the mass of life; yet clinging, leans;
And leaning, makes more dark the dread abyss
In which it fears to fall: beneath this crag,
Huge as despair, as if in weariness,
The melancholy mountain yawns . . . below,
You hear but see not an impetuous torrent
Raging among the caverns, and a bridge
Crosses the chasm; and high above there grow,   260
With intersecting trunks, from crag to crag,
Cedars, and yews, and pines; whose tangled hair
Is matted in one solid roof of shade
By the dark ivy's twine. At noonday here
'Tis twilight, and at sunset blackest night.

Orsino   Before you reach that bridge make some excuse
For spurring on your mules, or loitering
Until . . .

Beatrice   What sound is that?
Lucretia   Hark! No, it cannot be a servant's step;
It must be Cenci, unexpectedly   270
Returned . . . Make some excuse for being here.

Beatrice   [to ORSINO, as she goes out]
That step we hear approach must never pass
The bridge of which we spoke.

                            [Exeunt LUCRETIA and BEATRICE

Orsino   What shall I do?

Cenci must find me here, and I must bear
The imperious inquisition of his looks
As to what brought me hither: let me mask
Mine own in some inane and vacant smile.
     Enter GIACOMO, *in a hurried manner*
How! Have you ventured hither? Know you then
That Cenci is from home?

Giacomo   I sought him here;
And now must wait till he returns.

Orsino   Great God!   280
Weigh you the danger of this rashness?

Giacomo   Aye!
Does my destroyer know his danger? We
Are now no more, as once, parent and child,
But man to man; the oppressor to the oppressed;
The slanderer to the slandered; foe to foe.
He has cast Nature off, which was his shield,
And Nature casts him off, who is her shame;
And I spurn both. Is it a father's throat
Which I will shake, and say, I ask not gold;
I ask not happy years; nor memories   290
Of tranquil childhood; nor home-sheltered love;
Though all these hast thou torn from me, and more;
But only my fair fame; only one hoard
Of peace, which I thought hidden from thy hate,
Under the penury heaped on me by thee,
Or I will . . . God can understand and pardon,
Why should I speak with man?

Orsino   Be calm, dear friend.
Giacomo   Well, I will calmly tell you what he did.
This old Francesco Cenci, as you know,
Borrowed the dowry of my wife from me,   300
And then denied the loan; and left me so
In poverty, the which I sought to mend
By holding a poor office in the state.
It had been promised to me, and already
I bought new clothing for my ragged babes,
And my wife smiled; and my heart knew repose.
When Cenci's intercession, as I found,
Conferred this office on a wretch, whom thus

He paid for vilest service. I returned
With this ill news, and we sate sad together 310
Solacing our despondency with tears
Of such affection and unbroken faith
As temper life's worst bitterness; when he,
As he is wont, came to upbraid and curse,
Mocking our poverty, and telling us
Such was God's scourge for disobedient sons.
And then, that I might strike him dumb with shame,
I spoke of my wife's dowry; but he coined
A brief yet specious tale, how I had wasted
The sum in secret riot; and he saw 320
My wife was touched, and he went smiling forth.
And when I knew the impression he had made,
And felt my wife insult with silent scorn
My ardent truth, and look averse and cold,
I went forth too: but soon returned again;
Yet not so soon but that my wife had taught
My children her harsh thoughts, and they all cried,
'Give us clothes, father! Give us better food!
What you in one night squander were enough
For months!' I looked, and saw that home was hell. 330
And to that hell will I return no more
Until mine enemy has rendered up
Atonement, or, as he gave life to me
I will, reversing nature's law . . .

Orsino   Trust me,
The compensation which thou seekest here
Will be denied.

Giacomo   Then . . . Are you not my friend?
Did you not hint at the alternative,
Upon the brink of which you see I stand,
The other day when we conversed together?
My wrongs were then less. That word parricide, 340
Although I am resolved, haunts me like fear.

Orsino   It must be fear itself, for the bare word
Is hollow mockery. Mark, how wisest God
Draws to one point the threads of a just doom,
So sanctifying it: what you devise
Is, as it were, accomplished.

Giacomo	Is he dead?
Orsino	His grave is ready. Know that since we met
	Cenci has done an outrage to his daughter.
Giacomo	What outrage?
Orsino	That she speaks not, but you may

Conceive such half conjectures as I do,   350
From her fixed paleness, and the lofty grief
Of her stern brow bent on the idle air,
And her severe unmodulated voice,
Drowning both tenderness and dread; and last
From this: that whilst her stepmother and I,
Bewildered in our horror, talked together
With obscure hints; both self-misunderstood
And darkly guessing, stumbling, in our talk,
Over the truth, and yet to its revenge,
She interrupted us, and with a look   360
Which told before she spoke it, he must die: . . .

Giacomo   It is enough. My doubts are well appeased;
There is a higher reason for the act
Than mine; there is a holier judge than me,
A more unblamed avenger. Beatrice,
Who in the gentleness of thy sweet youth
Hast never trodden on a worm, or bruised
A living flower, but thou hast pitied it
With needless tears! Fair sister, thou in whom
Men wondered how such loveliness and wisdom   370
Did not destroy each other! Is there made
Ravage of thee? O heart, I ask no more
Justification! Shall I wait, Orsino,
Till he return, and stab him at the door?

Orsino   Not so; some accident might interpose
To rescue him from what is now most sure;
And you are unprovided where to fly,
How to excuse or to conceal. Nay, listen:
All is contrived; success is so assured
That . . .

Enter BEATRICE

Beatrice	'Tis my brother's voice! You know me not? 380
Giacomo	My sister, my lost sister!
Beatrice	Lost indeed!

I see Orsino has talked with you, and
That you conjecture things too horrible
To speak, yet far less than the truths Now, stay not,
He might return: yet kiss me; I shall know
That then thou hast consented to his death.
Farewell, farewell! Let piety to God,
Brotherly love, justice and clemency,
And all things that make tender hardest hearts,
Make thine hard, brother. Answer not . . . farewell.   390

[*Exeunt severally*]

SCENE II

A mean apartment in GIACOMO's *house.* GIACOMO *alone.*

Giacomo   'Tis midnight, and Orsino comes not yet.
[*Thunder, and the sound of a storm*]
What! can the everlasting elements
Feel with a worm like man? If so the shaft
Of mercy-winged lightning would not fall
On stones and trees. My wife and children sleep:
They are now living in unmeaning dreams:
But I must wake, still doubting if that deed
Be just which was most necessary. O
Thou unreplenished lamp! whose narrow fire
Is shaken by the wind, and on whose edge   10
Devouring darkness hovers! Thou small flame,
Which, as a dying pulse rises and falls,
Still flickerest up and down, how very soon,
Did I not feed thee, wouldst thou fail and be
As thou hadst never been! So wastes and sinks
Even now, perhaps, the life that kindled mine:
But that no power can fill with vital oil,
That broken lamp of flesh. Ha! 'tis the blood
Which fed these veins that ebbs till all is cold:
It is the form that moulded mine that sinks   20
Into the white and yellow spasms of death:
It is the soul by which mine was arrayed
In God's immortal likeness which now stands

Naked before Heaven's judgement seat!
                    [*A bell strikes*] One! Two!
The hours crawl on; and when my hairs are white,
My son will then perhaps be waiting thus,
Tortured between just hate and vain remorse;
Chiding the tardy messenger of news
Like those which I expect. I almost wish
He be not dead, although my wrongs are great;   30
Yet . . . 'tis Orsino's step . . .
                Enter ORSINO
                    Speak!

Orsino	I am come

To say he has escaped.

Giacomo	Escaped!
Orsino	And safe

Within Petrella. He past by the spot
Appointed for the deed an hour too soon.

Giacomo   Are we the fools of such contingencies?
And do we waste in blind misgivings thus
The hours when we should act? Then wind and thunder,
Which seemed to howl his knell, is the loud laughter
With which Heaven mocks our weakness! I henceforth
Will ne'er repent of aught designed or done   40
But my repentance.

Orsino   See, the lamp is out.

Giacomo   If no remorse is ours when the dim air
Has drank this innocent flame, why should we quail
When Cenci's life, that light by which ill spirits
See the worst deeds they prompt, shall sink for ever?
No, I am hardened.

Orsino   Why, what need of this?
Who feared the pale intrusion of remorse
In a just deed? Altho' our first plan failed,
Doubt not but he will soon be laid to rest.
But light the lamp: let us not talk i' the dark.   50

Giacomo   [*lighting the lamp*] And yet once quenched I cannot thus relume
My father's life: do you not think his ghost
Might plead that argument with God?

Orsino   Once gone
You cannot now recall your sister's peace;

Your own extinguished years of youth and hope;
Nor your wife's bitter words; nor all the taunts
Which, from the prosperous, weak misfortune takes;
Nor your dead mother; nor . . .

Giacomo   O, speak no more!
I am resolved, although this very hand
Must quench the life that animated it.   60

Orsino   There is no need of that. Listen: you know
Olimpio, the castellan of Petrella
In old Colonna's time; him whom your father
Degraded from his post? And Marzio,
That desperate wretch, whom he deprived last year
Of a reward of blood, well earned and due?

Giacomo   I knew Olimpio; and they say he hated
Old Cenci so, that in his silent rage
His lips grew white only to see him pass.
Of Marzio I know nothing.

Orsino   Marzio's hate   70
Matches Olimpio's. I have sent these men,
But in your name, and as at your request,
To talk with Beatrice and Lucretia.

Giacomo   Only to talk?

Orsino   The moments which even now
Pass onward to tomorrow's midnight hour
May memorise their flight with death: ere then
They must have talked, and may perhaps have done,
And made an end . . .

Giacomo   Listen! What sound is that?

Orsino   The house-dog moans, and the beams crack: nought else.

Giacomo   It is my wife complaining in her sleep: 80
I doubt not she is saying bitter things
Of me; and all my children round her dreaming
That I deny them sustenance.

Orsino   Whilst he
Who truly took it from them, and who fills
Their hungry rest with bitterness, now sleeps
Lapped in bad pleasures, and triumphantly
Mocks thee in visions of successful hate
Too like the truth of day.

Giacomo   If e'er he wakes

	Again, I will not trust to hireling hands . . .	
Orsino	Why, that were well. I must be gone; good-night!	90
	When next we meet may all be done!	
Giacomo	And all	
	Forgotten: Oh, that I had never been! [Exeunt	

END OF THE THIRD ACT

ACT IV, SCENE I

An apartment in the Castle of Petrella. Enter CENCI.

Cenci
She comes not; yet I left her even now
Vanquished and faint. She knows the penalty
Of her delay: yet what if threats are vain?
Am I not now within Petrella's moat?
Or fear I still the eyes and ears of Rome?
Might I not drag her by the golden hair?
Stamp on her? Keep her sleepless till her brain
Be overworn? Tame her with chains and famine?
Less would suffice. Yet so to leave undone
What I most seek! No, 'tis her stubborn will   10
Which by its own consent shall stoop as low
As that which drags it down.
Enter LUCRETIA
                              Thou loathed wretch!
Hide thee from my abhorrence; fly, begone!
Yet stay! Bid Beatrice come hither.

Lucretia   Oh,
Husband! I pray, for thine own wretched sake,
Heed what thou dost. A mall who walks like thee
Thro' crimes, and thro' the danger of his crimes,
Each hour may stumble o'er a sudden grave.
And thou art old; thy hairs are hoary grey;
As thou wouldst save thyself from death and hell,   20
Pity thy daughter; give her to some friend
In marriage: so that she may tempt thee not
To hatred, or worse thoughts, if worse there be.

Cenci
What! like her sister who has found a home
To mock my hate from with prosperity?
Strange ruin shall destroy both her and thee
And all that yet remain. My death may be
Rapid, her destiny outspeeds it. Go,
Bid her come hither, and before my mood
Be changed, lest I should drag her by the hair.   30

Lucretia
She sent me to thee, husband. At thy presence
She fell, as thou dost know, into a trance;

And in that trance she heard a voice which said,
'Cenci must die! Let him confess himself!
Even now the accusing Angel waits to hear
If God, to punish his enormous crimes,
Harden his dying heart!'

Cenci   Why – such things are . . .
No doubt divine revealings may be made.
'Tis plain I have been favoured from above,
For when I cursed my sons they died. – Aye . . . so . . .   40
As to the right or wrong, that's talk . . . repentance . . .
Repentance is an easy moment's work
And more depends on God than me. Well . . . well . . .
I must give up the greater point, which was
To poison and corrupt her soul.
[*A pause; Lucretia approaches anxiously, and then shrinks back
as he speaks*]   One, two;
Aye . . . Rocco and Cristofano my curse
Strangled: and Giacomo, I think, will find
Life a worse Hell than that beyond the grave:
Beatrice shall, if there be skill in hate,
Die in despair, blaspheming: to Bernardo,   50
He is so innocent, I will bequeath
The memory of these deeds, and make his youth
The sepulchre of hope, where evil thoughts
Shall grow like weeds on a neglected tomb.
When all is done, out in the wide Campagna,[109]
I will pile up my silver and my gold;
My costly robes, paintings and tapestries;
My parchments and all records of my wealth,
And make a bonfire in my joy, and leave
Of my possessions nothing but my name;   60
Which shall be an inheritance to strip
Its wearer bare as infamy. That done,
My soul, which is a scourge, will I resign
Into the hands of him who wielded it;
Be it for its own punishment or theirs,
He will not ask it of me till the lash
Be broken in its last and deepest wound;
Until its hate be all inflicted. Yet,
Lest death outspeed my purpose, let me make

Short work and sure . . . [*going*]

Lucretia [*stops him*] Oh, stay! It was a feint:
She had no vision, and she heard no voice.
I said it but to awe thee.

Cenci That is well.
Vile palterer with the sacred truth of God,
Be thy soul choked with that blaspheming lie!
For Beatrice worse terrors are in store
To bend her to my will.

Lucretia Oh! to what will?
What cruel sufferings more than she has known
Canst thou inflict?

Cenci Andrea! Go call my daughter,
And if she comes not tell her that I come.
What sufferings? I will drag her, step by step,
Thro' infamies unheard of among men:
She shall stand shelterless in the broad noon
Of public scorn, for acts blazoned abroad,
One among which shall be . . . What? Canst thou guess?
She shall become (for what she most abhors
Shall have a fascination to entrap
Her loathing will) to her own conscious self
All she appears to others; and when dead,
As she shall die unshrived and unforgiven,
A rebel to her father and her God,
Her corpse shall be abandoned to the hounds;
Her name shall be the terror of the earth;
Her spirit shall approach the throne of God
Plague-spotted with my curses. I will make
Body and soul a monstrous lump of ruin.

Enter ANDREA

Andrea The lady Beatrice . . .

Cenci Speak, pale slave! What
Said she?

Andrea My Lord, 'twas what she looked; she said:
'Go tell my father that I see the gulf
Of Hell between us two, which he may pass,
I will not.' [*Exit* ANDREA

Cenci Go thou quick, Lucretia,
Tell her to come; yet let her understand

Her coming is consent: and say, moreover.
That if she come not I will curse her.   [*Exit* LUCRETIA
                                  Ha!
With what but with a father's curse doth God
Panic-strike armed victory, and make pale
Cities in their prosperity? The world's Father
Must grant a parent's prayer against his child
Be he who asks even what men call me.
Will not the deaths of her rebellious brothers
Awe her before I speak? For I on them   110
Did imprecate quick ruin, and it came.
               Enter LUCRETIA
Well; what? Speak, wretch!

Lucretia   She said, 'I cannot come:
Go tell my father that I see a torrent
Of his own blood raging between us.'

Cenci   [*kneeling*]   God!
Hear me! If this most specious mass of flesh,
Which thou hast made my daughter; this my blood,
This particle of my divided being;
Or rather, this my bane and my disease,
Whose sight infects and poisons me; this devil
Which sprung from me as from a hell, was meant   120
To aught good use; if her bright loveliness
Was kindled to illumine this dark world;
If nursed by thy selectest dew of love
Such virtues blossom in her as should make
The peace of life, I pray thee for my sake,
As thou the common God and Father art
Of her, and me, and all; reverse that doom!
Earth, in the name of God, let her food be
Poison, until she be encrusted round
With leprous stains! Heaven, rain upon her head   130
The blistering drops of the Maremma's[110] dew,
Till she be speckled like a toad; parch up
Those love-enkindled lips, warp those fine limbs
To loathed lameness! All-beholding sun,
Strike in thine envy those life-darting eyes
With thine own blinding beams!

Lucretia   Peace! Peace!

For thine own sake unsay those dreadful words.
When high God grants, he punishes such prayers.

Cenci [*leaping up, and throwing his right hand towards heaven*]
He does his will, I mine! This in addition,
That if she have a child . . .

Lucretia   Horrible thought!   140

Cenci That if she ever have a child – and thou,
Quick Nature! I adjure thee by thy God,
That thou be fruitful in her, and increase
And multiply, fulfilling his command,
And my deep imprecation! – may it be
A hideous likeness of herself, that as
From a distorting mirror, she may see
Her image mixed with what she most abhors,
Smiling upon her from her nursing breast.
And that the child may from its infancy   150
Grow, day by day, more wicked and deformed,
Turning her mother's love to misery:
And that both she and it may live until
It shall repay her care and pain with hate,
Or what may else be more unnatural.
So he may hunt her through the clamorous scoffs
Of the loud world to a dishonoured grave.
Shall I revoke this curse? Go, bid her come,
Before my words are chronicled in heaven.

[*Exit* LUCRETIA

I do not feel as if I were a man,   160
But like a fiend appointed to chastise
The offences of some unremembered world.
My blood is running up and down my veins;
A fearful pleasure makes it prick and tingle:
I feel a giddy sickness of strange awe;
My heart is beating with an expectation
Of horrid joy.

Enter LUCRETIA
What? Speak!

Lucretia   She bids thee curse;
And if thy curses, as they cannot do,
Could kill her soul . . .

Cenci   She would not come. 'Tis well,

I can do both: first take what I demand,   170
And then extort concession. To thy chamber!
Fly ere I spurn thee: and beware this night
That thou cross not my footsteps. It were safer
To come between the tiger and his prey.

                                       [*Exit* LUCRETIA

It must be late; mine eyes grow weary dim
With unaccustomed heaviness of sleep.
Conscience! Oh, thou most insolent of lies!
They say that sleep, that healing dew of heaven,
Steeps not in balm the foldings of the brain
Which thinks thee an impostor. I will go   180
First to belie thee with an hour of rest,
Which will be deep and calm, I feel: and then . . .
O multitudinous Hell, the fiends will shake
Thine arches with the laughter of their joy!
There shall be lamentation heard in Heaven
As o'er an angel fallen; and upon Earth
All good shall droop and sicken, and ill things
Shall with a spirit of unnatural life
Stir and be quickened . . . even as I am now.

                                           [*Exit*

SCENE II

Before the Castle of Petrella. Enter BEATRICE *and* LUCRETIA
above on the ramparts.

Beatrice	They come not yet.
Lucretia	'Tis scarce midnight.
Beatrice	How slow
	Behind the course of thought, even sick with speed,
	Lags leaden-footed time!
Lucretia	The minutes pass . . .
	If he should wake before the deed is done?
Beatrice	O Mother! He must never wake again.
	What thou hast said persuades me that our act
	Will but dislodge a spirit of deep hell

	Out of a human form.	
Lucretia	'Tis true he spoke	

Lucretia   'Tis true he spoke
Of death and judgement with strange confidence
For one so wicked; as a man believing   10
In God, yet recking not of good or ill.
And yet to die without confession! . . .

Beatrice   Oh!
Believe that Heaven is merciful and just,
And will not add our dread necessity
To the amount of his offences.
     Enter OLIMPIO *and* MARZIO, *below*

Lucretia   See,
They come.

Beatrice   All mortal things must hasten thus
To their dark end. Let us go down.
      [*Exeunt* LUCRETIA *and* BEATRICE *from above*

Olimpio How feel you to this work?

Marzio   As one who thinks
A thousand crowns excellent market price
For an old murderer's life. Your cheeks are pale.   20

Olimpio It is the white reflection of your own,
Which you call pale.

Marzio   Is that their natural hue?

Olimpio Or 'tis my hate and the deferred desire
To wreak it which extinguishes their blood.

Marzio You are inclined then to this business?

Olimpio   Aye.
If one should bribe me with a thousand crowns
To kill a serpent which had stung my child,
I could not be more willing.
    Enter BEATRICE *and* LUCRETIA, *below*
            Noble ladies!

Beatrice Are ye resolved?

Olimpio   Is he asleep?

Marzio   Is all
Quiet?

Lucretia   I mixed an opiate with his drink: 30
He sleeps so soundly . . .

Beatrice   . . . that his death will be
But as a change of sin-chastising dreams,

A dark continuance of the Hell within him,
Which God extinguish! But ye are resolved?
Ye know it is a high and holy deed?

Olimpio   We are resolved.

Marzio   As to the how this act
Be warranted, it rests with you.

Beatrice   Well, follow!

Olimpio   Hush! Hark! What noise is that?

Marzio   Ha! someone comes!

Beatrice   Ye conscience-stricken cravens, rock to rest
Your baby hearts. It is the iron gate,   40
Which ye left open, swinging to the wind,
That enters whistling as in scorn. Come, follow!
And be your steps like mine, light, quick and bold.

                                              [*Exeunt*

SCENE III

An apartment in the castle. Enter BEATRICE *and* LUCRETIA.

Lucretia   They are about it now.

Beatrice   Nay, it is done.

Lucretia   I have not heard him groan.

Beatrice   He will not groan.

Lucretia   What sound is that?

Beatrice   List! 'tis the tread of feet
About his bed.

Lucretia   My God!
If he be now a cold stiff corpse . . .

Beatrice   O, fear not
What may be done, but what is left undone:
The act seals all.

                    Enter OLIMPIO *and* MARZIO
                            Is it accomplished?

Marzio   What?

Olimpio   Did you not call?

Beatrice   When?

Olimpio   Now.

Beatrice   I ask if all is over?

Olimpio	We dare not kill an old and sleeping man;
	His thin grey hair, his stern and reverent brow, 10
	His veined hands crossed on his heaving breast,
	And the calm innocent sleep in which he lay,
	Quelled me. Indeed, indeed. I cannot do it.
Marzio	But I was bolder; for I chid Olimpio,
	And bade him bear his wrongs to his own grave
	And leave me the reward. And now my knife
	Touched the loose wrinkled throat, when the old man
	Stirred in his sleep, and said. 'God! hear, O, hear,
	A father's curse! What art Thou not our father?'
	And then he laughed. I knew it was the ghost 20
	Of my dead father speaking through his lips,
	And could not kill him.

Beatrice   Miserable slaves!
Where, if ye dare not kill a sleeping man,
Found ye the boldness to return to me
With such a deed undone? Base palterers!
Cowards and traitors! Why, the very conscience
Which ye would sell for gold and for revenge
Is an equivocation: it sleeps over
A thousand daily acts disgracing men;
And when a deed where mercy insults heaven . . .   30
Why do I talk?
[*snatching a dagger from one of them and raising it*]
                        Hadst thou a tongue to say,
She murdered her own father, I must do it!
But never dream ye shall outlive him long!

Olimpio   Stop, for God's sake!
Marzio   I will go back and kill him.
Olimpio   Give me the weapon, we must do thy will.
Beatrice   Take it! Depart! Return!
                                [*Exeunt* OLIMPIO *and* MARZIO
                        How pale thou art!
We do but that which 'twere a deadly crime
To leave undone.

Lucretia   Would it were done!
Beatrice   Even whilst
That doubt is passing through your mind, the world
Is conscious of a change. Darkness and hell   40

Have swallowed up the vapour they sent forth
To blacken the sweet light of life. My breath
Comes, methinks, lighter, and the gellied blood
Runs freely thro' my veins. Hark!

Enter OLIMPIO *and* MARZIO

He is . . .

Olimpio   Dead!

Marzio   We strangled him that there might be no blood;
And then we threw his heavy corpse i' the garden
Under the balcony; 'twill seem it fell.

Beatrice   [*giving them a bag of coin*]
Here, take this gold and hasten to your homes.
And, Marzio, because thou wast only awed
By that which made me tremble, wear thou this!   50
[*clothes him in a rich mantle*]
It was the mantle which my grandfather
Wore in his high prosperity, and men
Envied his state: so may they envy thine.
Thou wert a weapon in the hand of God
To a just use. Live long and thrive! And, mark,
If thou hast crimes, repent: this deed is none.
[*A horn is sounded*]

Lucretia   Hark, 'tis the castle horn; my God! it sounds
Like the last trump.

Beatrice   Some tedious guest is coming.

Lucretia   The drawbridge is let down; there is a tramp
Of horses in the court; fly, hide yourselves!   60
[*Exeunt* OLIMPIO *and* MARZIO

Beatrice   Let us retire to counterfeit deep rest;
I scarcely need to counterfeit it now:
The spirit which doth reign within these limbs
Seems strangely undisturbed. I could even sleep
Fearless and calm: all ill is surely past.

[*Exeunt*

SCENE IV

Another apartment in the castle. Enter on one side the
Legate SAVELLA, *introduced by a servant, and on the*
other LUCRETIA *and* BERNARDO.

Savella	Lady, my duty to his Holiness
	Be my excuse that thus unseasonably
	I break upon your rest. I must speak with
	Count Cenci; doth he sleep?
Lucretia	[*in a hurried and confused manner*] I think he sleeps;
	Yet wake him not, pray, spare me awhile,
	He is a wicked and a wrathful man;
	Should he be roused out of his sleep tonight,
	Which is, I know, a hell of angry dreams,
	It were not well; indeed it were not well.
	Wait till daybreak . . . [*Aside*] O, I am deadly sick! 10
Savella	I grieve thus to distress you, but the Count
	Must answer charges of the gravest import,
	And suddenly; such my commission is.
Lucretia	[*with increased agitation*]
	I dare not rouse him: I know none who dare . . .
	'Twere perilous; . . . you might as safely waken
	A serpent; or a corpse in which some fiend
	Were laid to sleep.
Savella	Lady, my moments here
	Are counted. I must rouse him from his sleep,
	Since none else dare.
Lucretia	[*aside*] O, terror! O, despair!
	[*to Bernardo*] Bernardo, conduct you the Lord Legate to 20
	Your father's chamber. [*Exeunt* SAVELLA *and* BERNARDO
	Enter BEATRICE
Beatrice	'Tis a messenger
	Come to arrest the culprit who now stands
	Before the throne of unappealable God.
	Both Earth and Heaven, consenting arbiters,
	Acquit our deed.
Lucretia	Oh, agony of fear!
	Would that he yet might live! Even now I heard

The Legate's followers whisper as they passed
They had a warrant for his instant death.
All was prepared by unforbidden means
Which we must pay so dearly, having done.   30
Even now they search the tower, and find the body;
Now they suspect the truth; now they consult
Before they come to tax us with the fact;
O, horrible, 'tis all discovered!

Beatrice   Mother,
What is done wisely, is done well. Be bold
As thou art just. 'Tis like a truant child
To fear that others know what thou hast done,
Even from thine own strong consciousness, and thus
Write on unsteady eyes and altered cheeks
All thou wouldst hide. Be faithful to thyself,   40
And fear no other witness but thy fear.
For if, as cannot be, some circumstance
Should rise in accusation, we can blind
Suspicion with such cheap astonishment,
Or overbear it with such guiltless pride,
As murderers cannot feign. The deed is done,
And what may follow now regards not me.   50
I am as universal as the light;
Free as the earth-surrounding air; as firm
As the world's centre. Consequence, to me,
Is as the wind which strikes the solid rock
But shakes it not.
                  [*A cry within and tumult*]

Voices   Murder! Murder! Murder!
                  Enter BERNARDO and SAVELLA

Savella   [*to his followers*] Go search the castle round; sound the alarm;
Look to the gates that none escape!

Beatrice   What now?

Bernardo   I know not what to say . . . my father's dead.   60

Beatrice   How; dead! he only sleeps; you mistake, brother.
His sleep is very calm, very like death;
'Tis wonderful how well a tyrant sleeps.
He is not *dead*?

Bernardo   Dead; murdered.

Lucretia   [*with extreme agitation*].   Oh, no, no,

	He is not murdered though he may be dead;
	I have alone the keys of those apartments.
Savella	Ha! Is it so?
Beatrice	My Lord, I pray excuse us;
	We will retire; my mother is not well:
	She seems quite overcome with this strange horror.

                                                 [Exeunt LUCRETIA *and* BEATRICE

Savella	Can you suspect who may have murdered him?
Bernardo	I know not what to think.
Savella	Can you name any
	Who had an interest in his death?
Bernardo	Alas!
	I can name none who had not, and those most
	Who most lament that such a deed is done;
	My mother, and my sister, and myself. 70
Savella	'Tis strange! There were clear marks of violence.
	I found the old man's body in the moonlight
	Hanging beneath the window of his chamber,
	Among the branches of a pine: he could not
	Have fallen there, for all his limbs lay heaped
	And effortless; 'tis true there was no blood . . .
	Favour me, Sir – it much imports your house
	That all should be made clear – to tell the ladies
	That I request their presence.

                                                    [Exit BERNARDO

                    Enter GUARDS *bringing in* MARZIO

Guard	We have one.
Officer	My Lord, we found this ruffian and another 80
	Lurking among the rocks; there is no doubt
	But that they are the murderers of Count Cenci:
	Each had a bag of coin; this fellow wore
	A gold-inwoven robe, which, shining bright
	Under the dark rocks to the glimmering moon,
	Betrayed them to our notice: the other fell
	Desperately fighting.
Savella	What does he confess?
Officer	He keeps firm silence; but these lines found on him
	May speak.
Savella	Their language is at least sincere.
	[Reads]

To THE LADY BEATRICE   90
That the atonement of what my nature sickens to conjecture
may soon arrive, I send thee, at thy brother's desire, those
who will speak and do more than I dare write . . .
                                        Thy devoted servant, ORSINO

                    Enter LUCRETIA, BEATRICE *and* BERNARDO
                    Knowest thou this writing, Lady?
Beatrice   No.
Savella   Nor thou?
Lucretia   [*her conduct throughout the scene is marked by extreme agitation*]
                    Where was it found? What is it? It should be
                    Orsino's hand! It speaks of that strange horror
                    Which never yet found utterance, but which made
                    Between that hapless child and her dead father   100
                    A gulf of obscure hatred.
Savella   Is it so?
                    Is it true, Lady, that thy father did
                    Such outrages as to awaken in thee
                    Unfilial hate?
Beatrice   Not hate, 'twas more than hate:
                    This is most true, yet wherefore question me?
Savella   There is a deed demanding question done;
                    Thou hast a secret which will answer not.
Beatrice   What sayest? My Lord, your words are bold and rash.
Savella   I do arrest all present in the name
                    Of the Pope's Holiness. You must to Rome.   110
Lucretia   O, not to Rome! Indeed we are not guilty.
Beatrice   Guilty! Who dares talk of guilt? My Lord,
                    I am more innocent of parricide
                    Than is a child born fatherless . . . Dear Mother,
                    Your gentleness and patience are no shield
                    For this keen judging world, this two-edged lie,
                    Which seems, but is not. What! will human laws,
                    Rather will ye who are their ministers,
                    Bar all access to retribution first,
                    And then, when heaven doth interpose to do   120
                    What ye neglect, arming familiar things
                    To the redress of an unwonted crime,
                    Make ye the victims who demanded it

Culprits? 'Tis ye are culprits! That poor wretch
Who stands so pale, and trembling, and amazed,
If it be true he murdered Cenci, was
A sword in the right hand of justest God.
Wherefore should I have wielded it? Unless
The crimes which mortal tongue dare never name
God therefore scruples to avenge.

Savella   You own   130
That you desired his death?

Beatrice   It would have been
A crime no less than his, if for one moment
That fierce desire had faded in my heart.
'Tis true I did believe, and hope, and pray,
Aye, I even knew . . . for God is wise and just,
That some strange sudden death hung over him.
'Tis true that this did happen, and most true
There was no other rest for me on earth,
No other hope in Heaven . . . now what of this?

Savella   Strange thoughts beget strange deeds; and here are both:
I judge thee not.

Beatrice   And yet, if you arrest me,   141
You are the judge and executioner
Of that which is the life of life: the breath
Of accusation kills an innocent name,
And leaves for lame acquittal the poor life
Which is a mask without it. 'Tis most false
That I am guilty of foul parricide;
Although I must rejoice, for justest cause,
That other hands have sent my father's soul
To ask the mercy he denied to me.   150
Now leave us free, stain not a noble house
With vague surmises of rejected crime;
Add to our sufferings and your own neglect
No heavier sum: let them have been enough:
Leave us the wreck we have.

Savella   I dare not, Lady.
I pray that you prepare yourselves for Rome:
There the Pope's further pleasure will be known.

Lucretia   O, not to Rome! O, take us not to Rome!

Beatrice   Why not to Rome, dear mother? There as here

	Our innocence is as an armed heel	160

Our innocence is as an armed heel   160
To trample accusation. God is there
As here, and with his shadow ever clothes
The innocent, the injured and the weak;
And such are we. Cheer up, dear Lady, lean
On me: collect your wandering thoughts. My Lord,
As soon as you have taken some refreshment,
And had all such examinations made
Upon the spot, as may be necessary
To the full understanding of this matter,
We shall be ready. Mother; will you come?   170

Lucretia   Ha! they will bind us to the rack, and wrest
Self-accusation from our agony!
Will Giacomo be there? Orsino? Marzio?
All present; all confronted; all demanding
Each from the other's countenance the thing
Which is in every heart! O! misery!
[*She faints and is borne out*]

Savella   She faints: an ill appearance this.

Beatrice   My Lord,
She knows not yet the uses of the world.
She fears that power is as a beast which grasps
And loosens not: a snake whose look transmutes   180
All things to guilt which is its nutriment.
She cannot know how well the supine slaves
Of blind authority read the truth of things
When written on a brow of guilelessness:
She sees not yet triumphant Innocence
Stand at the judgement-seat of mortal man,
A judge and an accuser of the wrong
Which drags it there. Prepare yourself, my Lord:
Our suite will join yours in the court below.

                                                  [*Exeunt*

END OF THE FOURTH ACT

ACT V, SCENE I

An apartment in ORSINO's *palace. Enter* ORSINO *and* GIACOMO.

Giacomo	Do evil deeds thus quickly come to end?
	O, that the vain remorse which must chastise
	Crimes done, had but as loud a voice to warn
	As its keen sting is mortal to avenge!
	O, that the hour when present had cast off
	The mantle of its mystery, and shown
	The ghastly form with which it now returns
	When its scared game is roused, cheering the hounds
	Of conscience to their prey! Alas! Alas!
	It was a wicked thought, a piteous deed, 10
	To kill an old and hoary-headed father.
Orsino	It has turned out unluckily, in truth.
Giacomo	To violate the sacred doors of sleep;
	To cheat kind nature of the placid death
	Which she prepares for overwearied age;
	To drag from Heaven an unrepentant soul
	Which might have quenched in reconciling prayers
	A life of burning crimes . . .
Orsino	You cannot say
	I urged you to the deed.
Giacomo	O, had I never
	Found in thy smooth and ready countenance 20
	The mirror of my darkest thoughts; hadst thou
	Never with hints and questions made me look
	Upon the monster of my thought, until
	It grew familiar to desire . . .
Orsino	'Tis thus
	Men cast the blame of their unprosperous acts
	Upon the abettors of their own resolve;
	Or anything but their weak, guilty selves.
	And yet, confess the truth, it is the peril
	In which you stand that gives you this pale sickness
	Of penitence; confess 'tis fear disguised 30
	From its own shame that takes the mantle now
	Of thin remorse. What if we yet were safe?

Giacomo How can that be? Already Beatrice,
Lucretia and the murderer are in prison.
I doubt not officers are, whilst we speak,
Sent to arrest us.

Orsino I have all prepared
For instant flight. We can escape even now,
So we take fleet occasion by the hair.

Giacomo Rather expire in tortures, as I may.
What! will you cast by self-accusing flight
Assured conviction upon Beatrice?
She, who alone in this unnatural work,
Stands like God's angel ministered upon
By fiends; avenging such a nameless wrong
As turns black parricide to piety;
Whilst we for basest ends . . . I fear, Orsino,
While I consider all your words and looks,
Comparing them with your proposal now,
That you must be a villain. For what end
Could you engage in such a perilous crime,
Training me on with hints, and signs, and smiles,
Even to this gulf? Thou art no liar? No,
Thou art a lie! Traitor and murderer!
Coward and slave! But, no, defend thyself; [*drawing*]
Let the sword speak what the indignant tongue
Disdains to brand thee with.

Orsino Put up your weapon.
Is it the desperation of your fear
Makes you thus rash and sudden with a friend,
Now ruined for your sake? If honest anger
Have moved you, know that what I just proposed
Was but to try you. As for me, I think,
Thankless affection led me to this point,
From which, if my firm temper could repent,
I cannot now recede. Even whilst we speak
The ministers of justice wait below:
They grant me these brief moments. Now if you
Have any word of melancholy comfort
To speak to your pale wife, 'twere best to pass
Out at the postern, and avoid them so.

Giacomo O, generous friend! How canst thou pardon me?

Would that my life could purchase thine!

Orsino   That wish

Now comes a day too late. Haste; fare thee well!
Hear'st thou not steps along the corridor?   [*Exit* GIACOMO
I'm sorry for it; but the guards are waiting
At his own gate, and such was my contrivance
That I might rid me both of him and them.
I thought to act a solemn comedy
Upon the painted scene of this new world,
And to attain my own peculiar ends
By some such plot of mingled good and ill   80
As others weave; but there arose a Power
Which graspt and snapped the threads of my device
And turned it to a net of ruin . . . Ha! [*a shout is heard*]
[*A shout is heard*] Is that my name I hear proclaimed abroad?
But I will pass, wrapt in a vile disguise;
Rags on my back, and a false innocence
Upon my face, thro' the misdeeming crowd
Which judges by what seems. 'Tis easy then
For a new name and for a country new,
And a new life, fashioned on old desires,   190
To change the honours of abandoned Rome.
And these must be the masks of that within,
Which must remain unaltered . . . Oh, I fear
That what is past will never let me rest!
Why, when none else is conscious, but myself,
Of my misdeeds, should my own heart's contempt
Trouble me? Have I not the power to fly
My own reproaches? Shall I be the slave
Of . . . what? A word? which those of this false world
Employ against each other, not themselves;   100
As men wear daggers not for self-offence.
But if I am mistaken, where shall I
Find the disguise to hide me from myself,
As now I skulk from every other eye?

                                                    [*Exit*

SCENE II

A hall of justice. CAMILLO, JUDGES, *etc. are discovered seated;* MARZIO *is led in.*

First Judge	Accused, do you persist in your denial?
	I ask you, are you innocent, or guilty?
	I demand who were the participators
	In your offence? Speak truth and the whole truth.
Marzio	My God! I did not kill him; I know nothing;
	Olimpio sold the robe to me from which
	You would infer my guilt.
Second Judge	Away with him!
First Judge	Dare you, with lips yet white from the rack's kiss,
	Speak false? Is it so soft a questioner,
	That you would bandy lover's talk with it
	Till it wind out your life and soul? Away!
Marzio	Spare me! O, spare! I will confess.
First Judge	Then speak.
Marzio	I strangled him in his sleep.
First Judge	Who urged you to it?
Marzio	His own son Giacomo and the young prelate
	Orsino sent me to Petrella; there
	The ladies Beatrice and Lucretia
	Tempted me with a thousand crowns, and I
	And my companion forthwith murdered him.
	Now let me die.
First Judge	This sounds as bad as truth. Guards, there,
	Lead forth the prisoners!
	Enter LUCRETIA, BEATRICE *and* GIACOMO, *guarded*
	Look upon this man;
	When did you see him last?
Beatrice	We never saw him.
Marzio	You know me too well, Lady Beatrice.
Beatrice	I know thee! How? where? when?
Marzio	You know 'twas I
	Whom you did urge with menaces and bribes
	To kill your father. When the thing was done
	You clothed me in a robe of woven gold
	And bade me thrive: how I have thriven, you see.

10

20

You, my Lord Giacomo, Lady Lucretia,
You know that what I speak is true.
[BEATRICE *advances towards him; he covers his face, and*
shrinks back]   O, dart
The terrible resentment of those eyes   30
On the dead earth! Turn them away from me!
They wound: 'twas torture forced the truth. My Lords,
Having said this let me be led to death.

Beatrice   Poor wretch, I pity thee: yet stay awhile.

Camillo   Guards, lead him not away.

Beatrice   Cardinal Camillo.
You have a good repute for gentleness
And wisdom: can it be that you sit here
To countenance a wicked farce like this?
When some obscure and trembling slave is dragged
From sufferings which might shake the sternest heart   40
And bade to answer, not as he believes,
But as those may suspect or do desire
Whose questions thence suggest their own reply:
And that in peril of such hideous torments
As merciful God spares even the damned. Speak now
The thing you surely know, which is that you,
If your fine frame were stretched upon that wheel,
And you were told: 'Confess that you did poison
Your little nephew; that fair blue-eyed child
Who was the loadstar of your life:'— and though   50
All see, since his most swift and piteous death,
That day and night, and heaven and earth, and time,
And all the things hoped for or done therein
Are changed to you, through your exceeding grief,
Yet you would say, 'I confess anything:'
And beg from your tormentors, like that slave,
The refuge of dishonourable death.
I pray thee, Cardinal, that thou assert
My innocence.

Camillo   [*much moved*]   What shall we think, my Lords?
Shame on these tears! I thought the heart was frozen   60
Which is their fountain. I would pledge my soul
That she is guiltless.

Judge   Yet she must be tortured.

Camillo	I would as soon have tortured mine own nephew
	(If he now lived he would be just her age;
	His hair, too, was her colour, and his eyes
	Like hers in shape, but blue and not so deep)
	As that most perfect image of God's love
	That ever came sorrowing upon the earth.
	She is as pure as speechless infancy!
Judge	Well, be her purity on your head, my Lord, 70
	If you forbid the rack. His Holiness
	Enjoined us to pursue this monstrous crime
	By the severest forms of law; nay even
	To stretch a point against the criminals.
	The prisoners stand accused of parricide
	Upon such evidence as justifies
	Torture.
Beatrice	What evidence? This man's?
Judge	Even so.
Beatrice	[to MARZIO] Come near. And who art thou thus chosen forth
	Out of the multitude of living men
	To kill the innocent?
Marzio	I am Marzio, 80
	Thy father's vassal.
Beatrice	Fix thine eyes on mine;
	Answer to what I ask.
	[*Turning to the* JUDGES] I prithee mark
	His countenance: unlike bold calumny,
	Which sometimes dares not speak the thing it looks,
	He dares not look the thing he speaks, but bends
	His gaze on the blind earth.
	[*To* MARZIO] What! wilt thou say
	That I did murder my own father?
Marzio	Oh!
	Spare me! My brain swims round . . . I cannot speak . . .
	It was that horrid torture forced the truth. 90
	Take me away! Let her not look on me!
	I am a guilty miserable wretch;
	I have said all I know; now, let me die!
Beatrice	My Lords, if by my nature I had been
	So stern, as to have planned the crime alleged,
	Which your suspicions dictate to this slave,

And the rack makes him utter, do you think
I should have left this two-edged instrument
Of my misdeed; this man, this bloody knife,
With my own name engraven on the heft,
Lying unsheathed amid a world of foes,   100
For my own death? That with such horrible need
For deepest silence, I should have neglected
So trivial a precaution, as the making
His tomb the keeper of a secret written
On a thief's memory? What is his poor life?
What are a thousand lives? A parricide
Had trampled them like dust; and, see, he lives!
[*Turning to* MARZIO] And thou . . .

Marzio   Oh, spare me! Speak to me no more!
That stern yet piteous look, those solemn tones,
Wound worse than torture.
[*To the* JUDGES]   I have told it all;   110
For pity's sake lead me away to death.

Camillo   Guards, lead him nearer the Lady Beatrice,
He shrinks from her regard like autumn's leaf
From the keen breath of the serenest north.

Beatrice   Oh, thou who tremblest on the giddy verge
Of life and death, pause ere thou answerest me;
So mayst thou answer God with less dismay:
What evil have we done thee? I, alas!
Have lived but on this earth a few sad years
And so my lot was ordered, that a father   120
First turned the moments of awakening life
To drops, each poisoning youth's sweet hope; and then
Stabbed with one blow my everlasting soul;
And my untainted fame; and even that peace
Which sleeps within the core of the heart's heart;
But the wound was not mortal; so my hate
Became the only worship I could lift
To our great father, who in pity and love,
Armed thee, as thou dost say, to cut him off;
And thus his wrong becomes my accusation;   130
And art thou the accuser? If thou hopest
Mercy in heaven, show justice upon earth:
Worse than a bloody hand is a hard heart.

If thou hast done murders, made thy life's path
Over the trampled laws of God and man,
Rush not before thy Judge, and say: 'My maker,
I have done this and more; for there was one
Who was most pure and innocent on earth;
And because she endured what never any
Guilty or innocent endured before;   140
Because her wrongs could not be told, not thought;
Because thy hand at length did rescue her;
I with my words killed her and all her kin.'
Think, I adjure you, what it is to slay
The reverence living in the minds of men
Towards our ancient house, and stainless fame!
Think what it is to strangle infant pity,
Cradled in the belief of guileless looks,
Till it become a crime to suffer. Think
What tis to blot with infamy and blood   150
All that which shows like innocence, and is,
Hear me, great God! I swear, most innocent,
So that the world lose all discrimination
Between the sly, fierce, wild regard of guilt,
And that which now compels thee to reply
To what I ask: Am I or am I not
A parricide?

Marzio	Thou art not!
Judge	What is this?
Marzio	I here declare those whom I did accuse

Are innocent. 'Tis I alone am guilty.

Judge   Drag him away to torments; let them be   160
Subtle and long drawn out, to tear the folds
Of the heart's inmost cell. Unbind him not
Till he confess.

Marzio   Torture me as ye will:
A keener pang has wrung a higher truth
From my last breath. She is most innocent!
Bloodhounds, not men, glut yourselves well with me;
I will not give you that fine piece of nature
To rend and ruin.   [*Exit* MARZIO, *guarded*

Camillo   What say ye now, my Lords?
Judge   Let tortures strain the truth till it be white

	As snow thrice sifted by the frozen wind.	170
Camillo	Yet stained with blood.	
Judge	[*to* BEATRICE] Know you this paper, Lady?	
Beatrice	Entrap me not with questions. Who stands here	

As my accuser? Ha! wilt thou be he,
Who art my judge? Accuser, witness, judge,
What, all in one? Here is Orsino's name;
Where is Orsino? Let his eye meet mine.
What means this scrawl? Alas! Ye know not what,
And therefore on the chance that it may be
Some evil, will ye kill us?

Enter an OFFICER

Officer	Marzio's dead.	
Judge	What did he say?	
Officer	Nothing. As soon as we	180

Had bound him on the wheel, he smiled on us,
As one who baffles a deep adversary;
And holding his breath, died.

| *Judge* | There remains nothing | |

But to apply the question to those prisoners,
Who yet remain stubborn.

| *Camillo* | I overrule | |

Further proceedings, and in the behalf
Of these most innocent and noble persons
Will use my interest with the Holy Father.

| *Judge* | Let the Pope's pleasure then be done. Meanwhile | |

Conduct these culprits each to separate cells;   190
And be the engines ready: for this night
If the Pope's resolution be as grave,
Pious, and just as once, I'll wring the truth
Out of those nerves and sinews, groan by groan.

[*Exeunt*

SCENE III

The cell of a prison. BEATRICE *is discovered asleep on a couch;*
enter BERNARDO.

Bernardo	How gently slumber rests upon her face,
	Like the last thoughts of some day sweetly spent
	Closing in night and dreams, and so prolonged.
	After such torments as she bore last night,
	How light and soft her breathing comes. Ay, me!
	Methinks that I shall never sleep again.
	But I must shake the heavenly dew of rest
	From this sweet folded flower, thus . . . wake! awake!
	What, sister, canst thou sleep?
Beatrice	[*awaking*] I was just dreaming
	That we were all in Paradise. Thou knowest
	This cell seems like a kind of Paradise
	After our father's presence.
Bernardo	Dear, dear sister,
	Would that thy dream were not a dream! O, God!
	How shall I tell?
Beatrice	What wouldst thou tell, sweet brother?
Bernardo	Look not so calm and happy, or even whilst
	I stand considering what I have to say
	My heart will break.
Beatrice	See now, thou mak'st me weep:
	How very friendless thou wouldst be, dear child,
	If I were dead. Say what thou hast to say.
Bernardo	They have confessed; they could endure no more
	The tortures . . .
Beatrice	Ha! What was there to confess?
	They must have told some weak and wicked lie
	To flatter their tormentors. Have they said
	That they were guilty? O white innocence,
	That thou shouldst wear the mask of guilt to hide
	Thine awful and serenest countenance
	From those who know thee not!

Enter JUDGE *with* LUCRETIA *and* GIACOMO, *guarded*
                                       Ignoble hearts!

Line numbers in margin: 10 (at "This cell seems like a kind of Paradise"), 20 (at "They have confessed; they could endure no more").

    For some brief spasms of pain, which are at least
    As mortal as the limbs through which they pass,
    Are centuries of high splendour laid in dust?   30
    And that eternal honour which should live
    Sunlike, above the reek of mortal fame,
    Changed to a mockery and a byword? What!
    Will you give up these bodies to be dragged
    At horses' heels, so that our hair should sweep
    The footsteps of the vain and senseless crowd,
    Who, that they may make our calamity
    Their worship and their spectacle, will leave
    The churches and the theatres as void
    As their own hearts? Shall the light multitude   40
    Fling, at their choice, curses or faded pity,
    Sad funeral flowers to deck a living corpse,
    Upon us as we pass to pass away,
    And leave . . . what memory of our having been?
    Infamy, blood, terror, despair? O thou,
    Who wert a mother to the parentless,
    Kill not thy child! Let not her wrongs kill thee!
    Brother, lie down with me upon the rack,
    And let us each be silent as a corpse;
    It soon will be as soft as any grave.   50
    'Tis but the falsehood it can wring from fear
    Makes the rack cruel.

Giacomo   They will tear the truth
    Even from thee at last, those cruel pains:
    For pity's sake say thou art guilty now.

Lucretia   O, speak the truth! Let us all quickly die;
    And after death, God is our judge, not they;
    He will have mercy on us.

Bernardo   If indeed
    It can be true, say so, dear sister mine;
    And then the Pope will surely pardon you,
    And all be well.

Judge   Confess, or I will warp   60
    Your limbs with such keen tortures . . .

Beatrice   Tortures! Turn
    The rack henceforth into a spinning wheel!
    Torture your dog, that he may tell when last

He lapped the blood his master shed . . . not me!
My pangs are of the mind, and of the heart,
And of the soul; aye, of the inmost soul,
Which weeps within tears as of burning gall
To see, in this ill world where none are true,
My kindred false to their deserted selves.
And with considering all the wretched life   70
Which I have lived, and its now wretched end,
And the small justice shown by Heaven and Earth
To me or mine; and what a tyrant thou art,
And what slaves these; and what a world we make,
The oppressor and the oppressed . . . such pangs compel
My answer. What is it thou wouldst with me?

Judge   Art thou not guilty of thy father's death?

Beatrice   Or wilt thou rather tax high judging God
That he permitted such an act as that
Which I have suffered, and which he beheld;   80
Made it unutterable, and took from it
All refuge, all revenge, all consequence,
But that which thou hast called my father's death?
Which is or is not what men call a crime.
Which either I have done, or have not done;
Say what ye will. I shall deny no more.
If ye desire it thus, thus let it be,
And so an end of all. Now do your will;
No other pains shall force another word.

Judge   She is convicted, but has not confessed.   90
Be it enough. Until their final sentence
Let none have converse with them. You, young Lord,
Linger not here!

Beatrice   O, tear him not away!

Judge   Guards do your duty.

Bernardo   [*Embracing Beatrice*] Oh! would ye divide
Body from soul?

Officer   That is the headsman's business.
[*Exeunt all but* LUCRETIA, BEATRICE *and* GIACOMO

Giacomo   Have I confessed? Is it all over now?
No hope! No refuge! O weak, wicked tongue,
Which hast destroyed me, would that thou hadst been
Cut out and thrown to dogs first! To have killed

My father first, and then betrayed my sister;   100
Aye, thee! the one thing innocent and pure
In this black guilty world, to that which I
So well deserve! My wife! my little ones!
Destitute, helpless, and I . . . Father! God!
Canst thou forgive even the unforgiving,
When their full hearts break thus, thus! . . .
[covers his face and weeps]

Lucretia   O, my child!
To what a dreadful end are we all come!
Why did I yield? Why did I not sustain
Those torments? Oh, that I were all dissolved
Into these fast and unavailing tears,   110
Which flow and feel not!

Beatrice   What 'twas weak to do,
'Tis weaker to lament, once being done;
Take cheer! The God who knew my wrong, and made
Our speedy act the angel of his wrath,
Seems, and but seems to have abandoned us.
Let us not think that we shall die for this.
Brother, sit near me; give me your firm hand,
You had a manly heart. Bear up! Bear up!
O, dearest Lady, put your gentle head
Upon my lap, and try to sleep awhile: 120
Your eyes look pale, hollow and overworn
With heaviness of watching and slow grief.
Come, I will sing you some low, sleepy tune,
Not cheerful, nor yet sad; some dull old thing,
Some outworn and unused monotony,
Such as our country gossips sing and spin.
Till they almost forget they live: lie down!
So, that will do. Have I forgot the words?
Faith! They are sadder than I thought they were.

SONG

False friend, wilt thou smile or weep   130
When my life is laid asleep?
Little cares for a smile or a tear,
The clay-cold corpse upon the bier!
    Farewell! Heigho!

> What is this whispers low?
> There is a snake in thy smile, my dear;
> And bitter poison within thy tear.
>
> Sweet sleep, were death like to thee,
> Or if thou couldst mortal be,
> I would close these eyes of pain;   140
> When to wake? Never again.
>   O World! Farewell!
>   Listen to the passing bell!
> It says, thou and I must part,
> With a light and a heavy heart.   [*The scene closes*

SCENE IV

A hall of the prison. Enter CAMILLO *and* BERNARDO.

Camillo   The Pope is stern; not to be moved or bent.
               He looked as calm and keen as is the engine
               Which tortures and which kills, exempt itself
               From aught that it inflicts; a marble form,
               A rite, a law, a custom: not a man.
               He frowned, as if to frown had been the trick
               Of his machinery, on the advocates
               Presenting the defences, which he tore
               And threw behind, muttering with hoarse, harsh voice:
               'Which among ye defended their old father   10
               Killed in his sleep?' Then to another: 'Thou
               Dost this in virtue of thy place; 'tis well.'
               He turned to me then, looking deprecation,
               And said these three words, coldly: 'They must die.'
Bernardo   And yet you left him not?
Camillo   I urged him still;
               Pleading, as I could guess, the devilish wrong
               Which prompted your unnatural parent's death.
               And he replied: 'Paolo Santa Croce
               Murdered his mother yester evening,
               And he is fled. Parricide grows so rife   20
               That soon, for some just cause no doubt, the young
               Will strangle us all, dozing in our chairs.

	Authority, and power, and hoary hair
	Are grown crimes capital. You are my nephew,
	You come to ask their pardon; stay a moment;
	Here is their sentence; never see me more
	Till, to the letter, it be all fulfilled.'
Bernardo	O, God, not so! I did believe indeed
	That all you said was but sad preparation
	For happy news. O, there are words and looks
	To bend the sternest purpose! Once I knew them,
	Now I forget them at my dearest need.
	What think you if I seek him out, and bathe
	His feet and robe with hot and bitter tears?
	Importune him with prayers, vexing his brain
	With my perpetual cries, until in rage
	He strike me with his pastoral cross, and trample
	Upon my prostrate head, so that my blood
	May stain the senseless dust on which he treads,
	And remorse waken mercy? I will do it!
	O, wait till I return! [*rushes out*]
Camillo	Alas! poor boy!
	A wreck-devoted seaman thus might pray
	To the deaf sea.

Enter LUCRETIA, BEATRICE *and* GIACOMO, *guarded*

Beatrice	I hardly dare to fear
	That thou bring'st other news than a just pardon.
Camillo	May God in heaven be less inexorable
	To the Pope's prayers, than he has been to mine.
	Here is the sentence and the warrant.
Beatrice	[*wildly*] Oh,
	My God! Can it be possible I have
	To die so suddenly? So young to go
	Under the obscure, cold, rotting, wormy ground!
	To be nailed down into a narrow place;
	To see no more sweet sunshine; hear no more
	Blithe voice of living thing; muse not again
	Upon familiar thoughts, sad, yet thus lost –
	How fearful! to be nothing! Or to be . . .
	What? O, where am I? Let me not go mad!
	Sweet Heaven, forgive weak thoughts! If there should be
	No God, no Heaven, no Earth in the void world;

30

40

50

The wide, grey, lampless, deep, unpeopled world!
If all things then should be . . . my father's spirit,   60
His eye, his voice, his touch surrounding me;
The atmosphere and breath of my dead life!
If sometimes, as a shape more like himself,
Even the form which tortured me on earth,
Masked in grey hairs and wrinkles, he should come
And wind me in his hellish arms, and fix
His eyes on mine, and drag me down, down, down!
For was he not alone omnipotent
On Earth, and ever present? Even tho' dead,
Does not his spirit live in all that breathe,   70
And work for me and mine still the same ruin,
Scorn, pain, despair? Whoever yet returned
To teach the laws of death's untrodden realm?
Unjust perhaps as those which drive us now,
O, whither, whither?

Lucretia   Trust in God's sweet love,
The tender promises of Christ: ere night,
Think we shall be in Paradise.

Beatrice   'Tis past!
Whatever comes my heart shall sink no more.
And yet, I know not why, your words strike chill:
How tedious, false and cold seem all things. I   80
Have met with much injustice in this world;
No difference has been made by God or man,
Or any power moulding my wretched lot,
'Twixt good or evil, as regarded me.
I am cut off from the only world I know,
From light, and life, and love, in youth's sweet prime.
You do well telling me to trust in God,
I hope I do trust in him. In whom else
Can any trust? And yet my heart is cold.
[*During the latter speeches* GIACOMO *has retired conversing
with* CAMILLO, *who now goes out;* GIACOMO *advances*]

Giacomo   Know you not, Mother . . . Sister, know you not?   90
Bernardo even now is gone to implore
The Pope to grant our pardon.

Lucretia   Child, perhaps
It will be granted. We may all then live

       To make these woes a tale for distant years:
       O, what a thought! It gushes to my heart
       Like the warm blood.

Beatrice   Yet both will soon be cold.
       O, trample out that thought! Worse than despair,
       Worse than the bitterness of death, is hope:
       It is the only ill which can find place
       Upon the giddy, sharp and narrow hour   100
       Tottering beneath us. Plead with the swift frost
       That it should spare the eldest flower of spring:
       Plead with awakening earthquake, o'er whose couch
       Even now a city stands, strong, fair and free;
       Now stench and blackness yawn, like death. O, plead
       With famine, or wind-walking Pestilence,
       Blind lightning, or the deaf sea, not with man!
       Cruel, cold, formal man; righteous in words,
       In deeds a Cain. No, Mother, we must die:
       Since such is the reward of innocent lives;   110
       Such the alleviation of worst wrongs.
       And whilst our murderers live, and hard, cold men,
       Smiling and slow, walk thro' a world of tears
       To death as to life's sleep; 'twere just the grave
       Were some strange joy for us. Come, obscure Death,
       And wind me in thine all-embracing arms!
       Like a fond mother hide me in thy bosom,
       And rock me to the sleep from which none wake.
       Live ye, who live, subject to one another
       As we were once, who now . . .
                BERNARDO *rushes in*

Bernardo   Oh, horrible!   120
       That tears, that looks, that hope poured forth in prayer,
       Even till the heart is vacant and despairs,
       Should all be vain! The ministers of death
       Are waiting round the doors. I thought I saw
       Blood on the face of one . . what if 'twere fancy?
       Soon the heart's blood of all I love on earth
       Will sprinkle him, and he will wipe it off
       As if 'twere only rain. O life! O world!
       Cover me! let me be no more! To see
       That perfect mirror of pure innocence   130

Wherein I gazed, and grew happy and good,
Shivered to dust! To see thee, Beatrice,
Who made all lovely thou didst look upon . . .
Thee, light of life . . . dead, dark! while I say, sister,
To hear I have no sister; and thou, Mother,
Whose love was as a bond to all our loves . . .
Dead! The sweet bond broken!

Enter CAMILLO *and* GUARDS

                          They come! Let me
Kiss those warm lips before their crimson leaves
Are blighted . . . white . . . cold. Say farewell, before
Death chokes that gentle voice! O, let me hear   140
You speak!

Beatrice   Farewell, my tender brother. Think
Of our sad fate with gentleness, as now:
And let mild, pitying thoughts lighten for thee
Thy sorrow's load. Err not in harsh despair,
But tears and patience. One thing more, my child,
For thine own sake be constant to the love
Thou bearest us; and to the faith that I,
Tho' wrapt in a strange cloud of crime and shame,
Lived ever holy and unstained. And tho'
Ill tongues shall wound me, and our common name   150
Be as a mark stamped on thine innocent brow
For men to point at as they pass, do thou
Forbear, and never think a thought unkind
Of those, who perhaps love thee in their graves.
So mayest thou die as I do; fear and pain
Being subdued. Farewell! Farewell! Farewell!

Bernardo   I cannot say, farewell!

Camillo   O, Lady Beatrice!

Beatrice   Give yourself no unnecessary pain,
My dear Lord Cardinal. Here, Mother, tie
My girdle for me, and bind up this hair   160
In any simple knot; aye, that does well.
And yours I see is coming down. How often
Have we done this for one another; now
We shall not do it any more. My Lord,
We are quite ready. Well, 'tis very well.

THE END

The Mask of Anarchy

WRITTEN ON THE OCCASION OF
THE MASSACRE AT MANCHESTER

1

As I lay asleep in Italy
There came a voice from over the Sea,
And with great power it forth led me
To walk in the visions of Poesy.

2

I met Murder on the way –
He had a mask like Castlereagh[111] –
Very smooth he looked, yet grim;
Seven bloodhounds[112] followed him:

3

All were fat; and well they might
Be in admirable plight,   10
For one by one, and two by two,
He tossed them human hearts to chew
Which from his wide cloak he drew.

4

Next came Fraud, and he had on
Like Eldon,[113] an ermined gown;
His big tears, for he wept well,
Turned to millstones as they fell.

5

And the little children, who
Round his feet played to and fro,
Thinking every tear a gem,   20
Had their brains knocked out by them.

6

Clothed with the Bible, as with light,
And the shadows of the night,

Like Sidmouth,[114] next, Hypocrisy
On a crocodile rode by.

7

And many more Destructions played
In this ghastly masquerade,
All disguised, even to the eyes,
Like Bishops, lawyers, peers, or spies.

8

Last came Anarchy: he rode   30
On a white horse, splashed with blood;
He was pale even to the lips,
Like Death in the Apocalypse.

9

And he wore a kingly crown;
And in his grasp a sceptre shone;
On his brow this mark I saw –
'I AM GOD, AND KING, AND LAW!

10

With a pace stately and fast,
Over English land he past,
Trampling to a mire of blood   40
The adoring multitude.

11

And a mighty troop around,
With their trampling shook the ground,
Waving each a bloody sword,
For the service of their Lord.

12

And with glorious triumph, they
Rode thro' England proud and gay,
Drunk as with intoxication
Of the wine of desolation.

13

O'er fields and towns, from sea to sea,   50
Past the Pageant swift and free,
Tearing up, and trampling down;
Till they came to London town.

14

And each dweller, panic-stricken.
Felt his heart with terror sicken
Hearing the tempestuous cry
Of the triumph of Anarchy.

15

For with pomp to meet him came,
Clothed in arms like blood and flame,
The hired murderers, who did sing,   60
'Thou art God, and Law, and King.

16

'We have waited, weak and lone,
For thy coming, Mighty One!
Our purses are empty, our swords are cold,
Give us glory, and blood, and gold.'

17

Lawyers and priests, a motley crowd,
To the earth their pale brows bowed;
Like a bad prayer not over loud,
Whispering – 'Thou art Law and God.' –

18

Then all cried with one accord,   70
'Thou art King, and God, and Lord;
Anarchy, to thee we bow,
Be thy name made holy now!'

19

And Anarchy, the Skeleton,
Bowed and grinned to everyone,

As well as if his education
Had cost ten millions to the nation.

20

For he knew the Palaces
Of our Kings were rightly his;
His the sceptre, crown, and globe,   80
And the gold-inwoven robe.

21

So he sent his slaves before
To seize upon the Bank and Tower,[115]
And was proceeding with intent
To meet his pensioned Parliament,[116]

22

When one fled past, a maniac maid,
And her name was Hope, she said:
But she looked more like Despair,
And she cried out in the air:

23

'My father Time is weak and grey   90
With waiting for a better day;
See how idiot-like he stands,
Fumbling with his palsied hands!

24

'He has had child after child,
And the dust of death is piled
Over every one but me –
Misery, oh, Misery!'

25

Then she lay down in the street,
Right before the horses' feet,
Expecting, with a patient eye,   100
Murder, Fraud and Anarchy.

26

When between her and her foes
A mist, a light, an image rose,
Small at first, and weak and frail,
Like the vapour of a vale:

27

Till as clouds grow on the blast,
Like tower-crowned giants striding fast,
And glare with lightnings as they fly,
And speak in thunder to the sky,

28

It grew – a Shape arrayed in mail   110
Brighter than the viper's scale,
And upborne on wings whose grain
Was as the light of sunny rain.

29

On its helm, seen far away,
A planet, like the Morning's,[117] lay;
And those plumes its light rained thro'
Like a shower of crimson dew.

30

With step as soft as wind it past
O'er the heads of men – so fast
That they knew the presence there,   120
And looked, – and all was empty air.

31

As flowers beneath May's footstep waken,
As stars from Night's loose hair are shaken,
As waves arise when loud winds call,
Thoughts sprang where'er that step did fall.

32

And the prostrate multitude
Looked – and ankle-deep in blood,

Hope, that maiden most serene,
Was walking with a quiet mien:

33

And Anarchy, the ghastly birth,   130
Lay dead earth upon the earth;
The Horse of Death, tameless as wind,
Fled, and with his hoofs did grind
To dust the murderers thronged behind.

34

A rushing light of clouds and splendour,
A sense awakening, and yet tender,
Was heard and felt – and at its close
These words of joy and fear arose,

35

As if their own indignant Earth
Which gave the sons of England birth   140
Had felt their blood upon her brow,
And shuddering with a mother's throe

36

Had turned every drop of blood
By which her face had been bedewed
To an accent unwithstood, –
As if her heart had cried aloud:

37

'Men of England, heirs of Glory,
Heroes of unwritten story,
Nurslings of one mighty Mother,
Hopes of her, and one another;   150

38

'Rise like Lions after slumber
In unvanquishable number –
Shake your chains to earth like dew
Which in sleep had fallen on you –
Ye are many – they are few.

39

'What is Freedom? – ye can tell
That which slavery is, too well –
For its very name has grown
To an echo of your own.

40

' 'Tis to work and have such pay   160
As just keeps life from day to day
In your limbs, as in a cell
For the tyrants' use to dwell.

41

'So that ye for them are made,
Loom, and plough, and sword, and spade,
With or without your own will bent,
To their defence and nourishment.

42

' 'Tis to see your children weak
With their mothers pine and peak.
When the winter winds are bleak, –   170
They are dying whilst I speak.

43

' 'Tis to hunger for such diet
As the rich man in his riot
Casts to the fat dogs that lie
Surfeiting beneath his eye;

44

' 'Tis to let the Ghost of Gold
Take from Toil a thousandfold
More than ere its substance could
In the tyrannies of old.

45

'Paper coin – that forgery   180
Of the title deeds, which ye

Hold to something of the worth
Of the inheritance of Earth.

46

' 'Tis to be a slave in soul
And to hold no strong control
Over your own wills, but be
All that others make of ye.

47

'And at length when ye complain,
With a murmur weak and vain,
'Tis to see the Tyrant's crew   190
Ride over your wives and you –
Blood is on the grass like dew.

48

'Then it is to feel revenge
Fiercely thirsting to exchange
Blood for blood – and wrong for wrong –
Do not thus when ye are strong.

49

'Birds find rest in narrow nest,
When weary of their winged quest;
Beasts find fare in woody lair,
When storm and snow are in the air.   200

50

'Asses, swine, have litter spread
And with fitting food are fed;
All things have a home but one –
Thou, O Englishman, hast none!

51

'This is Slavery – savage men,
Or wild beasts within a den,
Would endure not as ye do –
But such ills they never knew.

52

'What art thou, Freedom? Oh! could slaves
Answering from their living graves   210
This demand – tyrants would flee
Like a dream's dim imagery:

53

'Thou art not, as impostors say,
A shadow soon to pass away,
A superstition, and a name
Echoing from the cave of Fame.

54

'For the labourer thou art bread
And a comely table spread,
From his daily labour come
To a neat and happy home.   220

55

'Thou art clothes, and fire, and food
For the trampled multitude –
No – in countries that are free
Such starvation cannot be
As in England now we see.

56

'To the rich thou art a check,
When his foot is on the neck
Of his victim, thou dost make
That he treads upon a snake.

57

'Thou art Justice – ne'er for gold   240
May the righteous laws be sold
As laws are in England – thou
Shield'st alike the high and low.

58

'Thou art Wisdom – Freemen never
Dream that God will damn for ever

All who think those things untrue
Of which Priests make such ado.

59

'Thou art Peace – never by thee
Would blood and treasure wasted be
As tyrants wasted them, when all   250
Leagued to quench thy flame in Gaul.[118]

60

'What if English toil and blood
Was poured forth, even as a flood?
It availed, O Liberty!
To dim, but not extinguish thee.

61

'Thou art Love – the rich have kist
Thy feet, and like him following Christ,
Give their substance to the free
And thro' the rough world follow thee,

62

'Or turn their wealth to arms, and make   260
War for thy beloved sake
On wealth, and war, and fraud – whence they
Drew the power which is their prey.

63

'Science, Poetry and Thought
Are the lamps; they make the lot
Of the dwellers in a cot
So serene, they curse it not.

64

'Spirit, Patience, Gentleness,
All that can adorn and bless,
Art thou – let deeds not words express   270
Thine exceeding loveliness.

65

'Let a great Assembly be
Of the fearless and the free
On some spot of English ground
Where the plains stretch wide around.

66

'Let the blue sky overhead,
The green earth on which ye tread.
All that must eternal be
Witness the solemnity.

67

'From the corners uttermost   280
Of the bounds of English coast;
From every hut, village and town
Where those who live and suffer moan
For others' misery or their own –

68

'From the workhouse and the prison
Where, pale as corpses newly risen,
Women, children, young and old
Groan for pain, and weep for cold –

69

'From the haunts of daily life
Where is waged the daily strife   290
With common wants and common cares
Which sows the human heart with tares –

70

'Lastly from the palaces
Where the murmur of distress
Echoes, like the distant sound
Of a wind alive around

71

'Those prison halls of wealth and fashion
Where some few feel such compassion

For those who groan, and toil, and wail
As must make their brethren pale –   300

72

'Ye who suffer woes untold,
Or to feel, or to behold
Your lost country bought and sold
With a price of blood and gold –

73

'Let a vast assembly be,
And with great solemnity
Declare with measured words that ye
Are, as God has made ye, free –

74

'Be your strong and simple words
Keen to wound as sharpened swords.   310
And wide as targes let them be,
With their shade to cover ye.

75

'Let the tyrants pour around
With a quick and startling sound,
Like the loosening of a sea,
Troops of armed emblazonry.

76

'Let the charged artillery drive
Till the dead air seems alive
With the clash of clanging wheels,
And the tramp of horses' heels.   320

77

'Let the fixed bayonet
Gleam with sharp desire to wet
Its bright point in English blood
Looking keen as one for food.

78

'Let the horsemen's scimitars
Wheel and flash, like sphereless stars
Thirsting to eclipse their burning
In a sea of death and mourning.

79

'Stand ye calm and resolute,
Like a forest close and mute,   330
With folded arms and looks which are
Weapons of unvanquished war,

80

'And let Panic, who outspeeds
The career of armed steeds,
Pass, a disregarded shade,
Thro' your phalanx undismayed.

81

'Let the laws of your own land,
Good or ill, between ye stand
Hand to hand, and foot to foot,
Arbiters of the dispute,   340

82

'The old laws of England – they
Whose reverend heads with age are grey,
Children of a wiser day;
And whose solemn voice must be
Thine own echo – Liberty!

83

'On those who first should violate
Such sacred heralds in their state
Rest the blood that must ensue,
And it will not rest on you.

84

'And if then the tyrants dare   350
Let them ride among you there,

Slash, and stab, and maim, and hew, –
What they like, that let them do.

85

'With folded arms and steady eyes,
And little fear, and less surprise,
Look upon them as they slay
Till their rage has died away.

86

'Then they will return with shame
To the place from which they came,
And the blood thus shed will speak   360
In hot blushes on their cheek.

87

'Every woman in the land
Will point at them as they stand –
They will hardly dare to greet
Their acquaintance in the street.

88

'And the bold, true warriors
Who have hugged Danger in wars
Will turn to those who would be free,
Ashamed of such base company.

89

'And that slaughter to the Nation   370
Shall steam up like inspiration,
Eloquent, oracular;
A volcano heard afar.

90

'And these words shall then become
Like oppression's thundered doom
Ringing thro' each heart and brain,
Heard again – again – again –

91

'Rise like Lions after slumber
In unvanquishable number –
Shake your chains to earth like dew   380
Which in sleep had fallen on you –
Ye are many – they are few.'

Ode to the West Wind*

1

O wild West Wind, thou breath of Autumn's being,
Thou from whose unseen presence the leaves dead
Are driven, like ghosts from an enchanter fleeing,

Yellow, and black, and pale, and hectic red,
Pestilence-stricken multitudes: O thou,
Who chariotest to their dark wintry bed

The winged seeds, where they lie cold and low,
Each like a corpse within its grave, until
Thine azure sister of the spring shall blow

Her clarion o'er the dreaming earth, and fill   10
(Driving sweet buds like flocks to feed in air)
With living hues and odours plain and hill:

Wild Spirit, which art moving everywhere;
Destroyer and preserver;[119] hear, Oh hear!

---

* This poem was conceived and chiefly written in a wood that skirts the Arno, near Florence, and on a day when that tempestuous wind, whose temperature is at once mild and animating, was collecting the vapours which pour down the autumnal rains. They began, as I foresaw, at sunset with a violent tempest of hail and rain, attended by that magnificent thunder and lightning peculiar to the Cisalpine regions.

The phenomenon alluded to at the conclusion of the third stanza is well known to naturalists. The vegetation at the bottom of the sea, of rivers, and of lakes, sympathises with that of the land in the change of seasons, and is consequently influenced by the winds which announce it.

2

Thou on whose stream, 'mid the steep sky's commotion,
Loose clouds like earth's decaying leaves are shed,
Shook from the tangled boughs of Heaven and Ocean,

Angels of rain and lightning: there are spread
On the blue surface of thine airy surge,
Like the bright hair uplifted from the head   20

Of some fierce Maenad,[120] even from the dim verge
Of the horizon to the zenith's height,
The locks of the approaching storm. Thou dirge

Of the dying year, to which this closing night
Will be the dome of a vast sepulchre,
Vaulted with all thy congregated might

Of vapours, from whose solid atmosphere
Black rain, and fire, and hail will burst: Oh hear!

3

Thou who didst waken from his summer dreams
The blue Mediterranean, where he lay,   30
Lulled by the coil of his crystalline streams,

Beside a pumice isle in Baiae's bay,[121]
And saw in sleep old palaces and towers
Quivering within the wave's intenser day,

All overgrown with azure moss and flowers
So sweet, the sense faints picturing them! Thou
For whose path the Atlantic's level powers

Cleave themselves into chasms, while far below
The sea-blooms and the oozy woods which wear
The sapless foliage of the ocean know   40

Thy voice, and suddenly grow grey with fear,
And tremble and despoil themselves: Oh hear!

4

If I were a dead leaf thou mightest bear;
If I were a swift cloud to fly with thee;
A wave to pant beneath thy power, and share

The impulse of thy strength, only less free
Than thou, O uncontrollable! If even
I were as in my boyhood, and could be

The comrade of thy wanderings over heaven,
As then, when to outstrip thy skiey speed   50
Scarce seemed a vision; I would ne'er have striven

As thus with thee in prayer in my sore need.
Oh! lift me as a wave, a leaf, a cloud!
I fall upon the thorns of life! I bleed!

A heavy weight of hours has chained and bowed
One too like thee: tameless, and swift, and proud.

5

Make me thy lyre, even as the forest is:
What if my leaves are falling like its own!
The tumult of thy mighty harmonies

Will take from both a deep, autumnal tone,   60
Sweet though in sadness. Be thou, spirit fierce,
My spirit! Be thou me, impetuous one!

Drive my dead thoughts over the universe
Like withered leaves to quicken a new birth!
And, by the incantation of this verse,

Scatter, as from an unextinguished hearth
Ashes and sparks, my words among mankind!
Be through my lips to unawakened earth

The trumpet of a prophecy! O Wind,
If Winter comes, can Spring be far behind?   70

Lines written during the Castlereagh Administration[122]

1

Corpses are cold in the tomb;
Stones on the pavement are dumb;
Abortions are dead in the womb,
And their mothers look pale – like the death-white shore
  Of Albion,[123] free no more.

2

Her sons are as stones in the way –
They are masses of senseless clay –
They are trodden, and move not away, –
The abortion with which she travaileth
  Is Liberty, smitten to death.   10

3

Then trample and dance, thou Oppressor!
For thy victim is no redresser;
Thou art sole lord and possessor
Of her corpses, and clods, and abortions – they pave
  Thy path to the grave.

4

Hearest thou the festival din
Of Death, and Destruction, and Sin,
And Wealth crying *Havoc!* within?
'Tis the bacchanal triumph which makes Truth dumb,
  Thine epithalamium.   20

5

Aye, marry thy ghastly wife!
Let Fear and Disquiet and Strife
Spread thy couch in the chamber of Life!
Marry Ruin, thou Tyrant! and God be thy guide
  To the bed of the bride!

Song to the Men of England

1

Men of England, wherefore plough
For the lords who lay ye low?
Wherefore weave with toil and care
The rich robes your tyrants wear?

2

Wherefore feed, and clothe, and save.
From the cradle to the grave,
Those ungrateful drones who would
Drain your sweat – nay, drink your blood?

3

Wherefore, Bees of England, forge
Many a weapon, chain, and scourge,   10
That these stingless drones may spoil
The forced produce of your toil?

4

Have ye leisure, comfort, calm,
Shelter, food, love's gentle balm?
Or what is it ye buy so dear
With your pain and with your fear?

5

The seed ye sow, another reaps;
The wealth ye find, another keeps;
The robes ye weave, another wears;
The arms ye forge, another bears.   20

6

Sow seed, – but let no tyrant reap;
Find wealth, – let no impostor heap;
Weave robes, – let not the idle wear;
Forge arms, – in your defence to bear.

7

Shrink to your cellars, holes, and cells;
In halls ye deck, another dwells.
Why shake the chains ye wrought? Ye see
The steel ye tempered glance on ye.

8

With plough and spade, and hoe and loom,
Trace your grave, and build your tomb,   30
And weave your winding-sheet, till fair
England be your sepulchre.

Similes for Two Political Characters of 1819 [124]

1

As from an ancestral oak
   Two empty ravens sound their clarion,
Yell by yell, and croak by croak,
When they scent the noonday smoke
      Of fresh human carrion: –

2

As two gibbering night-birds flit
   From their bowers of deadly yew
Through the night to frighten it,
When the moon is in a fit,
      And the stars are none, or few: –   10

3

As a shark and dogfish wait
   Under an Atlantic isle,
For the negro-ship, whose freight
Is the theme of their debate,
      Wrinkling their red gills the while –

4

Are ye, two vultures sick for battle,
  Two scorpions under one wet stone,
Two bloodless wolves whose dry throats rattle,
Two crows perched on the murrained cattle,
      Two vipers tangled into one.   20

England in 1819

An old, mad, blind, despised, and dying king,[125] –
Princes, the dregs of their dull race, who flow
Through public scorn, – mud from a muddy spring, –
Rulers, who neither see, nor feel, nor know,
But leech-like to their fainting country cling,
Till they drop, blind in blood, without a blow, –
A people starved and stabbed in the untilled field, –
An army, which liberticide and prey
Makes as a two-edged sword to all who wield, –
Golden and sanguine laws which tempt and slay;   10
Religion Christless, Godless – a book sealed;
A Senate, – Time's worst statute unrepealed, –
Are graves, from which a glorious Phantom may
Burst, to illumine our tempestuous day.

On the Medusa of Leonardo da Vinci
in the Florentine Gallery [126]

1

It lieth, gazing on the midnight sky,
    Upon the cloudy mountain peak supine;
Below, far lands are seen tremblingly;
    Its horror and its beauty are divine.
Upon its lips and eyelids seems to lie
    Loveliness like a shadow, from which shine,
Fiery and lurid, struggling underneath,
The agonies of anguish and of death.

2

Yet it is less the horror than the grace
    Which turns the gazer's spirit into stone   10
Whereon the lineaments of that dead face
    Are graven, till the characters be grown
Into itself, and thought no more can trace;
    'Tis the melodious hues of beauty thrown
Athwart the darkness and the glare of pain,
Which humanise and harmonise the strain.

3

And from its head as from one body grow,
    As [. . .] grass out of a watery rock,
Hairs which are vipers, and they curl and flow
    And their long tangles in each other lock,   20
And with unending involutions show
    Their mailed radiance, as it were to mock
The torture and the death within, and saw
The solid air with many a ragged jaw.

4

And, from a stone beside, a poisonous eft
    Peeps idly into those Gorgonian eyes;
Whilst in the air a ghastly bat, bereft
    Of sense, has flitted with a mad surprise

Out of the cave this hideous light had cleft,
   And he comes hastening like a moth that hies   30
After a taper; and the midnight sky
Flares, a light more dread than obscurity.

5

'Tis the tempestuous loveliness of terror;
   For from the serpents gleams a brazen glare
Kindled by that inextricable error
   Which makes a thrilling vapour of the air
Become a [. . .] and ever-shifting mirror
   Of all the beauty and the terror there –
A woman's countenance, with serpent-locks,
Gazing in death on heaven from those wet rocks.   40

Love's Philosophy

1

The fountains mingle with the river,
   And the rivers with the ocean;
The winds of heaven mix for ever
   With a sweet emotion;
Nothing in the world is single;
   All things by a law divine
In one spirit meet and mingle; –
   Why not I with thine?

2

See the mountains kiss high heaven,
   And the waves clasp one another;   10
No sister flower would be forgiven,
   If it disdained its brother;
And the sunlight clasps the earth
   And the moonbeams kiss the sea:
What is all this sweet work worth
   If thou kiss not me?

Peter Bell the Third

Part Third

HELL

Hell is like a city much like London –
   A populous and a smoky city;
There are all sorts of people undone,
And there is little or no fun done;   150
   Small justice shown, and still less pity.

There is a Castles, and a Canning
   A Cobbett, and a Castlereagh,[127]
All sorts of caitiff corpses planning
All sorts of cozening for trepanning
   Corpses less corrupt than they.

There is a Southey, who has lost
   His wits, or sold them, none knows which;
He walks about a double ghost,
And though as thin as Fraud almost –   160
   Ever grows more grim and rich.

There is a Chancery Court, a King
   A manufacturing mob; a set
Of thieves who by themselves are sent
Similar thieves to represent;
   An army; and a public debt.

Which last is a scheme of Paper money,
   And means – being interpreted –
'Bees, keep your wax – give us the honey
And we will plant while skies are sunny   170
   Flowers, which in winter serve instead.'

There is great talk of Revolution –
   And a great chance of despotism –
German soldiers – camps – confusion –
Tumults – lotteries – rage – delusion –
   Gin – suicide and methodism;

Taxes too, on wine and bread,
   And meat, and beer, and tea, and cheese,
From which those patriots pure are fed
Who gorge before they reel to bed   180
   The tenfold essence of all these.

There are mincing women, mewing
   (Like cats, who *amant miser*),*
Of there own virtue, and pursuing
Their gentler sisters to that ruin,
   Without which – what were chastity?†

Lawyers – judges – old hobnobbers
   Are there – Bailiffs – Chancellors –
Bishops – great and little robbers –
Rhymesters – pampleteers – stock-jobbers –   190
   Men of glory in the wars, –

Things whose trade is, over ladies
   To lean, and flirt, and stare, and simper,
Till all that is divine in women
Grows cruel, courteous, smooth, inhuman,
   Crucified 'twixt a smile and whimper.

Thrusting, toiling, wailing, moiling,
   Frowning, preaching – such a riot!
Each with never-ceasing labour
Whilst he thinks he cheats his neighbour   200
   Cheating his own heart of quiet.

---

* 'One of the attributes in Linnaeus's description of the Cat. To a similar cause the caterwauling of more than one species of this genus is to be referred; – except indeed that the poor quadruped is compelled to quarrel with its own pleasures, whilst the biped is supposed only to quarrel with those of others.'
† 'What would this husk and excuse for a Virtue be without its kernal prostitution, the kernal prostitution without this husk of a Virtue? I wonder the Women of the Town do not form an association, like the Society for the Suppression of Vice, for the support of what may be considered the "King, church, and Constitution" of their order. But this subject is almost too horrible for a joke.'

And all these meet at levees;
    Dinners convivial and political; –
Supers of epic poets; – teas,
Where small talk dies in agonies; –
    Breakfasts professional and critical;

Lunches and snacks so aldermanic
    That one would furnish forth ten dinners,
Where reigns a Cretan-tongued[128] panic
Lest news Russ, Dutch, or Alemannic[129]   210
    Should make some losers, and some winners

At conversazioni – balls –
    Conventicles and drawing-rooms.
Courts of law – committees – calls
Of a morning – clubs – book stalls –
    Churches – masquerades and tombs.

And this is Hell – and in this smother
    All are damnable and damned;
Each one damning, damns the other;
They are damned by one another,   220
    By none other are they damned.

'Tis a lie to say, 'God damns!'*
    Where was Heaven's Attorney General
When they first gave out such flams?
Let there be an end to shams,
    They are mines of poisonous mineral.

Statesmen damn themselves to be
    Cursed; and lawyers damn their souls
To the auction of a fee;
Churchmen damn themselves to see   230
    God's sweet love in burning coals.

---

* 'This libel on our national oath, and this accusation of all our countrymen of being in the daily practice of solemnly asseverating the most enormous falsehood, I fear deserves the notice of a more active Attorney General than that here alluded to.'

The rich are damned beyond all cure
    To taunt, and starve, and trample on
The weak and wretched: and the poor
Damn their broken hearts to endure
    Stripe on stripe, with groan on groan.

Sometimes the poor are damned indeed
    To take, – not means of being blessed, –
But Cobbett's snuff, revenge; that weed
From which the worms that it doth feed   240
    Squeeze less than they before possessed.

And some few, like we know who,
    Damned – but God alone knows why –
To believe their minds are given
To make this ugly Hell a Heaven;
    In which faith they live and die.

Thus, as in a Town, plague-stricken,
    Each man be he sound or no
Must indifferently sicken;
As when day begins to thicken   250
    None knows a pigeon from a crow, –

So good and bad, sane and mad,
    The oppressor and the oppressed;
Those who weep to see what others
Smile to inflict upon their brothers;
    Lovers, haters, worst and best;

All are damned – they breathe an air,
    Thick, infected, joy-dispelling:
Each pursues what seems most fair,
Mining like moles, through mind, and there   260
Scoop palace-caverns vast, where Care
    In throned state is ever dwelling.

Part Fourth

SIN

Lo, Peter in Hell's Grosvenor square,
   A footman in the Devil's service!
And the misjudging world would swear
That every man in service there
   To virtue would prefer vice.

But Peter, though now dammed, was not
   What Peter was before damnation.
Men oftentimes prepare a lot   270
Which ere it finds them, is not what
   Suits with their genuine station.

All things that Peter saw and felt
   Had a peculiar aspect to him;
And when they came within the belt
Of his own nature, seemed to melt
   Like cloud to cloud, into him.

And so the outward world uniting
   To that within him, he became
Considerably uninviting   280
To those who, meditation slighting,
   Were moulded in a different frame.

And he scorned them, and they scorned him;
   And he scorned all they did, and they
Did all that men of their own trim
Are wont to do to please their whim,
   Drinking, lying, swearing, play.

Such were his fellow servants; thus
   His virtue, like our own, was built
Too much on that indignant fuss   290
Hypocrite Pride stirs up in us
   To bully one another's guilt.

He had a mind which was somehow
   At once circumference and centre
Of all he might or feel or know;
Nothing went ever out, although
   Something did ever enter.

He had as much imagination
   As a pint-pot: – he never could
Fancy another situation   300
From which to dart his contemplation,
   Than that wherein he stood.

Yet his was individual mind,
   And new created all he saw
In a new manner, and refined
Those new creations, and combined
   Them, by a master-spirit's law,

Thus – though unimaginative,
   An apprehension clear, intense,
Of his mind's work, had made alive   310
The things it wrought on; I believe
   Wakening a sort of thought in sense.

But from the first 'twas Peter's drift
   To be a kind of moral eunuch,
He touched the hem of Nature's shift,
Felt faint – and never dared uplift
   The closest, all-concealing tunic.

She laughed the while, with an arch smile,
   And kissed him with a sister's kiss,
And said – 'My best Diogenes,[130]   320
I love you well – but, if you please,
   Tempt not again my deepest bliss.

' 'Tis you are cold – for I, not coy,
   Yield love for love, frank, warm and true:
And Burns, a Scottish Peasant boy, –
His errors prove it – knew my joy
   More, learned friend, than you.

'*Bocca baciata non perde ventura*
　　Anzi rinnuova come fa la luna: – 　　　　　　329
So thought Boccaccio, whose sweet words might cure a
Male prude like you from what you now endure, a
　　Low-tide in soul, like a stagnant laguna.'

Then Peter rubbed his eyes severe,
　　And smoothed his spacious forehead down
With his broad palm; – 'twixt love and fear,
He looked, as he no doubt felt, queer,
　　And in his dream sate down.

The Devil was no uncommon creature;
　　A leaden-witted thief – just huddled
Out of the dross and scum of nature; 　　　　　　340
A toadlike lump of limb and feature,
　　With mind, and heart, and fancy muddled.

He was that heavy, dull, cold thing
　　The spirit of evil well may be:
A drone too base to have a sting;
Who gluts, and grimes his lazy wing,
　　And calls lust, luxury.

Now he was quite the kind of wight
　　Round whom collect, at a fixed era,
Venison, turtle, hock and claret, – 　　　　　　350
Good cheer – and those who come to share it –
　　And best East Indian madeira!

It was his fancy to invite
　　Men of science, wit and learning,
Who came to lend each other Light: –
He proudly thought that his gold's might
　　Had set those spirits burning.

And men of learning, science, wit,
　　Considered him as you and I
Think of some rotten tree, and sit 　　　　　　360
Lounging and dining under it,
　　Exposed to the wide sky.

And all the while, with loose fat smile,
 The willing wretch sat winking there,
Believing 'twas his power that made
That jovial scene – and that all paid
 Homage to his unnoticed chair.

Though to be sure this place was Hell;
 He was the Devil – and all they –
What though the claret circled well,   370
And Wit, like ocean, rose and fell? –
 Were damned eternally.

Part Fifth

GRACE

Among the guests who often staid
 Till the Devil's petits soupers,
A man there came,[131] fair as a maid,
And Peter noted what he said,
 Standing behind his master's chair.

He was a mighty poet – and
 A subtle-souled Psychologist;
All things he seemed to understand   380
Of old or new – of sea or land –
 But his own mind – which was a mist.

This was a man who might have turned
 Hell into Heaven – and so in gladness
A Heaven unto himself have earned;
But he in shadows undiscerned
 Trusted, – and damned himself to madness.

He spoke of poetry, and how
 'Divine it was – a light – a love –
A spirit which like wind doth blow   390
As it listeth, to and fro;
 A dew rained down from God above,

'A power which comes and goes like dream,
    And which none can ever trace –
Heaven's light on Earth – Truth's brightest beam.'
And when he ceased there lay the gleam
    Of those words upon his face.

Now Peter, when he heard such talk
    Would, heedless of a broken pate,
Stand like a man asleep, or baulk   400
Some wishing guest of knife or fork,
    Or drop and break his master's plate.

At night oft would start and wake
    Like a lover, and began
In a wild measure songs to make
On moor, and glen, and rocky lake,
    And on the heart of man.

And on the universal sky –
    And the wide earth's bosom green, –
And the sweet, strange mystery   410
Of what beyond these things may lie
    And yet remain unseen.

For in his thought he visited
    The spots in which, ere dead and damned,
He his wayward life had led;
Yet knew not whence the thoughts were fed
    Which thus his fancy crammed.

And these obscure remembrances
    Stirred such harmony in Peter,
That, whensoever he should please,   420
He could speak of rocks and trees
    In poetic metre.

For though it was without a sense
    Of memory, yet he remembered well
Many a ditch and quickset fence;
Of lakes he had intelligence
    He knew something of heath and fell.

He had also dim recollections
   Of pedlars tramping on their rounds,
Milk pans and pails, and odd collections   430
Of saws, and proverbs, and reflections
   Old parsons make in burying-grounds.

But Peter's verse was clear, and came
   Announcing from the frozen hearth
Of a cold age, that none might tame
The soul of that diviner flame
   It augured to the Earth;

Like gentle rains, on the dry plains,
   Making that green which late was grey,
Or like the sudden moon, that stains   440
Some gloomy chamber's windowpanes
   With a broad light like day.

For language was in Peter's hand
   Like clay while he was yet a potter;
And he made songs for all the land
Sweet both to feel and understand
   As pipkins late to mountain Cotter.

And Mr ——,[132] the Bookseller,
   Gave twenty pounds for some: – then scorning
A footman's yellow coat to wear,   450
Peter, too proud of heart I fear,
   Instantly gave the Devil warning.

Whereat the Devil took offence,
   And swore in his soul a great oath then,
'That for his damned impertinence,
He'd bring him to a proper sense
   Of what was due to gentlemen!'

The Indian Girl's Song [133]

I

I arise from dreams of thee
In the first sweet sleep of night,
When the winds are breathing low,
And the stars are shining bright:
I arise from dreams of thee,
And a spirit in my feet
Hath led me – who knows how?
To thy chamber window, Sweet!

II

The wandering airs they faint
On the dark, the silent stream –   10
The Champak odours fail
Like sweet thoughts in a dream;
The nightingale's complaint,
It dies upon her heart; –
As I must on thine,
O beloved as thou art!

III

Oh! lift me from the grass!
I die! I faint! I fail!
Let thy love in kisses rain
On my lips and eyelids pale.   20
My cheek is cold and white, alas!
My heart beats loud and fast; –
Oh! press it to thine own again,
Where it will break at last.

Ode to Heaven [134]

CHORUS OF SPIRITS

First Spirit

Palace-roof of cloudless nights!
Paradise of golden lights!
  Deep, immeasurable, vast,
Which art now, and which wert then!
  Of the present and the past,
Of the eternal where and when,
  Presence-chamber, temple, home,
  Ever-canopying dome,
  Of acts and ages yet to come!

Glorious shapes have life in thee,   10
Earth, and all earth's company;
  Living globes which ever throng
Thy deep chasms and wildernesses;
  And green worlds that glide along;
And swift stars with flashing tresses;
  And icy moons most cold and bright,
  And mighty suns beyond the night,
  Atoms of intensest light.

Even thy name is as a god,
Heaven! for thou art the abode   20
  Of that power which is the glass
Wherein man his nature sees.
  Generations as they pass
Worship thee with bended knees.
  Their unremaining gods and they
  Like a river roll away:
  Thou remainest such alway.

Second Spirit

Thou art but the mind's first chamber,
Round which its young fancies clamber,
  Like weak insects in a cave,   30
Lighted up by stalactites;

But the portal of the grave,
Where a world of new delights
    Will make thy best glories seem
    But a dim and noonday gleam
    From the shadow of a dream!

Third Spirit

Peace! the abyss is wreathed with scorn
At your presumption, atom-born!
    What is heaven? and what are ye
Who its brief expanse inherit?   40
    What are suns and spheres which flee
    With the instinct of that spirit
    Of which ye are but a part?
    Drops which Nature's mighty heart
    Drives through thinnest veins! Depart!

What is heaven? a globe of dew,
Filling in the morning new
    Some eyed flower whose young leaves waken
On an unimagined world:
    Constellated suns unshaken.   50
Orbits measureless, are furled
    In that frail and fading sphere,
    With ten millions gathered there,
    To tremble, gleam, and disappear.

POEMS FROM 1820

The Sensitive Plant[135]

PART FIRST

A Sensitive Plant in a garden grew,
And the young winds fed it with silver dew,
And it opened its fan-like leaves to the light,
And closed them beneath the kisses of night.

And the Spring arose on the garden fair,
Like the Spirit of Love felt everywhere;
And each flower and herb on Earth's dark breast
Rose from the dreams of its wintry rest.

But none ever trembled and panted with bliss
In the garden, the field, or the wilderness,   10
Like a doe in the noontide with love's sweet want,
As the companionless[136] Sensitive Plant.

The snowdrop, and then the violet,
Arose from the ground with warm rain wet,
And their breath was mixed with fresh odour, sent
From the turf, like the voice and the instrument.

Then the pied wind-flowers and the tulip tall,
And narcissi, the fairest among them all,
Who gaze on their eyes in the stream's recess,
Till they die of their own dear loveliness;   20

And the Naiad-like[137] lily of the vale,
Whom youth makes so fair and passion so pale,
That the light of its tremulous bells is seen
Through their pavilions of tender green;

And the hyacinth purple, and white, and blue,
Which flung from its bells a sweet peal anew
Of music so delicate, soft, and intense,
It was felt like an odour within the sense;

And the rose like a nymph to the bath addrest,
Which unveiled the depth of her glowing breast,   30
Till, fold after fold, to the fainting air
The soul of her beauty and love lay bare:

And the wand-like lily, which lifted up,
As a Maenad,[138] its moonlight-coloured cup,
Till the fiery star, which is its eye,
Gazed through clear dew on the tender sky;

And the jessamine faint, and the sweet tuberose,
The sweetest flower for scent that blows;
And all rare blossoms from every clime
Grew in that garden in perfect prime.   40

And on the stream whose inconstant bosom
Was prankt under boughs of embowering blossom,
With golden and green light, slanting through
Their heaven of many a tangled hue,

Broad water-lilies lay tremulously,
And starry river-buds glimmered by,
And around them the soft stream did glide and dance
With a motion of sweet sound and radiance.

And the sinuous paths of lawn and of moss,
Which led through the garden along and across,   50
Some open at once to the sun and the breeze,
Some lost among bowers of blossoming trees,

Were all paved with daisies and delicate bells
As fair as the fabulous asphodels,
And flow'rets which drooping as day drooped too
Fell into pavilions, white, purple, and blue,
To roof the glow-worm from the evening dew.

And from this undefiled Paradise
The flowers (as an infant's awakening eyes
Smile on its mother, whose singing sweet   60
Can first lull, and at last must awaken it),

When Heaven's blithe winds had unfolded them,
As mine-lamps enkindle a hidden gem,
Shone smiling to Heaven, and every one
Shared joy in the light of the gentle sun;

For each one was interpenetrated
With the light and the odour its neighbour shed,
Like young lovers whom youth and love make dear
Wrapped and filled by their mutual atmosphere.

But the Sensitive Plant, which could give small fruit   70
Of the love which it felt from the leaf to the root,
Received more than all, it loved more than ever,
Where none wanted but it, could belong to the giver,

For the Sensitive Plant has no bright flower;
Radiance and odour are not its dower;
It loves, even like Love, its deep heart is full,
It desires what it has not, the beautiful!

The light winds which from unsustaining wings
Shed the music of many murmurings;
The beams which dart from many a star   80
Of the flowers whose hues they bear afar;

The plumed insects swift and free,
Like golden boats on a sunny sea,
Laden with light and odour, which pass
Over the gleam of the living grass;

The unseen clouds of the dew, which lie
Like fire in the flowers till the sun rides high,
Then wander like spirits among the spheres,
Each cloud faint with the fragrance it bears;

The quivering vapours of dim noontide,   90
Which like a sea o'er the warm earth glide,
In which every sound, and odour, and beam,
Move, as reeds in a single stream;

Each and all like ministering angels were
For the Sensitive Plant sweet joy to bear,
Whilst the lagging hours of the day went by
Like windless clouds o'er a tender sky.

And when evening descended from heaven above,
And the Earth was all rest, and the air was all love,
And delight, tho' less bright, was far more deep,   100
And the day's veil fell from the world of sleep,

And the beasts, and the birds, and the insects were drowned
In an ocean of dreams without a sound;
Whose waves never mark, tho' they ever impress
The light sand which paves it, consciousness;

(Only overhead the sweet nightingale
Ever sang more sweet as the day might fail,
And snatches of its Elysian[139] chant
Were mixed with the dreams of the Sensitive Plant.)

The Sensitive Plant was the earliest   110
Upgathered into the bosom of rest;
A sweet child weary of its delight,
The feeblest and yet the favourite,
Cradled within the embrace of night.

PART SECOND

There was a Power in this sweet place,
An Eve in this Eden; a ruling grace
Which to the flowers, did they waken or dream,
Was as God is to the starry scheme.

A Lady, the wonder of her kind,
Whose form was upborne by a lovely mind
Which, dilating, had moulded her mien and motion
Like a sea-flower unfolded beneath the ocean,

Tended the garden from morn to even:
And the meteors of that sublunar heaven,   10
Like the lamps of the air when night walks forth,
Laughed round her footsteps up from the Earth!

She had no companion of mortal race,
But her tremulous breath and her flushing face
Told, whilst the morn kissed the sleep from her eyes,
That her dreams were less slumber than Paradise:

As if some bright Spirit for her sweet sake
Had deserted heaven while the stars were awake,
As if yet around her he lingering were,
Tho' the veil of daylight concealed him from her.   20

Her step seemed to pity the grass it prest;
You might hear by the heaving of her breast,
That the coming and going of the wind
Brought pleasure there and left passion behind.

And wherever her airy footstep trod,
Her trailing hair from the grassy sod
Erased its light vestige, with shadowy sweep,
Like a sunny storm o'er the dark green deep.

I doubt not the flowers of that garden sweet
Rejoiced in the sound of her gentle feet;   30
I doubt not they felt the spirit that came
From her glowing fingers thro' all their frame.

She sprinkled bright water from the stream
On those that were faint with the sunny beam;
And out of the cups of the heavy flowers
She emptied the rain of the thunder showers.

She lifted their heads with her tender hands,
And sustained them with rods and osier bands;
If the flowers had been her own infants, she
Could never have nursed them more tenderly.   40

And all killing insects and gnawing worms,
And things of obscene and unlovely forms,
She bore in a basket of Indian woof,
Into the rough woods far aloof,

In a basket, of grasses and wildflowers full,
The freshest her gentle hands could pull
For the poor banished insects, whose intent,
Although they did ill, was innocent.

But the bee and the beamlike ephemeris,[140]
Whose path is the lightning's, and soft moths that kiss   50
The sweet lips of the flowers, and harm not, did she
Make her attendant angels be.

And many an antenatal tomb,
Where butterflies dream of the life to come,
She left clinging round the smooth and dark
Edge of the odorous cedar bark.

This fairest creature from earliest spring
Thus moved through the garden ministering
All the sweet season of summertide,
And ere the first leaf looked brown – she died!   60

PART THIRD

Three days the flowers of the garden fair
Like stars when the moon is awakened were,
Or the waves of Baiae,[141] ere luminous
She floats up through the smoke of Vesuvius.

And on the fourth, the Sensitive Plant
Felt the sound of the funeral chant,
And the steps of the bearers, heavy and slow,
And the sobs of the mourners deep and low;

The weary sound and the heavy breath,
And the silent motions of passing death,   10
And the smell, cold, oppressive, and dank,
Sent through the pores of the coffin plank;

The dark grass, and the flowers among the grass,
Were bright with tears as the crowd did pass;
From their sighs the wind caught a mournful tone,
And sate in the pines, and gave groan for groan.

The garden, once fair, became cold and foul,
Like the corpse of her who had been its soul,
Which at first was lovely as if in sleep,
Then slowly changed, till it grew a heap   20
To make men tremble who never weep.

Swift summer into the autumn flowed,
And frost in the mist of the morning rode,
Though the noonday sun looked clear and bright,
Mocking the spoil of the secret night.

The rose leaves, like flakes of crimson snow,
Paved the turf and the moss below.
The lilies were drooping, and white, and wan,
Like the head and the skin of a dying man.

And Indian plants, of scent and hue   30
The sweetest that ever were fed on dew,
Leaf by leaf, day after day,
Were massed into the common clay.

And the leaves, brown, yellow, and grey, and red,
And white with the whiteness of what is dead,
Like troops of ghosts on the dry wind past;
Their whistling noise made the birds aghast.

And the gusty winds waked the winged seeds,
Out of their birthplace of ugly weeds,
Till they clung round many a sweet flower's stem,   40
Which rotted into the earth with them.

The water-blooms under the rivulet
Fell from the stalks on which they were set;
And the eddies drove them here and there,
As the winds did those of the upper air.

Then the rain came down, and the broken stalks,
Were bent and tangled across the walks;
And the leafless network of parasite bowers
Massed into ruin; and all sweet flowers.

Between the time of the wind and the snow,   50
All loathliest weeds began to grow,
Whose coarse leaves were splashed with many a speck,
Like the water-snake's belly and the toad's back.

And thistles, and nettles, and darnels rank,
And the dock, and henbane, and hemlock[142] dank,
Stretched out its long and hollow shank,
And stifled the air till the dead wind stank.

And plants, at whose names the verse feels loath,
Filled the place with a monstrous undergrowth,
Prickly, and pulpous, and blistering, and blue,   60
Livid and starred with a lurid dew.

And agarics[143] and fungi, with mildew and mould
Started like mist from the wet ground cold;
Pale, fleshy, as if the decaying dead
With a spirit of growth had been animated!

Spawn, weeds, and filth, a leprous scum,
Made the running rivulet thick and dumb,
And at its outlet flags huge as stakes
Dammed it up with roots knotted like water snakes.

And hour by hour, when the air was still,   70
The vapours arose which have strength to kill:
At morn they were seen, at noon they were felt,
At night they were darkness no star could melt.

And unctuous meteors from spray to spray
Crept and flitted in broad noonday
Unseen; every branch on which they alit
By a venomous blight was burned and bit.

The Sensitive Plant, like one forbid,
Wept, and the tears within each lid
Of its folded leaves which together grew,   80
Were changed to a blight of frozen glue.

For the leaves soon fell, and the branches soon
By the heavy axe of the blast were hewn;
The sap shrank to the root through every pore
As blood to a heart that will beat no more.

For Winter came: the wind was his whip:
One choppy finger was on his lip:
He had torn the cataracts from the hills
And they clanked at his girdle like manacles;

His breath was a chain which without a sound   90
The earth, and the air, and the water bound;
He came, fiercely driven, in his chariot-throne
By the tenfold blasts of the arctic zone.

Then the weeds which were forms of living death
Fled from the frost to the earth beneath.
Their decay and sudden flight from frost
Was but like the vanishing of a ghost!

And under the roots of the Sensitive Plant
The moles and the dormice died for want:
The birds dropped stiff from the frozen air   100
And were caught in the branches naked and bare.

First there came down a thawing rain,
And its dull drops froze on the boughs again,
Then there steamed up a freezing dew
Which to the drops of the thaw-rain grew;

And a northern whirlwind, wandering about
Like a wolf that had smelt a dead child out,
Shook the boughs, thus laden, and heavy and stiff,
And snapped them off with his rigid griff.

When winter had gone and spring came back,   110
The Sensitive Plant was a leafless wreck;
But the mandrakes, and toadstools, and docks, and darnels,
Rose like the dead from their ruined charnels.

CONCLUSION

Whether the Sensitive Plant, or that
Which within its boughs like a spirit sat,
Ere its outward form had known decay,
Now felt this change, I cannot say.

Whether that lady's gentle mind,
No longer with the form combined
Which scattered love, as stars do light,
Found sadness, where it left delight,

I dare not guess; but in this life
Of error, ignorance, and strife,   10
Where nothing is, but all things seem,
And we the shadows of the dream,

It is a modest creed, and yet
Pleasant if one considers it,
To own that death itself must be,
Like all the rest, a mockery.

That garden sweet, that lady fair,
And all sweet shapes and odours there,
In truth have never passed away:
'Tis we, 'tis ours, are changed; not they.   20

For love, and beauty, and delight,
There is no death nor change: their might
Exceeds our organs,[144] which endure
No light, being themselves obscure.

Letter to Maria Gisborne

LEGHORN – *July 1, 1820*

The spider spreads her webs, whether she be
In poet's tower, cellar, or barn, or tree;
The silkworm in the dark green mulberry leaves
His winding sheet and cradle ever weaves;
So I, a thing whom moralists call worm,
Sit spinning still round this decaying form,
From the fine threads of rare and subtle thought –
No net of words in garish colours wrought
To catch the idle buzzers of the day –
But a soft cell, where when that fades away,   10
Memory may clothe in wings my living name
And feed it with the asphodels of fame,
Which in those hearts which must remember me
Grow, making love an immortality.

    Whoever should behold me now, I wist,
Would think I were a mighty mechanist,
Bent with sublime Archimedean art[145]
To breathe a soul into the iron heart
Of some machine portentous, or strange gin
Which by the force of figured spells might win   20
Its way over the sea, and sport therein;
For round the walls are hung dread engines, such
As Vulcan[146] never wrought for Jove to clutch
Ixion or the Titan: – or the quick
Wit of that man of God, St Dominic,[147]
To convince Atheist, Turk or Heretic;
Or those in philanthropic council[148] met,
Who thought to pay some interest for the debt
They owed to Jesus Christ for their salvation,
By giving a faint foretaste of damnation   30
To Shakespeare, Sidney, Spenser and the rest
Who made our land an island of the blest,
When lamp-like Spain, who now relumes her fire
On Freedom's hearth, grew dim with Empire: –
With thumbscrews, wheels, with tooth and spike and jag,

Which fishers found under the utmost crag
Of Cornwall and the storm-encompassed isles,[149]
Where to the sky the rude sea rarely smiles
Unless in treacherous wrath, as on the morn
When the exulting elements in scorn,   40
Satiated with destroyed destruction, lay
Sleeping in beauty on their mangled prey,
As panthers sleep; – and other strange and dread
Magical forms the brick floor overspread –
Proteus[150] transformed to metal did not make
More figures, or more strange; nor did he take
Such shapes of unintelligible brass,
Or heap himself in such a horrid mass
Of tin and iron not to be understood,
And forms of unimaginable wood,   50
To puzzle Tubal Cain[151] and all his brood:
Great screws, and cones, and wheels, and grooved blocks,
The elements of what will stand the shocks
Of wave and wind and time. Upon the table
More knacks and quips there be than I am able
To catalogise in this verse of mine: –
A pretty bowl of wood – not full of wine,
But quicksilver; that dew which the gnomes drink
When at their subterranean toil they swink,
Pledging the demons of the earthquake, who   60
Reply to them in lava – cry halloo!
And call out to the cities o'er their head, –
Roofs, towers, and shrines, the dying and the dead,
Crash through the chinks of earth – and then all quaff
Another rouse, and hold their sides and laugh.
This quicksilver no gnome has drunk – within
The walnut bowl it lies, veined and thin,
In colour like the wake of light that stains
The Tuscan deep, when from the moist moon rains
The inmost shower of its white fire – the breeze   70
Is still – blue heaven smiles over the pale seas.
And in this bowl of quicksilver – for I
Yield to the impulse of an infancy
Outlasting manhood – I have made to float
A rude idealism of a paper boat –

A hollow screw with cogs – Henry will know
The thing I mean and laugh at me, – if so
He fears not I should do more mischief. – Next
Lie bills and calculations much perplext,
With steamboats, frigates, and machinery quaint   80
Traced over them in blue and yellow paint.
Then comes a range of mathematical
Instruments, for plans nautical and statical;
A heap of rosin, a queer broken glass
With ink in it: – a china cup that was
What it will never be again, I think,
A thing from which sweet lips were wont to drink
The liquor doctors rail at – and which I
Will quaff in spite of them – and when we die
We'll toss up who died first of drinking tea,   90
And cry out, – heads or tails? where'er we be.
Near that a dusty paintbox, some odd hooks,
A half-burnt match, an ivory block, three books,
Where conic sections, spherics, logarithms,
To great Laplace,[152] from Saunderson and Sims,
Lie heaped in their harmonious disarray
Of figures, – disentangle them who may.
Baron de Tott's Memoirs[153] beside them lie,
And some odd volumes of old chemistry.
Near those a most inexplicable thing,   100
With lead in the middle – I'm conjecturing
How to make Henry understand; but no –
I'll leave, as Spenser says, with many mo,
This secret in the pregnant womb of time,
Too vast a matter for so weak a rhyme.

And here like some weird Archimage[154] sit I,
Plotting dark spells, and devilish enginery,
The self-impelling steam-wheels of the mind
Which pump up oaths from clergymen, and grind
The gentle spirit of our meek reviews   110
Into a powdery foam of salt abuse,
Ruffling the ocean of their self-content; –
I sit – and smile or sigh as is my bent,
But not for them – Libeccio[155] rushes round

With an inconstant and an idle sound,
I heed him more than them – the thunder-smoke
Is gathering on the mountains, like a cloak
Folded athwart their shoulders broad and bare;
The ripe corn under the undulating air
Undulates like an ocean; – and the vines   120
Are trembling wide in all their trellised lines –
The murmur of the awakening sea doth fill
The empty pauses of the blast; –the hill
Looks hoary through the white electric rain,
And from the glens beyond, in sullen strain,
The interrupted thunder howls; above
One chasm of heaven smiles, like the eye of Love
On the unquiet world; – while such things are,
How could one worth your friendship heed the war
Of worms? the shriek of the world's carrion jays,   130
Their censure, or their wonder, or their praise?

You are not here! the quaint witch Memory sees,
In vacant chairs, your absent images,
And points where once you sat, and now should be
But are not. – I demand if ever we
Shall meet as then we met; – and she replies,
Veiling in awe her second-sighted eyes:
'I know the past alone – but summon home
My sister Hope, – she speaks of all to come.'
But 1, an old diviner, who knew well   140
Every false verse of that sweet oracle,
Turned to the sad enchantress once again,
And sought a respite from my gentle pain,
In citing every passage o'er and o'er
Of our communion – how on the sea-shore
We watched the ocean and the sky together,
Under the roof of blue Italian weather;
How I ran home through last year's thunderstorm,
And felt the transverse lightning linger warm
Upon my cheek – and how we often made   150
Feasts for each other, where good will outweighed
The frugal luxury of our country cheer,
As well it might, were it less firm and clear

Than ours must ever be; – and how we spun
A shroud of talk to hide us from the sun
Of this familiar life, which seems to be
But is not – or is but quaint mockery
Of all we would believe; and sadly blame
The jarring and inexplicable frame
Of this wrong world: – and then anatomise   160
The purposes and thoughts of men whose eyes
Were closed in distant years; – or widely guess
The issue of the earth's great business,
When we shall be as we no longer are; –
Like babbling gossips safe, who hear the war
Of winds, and sigh, but tremble not; – or how
You listened to some interrupted flow
Of visionary rhyme, – in joy and pain
Struck from the inmost fountains of my brain,
With little skill perhaps; – or how we sought   170
Those deepest wells of passion or of thought
Wrought by wise poets in the waste of years,
Staining their sacred waters with our tears:
Quenching a thirst ever to be renewed!
Or how I, wisest lady! then indued
The language of a land which now is free,[156]
And winged with thoughts of truth and majesty,
Flits round the tyrant's sceptre like a cloud,
And bursts the peopled prisons, and cries aloud,
My name is Legion! – that majestic tongue   180
Which Calderon over the desert flung
Of ages and of nations; and which found
An echo in our hearts, and with the sound
Startled oblivion; – thou wert then to me
As is a nurse – when inarticulately
A child would talk as its grown parents do.
If living winds the rapid clouds pursue,
If hawks chase doves through the ethereal way,
Huntsmen the innocent deer, and beasts their prey,
Why should not we rouse with the spirit's blast   190
Out of the forest of the pathless past
These recollected pleasures?
                              You are now

In London, that great sea, whose ebb and flow
At once is deaf and loud, and on the shore
Vomits its wrecks, and still howls on for more.
Yet in its depth what treasures! You will see
That which was Godwin,[157] – greater none than he
Though fallen – and fallen on evil times – to stand
Among the spirits of our age and land,
Before the dread tribunal of *to come*   200
The foremost, – while Rebuke cowers pale and dumb.
You will see Coleridge – he who sits obscure
In the exceeding lustre, and the pure
Intense irradiation of a mind,
Which, with its own internal lightning blind,
Flags wearily through darkness and despair –
A cloud-encircled meteor of the air,
A hooded eagle among blinking owls. –
You will see Hunt[158] – one of those happy souls
Which are the salt of the earth, and without whom   210
This world would smell like what it is – a tomb:
Who is, what others seem; his room no doubt
Is still adorned by many a cast from Shout,[159]
With graceful flowers tastefully placed about;
And coronals of bay from ribbons hung,
And brighter wreaths in neat disorder flung;
The gifts of the most learn'd among some dozens
Of female friends, sisters-in-law and cousins.
And there is he with his eternal puns,
Which beat the dullest brain for smiles, like duns   220
Thundering for money at a poet's door;
Alas! it is no use to say, 'I'm poor!'
Or oft in graver mood, when he will look
Things wiser than were ever read in book.
Except in Shakespeare's wisest tenderness. –
You will see Hogg,[160] – and I cannot express
His virtues, – though I know that they are great
Because he locks, then barricades, the gate
Within which they inhabit; – of his wit
And wisdom, you'll cry out when you are bit.   230
He is a pearl within an oyster shell,
One of the richest of the deep; – and there

Is English Peacock[161] with his mountain fair
Turned into a Flamingo; – that shy bird
That gleams i' the Indian air – have you not heard
When a man marries, dies, or turns Hindoo,
His best friends hear no more of him? – but you
Will see him, and will like him too, I hope,
With the milk-white Snowdonian Antelope
Matched with this cameleopard; his fine wit   240
Makes such a wound, the knife is lost in it;
A strain too learned for a shallow age,
Too wise for selfish bigots; let his page,
Which charms the chosen spirits of the time,
Fold itself up for the serener clime
Of years to come, and find its recompense
In that just expectation.– Wit and sense,
Virtue and human knowledge; all that might
Make this dull world a business of delight,
Are all combined in Horace Smith.[162] – And these,   250
With some exceptions, which I need not tease
Your patience by descanting on, – are all
You and I know in London.
      I recall
My thoughts, and bid you look upon the night.
As water does a sponge, so the moonlight
Fills the void, hollow, universal air –
What see you? – unpavilioned heaven is fair,
Whether the moon, into her chamber gone,
Leaves midnight to the golden stars, or wan,
Climbs with diminished beams the azure steep;   260
Or whether clouds sail o'er the inverse deep,
Piloted by the many-wandering blast,
And the rare stars rush through them dim and fast: –
All this is beautiful in every land. –
But what see you beside? – a shabby stand
Of Hackney coaches – a brick house or wall
Fencing some lonely court, white with the scrawl
Of our unhappy politics; – or worse –
A wretched woman reeling by, whose curse
Mixed with the watchman's, partner of her trade?   270
You must accept in place of serenade –

Or yellow-haired Pollonia[163] murmuring
To Henry, some unutterable thing.
I see a chaos of green leaves and fruit
Built round dark caverns, even to the root
Of the living stems that feed them – in whose bowers
There sleep in their dark dew the folded flowers;
Beyond, the surface of the unsickled corn
Trembles not in the slumbering air, and borne
In circles quaint, and ever-changing dance,   280
Like winged stars the fireflies flash and glance,
Pale in the open moonshine, but each one
Under the dark trees seems a little sun,
A meteor tamed; a fixed star gone astray
From the silver regions of the Milky Way; –
Afar the Contadino's song is heard,
Rude, but made sweet by distance – and a bird
Which cannot be the Nightingale, and yet
I know none else that sings so sweet as it
At this late hour; – and then all is still: –   290
Now Italy or London, which you will!

    Next winter you must pass with me; I'll have
My house by that time turned into a grave
Of dead despondence and low-thoughted care,
And all the dreams which our tormenters are;
Oh! that Hunt, Hogg, Peacock and Smith were there,
With everything belonging to them fair! –
We will have books, Spanish, Italian, Greek;
And ask one week to make another week
As like his father, as I'm unlike mine,   300
Which is not his fault, as you may divine.
Though we eat little flesh and drink no wine,
Yet let's be merry: we'll have tea and toast;
Custards for supper, and an endless host
Of syllabubs and jellies and mince-pies,
And other such ladylike luxuries, –
Feasting on which we will philosophise!
And we'll have fires out of the Grand Duke's wood,
To thaw the six weeks' winter in our blood.
And then we'll talk; – what shall we talk about?   310

Oh! there are themes enough for many a bout
Of thought-entangled descant; – as to nerves –
With cones and parallelograms and curves
I've sworn to strangle them if once they dare
To bother me – when you are with me there.
And they shall never more sip laudanum,
From Helicon or Himeros;[164] – well, come,
And, in despite of God and of the devil,
We'll make our friendly philosophic revel
Outlast the leafless time; till buds and flowers   320
Warn the obscure inevitable hours
Sweet meeting by sad parting to renew: –
'Tomorrow to fresh woods and pastures new.'[165]

The Witch of Atlas

TO MARY

*(On her objecting to the following poem, upon
the score of its containing no human interest)*

1

How, my dear Mary, are you critic-bitten
    (For vipers kill, though dead), by some review,
That you condemn these verses I have written,
    Because they tell no story, false or true!
What, though no mice are caught by a young kitten,
    May it not leap and play as grown cats do,
Till its claws come? Prithee, for this one time,
Content thee with a visionary rhyme.

2

What hand would crush the silken-winged fly,
    The youngest of inconstant April's minions,   10
Because it cannot climb the purest sky,
    Where the swan sings, amid the sun's dominions?
Not thine. Thou knowest 'tis its doom to die,
    When day shall hide within her twilight pinions,
The lucent eyes, and the eternal smile,
Serene as thine, which lent it life awhile.

3

To thy fair feet a winged Vision came,
    Whose date should have been longer than a day,
And o'er thy head did beat its wings for fame,
    And in thy sight its fading plumes display;   20
The watery bow burned in the evening flame,
    But the shower fell, the swift sun went his way –
And that is dead. – O, let me not believe
That anything of mine is fit to live!

4

Wordsworth informs us he was nineteen years
    Considering and retouching Peter Bell;[166]

Watering his laurels with the killing tears
  Of slow, dull care, so that their roots to hell
Might pierce, and their wide branches blot the spheres
  Of heaven, with dewy leaves and flowers; this well   30
May be, for Heaven and Earth conspire to foil
The over-busy gardener's blundering toil.

5

My Witch indeed is not so sweet a creature
  As Ruth or Lucy,[167] whom his graceful praise
Clothes for our grandsons – but she matches Peter,
  Though he took nineteen years, and she three days
In dressing. Light the vest of flowing metre
  She wears; he, proud as dandy with his stays,
Has hung upon his wiry limbs a dress
Like King Lear's 'looped and windowed raggedness'.   40

6

If you strip Peter, you will see a fellow
  Scorched by Hell's hyperequatorial climate
Into a kind of a sulphureous yellow:
  A lean mark, hardly fit to fling a rhyme at;
In shape a Scaramouch,[168] in hue Othello,
  If you unveil my Witch, no priest nor primate
Can shrive you of that sin, – if sin there be
In love, when it becomes idolatry.

The Witch of Atlas

1

Before those cruel Twins, whom at one birth
  Incestuous Change bore to her father Time,   50
Error and Truth, had hunted from the Earth
  All those bright natures which adorned its prime,
And left us nothing to believe in, worth
  The pains of putting into learned rhyme,
A lady-witch there lived on Atlas' mountain[169]
Within a cavern, by a secret fountain.

2

Her mother was one of the Atlantides:[170]
    The all-beholding Sun had ne'er beholden
In his wide voyage o'er continents and seas
    So fair a creature, as she lay enfolden   60
In the warm shadow of her loveliness; –
    He kissed her with his beams, and made all golden
The chamber of grey rock in which she lay –
She, in that dream of joy, dissolved away.

3

'Tis said, she first was changed into a vapour,
    And then into a cloud, such clouds as flit,
Like splendour-winged moths about a taper,
    Round the red west when the sun dies in it:
And then into a meteor, such as caper
    On hill-tops when the moon is in a fit: 70
Then, into one of those mysterious stars
Which hide themselves between the Earth and Mars.

4

Ten times the Mother of the Months had bent
    Her bow beside the folding-star,[171] and bidden
With that bright sign the billows to indent
    The sea-deserted sand – like children chidden,
At her command they ever came and went –
    Since in that cave a dewy splendour hidden
Took shape and motion: with the living form
Of this embodied Power, the cave grew warm.   80

5

A lovely lady garmented in light
    From her own beauty – deep her eyes, as are
Two openings of unfathomable night
    Seen through a Temple's cloven roof – her hair
Dark – the dim brain whirls dizzy with delight,
    Picturing her form; her soft smiles shone afar,
And her low voice was heard like love, and drew
All living things towards this wonder new.

6

And first the spotted cameleopard came,   90
   And then the wise and fearless elephant:
Then the sly serpent, in the golden flame
   Of his own volumes intervolved; – all gaunt
And sanguine beasts her gentle looks made tame.
   They drank before her at her sacred fount;
And every beast of beating heart grew bold,
Such gentleness and power even to behold.

7

The brinded lioness led forth her young,
   That she might teach them how they should forego
Their inborn thirst of death; the pard unstrung   100
   His sinews at her feet, and sought to know,
With looks whose motions spoke without a tongue,
   How he might be as gentle as the doe.
The magic circle of her voice and eyes
All savage natures did imparadise.

8

And old Silenus,[172] shaking a green stick
   Of lilies, and the wood-gods in a crew
Came, blithe, as in the olive copses thick
   Cicadae are, drunk with the noonday dew:
And Dryope and Faunus[173] followed quick,
   Teasing the God to sing them something new;   110
Till in this cave they found the lady lone,
Sitting upon a seat of emerald stone.

9

And universal Pan,[174] 'tis said, was there,
   And though none saw him, – through the adamant
Of the deep mountains, through the trackless air,
   And through those living spirits, like a want,[175]
He past out of his everlasting lair
   Where the quick heart of the great world doth pant,
And felt that wondrous lady all alone, –
And she felt him, upon her emerald throne.   120

10

And every nymph of stream and spreading tree,
    And every shepherdess of Ocean's flocks,
Who drives her white waves over the green sea,
    And Ocean with the brine on his grey locks,
And quaint Priapus[176] with his company,
    All came, much wondering how the enwombed rocks
Could have brought forth so beautiful a birth; –
Her love subdued their wonder and their mirth.

11

The herdsmen and the mountain maidens came,
    And the rude kings of pastoral Garamant[177] –   130
Their spirits shook within them, as a flame
    Stirred by the air under a cavern gaunt:
Pigmies, and Polyphemes,[178] by many a name,
    Centaurs and Satyrs,[179] and such shapes as haunt
Wet clefts, – and lumps neither alive nor dead,
Dog-headed, bosom-eyed, and bird-footed.

12

For she was beautiful – her beauty made
    The bright world dim, and everything beside
Seemed like the fleeting image of a shade:
    No thought of living spirit could abide,   140
Which to her looks had ever been betrayed,
    On any object in the world so wide,
On any hope within the circling skies,
But on her form, and in her inmost eyes.

13

Which when the lady knew, she took her spindle
    And twined three threads of fleecy mist, and three
Long lines of light, such as the dawn may kindle
    The clouds and waves and mountains with; and she
As many star-beams, ere their lamps could dwindle
    In the belated moon, wound skilfully;   150
And with these threads a subtle veil she wove –
A shadow for the splendour of her love.

14

The deep recesses of her odorous dwelling
    Were stored with magic treasures – sounds of air,
Which had the power all spirits of compelling,
    Folded in cells of chrystal silence there;
Such as we hear in youth, and think the feeling
    Will never die – yet ere we are aware,
The feeling and the sound are fled and gone,
And the regret they leave remains alone.   160

15

And there lay Visions swift, and sweet, and quaint,
    Each in its thin sheath, like a chrysalis,
Some eager to burst forth, some weak and faint
    With the soft burthen of intensest bliss;
It was its work to bear to many a saint
    Whose heart adores the shrine which holiest is,
Even Love's: – and others white, green, grey and black,
And of all shapes – and each was at her beck.

16

And odours in a kind of aviary
    Of ever-blooming Eden trees she kept,   170
Clipt in a floating net, a lovesick Fairy
    Had woven from dew-beams while the moon yet slept;
As bats at the wired window of a dairy,
    They beat their vans; and each was an adept,
When loosed and missioned, making wings of winds,
To stir sweet thoughts or sad, in destined minds.

17

And liquors clear and sweet, whose healthful might
    Could medicine the sick soul to happy sleep,
And change eternal death into a night
    Of glorious dreams – or if eyes needs must weep,   180
Could make their tears all wonder and delight,
    She in her chrystal vials did closely keep:
If men could drink of those clear vials, 'tis said
The living were not envied of the dead.

18

Her cave was stored with scrolls of strange device,
   The works of some Saturnian Archimage,[180]
Which taught the expiations at whose price
   Men from the Gods might win that happy age
Too lightly lost, redeeming native vice;
   And which might quench the Earth-consuming rage   190
Of gold and blood – till men should live and move
Harmonious as the sacred stars above.

19

And how all things that seem untameable,
   Not to be checked and not to be confined,
Obey the spells of wisdom's wizard skill;
   Time, earth and fire – the ocean and the wind,
And all their shapes – and man's imperial will;
   And other scrolls whose writings did unbind
The inmost lore of Love – let the profane
Tremble to ask what secrets they contain.   200

20

And wondrous works of substances unknown,
   To which the enchantment of her father's power
Had changed those ragged blocks of savage stone,
   Were heaped in the recesses of her bower;
Carved lamps and chalices, and phials which shone
   In their own golden beams – each like a flower,
Out of whose depth a firefly shakes his light
Under a cypress in a starless night.

21

At first she lived alone in this wild home,
   And her own thoughts were each a minister,   210
Clothing themselves, or with the ocean foam,
   Or with the wind, or with the speed of fire,
To work whatever purposes might come
   Into her mind; such power her mighty Sire
Had girt them with, whether to fly or run,
Through all the regions which he shines upon.

22

The Ocean-nymphs and Hamadryades,
   Oreads and Naiads,[181] with long weedy locks,
Offered to do her bidding through the seas,
   Under the earth, and in the hollow rocks,   220
And far beneath the matted roots of trees,
   And in the knarled heart of stubborn oaks,
So they might live for ever in the light
Of her sweet presence – each a satellite.

23

'This may not be,' the wizard maid replied;
   'The fountains where the Naiads bedew
Their shining hair, at length are drained and dried;
   The solid oaks forget their strength, and strew
Their latest leaf upon the mountains wide;
   The boundless ocean like a drop of dew   230
Will be consumed – the stubborn centre must
Be scattered, like a cloud of summer dust.

24

'And ye with them will perish, one by one; –
   If I must sigh to think that this shall be,
If I must weep when the surviving Sun
   Shall smile on your decay – Oh, ask not me
To love you till your little race is run;
   I cannot die as ye must – over me
Your leaves shall glance – the streams in which ye dwell
Shall be my paths henceforth, and so – farewell!'   240

25

She spoke and wept: – the dark and azure well
   Sparkled beneath the shower of her bright tears,
And every little circlet where they fell
   Flung to the cavern-roof inconstant spheres
And intertangled lines of light: – a knell
   Of sobbing voices came upon her ears
From those departing Forms, o'er the serene
Of the white streams and of the forest green.

26

All day the wizard lady sate aloof,
   Spelling out scrolls of dread antiquity,   250
Under the cavern's fountain-lighted roof;
   Or broidering the pictured poesy
Of some high tale upon her growing woof,
   Which the sweet splendour of her smiles could dye
In hues outshining Heaven – and ever she
Added some grace to the wrought poesy.

27

While on her hearth lay blazing many a piece
   Of sandalwood, rare gums and cinnamon;
Men scarcely know how beautiful fire is –
   Each flame of it is as a precious stone   260
Dissolved in ever-moving light, and this
   Belongs to each and all who gaze upon.
The Witch beheld it not, for in her hand
She held a woof that dimmed the burning brand.

28

This lady never slept, but lay in trance
   All night within the fountain – as in sleep.
Its emerald crags glowed in her beauty's glance;
   Through the green splendour of the water deep
She saw the constellations reel and dance
   Like fireflies – and withal did ever keep   270
The tenour of her contemplations calm,
With open eyes, closed feet, and folded palm.

29

And when the whirlwinds and the clouds descended
   From the white pinnacles of that cold hill,
She passed at dewfall to a space extended,
   Where in a lawn of flowering asphodel,
Amid a wood of pines and cedars blended,
   There yawned an inextinguishable well
Of crimson fire – full even to the brim,
And overflowing all the margin trim.   280

30

Within the which she lay when the fierce war
   Of wintry winds shook that innocuous liquor
In many a mimic moon and bearded star
   O'er woods and lawns; – the serpent heard it flicker
In sleep, and dreaming still, he crept afar –
   And when the windless snow descended thicker
Than autumn leaves, she watched it as it came
Melt on the surface of the level flame.

31

She had a Boat, which some say Vulcan[182] wrought
   For Venus, as the chariot of her star;   290
But it was found too feeble to be fraught
   With all the ardours in that sphere which are,
And so she sold it, and Apollo[183] bought
   And gave it to this daughter: from a car
Changed to the fairest and the lightest boat
Which ever upon mortal stream did float.

32

And others say that, when but three hours old,
   The first-born Love out of his cradle leapt,
And clove dun Chaos with his wings of gold,
   And like an horticultural adept,   300
Stole a strange seed, and wrapt it up in mould,
   And sowed it in his mother's star, and kept
Watering it all the summer with sweet dew,
And with his wings fanning it as it grew.

33

The plant grew strong and green, the snowy flower
   Fell, and the long and gourd-like fruit began
To turn the light and dew by inward power
   To its own substance; woven tracery ran
Of light firm texture, ribbed and branching, o'er
   The solid rind, like a leaf's veined fan –   310
Of which Love scooped this boat – and with soft motion
Piloted it round the circumfluous ocean.

34

This boat she moored upon her fount, and lit
   A living spirit within all its frame,
Breathing the soul of swiftness into it.
   Couched on the fountain like a panther tame,
One of the twain at Evan's[184] feet that sit –
   Or as on Vesta's[185] sceptre a swift flame –
Or on blind Homer's heart a winged thought, –
In joyous expectation lay the boat.   320

35

Then by strange art she kneaded fire and snow
   Together, tempering the repugnant mass
With liquid love – all things together grow
   Through which the harmony of love can pass;
And a fair Shape out of her hands did flow –
   A living Image, which did far surpass
In beauty that bright shape of vital stone
Which drew the heart out of Pygmalion.[186]

36

A sexless thing[187] it was, and in its growth
   It seemed to have developed no defect   330
Of either sex, yet all the grace of both, –
   In gentleness and strength its limbs were decked;
The bosom swelled lightly with its full youth,
   The countenance was such as might select
Some artist that his skill should never die,
Imaging forth such perfect purity.

37

From its smooth shoulders hung two rapid wings,
   Fit to have borne it to the seventh sphere,
Tipped with the speed of liquid lightenings.
   Dyed in the ardours of the atmosphere: 340
She led her creature to the boiling springs
   Where the light boat was moored, and said: 'Sit here!'
And pointed to the prow, and took her seat
Beside the rudder, with opposing feet.

38

And down the streams which clove those mountains vast,
   Around their inland islets, and amid
The panther-peopled forests, whose shade cast
   Darkness and odours, and a pleasure hid
In melancholy gloom, the pinnace past;
   By many a star-surrounded pyramid   350
Of icy crag cleaving the purple sky,
And caverns yawning round unfathomably.

39

The silver noon into that winding dell,
   With slanted gleam athwart the forest tops,
Tempered like golden evening, feebly fell;
   A green and glowing light, like that which drops
From folded lilies in which glow-worms dwell,
   When earth over her face night's mantle wraps;
Between the severed mountains lay on high
Over the stream, a narrow rift of sky.   360

40

And ever as she went, the Image lay
   With folded wings and unawakened eyes:
And o'er its gentle countenance did play
   The busy dreams, as thick as summer flies,
Chasing the rapid smiles that would not stay,
   And drinking the warm tears, and the sweet sighs
Inhaling, which, with busy murmur vain,
They had aroused from the full heart and brain.

41

And ever down the prone vale, like a cloud
   Upon a stream of wind, the pinnace went: 370
Now lingering on the pools, in which abode
   The calm and darkness of the deep content
In which they paused; now o'er the shallow road
   Of white and dancing waters, all besprent
With sand and polished pebbles: – mortal boat
In such a shallow rapid could not float.

42

And down the earthquaking cataracts which shiver
 Their snow-like waters into golden air,
Or under chasms unfathomable ever
 Sepulchre them, till in their rage they tear   380
A subterranean portal for the river,
 It fled – the circling sunbows did upbear
Its fall down the hoar precipice of spray,
Lighting it far upon its lampless way.

43

And when the wizard lady would ascend
 The labyrinths of some many-winding vale,
Which to the inmost mountain upward tend –
 She called, 'Hermaphroditus!' – and the pale
And heavy hue which slumber could extend
 Over its lips and eyes, as on the gale   390
A rapid shadow from a slope of grass,
Into the darkness of the stream did pass.

44

Anti it unfurled its heaven-coloured pinions,
 With stars of fire spotting the stream below;
And from above into the Sun's dominions
 Flinging a glory, like the golden glow
In which spring clothes her emerald-winged minions,
 All interwoven with fine feathery snow
And moonlight splendour of intensest rime,
With which frost paints the pines in wintertime. 400

45

And then it winnowed the Elysian[188] air
 Which ever hung about that lady bright,
With its ethereal vans – and speeding there,
 Like a star up the torrent of the night,
Or a swift eagle in the morning glare
 Breasting the whirlwind with impetuous flight,
The pinnace, oared by those enchanted wings,
Clove the fierce streams towards their upper springs.

46

The water flashed like sunlight, by the prow
   Of a noon-wandering meteor flung to Heaven;   410
The still air seemed as if its waves did flow
   In tempest down the mountains; loosely driven
The lady's radiant hair streamed to and fro:
   Beneath, the billows having vainly striven
Indignant and impetuous, roared to feel
The swift and steady motion of the keel.

47

Or, when the weary moon was in the wane.
   Or in the noon of interlunar night,
The lady-witch in visions could not chain
   Her spirit; but sailed forth under the light   420
Of shooting stars, and bade extend amain
   Its storm-outspeeding wings, the Hermaphrodite;
She to the Austral[189] waters took her way,
Beyond the fabulous Thamondocana.[190]

48

Where, like a meadow which no scythe has shaven,
   Which rain could never bend, or whirl-blast shake,
With the Antarctic constellations paven,
   Canopus[191] and his crew, lay the Austral lake –
There she would build herself a windless haven
   Out of the clouds whose moving turrets make   430
The bastions of the storm, when through the sky
The spirits of the tempest thundered by.

49

A haven beneath whose translucent floor
   The tremulous stars sparkled unfathomably,
And around which the solid vapours hoar,
   Based on the level waters, to the sky
Lifted their dreadful crags, and like a shore
   Of wintry mountains, inaccessibly
Hemmed in with rifts and precipices grey,
And hanging crags, many a cove and bay.   440

50

And whilst the outer lake beneath the lash
    Of the wind's scourge, foamed like a wounded thing;
And the incessant hail with stony clash
    Ploughed up the waters, and the flagging wing
Of the roused cormorant in the lightning flash
    Looked like the wreck of some wind-wandering
Fragment of inky thunder-smoke – this haven
Was as a gem to copy Heaven engraven.

51

On which that lady played her many pranks,
    Circling the image of a shooting star,   450
Even as a tiger on Hydaspes'[192] banks
    Outspeeds the antelopes which speediest are,
In her light boat; and many quips and cranks
    She played upon the water, till the car
Of the late moon, like a sick matron wan,
To journey from the misty east began.

52

And then she called out of the hollow turrets
    Of those high clouds, white, golden and vermilion,
The armies of her ministering spirits –
    In mighty legions, million after million,   460
They came, each troop emblazoning its merits
    On meteor flags; and many a proud pavilion
Of the intertexture of the atmosphere
They pitched upon the plain of the calm mere.

53

They framed the imperial tent of their great Queen
    Of woven exhalations, underlaid
With lambent lightning-fire, as may be seen
    A dome of thin and open ivory inlaid
With crimson silk – cressets from the serene
    Hung there, and on the water for her tread   470
A tapestry of fleece-like mist was strewn,
Dyed in the beams of the ascending moon.

54

And on a throne o'erlaid with starlight, caught
　　Upon those wandering isles of aery dew,
Which highest shoals of mountain shipwreck not,
　　She sate, and heard all that had happened new
Between the earth and moon, since they had brought
　　The last intelligence – and now she grew
Pale as that moon, lost in the watery night –
And now she wept, and now she laughed outright.   480

55

These were tame pleasures: she would often climb
　　The steepest ladder of the crudded rack
Up to some beaked cape of cloud sublime,
　　And like Arion[193] on the dolphin's back
Ride singing through the shoreless air; – oft time,
　　Following the serpent lightning's winding track,
She ran upon the platforms of the wind,
And laughed to hear the fireballs roar behind.

52

And sometimes to those streams of upper air
　　Which whirl the earth in its diurnal round,   490
She would ascend, and win the spirits there
　　To let her join their chorus. Mortals found
That on those days the sky was calm and fair,
　　And mystic snatches of harmonious sound
Wandered upon the earth where'er she past,
And happy thoughts of hope, too sweet to last.

57

But her choice sport was, in the hours of sleep,
　　To glide adown old Nilus,[194] where he threads
Egypt and Ethiopia, from the steep
　　Of utmost Axumè,[195] until he spreads,   500
Like a calm flock of silver-fleeced sheep,
　　His waters on the plain: and crested heads
Of cities and proud temples gleam amid,
And many a vapour-belted pyramid.

58

By Moeris and the Mareotid[196] lakes,
　　Strewn with faint blooms like bridal-chamber floors;
Where naked boys bridling tame water-snakes,
　　Or charioteering ghastly alligators,
Had left on the sweet waters mighty wakes
　　Of those huge forms – within the brazen doors   510
Of the great Labyrinth slept both boy and beast,
Tired with the pomp of their Osirian[197] feast.

59

And where within the surface of the river
　　The shadows of the massy temples lie,
And never are erased – but tremble ever
　　Like things which every cloud can doom to die,
Through lotus-pav'n canals, and wheresoever
　　The works of man pierced that serenest sky
With tombs, and towers, and fanes, 'twas her delight
To wander in the shadow of the night.   520

60

With motion like the spirit of that wind
　　Whose soft step deepens slumber, her light feet
Passed through the peopled haunts of human kind,
　　Scattering sweet visions from her presence sweet,
Through fane, and palace-court, and labyrinth mined
　　With many a dark and subterranean street
Under the Nile, through chambers high and deep
She passed, observing mortals in their sleep.

61

A pleasure sweet doubtless it was to see
　　Mortals subdued in all the shapes of sleep.   530
Here lay two sister twins in infancy;
　　There, a lone youth who in his dreams did weep;
Within, two lovers linked innocently
　　In their loose locks which over both did creep
Like ivy from one stem; – and there lay calm
Old age with snow-bright hair and folded palm.

62

But other troubled forms of sleep she saw,
   Not to be mirrored in a holy song –
Distortions foul of supernatural awe,
   And pale imaginings of visioned wrong;   540
And all the code of custom's lawless law
   Written upon the brows of old and young:
'This,' said the wizard maiden, 'is the strife
Which stirs the liquid surface of man's life.'

63

And little did the sight disturb her soul. –
   We, the weak mariners of that wide lake
Where'er its shores extend or billows roll,
   Our course unpiloted and starless make
O'er its wild surface to an unknown goal: –
   But she in the calm depths her way could take,   550
Where in bright bowers immortal forms abide
Beneath the weltering of the restless tide.

64

And she saw princes couched under the glow
   Of sunlike gems: and round each temple-court
In dormitories ranged, row after row,
   She saw the priests asleep – all of one sort –
For all were educated to be so. –
   The peasants in their huts, and in the port
The sailors she saw cradled on the waves,
And the dead lulled within their dreamless graves.   560

65

And all the forms in which those spirits lay
   Were in her sight like the diaphanous
Veils, in which those sweet ladies oft array
   Their delicate limbs, who would conceal from us
Only their scorn of all concealment: they
   Move in the light of their own beauty thus.
But these and all now lay with sleep upon them,
And little thought a Witch was looking on them.

66

She, all those human figures breathing there,
   Beheld as living spirits – to her eyes   570
The naked beauty of the soul lay bare,
   And often through a rude and worn disguise
She saw the inner form most bright and fair –
   And then she had a charm of strange device,
Which, murmured on mute lips with tender tone,
Could make that spirit mingle with her own.

67

Alas! Aurora,[198] what wouldst thou have given
   For such a charm when Tithon became grey?
Or how much, Venus, of thy silver Heaven
   Wouldst thou have yielded, ere Proserpina[199]   580
Had half (oh! why not all?) the debt forgiven
   Which dear Adonis had been doomed to pay,
To any witch who would have taught you it?
The Heliad[200] doth not know its value yet.

68

'Tis said in after times her spirit free
   Knew what love was, and felt itself alone –
But holy Dian[201] could not chaster be
   Before she stooped to kiss Endymion
Than now this lady – like a sexless bee
   Tasting all blossoms, and confined to none –   590
Among those mortal forms, the wizard-maiden
Passed with an eye serene and heart unladen.

69

To those she saw most beautiful, she gave
   Strange panacea in a crystal bowl: –
They drank in their deep sleep of that sweet wave,
   And lived thenceforward as if some control,
Mightier than life, were in them; and the grave
   Of such, when death oppressed the weary soul,
Was as a green and overarching bower
Lit by the gems of many a starry flower.   600

70

For on the night that they were buried, she
    Restored the embalmers' ruining, and shook
The light out of the funeral lamps, to be
    A mimic day within that deathy nook;
And she unwound the woven imagery
    Of second childhood's swaddling bands, and took
The coffin, its last cradle, from its niche,
And threw it with contempt into a ditch.

71

And there the body lay, age after age,
    Mute, breathing, beating, warm, and undecaying,   610
Like one asleep in a green hermitage,
    With gentle smiles about its eyelids playing,
And living in its dreams beyond the rage
    Of death or life; while they were still arraying
In liveries ever new, the rapid, blind
And fleeting generations of mankind.

72

And she would write strange dreams upon the brain
    Of those who were less beautiful, and make
All harsh and crooked purposes more vain
    Than in the desert is the serpent's wake   620
Which the sand covers, – all his evil gain
    The miser in such dreams would rise and shake
Into a beggar's lap; – the lying scribe
Would his own lies betray without a bribe.

73

The priests would write an explanation full,
    Translating hieroglyphics into Greek,
How the God Apis[202] really was a bull,
    And nothing more; and bid the herald stick
The same against the temple doors, and pull
    The old cant down; they licensed all to speak   630
Whate'er they thought of hawks, and cats, and geese,
By pastoral letters to each diocese.

74

The king would dress an ape up in his crown
  And robes, and seat him on his glorious seat,
And on the right hand of the sunlike throne
  Would place a gaudy mock-bird to repeat
The chatterings of the monkey. – Every one
  Of the prone courtiers crawled to kiss the feet
Of their great Emperor, when the morning came,
And kissed – alas, how many kiss the same!   640

75

The soldiers dreamed that they were blacksmiths, and
  Walked out of quarters in somnambulism;
Round the red anvils you might see them stand
  Like Cyclopses in Vulcan's[203] sooty abysm,
Beating their swords to ploughshares; – in a band
  The gaolers sent those of the liberal schism
Free through the streets of Memphis, much, I wis,
To the annoyance of king Amasis.[204]

76

And timid lovers who had been so coy,
  They hardly knew whether they loved or not,   650
Would rise out of their rest, and take sweet joy,
  To the fulfilment of their inmost thought;
And when next day the maiden and the boy
  Met one another, both, like sinners caught,
Blushed at the thing which each believed was done
Only in fancy – till the tenth moon shone;

77

And then the Witch would let them take no ill:
  Of many thousand schemes which lovers find,
The Witch found one, – and so they took their fill
  Of happiness in marriage warm and kind.   660
Friends who, by practice of some envious skill,
  Were torn apart, a wide wound, mind from mind!
She did unite again with visions clear
Of deep affection and of truth sincere.

78

These were the pranks she played among the cities
    Of mortal men, and what she did to sprites
And Gods, entangling them in her sweet ditties
    To do her will, and show their subtle slights,
I will declare another time; for it is
    A tale more fit for the weird winter nights   670
Than for these garish summer days, when we
Scarcely believe much more than we can see.

Hymn of Apollo [205]

1

The sleepless Hours who watch me as I lie,
    Curtained with star-inwoven tapestries
From the broad moonlight of the sky,
    Fanning the busy dreams from my dim eyes, –
Waken me when their Mother, the grey Dawn,
Tells them that dreams and that the moon is gone.

2

Then I arise, and climbing Heaven's blue dome,
    I walk over the mountains and the waves,
Leaving my robe upon the ocean foam;
    My footsteps pave the clouds with fire; the caves   10
Are filled with my bright presence, and the air
Leaves the green earth to my embraces bare.

3

The sunbeams are my shafts, with which I kill
    Deceit, that loves the night and fears the day;
All men who do or even imagine ill
    Fly me, and from the glory of my ray
Good minds and open actions take new might,
Until diminished by the reign of night.

4

I feed the clouds, the rainbows and the flowers
   With their ethereal colours; the moon's globe   20
And the pure stars in their eternal bowers
   Are cinctured with my power as with a robe;
Whatever lamps on Earth or Heaven may shine
Are portions of one power, which is mine.

5

I stand at noon upon the peak of Heaven,
   Then with unwilling steps I wander down
Into the clouds of the Atlantic even;
   For grief that I depart they weep and frown:
What look is more delightful than the smile
With which I soothe them from the western isle?   30

6

I am the eye with which the Universe
   Beholds itself and knows itself divine;
All harmony of instrument or verse,
   All prophecy, all medicine are mine,
All light of art or nature; – to my song,
Victory and praise in its own right belong.

Hymn of Pan [206]

1

From the forests and highlands
   We come, we come;
From the river-girt islands,
   Where loud waves are dumb
     Listening to my sweet pipings.
The wind in the reeds and the rushes,
   The bees on the bells of thyme,
The birds on the myrtle bushes,
   The cicale above in the lime,

And the lizards below in the grass,   10
Were as silent as ever old Tmolus[207] was,
     Listening to my sweet pipings.

2

Liquid Peneus was flowing,
   And all dark Tempe lay
In Pelion's[208] shadow, outgrowing
   The light of the dying day,
      Speeded by my sweet pipings.
The Sileni, and Sylvans, and Fauns,[209]
   And the Nymphs of the woods and the waves,
To the edge of the moist river-lawns,   20
   And the brink of the dewy caves,
And all that did then attend and follow,
Were silent with love, as you now, Apollo,
      With envy of my sweet pipings.

3

I sang of the dancing stars,
   I sang of the daedal[210] Earth,
And of Heaven – and the giant wars,[211]
   And Love, and Death, and Birth, –
      And then I changed my pipings, –
Singing how down the vale of Maenalus   30
   I pursued a maiden and clasped a reed:[212]
Gods and men, we are all deluded thus!
   It breaks in our bosom and then we bleed:
All wept, as I think both ye[213] now would,
If envy or age had not frozen your blood,
      At the sorrow of my sweet pipings.

Song

1

Rarely, rarely, comest thou,
   Spirit of Delight!
Wherefore hast thou left me now
   Many a day and night?
Many a weary night and day
'Tis since thou art fled away.

2

How shall ever one like me
   Win thee back again?
With the joyous and the free
   Thou wilt scoff at pain.   10
Spirit false! thou hast forgot
All but those who need thee not.

3

As a lizard with the shade
   Of a trembling leaf,
Thou with sorrow art dismayed;
   Even the sighs of grief
Reproach thee, that thou art not near,
And reproach thou wilt not hear.

4

Let me set my mournful ditty
   To a merry measure,   20
Thou wilt never come for pity,
   Thou wilt come for pleasure.
Pity then will cut away
Those cruel wings, and thou wilt stay.

5

I love all that thou lovest,
   Spirit of Delight!

The fresh Earth in new leaves drest,
   And the starry night;
Autumn evening, and the morn
When the golden mists are born. 30

6

I love snow, and all the forms
   Of the radiant frost;
I love waves, and winds, and storms –
   Everything almost
Which is Nature's, and may be
Untainted by man's misery.

7

I love tranquil solitude,
   And such society
As is quiet, wise and good;
   Between thee and me 40
What difference? but thou dost possess
The things I seek, not love them less.

8

I love Love – though he has wings,
   And like light can flee,
But above all other things,
   Spirit, I love thee –
Thou art love and life! O come,
Make once more my heart thy home.

The Tower of Famine

Amid the desolation of a city,
Which was the cradle, and is now the grave
Of an extinguished people; so that pity

Weeps o'er the shipwrecks of oblivion's wave,
There stands the Tower of Famine. It is built
Upon some prison homes, whose dwellers rave

For bread, and gold, and blood: pain, linked to guilt,
Agitates the light flame of their hours,
Until its vital oil is spent or spilt:

There stands the pile, a tower amid the towers   10
And sacred domes; each marble-ribbed roof,
The brazen-gated temples, and the bowers

Of solitary wealth; the tempest-proof
Pavilions of the dark Italian air
Are by its presence dimmed – they stand aloof,

And are withdrawn – so that the world is bare,
As if a spectre wrapt in shapeless terror
Amid a company of ladies fair

Should glide and glow, till it became a mirror
Of all their beauty, and their hair and hue,   20
The life of their sweet eyes, with all its error,
Should be absorbed, till they to marble grew.

To a Skylark

Hail to thee, blithe spirit!
   Bird thou never wert,
That from heaven, or near it,
   Pourest thy full heart
In profuse strains of unpremeditated art.

Higher still and higher
   From the earth thou springest
Like a cloud of fire;
   The blue deep thou wingest,
And singing still dost soar, and soaring ever singest.   10

In the golden lightning
   Of the sunken sun,
O'er which clouds are brightning,
   Thou dost float and run;
Like an unbodied joy whose race is just begun.

The pale purple even
   Melts around thy flight;
Like a star of heaven,[214]
   In the broad daylight
Thou art unseen, but yet I hear thy shrill delight,   20

Keen as are the arrows
   Of that silver sphere,[215]
Whose intense lamp narrows
   In the white dawn clear,
Until we hardly see, we feel that it is there.

All the earth and air
   With thy voice is loud,
As, when night is bare,
   From one lonely cloud
The moon rains out her beams, and heaven
                   is overflowed.   30

What thou art we know not;
     What is most like thee?
From rainbow clouds there flow not
     Drops so bright to see,
As from thy presence showers a rain of melody.

Like a poet hidden
     In the light of thought,
Singing hymns unbidden,
     Till the world is wrought
To sympathy with hopes and fears it heeded not: 40

Like a high-born maiden
     In a palace-tower,
Soothing her love-laden
     Soul in secret hour
With music sweet as love, which overflows her bower:

Like a glow-worm golden
     In a dell of dew,
Scattering unbeholden
     Its aerial hue   49
Among the flowers and grass, which screen it from the view:

Like a rose embowered
     In its own green leaves,
By warm winds deflowered,
     Till the scent it gives
Makes faint with too much sweet these heavy-winged
                                   thieves:

Sound of vernal showers
     On the twinkling grass,
Rain-awakened flowers,
     All that ever was
Joyous, and clear, and fresh, thy music doth surpass.   60

Teach us, sprite or bird,
    What sweet thoughts are thine:
I have never heard
    Praise of love or wine
That panted forth a flood of rapture so divine.

Chorus Hymeneal,[216]
    Or triumphal chaunt,
Matched with thine would be all
    But an empty vaunt,
A thing wherein we feel there is some hidden want.   70

What objects are the fountains
    Of thy happy strain?
What fields, or waves, or mountains?
    What shapes of sky or plain?
What love of thine own kind? what ignorance of pain?

With thy clear keen joyance
    Languor cannot be:
Shadow of annoyance
    Never came near thee:
Thou lovest; but ne'er knew love's sad satiety.   80

Waking or asleep,
    Thou of death must deem
Things more true and deep
    Than we mortals dream,
Or how could thy notes flow in such a crystal stream?

We look before and after,
    And pine for what is not:
Our sincerest laughter
    With some pain is fraught;
Our sweetest songs are those that tell of saddest thought.   90

Yet if we could scorn
  Hate, and pride, and fear;
If we were things born
  Not to shed a tear,
I know not how thy joy we ever should come near.

Better than all measures
  Of delightful sound,
Better than all treasures
  That in books are found,
Thy skill to poet were, thou scorner of the ground!   100

Teach me half the gladness
  That thy brain must know,
Such harmonious madness
  From my lips would flow,
The world should listen then, as I am listening now.

Ode to Liberty[217]

> Yet, Freedom, yet, thy banner, torn but flying,
> Streams like a thunderstorm against the wind.
>
> BYRON[218]

1

A glorious people vibrated again
    The lightning of the nations: Liberty
From heart to heart, from tower to tower, o'er Spain,
    Scattering contagious fire into the sky,
Gleamed. My soul spurned the chains of its dismay,
        And, in the rapid plumes of song,
        Clothed itself, sublime and strong;
As a young eagle soars the morning clouds among,
    Hovering inverse o'er its accustomed prey;
      Till from its station in the heaven of fame   10
    The Spirit's whirlwind rapt it, and the ray
    Of the remotest sphere of living flame
Which paves the void was from behind it flung,
    As foam from a ship's swiftness, when there came
    A voice out of the deep: I will record the same.

2

The Sun and the serenest Moon sprang forth:
    The burning stars of the abyss were hurled
Into the depths of heaven. The daedal[219] earth,
    That island in the ocean of the world,
Hung in its cloud of all-sustaining air: 20
        But this divinest universe
        Was yet a chaos and a curse,
For thou wert not: but power from worst producing worse,
    The spirit of the beasts was kindled there,
      And of the birds, and of the watery forms,
    And there was war among them, and despair
      Within them, raging without truce or terms:
The bosom of their violated nurse
    Groan'd, for beasts warr'd on beasts, and worms on worms,
    And men on men; each heart was as a hell of storms.   30

3

Man, the imperial shape, then multiplied
   His generations under the pavilion
Of the Sun's throne: palace and pyramid,
   Temple and prison, to many a swarming million
Were as to mountain-wolves their ragged caves.
        This human living multitude
        Was savage, cunning, blind, and rude,
For thou wert not; but o'er the populous solitude,
   Like one fierce cloud over a waste of waves
    Hung tyranny; beneath, sate deified   40
   The sister-pest, congregator of slaves;
    Into the shadow of her pinions wide
Anarchs and priests who feed on gold and blood,
   Till with the stain their inmost souls are dyed,
   Drove the astonished herds of men from every side.

4

The nodding promontories, and blue isles,
   And cloud-like mountains, and dividuous waves
Of Greece, basked glorious in the open smiles
   Of favouring heaven: from their enchanted caves
Prophetic echoes flung dim melody   50
        On the unapprehensive wild.
        The vine, the corn, the olive mild,
Grew savage yet, to human use unreconciled;
   And, like unfolded flowers beneath the sea,
    Like the man's thought dark in the infant's brain,
   Like aught that is which wraps what is to be,
    Art's deathless dreams lay veiled by many a vein
Of Parian stone;[220] and yet a speechless child,
   Verse murmured, and Philosophy did strain
   Her lidless eyes for thee: when o'er the Aegean main   60

5

Athens arose: a city such as vision
    Builds from the purple crags and silver towers
Of battlemented cloud, as in derision
    Of kingliest masonry: the ocean-floors
Pave it; the evening sky pavilions it;
        Its portals are inhabited
        By thunder-zoned winds, each head
Within its cloudy wings with sunfire garlanded,
    A divine work! Athens diviner yet
        Gleamed with its crest of columns, on the will   70
    Of man, as on a mount of diamond, set;
        For thou[221] wert, and thine all-creative skill
Peopled with forms that mock the eternal dead
    In marble immortality, that hill[222]
    Which was thine earliest throne and latest oracle.

6

Within the surface of Time's fleeting river
    Its wrinkled image lies, as then it lay
Immoveably unquiet, and for ever
    It trembles, but it cannot pass away!
The voices of thy bards and sages thunder   80
        With an earth-awakening blast
        Through the caverns of the past;
Religion veils her eyes; Oppression shrinks aghast:
    A winged sound of joy, and love, and wonder,
        Which soars where Expectation never flew,
    Rending the veil of space and time asunder!
        One ocean feeds the clouds, and streams, and dew;
One sun illumines heaven; one spirit vast
    With life and love makes chaos ever new,
    As Athens doth the world with thy delight renew.   90

* See the *Bacchae* of Euripides.

7

Then Rome was, and from thy deep bosom fairest,
   Like a wolf-cub from a Cadmaean Maenad,[223]
She drew the milk of greatness, though thy dearest
   From that Elysian[224] food was yet unweaned;
And many a deed of terrible uprightness
      By thy sweet love was sanctified;
      And in thy smile, and by thy side,
Saintly Camillus lived, and firm Atilius[225] died.
   But when tears stained thy robe of vestal whiteness,
     And gold profaned thy Capitolian[226] throne,   100
   Thou didst desert, with spirit-winged lightness,
     The senate of the tyrants: they sunk prone
Slaves of one tyrant: Palatinus[227] sighed
   Faint echoes of Ionian song; that tone
   Thou didst delay to hear, lamenting to disown.

8

From what Hyrcanian[228] glen or frozen hill,
   Or piny promontory of the Arctic main,
Or utmost islet inaccessible,
   Didst thou lament the ruin of thy reign,
Teaching the woods and waves, and desert rocks,   110
      And every Naiad's[229] ice-cold urn,
      To talk in echoes sad and stern,
Of that sublimest lore which man had dared unlearn?
   For neither didst thou watch the wizard flocks
     Of the Scald's dreams, nor haunt the Druid's[230] sleep.
   What if the tears rained through thy shattered locks
     Were quickly dried? for thou didst groan, not weep,
When from its sea of death to kill and burn,
   The Galilean serpent[231] forth did creep,
   And made thy world an undistinguishable heap.   120

9

A thousand years the Earth cried, Where art thou?
    And then the shadow of thy coming fell
On Saxon Alfred's[232] olive-cinctured brow:
    And many a warrior-peopled citadel,
Like rocks which fire lifts out of the flat deep,
        Arose in sacred Italy,
        Frowning o'er the tempestuous sea
Of kings, and priests, and slaves, in tower-crowned majesty;
    That multitudinous anarchy did sweep
        And burst around their walls, like idle foam,   130
    Whilst from the human spirit's deepest deep
        Strange melody with love and awe struck dumb
Dissonant arms; and Art, which cannot die,
    With divine wand traced on our earthly home
    Fit imagery to pave heaven's everlasting dome.

10

Thou huntress swifter than the Moon![233] thou terror
    Of the world's wolves! thou bearer of the quiver,
Whose sunlike shafts pierce tempest-winged Error,
    As light may pierce the clouds when they dissever
In the calm regions of the orient day!   140
        Luther caught thy wakening glance,
        Like lightning, from his leaden lance
Reflected, it dissolved the visions of the trance
    In which, as in a tomb, the nations lay;
        And England's prophets hailed thee as their queen,
    In songs whose music cannot pass away,
        Though it must flow for ever: not unseen
Before the spirit-sighted countenance
    Of Milton didst thou pass, from the sad scene
    Beyond whose night he saw, with a dejected mien.   150

11

The eager hours and unreluctant years
  As on a dawn-illumined mountain stood,
Trampling to silence their loud hopes and fears,
  Darkening each other with their multitude,
And cried aloud, Liberty! Indignation
      Answered Pity from her cave;
      Death grew pale within the grave,
And Desolation howled to the destroyer, Save!
  When, like heaven's sun girt by the exhalation
    Of its own glorious light, thou didst arise,   160
  Chasing thy foes from nation unto nation
    Like shadows: as if day had cloven the skies
At dreaming midnight o'er the western wave,
  Men started, staggering with a glad surprise,
  Under the lightnings of thine unfamiliar eyes.

12

Thou heaven of earth! what spells could pall thee then
  In ominous eclipse? a thousand years
Bred from the slime of deep oppression's den,
  Dyed all thy liquid light with blood and tears,
Till thy sweet stars could weep the stain away;   170
      How like Bacchanals[234] of blood
      Round France,[235] the ghastly vintage, stood
Destruction's sceptred slaves, and Folly's mitred brood!
  When one, like them, but mightier far than they,
    The Anarch[236] of thine own bewildered powers
  Rose: armies mingled in obscure array,
    Like clouds with clouds, darkening the sacred bowers
Of serene heaven. He, by the past pursued,
  Rests with those dead, but unforgotten hours,
  Whose ghosts scare victor kings in their ancestral towers.   180

13

England yet sleeps: was she not called of old?
   Spain calls her now, as with its thrilling thunder
Vesuvius wakens Etna,[237] and the cold
   Snow-crags by its reply are cloven in sunder:
O'er the lit waves every Aeolian isle[238]
      From Pithecusa to Pelorus[239]
      Howls, and leaps, and glares in chorus:
They cry, Be dim; ye lamps of heaven suspended o'er us.
   Her chains are threads of gold, she need but smile
     And they dissolve; but Spain's were links of steel,   190
   Till bit to dust by virtue's keenest file.
     Twins of a single destiny! appeal
To the eternal years enthroned before us,
   In the dim West; impress as from a seal
   All ye have thought and done! Time cannot dare conceal.

14

Tomb of Arminius![240] render up thy dead
   Till, like a standard from a watch-tower's staff,
His soul may stream over the tyrant's head;
   Thy victory shall be his epitaph,
Wild Bacchanal of truth's mysterious wine,   200
      King-deluded Germany,
      His dead spirit lives in thee.
Why do we fear or hope? thou art already free!
   And thou, lost Paradise of this divine
    And glorious world! thou flowery wilderness!
   Thou island of eternity! thou shrine
    Where desolation clothed with loveliness,
Worships the thing thou wert! O Italy,
   Gather thy blood into thy heart; repress
   The beasts who make their dens thy sacred palaces.   210

15

O, that the free would stamp the impious name
    Of KING into the dust! or write it there,
So that this blot upon the page of fame
    Were as a serpent's path, which the light air
Erases, and the flat sands close behind!
        Ye the oracle have heard:
        Lift the victory-flashing sword,
And cut the snaky knots of this foul gordian word,
    Which weak itself as stubble, yet can bind
      Into a mass, irrefragably firm,   220
    The axes and the rods which awe mankind;
      The sound has poison in it, 'tis the sperm
Of what makes life foul, cankerous, and abhorred;
    Disdain not thou, at thine appointed term,
    To set thine armed heel on this reluctant worm.

16

O, that the wise from their bright minds would kindle
    Such lamps within the dome of this dim world,
That the pale name of PRIEST might shrink and dwindle
    Into the hell from which it first was hurled,
A scoff of impious pride from fiends impure;   230
        Till human thoughts might kneel alone
        Each before the judgement-throne
Of its own aweless soul, or of the power unknown!
    O, that the words which make the thoughts obscure
      From which they spring, as clouds of glimmering dew
From a white lake blot heaven's blue portraiture,
    Were stript of their thin masks and various hue
And frowns and smiles and splendours not their own,
    Till in the nakedness of false and true
    They stand before their Lord, each to receive its due.   240

17

He who taught man to vanquish whatsoever
  Can be between the cradle and the grave
Crowned him the King of Life. O vain endeavour!
  If on his own high will, a willing slave,
He has enthroned the oppression and the oppressor.
        What if earth can clothe and feed
        Amplest millions at their need,
And power in thought be as the tree within the seed?
  Or what if Art, an ardent intercessor,
    Driving on fiery wings to Nature's throne,   250
  Checks the great mother stooping to caress her,
    And cries: Give me, thy child, dominion
Over all height and depth? if Life can breed
  New wants, and wealth from those who toil and groan,
  Rend of thy gifts and hers a thousandfold for one.

18

Come Thou, but lead out of the inmost cave
  Of man's deep spirit, as the morning-star
Beckons the Sun from the Eoan[241] wave,
  Wisdom. I hear the pennons of her car
Self-moving, like cloud charioted by flame;   260
        Comes she not, and come ye not,
        Rulers of eternal thought,
To judge, with solemn truth, life's ill-apportioned lot,
  Blind Love, and equal Justice, and the Fame
    Of what has been, the Hope of what will be?
  O Liberty! if such could be thy name
    Wert thou disjoined from these, or they from thee:
If thine or theirs were treasures to be bought
  By blood or tears, have not the wise and free   269
  Wept tears, and blood like tears? The solemn harmony

19

Paused, and the spirit of that mighty singing
  To its abyss was suddenly withdrawn;
Then, as a wild swan, when sublimely winging
  Its path athwart the thunder-smoke of dawn,
Sinks headlong through the aerial golden light
    On the heavy-sounding plain,
    When the bolt has pierced its brain;
As summer clouds dissolve, unburthened of their rain;
  As a far taper fades with fading night,
    As a brief insect dies with dying day,   280
  My song, its pinions disarrayed of might,
    Drooped; o'er it closed the echoes far away
Of the great voice which did its flight sustain,
  As waves which lately paved his watery way
  Hiss round a drowner's head in their tempestuous play.

To the Lord Chancellor[242]

1

Thy country's curse is on thee, darkest crest
  Of that foul, knotted, many-headed worm
Which rends our Mother's bosom – Priestly Pest!
  Masked Resurrection of a buried Form!

2

Thy country's curse is on thee! Justice sold,
  Truth trampled, Nature's landmarks overthrown,
And heaps of fraud-accumulated gold,
  Plead, loud as thunder, at Destruction's throne.

3

And, whilst that sure slow Angel which aye stands
  Watching the beck of Mutability   10
Delays to execute her high commands,
  And, though a nation weeps, spares thine and thee.

4

Oh let a father's curse be on thy soul,
 And let a daughter's hope be on thy tomb;
Be both, on thy grey head, a leaden cowl
 To weigh thee down to thine approaching doom.

5

I curse thee by a parent's outraged love,
 By hopes long cherished and too lately lost,
By gentle feelings thou couldst never prove,
 By griefs which thy stern nature never crost;   20

6

By those infantine smiles of happy light,
 Which were a fire within a stranger's hearth,
Quenched even when kindled, in untimely night,
 Hiding the promise of a lovely birth;

7

By those unpractised accents of young speech,
 Which he who is a father thought to frame
To gentlest lore, such as the wisest teach –
 Thou strike the lyre of mind! – O grief and shame!

8

By all the happy see in children's growth –
 That undeveloped flower of budding years –
Sweetness and sadness interwoven both,   30
 Source of the sweetest hopes and saddest fears –

9

By all the days under an hireling's care,
 Of dull constraint and bitter heaviness, –
O wretched ye if ever any were, –
 Sadder than orphans, yet not fatherless!

10

By the false cant which on their innocent lips
 Must hang like poison on an opening bloom,
By the dark creeds which cover with eclipse
 Their pathway from the cradle to the tomb –   40

11

By thy most impious Hell, and all its terror;
    By all the grief, the madness, and the guilt
Of thine impostures, which must be their error –
    That sand on which thy crumbling power is built –

12

By thy complicity with lust and hate –
    Thy thirst for tears – thy hunger after gold –
The ready frauds which ever on thee wait –
    The servile arts in which thou hast grown old –

13

By thy most killing sneer, and by thy smile –
    By all the snares and arts of thy black den,   50
And – for thou canst outweep the crocodile[243] –
    By thy false tears – those millstones braining men –

14

By all the hate which checks a father's love –
    By all the scorn which kills a father's care –
By those most impious hands that dared remove
    Nature's high bounds – by thee – and by despair –

15

Yes, the despair which bids a father groan,
    And cry – my children are no longer mine –
The blood within those veins may be mine own,
    But – Tyrant – their polluted souls are thine; –   60

16

I curse thee – though I hate thee not – O slave!
    If thou couldst quench the earth-consuming Hell
Of which thou art a demon, on thy grave
    This curse should be a blessing. Fare thee well!

The Cloud

I bring fresh showers for the thirsting flowers,
    From the seas and the streams;
I bear light shade for the leaves when laid
    In their noonday dreams.
From my wings are shaken the dews that waken
    The sweet buds every one,
When rocked to rest on their mother's breast,
    As she dances about the sun.
I wield the flail of the lashing hail,
    And whiten the green plains under,   10
And then again I dissolve it in rain,
    And laugh as I pass in thunder.

I sift the snow on the mountains below,
    And their great pines groan aghast;
And all the night 'tis my pillow white,
    While I sleep in the arms of the blast.
Sublime on the towers of my skiey bowers,
    Lightning my pilot sits;
In a cavern under is fettered the thunder,
    It struggles and howls at fits;   20
Over earth and ocean, with gentle motion,
    This pilot is guiding me,
Lured by the love of the genii that move
    In the depths of the purple sea;
Over the rills, and the crags, and the hills,
    Over the lakes and the plains,
Wherever he dream, under mountain or stream,
    The Spirit he loves remains;
And I all the while bask in heaven's blue smile,
    Whilst he is dissolving in rains.   30

The sanguine sunrise, with his meteor eyes,
    And his burning plumes outspread,
Leaps on the back of my sailing rack,
    When the morning star shines dead.

As on the jag of a mountain crag,
 Which an earthquake rocks and swings,
An eagle alit one moment may sit
 In the light of its golden wings.
And when sunset may breathe, from the lit sea beneath,
 Its ardours of rest and of love,   40
And the crimson pall of eve may fall
 From the depth of heaven above,
With wings folded I rest, on mine airy nest,
 As still as a brooding dove.

That orbed maiden with white fire laden,
 Whom mortals call the moon,
Glides glimmering o'er my fleece-like floor,
 By the midnight breezes strewn;
And wherever the beat of her unseen feet,
 Which only the angels hear,   50
May have broken the woof of my tent's thin roof,
 The stars peep behind her and peer;
And I laugh to see them whirl and flee,
 Like a swarm of golden bees,
When I widen the rent in my wind-built tent,
 Till the calm rivers, lakes, and seas,
Like strips of the sky fallen through me on high,
 Are each paved with the moon and these.

I bind the sun's throne with a burning zone,
 And the moon's with a girdle of pearl; 60
The volcanoes are dim, and the stars reel and swim,
 When the whirlwinds my banner unfurl.
From cape to cape, with a bridge-like shape,
 Over a torrent sea,
Sunbeam-proof, I hang like a roof,
 The mountains its columns be.
The triumphal arch through which I march
 With hurricane, fire, and snow,
When the powers of the air are chained to my chair,
 Is the million-coloured bow;   70
The sphere-fire above its soft colours wove,
 While the moist earth was laughing below.

I am the daughter of earth and water,
    And the nursling of the sky;
I pass through the pores of the ocean and shores;
    I change, but I cannot die.
For after the rain when with never a stain
    The pavilion of heaven is bare,
And the winds and sunbeams, with their convex gleams,
    Build up the blue dome of air,   80
I silently laugh at my own cenotaph,
    And out of the caverns of rain,
Like a child from the womb, like a ghost from the tomb,
    I arise and unbuild it again.

POEMS FROM 1821

Epipsychidion[244]

*Verses addressed to the Noble and Unfortunate Lady Emilia V—
now imprisoned in the Convent of —*

L'anima amante si slancia fuori del creato, e si crea nel infinito un Mondo
tutto per essa, diverso assai da questo oscuro e pauroso baratro.

HER OWN WORDS[245]

My Song, I fear that thou wilt find but few
Who fitly shall conceive thy reasoning,
Of such hard matter dost thou entertain;
Whence, if by misadventure, chance should bring
Thee to base company (as chance may do),
Quite unaware of what thou dost contain,
I prithee, comfort thy sweet self again,
My last delight! tell them that they are dull,
And bid them own that thou art beautiful.

ADVERTISEMENT[246]

The writer of the following lines died at Florence, as he was preparing for a
voyage to one of the wildest of the Sporades, which he had bought, and
where he had fitted up the ruins of an old building, and where it was his
hope to have realised a scheme of life, suited perhaps to that happier and
better world of which he is now an inhabitant, but hardly practicable in
this. His life was singular; less on account of the romantic vicissitudes
which diversified it, than the ideal tinge which it received from his own
character and feelings. The present Poem, like the *Vita Nuova* of Dante, is
sufficiently intelligible to a certain class of readers without a matter-of-fact
history of the circumstances to which it relates; and to a certain other class
it must ever remain incomprehensible, from a defect of a common organ of
perception for the ideas of which it treats. Not but that, *gran vergogna
sarebbe a colui, che rimasse cosa sotto veste di figura, o di colore rettorico: e
domandato non sapesse denudare le sue parole da cotal veste, in guisa che
avessero verace intendimento.*

The present poem appears to have been intended by the Writer as the dedication to some longer one. The stanza on the opposite page is almost a literal translation from Dante's famous Canzone

Voi, ch' intendendo, il terzo ciel movete, &c.

The presumptuous application of the concluding lines to his own composition will raise a smile at the expense of my unfortunate friend: be it a smile not of contempt, but pity.   S.

Sweet Spirit! Sister of that orphan one,
Whose empire is the name thou weepest on,
In my heart's temple I suspend to thee
These votive wreaths of withered memory.

Poor captive bird! who, from thy narrow cage,
Pourest such music, that it might assuage
The rugged hearts of those who prisoned thee,
Were they not deaf to all sweet melody;
This song shall be thy rose: its petals pale
Are dead, indeed, my adored Nightingale!   10
But soft and fragrant is the faded blossom,
And it has no thorn left to wound thy bosom.

High, spirit-winged Heart! who dost for ever
Beat thine unfeeling bars with vain endeavour,
Till those bright plumes of thought, in which arrayed
It over-soared this low and worldly shade,
Lie shattered; and thy panting, wounded breast
Stains with dear blood its unmaternal nest!
I weep vain tears: blood would less bitter be,
Yet poured forth gladlier, could it profit thee.   20

Seraph of Heaven! too gentle to be human,
Veiling beneath that radiant form of Woman
All that is insupportable in thee
Of light, and love, and immortality!
Sweet Benediction in the eternal Curse!
Veiled Glory of this lampless Universe!

Thou Moon beyond the clouds! Thou living Form
Among the Dead! Thou Star above the Storm!
Thou Wonder, and thou Beauty, and thou Terror!
Thou Harmony of Nature's art! Thou Mirror   30
In whom, as in the splendour of the Sun,
All shapes look glorious which thou gazest on!
Ay, even the dim words which obscure thee now
Flash, lightning-like, with unaccustomed glow;
I pray thee that thou blot from this sad song
All of its much mortality and wrong,
With those clear drops, which start like sacred dew
From the twin lights thy sweet soul darkens through,
Weeping, till sorrow becomes ecstasy:
Then smile on it, so that it may not die.   40

   I never thought before my death to see
Youth's vision thus made perfect. Emily,
I love thee; though the world by no thin name
Will hide that love, from its unvalued shame.
Would we two had been twins of the same mother!
Or, that the name my heart lent to another
Could be a sister's bond for her and thee,
Blending two beams of one eternity!
Yet were one lawful and the other true,
These names, though dear, could paint not, as is due,   50
How beyond refuge I am thine. Ah me!
I am not thine: I am a part of *thee*.

   Sweet Lamp! my moth-like Muse has burned its wings;
Or, like a dying swan who soars and sings,
Young Love should teach Time, in his own grey style,
All that thou art. Art thou not void of guile,
A lovely soul formed to be blest and bless?
A well of sealed and secret happiness,
Whose waters like blithe light and music are,
Vanquishing dissonance and gloom? A Star   60
Which moves not in the moving Heavens, alone?
A smile amid dark frowns? a gentle tone
Amid rude voices? a beloved light?
A Solitude, a Refuge, a Delight?

A Lute, which those whom love has taught to play
Make music on, to soothe the roughest day
And lull fond grief asleep? a buried treasure?
A cradle of young thoughts of wingless pleasure;
A violet-shrouded grave of Woe? – I measure
The world of fancies, seeking one like thee,   70
And find – alas! mine own infirmity.

  She met me, Stranger,[247] upon life's rough way,
And lured me towards sweet Death; as Night by Day,
Winter by Spring, or Sorrow by swift Hope,
Led into light, life, peace. An antelope,
In the suspended impulse of its lightness,
Were less ethereally light: the brightness
Of her divinest presence trembles through
Her limbs, as underneath a cloud of dew
Embodied in the windless Heaven of June   80
Amid the splendour-winged stars, the Moon
Burns, inextinguishably beautiful:
And from her lips, as from a hyacinth full
Of honey-dew, a liquid murmur drops,
Killing the sense with passion; sweet as stops
Of planetary music heard in trance.
In her mild lights the starry spirits dance,
The sunbeams of those wells which ever leap
Under the lightnings of the soul – too deep
For the brief fathom-line of thought or sense.   90
The glory of her being, issuing thence,
Stains the dead, blank, cold air with a warm shade
Of unentangled intermixture, made
By Love, of light and motion: one intense
Diffusion, one serene Omnipresence,
Whose flowing outlines mingle in their flowing.
Around her cheeks and utmost fingers glowing
With the unintermitted blood, which there
Quivers (as in a fleece of snow-like air
The crimson pulse of living morning quiver),   100
Continuously prolonged, and ending never,
Till they are lost, and in that Beauty furled
Which penetrates and clasps and fills the world;

Scarce visible from extreme loveliness.
Warm fragrance seems to fall from her light dress,
And her loose hair; and where some heavy tress
The air of her own speed has disentwined,
The sweetness seems to satiate the faint wind;
And in the soul a wild odour is felt,
Beyond the sense, like fiery dews that melt   110
Into the bosom of a frozen bud. –
See where she stands! a mortal shape indued
With love and life and light and deity,
And motion which may change but cannot die;
An image of some bright Eternity;
A shadow of some golden dream; a Splendour
Leaving the third sphere pilotless; a tender
Reflection of the eternal Moon of Love
Under whose motions life's dull billows move;
A Metaphor of Spring and Youth and Morning;   120
A Vision like incarnate April, warning,
With smiles and tears, Frost the Anatomy
Into his summer grave.

               Ah, woe is me!
What have I dared? where am I lifted? how
Shall I descend, and perish not? I know
That Love makes all things equal: I have heard
By mine own heart this joyous truth averred:
The spirit of the worm beneath the sod
In love and worship, blends itself with God.

  Spouse! Sister! Angel! Pilot of the Fate   130
Whose course has been so starless! O too late
Beloved! O too soon adored, by me!
For in the fields of immortality
My spirit should at first have worshipped thine,
A divine presence in a place divine;
Or should have moved beside it on this earth,
A shadow of that substance, from its birth;
But not as now: – I love thee; yes, I feel
That on the fountain of my heart a seal
Is set, to keep its waters pure and bright   140
For thee, since in those *tears* thou hast delight.

We – are we not formed, as notes of music are,
For one another, though dissimilar;
Such difference without discord, as can make
Those sweetest sounds, in which all spirits shake
As trembling leaves in a continuous air?

   Thy wisdom speaks in me, and bids me dare
Beacon the rocks on which high hearts are wreckt.
I never was attached to that great sect,
Whose doctrine is, that each one should select   150
Out of the crowd a mistress or a friend,
And all the rest, though fair and wise, commend
To cold oblivion, though it is in the code
Of modern morals, and the beaten road
Which those poor slaves with weary footsteps tread,
Who travel to their home among the dead
By the broad highway of the world, and so
With one chained friend, perhaps a jealous foe,
The dreariest and the longest journey go.

   True Love in this differs from gold and clay,   160
That to divide is not to take away.
Love is like understanding, that grows bright,
Gazing on many truths; 'tis like thy light,
Imagination! which from earth and sky,
And from the depths of human phantasy,
As from a thousand prisms and mirrors, fills
The Universe with glorious beams, and kills
Error, the worm, with many a sun-like arrow
Of its reverberated lightning. Narrow
The heart that loves, the brain that contemplates,   170
The life that wears, the spirit that creates
One object, and one form, and builds thereby
A sepulchre for its eternity.

   Mind from its object differs most in this:
Evil from good; misery from happiness;
The baser from the nobler; the impure
And frail, from what is clear and must endure.
If you divide suffering and dross, you may

Diminish till it is consumed away;
If you divide pleasure and love and thought,   180
Each part exceeds the whole; and we know not
How much, while any yet remains unshared,
Of pleasure may be gained, of sorrow spared:
This truth is that deep well, whence sages draw
The unenvied light of hope; the eternal law
By which those live, to whom this world of life
Is as a garden ravaged, and whose strife
Tills for the promise of a later birth
The wilderness of this Elysian earth.

There was a Being whom my spirit oft   190
Met on its visioned wanderings, far aloft,
In the clear golden prime of my youth's dawn,
Upon the fairy isles of sunny lawn,
Amid the enchanted mountains, and the caves
Of divine sleep, and on the air-like waves
Of wonder-level dream, whose tremulous floor
Paved her light steps; – on an imagined shore,
Under the grey beak of some promontory
She met me, robed in such exceeding glory,
That I beheld her not. In solitudes   200
Her voice came to me through the whispering woods,
And from the fountains, and the odours deep
Of flowers, which, like lips murmuring in their sleep
Of the sweet kisses which had lulled them there,
Breathed but of *her* to the enamoured air;
And from the breezes whether low or loud,
And from the rain of every passing cloud,
And from the singing of the summer-birds,
And from all sounds, all silence. In the words
Of antique verse and high romance, – in form   210
Sound, colour – in whatever checks that Storm
Which with the shattered present chokes the past;
And in that best philosophy, whose taste
Makes this cold common hell, our life, a doom
As glorious as a fiery martyrdom;
Her Spirit was the harmony of truth. –

Then, from the caverns of my dreamy youth
I sprang, as one sandalled with plumes of fire,
And towards the loadstar of my one desire.
I flitted, like a dizzy moth, whose flight   220
Is as a dead leaf's in the owlet light,
When it would seek in Hesper's[248] setting sphere
A radiant death, a fiery sepulchre,
As if it were a lamp of earthly flame. –
But She, whom prayers or tears then could not tame,
Passed, like a God throned on a winged planet.
Whose burning plumes to tenfold swiftness fan it,
Into the dreary cone of our life's shade;
And as a man with mighty loss dismayed,
I would have followed, though the grave between   230
Yawned like a gulf whose spectres are unseen:
When a voice said: – 'O thou of hearts the weakest,
The phantom is beside thee whom thou seekest.'
Then I – 'Where?' – the world's echo answered, 'Where!'
And in that silence, and in my despair,
I questioned every tongueless wind that flew
Over my tower of mourning, if it knew
Whither 'twas fled, this soul out of my soul;
And murmured names and spells which have control
Over the sightless tyrants of our fate;   240
But neither prayer nor verse could dissipate
The night which closed on her; nor uncreate
That world within this Chaos, mine and me,
Of which she was the veiled Divinity,
The world I say of thoughts that worshipped her:
And therefore I went forth, with hope and fear
And every gentle passion sick to death,
Feeding my course with expectation's breath,
Into the wintry forest of our life;
And struggling through its error with vain strife,   250
And stumbling in my weakness and my haste,
And half bewildered by new forms, I passed,
Seeking among those untaught foresters
If I could find one form resembling hers,
In which she might have masked herself from me.
There, – One whose voice was venomed melody

Sate by a well, under blue night-shade bowers;
The breath of her false mouth was like faint flowers,
Her touch was as electric poison, – flame
Out of her looks into my vitals came,   260
And from her living cheeks and bosom flew
A killing air, which pierced like honey-dew
Into the core of my green heart, and lay
Upon its leaves; until, as hair grown grey
O'er a young brow, they hid its unblown prime
With ruins of unseasonable time.

   In many mortal forms I rashly sought
The shadow of that idol of my thought.
And some were fair – but beauty dies away:
Others were wise – but honeyed words betray: 270
And One was true – oh! why not true to me?
Then, as a hunted deer that could not flee,
I turned upon my thoughts, and stood at bay,
Wounded and weak and panting; the cold day
Trembled, for pity of my strife and pain.
When, like a noonday dawn, there shone again
Deliverance. One stood on my path who seemed
As like the glorious shape which I had dreamed,
As is the Moon, whose changes ever run
Into themselves, to the eternal Sun;   280
The cold chaste Moon, the Queen of Heaven's bright isles,
Who makes all beautiful on which she smiles.
That wandering shrine of soft yet icy flame
Which ever is transformed, yet still the same,
And warms not but illumines. Young and fair
As the descended Spirit of that sphere,
She hid me, as the Moon may hide the night
From its own darkness, until all was bright
Between the Heaven and Earth of my calm mind,
And, as a cloud charioted by the wind,   290
She led me to a cave in that wild place,
And sate beside me, with her downward face
Illumining my slumbers, like the Moon
Waxing and waning over Endymion.[249]
And I was laid asleep, spirit and limb,

And all my being became bright or dim
As the Moon's image in a summer sea,
According as she smiled or frowned on me;
And there I lay, within a chaste cold bed:
Alas, I then was nor alive nor dead: –   300
For at her silver voice came Death and Life,
Unmindful each of their accustomed strife,
Masked like twin babes, a sister and a brother,
The wandering hopes of one abandoned mother,
And through the cavern without wings they flew,
And cried, 'Away! he is not of our crew.'
I wept, and though it be a dream, I weep.

    What storms then shook the ocean of my sleep,
Blotting that Moon, whose pale and waning lips
Then shrank as in the sickness of eclipse; –   310
And how my soul was as a lampless sea,
And who was then its Tempest; and when She,
The Planet of that hour was quenched, what frost
Crept o'er those waters, 'till from coast to coast
The moving billows of my being fell
Into a death of ice, immovable; –
And then – what earthquakes made it gape and split,
The white Moon smiling all the while on it,
These words conceal: – If not, each word would be
The key of staunchless tears. Weep not for me!   320

    At length, into the obscure Forest came
The Vision I had sought through grief and shame.
Athwart that wintry wilderness of thorns
Flashed from her motion splendour like the Morn's,
And from her presence life was radiated
Through the grey earth and branches bare and dead;
So that her way was paved and roofed above
With flowers as soft as thoughts of budding love;
And music from her respiration spread
Like light, – all other sounds were penetrated   330
By the small, still, sweet spirit of that sound,
So that the savage winds hung mute around;
And odours warm and fresh fell from her hair

Dissolving the dull cold in the frore air:
Soft as an Incarnation of the Sun,
When light is changed to love, this glorious One
Floated into the cavern where I lay,
And called my Spirit, and the dreaming clay
Was lifted by the thing that dreamed below
As smoke by fire, and in her beauty's glow   340
I stood, and felt the dawn of my long night
Was penetrating me with living light:
I knew it was the Vision veiled from me
So many years – that it was Emily.

   Twin Spheres of light who rule this passive Earth,
This world of love, this *me*; and into birth
Awaken all its fruits and flowers, and dart
Magnetic might into its central heart;
And lift its billows and its mists, and guide
By everlasting laws, each wind and tide   350
To its fit cloud, and its appointed cave;
And lull its storms, each in the craggy grave
Which was its cradle, luring to faint bowers
The armies of the rainbow-winged showers;
And, as those married lights, which from the towers
Of Heaven look forth and fold the wandering globe
In liquid sleep and splendour, as a robe;
And all their many-mingled influence blend,
If equal, yet unlike, to one sweet end; –
So ye, bright regents, with alternate sway   360
Govern my sphere of being, night and day!
Thou, not disdaining even a borrowed might;
Thou, not eclipsing a remoter light;
And, through the shadow of the seasons three,
From Spring to Autumn's sere maturity,
Light it into the Winter of the tomb,
Where it may ripen to a brighter bloom.
Thou too, O Comet beautiful and fierce,
Who drew the heart of this frail Universe
Towards thine own; till, wreckt in that convulsion, 370
Alternating attraction and repulsion,
Thine went astray and that was rent in twain;

Oh, float into our azure heaven again!
Be there love's folding-star at thy return;
The living Sun will feed thee from its urn
Of golden fire; the Moon will veil her horn
In thy last smiles; adoring Even and Morn
Will worship thee with incense of calm breath
And lights and shadows; as the star of Death
And Birth is worshipped by those sisters wild   380
Called Hope and Fear – upon the heart are piled
Their offerings, – of this sacrifice divine
A World shall be the altar.
                              Lady mine,
Scorn not these flowers of thought, the fading birth
Which from its heart of hearts that plant puts forth,
Whose fruit, made perfect by thy sunny eyes,
Will be as of the trees of Paradise.

    The day is come, and thou wilt fly with me.
To whatsoe'er of dull mortality
Is mine, remain a vestal sister still;   390
To the intense, the deep, the imperishable,
Not mine but me, henceforth be thou united
Even as a bride, delighting and delighted.
The hour is come: – the destined Star has risen
Which shall descend upon a vacant prison.
The walls are high, the gates are strong, thick set
The sentinels – but true love never yet
Was thus constrained: it overleaps all fence:
Like lightning, with invisible violence
Piercing its continents; like Heaven's free breath,   400
Which he who grasps can hold not; liker Death,
Who rides upon a thought, and makes his way
Through temple, tower, and palace, and the array
Of arms: more strength has Love than he or they;
For it can burst his charnel, and make free
The limbs in chains, the heart in agony,
The soul in dust and chaos.
                              Emily,
A ship is floating in the harbour now,
A wind is hovering o'er the mountain's brow;

There is a path on the sea's azure floor,   410
No keel has ever ploughed that path before;
The halcyons brood around the foamless isles;
The treacherous Ocean has forsworn its wiles;
The merry mariners are bold and free:
Say, my heart's sister, wilt thou sail with me?
Our bark is as an albatross, whose nest
Is a far Eden of the purple East;
And we between her wings will sit, while Night
And Day, and Storm, and Calm, pursue their flight.
Our ministers, along the boundless Sea,   420
Treading each other's heels, unheededly.
It is an isle under Ionian skies,
Beautiful as a wreck of Paradise,
And, for the harbours are not safe and good,
This land would have remained a solitude
But for some pastoral people native there,
Who from the Elysian, clear, and golden air
Draw the last spirit of the age of gold,
Simple and spirited; innocent and bold.
The blue Aegean girds this chosen home,   430
With ever-changing sound and light and foam,
Kissing the sifted sands, and caverns hoar;
And all the winds wandering along the shore
Undulate with the undulating tide:
There are thick woods where sylvan forms abide;
And many a fountain, rivulet, and pond,
As clear as elemental diamond,
Or serene morning air; and far beyond,
The mossy tracks made by the goats and deer
(Which the rough shepherd treads but once a year)   440
Pierce into glades, caverns, and bowers, and halls
Built round with ivy, which the waterfalls
Illumining, with sound that never fails
Accompany the noonday nightingales;
And all the place is peopled with sweet airs;
The light clear element which the isle wears
Is heavy with the scent of lemon-flowers,
Which floats like mist laden with unseen showers,
And falls upon the eyelids like faint sleep;

And from the moss violets and jonquils peep,   450
And dart their arrowy odour through the brain
Till you might faint with that delicious pain.
And every motion, odour, beam, and tone,
With that deep music is in unison:
Which is a soul within the soul – they seem
Like echoes of an antenatal dream. –
It is an isle 'twixt Heaven, Air, Earth, and Sea,
Cradled, and hung in clear tranquillity;
Bright as that wandering Eden Lucifer,
Washed by the soft blue Oceans of young air.   460
It is a favoured place. Famine or Blight,
Pestilence, War and Earthquake, never light
Upon its mountain-peaks; blind vultures, they
Sail onward far upon their fatal way:
The winged storms, chaunting their thunder-psalm
To other lands, leave azure chasms of calm
Over this isle, or weep themselves in dew,
From which its fields and woods ever renew
Their green and golden immortality.
And from the sea there rise, and from the sky   470
There fall, clear exhalations, soft and bright.
Veil after veil, each hiding some delight,
Which Sun or Moon or zephyr draw aside,
Till the isle's beauty, like a naked bride
Glowing at once with love and loveliness,
Blushes and trembles at its own excess:
Yet, like a buried lamp, a Soul no less
Burns in the heart of this delicious isle,
An atom of th' Eternal, whose own smile
Unfolds itself, and may be felt not seen   480
O'er the grey rocks, blue waves, and forests green,
Filling their bare and void interstices. –
But the chief marvel of the wilderness
Is a lone dwelling, built by whom or how
None of the rustic island-people know:
'Tis not a tower of strength, though with its height
It overtops the woods; but, for delight,
Some wise and tender Ocean-King, ere crime
Had been invented, in the world's young prime,

Reared it, a wonder of that simple time,   490
An envy of the isles, a pleasure-house
Made sacred to his sister and his spouse.
It scarce seems now a wreck of human art,
But, as it were Titanic; in the heart
Of Earth having assumed its form, then grown
Out of the mountains, from the living stone,
Lifting itself in caverns light and high:
For all the antique and learned imagery
Has been erased, and in the place of it
The ivy and the wild-vine interknit   500
The volumes of their many twining stems;
Parasite flowers illume with dewy gems
The lampless halls, and when they fade, the sky
Peeps through their winter-woof of tracery
With moonlight patches, or star atoms keen,
Or fragments of the day's intense serene; –
Working mosaic on their Parian[250] floors.
And, day and night, aloof, from the high towers
And terraces, the Earth and Ocean seem
To sleep in one another's arms, and dream   510
Of waves, flowers, clouds, woods, rocks, and all that we
Read in their smiles, and call reality.

    This isle and house are mine, and I have vowed
Thee to be lady of the solitude. –
And I have fitted up some chambers there
Looking towards the golden Eastern air,
And level with the living winds, which flow
Like waves above the living waves below. –
I have sent books and music there, and all
Those instruments with which high spirits call   520
The future from its cradle, and the past
Out of its grave, and make the present last
In thoughts and joys which sleep, but cannot die,
Folded within their own eternity.
Our simple life wants little, and true taste
Hires not the pale drudge Luxury, to waste
The scene it would adorn, and therefore still,
Nature with all her children, haunts the hill.

The ring-dove, in the embowering ivy, yet
Keeps up her love-lament, and the owls flit 530
Round the evening tower, and the young stars glance
Between the quick bats in their twilight dance;
The spotted deer bask in the fresh moonlight
Before our gate, and the slow, silent night
Is measured by the pants of their calm sleep.
Be this our home in life, and when years heap
Their withered hours, like leaves, on our decay,
Let us become the over-hanging day,
The living soul of this Elysian isle,
Conscious, inseparable, one. Meanwhile 540
We two will rise, and sit, and walk together,
Under the roof of blue Ionian weather,
And wander in the meadows, or ascend
The mossy mountains, where the blue heavens bend
With lightest winds, to touch their paramour;
Or linger, where the pebble-paven shore,
Under the quick, faint kisses of the sea
Trembles and sparkles as with ecstasy, –
Possessing and possest by all that is
Within that calm circumference of bliss, 550
And by each other, till to love and live
Be one: – or, at the noontide hour, arrive
Where some old cavern hoar seems yet to keep
The moonlight of the expired night asleep,
Through which the awakened day can never peep;
A veil for our seclusion, close as Night's,
Where secure sleep may kill thine innocent lights;
Sleep, the fresh dew of languid love, the rain
Whose drops quench kisses till they burn again.
And we will talk, until thought's melody 560
Become too sweet for utterance, and it die
In words, to live again in looks, which dart
With thrilling tone into the voiceless heart,
Harmonising silence without a sound.
Our breath shall intermix, our bosoms bound
And our veins beat together; and our lips,
With other eloquence than words, eclipse
The soul that burns between them, and the wells

Which boil under our being's inmost cells,
The fountains of our deepest life, shall be   570
Confused in passion's golden purity,
As mountain-springs under the morning Sun.
We shall become the same, we shall be one
Spirit within two frames, oh! wherefore two?
One passion in twin-hearts, which grows and grew,
Till like two meteors of expanding flame,
Those spheres instinct with it become the same,
Touch, mingle, are transfigured; ever still
Burning, yet ever inconsumable:
In one another's substance finding food,   580
Like flames too pure and light and unimbued
To nourish their bright lives with baser prey,
Which point to Heaven and cannot pass away:
One hope within two wills, one will beneath
Two overshadowing minds, one life, one death,
One Heaven, one Hell, one immortality,
And one annihilation. Woe is me!
The winged words on which my soul would pierce
Into the height of Love's rare Universe,
Are chains of lead around its flight of fire. –   590
I pant, I sink, I tremble, I expire!

    Weak Verses, go, kneel at your Sovereign's[251] feet,
And say: – 'We are the masters of thy slave;
What wouldest thou with us and ours and thine?'
Then call your sisters from Oblivion's cave,
All singing loud: 'Love's very pain is sweet,
But its reward is in the world divine
Which, if not here, it builds beyond the grave.'
So shall ye live when I am there. Then haste
Over the hearts of men, until ye meet   600
Marina, Vanna, Primus,[252] and the rest,
And bid them love each other and be blest:
And leave the troop which errs, and which reproves,
And come and be my guest, – for I am Love's.

Adonais[253]

An Elegy on the Death of John Keats,
Author of Endymion, Hyperion, *etc.*

Ἀστὴρ ἠρὶν μὲν ἔλαμπες ἐνὶ ζωοῖσιν Ἑῷος.
νῦν δὲ θανὼν λάμπεις Ἕσπερος ἐν φθιμένοις

PLATO

PREFACE

Φάρμακον ἦλθε, Βίων, ποτὶ σὸν στόμα, φάρμακον εἶδες.
πῶς τευ τοῖς χείλεσσι ποτέδραμε, κοὐκ ἐγλυκάνθη;
τίς δὲ βροτὸς τοσσοῦτον ἀνάμεροσ, ἢ κεράσαι τοι,
ἢ δοῦναι λαλέοντι τὸ φάρμακον; ἐκφυγεν ᾠδάν.

MOSCHUS, EPITAPH. BION.[254]

It is my intention to subjoin to the London edition of this poem, a criticism upon the claims of its lamented object to be classed among the writers of the highest genius who have adorned our age. My known repugnance to the narrow principles of taste on which several of his earlier compositions were modelled, proves at least that I am an impartial judge. I consider the fragment of *Hyperion* as second to nothing that was ever produced by a writer of the same years.

John Keats died at Rome of a consumption, in his twenty-fourth year, on the — of — 1821, and was buried in the romantic and lonely cemetery of the protestants in that city, under the pyramid which is the tomb of Cestius, and the massy walls and towers, now mouldering and desolate, which formed the circuit of ancient Rome. The cemetery is an open space along the ruins covered in winter with violets and daises. It might make one in love with death to think that one should be buried in so sweet a place.

The genius of the lamented person to whose memory I have dedicated these unworthy verses, was not less delicate and fragile than it was beautiful; and where canker-worms abound, what wonder if its young flower was blighted in the bud? The savage criticism on his *Endymion*, which appeared in the *Quarterly Review*, produced the most violent effect on his susceptible mind; the agitation thus originated ended in the rupture of a blood-vessel in the lungs; a rapid consumption ensued, and the succeeding acknowledgements from more candid critics, of the true greatness of his powers, were ineffectual to heal the wound thus wantonly inflicted.

It may be well said, that these wretched men know not what they do. They scatter their insults and their slanders without heed as to whether the poisoned shaft lights on a heart made callous by many blows, or one, like Keats's, composed of more penetrable stuff. One of their associates is, to my knowledge, a most base and unprincipled calumniator. As to *Endymion*, was it a poem, whatever might be its defects, to be treated contemptuously by those who had celebrated, with various degrees of complacency and panegyric, *Paris*, and *Woman*, and *A Syrian Tale*, and Mrs Lefanu, and Mr Barrett, and Mr Howard Payne, and a long list of the illustrious obscure? Are these the men who, in their venal good nature, presumed to draw a parallel between the Revd Mr Milman and Lord Byron? What gnat did they strain at here, after having swallowed all those camels? Against what woman taken in adultery dares the foremost of these literary prostitutes to cast his opprobrious stone? Miserable man! you, one of the meanest, have wantonly defaced one of the noblest specimens of the workmanship of God. Nor shall it be your excuse, that, murderer as you are, you have spoken daggers, but used none.

The circumstances of the closing scene of poor Keats's life were not made known to me until the Elegy was ready for the press. I am given to understand that the wound which his sensitive spirit had received from the criticism of *Endymion* was exasperated by the bitter sense of unrequited benefits; the poor fellow seems to have been hooted from the stage of life, no less by those on whom he had wasted the promise of his genius, than those on whom he had lavished his fortune and his care. He was accompanied to Rome, and attended in his last illness, by Mr Severn, a young artist of the highest promise, who, I have been informed, 'almost risked his own life, and sacrificed every prospect to unwearied attendance upon his dying friend'. Had I known these circumstances before the completion of my poem, I should have been tempted to add my feeble tribute of applause to the more solid recompense which the virtuous man finds in the recollection of his own motives. Mr Severn can dispense with a reward from 'such stuff as dreams are made of'. His conduct is a golden augury of the success of his future career – may the unextinguished Spirit of his illustrious friend animate the creations of his pencil, and plead against Oblivion for his name!

Adonais

1

I weep for Adonais – he is dead!
O, weep for Adonais! though our tears
Thaw not the frost which binds so dear a head!
And thou, sad Hour, selected from all years
To mourn our loss, rouse thy obscure compeers,
And teach them thine own sorrow, say: With me
Died Adonais; till the Future dares
Forget the Past, his fate and fame shall be
An echo and a light unto eternity!

2

Where wert thou mighty Mother, when he lay,   10
When thy Son lay, pierced by the shaft which flies
In darkness? where was lorn Urania[255]
When Adonais died? With veiled eyes,
'Mid listening Echoes, in her Paradise
She sate, while one, with soft enamoured breath,
Rekindled all the fading melodies,
With which, like flowers that mock the corse beneath,
He had adorned and hid the coming bulk of death.

3

O, weep for Adonais – he is dead!
Wake, melancholy Mother, wake and weep!   20
Yet wherefore? Quench within their burning bed
Thy fiery tears, and let thy loud heart keep
Like his, a mute and uncomplaining sleep;
For he is gone, where all things wise and fair
Descend; – oh, dream not that the amorous Deep
Will yet restore him to the vital air;
Death feeds on his mute voice, and laughs at our despair

4

Most musical of mourners, weep again!
Lament anew, Urania! – He died,[256]
Who was the Sire of an immortal strain,   30
Blind, old, and lonely, when his country's pride,
The priest, the slave, and the liberticide,
Trampled and mocked with many a loathed rite
Of lust and blood; he went, unterrified,
Into the gulf of death; but his clear Sprite
Yet reigns o'er earth; the third among the sons of light.[257]

5

Most musical of mourners, weep anew!
Not all to that bright station dared to climb;
And happier they their happiness who knew,
Whose tapers yet burn through that night of time   40
In which suns perished; others more sublime,
Struck by the envious wrath of man or God,
Have sunk, extinct in their refulgent prime;
And some yet live, treading the thorny road,
Which leads, through toil and hate, to Fame's serene abode.

6

But now, thy youngest, dearest one, has perished
The nursling of thy widowhood, who grew,
Like a pale flower by some sad maiden cherished,
And fed with true love tears, instead of dew;
Most musical of mourners, weep anew!   50
Thy extreme hope, the loveliest and the last,
The bloom, whose petals nipt before they blew
Died on the promise of the fruit, is waste;
The broken lily lies – the storm is overpast.

7

To that high Capital,[258] where kingly Death
Keeps his pale court in beauty and decay,
He came; and bought, with price of purest breath,
A grave among the eternal. – Come away!
Haste, while the vault of blue Italian day

Is yet his fitting charnel-roof! while still   60
He lies, as if in dewy sleep he lay;
Awake him not! surely he takes his fill
Of deep and liquid rest, forgetful of all ill.

8

He will awake no more, oh, never more! –
Within the twilight chamber spreads apace,
The shadow of white Death, and at the door
Invisible Corruption waits to trace
His extreme way to her dim dwelling-place;
The eternal Hunger sits, but pity and awe
Soothe her pale rage, nor dares she to deface   70
So fair a prey, till darkness, and the law
Of change, shall o'er his sleep the mortal curtain draw.

9

O, weep for Adonais! – The quick Dreams,
The passion-winged Ministers of thought,
Who were his flocks, whom near the living streams
Of his young spirit he fed, and whom he taught
The love which was its music, wander not, –
Wander no more, from kindling brain to brain,
But droop there, whence they sprung: and mourn their lot
Round the cold heart, where, after their sweet pain,   80
They ne'er will gather strength, or find a home again.

10

And one with trembling hands clasps his cold head,
And fans him with her moonlight wings, and cries:
'Our love, our hope, our sorrow, is not dead;
See, on the silken fringe of his faint eyes,
Like dew upon a sleeping flower, there lies
A tear some Dream has loosened from his brain.'
Lost Angel of a ruined Paradise!
She knew not 'twas her own; as with no stain
She faded, like a cloud which had outwept its rain.   90

11

One from a lucid urn of starry dew
Washed his light limbs as if embalming them;
Another clipt her profuse locks, and threw
The wreath upon him, like an anadem,[259]
Which frozen tears instead of pearls begem;
Another in her wilful grief would break
Her bow and winged reeds, as if to stem
A greater loss with one which was more weak;
And dull the barbed fire against his frozen cheek.

12

Another Splendour on his mouth alit,   100
That mouth, whence it was wont to draw the breath
Which gave it strength to pierce the guarded wit,
And pass into the panting heart beneath
With lightning and with music: the damp death
Quenched its caress upon his icy lips;
And, as a dying meteor stains a wreath
Of moonlight vapour, which the cold night clips,
It flushed through his pale limbs, and past to its eclipse.

13

And others came . . . Desires and Adorations,
Winged Persuasions and veiled Destinies,   110
Splendours, and Glooms, and glimmering Incarnations
Of hopes and fears, and twilight Phantasies;
And Sorrow, with her family of Sighs,
And Pleasure, blind with tears, led by the gleam
Of her own dying smile instead of eyes,
Came in slow pomp; – the moving pomp might seem
Like pageantry of mist on an autumnal stream.

14

All he had loved, and moulded into thought,
From shape, and hue, and odour, and sweet sound,
Lamented Adonais. Morning sought   120
Her eastern watch-tower, and her hair unbound,
Wet with the tears which should adorn the ground,

Dimmed the aerial eyes that kindle day;
Afar the melancholy thunder moaned,
Pale Ocean in unquiet slumber lay,
And the wild winds flew round, sobbing in their dismay.

15

Lost Echo sits amid the voiceless mountains,
And feeds her grief with his remembered lay,
And will no more reply to winds or fountains,
Or amorous birds perched on the young green spray.   130
Or herdsman's horn, or bell at closing day;
Since she can mimic not his lips, more dear
Than those for whose disdain she pined away
Into a shadow of all sounds: – a drear
Murmur, between their songs, is all the woodmen hear.

16

Grief made the young Spring wild, and she threw down
Her kindling buds, as if she Autumn were,
Or they dead leaves; since her delight is flown,
For whom should she have waked the sullen year?
To Phoebus was not Hyacinth so dear   140
Nor to himself Narcissus,[260] as to both
Thou Adonais: wan they stand and sere
Amid the drooping comrades of their youth,
With dew all turned to tears; odour, to sighing ruth.

17

Thy spirit's sister, the lorn nightingale
Mourns not her mate with such melodious pain;
Not so the eagle, who like thee could scale
Heaven, and could nourish in the sun's domain
Her mighty youth with morning, doth complain,
Soaring and screaming round her empty nest,   150
As Albion wails for thee: the curse of Cain
Light on his head who pierced thy innocent breast,
And scared the angel soul that was its earthly guest!

18

Ah, woe is me! Winter is come and gone,
But grief returns with the revolving year;
The airs and streams renew their joyous tone;
The ants, the bees, the swallows reappear;
Fresh leaves and flowers deck the dead Seasons' bier;
The amorous birds now pair in every brake,
And build their mossy homes in field and brere;   160
And the green lizard, and the golden snake,
Like unimprisoned flames, out of their trance awake.

19

Through wood and stream and field and hill and Ocean,
A quickening life from the Earth's heart has burst
As it has ever done, with change and motion,
From the great morning of the world when first
God dawned on Chaos; in its steam immersed
The lamps of Heaven flash with a softer light;
All baser things pant with life's sacred thirst;
Diffuse themselves; and spend in love's delight,   170
The beauty and the joy of their renewed might.

20

The leprous corpse touched by this spirit tender
Exhales itself in flowers of gentle breath;
Like incarnations of the stars, when splendour
Is changed to fragrance, they illumine death
And mock the merry worm that wakes beneath;
Nought we know, dies. Shall that alone which knows
Be as a sword consumed before the sheath
By sightless lightning? – th' intense atom glows
A moment, then is quenched in a most cold repose.   180

21

Alas! that all we loved of him should be,
But for our grief, as if it had not been,
And grief itself be mortal! Woe is me!
Whence are we, and why are we? of what scene
The actors or spectators? Great and mean

Meet massed in death, who lends what life must borrow.
As long as skies are blue, and fields are green,
Evening must usher night, night urge the morrow,
Month follow month with woe, and year wake year to sorrow.

22

He will awake no more, oh, never more!   190
'Wake thou,' cried Misery, 'childless Mother, rise
Out of thy sleep, and slake, in thy heart's core,
A wound more fierce than his with tears and sighs.'
And all the Dreams that watched Urania's eyes,
And all the Echoes whom their sister's song
Had held in holy silence, cried: 'Arise!'
Swift as a Thought by the snake Memory stung,
From her ambrosial rest the fading Splendour sprung.

23

She rose like an autumnal Night, that springs
Out of the East, and follows wild and drear   200
The golden Day, which, on eternal wings,
Even as a ghost abandoning a bier,
Had left the Earth a corpse. Sorrow and fear
So struck, so roused, so rapt Urania;
So saddened round her like an atmosphere
Of stormy mist; so swept her on her way,
Even to the mournful place where Adonais lay.

24

Out of her secret Paradise she sped,
Through camps and cities rough with stone, and steel,
And human hearts, which to her aery tread   210
Yielding not, wounded the invisible
Palms of her tender feet where'er they fell:
And barbed tongues, and thoughts more sharp than they
Rent the soft Form they never could repel,
Whose sacred blood, like the young tears of May,
Paved with eternal flowers that undeserving way.

25

In the death chamber for a moment Death,
Shamed by the presence of that living Might,
Blushed to annihilation, and the breath
Revisited those lips, and life's pale light   220
Flashed through those limbs, so late her dear delight.
'Leave me not wild and drear and comfortless,
As silent lightning leaves the starless night!
Leave me not!' cried Urania: her distress
Roused Death: Death rose and smiled, and met her vain caress.

26

'Stay yet awhile! speak to me once again;
Kiss me, so long but as a kiss may live;
And in my heartless breast and burning brain
That word, that kiss shall all thoughts else survive,
With food of saddest memory kept alive,   230
Now thou art dead, as if it were a part
Of thee, my Adonais! I would give
All that I am to be as thou now art!
But I am chained to Time, and cannot thence depart!

27

'Oh gentle child, beautiful as thou wert,
Why didst thou leave the trodden paths of men
Too soon, and with weak hands though mighty heart
Dare the unpastured dragon in his den?
Defenceless as thou wert, oh, where was then
Wisdom the mirrored shield, or scorn the spear?   240
Or hadst thou waited the full cycle, when
Thy spirit should have filled its crescent sphere,
The monsters of life's waste had fled from thee like deer.

28

'The herded wolves, bold only to pursue;
The obscene ravens, clamorous o'er the dead;
The vultures to the conqueror's banner true
Who feed where Desolation first has fed,
And whose wings rain contagion; – how they fled,

When like Apollo, from his golden bow,
The Pythian of the age[261] one arrow sped   250
And smiled! – The spoilers tempt no second blow,
They fawn on the proud feet that spurn them as they go.

29

'The sun comes forth, and many reptiles spawn;
He sets, and each ephemeral insect then
Is gathered into death without a dawn,
And the immortal stars awake again;
So is it in the world of living men:
A godlike mind soars forth, in its delight
Making earth bare and veiling heaven, and when
It sinks, the swarms that dimmed or shared its light   260
Leave to its kindred lamps the spirit's awful night.'

30

Thus ceased she: and the mountain shepherds came
Their garlands sere, their magic mantles rent;
The Pilgrim of Eternity,[262] whose fame
Over his living head like Heaven is bent,
An early but enduring monument,
Came, veiling all the lightnings of his song
In sorrow; from her wilds Ierne sent
The sweetest lyrist[263] of her saddest wrong,
And love taught grief to fall like music from his tongue.   270

31

Midst others of less note, came one frail Form,[264]
A phantom among men; companionless
As the last cloud of an expiring storm
Whose thunder is its knell; he, as I guess,
Had gazed on Nature's naked loveliness,
Actaeon-like,[265] and now he fled astray
With feeble steps o'er the world's wilderness,
And his own thoughts, along that rugged way,
Pursued, like raging hounds, their father and their prey.

32

A pardlike Spirit beautiful and swift –   280
A Love in desolation masked; – a Power
Girt round with weakness; – it can scarce uplift
The weight of the superincumbent hour;
It is a dying lamp, a falling shower,
A breaking billow; even whilst we speak
Is it not broken? On the withering flower
The killing sun smiles brightly: on a cheek
The life can burn in blood, even while the heart may break.

33

His head was bound with pansies overblown,
And faded violets, white, and pied, and blue;   290
And a light spear topped with a cypress cone,
Round whose rude shaft dark ivy tresses grew
Yet dripping with the forest's noonday dew,
Vibrated, as the ever-beating heart
Shook the weak hand that grasped it; of that crew
He[266] came the last, neglected and apart;
A herd-abandoned deer struck by the hunter's dart.

34

All stood aloof, and at his partial moan
Smiled through their tears; well knew that gentle band
Who in another's fate now wept his own,   300
As in the accents of an unknown land
He sung new sorrow; sad Urania scanned
The Stranger's mien, and murmured: 'Who art thou?'
He answered not, but with a sudden hand
Made bare his branded and ensanguined brow,
Which was like Cain's or Christ's – oh! that it should be so!

35

What softer voice is hushed over the dead?
Athwart what brow is that dark mantle thrown?
What form leans sadly o'er the white deathbed,
In mockery of monumental stone,   310
The heavy heart heaving without a moan?

If it be He, who, gentlest of the wise,
   Taught, soothed, loved, honoured the departed one;
   Let me not vex, with inharmonious sighs,
The silence of that heart's accepted sacrifice.

36

Our Adonais has drunk poison – oh!
   What deaf and viperous murderer[267] could crown
   Life's early cup with such a draught of woe?
   The nameless worm would now itself disown:
   It felt, yet could escape the magic tone   320
   Whose prelude held all envy, hate, and wrong,
   But what was howling in one breast alone,
   Silent with expectation of the song,
Whose master's hand is cold, whose silver lyre unstrung.

37

Live thou, whose infamy is not thy fame!
   Live! fear no heavier chastisement from me,
   Thou noteless blot on a remembered name!
   But be thyself, and know thyself to be!
   And ever at thy season be thou free
   To spill the venom when thy fangs o'erflow: 330
   Remorse and Self-contempt shall cling to thee;
   Hot Shame shall burn upon thy secret brow,
And like a beaten hound tremble thou shalt – as now.

38

Nor let us weep that our delight is fled
   Far from these carrion kites that scream below;
   He wakes or sleeps with the enduring dead;
   Thou canst not soar where he is sitting now. –
   Dust to the dust! but the pure spirit shall flow
   Back to the burning fountain whence it came,
   A portion of the Eternal, which must glow   340
   Through time and changes, unquenchably the same,
Whilst thy cold embers choke the sordid hearth of shame.

39

Peace, peace! he is not dead, he doth not sleep
He hath awakened from the dream of life –
'Tis we, who lost in stormy visions, keep
With phantoms an unprofitable strife,
And in mad trance, strike with our spirit's knife
Invulnerable nothings. – *We* decay
Like corpses in a charnel; fear and grief
Convulse us and consume us day by day,   350
And cold hopes swarm like worms within our living clay.

40

He has outsoared the shadow of our night;
Envy and calumny and hate and pain,
And that unrest which men miscall delight,
Can touch him not and torture not again;
From the contagion of the world's slow stain
He is secure, and now can never mourn
A heart grown cold, a head grown grey in vain;
Nor, when the spirit's self has ceased to burn,
With sparkless ashes load an unlamented urn.   360

41

He lives, he wakes – 'tis Death is dead, not he;
Mourn not for Adonais. – Thou young Dawn,
Turn all thy dew to splendour, for from thee
The spirit thou lamentest is not gone;
Ye caverns and ye forests, cease to moan!
Cease, ye faint flowers and fountains, and thou Air,
Which like a mourning veil thy scarf hadst thrown
O'er the abandoned Earth, now leave it bare
Even to the joyous stars which smile on its despair!

42

He is made one with Nature: there is heard   370
His voice in all her music, from the moan
Of thunder, to the song of night's sweet bird;
He is a presence to be felt and known
In darkness and in light, from herb and stone,

Spreading itself where'er that Power may move
Which has withdrawn his being to its own;
Which wields the world with never-wearied love,
Sustains it from beneath, and kindles it above.

43

He is a portion of the loveliness
Which once he made more lovely: he doth bear   380
His part, while the one Spirit's plastic stress
Sweeps through the dull dense world, compelling there,
All new successions to the forms they wear;
Torturing th' unwilling dross that checks its flight
To its own likeness, as each mass may bear;
And bursting in its beauty and its might
From trees and beasts and men into the Heaven's light.

44

The splendours of the firmament of time
May be eclipsed, but are extinguished not;
Like stars to their appointed height they climb   390
And death is a low mist which cannot blot
The brightness it may veil. When lofty thought
Lifts a young heart above its mortal lair,
And love and life contend in it, for what
Shall be its earthly doom, the dead live there
And move like winds of light on dark and stormy air.

45

The inheritors of unfulfilled renown
Rose from their thrones, built beyond mortal thought,
Far in the Unapparent. Chatterton[268]
Rose pale, his solemn agony had not   400
Yet faded from him; Sidney,[269] as he fought
And as he fell and as he lived and loved,
Sublimely mild, a Spirit without spot,
Arose; and Lucan,[270] by his death approved:
Oblivion as they rose shrank like a thing reproved.

46

And many more, whose names on Earth are dark
But whose transmitted effluence cannot die
So long as fire outlives the parent spark,
Rose, robed in dazzling immortality.
'Thou art become as one of us,' they cry,   410
'It was for thee yon kingless sphere has long
Swung blind in unascended majesty,
Silent alone amid a Heaven of Song.
Assume thy winged throne, thou Vesper of our throng!'

47

Who mourns for Adonais? Oh, come forth,
Fond wretch! and know thyself and him aright.
Clasp with thy panting soul the pendulous Earth;
As from a centre, dart thy spirit's light
Beyond all worlds, until its spacious might
Satiate the void circumference: then shrink   420
Even to a point within our day and night;
And keep thy heart light lest it make thee sink
When hope has kindled hope, and lured thee to the brink.

48

Or go to Rome, which is the sepulchre,
O, not of him, but of our joy: 'tis nought
That ages, empires, and religions there
Lie buried in the ravage they have wrought;
For such as he can lend, – they borrow not
Glory from those who made the world their prey;
And he is gathered to the kings of thought   430
Who waged contention with their time's decay,
And of the past are all that cannot pass away.

49

Go thou to Rome, – at once the Paradise,
The grave, the city, and the wilderness;
And where its wrecks like shattered mountains rise,
And flowering weeds, and fragrant copses dress
The bones of Desolation's nakedness

Pass, till the spirit of the spot shall lead
Thy footsteps to a slope of green access
Where, like an infant's smile, over the dead,   440
A light of laughing flowers along the grass is spread.

50

And grey walls[271] moulder round, on which dull Time
Feeds, like slow fire upon a hoary brand;
And one keen pyramid[272] with wedge sublime,
Pavilioning the dust of him who planned
This refuge for his memory, doth stand
Like flame transformed to marble; and beneath,
A field is spread, on which a newer band
Have pitched in Heaven's smile their camp of death,
Welcoming him we lose with scarce extinguished breath.   450

51

Here pause: these graves are all too young as yet
To have outgrown the sorrow which consigned
Its charge to each; and if the seal is set,
Here, on one fountain of a mourning mind,
Break it not thou! too surely shalt thou find
Thine own well full, if thou returnest home,
Of tears and gall. From the world's bitter wind
Seek shelter in the shadow of the tomb.
What Adonais is, why fear we to become?

52

The One remains, the many change and pass;   460
Heaven's light forever shines. Earth's shadows fly;
Life, like a dome of many-coloured glass,
Stains the white radiance of Eternity,
Until Death tramples it to fragments. – Die.
If thou wouldst be with that which thou dost seek!
Follow where all is fled! – Rome's azure sky,
Flowers, ruins, statues, music, words are weak
The glory they transfuse with fitting truth to speak.

53

Why linger, why turn back, why shrink, my Heart?
Thy hopes are gone before: from all things here   470
They have departed; thou shouldst now depart!
A light is past from the revolving year,
And man, and woman; and what still is dear
Attracts to crush, repels to make thee wither.
The soft sky smiles, – the low wind whispers near:
'Tis Adonais calls! oh, hasten thither,
No more let Life divide what Death can join together.

54

That Light whose smile kindles the Universe,
That Beauty in which all things work and move,
That Benediction which the eclipsing Curse   480
Of birth can quench not, that sustaining Love
Which through the web of being blindly wove
By man and beast and earth and air and sea
Burns bright or dim, as each are mirrors of
The fire for which all thirst, now beams on me,
Consuming the last clouds of cold mortality.

55

The breath whose might I have invoked in song
Descends on me; my spirit's bark is driven,
Far from the shore, far from the trembling throng
Whose sails were never to the tempest given;   490
The massy earth and sphered skies are riven!
I am borne darkly, fearfully, afar;
Whilst burning through the inmost veil of Heaven,
The soul of Adonais, like a star,
Beacons from the abode where the Eternal are.

Written on Hearing the News of the Death of Napoleon[273]

What! alive and so bold, O Earth?
  Art thou not overbold?
  What! leapest thou forth as of old
In the light of thy morning mirth,
The last of the flock of the starry fold?
Ha! leapest thou forth as of old?
Are not the limbs still when the ghost is fled,
And canst thou move, Napoleon being dead?

How! is not thy quick heart cold?
  What spark is alive on thy hearth?   10
How! is not *his* death-knell knolled?
  And livest *thou* still, Mother Earth?
Thou wert warming thy fingers old
O'er the embers covered and cold
Of that most fiery spirit, when it fled –
What, Mother, do you laugh now he is dead?

'Who has known me of old,' replied Earth,
  'Or who has my story told?
  It is thou who art overbold.'
And the lightning of scorn laughed forth   20
As she sung, 'To my bosom I fold
All my sons when their knell is knolled,
And so with living motion all are fed,
And the quick spring like weeds out of the dead.

'Still alive and still bold,' shouted Earth,
  'I grow bolder and still more bold.
  The dead fill me ten thousand fold
Fuller of speed, and splendour, and mirth,
I was cloudy, and sullen, and cold,
Like a frozen chaos uprolled,   30
Till by the spirit of the mighty dead
My heart grew warm. I feed on whom I fed.

'Aye, alive and still bold,' muttered Earth,
    'Napoleon's fierce spirit rolled,
    In terror and blood and gold,
A torrent of ruin to death from his birth.
Leave the millions who follow to mould
The metal before it be cold;
And weave into his shame, which like the dead
Shrouds me, the hopes that from his glory fled.'   40

To Night

1

Swiftly walk over the western wave,
        Spirit of Night!
Out of the misty eastern cave,
Where, all the long and lone daylight,
Thou wovest dreams of joy and fear,
Which make thee terrible and dear, –
        Swift be thy flight!

2

Wrap thy form in a mantle grey,
        Star-inwrought!
Blind with thine hair the eyes of day;   10
Kiss her until she be wearied out,
Then wander o'er city, and sea, and land,
Touching all with thine opiate wand –
        Come, long sought!

3

When I arose and saw the dawn,
        I sighed for thee;
When light rode high, and the dew was gone,
And noon lay heavy on flower and tree,
And the weary Day turned to his rest,
Lingering like an unloved guest,   20
        I sighed for thee.

4

Thy brother Death came, and cried,
        Wouldst thou me?
Thy sweet child Sleep, the filmy-eyed,
Murmured like a noontide bee,
Shall I nestle near thy side?
Wouldst thou me? – And I replied,
        No, not thee!

5

Death will come when thou art dead,
        Soon, too soon –   30
Sleep will come when thou art fled;
Of neither would I ask the boon
I ask thee, beloved Night –
Swift be thine approaching flight,
        Come soon, soon!

To —

One word is too often profaned
    For me to profane it,
One feeling too falsely disdained
    For thee to disdain it.
One hope is too like despair
    For prudence to smother,
And pity from thee more dear
    Than that from another.

I can give not what men call love,
    But wilt thou accept not   10
The worship the heart lifts above
    And the Heavens reject not,
The desire of the moth for the star
    Of the night for the morrow,
The devotion to something afar
    From the sphere of our sorrow?

To —

Music, when soft voices die,
Vibrates in the memory –
Odours, when sweet violets sicken,
Live within the sense they quicken.
Rose leaves, when the rose is dead,
Are heaped for the beloved's bed;
And so thy thoughts, when thou art gone,
Love itself shall slumber on.

Political Greatness[274]

Nor happiness, nor majesty, nor fame,
Nor peace, nor strength, nor skill in arms or arts,
Shepherd those herds whom tyranny makes tame;
Verse echoes not one beating of their hearts,
History is but the shadow of their shame,
Art veils her glass, or from the pageant starts
As to oblivion their blind millions fleet,
Staining that Heaven with obscene imagery
Of their own likeness. What are numbers knit
By force or custom? Man who man would be,   10
Must rule the empire of himself; in it
Must be supreme, establishing his throne
On vanquished will, quelling the anarchy
Of hopes and fears, being himself alone.

Evening: *Ponte al Mare, Pisa*

1

The sun is set: the swallows are asleep;
    The bats are flitting fast in the grey air;
The slow soft toads out of damp corners creep,
    And evening's breath, wandering here and there
Over the quivering surface of the stream,
Wakes not one ripple from its summer dream.

2

There is no dew on the dry grass tonight,
    Nor damp within the shadow of the trees;
The wind is intermitting, dry, and light;
    And in the inconstant motion of the breeze   10
The dust and straws are driven up and down,
And whirled about the pavement of the town.

3

Within the surface of the fleeting river
    The wrinkled image of the city lay,
Immovably unquiet, and for ever
    It trembles, but it never fades away;
Go to the . . .
You, being changed, will find it then as now.

4

The chasm in which the sun has sunk is shut
    By darkest barriers of cinereous cloud,   20
Like mountain over mountain huddled – but
    Growing and moving upwards in a crowd,
And over it a space of watery blue,
Which the keen evening star is shining through.

POEMS FROM 1822

Lines

1

When the lamp is shattered
The light in the dust lies dead –
   When the cloud is scattered
The rainbow's glory is shed.
   When the lute is broken,
Sweet tones are remembered not;
   When the lips have spoken,
Loved accents are soon forgot.

2

   As music and splendour
Survive not the lamp and the lute,   10
   The heart's echoes render
No song when the spirit is mute: –
   No song but sad dirges,
Like the wind through a ruined cell,
   Or the mournful surges
That ring the dead seaman's knell.

3

   When hearts have once mingled
Love first leaves the well-built nest;
   The weak one is singled
To endure what it once possest.   20
   O Love! who bewailest
The frailty of all things here,
   Why choose you the frailest
For your cradle, your home, and your bier?

4

   Its passions will rock thee
As the storms rock the ravens on high:
   Bright reason will mock thee,
Like the sun from a wìntry sky.

From thy nest every rafter
Will rot, and thine eagle home   30
    Leave thee naked to laughter,
When leaves fall and cold winds come.

To Jane: The Invitation

Best and brightest, come away!
Fairer far than this fair Day,
Which, like thee to those in sorrow,
Comes to bid a sweet good-morrow
To the rough Year just awake
In its cradle on the brake.

The brightest hour of unborn Spring,
Through the winter wandering,
Found, it seems, the halcyon Morn
To hoar February born;   10
Bending from Heaven, in azure mirth,
It kissed the forehead of the Earth,
And smiled upon the silent sea,
And bade the frozen streams be free,
And waked to music all their fountains,
And breathed upon the frozen mountains,
And like a prophetess of May
Strewed flowers upon the barren way,
Making the wintry world appear
Like one on whom thou smilest, dear.   20

Away, away, from men and towns,
To the wild wood and the downs –
To the silent wilderness
Where the soul need not repress
Its music lest it should not find
An echo in another's mind,
While the touch of Nature's art
Harmonises heart to heart.
I leave this notice on my door
For each accustomed visitor: –   30

'I am gone into the fields
To take what this sweet hour yields; –
Reflection, you may come tomorrow,
Sit by the fireside with Sorrow. –
You with the unpaid bill, Despair, –
You, tiresome verse-reciter, Care,–
I will pay you in the grave, –
Death will listen to your stave.
Expectation too, be off!
Today is for itself enough;   40
Hope, in pity mock not Woe
With smiles, nor follow where I go;
Long having lived on thy sweet food.
At length I find one moment's good
After long pain – with all your love,
This you never told me of.'

Radiant Sister of the Day,
Awake! arise! and come away!
To the wild woods and the plains,
And the pools where winter rains   50
Image all their roof of leaves,
Where the pine its garland weaves
Of sapless green and ivy dun
Round stems that never kiss the sun;
Where the lawns and pastures be,
And the sandhills of the sea; –
Where the melting hoar-frost wets
The daisy-star that never sets,
And wind-flowers, and violets,
Which yet join not scent to hue,   60
Crown the pale year weak and new;
When the night is left behind
In the deep east, dun and blind,
And the blue noon is over us,
And the multitudinous
Billows murmur at our feet,
Where the earth and ocean meet,
And all things seem only one
In the universal sun.

To Jane: The Recollection

1

Now the last day of many days,
　　All beautiful and bright as thou,
　　　　The loveliest and the last, is dead,
Rise, Memory, and write its praise!
　　Up to thy wonted work! come, trace
　　　　The epitaph of glory fled, –
For now the Earth has changed its face,
　　A frown is on the Heaven's brow.

2

We wandered to the Pine Forest
　　That skirts the Ocean's foam,   10
The lightest wind was in its nest,
　　The tempest in its home.
The whispering waves were half asleep,
　　The clouds were gone to play,
And on the bosom of the deep,
　　The smile of Heaven lay;
It seemed as if the hour were one
　　Sent from beyond the skies,
Which scattered from above the sun
　　A light of Paradise.   20

3

We paused amid the pines that stood
　　The giants of the waste,
Tortured by storms to shapes as rude
　　As serpents interlaced,
And soothed by every azure breath,
　　That under heaven is blown,
To harmonies and hues beneath,
　　As tender as its own;
Now all the treetops lay asleep,
　　Like green waves on the sea,   30
As still as in the silent deep
　　The ocean woods may be.

4

How calm it was! – the silence there
  By such a chain was bound
That even the busy woodpecker
  Made stiller by her sound
The inviolable quietness;
  The breath of peace we drew
With its soft motion made not less
  The calm that round us grew.   40
There seemed from the remotest seat
  Of the white mountain waste,
To the soft flower beneath our feet,
  A magic circle traced, –
A spirit interfused around,
  A thrilling silent life, –
To momentary peace it bound
  Our mortal nature's strife; –
And still I felt the centre of
  The magic circle there,   50
Was one fair form that filled with love
  The lifeless atmosphere.

5

We paused beside the pools that lie
  Under the forest bough,
Each seemed as 'twere a little sky
  Gulfed in a world below;
A firmament of purple light,
  Which in the dark earth lay,
More boundless than the depth of night,
  And purer than the day –   60
In which the lovely forests grew
  As in the upper air,
More perfect both in shape and hue
  Than any spreading there.
There lay the glade and neighbouring lawn,
  And through the dark green wood
The white sun twinkling like the dawn
  Out of a speckled cloud.
Sweet views, which in our world above

Can never well be seen,   70
Were imaged by the water's love
    Of that fair forest green.
And all was interfused beneath
    With an elysian glow,
An atmosphere without a breath,
    A softer day below.
Like one beloved the scene had lent
    To the dark water's breast,
Its every leaf and lineament
    With more than truth exprest;   80
Until an envious wind crept by,
    Like an unwelcome thought,
Which from the mind's too faithful eye
    Blots one dear image out.
Though thou art ever fair and kind,
    The forests ever green,
Less oft is peace in Shelley's mind,
    Than calm in waters seen.

With a Guitar, to Jane[275]

Ariel to Miranda[276] – Take
This slave of Music, for the sake
Of him who is the slave of thee,
And teach it all the harmony
In which thou canst, and only thou,
Make the delighted spirit glow,
Till joy denies itself again,
And, too intense, is turned to pain;
 For by permission and command
Of thine own Prince Ferdinand,   10
Poor Ariel sends this silent token
Of more than ever can be spoken;
Your guardian spirit, Ariel, who,
From life to life, must still pursue
Your happiness; – for thus alone
Can Ariel ever find his own.

From Prospero's enchanted cell,
As the mighty verses tell,
To the throne of Naples, he
Lit you o'er the trackless sea,   20
 Flitting on, your prow before,
Like a living meteor.
When you die, the silent Moon,
In her interlunar swoon,
Is not sadder in her cell
Than deserted Ariel.
When you live again on earth,
Like an unseen star of birth,
Ariel guides you o'er the sea
Of life from your nativity.   30
Many changes have been run,
Since Ferdinand and you begun
Your course of love, and Ariel still
Has tracked your steps, and served your will;
Now, in humbler, happier lot,
This is all remembered not;
And now, alas! the poor sprite is
Imprisoned, for some fault of his,
In a body like a grave; –
From you he only dares to crave,   40
For his service and his sorrow,
A smile today, a song tomorrow.

The artist who this idol wrought,
To echo all harmonious thought,
Felled a tree, while on the steep
The woods were in their winter sleep,
Rocked in that repose divine
On the windswept Apennine;
And dreaming, some of Autumn past,
And some of Spring approaching fast.   50
And some of April buds and showers,
And some of songs in July bowers,
And all of love; and so this tree, –
O that such our death may be! –
Died in sleep, and felt no pain,

To live in happier form again:
From which, beneath Heaven's fairest star,
The artist wrought this loved Guitar,
And taught it justly to reply,
To all who question skilfully,   60
In language gentle as thine own;
Whispering in enamoured tone
Sweet oracles of woods and dells,
And summer winds in sylvan cells;
For it had learnt all harmonies
Of the plains and of the skies,
Of the forests and the mountains,
And the many-voiced fountains;
The clearest echoes of the hills,
The softest notes of falling rills,   70
The melodies of birds and bees,
The murmuring of summer seas,
And pattering rain, and breathing dew,
And airs of evening; and it knew
That seldom-heard mysterious sound,
Which, driven on its diurnal round,
As it floats through boundless day,
Our world enkindles on its way –
All this it knows, but will not tell
To those who cannot question well   80
The spirit that inhabits it;
It talks according to the wit
Of its companions; and no more
Is heard than has been felt before,
By those who tempt it to betray
These secrets of an elder day:
But sweetly as its answers will
Flatter hands of perfect skill,
It keeps its highest, holiest tone
For our beloved Jane alone.   90

To Jane

1

The keen stars were twinkling,
And the fair moon was rising among them,
    Dear Jane!
    The guitar was tinkling,
But the notes were not sweet till you sung them
    Again.

2

    As the moon's soft splendour
O'er the faint cold starlight of Heaven
    Is thrown,
    So your voice most tender   10
To the strings without soul had then given
    Its own.

3

    The stars will awaken,
Though the moon sleep a full hour later,
    Tonight;
    No leaf will be shaken
Whilst the dews of your melody scatter
    Delight.

4

    Though the sound overpowers,
Sing again, with your dear voice revealing   20
    A tone
    Of some world far from ours,
Where music and moonlight and feeling
    Are one.

Lines written in the Bay of Lerici[277]

She left me at the silent time
When the moon had ceased to climb
The azure path of Heaven's steep,
And, like an albatross asleep,
Balanced on her wings of light,
Hovered in the purple night,
Ere she sought her ocean nest
In the chambers of the west.
She left me, and I stayed alone,
Thinking over every tone,   10
Which, though silent to the ear,
The enchanted heart could hear,
Like notes which die when born, but still
Haunt the echoes of the hill;
And feeling ever – O too much ! –
The soft vibration of her touch,
As if her gentle hand even now
Lightly trembled on my brow;
And thus, although she absent were,
Memory gave me all of her   20
That even Fancy dares to claim: –
Her presence had made weak and tame
All passions, and I lived alone
In the time which is our own;
The past and future were forgot,
As they had been, and would be, not.
But soon, the guardian angel gone,
The daemon reassumed his throne
In my faint heart. I dare not speak
My thoughts; but thus disturbed and weak   30
I sat, and saw the vessels glide
Over the ocean bright and wide,
Like spirit-winged chariots sent
O'er some serenest element
For ministrations strange and far;
As if to some Elysian star
Sailed for drink to medicine

Such sweet and bitter pain as mine.
And the wind that winged their flight
From the land came fresh and light;　　　　　　40
And the scent of winged flowers,
And the coolness of the hours
Of dew, and sweet warmth left by day,
Were scattered o'er the twinkling bay;
And the fisher, with his lamp
And spear, about the low rocks damp
Crept, and struck the fish which came
To worship the delusive flame.
Too happy they, whose pleasure sought
Extinguishes all sense and thought　　　　　　50
Of the regret that pleasure leaves,
Destroying life alone, not peace!

The Triumph of Life

Swift as a spirit hastening to his task
Of glory and of good, the Sun sprang forth
Rejoicing in his splendour, and the mask

Of darkness fell from the awakened Earth –
The smokeless altars of the mountain snows
Flamed above crimson clouds, and at the birth

Of light, the Ocean's orison arose,
To which the birds tempered their matin lay.
All flowers in field or forest which unclose

Their trembling eyelids to the kiss of day,　　　　　10
Swinging their censers in the element,
With orient incense lit by the new ray

Burned slow and inconsumably, and sent
Their odorous sighs up to the smiling air;
And, in succession due, did continent,

Isle, ocean, and all things that in them wear
The form and character of mortal mould,
Rise as the sun their father rose, to bear

Their portion of the toil, which he of old
Took as his own, and then imposed on them: 20
But I, whom thoughts which must remain untold

Had kept as wakeful as the stars that gem
The cone of night,[278] now they were laid asleep
Stretched my faint limbs beneath the hoary stem

Which an old chestnut flung athwart the steep
Of a green Apennine:[279] before me fled
The night; behind me rose the day; the deep

Was at my feet, and Heaven above my head,
When a strange trance over my fancy grew
Which was not slumber, for the shade it spread   30

Was so transparent, that the scene came through
As clear as when a veil of light is drawn
O'er evening hills they glimmer; and I knew

That I had felt the freshness of that dawn
Bathe in the same cold dew my brow and hair,
And sate as thus upon that slope of lawn

Under the selfsame bough, and heard as there
The birds, the fountains and the ocean hold
Sweet talk in music through the enamoured air,
And then a vision on my brain was rolled.   40

                    *   *   *

As in that trance of wondrous thought I lay,
This was the tenour of my waking dream: –
Methought I sate beside a public way

Thick strewn with summer dust, and a great stream
Of people there was hurrying to and fro,
Numerous as gnats upon the evening gleam,

All hastening onward, yet none seemed to know
Whither he went, or whence he came, or why
He made one of the multitude, and so

Was borne amid the crowd, as through the sky   50
One of the million leaves of summer's bier;
Old age and youth, manhood and infancy,

Mixed in one mighty torrent did appear,
Some flying from the thing they feared, and some
Seeking the object of another's fear;

And others as with steps towards the tomb,
Pored on the trodden worms that crawled beneath,
And others mournfully within the gloom

Of their own shadow walked and called it death;
And some fled from it as it were a ghost,   60
Half fainting in the affliction of vain breath:

But more, with motions which each other crost,
Pursued or shunned the shadows the clouds threw
Or birds within the noonday ether lost,

Upon that path where flowers never grew, –
And, weary with vain toil and faint for thirst,
Heard not the fountains, whose melodious dew

Out of their mossy cells for ever burst;
Nor felt the breeze which from the forest told
Of grassy paths and wood-lawns interspersed   70

With overarching elms and caverns cold,
And violet banks where sweet dreams brood, but they
Pursued their serious folly as of old.

And as I gazed, methought that in the way
The throng grew wilder, as the woods of June
When the south wind shakes the extinguished day,

And a cold glare, intenser than the noon,
But icy cold, obscured with blinding light
The sun, as he the stars. Like the young moon

When on the sunlit limits of the night   80
Her white shell trembles amid crimson air,
And whilst the sleeping tempest gathers might,

Doth, as the herald of its coming, bear
The ghost of its dead mother, whose dim form
Bends in dark ether from her infant's chair, –

So came a chariot on the silent storm
Of its own rushing splendour, and a Shape
So sate within, as one whom years deform,

Beneath a dusky hood and double cape,
Crouching within the shadow of a tomb;   90
And o'er what seemed the head a cloud-like crape

Was bent, a dun and faint ethereal gloom
Tempering the light. Upon the chariot beam
A Janus-visaged[280] Shadow did assume

The guidance of that wonder-winged team;
The shapes which drew it in thick light[e]nings
Were lost: – I heard alone on the air's soft stream

The music of their ever-moving wings.
All the four faces of that charioteer
Had their eyes banded; little profit brings   100

Speed in the van and blindness in the rear,
Nor then avail the beams that quench the sun
Or that with banded eyes could pierce the sphere

Of all that is, has been or will be done;
So ill was the car guided – but it past
With solemn speed majestically on.

The crowd gave way, and I arose aghast,
Or seemed to rise, so mighty was the trance,
And saw, like clouds upon the thunder blast,

The million with fierce song and maniac dance   110
Raging around – such seemed the jubilee
As when to greet some conqueror's advance

Imperial Rome[281] poured forth her living sea
From senate-house, and forum, and theatre,
When Freedom left those who upon the free

Had bound a yoke, which soon they stooped to bear.
Nor wanted here the just similitude
Of a triumphal pageant, for where'er

The chariot rolled, a captive multitude
Was driven; – all those who had grown old in power   120
Or misery, – all who had their age subdued

By action or by suffering, and whose hour
Was drained to its last sand in weal or woe,
So that the trunk survived both fruit and flower; –

All those whose fame or infamy must grow
Till the great winter lay the form and name
Of this green earth with them for ever low; –

All but the sacred few who could not tame
Their spirits to the conqueror – but as soon
As they had touched the world with living flame,   130

Fled back like eagles to their native noon,
Or those who put aside the diadem
Of earthly thrones or gems, till the last one

Were there; for they of Athens and Jerusalem[282]
Were neither mid the mighty captives seen,
Nor mid the ribald crowd that followed them,

Nor those who went before fierce and obscene.
The wild dance maddens in the van, and those
Who lead it – fleet as shadows on the green,

Outspeed the chariot, and without repose   140
Mix with each other in tempestuous measure
To savage music, wilder as it grows;

They, tortured by their agonising pleasure,
Convulsed and on the rapid whirlwinds spun
Of that fierce spirit, whose unholy leisure

Was soothed by mischief since the world begun,
Throw back their heads and loose their streaming hair;
And in their dance round her who dims the sun,

Maidens and youths fling their wild arms in air
As their feet twinkle; they recede, and now   150
Bending within each other's atmosphere

Kindle invisibly – and as they glow,
Like moths by light attracted and repelled,
Oft to their bright destruction come and go,

Till like two clouds into one vale impelled
That shake the mountains when their lightnings mingle
And die in rain – the fiery band which held

Their natures, snaps – while the shock still may tingle –
One falls and then another in the path
Senseless – nor is the desolation single,   160

Yet ere I can say *where* – the chariot hath
Past over them – nor other trace I find
But as of foam after the ocean's wrath

Is spent upon the desert shore; – behind,
Old men and women foully disarrayed,
Shake their gray hairs in the insulting wind,

And follow in the dance, with limbs decayed,
Seeking to reach the light which leaves them still
Farther behind and deeper in the shade.

But not the less with impotence of will   170
They wheel, though ghastly shadows interpose
Round them and round each other, and fulfil

Their work, and in the dust from whence they rose
Sink, and corruption veils them as they lie,
And frost in these performs what fire in those.

Struck to the heart by this sad pageantry.
Half to myself I said – And what is this?
Whose shape is that within the car? And why –

I would have added – is all here amiss? –
But a voice answered – 'Life!' – I turned, and knew   180
(O Heaven, have mercy on such wretchedness!)

That what I thought was an old root which grew
To strange distortion out of the hillside,
Was indeed one of those deluded crew,

And that the grass, which methought hung so wide
And white, was but his thin discoloured hair,
And that the holes it vainly sought to hide,

Were or had been eyes: 'If thou canst, forbear
To join the dance, which I had well forborne,'
Said the grim Feature,[283] of my thought aware,   190

'I will unfold that which to this deep scorn
Led me and my companions, and relate
The progress of the pageant since the morn;

'If thirst of knowledge shall not then abate,
Follow it thou even to the night, but I
Am weary.' – Then like one who with the weight

Of his own words is staggered, wearily
He paused; and ere he could resume, I cried:
'First, who art thou?' – 'Before thy memory,

'I feared, loved, hated, suffered, did and died,   200
And if the spark with which Heaven lit my spirit
Had been with purer nutriment supplied,

'Corruption would not now thus much inherit
Of what was once Rousseau, – nor this disguise
Stain that which ought to have disdained to wear it;

'If I have been extinguished, yet there rise
A thousand beacons from the spark I bore' –
'And who are those chained to the car?' – 'The wise,

'The great, the unforgotten, – they who wore
Mitres and helms and crowns, or wreaths of light,   210
Signs of thought's empire over thought – their lore

'Taught them not this, to know themselves; their might
Could not repress the mystery within,
And for the morn of truth they feigned, deep night

'Caught them ere evening.' – 'Who is he with chin
Upon his breast, and hands crost on his chain?' –
'The Child of a fierce hour;[284] he sought to win

'The world, and lost all that it did contain
Of greatness, in its hope destroyed; and more
Of fame and peace than virtue's self can gain   220

'Without the opportunity which bore
Him on its eagle pinions to the peak
From which a thousand climbers have before

'Fallen, as Napoleon fell' – I felt my cheek
Alter, to see the shadow pass away,
Whose grasp had left the giant world so weak,

That every pigmy kicked it as it lay;
And much I grieved to think how power and will
In opposition rule our mortal day,

And why God made irreconcilable   230
Good and the means of good; and for despair
I half disdained mine eyes' desire to fill

With the spent vision of the times that were
And scarce have ceased to be. – 'Dost thou behold,'
Said my guide, 'those spoilers spoiled, Voltaire,

'Frederick, and Paul, Catherine, and Leopold,[285]
And hoary anarchs, demagogues, and sage –
[. . .] names which the world thinks always old,

'For in the battle life and they did wage,
She remained conqueror. I was overcome   240
By my own heart alone, which neither age.

'Nor tears, nor infamy, nor now the tomb
Could temper to its object.' – 'Let them pass,'
I cried, 'the world and its mysterious doom

'Is not so much more glorious than it was,
That I desire to worship those who drew
New figures on its false and fragile glass

'As the old faded.' – 'Figures ever new
Rise on the bubble, paint them as you may;
We have but thrown as those before us threw,   250

'Our shadows on it as it past away.
But mark how chained to the triumphal chair
The mighty phantoms of an elder day;

'All that is mortal of great Plato[286] there
Expiates the joy and woe his master knew not;
The star that ruled his doom was far too fair,

'And life, where long that flower of Heaven grew not,
Conquered that heart by love, which gold, or pain,
Or age, or sloth, or slavery could subdue not.

'And near him walk the [. . .] twain,   260
The tutor and his pupil, whom Dominion
Followed as tame as vulture in a chain.

'The world was darkened beneath either pinion
Of him whom from the flock of conquerors
Fame singled out for her thunder-beating minion;

'The other long outlived both woes and wars,
Throned in the thoughts of men, and still had kept
The jealous key of truth's eternal doors,

'If Bacon's eagle spirit[287] had not leapt
Like lightning out of darkness – he compelled   270
The Proteus[288] shape of Nature as it slept

'To wake, and lead him to the caves that held
The treasure of the secrets of its reign.
See the great bards of elder time, who quelled

'The passions which they sung, as by their strain
May well be known: their living melody
Tempers its own contagion to the vein

'Of those who are infected with it – I
Have suffered what I wrote, or viler pain!
And so my words have seeds of misery –   280

'Even as the deeds of others, not as theirs.'
And then he pointed to a company,

'Midst whom I quickly recognised the heirs
Of Caesar's crime, from him to Constantine;[289]
The anarch chiefs, whose force and murderous snares

Had founded many a sceptre-bearing line,
And spread the plague of gold and blood abroad:
And Gregory and John,[290] and men divine,

Who rose like shadows between man and God;
Till that eclipse, still hanging over heaven,   290
Was worshipped by the world o'er which they strode,

For the true sun it quenched – 'Their power was given
But to destroy,' replied the leader: – 'I
Am one of those who have created, even

'If it be but a world of agony.' –
'Whence camest thou and whither goest thou?
How did thy course begin,' I said, 'and why?

'Mine eyes are sick of this perpetual flow
Of people, and my heart sick of one sad thought –
Speak!' – 'Whence I am! I partly seem to know,   300

'And how and by what paths I have been brought
To this dread pass, methinks even thou mayst guess; –
Why this should be, my mind can compass not;

'Whither the conqueror hurries me, still less; –
But follow thou, and from spectator turn
Actor or victim in this wretchedness,

'And what thou wouldst be taught I then may learn
From thee. Now listen: – In the April prime,
When all the forest tips began to burn

'With kindling green, touched by the azure clime   310
Of the young season, I was laid asleep
Under a mountain, which from unknown time

'Had yawned into a cavern, high and deep;
And from it came a gentle rivulet,
Whose water, like clear air, in its calm sweep

'Bent the soft grass, and kept for ever wet
The stems of the sweet flowers, and filled the grove
With sounds, which whoso hears must needs forget

'All pleasure and all pain, all hate and love,
Which they had known before that hour of rest;   320
A sleeping mother then would dream not of

'Her only child who died upon the breast
At eventide – a king would mourn no more
The crown of which his brows were dispossest

'When the sun lingered o'er his ocean floor,
To gild his rival's new prosperity.
Thou wouldst forget thus vainly to deplore

'Ills, which if ills can find no cure from thee,
The thought of which no other sleep will quell,
Nor other music blot from memory,   330

'So sweet and deep is the oblivious spell;
And whether life had been before that sleep
The heaven which I imagine, or a hell

'Like this harsh world in which I wake to weep,
I know not. I arose, and for a space
The scene of woods and waters seemed to keep,

'Though it was now broad day, a gentle trace
Of light diviner than the common sun
Sheds on the common earth, and all the place

'Was filled with magic sounds woven into one   340
Oblivious melody, confusing sense
Amid the gliding waves and shadows dun;

'And, as I looked, the bright omnipresence
Of morning through the orient cavern flowed,
And the sun's image radiantly intense

'Burned on the waters of the well that glowed
Like gold, and threaded all the forest's maze
With winding paths of emerald fire; there stood

'Amid the sun, as he amid the blaze
Of his own glory, on the vibrating   350
Floor of the fountain, paved with flashing rays,

'A Shape all light, which with one hand did fling
Dew on the earth, as if she were the dawn,
And the invisible rain did ever sing

'A silver music on the mossy lawn;
And still before me on the dusky grass,
Iris[291] her many-coloured scarf had drawn:

'In her right hand she bore a crystal glass,
Mantling with bright Nepenthe;[292] the fierce splendour
Fell from her as she moved under the mass   360

'Of the deep cavern, and with palms so tender,
Their tread broke not the mirror of its billow,
Glided along the river, and did bend her

'Head under the dark boughs, till like a willow
Her fair hair swept the bosom of the stream
That whispered with delight to be its pillow.

'As one enamoured is upborne in dream
O'er lily-paven lakes 'mid silver mist,
To wondrous music, so this shape might seem

'Partly to tread the waves with feet which kissed   370
The dancing foam; partly to glide along
The air which roughened the moist amethyst,

'Or the faint morning beams that fell among
The trees, or the soft shadows of the trees;
And her feet, ever to the ceaseless song

'Of leaves, and winds, and waves, and birds, and bees,
And falling drops, moved in a measure new
Yet sweet, as on the summer evening breeze,

'Up from the lake a shape of golden dew
Between two rocks, athwart the rising moon,   380
Dances i' the wind, where never eagle flew;

'And still her feet, no less than the sweet tune
To which they moved, seemed as they moved to blot
The thoughts of him who gazed on them; and soon

'All that was, seemed as if it had been not;
And all the gazer's mind was strewn beneath
Her feet like embers; and she, thought by thought,

'Trampled its sparks into the dust of death;
As day upon the threshold of the east
Treads out the lamps of night, until the breath   390

'Of darkness re-illumine even the least
Of heaven's living eyes – like day she came,
Making the night a dream and ere she ceased

'To move, as one between desire and shame
Suspended, I said – If, as it doth seem,
Thou comest from the realm without a name,

'Into this valley of perpetual dream,
Show whence I came, and where I am, and why –
Pass not away upon the passing stream.

' "Arise and quench thy thirst," was her reply.   400
And as a shut lily stricken by the wand
Of dewy morning's vital alchemy,

'I rose; and, bending at her sweet command,
Touched with faint lips the cup she raised,
And suddenly my brain became as sand

'Where the first wave had more than half erased
The track of deer on desert Labrador;
Whilst the wolf, from which they fled amazed,

'Leaves his stamp visibly upon the shore,
Until the second bursts; so on my sight   410
Burst a new vision, never seen before,

'And the fair shape waned in the coming light,
As veil by veil the silent splendour drops
From Lucifer,[293] amid the chrysolite

'Of sunrise, ere it tinge the mountain tops;
And as the presence of that fairest planet,
Although unseen, is felt by one who hopes

'That his day's path may end as he began it,
In that star's smile, whose light is like the scent
Of a jonquil when evening breezes fan it,   420

'Or the soft note in which his dear lament
The Brescian shepherd[294] breathes, or the caress
That turned his weary slumber to content;

'So knew I in that light's severe excess
The presence of that shape which on the stream
Moved, as I moved along the wilderness,

'More dimly than a day-appearing dream,
The ghost of a forgotten form of sleep;
A light of heaven, whose half-extinguished beam,

'Through the sick day in which we wake to weep,   430
Glimmers, for ever sought, for ever lost;
So did that shape its obscure tenour keep

'Beside my path, as silent as a ghost;
But the new Vision, and the cold bright car,
With solemn speed and stunning music, crost

'The forest, and as if from some dread war
Triumphantly returning, the loud million
Fiercely extolled the fortune of her star.

'A moving arch of victory, the vermilion
And green and azure plumes of Iris had   440
Built high over her wind-winged pavilion,

'And underneath ethereal glory clad
The wilderness, and far before her flew
The tempest of the splendour, which forbade

'Shadow to fall from leaf and stone; the crew
Seemed in that light, like atomies to dance
Within a sunbeam; – some upon the new

'Embroidery of flowers, that did enhance
The grassy vesture of the desert, played,
 Forgetful of the chariot's swift advance;   450

'Others stood gazing, till within the shade
Of the great mountain its light left them dim;
Others outspeeded it; and others made

'Circles around it, like the clouds that swim
Round the high moon in a bright sea of air;
And more did follow, with exulting hymn,

'The chariot and the captives fettered there: –
But all like bubbles on an eddying flood
Fell into the same track at last, and were

'Borne onward. I among the multitude   460
Was swept – me, sweetest flowers delayed not long;
Me, not the shadow nor the solitude;

'Me, not that falling stream's Lethean[295] song;
Me, not the phantom of that early Form
Which moved upon its motion – but among

'The thickest billows of that living storm
I plunged, and bared my bosom to the clime
Of that cold light, whose airs too soon deform.

'Before the chariot had begun to climb
The opposing steep of that mysterious dell,   470
Behold a wonder worthy of the rhyme

'Of him who from the lowest depths of hell,[296]
Through every paradise and through all glory,
Love led serene, and who returned to tell

'In words of hate and awe; the wondrous story
How all things are transfigured except Love;
For deaf as is a sea, which wrath makes hoary,

'The world can hear not the sweet notes that move
The sphere whose light is melody to lovers –
A wonder worthy of his rhyme – the grove   480

'Grew dense with shadows to its inmost covers,
The earth was grey with phantoms, and the air
Was peopled with dim forms, as when there hovers

'A flock of vampire-bats before the glare
Of the tropic sun, bringing, ere evening,
Strange night upon some Indian isle; – thus were

'Phantoms diffused around; and some did fling
Shadows of shadows, yet unlike themselves,
Behind them; some like eaglets on the wing

'Were lost in the white day; others like elves   490
Danced in a thousand unimagined shapes
Upon the sunny streams and grassy shelves;

'And others sate chattering like restless apes
On vulgar hands and voluble like fire;
Some made a cradle of the ermined capes

'Of kingly mantles; some across the tire
Of pontiffs sate like vultures; others played
Under the crown which girt with empire

'A baby's or an idiot's brow, and made
Their nests in it. The old anatomies   500
Sate hatching their bare broods under the shade

'Of demon wings, and laughed from their dead eyes
To reassume the delegated power,
Arrayed in which those worms did monarchise,

'Who made this earth their charnel. Others more
Humble, like falcons, sate upon the fist
Of common men, and round their heads did soar;

'Or like small gnats and flies, as thick as mist
On evening marshes, thronged about the brow
Of lawyers, statesmen, priest and theorist; –   510

'And others, like discoloured flakes of snow
On fairest bosoms and the sunniest hair,
Fell, and were melted by the youthful glow

'Which they extinguished; and, like tears, they were
A veil to those from whose faint lids they rained
In drops of sorrow. I became aware

'Of whence those forms proceeded which thus stained
The track in which we moved. After brief space,
From every form the beauty slowly waned;

'From every firmest limb and fairest face   520
The strength and freshness fell like dust, and left
The action and the shape without the grace

'Of life. The marble brow of youth was cleft
With care; and in those eyes where once hope shone,
Desire, like a lioness bereft

'Of her last cub, glared ere it died; each one
Of that great crowd sent forth incessantly
These shadows, numerous as the dead leaves blown

'In autumn evening from a poplar tree.
Each like himself and like each other were   530
At first; but some distorted seemed to be

'Obscure clouds, moulded by the casual air:
And of this stuff the car's creative ray
Wrought all the busy phantoms that were there,

'As the sun shapes the clouds: thus on the way
Mask after mask fell from the countenance
And form of all; and long before the day

'Was old, the joy which waked like heaven's glance
The sleepers in the oblivious valley, died;
And some grew weary of the ghastly dance.   540

'And fell, as I have fallen, by the wayside; –
Those soonest from whose forms most shadows past,
And least of strength and beauty did abide.

'Then, what is life?' I cried.

PROSE

Declaration of Rights

1

Government has no rights; it is a delegation from several individuals for the purpose of securing their own. It is therefore just, only so far as it exists by their consent, useful only so far as it operates to their well-being.

2

If these individuals think that the form of government which they, or their forefathers, constituted is ill adapted to produce their happiness, they have a right to change it.

3

Government is devised for the security of rights. The rights of man are liberty, and an equal participation of the commonage of nature.

4

As the benefit of the governed is, or ought to be, the origin of government, no men can have any authority that does not expressly emanate from their will.

5

Though all governments are not so had as that of Turkey, yet none are so good as they might be; the majority of every country have a right to perfect their government; the minority should not disturb them, they ought to secede, and form their own system in their own way.

6

All have a right to an equal share in the benefits, and burdens of Government. Any disabilities for opinion, imply by their existence, barefaced tyranny on the side of government, ignorant slavishness on the side of the governed.

7

The rights of man in the present state of society are only to be secured by some degree of coercion to be exercised on their violator. The sufferer has a right that the degree of coercion employed be as slight as possible.

8

It may be considered as a plain proof of the hollowness of any proposition, if power be used to enforce instead of reason to persuade its admission. Government is never supported by fraud until it cannot be supported by reason.

9

No man has a right to disturb the public peace by personally resisting the execution of a law however bad. He ought to acquiesce, using at the same time the utmost powers of his reason to promote its repeal.

10

A man must have a right to act in a certain manner before it can be his duty. He may, before he ought.

11

A man has a right to think as his reason directs, it is a duty he owes to himself to think with freedom, that he may act from conviction.

12

A man has a right to unrestricted liberty of discussion; falsehood is a scorpion that will sting itself to death.

13

A man has not only a right to express his thoughts but it is his duty to do so.

14

No law has a right to discourage the practice of truth. A man ought to speak the truth on every occasion, a duty can never be criminal, what is not criminal cannot be injurious.

15

Law cannot make what is in its nature virtuous or innocent to be criminal, any more than it can make what is criminal to be innocent. Government cannot make a law, it can only pronounce that which was the law before its organisation, viz. the moral result of the imperishable relations of things.

16

The present generation cannot bind their posterity. The few cannot promise for the many.

17

No man has a right to do an evil thing that good may come.

18

Expediency is inadmissible in morals. Politics are only sound when conducted on principles of morality. They are, in fact, the morals of nations.

19

Man has no right to kill his brother, it is no excuse that he does so in uniform. He only adds the infamy of servitude to the crime of murder.

20

Man, whatever be his country, has the same rights in one place as another, the rights of universal citizenship.

21

The government of a country ought to he perfectly indifferent to every opinion. Religious differences, the bloodiest and most rancorous of all, spring from partiality.

22

A delegation of individuals, for the purpose of securing their rights, can have no undelegated power of restraining the expression of their opinion.

23

Belief is involuntary; nothing involuntary is meritorious or reprehensible. A man ought not to be considered worse or better for his belief.

24

A Christian, a Deist, a Turk, and a Jew, have equal rights: they are men and brethren.

25

If a person's religious ideas correspond not with your own, love him nevertheless. How different would yours have been had the chance of birth placed you in Tartary or India!

26

Those who believe that Heaven is what earth has been, a monopoly in the hands of a favoured few, would do well to reconsider their opinion: if they find that it came from their priest or their grandmother, they could not do better than reject it.

27

No man has a right to be respected for any other possessions but those of virtue and talents. Titles are tinsel, power a corruptor, glory a bubble, and excessive wealth, a libel on its possessor.

28

No man has a right to monopolise more than he can enjoy; what the rich give to the poor, whilst millions are starving, is not a perfect favour, but an imperfect right.

29

Every man has a right to a certain degree of leisure and liberty, because it is his duty to attain a certain degree of knowledge. He may before he ought.

30

Sobriety of body and mind is necessary to those who would be free, because without sobriety a high sense of philanthropy cannot actuate the heart, nor cool and determined courage execute its dictates.

31

The only use of government is to repress the vices of man. If man were today sinless, tomorrow he would have a right to demand that government and all its evils should cease.

Man! thou whose rights are here declared, be no longer forgetful of the loftiness of thy destination. Think of thy rights; of those possessions which will give thee virtue and wisdom, by which thou mayest arrive at happiness and freedom. They are declared to thee by one who knows thy dignity, for every hour does his heart swell with honourable pride in the contemplation of what thou mayest attain, by one who is not forgetful of thy degeneracy, for every moment brings home to him the bitter conviction of what thou art.

Awake! – arise![297] *– or be for ever fallen.*

A Letter to Lord Ellenborough

ADVERTISEMENT

I have waited impatiently for these last four months in the hopes that some pen fitter for the important task would have spared me the perilous pleasure of becoming the champion of an innocent man. – This may serve as an excuse for delay, to those who think that I have let pass the aptest opportunity – but it is not to be supposed that in four short months the public indignation raised by Mr Eaton's unmerited suffering can have subsided.

LETTER

MY LORD,

As the station to which you have been called by your country is important, so much the more awful is your responsibility, so much the more does it become you to watch lest you inadvertently punish the virtuous and reward the vicious.

You preside over a court which is instituted for the suppression of crime, and to whose authority the people submit on no other conditions than that its decrees should be conformable to justice.

If it should be demonstrated that a judge had condemned an innocent man, the bare existence of laws in conformity to which the accused is punished would but little extenuate his offence. The inquisitor when he burns an obstinate heretic may set up a similar plea, yet few are sufficiently blinded by intolerance to acknowledge its validity. It will less avail such a judge to assert the policy of punishing one who has committed no crime. Policy and morality ought to be deemed synonymous in a court of justice, and he whose conduct has been regulated by the latter principle is not justly amenable to any penal law for a supposed violation of the former. It is true, my Lord, laws exist which suffice to screen you from the animadversion of any constituted power, in consequence of the unmerited sentence which you have passed upon Mr Eaton; but there are no laws which screen you from the reproof of a nation's disgust, none which ward off the just judgement of posterity, if that posterity will deign to recollect you.

By what right do you punish Mr Eaton? What but antiquated precedents, gathered from times of priestly and tyrannical domination, can be adduced in palliation of an outrage so insulting to humanity and justice? Whom has he injured? What crime has he committed? Wherefore may he not walk abroad like other men and follow his accustomed pursuits? What end is proposed in confining this man, charged with the commission of no dishonourable action? Wherefore did his aggressor avail himself of popular prejudice, and return no answer but one of commonplace contempt, to a defence of plain and simple sincerity? Lastly, when the prejudices of the jury, as Christians, were strongly and unfairly inflamed* against this injured man as a Deist, wherefore did not you, my Lord, check such unconstitutional pleading, and desire the jury to pronounce the accused innocent or criminal[†] without reference to the particular faith which he professed?

In the name of justice, what answer is there to these questions? The answer which heathen Athens made to Socrates is the same with which Christian England must attempt to silence the advocates of this injured man – 'He has questioned established opinions.' – Alas! the crime of enquiry is one which religion never has forgiven. Implicit faith and fearless enquiry have in all ages been irreconcilable enemies. Unrestrained philosophy has in every age opposed itself to the reveries of credulity and fanaticism. – The truths of astronomy demonstrated by Newton have superseded astrology; since the modern discoveries in chemistry the philosopher's stone has no longer been deemed attainable. Miracles of every kind have become rare, in proportion to the hidden principles which those who study nature have developed. That which is false will ultimately be controverted by its own falsehood. That which is true needs but publicity to be acknowledged. It is ever a proof that the falsehood of a proposition is felt by those who use power and coercion, not reasoning and persuasion, to procure its admission. – Falsehood skulks in holes and corners, 'it lets I dare not wait upon I would, like the poor cat in the adage',[‡] except when it has power, and then, as it was a coward, it is a tyrant; but the eagle-eye of truth darts thro' the undazzling sunbeam of the immutable and just, gathering thence wherewith to vivify and illuminate a universe!

Wherefore, I repeat, is Mr Eaton punished? – Because he is a Deist? – And what are you, my Lord? – A Christian. Ha then! the mask is fallen off; you persecute him because his faith differs from yours. You copy the persecutors of Christianity in your actions? and are an additional proof that your religion is as bloody, barbarous, and intolerant as theirs. – If some deistical bigot in power (supposing such a character for the sake of

---

* See the Attorney General's speech.
† By Mr Fox's bill (1791) juries are, in cases of libel, judges both of the law and the fact.
‡ Shakespeare

illustration) should in dark and barbarous ages have enacted a statute, making the profession of christianity criminal, if you my Lord were a christian bookseller and Mr Eaton a judge, those arguments which you consider adequate to justify yourself for the sentence which you have passed must likewise suffice in this suppositionary case to justify Mr Eaton in sentencing you to Newgate and the pillory for being a Christian. Whence is any right derived but that which power confers for persecution? Do you think to convert Mr Eaton to your religion by embittering his existence? You might force him by torture to profess your tenets, but he could not believe them, except you should make them credible, which perhaps exceeds your power. Do you think to please the God you worship by this exhibition of your zeal? If so, the Demon to whom some nations offer human hecatombs is less barbarous than the Deity of civilised society.

You consider man as an accountable being – but he can only be accountable for those actions which are influenced by his will.

Belief and disbelief are utterly distinct from and unconnected with volition. They are the apprehension of the agreement or disagreement of the ideas which compose any proposition. Belief is an involuntary operation of the mind, and, like other passions, its intensity is precisely proportionate to the degrees of excitement. – Volition is essential to merit or demerit. How then can merit or demerit be attached to what is distinct from that faculty of the mind whose presence is essential to their being? I am aware that religion is founded on the voluntariness of belief, as it makes it a subject of reward and punishment; but before we extinguish the steady ray of reason and common sense, it is fit that we should discover, which we cannot do without their assistance, whether or no there be any other which may suffice to guide us through the labyrinth of life.

If the law *de heretico comburendo*[298] has not been formally repealed, I conceive that from the promise held out by your Lordship's zeal, we need not despair of beholding the flames of persecution rekindled in Smithfield. Even now the lash that drove Descartes and Voltaire from their native country, the chains which bound Galileo, the flames which burned Vanini,[299] again resound: – And where? in a nation that presumptuously calls itself the sanctuary of freedom. Under a government which, whilst it infringes the very right of thought and speech, boasts of permitting the liberty of the press; in a civilised and enlightened country, a man is pilloried and imprisoned because he is a Deist, and no one raises his voice in the indignation of outraged humanity. Does the Christian God, whom his followers eulogise as the Deity of humility and peace; he, the regenerator of the world, the meek reformer, authorise one man to rise against another, and because lictors are at his beck, to chain and torture him as an Infidel?

When the Apostles went abroad to convert the nations, were they enjoined to stab and poison all who disbelieved the divinity of Christ's mission; assuredly they would have been no more justifiable in this case, than he is at present who puts into execution the law which inflicts pillory and imprisonment on the Deist.

Has not Mr Eaton an equal right to call your Lordship an Infidel, as you have to imprison him for promulgating a different doctrine from that which you profess? – What do I say! – Has he not even a stronger plea? – The word *Infidel* can only mean anything when applied to a person who professes that which he disbelieves. The test of truth is an undivided reliance on its inclusive powers; – the test of conscious falsehood is the variety of the forms under which it presents itself, and its tendency towards employing whatever coercive means may be within its command in order to procure the admission of what is unsusceptible of support from reason or persuasion. A dispassionate observer would feel himself more powerfully interested in favour of a man who, depending on the truth of his opinions, simply stated his reasons for entertaining them, than in that of his aggressor, who daringly avowing his unwillingness to answer them by argument, proceeded to repress the activity and break the spirit of their promulgator by that torture and imprisonment whose infliction he could command.

I hesitate not to affirm that the opinions which Mr Eaton sustained, when undergoing that mockery of a trial at which your Lordship presided, appear to me more true and good than those of his accuser; – but were they false as the visions of a Calvinist, it still would be the duty of those who love liberty and virtue to raise their voice indignantly against a reviving system of persecution, against the coercively repressing any opinion which, if false, needs but the opposition of truth; which if true, in spite of force, must ultimately prevail.

Mr Eaton asserted that the scriptures were, from beginning to end, a fable and imposture,* that the Apostles were liars and deceivers. He denied the miracles, resurrection, and ascension of Jesus Christ. – He did so, and the Attorney General denied the propositions which he asserted, and asserted those which he denied. What singular conclusion is deducible from this fact? None, but that the Attorney General and Mr Eaton sustained two opposite opinions. The Attorney General puts some obsolete and tyrannical laws in force against Mr Eaton, because he publishes a book tending to

---

* See the Attorney General's speech.

prove that certain supernatural events, which are supposed to have taken place eighteen centuries ago, in a remote corner of the world, did not actually take place. But how are the truth or falsehood of the facts in dispute relevant to the merit or demerit attachable to the advocates of the two opinions? No man is accountable for his belief, because no man is capable of directing it. Mr Eaton is therefore totally blameless. What are we to think of the justice of a sentence which punishes an individual against whom it is not even attempted to attach the slightest stain of criminality?

It is asserted that Mr Eaton's opinions are calculated to subvert morality – How? What moral truth is spoken of with irreverence or ridicule in the book which he published? Morality, or the duty of a man and a citizen, is founded on the relations which arise from the association of human beings, and which vary with the circumstances produced by the different states of this association. – This duty in similar situations must be precisely the same in all ages and nations. – The opinion contrary to this has arisen from a supposition that the will of God is the source or criterion of morality. It is plain that the utmost exertion of Omnipotence could not cause that to be virtuous which actually is vicious. An all powerful Demon might indubitably annex punishments to virtue and rewards to vice, but could not by these means effect the slightest change in their abstract and immutable natures. – Omnipotence could vary by a providential interposition the relations of human society; – in this latter case, what before was virtuous would become vicious, according to the necessary and natural result of the alteration; but the abstract natures of the opposite principles would have sustained not the slightest change; for instance, the punishment with which society restrains the robber, the assassin, and the ravisher is just, laudable, and requisite. We admire and respect the institutions which curb those who would defeat the ends for which society was established; – but, should a precisely similar coercion be exercised against one who merely expressed his disbelief of a system admitted by those entrusted with the executive power, using at the same time no methods of promulgation but those afforded by reason, certainly this coercion would be eminently inhuman and immoral; and the supposition that any revelation from an unknown power avails to palliate a persecution so senseless, unprovoked, and indefensible is at once to destroy the barrier which reason places between vice and virtue, and leave to unprincipled fanaticism a plea whereby it may excuse every act of frenzy which its own wild passions, not the inspirations of the Deity, have engendered.

Moral qualities are such as only a human being can possess. To attribute them to the Spirit of the Universe, or to suppose that it is capable of altering them, is to degrade God into man, and to annex to this incomprehensible being qualities incompatible with any *possible* definition of his nature. – It may here be objected – ought not the Creator to possess the perfections of the creature? No. To attribute to God the moral qualities of man is to suppose him susceptible of passions which, arising out of corporeal organisation, it is plain that a pure spirit cannot possess. A bear is not perfect except he is rough, a tiger is not perfect if he be not voracious, an elephant is not perfect if otherwise than docile. How *deep* an argument must that not be which proves that the Deity is as rough as a bear, as voracious as a tiger, and as docile as an elephant! But even suppose, with the vulgar, that God is a venerable old man, seated on a throne of clouds, his breast the theatre of various passions, analogous to those of humanity, his will changeable and uncertain as that of an earthly king, – still goodness and justice are qualities seldom nominally denied him, and it will be admitted that he disapproves of any action incompatible with these qualities. Persecution for opinion is unjust. With what consistency, then, can the worshippers of a Deity whose benevolence they boast, embitter the existence of their fellow being because his ideas of that Deity are different from those which they entertain. – Alas! there is no consistency in those persecutors who worship a benevolent Deity; those who worship a Demon would alone act consonantly to these principles, by imprisoning and torturing in his name.

Persecution is the only name applicable to punishment inflicted on an individual in consequence of his opinions. – What end is persecution designed to answer? Can it convince him whom it injures? Can it prove to the people the falsehood of his opinions? It may make him a hypocrite, and them cowards, but bad means can promote no good end. The unprejudiced mind looks with suspicion on a doctrine that needs the sustaining hand of power.

Socrates was poisoned because he dared to combat the degrading superstitions in which his countrymen were educated. Not long after his death, Athens recognised the injustice of his sentence; his accuser Melitus was condemned, and Socrates became a demigod.

Jesus Christ was crucified because he attempted to supersede the ritual of Moses with regulations more moral and humane – his very judge made public acknowledgment of his innocence, but a bigoted and ignorant mob demanded the deed of horror. Barabbas the murderer and traitor was released. The meek reformer Jesus was immolated to the sanguinary Deity of the Jews. Time rolled on, time changed the situations, and with them, the opinions of men.

The vulgar, ever in extremes, became persuaded that the crucifixion of Jesus was a supernatural event, and testimonies of miracles, so frequent in unenlightened ages, were not wanting to prove that he was something divine. This belief rolling through the lapse of ages, acquired force and extent, until the divinity of Jesus became a dogma, which to dispute was death, which to doubt was infamy.

Christianity is now the established religion; he who attempts to disprove it must behold murderers and traitors take precedence of him in public opinion, tho', if his genius be equal to his courage, and assisted by a peculiar coalition of circumstances, future ages may exalt him to a divinity, and persecute others in his name, as he was persecuted in the name of his predecessor, in the homage of the world.

The same means that have supported every other popular belief have supported Christianity. War, imprisonment, murder, and falsehood; deeds of unexampled and incomparable atrocity have made it what it is. We derive from our ancestors a belief thus fostered and supported. – We quarrel, persecute, and hate for its maintenance. – Does not analogy favour the opinion that as like other systems it has arisen and augmented, so like them it will decay and perish; that as violence and falsehood, not reasoning and persuasion, have procured its admission among mankind: so, when enthusiasm has subsided, and time, that infallible controverter of false opinions, has involved its pretended evidences in the darkness of antiquity, it will become obsolete, and that men will then laugh as heartily at grace, faith, redemption, and original sin, as they now do at the metamorphosis of Jupiter, the miracles of Romish Saints, the efficacy of witchcraft, and the appearance of departed spirits.

Had the Christian religion commenced and continued by the mere force of reasoning and persuasion, by its self-evident excellence and fitness, the preceding analogy would be inadmissible. We should never speculate upon the future obsoleteness of a system perfectly conformable to nature and reason. It would endure as long as they endured, it would be a truth as indisputable as the light of the sun, the criminality of murder, and other facts, physical and moral, which, depending on our organisation, and relative situations, must remain acknowledged so long as man is man. – It is an incontrovertible fact, the consideration of which ought to repress the hasty conclusions of credulity, or moderate its obstinacy in maintaining them, that had the Jews not been a barbarous and fanatical race of men, had even the resolution of Pontius Pilate been equal to his candour, the Christian religion never could have prevailed, it could not even have existed. Man! the very existence of whose most cherished opinions depends from a thread so feeble, arises out of a source so equivocal, learn at least humility; own at least that it is possible for thyself also to have been seduced by education and circumstance into the admission of tenets destitute of rational proof, and the truth of which has not yet been satisfactorily demonstrated. Acknowledge at least that the falsehood of thy brother's opinions is no sufficient reason for his meriting thy hatred. – What! because a fellow being disputes the reasonableness of thy faith, wilt thou punish him with torture and imprisonment? If persecution for religious opinions were admitted by the moralist, how wide a door would not be opened by which convulsionists of every kind might make inroads on the peace of society! How many deeds of barbarism and blood would not receive a sanction! – But I will demand if that man is not rather entitled to the respect than the discountenance of society who, by disputing a received doctrine, either proves its falsehood and inutility, thereby aiming at the abolition of what is false and useless, or giving to its adherents an opportunity of establishing its excellence and truth. – Surely this can be no crime. Surely the individual who devotes his time to fearless and unrestricted enquiry into the grand questions arising out of our moral nature, ought rather to receive the patronage, than encounter the vengeance, of an enlightened legislature. I would have you to know, my Lord, that fetters of iron cannot bind or subdue the soul of virtue. From the damps and solitude of its dungeon it ascends free and undaunted, whither thine, from the pompous seat of judgement, dare not soar. I do not warn you to beware lest your profession as a Christian should make you forget that you are a man; – but I warn you against festinating that period which, under the present coercive system, is too rapidly maturing, when the seats of justice shall be the seats of venality and slavishness, and the cells of Newgate become the abode of all that is honourable and true.

I mean not to compare Mr Eaton with Socrates or Jesus; he is a man of blameless and respectable character, he is a citizen unimpeached with crime; if, therefore, his rights as a citizen and a man have been infringed, they have been infringed by illegal and immoral violence. But I will assert that should a second Jesus arise among men; should such a one as Socrates again enlighten the earth, lengthened imprisonment and infamous punishment (according to the regimen of persecution revived by your Lordship) would effect what hemlock and the cross have heretofore effected, and the stain on the national character, like that on Athens and Judea, would remain indelible, but by the destruction of the history in which it is recorded. When the Christian Religion shall have faded from the earth, when its memory like that of Polytheism now shall remain, but remain only as the subject of ridicule and wonder, indignant posterity would attach immortal infamy to such an outrage; like the murder of Socrates, it would secure the execration of every age.

The horrible and wide wasting enormities which gleam like comets thro' the darkness of gothic and superstitious ages are regarded by the moralist as no more than the necessary effects of known causes; but when an enlightened age and nation signalises itself by a deed, becoming none but barbarians and fanatics, Philosophy itself is even induced to doubt whether human nature will ever emerge from the pettishness and imbecility of its childhood. The system of persecution at whose new birth, you, my Lord, are one of the presiding midwives, is not more impotent and wicked than inconsistent. The press is loaded with what are called (ironically I should conceive) *proofs* of the Christian Religion: these books are replete with invective and calumny against Infidels, they presuppose that he who rejects Christianity must be utterly divested of reason and feeling. They advance the most unsupported assertions and take as first principles the most revolting dogmas. The inferences drawn from these assumed premises are imposingly logical and correct; but if a foundation is weak, no architect is needed to foretell the instability of the superstructure. – If the truth of Christianity is not disputable, for what purpose are these books written? If they are sufficient to prove it, what further need of controversy? *If God has spoken, why is not the universe convinced?*[300] If the Christian Religion needs deeper learning, more painful investigation, to establish its genuineness, wherefore attempt to accomplish that by force which the human mind can alone effect with satisfaction to itself? If, lastly, its truth *cannot* be demonstrated, wherefore impotently attempt to snatch from God the government of his creation, and impiously assert that the Spirit of Benevolence has left that knowledge most essential to the well being of man, the only one which, since its promulgation, has been the subject of unceasing cavil, the cause of irreconcilable hatred? – Either the Christian Religion is true, or it is not. If true, it comes from God, and its authenticity can admit of doubt and dispute no further than its Omnipotent Author is willing to allow; – if true, it admits of rational proof, and is capable of being placed equally beyond controversy, as the principles which have been established concerning matter and mind by Locke and Newton; and in proportion to the usefulness of the fact in dispute, so must it be supposed that a benevolent being is anxious to procure the diffusion of its knowledge on the earth. – If false, surely no enlightened legislature would punish the reasoner who opposes a system so much the more fatal and pernicious as it is extensively admitted; so much the more productive of absurd and ruinous consequences, as it is entwined by education, with the prejudices and affections of the human heart, in the shape of a popular belief.

Let us suppose that some half-witted philosopher should assert that the earth was the centre of the universe, or that ideas could enter the human mind independently of sensation or reflection. This man would assert what is demonstrably incorrect; – he would promulgate a false opinion. Yet would he therefore deserve pillory and imprisonment? By no means; probably few would discharge more correctly the duties of a citizen and a man. I admit that the case above stated is not precisely in point. The thinking part of the community has not received as indisputable the truth of Christianity as they have that of the Newtonian system. A very large portion of society, and that powerfully and extensively connected, derives its sole emolument from the belief of Christianity, as a popular faith.

To torture and imprison the asserter of a dogma, however ridiculous and false, is highly barbarous and impolitic: – how then, does not the cruelty of persecution become aggravated when it is directed against the opposer of an opinion *yet under dispute* and which men of unrivalled acquirements, penetrating genius, and stainless virtue, have spent, and at last sacrificed, their lives in combating.

The time is rapidly approaching – I hope, that you, my Lord, may live to behold its arrival – when the Mahometan, the Jew, the Christian, the Deist, and the Atheist will live together in one community, equally sharing the benefits which arise from its association, and united in the bonds of charity and brotherly love. —My Lord, you have condemned an innocent man, – no crime was imputed to him – and you sentenced him to torture and imprisonment. I have not addressed this letter to you with the hopes of convincing you that you have acted wrong. The most unprincipled and barbarous of men are not unprepared with sophisms to prove that they would have acted in no other manner, and to show that vice is virtue. But I raise my solitary voice, to express my disapprobation, so far as it goes, of the cruel and unjust sentence you passed upon Mr Eaton; to assert, so far as I am capable of influencing, those rights of humanity, which you have wantonly and unlawfully infringed.

My Lord,

Yours, etc.

A Vindication of Natural Diet

I hold that the depravity of the physical and moral nature of man originated in his unnatural habits of life. The origin of man, like that of the universe of which he is a part, is enveloped in impenetrable mystery. His generations either had a beginning, or they had not. The weight of evidence in favour of each of these suppositions seems tolerably equal; and it is perfectly unimportant to the present argument which is assumed. The language spoken however by the mythology of nearly all religions seems to prove that at some distant period man forsook the path of nature, and sacrificed the purity and happiness of his being to unnatural appetites. The date of this event seems to have also been that of some great change in the climates of the earth, with which it has an obvious correspondence. The allegory of Adam and Eve eating of the tree of evil, and entailing upon their posterity the wrath of God, and the loss of everlasting life, admits of no other explanation than the disease and crime that have flowed from unnatural diet. Milton was so well aware of this, that he makes Raphael thus exhibit to Adam the consequence of his disobedience:

> – Immediately a place,
> Before his eyes appeared; sad, noisome, dark:
> A lazar-house it seem'd; wherein were laid
> Numbers of all diseased: all maladies
> Of ghastly spasms or racking torture, qualms
> Of heartsick agony, all feverous kinds,
> Convulsions, epilepsies, fierce catarrhs,
> Intestine stone and ulcer, cholic pangs,
> Demoniac frenzy, moping melancholy,
> And moonstruck madness, pining atrophy,
> Marasmus, and wide-wasting pestilence,
> Dropsies, and asthmas, and joint-racking rheums.[301]

– And how many thousands more might not be added to this frightful catalogue!

The story of Prometheus is one likewise which, although universally admitted to be allegorical, has never been satisfactorily explained. Prometheus stole fire from heaven, and was chained for this crime to Mount Caucasus, where a vulture continually devoured his liver, that grew to meet its hunger. – Hesiod says, that before the time of Prometheus, mankind were exempt from suffering; that they enjoyed a vigorous youth, and that death, when at length it came, approached like sleep, and gently closed their eyes. – Again, so general was this opinion, that Horace,[302] a poet of the Augustan age, writes

> Audax omnia perpeti,
> Gens humana ruit per vetitum nefas,
>   Audax Iapeti genus,
> Ignem fraude mala gentibus intulit,
>   Post ignem aetherea domo,
> Subductum, macies et nova febrium.
>   Terris incubuit cohors
> Semotiq prius tarda necessitas,
>   Lethi corripuit gradum –

How plain a language is spoken by all this. – Prometheus (who represents the human race) effected some great change in the condition of his nature, and applied fire to culinary purposes; thus inventing an expedient for screening from his disgust the horrors of the shambles. From this moment his vitals were devoured by the vulture of disease. It consumed his being in every shape of its loathsome and infinite variety, inducing the soul-quelling sinkings of premature and violent death. All vice arose from the ruin of healthful innocence. Tyranny, superstition, commerce and inequality were then first known, when reason vainly attempted to guide the wanderings of exacerbated passion. I conclude this part of the subject with an extract from Mr Newton's *Defence of Vegetable Regimen*, from whom I have borrowed this interpretation of the fable of Prometheus.

'Making allowance for such transposition of the events of the allegory, as time might produce after the important truths were forgotten, which the portion of the ancient mythology was intended to transmit, the drift of the fable seems to be this: Man at his creation was endowed with the gift of perpetual youth: that is, he was not formed to be a sickly suffering creature as we now see him, but to enjoy health, and to sink by slow degrees into the bosom of his parent earth without disease or pain. Prometheus first taught the use of animal food (primus bovem occidit Prometheus)* and of fire, with which to render it more digestible and pleasing to the taste. Jupiter, and the rest of the gods, foreseeing the consequences of the inventions, were amused or irritated at the short-sighted devices of the newly-formed creature, and left him to experience the sad effects of them.

* Pliny, *Nat. Hist.*, Lib.vii, section 57

Thirst, the necessary concomitant of a flesh diet [perhaps of all diet vitiated by culinary preparation], ensued; water was resorted to, and man forfeited the inestimable gift of health which he had received from heaven: he became diseased, the partaker of a precarious existence, and no longer descended slowly to his grave.'

> But just disease to luxury succeeds,
> And every death its own avenger breeds;
> The fury passions from that blood began,
> And turn'd on man a fiercer savage – Man.[303]

Man, and the animals whom he has infected with his society, or depraved by his dominion, are alone diseased. The wild hog, the mouflon, the bison, and the wolf, are perfectly exempt from malady, and invariably die either from external violence, or natural old age. But the domestic hog, the sheep, the cow, and the dog, are subject to an incredible variety of distempers; and, like the corrupters of their nature, have physicians who thrive upon their miseries. The supereminence of man is like Satan's, a supereminence of pain; and the majority of his species, doomed to penury, disease, and crime, have reason to curse the untoward event that, by enabling him to communicate his sensations, raised him above the level of his fellow animals. But the steps that have been taken are irrevocable. The whole of human science is comprised in one question: – How can the advantages of intellect and civilisation, be reconciled with the liberty and pure pleasures of natural life? How can we take the benefits and reject the evils of the system which is now interwoven with all the fibres of our being? – I believe that abstinence from animal food and spirituous liquors would in a great measure capacitate us for the solution of this important question.

Comparative anatomy teaches us that man resembles frugivorous animals in everything, and carnivorous in nothing; he has neither claws wherewith to seize his prey, nor distinct and pointed teeth to tear the living fibre. A Mandarin of the first class, with nails two inches long, would probably find them alone inefficient to hold even a hare. After every subterfuge of gluttony, the bull must be degraded into the ox, and the ram into the wether, by an unnatural and inhuman operation, that the flaccid fibre may offer a fainter resistance to rebellious nature. It is only by softening and disguising dead flesh by culinary preparation that it is rendered susceptible of mastication or digestion, and that the sight of its bloody juices and raw horror does not excite intolerable loathing and disgust. Let the advocate of animal food force himself to a decisive experiment on its fitness, and as Plutarch recommends, tear a living lamb with his teeth, and plunging his head into its vitals, slake his thirst with the steaming blood; when fresh from the deed of horror let him revert to the irresistible instincts of nature that would rise in judgement against it, and say, Nature formed me for such work as this. Then, and then only, would he be consistent.

Man resembles no carnivorous animal. There is no exception, except man be one, to the rule of herbivorous animals having cellulated colons.

The orang-outang perfectly resembles man both in the order and number of his teeth. The orang-outang is the most anthropomorphous of the ape tribe, all of which are strictly frugivorous. There is no other species of animals in which this analogy exists.* In many frugivorous animals, the canine teeth are more pointed and distinct than those of man. The resemblance also of the human stomach to that of the orang-outang is greater than to that of any other animal.

The intestines are also identical with those of herbivorous animals, which present a larger surface for absorption, and have ample and cellulated colons. The coecum also, though short, is larger than that of carnivorous animals; and even here the orang-outang retains its accustomed similarity. The structure of the human frame then is that of one fitted to a pure vegetable diet, in every essential particular. It is true, that the reluctance to abstain from animal food, in those who have been long accustomed to its stimulus, is so great in some persons of weak minds, as to be scarcely overcome; but this is far from bringing any argument in its favour. – A lamb, which was fed for some time on flesh by a ship's crew, refused its natural diet at the end of the voyage. There are numerous instances of horses, sheep, oxen, and even wood-pigeons, having been taught to live upon flesh, until they have loathed their accustomed aliment. Young children evidently prefer pastry, oranges, apples, and other fruit, to the flesh of animals; until, by the gradual depravation of the digestive organs, the free use of vegetables has for a time produced serious inconveniences; *for a time,* I say, since there never was an instance wherein a change from spirituous liquors and animal food, to vegetables and pure water, has failed ultimately to invigorate the body, by rendering its juices bland and consentaneous, and to restore to the mind that cheerfulness and elasticity which not one in fifty possess on the present system. A love of strong liquors is also with difficulty taught to infants. Almost everyone remembers the wry faces which the first glass of port produced. Unsophisticated instinct is invariably unerring; but to decide on the fitness of animal food,

---

* Cuvier, *Leçons d'Anat. Comp.*, tom. iii, pp. 169, 373, 448, 465, 480. Ree's *Cyclopaedia*, article Man.

from the perverted appetites which its constrained adoption produces, is to make the criminal a judge in his own cause: – it is even worse, it is appealing to the infatuated drunkard in a question of the salubrity of brandy.

What is the cause of morbid action in the animal system? Not the air we breathe, for our fellow denizens of nature breathe the same uninjured; not the water we drink (if remote from the pollutions of man and his inventions),* for the animals drink it too; not the earth we tread upon; not the unobscured sight of glorious nature, in the wood, the field, or the expanse of sky and ocean; nothing that we are or do in common with the undiseased inhabitants of the forest. Something then wherein we differ from them: our habit of altering our food by fire, so that our appetite is no longer a just criterion for the fitness of its gratification. Except in children, there remain no traces of that instinct which determines in all other animals what aliment is natural or otherwise, and so perfectly obliterated are they in the reasoning adults of our species, that it has become necessary to urge considerations drawn from comparative anatomy to prove that we are naturally frugivorous.

Crime is madness. Madness is disease. Whenever the cause of disease shall be discovered, the root from which all vice and misery have so long overshadowed the globe will lie bare to the axe. All the exertions of man from that moment may be considered as tending to the clear profit of his species. No sane mind in a sane body resolves upon a real crime. It is a man of violent passions, bloodshot eyes, and swollen veins, that alone can grasp the knife of murder. The system of a simple diet promises no Utopian advantages. It is no mere reform of legislation, whilst the furious passions and evil propensities of the human heart, in which it had its origin, are still unassuaged. It strikes at the root of all evil, and is an experiment which may be tried with success, not alone by nations, but by small societies, families, and even individuals. In no cases has a return to vegetable diet produced the slightest injury; in most it has been attended with changes undeniably beneficial. Should ever a physician be born with the genius of Locke, I am persuaded that he might trace all bodily and mental derangements to our unnatural habits, as clearly as that philosopher has traced all knowledge to sensation. What prolific sources of disease are not

---

* The necessity of resorting to some means of purifying water, and the disease which arises from its adulteration in civilised countries, is sufficiently apparent – see Dr Lambe's Reports on Cancer. I do not assert that the use of water is in itself unnatural, but that the unperverted palate would swallow no liquid capable of occasioning disease.

those mineral and vegetable poisons that have been introduced for its extirpation! How many thousands have become murderers and robbers, bigots and domestic tyrants, dissolute and abandoned adventurers, from the use of fermented liquors; who, had they slaked their thirst only at the mountain stream, would have lived but to diffuse the happiness of their own unperverted feelings. How many groundless opinions and absurd institutions have not received a general sanction from the sottishness and intemperance of individuals! Who will assert that had the populace of Paris drank at the pure source of the Seine, and satisfied their hunger at the ever-furnished table of vegetable nature, they would have lent their brutal suffrage to the proscription list of Robespierre? Could a set of men, whose passions were not perverted by unnatural stimuli, look with coolness on an *auto-da-fé*?[304] Is it to be believed that a being of gentle feelings, rising from his meal of roots, would take delight in sports of blood ? Was Nero a man of temperate life? could you read calm health in his cheek, flushed with ungovernable propensities of hatred for the human race? Did Muley Ismael's[305] pulse beat evenly, was his skin transparent, did his eyes beam with healthfulness, and its invariable concomitants cheerfulness and benignity? Though history has decided none of these questions, a child could not hesitate to answer in the negative. Surely the bile-suffused cheek of Bonaparte, his wrinkled brow, and yellow eye, the ceaseless inquietude of his nervous system, speak no less plainly the character of his unresting ambition than his murders and his victories. It is impossible that had Bonaparte descended from a race of vegetable feeders, he could have had either the inclination or the power to ascend the throne of the Bourbons. The desire of tyranny could scarcely be excited in the individual, the power to tyrannise would certainly not be delegated by a society, neither frenzied by inebriation, nor rendered impotent and irrational by disease. Pregnant indeed with inexhaustible calamity is the renunciation of instinct, as it concerns our physical nature; arithmetic cannot enumerate, nor reason perhaps suspect, the multitudinous sources of disease in civilised life. Even common water, that apparently innoxious pabulum, when corrupted by the filth of populous cities is a deadly and insidious destroyer.* Who can wonder that all the inducements held out by God himself in the Bible to virtue should have been vainer than a nurse's tale; and that those dogmas apparently favourable to the intolerant and angry passions should have alone been deemed essential whilst Christians are in the daily practice of all those habits which have infected with disease and crime, not only the

* Lambe's Reports on Cancer

reprobate sons, but these favoured children of the common Father's love? Omnipotence itself could not save them from the consequences of this original and universal sin.

There is no disease, bodily or mental, which adoption of vegetable diet and pure water has not infallibly mitigated, wherever the experiment has been fairly tried. Debility is gradually converted into strength, disease into healthfulness; madness in all its hideous variety, from the ravings of the fettered maniac, to the unaccountable irrationalities of ill temper, that make a hell of domestic life, into a calm and considerate evenness of temper, that alone might offer a certain pledge of the future moral reformation of society. On a natural system of diet, old age would be our last and our only malady; the term of our existence would be protracted; we should enjoy life and no longer preclude others from the enjoyment of it. All sensational delights would be infinitely more exquisite and perfect. The very sense of being would then be a continued pleasure, such as we now feel it in some few and favoured moments of youth. By all that is sacred in our hopes for the human race, I conjure those who love happiness and truth to give a fair trial to the vegetable system. Reasoning is surely superfluous on a subject whose merits an experience of six months would set for ever at rest. But it is only among the enlightened and benevolent that so great a sacrifice of appetite and prejudice can be expected, even though its ultimate excellence should not admit of dispute. It is found easier, by the short-sighted victims of disease, to palliate their torments by medicine than to prevent them by regimen. The vulgar of all ranks are invariably sensual and indocile; yet I cannot but feel myself persuaded that when the benefits of vegetable diet are mathematically proved; when it is as clear that those who live naturally are exempt from premature death as that nine is not one, the most sottish of mankind will feel a preference towards a long and tranquil, contrasted with a short and painful, life. On the average, out of sixty persons, four die in three years. In April 1814, a statement will be given that sixty persons, all having lived more than three years on vegetables and pure water, are then *in perfect health*. More than two years have now elapsed; *not one of them has died*; no such example will be found in any sixty persons taken at random. Seventeen persons of all ages (the families of Dr Lambe and Mr Newton) have lived for seven years on this diet, without a death and almost without the slightest illness. Surely when we consider that some of these were infants, and one a martyr to asthma now nearly subdued, we may challenge any seventeen persons taken at random in this city to exhibit a parallel case. Those who may have been excited to question the rectitude of established habits of diet by these loose remarks should consult Mr Newton's luminous and eloquent essay.* It is from that book, and from the conversation of its excellent and enlightened author, that I have derived the materials which I here present to the public.

When these proofs come fairly before the world, and are clearly seen by all who understand arithmetic, it is scarcely possible that abstinence from aliments demonstrably pernicious should not become universal. In proportion to the number of proselytes, so will be the weight of evidence, and when a thousand persons can be produced living on vegetables and distilled water, who have to dread no disease but old age, the world will be compelled to regard animal flesh and fermented liquors as slow but certain poisons. The change which would be produced by simpler habits on political economy is sufficiently remarkable. The monopolising eater of animal flesh would no longer destroy his constitution by devouring an acre at a meal, and many loaves of bread would cease to contribute to gout, madness and apoplexy, in the shape of a pint of porter, or a dram of gin, when appeasing the long-protracted famine of the hard-working peasant's hungry babes. The quantity of nutritious vegetable matter consumed in fattening the carcase of an ox would afford ten times the sustenance, undepraving indeed, and incapable of generating disease, if gathered immediately from the bosom of the earth. The most fertile districts of the habitable globe are now actually cultivated by men for animals, at a delay and waste of aliment absolutely incapable of calculation. It is only the wealthy that can, to any great degree, even now, indulge the unnatural craving for dead flesh, and they pay for the greater licence of the privilege by subjection to supernumerary diseases. Again, the spirit of the nation that should take the lead in this great reform would insensibly become agricultural; commerce, with all its vices, selfishness and corruption, would gradually decline; more natural habits would produce gentler manners, and the excessive complication of political relations would be so far simplified that every individual might feel and understand why he loved his country and took a personal interest in its welfare. How would England, for example, depend on the caprices of foreign rulers if she contained within herself all the necessaries, and despised whatever they possessed of the luxuries of life? How could they starve her into compliance with their views? Of what consequence would it be that they refused to take her woollen manufactures, when large and fertile tracts of the island ceased to be allotted to the waste of pasturage? On a natural system of diet, we should require no spices from India; no wines from Portugal, Spain, France,

* _Return to Nature, or Defence of Vegetable Regimen_, Cadell, 1811

or Madeira; none of those multitudinous articles of luxury, for which every corner of the globe is rifled, and which are the causes of so much individual rivalship, such calamitous and sanguinary national disputes. In the history of modern times, the avarice of commercial monopoly, no less than the ambition of weak and wicked chiefs, seems to have fomented the universal discord, to have added stubbornness to the mistakes of cabinets, and indocility to the infatuation of the people. Let it ever be remembered that it is the direct influence of commerce to make the interval between the richest and the poorest man wider and more unconquerable. Let it be remembered that it is a foe to everything of real worth and excellence in the human character. The odious and disgusting aristocracy of wealth is built upon the ruins of all that is good in chivalry or republicanism; and luxury is the forerunner of a barbarism scarce capable of cure. Is it impossible to realise a state of society where all the energies of man shall be directed to the production of his solid happiness? Certainly if this advantage (the object of all political speculation) be in any degree attainable, it is attainable only by a community which holds out no factitious incentives to the avarice and ambition of the few, and which is internally organised for the liberty, security and comfort of the many. None must be entrusted with power (and money is the completest species of power) who do not stand pledged to use it exclusively for the general benefit. But the use of animal flesh and fermented liquors directly militates with this equality of the rights of man. The peasant cannot gratify these fashionable cravings without leaving his family to starve. Without disease and war, those sweeping curtailers of population, pasturage would include a waste too great to be afforded. The labour requisite to support a family is far lighter* than is usually supposed. The peasantry work, not only for themselves, but for the aristocracy, the army and the manufacturers.

The advantage of a reform in diet is obviously greater than that of any other. It strikes at the root of the evil. To remedy the abuses of legislation, before we annihilate the propensities by which they are produced, is to suppose that by taking away the effect the cause will cease to operate. But the efficacy of this system depends entirely on the proselytism of individuals, and grounds its merits as a benefit to the community upon the total change

---

* It has come under the author's experience that some of the workmen on an embankment in North Wales, who, in consequence of the inability of the proprietor to pay them, seldom received their wages, have supported large families by cultivating small spots of sterile ground by moonlight. In the notes to Pratt's poem 'Bread, or the Poor', is an account of an industrious labourer, who, by working in a small garden before and after his day's task, attained to an enviable state of independence.

of the dietetic habits in its members. It proceeds securely from a number of particular cases, to one that is universal, and has this advantage over the contrary mode, that one error does not invalidate all that has gone before.

Let not too much however be expected from this system. The healthiest among us is not exempt from hereditary disease. The most symmetrical, athletic, and long-lived, is a being inexpressibly inferior to what he would have been had not the unnatural habits of his ancestors accumulated for him a certain portion of malady and deformity. In the most perfect specimen of civilised man, something is still found wanting by the physiological critic. Can a return to nature, then, instantaneously eradicate predispositions that have been slowly taking root in the silence of innumerable ages? – Indubitably not. All that I contend for is that from the moment of the relinquishing all unnatural habits, no new disease is generated; and that the predisposition to hereditary maladies gradually perishes for want of its accustomed supply. In cases of consumption, cancer, gout, asthma and scrofula, such is the invariable tendency of a diet of vegetables and pure water.

Those who may be induced by these remarks to give the vegetable system a fair trial should, in the first place, date the commencement of their practice from the moment of their conviction. All depends upon breaking through a pernicious habit, resolutely and at once. Dr Trotter* asserts that no drunkard was ever reformed by gradually relinquishing his dram. Animal flesh in its effects on the human stomach is analogous to a dram. It is similar in the kind, though differing in the degree, of its operation. The proselyte to a pure diet must be warned to expect a temporary diminution of muscular strength. The subtraction of a powerful stimulus will suffice to account for this event. But it is only temporary, and is succeeded by an equable capability for exertion, far surpassing his former various and fluctuating strength. Above all, he will acquire an easiness of breathing, by which the same exertion is performed with a remarkable exemption from that painful and difficult panting now felt by almost everyone after hastily climbing an ordinary mountain. He will be equally capable of bodily exertion, or mental application, after as before his simple meal. He will feel none of the narcotic effects of ordinary diet. Irritability, the direct consequence of exhausting stimuli, would yield to the power of natural and tranquil impulses. He will no longer pine under the lethargy of ennui, that unconquerable weariness of life more dreaded than death itself. He will escape the epidemic madness that broods over its own injurious notions of

* See Trotter on the Nervous Temperament.

th Deity, and 'realises the hell that priests and beldams feign'. Every man forms as it were his god from his own character; to the divinity of one of simple habits no offering would be more acceptable than the happiness of his creatures. He would be incapable of hating or persecuting others for the love of God. He will find, moreover, a system of simple diet to be a system of perfect epicurism. He will no longer be incessantly occupied in blunting and destroying those organs from which he expects his gratification. The pleasures of taste to be derived from a dinner of potatoes, beans, peas, turnips, lettuce, with a dessert of apples, gooseberries, strawberries, currants, raspberries, and in winter, oranges, apples and pears, is far greater than supposed. Those who wait until they can eat this plain fare, with the sauce of appetite, will scarcely join with the hypocritical sensualist at a lord mayor's feast who declaims against the pleasures of the table. Solomon kept thousand concubines, and owned in despair that all was vanity. The man whose happiness is constituted by the society of one amiable woman would find some difficulty in sympathising with the disappointment of this venerable debauchee.

I access myself not only to the young enthusiast: the ardent devotee of truth and virtue; the pure and passionate moralist, yet unvitiated by the contagion of the world. He will embrace a pure system, from its abstract truth, its beauty, its simplicity, and its promise of wide-extended benefit; unless custom has turned poison into food, he will hate the brutal pleasure of the chase by instinct; it will be a contemplation full of horror and disappointment to his mind, that beings capable of the gentlest and most adorable sympathies, should take delight in the death-pangs and last convulsions of dying animals. The elderly man, whose youth has been poisoned by intemperance, or who has lived with apparent moderation and is afflicted with a variety of painful maladies, would find his account in a beneficial change produced without the risk of poisonous medicines. The mother, whom the perpetual restlessness of disease, and unaccountable deaths incident to her children, are the causes of incurable unhappiness, would on this diet experience the satisfaction of beholding their perpetual health and natural playfulness.* The most valuable lives are daily destroyed

* See Mr Non's book. His children are the most beautiful and healthy creatures it is
  possible conceive; the girls are perfect models for a sculptor – their dispositions are
  also the gentle and conciliating; the judicious treatment, which they experience
  in other is, may be a correlative cause of this. In the first five years of their life, of
  18,000 cn that are born, 7,500 die of various diseases; and how many more of
  those that vive are not rendered miserable by maladies not immediately mortal?
  The qual d quantity of a woman's milk are materially injured by the use of dead

by diseases that it is dangerous to palliate and impossible to cure by medicine. How much longer will man continue to pimp for the gluttony of death, his most insidious, implacable, and eternal foe?

The proselyte to a simple and natural diet who desires health must from the moment of his conversion attend to these rules –

> NEVER TAKE ANY SUBSTANCE INTO THE STOMACH THAT ONCE HAD LIFE. DRINK NO LIQUID BUT WATER RESTORED TO ITS ORIGINAL PURITY BY DISTILLATION.

APPENDIX

Persons on vegetable diet have been remarkable for longevity. The first Christians practised abstinence from animal flesh on a principle of self-mortification.

Old Parr*	152	St Anthony	105
Mary Patten†	136	James the Hermit	104
A shepherd in Hungary‡	126	Arsenius	120
Patrick O'Neale§	113	St Epiphanius	115
Joseph Elkins¶	103	Simeon	112
Elizabeth de Val**	101	Rombald	120
Aurungzebe††	100		

Mr Newton's mode of reasoning on longevity is ingenious and conclusive: 'Old Parr, healthy as the wild animals, attained to the age of 152 years. All men might be as healthy as the wild animals. Therefore all men might attain to the age of 152 years.'§§ The conclusion is sufficiently modest. Old

---

flesh. In an island near Iceland, where no vegetables are to be got the children invariably die of tetanus before they are three weeks old, and the population is supplied from the mainland. Sir G. Mackenzie's *Hist. of Iceland.* also Emile, pp. 53, 54 and 56.

* Cheyne's *Essay on Health*, p. 62
† *Gentleman's Magazine*, vii, p. 449
‡ *Morning Post*, January 28, 1800
§ Emile, i, p. 44
¶ He died at Coombe in Northumberland.
** *Scot's Magazine*, xxxiv, p. 696
†† Aurungzebe, from the time of his usurpation, adhered strictly to the Vegetable System.
§§ *Return to Nature*

Parr cannot be supposed to have escaped the inheritance of disease, amassed by the unnatural habits of his ancestors. The term of human life may be expected to be infinitely greater, taking into the consideration all the circumstances that must have contributed to abridge even that of Parr.

It may be here remarked that the author and his wife have lived on vegetables for eight months. The improvement of health and temper here stated is the result of his own experience.

An Address to the People on the Death of the Princess Charlotte

BY THE HERMIT OF MARLOW

We pity the plumage, but forget the dying bird.[306]

1

The Princess Charlotte is dead. She no longer moves, nor thinks, nor feels. She is as inanimate as the clay with which she is about to mingle. It is a dreadful thing to know that she is a putrid corpse, who but a few days since was full of life and hope: a woman young, innocent, and beautiful, snatched from the bosom of domestic peace, and leaving that single vacancy which none can die and leave not.

2

Thus much the death of the Princess Charlotte has in common with the death of thousands. How many women die in childbed and leave their families of motherless children and their husbands to live on, blighted by the remembrance of that heavy loss? How many women of active and energetic virtues; mild, affectionate, and wise, whose life is as a chain of happiness and union, which once being broken, leaves those whom it bound to perish, have died, and have been deplored with bitterness, which is too deep for words? Some have perished in penury or shame, and their orphan baby has survived, a prey to the scorn and neglect of strangers. Men have watched by the bedside of their expiring wives, and have gone mad when the hideous death-rattle was heard within the throat, regardless of the rosy child sleeping in the lap of the unobservant nurse. The countenance of the physician had been read by the stare of this distracted husband, till the legible despair sunk into his heart. All this has been and is. You walk with a merry heart through the streets of this great city, and think not that such are the scenes acting all round you. You do not number in your thought the mothers who die in childbed. It is the most horrible of ruins: – in sickness, in old age, in battle, death comes as to his own home; but in the season of joy and hope, when life should succeed to life, and the assembled family expects one more, the youngest and the best beloved, that the wife, the mother – she for whom each member of the family was so dear to one another, should die! – Yet thousands of the poorest poor, whose misery is aggravated by what cannot be spoken now, suffer this. And have they no affections? Do not their hearts beat in their bosoms, and the tears gush from their eyes? Are they not human flesh and blood? Yet none weep for them – none mourn for them – none when their coffins are carried to the grave (if indeed the parish furnishes a coffin for all) turn aside and moralise upon the sadness they have left behind.

3

The Athenians did well to celebrate with public mourning the death of those who had guided the republic with their valour and their understanding or illustrated it with their genius. Men do well to mourn for the dead: it proves that we love something beside ourselves: and he must have a hard heart who can see his friend depart to rottenness and dust, and speed him without emotion on his voyage to 'that bourne whence no traveller returns'.[307] To lament for those who have benefited the state is a habit of piety yet more favourable to the cultivation of our best affections. When Milton died it had been well that the universal English nation had been clothed in solemn black, and that the muffled bells had tolled from town to town. The French nation should have enjoined a public mourning at the deaths of Rousseau and Voltaire. We cannot truly grieve for everyone who dies beyond the circle of those especially dear to us; yet in the extinction of the objects of public love and admiration, and gratitude, there is something, if we enjoy a liberal mind, which has departed from within that circle. It were well done also that men should mourn for any public calamity which has befallen their country or the world, though it be not death. This helps to maintain that connection between one man and another, and all men considered as a whole, which is the bond of social life. There should be public mourning when those events take place which make all good men mourn in their hearts, – the rule of foreign or domestic tyrants, the abuse of public faith, the wresting of old and venerable laws to the murder of the innocent, the established insecurity of all those, the flower of the nation, who cherish an unconquerable enthusiasm for public good. Thus, if Horne Tooke and Hardy[308] had been convicted of high treason, it had been good that there had been not only the sorrow and the indignation which would have filled all hearts, but the external symbols of grief. When the French Republic was extinguished, the world ought to have mourned.

4

But this appeal to the feelings of men should not be made lightly, or in any manner that tends to waste, on inadequate objects, those fertilising streams of sympathy, which a public mourning should be the occasion of pouring forth. This solemnity should be used only to express a wide and intelligible calamity, and one which is felt to be such by those who feel for their country and for mankind; its character ought to be universal, not particular.

5

The news of the death of the Princess Charlotte, and of the execution of Brandreth, Ludlam and Turner, arrived nearly at the same time. If beauty, youth, innocence, amiable manners and the exercise of the domestic virtues could alone justify public sorrow when they are extinguished for ever, this interesting Lady would well deserve that exhibition. She was the last and the best of her race. But there were thousands of others equally distinguished as she, for private excellencies, who have been cut off in youth and hope. The accident of her birth neither made her life more virtuous nor her death more worthy of grief. For the public she had done nothing either good or evil; her education had rendered her incapable of either in a large and comprehensive sense. She was born a Princess; and those who are destined to rule mankind are dispensed with acquiring that wisdom and that experience which is necessary even to rule themselves. She was not like Lady Jane Grey, or Queen Elizabeth, a woman of profound and various learning. She had accomplished nothing, and aspired to nothing, and could understand nothing respecting those great political questions which involve the happiness of those over whom she was destined to rule. Yet this should not be said in blame, but in compassion: let us speak no evil of the dead. Such is the misery, such the impotence of royalty. – Princes are prevented from the cradle from becoming anything which may deserve that greatest of all rewards next to a good conscience, public admiration and regret.

6

The execution of Brandreth, Ludlam and Turner is an event of quite a different character from the death of the Princess Charlotte. These men were shut up in a horrible dungeon, for many months, with the fear of a hideous death and of everlasting hell thrust before their eyes; and at last were brought to the scaffold and hung. They too had domestic affections, and were remarkable for the exercise of private virtues. Perhaps their low station permitted the growth of those affections in a degree not consistent with a more exalted rank. They had sons, and brothers, and sisters, and fathers, who loved them, it should seem, more than the Princess Charlotte could be loved by those whom the regulations of her rank had held in perpetual estrangement from her. Her husband was to her as father, mother, and brethren. Ludlam and Turner were men of mature years, and the affections were ripened and strengthened within them. What these sufferers felt shall not be said. But what must have been the long and various agony of their kindred may be inferred from Edward Turner, who, when he saw his brother dragged along upon the hurdle, shrieked horribly and fell in a fit, and was carried away like a corpse by two men. How fearful must have been their agony, sitting in solitude on that day when the tempestuous voice of horror from the crowd, told them that the head so dear to them was severed from the body! Yes – they listened to the maddening shriek which burst from the multitude: they heard the rush of ten thousand terror-stricken feet, the groans and the hootings which told them that the mangled and distorted head was then lifted into the air. The sufferers were dead. What is death? Who dares to say that which will come after the grave?* Brandreth was calm, and evidently believed that the consequences of our errors were limited by that tremendous barrier. Ludlam and Turner were full of fears, lest God should plunge them in everlasting fire. Mr Pickering, the clergyman, was evidently anxious that Brandreth should not by a false confidence lose the single opportunity of reconciling himself with the Ruler of the future world. None knew what death was, or could know. Yet these men were presumptuously thrust into that unfathomable gulf, by other men, who knew as little and who reckoned not the present or the future sufferings of their victims. Nothing is more horrible than that man should for any cause shed the life of man. For all other calamities there is a remedy or a consolation. When that Power through which we live ceases to maintain the life which it has conferred, then is grief and agony, and the burthen which must be borne; such sorrow improves the heart. But when man sheds the blood of man, revenge, and hatred, and a long train of executions, and assassinations, and proscriptions, is perpetuated to remotest time.

7

Such are the particular and some of the general considerations depending on the death of these men. But however deplorable, if it were a mere private or customary grief, the public, as the public, should not mourn. But it is more than this. The events which led to the death of those unfortunate men are a public calamity. I will not impute blame to the jury who pronounced them guilty of high treason, perhaps the law requires that such should be

* 'Your death has eyes in his head – mine is not painted so.' – *Cymbeline*

the denomination of their offence. Some restraint ought indeed to be imposed on those thoughtless men who imagine they can find in violence a remedy for violence, even if their oppressors had tempted them to this occasion of their ruin. They are instruments of evil, not so guilty as the hands that wielded them, but fit to inspire caution. But their death, by hanging and beheading, and the circumstances of which it is the characteristic and the consequence, constitute a calamity such as the English nation ought to mourn with an unassuageable grief.

8

Kings and their ministers have in every age been distinguished from other men by a thirst for expenditure and bloodshed. There existed in this country, until the American war, a check, sufficiently feeble and pliant indeed, to this desolating propensity. Until America proclaimed itself a republic, England was perhaps the freest and most glorious nation subsisting on the surface of the earth. It was not what is to the full desirable that a nation should be, but all that it can be, when it does not govern itself. The consequences however of that fundamental defect soon became evident. The government which the imperfect constitution of our representative assembly threw into the hands of a few aristocrats, improved the method of anticipating the taxes by loans, invented by the ministers of William III, until an enormous debt had been created. In the war against the republic of France, this policy was followed up, until now, the *mere interest* of the public debt amounts to more than twice as much as the lavish expenditure of the public treasure, for maintaining the standing army, and the royal family, and the pensioners, and the placemen. The effect of this debt is to produce such an unequal distribution of the means of living as saps the foundation of social union and civilised life. It creates a double aristocracy, instead of one which was sufficiently burthensome before, and gives twice as many people the liberty of living in luxury and idleness on the produce of the industrious and the poor. And it does not give them this because they are more wise and meritorious than the rest, or because their leisure is spent in schemes of public good, or in those exercises of the intellect and the imagination whose creations ennoble or adorn a country. They are not, like the old aristocracy, men of pride and honour, *sans peur et sans tache,*[309] but petty piddling slaves who have gained a right to the title of public creditors either by gambling in the funds or by subserviency to government or some other villainous trade. They are not the 'Corinthian capital of polished society', but the petty and creeping weeds which deface the rich tracery of its sculpture. The effect of this system is that the day labourer gains no more now by working sixteen hours a day than he gained before by working eight. I put the thing in its simplest and most intelligible shape. The labourer, he that tills the ground and manufactures cloth, is the man who has to provide, out of what he would bring home to his wife and children, for the luxuries and comforts of those whose claims are represented by an annuity of forty-four millions a year levied upon the English nation. Before, he supported the army and the pensioners, and the royal family, and the landholders; and this is a hard necessity to which it was well that he should submit. Many and various are the mischiefs flowing from oppression, but this is the representative of them all; namely, that one man is forced to labour for another in a degree not only not necessary to the support of the subsisting distinctions among mankind, but so as by the excess of the injustice to endanger the very foundations of all that is valuable in social order, and to provoke that anarchy which is at once the enemy of freedom, and the child and the chastiser of misrule. The nation, tottering on the brink of two chasms, began to be weary of a continuance of such dangers and degradations, and the miseries which are the consequence of them; the public voice loudly demanded a free representation of the people. It began to be felt that no other constituted body of men could meet the difficulties which impend. Nothing but the nation itself dares to touch the question as to whether there is any remedy or no to the annual payment of forty-four millions a year, beyond the necessary expenses of state, for ever and for ever. A nobler spirit also went abroad, and the love of liberty, and patriotism, and the self-respect attendant on those glorious emotions, revived in the bosoms of men. The government had a desperate game to play.

9

In the manufacturing districts of England discontent and disaffection had prevailed for many years; this was the consequence of that system of double aristocracy produced by the causes before mentioned. The manufacturers, the helots of our luxury, are left by this system famished, without affections, without health, without leisure or opportunity for such instruction as might counteract those habits of turbulence and dissipation produced by the precariousness and insecurity of poverty. Here was a ready field for any adventurer who should wish for whatever purpose to incite a few ignorant men to acts of illegal outrage. So soon as it was plainly seen that the demands of the people for a free representation must be conceded if some intimidation and prejudice were not conjured up, a conspiracy of the most horrible atrocity was laid in train. It is impossible to know how far the higher members of the government are involved in the guilt of their infernal agents. It is impossible to know how numerous or how active they have been, or by what false hopes they are yet inflaming the untutored multitude to put their necks under the axe and into the halter. But thus much is known, that so as the whole nation lifted up its voice for parliamentary reform, spies were sent forth. These were selected from the most worthless and infamous of mankind, and dispersed among the multitude of famished and illiterate labourers. It was their business if they found no discontent to create it. It was their business to find victims, no matter whether right or wrong. It was their business to produce upon the public an impression that if any attempt to attain national freedom, or to diminish the burthens of debt and taxation under which we groan, were successful, the starving multitude would rush in and confound all orders and distinctions, and institutions and laws, in common ruin. The inference with which they were required to arm the ministers was that despotic power ought to be eternal. To produce this salutary impression, they betrayed some innocent and unsuspecting rustics into a crime whose penalty is a hideous death. A few hungry and ignorant manufacturers seduced by the splendid promises of these remorseless blood-conspirators, collected together in what is called rebellion against the state. All was prepared, and the eighteen dragoons, assembled in readiness no doubt, conducted their astonished victims to that dungeon which they left only to be mangled by the executioner's hand. The cruel instigators of their ruin retired to enjoy the great revenues which they had earned by a life of villainy. The public voice was overpowered by the timid and the selfish, who threw the weight of fear into the scale of public opinion, and parliament confided anew to the executive government those extraordinary powers which may never be laid down, or which may be laid down in blood, or which the regularly constituted assembly of the nation must wrest out of their hands. Our alternatives are a despotism, a revolution, or reform.

10

On the 7th of November, Brandreth, Turner and Ludlam ascended the scaffold. We feel for Brandreth the less, because it seems he killed a man. But recollect who instigated him to the proceedings which led to murder. On the word of a dying man, Brandreth tells us that, 'OLIVER *brought him to this*' – that, '*but for* OLIVER *he would not have been there*'. See, too, Ludlam and Turner, with their sons and brothers and sisters, how they kneel together in a dreadful agony of prayer. Hell is before their eyes, and they shudder and feel sick with fear, lest some unrepented or some wilful sin should seal their doom in everlasting fire. With that dreadful penalty before their eyes – with that tremendous sanction for the truth of all he spoke, Turner exclaimed loudly and distinctly, *while the executioner was putting the rope round his neck,* 'THIS IS ALL OLIVER AND THE GOVERNMENT.' What more he might have said we know not, because the chaplain prevented any further observations. Troops of horse, with keen and glittering swords, hemmed in the multitudes collected to witness this abominable exhibition. 'When the stroke of the axe was heard, there was a burst of horror from the crowd. The instant the head was exhibited, there was a tremendous shriek set up, and the multitude ran violently in all directions, as if under the impulse of sudden frenzy. Those who resumed their stations, groaned and hooted.'* It is a national calamity that we endure men to rule over us who sanction for whatever ends a conspiracy which is to arrive at its purpose through such a frightful pouring forth of human blood and agony. But when that purpose is to trample upon our rights and liberties for ever, to present to us the alternatives of anarchy and oppression, and triumph when the astonished nation accepts the latter at their hands, to maintain a vast standing army, and add, year by year, to a public debt, which, already, they know, cannot be discharged; and which, when the delusion that supports it fails, will produce as much misery and confusion through all classes of society as it has continued to produce of famine and degradation to the undefended poor; to imprison and calumniate those who may offend them, at will; when this, if not the purpose, is the effect of that conspiracy, how ought we not to mourn?

11

Mourn then People of England. Clothe yourselves in solemn black. Let the bells be tolled. Think of mortality and change. Shroud yourselves in solitude and the gloom of sacred sorrow. Spare no symbol of universal grief. Weep – mourn – lament. Fill the great City, fill the boundless fields, with lamentation and the echo of groans. A beautiful Princess is dead: – she who should have been the Queen of her beloved nation, and whose posterity should have ruled it for ever. She loved the domestic affections, and cherished arts which adorn and valour which defends. She was amiable and would have become wise, but she was young, and in the flower of youth the despoiler came. LIBERTY is dead. Slave! I charge thee disturb not the depth and solemnity of our grief by any meaner sorrow. If One has died who was

* These expressions are taken from the *Examiner*, Sunday, November 9th.

like her that should have ruled over this land, like Liberty, young, innocent, and lovely, know that the power through which that one perished was God, and that it was a private grief. But *man* has murdered Liberty, and whilst the life was ebbing from its wound, there descended on the heads and on the hearts of every human thing the sympathy of a universal blast and curse. Fetters heavier than iron weigh upon us, because they bind our souls. We move about in a dungeon more pestilential than damp and narrow walls, because the earth is its floor and the heavens are its roof. Let us follow the corpse of British Liberty slowly and reverentially to its tomb: and if some glorious Phantom should appear, and make its throne of broken swords and sceptres and royal crowns trampled in the dust, let us say that the Spirit of Liberty has arisen from its grave and left all that was gross and mortal there, and kneel down and worship it as our Queen.

A Philosophical View of Reform

CHAPTER 1

Introduction

From the dissolution of the Roman Empire, that vast and successful scheme for the enslaving [of] the most civilised portion of mankind, to the epoch of the present year have succeeded a series of schemes on a smaller scale, operating to the same effect. Names borrowed from the life and opinions of Jesus Christ were employed as symbols of domination and imposture, and a system of liberty and equality (for such was the system preached by that great Reformer) was perverted to support oppression – not his doctrines, for they are too simple and direct to be susceptible of such perversion, but the mere names. Such was the origin of the Catholic Church, which, together with the several dynasties then beginning to consolidate themselves in Europe, means, being interpreted, a plan according to which the cunning and selfish few have employed the fears and hopes of the ignorant many to the establishment of their own power and the destruction of the real interest of all.

The republics and municipal governments of Italy opposed for some time a systematic and effectual resistance to the all-surrounding tyranny. The Lombard League defeated the armies of the despot in open field, and until Florence was betrayed to those flattered traitors [and] polished tyrants, the Medici, Freedom had one citadel wherein it could find refuge from a world which was its enemy. Florence long balanced, divided, and weakened the strength of the Empire and the Popedom. To this cause, if to anything, was due the undisputed superiority of Italy in literature and the arts over all its contemporary nations, that union of energy and of beauty which distinguish[es] from all other poets the writings of Dante, that restlessness of fervid power which expressed itself in painting and sculpture and in daring architectural forms, and from which, and conjointly from the creations of Athens, its predecessor and its image, Raphael and Michel Angelo drew the inspiration which created those forms and colours now the astonishment of the world. The father of our own literature, Chaucer, wrought from the simple and powerful language of a nursling of this republic the basis of our own literature. And thus we owe among other causes the exact condition belonging to [our own] intellectual existence to the generous disdain of submission which burned in the bosoms of men who filled a distant generation and inhabited another land.

When this resistance was overpowered (as what resistance to fraud and [tyranny] has not been overpowered?) another was even then maturing. The progress of philosophy and civilisation which ended in that imperfect emancipation of mankind from the yoke of priests and kings called the Reformation had already commenced. Exasperated by their long sufferings, inflamed by the spark of that superstition from the flames of which they were emerging, the poor rose against their natural enemies, the rich, and repaid with bloody interest the tyranny of ages. One of the signs of the times was that the oppressed peasantry rose like the negro slaves of West Indian plantations and murdered their tyrants when they were unaware. For so dear is power that the tyrants themselves neither then, nor now, nor ever, left or leave a path to freedom but through their own blood. The contest then waged under the names of religion – which have seldom been any more [than] the popular and visible symbols which express the degree of power in some shape or other asserted by one party and disclaimed by the other – ended; and the result, though partial and imperfect, is perhaps the most animating that the philanthropist can contemplate in the history of man. The Republic of Holland, which has been so long an armoury of arrows of learning by which superstition has been wounded even to death, was established by this contest. What though the name of Republic – and by whom but by conscience-stricken tyrants could it be extinguished – is no more? The Republics of Switzerland derived from this event their consolidation and their union. From England then first began to pass away the strain of conquest. The exposition of a certain portion of religious imposture drew with it an enquiry into political imposture and was attended with an extraordinary exertion of the energies of intellectual power. Shakespeare and Lord Bacon and the great writers of the age of Elizabeth and James I were at once the effects of the new spirit in men's minds and the causes of its more complete development. By rapid gradation the nation was conducted to the temporary abolition of aristocracy and episcopacy, and [to] the mighty example which, 'in teaching nations how to live', England afforded to the world – of bringing to public justice one of those chiefs of a conspiracy of privileged murderers and robbers whose impunity has been the consecration of crime [the execution of Charles I].[310]

After the selfish passions and compromising interests of men had enlisted themselves to produce and establish the restoration of Charles II, the unequal combat was renewed under the reign of his successor [James

II], and that compromise between the inextinguishable spirit of Liberty and the ever-watchful spirit of fraud and tyranny, called the Revolution [of 1688],[311] had place. On this occasion monarchy and aristocracy and episcopacy were at once established and limited by law. Unfortunately they lost no more in extent of power than they gained in security of possession. Meanwhile those by whom they were established acknowledged and declared that the will of the people was the source from which these powers, in this instance, derived the right to subsist. A man has no right to be a king or lord or a bishop but so long as it is for the benefit of the people and so long as the people judge that it is for their benefit that he should impersonate that character. The solemn establishment of this maxim as the basis of our constitutional law more than any beneficial and energetic application of it to the circumstances of this era of its promulgation was the fruit of that vaunted event. Correlative with this series of events in England was the commencement of a new epoch in the history of the progress of civilisation and society.

That superstition which had disguised itself under the name of the religion of Jesus subsisted under all its forms, even where it had been separated from those things especially considered as abuses by the multitude, in the shape of intolerant and oppressive hierarchies. Catholics massacred Protestants and Protestants proscribed Catholics, and extermination was the sanction of each faith within the limits of the power of its professors. The New Testament is in everyone's hand, and the few who ever read it with the simple sincerity of an unbiased judgement may perceive how distinct from the opinions of any of those professing themselves establishers [of churches] were the doctrines and the actions of Jesus Christ. At the period of the Reformation this test was applied, and this judgement formed of the then existing hierarchy, and the same compromise was then made between the spirit of truth and the spirit of imposture after [the] struggle which ploughed up the area of the human mind as was made in the particular instance of England between the spirit of freedom and the spirit of tyranny at that event called the Revolution [of 1688]. In both instances the maxims so solemnly recorded remain as trophies of our difficult and incomplete victory, planted in the enemies' land. *The will of the people to change their government is an acknowledged right in the Constitution of England.* The protesting against religious dogmas which present themselves to his mind as false is the inalienable prerogative of every human being.

The new epoch was marked by the commencement of deeper enquiries into the forms of human nature than are compatible with an unreserved belief in any of those popular mistakes upon which popular systems of faith with respect to the cause and agencies of the universe, with all their superstructure of political and religious tyranny, are built. Lord Bacon, Spinoza, Hobbes, Bayle, Montaigne regulated the reasoning powers, criticised the past history, exposed the errors by illustrating their causes and their connection, and anatomised the inmost nature of social man. Then, with a less interval of time than of genius, followed [Locke] and the philosophers of his exact and intelligible but superficial school. Their illustrations of some of the minor consequences of the doctrines established by the sublime genius of their predecessors were correct, popular, simple, and energetic. Above all, they indicated inferences the most incompatible with the popular religions and the established governments of Europe. [Philosophy went forth into the enchanted forest of the demons of worldly power as the pioneer of the over-growth of ages.] Berkeley, and Hume, [and] Hartley [at a] later age, following the traces of these inductions, have clearly established the certainty of our ignorance with respect to those obscure questions which under the name of religious truths have been the watchwords of contention and the symbols of unjust power ever since they were distorted by the narrow passions of the immediate followers of Jesus from that meaning to which philosophers are even now restoring them. A crowd of writers in France seized upon the most popular portions of the new philosophy which conducted to inferences at war with the dreadful oppressions under which the country groaned and made familiar to mankind the falsehood of their religious mediators and political oppressors. Considered as philosophers, their error seems to have consisted chiefly of a limitedness of view; they told the truth, but not the whole truth. This might have arisen from the terrible sufferings of their countrymen inviting them rather to apply a portion of what had already been discovered to their immediate relief than to pursue one interest, the abstractions of thought, as the great philosophers who preceded them had done, for the sake of a future and more universal advantage. While that philosophy which, burying itself in the obscure part of our nature, regards the truth and falsehood of dogmas relating to the cause of the universe and the nature and manner of man's relation with it, was thus stripping power of its darkest mask, political philosophy, or that which considers the relations of man as a social being, was assuming a precise form. This philosophy indeed sprang from and maintained a connection with that other as its parent. What would Swift and Bolingbroke and Sidney [Algernon] and Locke and Montesquieu, or even Rousseau, not to speak of political philosophers of our own age, Godwin and Bentham, have been but for Lord Bacon, Montaigne, and Spinoza, and other great luminaries of the preceding epoch? Something excellent and eminent, no doubt, the least of these would have been, but something different from and inferior to what they are. A series of these writers illustrated with more or less success the principles of human nature as applied to man in political society. A thirst for accommodating the existing forms according to which mankind are found divided to those rules of freedom and equality which are thus discovered as being the elementary principles according to which the happiness resulting from the social union ought to be produced and distributed was kindled by these enquiries. Contemporary with this condition of the intellect all the powers of man seemed, though in most cases under forms highly inauspicious, to develop themselves with uncommon energy. The mechanical sciences attained to a degree of perfection which, though obscurely foreseen by Lord Bacon, it had been accounted madness to have prophesied in a preceding age. Commerce was pursued with a perpetually increasing vigour, and the same area of the earth was perpetually compelled to furnish more and more subsistence. The means and sources of knowledge were thus increased, together with knowledge itself and the instruments of knowledge. The benefit of this increase of the powers of man became, in consequence of the inartificial forms into which society came to be distributed, an instrument of his additional evil. The capabilities of happiness were increased and applied to the augmentation of misery. Modern society is thus an engine assumed to be for useful purposes, whose force is by a system of subtle mechanism augmented to the highest pitch, but which, instead of grinding corn or raising water, acts against itself and is perpetually wearing away or breaking to pieces the wheels of which it is composed. The result of the labours of the political philosophers has been the establishment of the principle of utility as the substance, and liberty and equality as the forms, according to which the concerns of human life ought to be administered. By this test the various institutions regulating political society have been tried and, as the undigested growth of the private passions, errors, and interests of barbarians and oppressors, have been condemned. And many new theories, more or less perfect, but all superior to the mass of evil which they would supplant, have been given to the world.

The system of government in the United States of America was the first practical illustration of the new philosophy. Sufficiently remote, it will be confessed, from the accuracy of ideal excellence is that representative system which will soon cover the extent of that vast Continent. But it is scarcely less remote from the insolent and contaminating tyrannies under which, with some limitation of these terms as regards England, Europe groaned at the period of the successful rebellion of America. America holds forth the victorious example of an immensely populous and, as far as the external arts of life are concerned, a highly civilised community administered according to republican forms. It has no king; that is, it has no officer to whom wealth and from whom corruption flows. It has no hereditary oligarchy; that is, it acknowledges no order of men privileged to cheat and insult the rest of the members of the state and who inherit a right of legislating and judging which the principles of human nature compel them to exercise to their own profit and to the detriment of those not included within their peculiar class. It has no established church; that is, it has no system of opinions respecting the abstrusest questions which can be topics of human thought founded in an age of error and fanaticism and opposed by law to all other opinions, defended by prosecutions and sanctioned by enormous bounties given to idle priests and forced through the unwilling hands of those who have an interest in the cultivation and improvement of the soil. It has no false representation, whose consequences are captivity, confiscation, infamy, and ruin, but a true representation. The will of the many is represented by the few in the assemblies of legislation and by the officers of the executive entrusted with the administration of the executive power almost as directly as the will of one person can be represented by the will of another. (This is not the place for dilating upon the inexpressible advantages [if such advantages require any manifestation] of self-governing society, or one which approaches it in the degree of the Republic of the United States.) Lastly, it has an institution by which it is honourably distinguished from all other governments which ever existed. It constitutionally acknowledges the progress of human improvement and is framed under the limitation of the probability of more simple views of political science being rendered applicable to human life. There is a law by which the constitution is reserved for revision every ten years. [*Editor's note:* Such a clause was proposed but not adopted.] Every other set of men who have assumed the office of legislation and framing institutions for future ages, with far less right to such an assumption than the founders of the American Republic, assumed that their work was the wisest and the best that could possibly have been produced; these illustrious men [on the other hand] looked upon the past history of their species and saw that it was the history of his mistakes and his sufferings arising from his mistakes; they observed the superiority of their own work to all the works which had preceded it, and they judged it probable that other political institutions would be discovered bearing the same relation to those which they had established which they bear to those which have preceded them. They provided therefore for the application of these contingent discoveries to the social state without the violence and misery attendant upon such change in less modest and more imperfect governments. The United States, as we would have expected from theoretical deduction, affords an example, compared with the old governments of Europe and Asia, of a free, happy, and strong people. Nor let it be said that they owe their superiority rather to the situation than to their government. Give them a king, and let that king waste in luxury, riot and bribery the same sum which now serves for the entire expenses of their government. Give them an aristocracy, and let that aristocracy legislate for the people. Give them a priesthood, and let them bribe with a tenth of the produce of the soil a certain set of men to say a certain set of words. Pledge the larger part of them by financial subterfuge to pay the half of their property or earnings to another portion, and let the proportion of those who enjoy the fruits of the toil of others without toiling themselves be three instead of one. Give them a Court of Chancery, and let the property, the liberty, and the interest in the dearest concerns of life, the exercise of the most sacred rights of a social being, depend upon the will of one of the most servile creature[s] of that kingly and oligarchical and priestly power to which every man in proportion as he is of an enquiring and philosophical mind and of a sincere and honourable disposition is a natural, a necessary enemy. Give them, as you must if you give them these things, a great standing army to cut down the people if they murmur. If any American should see these words, his blood would run cold at the imagination of such a change. He well knows that the prosperity and happiness of the United States if subjected to such institutions [would] be no more.

The just and successful revolt of America corresponded with a state of public opinion in Europe of which it was the first result. The French Revolution was the second. The oppressors of mankind had enjoyed (Oh that we could say suffered) a long and undisturbed reign in France, and to the pining famine, the shelterless destitution of the inhabitants of that country had been added and heaped-up insult harder to endure than misery. For the feudal system (the immediate causes and conditions of its institution having become obliterated) had degenerated into an instrument not only of oppression but of contumely, and both were unsparingly inflicted. Blind in the possession of strength, drunken as with the intoxication of ancestral greatness, the rulers perceived not that increase of knowledge in their subjects which made its exercise insecure. They called soldiers to hew down the people when their power was already past. The tyrants were, as usual, the aggressors. Then the oppressed, having being rendered brutal, ignorant, servile and bloody by long slavery, having had the intellectual thirst excited in them by the progress of civilisation satiated from fountains of literature poisoned by the spirit and the form of monarchy, arose and took a dreadful revenge upon their oppressors. Their desire to wreak revenge to this extent, in itself a mistake, a crime, a calamity, arose from the same source as their other miseries and errors and affords an additional proof of the necessity of that long-delayed change which it accompanied and disgraced. If a just and necessary revolution could have been accomplished with as little expense of happiness and order in a country governed by despotic as [in] one governed by free laws, equal liberty and justice would lose their chief recommendations and tyranny be divested of its most revolting attributes. Tyranny entrenches itself within the existing interests of the most refined citizens of a nation and says, 'If you dare trample upon these, be free.' Though this terrible condition shall not be evaded, the world is no longer in a temper to decline the challenge.

The French were what their literature is (excluding Montaigne and Rousseau, and some few leaders of the [. . .]) – weak, superficial, vain, with little imagination, and with passions as well as judgements cleaving to the external form of things. Not that [they] are organically different from the inhabitants of the nations who have become [. . .] or rather not that their organical differences, whatever they may amount to, incapacitate them from arriving at the exercise of the highest powers to be attained by man. Their institutions made them what they were. Slavery and superstition, contumely and the tame endurance of contumely, and the habits engendered from generation to generation out of this transmitted inheritance of wrong, created this thing which has extinguished what has been called the likeness of God in man. The Revolution in France overthrew the hierarchy, the aristocracy, and the monarchy, and the whole of that peculiarly insolent and oppressive system on which they were based. But as it only partially extinguished those passions which are the spirit of these forms, a reaction took place which has restored in a certain limited degree the old system – in a degree, indeed, exceedingly limited, and stripped of all its ancient terrors. The hope of the monarchy of France, with his teeth drawn and his claws pared, was its maintaining the formal likeness of most imperfect and insecure dominion. The usurpation of Bonaparte and then the Restoration of the Bourbons were the shapes in which this reaction clothed itself, and the heart of every lover of liberty was struck as with palsy by the succession of these events. But reversing the proverbial expression of Shakespeare, it may be the good which the Revolutionists did lives after them, their ills are interred with their bones. But the military project of government of the great tyrant having failed, and there being even no attempt – and, if there were any attempt, there being not the remotest possibility of re-establishing the enormous system of tyranny abolished by the Revolution – France is, as it were, regenerated. Its legislative assemblies are in a certain limited degree representations of the popular will, and the executive power is hemmed in by jealous laws. France occupies in this respect the same situation as was occupied by England at the Restoration of Charles II. It has undergone a revolution (unlike in the violence and calamities which attended it, because unlike in the abuses which it was excited to put down) which may be paralleled with that in our own country which ended in the death of Charles I. The authors of both revolutions proposed a greater and more glorious object than the degraded passions of their countrymen permitted them to attain. But in both cases abuses were abolished which never since have dared to show their face.

There remains in the natural order of human things that the tyranny and perfidy of the reigns of Charles II and James II (for these were less the result of the disposition of particular men than the vices which would have been engendered in any but an extraordinary man by the natural necessities of their situation) perhaps under a milder form and within a shorter period should produce the institution of a government in France which may bear the same relation to the state of political knowledge existing at the present day as the Revolution under William III bore to the state of political knowledge existing at that period.

Germany, which is among the great nations of Europe one of the latest civilised with the exception of Russia, is rising with the fervour of a vigorous youth in the assertion of those rights for which it has that desire arising from knowledge, the surest pledge of victory. The deep passion and the bold and Aeschylean vigour of the imagery of their poetry; the enthusiasm, however distorted, of their religious sentiments; the flexibility and comprehensiveness of their language, which is a many-sided mirror of every changing thought; their severe, bold, and liberal spirit of criticism; their subtle and deep philosophy, however erroneous and illogical [in] mingling fervid intuitions into truth with obscure error (for the period of just distinction is yet to come), and their taste and power in the plastic arts, prove that they are a great people. And every great people either has been, or is, or will be free. The panic-stricken tyrants of that country promised to their subjects that their governments should be administered according to republican forms, they retaining merely the right of hereditary chief magistracy in their families. This promise, made in danger, the oppressors dream that they can break in security. And everything in consequence wears in Germany the aspect of rapidly maturing revolution.

In Spain and in the dependencies of Spain good and evil in the forms of despair and tyranny are struggling foot to foot. That great people have been delivered bound hand and foot to be trampled upon and insulted by a traitorous and sanguinary tyrant, a wretch who makes credible all that might have been doubted in the history of Nero, Christiern, Muley Ismael, or Ezzelin[312] – the persons who have thus delivered them were that hypocritical knot of conspiring tyrants who proceeded upon the credit they gained by putting down the only tyrant among them who was not a hypocrite to undertake the administration of those *arrondissements* of consecrated injustice and violence which they deliver to those who the nearest resemble them under the name of the kingdoms of the earth. This action signed a sentence of death, confiscation, exile, or captivity against every philosopher and patriot in Spain. The tyrant Ferdinand, he whose name is changed into a proverb of execration, found natural allies in all the priests and a few of the most dishonourable military chiefs of that devoted country. And the consequences of military despotism and the black, stagnant, venomous hatred which priests in common with eunuchs seek every opportunity to wreak upon the portion of mankind exempt from their own unmanly disqualifications is slavery. And what is slavery – in its mildest form hideous and, so long as one amiable or great attribute survives in its victims, rankling and intolerable, but in its darkest shape [as] it now exhibits itself in Spain it is the presence of all and more than all the evils for the sake of an exemption from which mankind submit to the mighty calamity of government. It is a system of insecurity of property, and of person, of prostration of conscience and understanding, of famine heaped upon the greater number, and contumely heaped upon all, defended by unspeakable tortures employed not merely as punishments but as precautions, by want, death, and captivity, and the application to political purposes of the execrated and enormous instruments of religious cruelty. Those men of understanding, integrity, and courage who rescued their country from one tyrant are exiled from it by his successor and his enemy and their legitimate king. Tyrants, however they may squabble among themselves, have common friends and foes. The taxes are levied at the point of the sword. Armed insurgents occupy all the defensible mountains of the country. The dungeons are peopled thickly, and persons of every sex and age have the fibres of their frame torn by subtle torments. Boiling water (such is an article in the last news from Spain) is poured upon the legs of a noble Spanish lady newly delivered, slowly and cautiously, that she may confess what she knows of a conspiracy against the tyrant, and she dies, as constant as the slave Epicharis, imprecating curses upon her torturers and passionately calling upon her children These events, in the present condition of the understanding and sentiment of mankind, are the rapidly passing shadows which forerun successful insurrection, the ominous comets of our republican poet[313] perplexing great monarchs with fear of change. Spain, having passed through an ordeal severe in proportion to the wrongs and errors which it is kindled to erase, must of necessity be renovated. [The country which] produced Calderon and Cervantes, what else did it but breathe through the tumult of the despotism and superstition which invested them, the prophecy of a glorious consummation?

The independents of South America are as it were already free. Great republics are about to consolidate themselves in a portion of the globe sufficiently vast and fertile to nourish more human beings than at present occupy, with the exception perhaps of China, the remainder of the inhabited earth, Some indefinite arrears of misery and blood remain to be paid to the Moloch of oppression, These, to the last drop and groan, it will implacably exact, But not the less are [they] inevitably enfranchised. The great monarchies of Asia cannot, let us confidently hope, remain unshaken by the earthquake which shatters to dust the mountainous strongholds of the tyrants of the western world.

Revolutions in the political and religious state of the Indian peninsula seem to be accomplishing, and it cannot be doubted but the zeal of the missionaries of what is called the Christian faith will produce beneficial innovation there, even by the application of dogmas and forms of what is here an outworn incumbrance. The Indians have been enslaved and cramped in the most severe and paralysing forms which were ever devised by man; some of this new enthusiasm ought to be kindled among them to consume it and leave them free, and even if the doctrines of Jesus do not penetrate through the darkness of that which those who profess to be his followers call Christianity, there will yet be a number of social forms modelled upon those European feelings from which it has taken its colour substituted to those according to which they are at present cramped, and from which, when the time for complete emancipation shall arrive, their disengagement may be less difficult, and under which their progress to it may be the less imperceptibly slow. Many native Indians have acquired, it is said, a competent knowledge in the arts and philosophy of Europe, and Locke and Hume and Rousseau are familiarly talked about in Brahminical society. But the thing to be sought is that they should as they would if they were free to attain to a system of arts and literature of their own. Of Persia we know little but that it has been the theatre of sanguinary contests for power, and that it is now at peace. The Persians appear to be from organisation a beautiful, refined, and impassioned people and would probably soon be infected by the contagion of good. The Jews, that wonderful people which has preserved so long the symbols of their union, may reassume their ancestral seats. The Turkish Empire is in its last stage of ruin, and it cannot be doubted but that the time is approaching when the deserts of Asia Minor and of Greece will be colonised by the overflowing population of countries less enslaved and debased, and that the climate and the scenery which was the birthplace of all that is wise and beautiful will not remain forever the spoil of wild beasts and unlettered Tartars. In Syria and Arabia the spirit of human intellect has roused a sect of people called Wahabees,[314] who maintain the Unity of God, and the equality of man, and their enthusiasm must go on 'conquering and to conquer' even if it must be repressed in its present shape. Egypt having but a nominal dependence upon Constantinople is under the government of Ottoman Bey,[315] a person of enlightened views, who is introducing European literature and arts, and is thus beginning that change which Time, the great innovator, will accomplish in that degraded country; [and] by the same means its sublime enduring monuments may excite lofty emotions in the hearts of the posterity of those who now contemplate them without admiration.

Lastly, in the West Indian islands, first from the disinterested yet necessarily callous measures of the English nation, and then from the infection of the spirit of Liberty in France, the deepest stain upon civilised man is fading away. Two nations of free negroes[316] are already established; one, in pernicious mockery of the usurpation over France, an empire, the other a republic– both animating yet terrific spectacles to those who inherit around them the degradation of slavery and the peril of dominion.

Such is a slight sketch of the general condition of the human race to which they have been conducted after the obliteration of the Greek republics by the successful external tyranny of Rome – its internal liberty having been first abolished – and by those miseries and superstitions consequent upon this event which compelled the human race to begin anew its difficult and obscure career of producing, according to the forms of society, the great portion of good.

Meanwhile England, the particular object for the sake of which these general considerations have been stated on the present occasion, has arrived like the nations which surround it at a crisis in its destiny. The literature of England, an energetic development of which has ever followed or preceded a great and free development of the national will, has arisen, as it were, from a new birth. In spite of that low-thoughted envy which would undervalue, through a fear of comparison with its own insignificance, the eminence of contemporary merit, it is *felt by the British* [that] ours is in intellectual achievements a memorable age, and we live among such philosophers and poets as surpass beyond comparison any who have appeared in our nation since its last struggle for Liberty. For the most unfailing herald, or companion, or follower, of a universal employment of the sentiments of a nation to the production of beneficial change is poetry, meaning by poetry an intense and impassioned power of communicating intense and impassioned impressions respecting man and nature. The persons in whom this power takes its abode may often, as far as regards many portions of their nature, have little tendency [to] the spirit of good of which it is the minister. But although they may deny and abjure, they are yet compelled to serve that which is seated on the throne of their own soul. And whatever systems they may [have] professed to support, they actually advance the interests of liberty. It is impossible to read the productions of our most celebrated writers, whatever may be their system relating to thought or expression, without being startled by the electric life which there is in their words. They measure the circumference or sound the depths of human nature with a comprehensive and all-penetrating spirit at which they are themselves perhaps most sincerely astonished, for it [is] less their own spirit than the spirit of their age. They are the priests of an unapprehended inspiration, the mirrors of gigantic shadows which futurity casts upon the present; the words which express what they conceive not; the trumpet which sings to battle and feels not what it inspires; the influence which is moved not, but moves. Poets and philosophers are the unacknowledged legislators[317] of the world.

But, omitting these more abstracted considerations, has there not been and is there not in England a desire of change arising from the profound sentiment of the exceeding inefficiency of the existing institutions to provide for the physical and intellectual happiness of the people? It is proposed in this work (1) to state and examine the present condition of this desire, (2) to elucidate its causes and its object, (3) to then show the practicability and utility, nay the necessity of change, (4) to examine the state of parties as regards it, and (5) to state the probable, the possible, and the desirable mode in which it should be accomplished.

CHAPTER 2

On the Sentiment of the Necessity of Change

Two circumstances arrest the attention of those who turn their regard to the present political condition of the English nation – first, that there is an almost universal sentiment of the approach of some change to be wrought in the institutions of the government, and secondly, the necessity and desirableness of such a change. From the first of these propositions, it being matter of fact, no person addressing the public can dissent. The latter, from a general belief in which the former flows and on which it depends, is matter of opinion, but [one] which to the mind of all, excepting those interested in maintaining the contrary, is a doctrine so clearly established that even they, admitting that great abuses exist, are compelled to impugn it by insisting upon the specious topic, that popular violence, by which they alone could be remedied, would be more injurious than the continuance of these abuses. But as those who argue thus derive for the most part great advantage and convenience from the continuance of these abuses, their estimation of the mischiefs of uprising [and] popular violence as compared with the mischiefs of tyrannical and fraudulent forms of government are likely, from the known principles of human nature, to be exaggerated.

[*The following passage is omitted in Mary Shelley's transcription*: According to the principles of human nature as modified by the existing opinions and institutions of society, a man loves himself with an overweening love. The generous emotions of disinterested affection which the records of human nature and our experience teach us that the human heart is highly susceptible of are confined within the narrow circle of our kindred and friends. And therefore there is a class of men, considerable from talents, influence and station, who of necessity are enemies to Reform.

For Reform would benefit the nation at their expense instead of suffering them to benefit themselves at the expense of the nation. If a reform however mild were to take place, they must submit to a diminution of those luxuries and vanities in the idolatry of which they have been trained. Not only they but, what in most cases would be esteemed a harder necessity, their wives and children and dependants must be comprehended in the same restrictions. That degree of pain, which, however it is to be regretted, is necessarily attached to the relinquishment of the habits of particular persons at war with the general permanent advantage, must be inflicted by the mildest reform. It is not alleged that every person whose interest is directly or indirectly concerned in the maintaining things as they are, is therefore necessarily interested. There are individuals who can be just judges even against themselves, and by study and self-examination have established a severe tribunal within themselves to which these principles which demand the advantages of the greater number are admitted to appeal. With some it assumes the mark of fear, with others that of hope – with all it is expectation.]

Such an estimate comes too with a worse grace from them who, if they would in opposition to their own unjust advantage take the lead in reform, might spare the nation from the inconveniences of the temporary dominion of the poor, who by means of that degraded condition which their insurrection would be designed to ameliorate are sufficiently incapable of discerning their own genuine and permanent advantage, though surely less incapable than those whose interests consist in proposing to themselves an object perfectly opposite [to] and wholly incompatible with that advantage: all public functionaries who are overpaid either in money or in power for their public services, beginning with the person invested with the royal authority and ending with the turnkey who extorts his last shilling from his starving prisoner; all members of the House of Lords who tremble lest the annihilation of their borough interest might not involve the risk of their hereditary legislative power and of those distinctions which considered in a pecuniary point of view are injurious to those beyond the pale of their caste in proportion as they are beneficial to those within; an immense majority of the assembly called the House of Commons, who would be reduced, if they desired to administer public business, to consult the interest of their electors and conform themselves. The functionaries who know that their claims to several millions yearly of the produce of the soil for the services of certain dogmas, which if necessary other men would enforce as effectually for as many thousands, would undergo a very severe examination [in the event of general Reform]. These persons propose to us the dilemma of submitting to a despotism which is notoriously gathering like an avalanche year by year, or taking the risk of something which it must be confessed bears the aspect of revolution. To this alternative we are reduced by the selfishness of those who taunt us with it.

[*The following passage is omitted in Mary Shelley's transcription*: It is of no avail that they call this selfishness principle or that they are self-deluded by the same sophism with which they would deceive others. To attach another name to the same idea to which those principles which demand the advantage of the greater number are admitted to appeal may puzzle the hearer but can in no manner change the import of it. But these, even should they be few, would yet be few among the many.]

And the history of the world teaches us not to hesitate an instant in the decision, if indeed the power of decision be not already past.

The establishment of King William III on the throne of England has already been referred to as a compromise between liberty and despotism. The Parliament of which that event was the act had ceased to be in an emphatic sense a representation of the people. The Long Parliament, questionless, was the organ of all classes of people in England since it effected the complete revolution in a tyranny consecrated by time. But since its meeting and since its dissolution a great change had taken place in England. Feudal manners and institutions having become obliterated, monopolies and patents having been abolished, property and personal liberty having been rendered secure, the nation advanced rapidly towards the acquirement of the elements of national prosperity. Population increased, a greater number of hands were employed in the labours of agriculture and commerce, towns arose where villages had been, and the proportion borne by those whose labour produces the materials of subsistence and enjoyment to those who claim for themselves a superfluity of these materials began to increase indefinitely. A fourth class therefore appeared in the nation, the unrepresented multitude. Nor was it so much that villages which sent no members to Parliament became great cities, and that towns which had been considerable enough to send members dwindled from local circumstances into villages. This cause no doubt contributed to the general effect of rendering the Commons House a less complete representation of the people. Yet had this been all, though it had ceased to be a legal and actual, it might still have been a virtual representation of the people. But the nation universally became multiplied into a denomination which had no constitutional presence in the state. This denomination had not existed before, or had existed only to a degree in which its interests were sensibly interwoven with that of those who enjoyed a constitutional presence. Thus, the proportion borne by the Englishmen who possessed [the] faculty of suffrage to those who were excluded from that faculty at the several periods of 1641 and 1688 had changed by the operation of these causes from 1 to 8 to 1 to 20. The rapid and effectual progress by which it changed from 1 to 20 to one to many hundreds in the interval between 1688 and 1819 is a process, to those familiar with history of the political economy of that period, which is rendered by these principles sufficiently intelligible. The number therefore of those who have influence on the government, even if numerically the same as at the former period, was relatively different. And a sufficiently just measure is afforded of the degree in which a country is enslaved or free by the consideration of the relative number of individuals who are admitted to the exercise of political rights. Meanwhile another cause was operating of a deeper and more extensive nature. The class who compose the Lords must, by the advantage of their situation as the great landed proprietors, possess a considerable influence over nomination to the Commons. This influence from an original imperfection in the equal distribution of suffrage was always enormous, but it is only since it has been combined with the cause before stated that it has appeared to be fraught with consequences incompatible with public liberty. In 1641 this influence was almost wholly [inoperative to] pervert the counsels of the nation from its own advantage. But at that epoch the enormous tyranny of the agents of the royal power weighed equally upon all denominations of men and united all counsels to extinguish it; add to which, the nation was as stated before in a very considerable degree fairly represented In Parliament. [The] common danger which was the bond of union between the aristocracy and the people having been destroyed, the former systematised their influence through the permanence of hereditary right, while the latter were losing power by the inflexibility of the institutions which forbade a just accommodation to their numerical increase. After the operations of these causes had commenced, the accession of William III placed a seal upon forty years of Revolution.

The government of this country at the period of 1688 was regal, tempered by aristocracy, for what conditions of democracy attach to an assembly one portion of which [was] imperfectly nominated by less than a twentieth part of the people, and another perfectly nominated by the nobles? For the nobility, having by the assistance of the people imposed close limitations upon the royal power, finding that power to be its natural ally and the people (for the people from the increase of their numbers acquired greater and more important rights while the organ through which those rights might be asserted grew feebler in proportion to the increase of the cause of those rights and of their importance) its natural enemy, made the Crown the mask and pretence of their own authority. At this period began that despotism of the oligarchy of party, and under colour of administering the executive power lodged in the king, represented in truth the interests of the rich. When it is said by political reasoners, speaking of the interval between 1688 and the present time, that the royal power progressively increased, they use an expression which suggests a very imperfect and partial idea. The power which has increased is that entrusted with the administration of affairs, composed of men responsible to the aristocratic assemblies, or to the reigning party in those assemblies which represents those orders of the nation which are privileged, and will retain power as long as it pleases them, and must be divested of power as soon as it ceases to please them. The power which has increased therefore is the [pow]er of the rich. The name and office of king is merely a mask of this power and is a kind of stalking-horse used to conceal these 'catchers of men', while they lay their nets. Monarchy is only the string which ties the robber's bundle. Though less contumelious and abhorrent from the dignity of human nature than an absolute monarchy, an oligarchy of this nature exacts more of suffering from the people because it reigns both by opinion generated by imposture and the force which that opinion places within its grasp.

At the epoch adverted to, the device of public credit was first systematically applied as an instrument of government. It was employed at the accession of William III less as a resource for meeting the financial exigencies of the state than as a bond to connect those in the possession of property with those who had, by taking advantage of an accident of party, acceded to power. In the interval elapsed since that period, it has accurately fulfilled the intention of its establishment and has continued to add strength to the government even until the present crisis. Now this advice is one of those execrable contrivances of misrule which overbalance the materials of common advantage produced by the progress of civilisation and increase the number of those who are idle in proportion to those who work, while it increases, through the factitious wants of those indolent, privileged persons, the quantity of work to be done. The rich, no longer being able to rule by force, have invented this scheme that they may rule by fraud.

The most despotic governments of antiquity were strangers to this invention, which is a compendious method of extorting from the people far more than praetorian guards and arbitrary tribunals and excise officers, created judges in the last resort, could ever wring. Neither the Persian monarchy nor the Roman Empire, where the will of one person was acknowledged as unappealable law, ever extorted a twentieth part the proportion now extorted from the property and labour of the inhabitants of Great Britain. The precious metals have been from the earliest records of civilisation employed as the signs of labour and the titles to an unequal distribution of its produce. The [government of] a country is necessarily entrusted with the affixing to certain portions of these metals a stamp by which to mark their genuineness; no other is considered as current coin, nor can be legal tender. The reason for this is that no alloyed coin should pass current and thereby depreciate the genuine, and by augmenting the price of the articles which are the produce of labour, defraud the holders of that which is genuine of the advantages legally belonging to them. If the government itself abuses the trust reposed in it to debase the coin in order that it may derive advantage from the unlimited multiplication of the mark entitling the holder to command the labour and property of others, the gradations by which it sinks, as labour rises, to the level of their comparative values, produces public confusion and misery. The foreign exchange meanwhile instructs the government how temporary was its resource. This mode of making the distribution of the sign of labour a source of private aggrandisement at the expense of public confusion and loss was not wholly unknown to the nations of antiquity,

But the modern scheme of public credit is a far subtler and more complicated contrivance of misrule. All great transactions of personal property in England are managed by signs and that is by the authority of the possessor expressed upon paper, thus representing in a compendious form his right to so much gold, which represents his right to so much labour. A man may write on a piece of paper what he pleases; he may say he is worth a thousand when he is not worth a hundred pounds. If he can make others believe this, he has credit for the sum to which his name is attached. And so long as this credit lasts, he can enjoy all the advantages which would arise out of the actual possession of the sum he is believed to possess. He can lend two hundred to this man and three to that other, and his bills, among those who believe that he possesses this sum, pass like money. Of course in the same proportion as bills of this sort, beyond the actual goods or gold and silver possessed by the drawer, pass current, they defraud those who have gold and silver and goods of the advantages legally attached to the possession of them, and they defraud the labourer and artisan of the advantage attached to increasing the nominal price of labour, and such a participation in them as their industry *might* command, while they render wages fluctuating and add to the toil of the cultivator and manufacturer.

The existing government of England in substituting a currency of paper [for] one of gold has had no need to depreciate the currency by alloying the coin of the country; they have merely fabricated pieces of paper on which they promise to pay a certain sum. The holders of these papers came for payment in some representation of property universally exchangeable. They then declared that the persons who held the office for that payment could not be forced by law to pay. They declared subsequently that these pieces of paper were the legal coin of the country. Of this nature are all such transactions of companies and banks as consist in the circulation of promissory notes to a greater amount than the actual property possessed by those whose names they bear. They have the effect of augmenting the prices of provision and of benefiting at the expense of the community the speculators in this traffic. One of the vaunted effects of this system is to increase the national industry: that is, to increase the labours of the poor and those luxuries of the rich which they supply; to make a manufacturer work sixteen hours where he only worked eight; to turn children into lifeless and bloodless machines at an age when otherwise they would be at play before the cottage doors of their parents; to augment indefinitely the proportion of those who enjoy the profit of the labour of others as compared with those who exercise this labour [. . .]

The consequences of this transaction have been the establishment of a new aristocracy, which has its basis in fraud as the old one had its basis in force. The hereditary landowners in England derived their title from royal grants – they are fiefs bestowed by conquerors, or church-lands, or they have been bought by bankers and merchants from those persons. Now bankers and merchants are persons whose [. . .] Since usage has consecrated the distinction of the word aristocracy from its primitive meaning [. . .] Let me be assumed to employ the word *aristocracy* in that ordinary sense which signifies that class of persons who possess a right to the produce of the labour of others, without dedicating to the common service any labour in return. This class of persons, whose existence is a prodigious anomaly in the social system, has ever constituted an inseparable portion of it, and there has never been an approach in practice towards any plan of political society modelled on equal justice, at least in the complicated mechanism of modern life. Mankind seem to acquiesce, as in a necessary condition of the imbecility of their own will and reason, in the existence of an aristocracy. With reference to this imbecility, it has doubtless been the instrument of great social advantage, although that advantage would have been greater which might have been produced according to the forms of a just distribution of the goods and evils of life. The object therefore of all enlightened legislation and administration is to enclose within the narrowest practicable limits this order of drones. The effect of the financial impostures of the modern rulers of England has been to increase the numbers of the drones. Instead of one aristocracy the condition [to] which, in the present state of human affairs, the friends of justice and liberty are willing to subscribe as to an inevitable evil, they have supplied us with two aristocracies: the one, consisting [of] great land proprietors and merchants who receive and interchange the produce of this country with the produce of other countries; in this, because all other great communities have as yet acquiesced in it, we acquiesce. Connected with the members of [it] is a certain generosity and refinement of manners and opinion which, although neither philosophy nor virtue has been that acknowledged substitute for them, at least is a religion which makes respected those venerable names. The other is an aristocracy of attorneys and excisemen and directors and government pensioners, usurers, stock jobbers, country bankers, with their dependants and descendants. These are a set of pelting wretches in whose employment there is nothing to exercise, even to their distortion, the more majestic faculties of the soul. Though at the bottom it is all trick, there is something frank and magnificent in the chivalrous disdain of infamy connected with a gentleman. There is something to which – until you see through the base falsehood upon which all inequality is founded – it is difficult for the imagination to refuse its respect in the faithful and direct dealings of the substantial merchant. But in the habits and lives of this new aristocracy created out of an increase [in] the public calamities, and whose existence must be determined by their termination, there is nothing to qualify our disapprobation. They eat and drink and sleep and, in the intervals of those things performed with most ridiculous ceremony and accompaniments, they cringe and lie. They poison the literature of the age in which they live by requiring either the antitype of their own mediocrity in books, or such stupid and distorted and inharmonious idealisms as alone have the power to stir their torpid imaginations. Their hopes and fears are of the narrowest description. Their domestic affections are feeble, and they have no others. They think of any commerce with their species but as a means, never as an end, and as a means to the basest forms of personal advantage.

If this aristocracy had arisen from a false and depreciated currency to the exclusion of the other, its existence would have been a moral calamity and disgrace, but it would not have constituted an oppression. But the hereditary aristocracy who held the political administration of affairs took the measures which created this other for purposes peculiarly its own. Those measures were so contrived as in no manner to diminish the wealth and power of the contrivers. The lord does not spare himself one luxury, but the peasant and artisan are assured of many needful things. To support the system of social order according to its supposed unavoidable constitution, those from whose labour all those external accommodations which distinguish a civilised being from a savage arise, worked, before the institution of this double aristocracy, eight hours. And of these only the healthy were compelled to labour, the efforts of the old, the sick, and the immature being dispensed with, and they being maintained by the labour of the sane, for such is the plain English of the poor-rates. That labour procured a competent share of the decencies of life, and society seemed to extend the benefits of its institution even to its most unvalued instruments. Although deprived of those resources of sentiment and knowledge which might have been their lot could the wisdom of the institutions of social forms have established a system of strict justice, yet they earned by their labour a competency in those external materials of life which, and not the loss of moral and intellectual excellence, is supposed to be the legitimate object of the desires and murmurs of the poor. Since the institution of this double aristocracy, however, they have often worked not ten but twenty hours a day. Not that all the poor have rigidly worked twenty hours, but that the worth of the labour of twenty hours now, in food and clothing, is equivalent to the worth of ten hours then. And because twenty hours labour cannot, from the nature of the human frame, be exacted from those who before performed ten, the aged and the sickly are compelled either to work or starve. Children who were exempted from labour are put in requisition, and the vigorous promise of the coming generation blighted by premature exertion. For fourteen hours labour which they do perform, they receive – no matter in what nominal amount – the price of seven. They eat less bread, wear worse clothes, are more ignorant, immoral, miserable, and desperate. This, then, is the condition of the lowest and the largest class from whose labour the whole materials of life are wrought, of which the others are only the receivers or the consumers. They are more superstitious, for misery on earth begets a diseased expectation and panic-stricken faith in miseries beyond the grave. God, they argue, rules this world as well as that; and assuredly since his nature is immutable, and his powerful will unchangeable, he rules them by the same laws. The gleams of hope which speak of Paradise seem like the flames in Milton's hell only to make darkness visible, and all things take [their] colour from what surrounds them. They become revengeful [. . .]

But the condition of all classes of society, excepting those within the privileged pale, is singularly unprosperous, and even they experience the reaction of their own short-sighted tyranny in all those sufferings and deprivations which are not of a distinctly physical nature, in the loss of dignity, simplicity and energy, and in the possession of all those qualities which distinguish a slave-driver from a proprietor. Right government being an institution for the purpose of securing such a moderate degree of happiness to men as has been experimentally practicable, the sure character of misgovernment is misery, and first discontent and, if that be despised, then insurrection, as the legitimate expression of that misery. The public ought to demand happiness; the labouring classes, when they cannot get food for their labour, are impelled to take it by force. Laws and assemblies and courts of justice and delegated powers placed in balance or in opposition are the means and the form, but public happiness is the substance and the end of political institution. Whenever this is attained in a nation, not from external force but from the internal arrangement and divisions of the common burthens of defence and maintenance, then there is oppression. And then arises an alternative between reform and the institution of a military despotism or a revolution in which these two parties, one starving after ill-digested systems of democracy, and the other clinging to the outworn abuses of power, leave the few who aspire to more than the former and who would overthrow the latter at whatever expense to wait until that modified advantage which results from this conflict produces a small portion of that social improvement which, with the temperance and the toleration which both regard as a crime, might have resulted from the occasion which they let pass in a far more signal manner.

The propositions which are the consequences or the corollaries to which the preceding reasoning seems to have conducted us are:

That the majority [of] the people of England are destitute and miserable, ill-clothed, ill-fed, ill-educated.

That they know this, and that they are impatient to procure a reform of the cause of their abject and wretched state.

That the cause of this peculiar misery is the unequal distribution which, under the form of the national debt, has been surreptitiously made of the products of their labour and the products of the labour of their ancestors; for all property is the produce of labour.

That the cause of that cause is a defect in the government.

That if they knew nothing of their condition, but believed that all they endured and all [they] were deprived of arose from the unavoidable condition of human life, this belief being an error, and [one] the endurance of [which] enforces an injustice, every enlightened and honourable person, whatever may be the imagined interest of his peculiar class, ought to excite them to the discovery of the true state of the case and to the temperate but irresistible vindication of their rights.

It is better that they should be instructed in the whole truth, that they should see the clear grounds of their rights, the objects to which they ought to tend; and be impressed with the first persuasion that patience and reason and endurance, and a calm yet invisible progress [. . .]

A reform in England is most just and necessary. What ought to be that reform?

A writer of the present day[318] [Thomas Malthus] (a priest of course, for his doctrines are those of a eunuch and of a tyrant) has stated that the evils of the poor arise from an excess of population, and that after they have been stripped naked by the tax-gatherer and reduced to bread and tea and fourteen hours of hard labour by their masters, and after the frost has bitten their defenceless limbs, and the cramp has wrung like a disease within their bones, and hunger – and the suppressed revenge of hunger – has stamped the ferocity of want like the mark of Cain upon their countenance, that the last tie by which Nature holds them to benignant earth whose plenty is garnered up in the strongholds of their tyrants, is to be divided; that the single alleviation of their sufferings and their scorns, the one thing which made it impossible to degrade them below the beasts, which amid all their crimes and miseries yet separated a cynical and unmanly contamination, an anti-social cruelty, from all soothing, elevating, and harmonious gentleness of the sexual intercourse and the humanising charities of domestic life which are its appendages – that this is to be obliterated. They are required to abstain from marrying under penalty of starvation. And it is threatened to deprive them of that property which is as strictly their birthright as a gentleman's land is his birthright, without giving them any compensation but the insulting advice to conquer, with minds undisciplined in the habits of higher gratification, a propensity which persons of the most consummate wisdom have been unable to resist, and which it is difficult to admire a person for having resisted. The doctrine of this writer is that the principle of population when under no dominion of moral restraint [is] outstripping the sustenance produced by the labour of man, and that not in proportion to the number of inhabitants, but operating equally in a thinly peopled community as in one where the population is enormous, being not a prevention but a check. So far a man might have been conducted by a train of reasoning which, though it may be shown to be defective, would argue in the reasoner no selfish and slavish feelings. But he has the hardened insolence to propose as a remedy that the poor should be compelled (for what except compulsion is a threat of the confiscation of those funds which by the institutions of their country had been set apart for their sustenance in sickness or destitution?) to abstain from sexual intercourse, while the rich are to be permitted to add as many mouths to consume the products of the labour of the poor as they please. The rights of all men are intrinsically and originally equal and they forgo the assertion of all of them only that they may the more securely enjoy a portion. If any new disadvantages are found to attach to the condition of social existence, those disadvantages ought not to be borne exclusively by one class of men, nor especially by that class whose ignorance leads them to exaggerate the advantages of sensual enjoyment, whose callous habits render domestic endearments more important to dispose them to resist the suggestions to violence and cruelty by which their situation ever exposes them to be tempted, and all whose other enjoyments are limited and few, while their sufferings are various and many. In this sense I cannot imagine how the advocates of equality would so readily have conceded that the unlimited operation of the principle of population affects the truth of these theories. On the contrary, the more heavy and certain are the evils of life, the more injustice is there in casting the burden of them exclusively on one order in the community. They seem to have conceded it merely because their opponents have insolently assumed it. Surely it is enough that the rich should possess to the exclusion of the poor all other luxuries and comforts, and wisdom, and refinement, the least envied but the most deserving of envy among all their privileges.

What is the reform that we desire? Before we aspire after theoretical perfection in the amelioration of our political state, it is necessary that we possess those advantages which we have been cheated of and to which the experience of modern times has proved that nations even under the present [conditions] are susceptible:

First, we would regain these; second, we would establish some form of government which might secure us against such a series of events as have conducted us to a persuasion that the forms according to which it is now administered are inadequate to that purpose.
We would abolish the national debt.
We would disband the standing army.
We would, with every possible regard to the existing interests of the holders, abolish sinecures.
We would, with every possible regard to the existing interests of the holders, abolish tithes, and make all religions, all forms of opinion respecting the origin and government of the universe, equal in the eye of the law.
We would make justice cheap, certain, and speedy, and extend the institution of juries to every possible occasion of jurisprudence.

The national debt was chiefly contracted in two libertine wars, undertaken by the privileged classes of the country – the first, for the ineffectual purpose of tyrannising over one portion of their subjects; the second, in order to extinguish the resolute spirit of obtaining their rights, in another. The labour which this money represents, and that which is represented by the money wrung, for purposes of the same detestable character, out of the people since the commencement of the American War would, if properly employed, have covered our land with monuments of architecture exceeding the sumptuousness and the beauty of Egypt and Athens; it might have made every peasant's cottage, surrounded with its garden, a little paradise of comfort, with every convenience desirable in civilised life; neat tables and chairs, and good beds, and a nice collection of useful books; and our ships, manned by sailors well paid and well clothed, might have kept watch round this glorious island against the less enlightened nations which assuredly would have envied, until they could have imitated, its prosperity. But the labour which is expressed by these sums has been diverted from these purposes of human happiness to the promotion of slavery, or the attempt at dominion, and a great portion of the sum in question is debt and must be paid. Is it to remain unpaid for ever, an eternal rent-charge upon the sacred soil from which the inhabitants of these islands draw their subsistence? This were to pronounce the perpetual institution of two orders of aristocracy, and men are in a temper to endure one with some reluctance. Is it to be paid now? If so what are the funds, or when and how is it to be paid? The fact is that the national debt is a debt not contracted by the whole nation towards a portion of it, but a debt contracted by the whole mass of the privileged classes towards one particular portion of those classes. If the principal were paid, the whole property of those who possess property must be valued and the public creditor, whose property would have been included in this estimate, satisfied out of the proceeds, it has been said that all the land in the nation is mortgaged for the amount of the national debt. This is a partial statement; not only all the land in the nation but all the property of whatever denomination, all the houses and the furniture and the goods and every article of merchandise, and the property which is represented by the very money lent by the fund-holder, who is bound to pay a certain portion as debtor while he is to receive another certain portion as creditor. The property of the rich is mortgaged: to use the language of the law, let the mortgagee foreclose.

If the principal of this debt were paid, after such reductions had been made so as to make an equal value, taking corn for the standard, be given as was received, it would be the rich who alone could, as justly they ought to, pay it. It would be a mere transfer among persons of property. Such a gentleman must lose a third of his estate, such a citizen a fourth of his money in the funds; the persons who borrowed would have paid, and the juggling and complicated system of paper finance be suddenly at an end. As it is, the interest is chiefly paid by those who had no hand in the borrowing and who are sufferers in other respects from the consequences of those transactions in which the money was spent.

The payment of the principal of what is called the national debt, which it is pretended is so difficult a problem, is only difficult to those who do not see who is the creditor and who the debtor, and who are the wretched sufferers from whom they both wring taxes which under the form of interest is given by the former [latter] and accepted by the latter [former]. It is from the labour of those who have no property that all the persons who possess property think to extort the perpetual interest of a debt, the whole of them to the part, which the latter [former] know they could not persuade the former [latter] to pay, but by conspiring with them in an imposture which makes the third class pay what the first [second] neither received by their sanction nor spent for their benefit, and what the second [first] never lent to them. They would both shift to the labour of the present and of all succeeding generations the payment of the interest of their own debt, from themselves and their posterity, because the payment of the principal would be no more than a compromise and transfer of property between each other by which the nation would be spared forty-four millions a year, which now is paid to maintain in luxury and indolence the public debtors and to protect them from the demand of their creditors upon them, who, being part of the same body and owing as debtors while they possess a claim as creditors, agree to abstain from demanding the principal which they must all unite to pay, for the sake of receiving an enormous interest which is principally wrung out of those who had no concern whatever in the transaction. One of the first acts of a reformed government would undoubtedly be an effectual scheme for compelling these to compromise their debt between themselves.

When I speak of persons of property, I mean not every man who possesses any right of property; I mean the rich. Every man whose scope in society has a plebeian and intelligible utility, whose personal exertions are more valuable to him than his capital; every tradesman who is not a monopolist, all surgeons and physicians and those mechanics and editors and literary men and artists, and farmers, all those persons whose profits spring from honourably and honestly exerting their own skill or wisdom or strength in greater abundance than from the employment of money to take advantage of the necessity of the starvation of their fellow citizens for their profit, or those who pay, as well as those more obviously understood by the labouring classes, the interest of the national debt. It is the interest of all these persons as well as that of the poor to insist upon the payment of the principal.

For this purpose the form ought to be as simple and succinct as possible. The operations deciding who was to pay, at what time and how much and to whom are, divested of financial chicanery, problems readily to be determined. The common tribunals may possess a legal jurisdiction to award the proportion due upon the several claim of each.

There are two descriptions of property which, without entering into the subtleties of a more refined moral theory as applicable to the existing forms of society, are entitled to two very different measures of forbearance and regard. And this forbearance and regard have by political institutions usually been accorded in an inverse reason from what is just and natural. Labour, industry, economy, skill, genius, or any similar powers honourably and innocently exerted, are the foundations of one description of property, and all true political institutions ought to defend every man in the exercise of his discretion with respect to property so acquired. Of this kind is the principal part of the property enjoyed by those who are but one degree removed from the class which subsists by daily labour. Yet there are instances of persons in this class who have procured their property by fraudulent and violent means, as there are instances in the other of persons who have acquired their property by innocent or honourable exertion. All political science abounds with limitations and exceptions. Property thus acquired, men leave to their children. Absolute right becomes weakened by descent, first because it is only to avoid the greater evil of arbitrarily interfering with the discretion of any man in matters of property that the great evil of acknowledging any person to have an exclusive right to property who has not created it by his skill or labour is admitted, and secondly because the mode of its having been originally acquired is forgotten, and it is confounded with the property acquired in a very different manner; and the principle upon which all property justly rests, after the great principle of the general advantage, becomes thus disregarded and misunderstood. Yet the privilege of disposing of property by will is one necessarily connected with the existing forms of domestic life, and exerted merely by those who have acquired property by industry or who have preserved it by economy it would never produce any great and invidious inequality of fortune. A thousand accidents would perpetually tend to level the accidental elevation and the signs of property would perpetually recur to those whose deserving skill might attract or whose labour might create it.

But there is another species of property which has its foundation in usurpation or imposture or violence without which by the nature of things immense possessions of gold or land could never have been accumulated. Of this nature is the principal part of the property enjoyed by the aristocracy and by the great fund-holders, the great majority of whose ancestors never either deserved it by their skill and talents or acquired and created it by their personal labour. It could not be that they deserved it, for if the honourable exertion of the most glorious imperial faculties of our nature had been the criterion of the possession of property, the posterity of Shakespeare, of Milton, of Hampden, of Lor[d Bacon] would be the wealthiest proprietors in England. It could not be that they acquired it by legitimate industry, for, besides that the real mode of acquisition is a matter of history, no honourable profession or honest trade, nor the hereditary exercise of it, ever in such numerous instances accumulated masses of property so vast as those enjoyed by the ruling orders in England. They were either grants from the feudal sovereigns whose right to what they granted was founded upon conquest or oppression, both a denial of all right; or they were the lands of the ancient Catholic clergy which, according to the most acknowledged principles of public justice, reverted to the nation at their suppression; or they were the products of patents and monopolies, an exercise of sovereignty more pernicious than direct violence to the interests of a commercial nation; or in later times such property has been accumulated by dishonourable cunning and the taking advantage of a fictitious paper currency to obtain an unfair power over labour and the fruits of labour.

Property thus accumulated being transmitted from father to son acquires, as property of the more legitimate kind loses, force and sanction, but in a more limited manner. For not only on an examination and recurrence to first principles is it seen to have been founded on a violation of all that to which the latter owes its sacredness, but it is felt in its existence and perpetuation as a public burthen, and known as a rallying point to the ministers of tyranny, having the property of a snowball, gathering as it rolls, and rolling until it bursts. [It] is astonishing that political theorists have not branded [it] as the most pernicious and odious. [Yet] there are three sets of people: one who can place a thing to another in an intelligible light, another who can understand it when so communicated, and a third who can neither discover [n]or understand it.

Labour and skill and the immediate wages of labour and skill is a property of the most sacred and indisputable right and the foundation of all other property. And the right of a man [to] property in the exertion of his own bodily and mental faculties, or to the produce and free reward from and for that exertion, is the most [inalienable of rights]. If, however, he takes by violence, or appropriates to himself through fraudulent cunning, or receives from another property so acquired, his claim to that property is of a far inferior force. We may acquiesce, if we evidently perceive an overbalance of public advantage in submission under this claim; but if any public emergency should arise, at which it might be necessary as at present by a tax on capital to satisfy the claims of a part of the nation by a contribution from such national resources as may with the least injustice be appropriated to that purpose, assuredly it would not be on labour and skill, the foundation of all property, nor on the profits and savings of labour and skill, which are property itself, but on such possession which can only be called property in a modified sense, as have from their magnitude and their nature an evident origin in violence or imposture.

The national debt, as has been stated, is a debt contracted by the whole of a particular class in the nation towards a portion of that class. It is sufficiently clear that this debt was not contracted for the purpose of the public advantage. Besides there was no authority in the nation competent to a measure of this nature. The usual vindication of national debts is that, [since] they are contracted in an overwhelming measure for the purpose of defence against a common danger, for the vindication of the rights and liberties of posterity, it is just that posterity should bear the burthen of payment. This reasoning is most fallacious. The history of nations presents us with a succession of extraordinary emergencies, and through their present imperfect organisation their existence is perpetually threatened by new and unexpected combinations and developments of foreign or internal force. Imagine a situation of equal emergency to occur to England as that which the ruling party assume to have occurred as their excuse for burthening the nation with the perpetual payment of £45,000,000 annually. Suppose France, Russia and America were to enter into a league against England, the first to revenge [avenge] its injuries, the second to satisfy its ambition, the third to soothe its jealousy. Could the nation bear £90,000,000 of yearly interest? Must there be twice as many luxurious and idle persons? Must the labourer receive for twenty-eight hours' work what he now receives for fourteen, as he now receives for fourteen what he once received for seven? But this argument [. . .]

What is meant by a reform of Parliament? If England were a republic governed by one assembly; if there were no chamber of hereditary aristocracy which is at once an actual and a virtual representation of all who claim through rank or wealth superiority over their countrymen; if there were no king who is as the rallying point of those whose tendency is at once to [gather] and to confer that power which is consolidated at the expense of the nation, then [. . .]

The advocates of universal suffrage have reasoned correctly that no individual who is governed can be denied a direct share in the government of his country without supreme justice. If we pursue the train of reasonings which have conducted to this conclusion, we discover that systems of social order still more incompatible than universal suffrage with any reasonable hope of instant accomplishment appear to be that which should result from a just combination of the elements of social life. I do not understand why those reasoners who propose at any price an immediate appeal to universal suffrage, because it is that which it is injustice to withhold, do not insist on the same ground on the immediate abolition, for instance, of monarchy and aristocracy, and the levelling of inordinate wealth, and an agrarian distribution, including the parks and chases of the rich, of the uncultivated districts of the country. No doubt the institution of universal suffrage would by necessary consequence *immediately* tend to the *temporary* abolition of these forms; because it is impossible that the people, having attained power, should fail to see what the demagogues now conceal from them – the legitimate consequence of the doctrines through which they had attained it. A republic, however just in its principle and glorious in its object, would through violence and sudden change which must attend it incur a great risk of being as rapid in its decline as in its growth. It is better that they should be instructed in the whole truth; that they should see the clear grounds of their rights, the objects to which they ought to tend; and be impressed with the just persuasion that patience and reason and endurance [are the means of] a calm yet irresistible progress. A civil war, which might be engendered by the passions attending on this mode of reform, would confirm in the mass of the nation those military habits which have been already introduced by our tyrants and with which liberty is incompatible. From the moment that a man is a soldier, he becomes a slave. He is taught obedience; his will is no longer – which is the most sacred prerogative of man – guided by his own judgement. He is taught to despise human life and human suffering; this is the universal distinction of slaves. He is more degraded than a murderer; he is like the bloody knife which has stabbed and feels not; a murderer we may abhor and despise, a soldier is by profession beyond abhorrence and below contempt.

CHAPTER 3

Probable Means

That Commons should reform itself, uninfluenced by any fear that the people would, on their refusal, assume to itself that office, seems a contradiction. What need of reform if it expresses the will and watches over the interests of the public? And if, as is sufficiently evident, it despises that will and neglects that interest, what motives would incite it to institute a reform which the aspect of the times renders indeed sufficiently perilous, but without which there will speedily be no longer anything in England to distinguish it from the basest and most abject community of slaves that ever existed?

The great principle of reform consists in every individual of mature age and perfect understanding giving his consent to the institution and the continued existence of the social system which is instituted for his advantage and for the advantage of others in his situation. As in a great nation this is practically impossible, masses of individuals consent to qualify other individuals, whom they delegate to superintend their concerns. These delegates have constitutional authority to exercise the functions of sovereignty; they unite in the highest degree the legislature and executive functions. A government that is founded on any other basis is a government of fraud or force and ought on the first convenient occasion to be overthrown. The broad principle of political reform is the natural equality of men, not with relation to their property but to their rights. That equality in possessions which Jesus Christ so passionately taught is a moral rather than political truth and is such as social institutions cannot without mischief inflexibly secure. Morals and politics can only be considered as portions of the same science, with relation to a system of such absolute perfection as Christ and Plato and Rousseau and other reasoners have asserted, and as Godwin has, with irresistible eloquence, systematised and developed. Equality in possessions must be the last result of the utmost refinements of civilisation; it is one of the conditions of that system of society towards which, with whatever hope of ultimate success, it is our duty to tend. We may and ought to advert to it as to the elementary principle, as to the goal, unattainable perhaps by us, but which, as it were, we revive in our posterity to pursue. We derive tranquillity and courage and grandeur of soul from contemplating an object which is because we will it, and may be because we hope and desire it, and must be if succeeding generations of the enlightened sincerely and earnestly seek it. We should with sincere and patient as [. . .]

But our present business is with the difficult and unbending realities of actual life, and when we have drawn inspiration from the great object of our hopes it becomes us with patience and resolution to apply ourselves to accommodating our theories to immediate practice.

That representative assembly called the House of Commons ought questionless to be *immediately* nominated by the great mass of the people. The aristocracy and those who unite in their own persons the vast privileges conferred by the possession of inordinate wealth are sufficiently represented by the House of Peers and by the King. Those theorists who admire and would put into action the mechanism of what is called the British Constitution would acquiesce in this view of the question. For if the House of Peers be a permanent representative of the privileged classes, if the regal power be no more than another form, and a form still more jealousy to be regarded, of the same representation, while the House of Commons be not chosen by the mass of the population, what becomes of that democratic element, upon the presence of which it has been supposed that the waning superiority of England over the surrounding nations has depended?

Any sudden attempt at universal suffrage would produce an immature attempt at a republic. It [is better] that [an] object so inexpressibly great and sacred should never have been attempted than that it should be attempted and fail. It is no prejudice to the ultimate establishment of the boldest political innovations that we temporise so as, when they shall be accomplished, they may be rendered permanent.

Considering the population of Great Britain and Ireland as twenty millions and the representative assembly as five hundred, each member ought to be the expression of the will of 40,000 persons; of these two-thirds would [consist of] women and children and persons under age; the actual number of voters therefore for each member would be 13,333. The whole extent of the empire might be divided into five hundred electoral departments or parishes, and the inhabitants assemble on a certain day to exercise their rights of suffrage.

Mr Bentham and other writers have urged the admission of females to the right of suffrage; this attempt seems somewhat immature. Should my opinion be the result of despondency, the writer of these pages would be the last to withhold his vote from any system which might tend to an equal and full development of the capacities of all living beings.

The system of voting by ballot which some reasoners have recommended is attended with obvious inconveniences. [It withdraws the elector from the regard of his country, and] his neighbours, and permits him to conceal the motives of his vote, which, if concealed, cannot but be dishonourable; when, if he had known that he had to render a public account of his conduct, he would never have permitted them to guide him. There is in this system of voting by ballot, and of electing a member of the *Representative Assembly* as a churchwarden is elected, something too mechanical. The elector and the elected ought to meet one another face to face and interchange the meanings of actual presence and share some common impulses and, in a degree, understand each other. There ought to be the common sympathy of the excitements of a popular assembly among the electors themselves. The imagination would thus be strongly excited, and a mass of generous and enlarged and popular sentiments be awakened, which would give the vitality of [. . .]

That republican boldness of censuring and judging one another, which has indeed [been] exerted in England under the title of public opinion, though perverted from its true uses into an instrument of prejudice and calumny, would then be applied to its genuine purposes. Year by year the people would become more susceptible of assuming forms of government more simple and beneficial.

It is in this publicity of the exercise of sovereignty that the difference between the republics of Greece and the monarchies of Asia consisted. The actions of the times [. . .]

If the existing government shall compel the nation to take the task of reform into its own hands, one of the most obvious consequences of such a circumstance would be the abolition of monarchy and aristocracy. Why, it will then be argued, if the subsisting condition of social forms is to be thrown into confusion, should these things be endured? Then why do we now endure them? Is it because we think that an hereditary King is cheaper and wiser than an elected President, or a House of Lords and a Bench of Bishops are institutions modelled by the wisdom of the most refined and civilised periods, beyond which the wit of mortal man can furnish nothing more perfect? In case the subsisting government should compel the people to revolt to establish a representative assembly in defiance of them and to assume in that assembly an attitude of resistance and defence, this question would probably be answered in a very summary manner. No friend of mankind and of his country can desire that such a crisis should suddenly arrive; but still less, once having arrived, can he hesitate under what banner to array his person and his power. At the peace, the people would have been contented with strict economy and severe retrenchment, and some direct and intelligible plan for producing that equilibrium between the capitalists and the land holders which is delusively styled the payment of the national debt; had this system been adopted, they probably would have refrained from exacting Parliamentary reform, the only secure guarantee that it would have been pursued. Two years ago it might still have been possible to have commenced a system of gradual reform. The people were then insulted, tempted and betrayed, and *the petitions of a million* of men rejected with disdain. Now they are more miserable, more hopeless, more impatient of their misery. Above all, they have become more universally aware of the true sources of their misery. It is possible that the period of conciliation is past, and that after having played with the confidence and cheated the expectations of the people, their passions will be too little under discipline to allow them to wait the slow, gradual and certain operation of such a reform as we can imagine the constituted authorities to concede.

Upon the issue of this question depends the species of reform which a philosophical mind should regard with approbation. If reform shall be begun by the existing government, let us be contented with a limited *beginning*, with any whatsoever opening; let the rotten boroughs be disfranchised and their rights transferred to the unrepresented cities and districts of the nation; it is no matter how slow, gradual and cautious be the change; we shall demand more and more with firmness and moderation, never anticipating, but never deferring the moment of successful opposition, so that the people may become habituated [to] exercising the functions of sovereignty, in proportion as they acquire the possession of it. If reform could begin from within the Houses of Parliament, as constituted at present, it appears to me that what is called moderate reform, that is a suffrage whose qualification should be the possession of a certain small property, and triennial parliaments, would be principles – a system in which, for the sake of obtaining without bloodshed or confusion ulterior improvements of a more important character, all reformers ought to acquiesce. Not that such are first principles, or that they would produce a system of perfect social institutions or one approaching to [such]. But nothing is more idle than to reject a limited benefit because we cannot without great sacrifices obtain an unlimited one. We might thus reject a representative republic, if it were obtainable, on the plea that the imagination of man can conceive of something more absolutely perfect. Towards whatsoever we regard as perfect, undoubtedly it is no less our duty than it is our nature to press forward; this is the generous enthusiasm which accomplishes not indeed the consummation after which it aspires, but one which approaches it in a degree far nearer than if the whole powers had not been developed by a delusion. It is in politics rather than in religion that faith is meritorious.

If the Houses of Parliament obstinately and perpetually refuse to concede any reform to the people, my vote is for universal suffrage and equal representation. My vote is – but, it is asked, how shall this be accomplished, in defiance of and in opposition to the constituted authorities of the nation, they who possess whether with or without its consent the command of a standing army and of a legion of spies and police officers and hold all the strings of that complicated mechanism with which the hopes and fears of men are moved like puppets? They would disperse any assembly really chosen by the people; they would shoot and hew down any multitude, without regard to sex or age as the Jews did the Canaanites, which might be collected in its defence; they would calumniate, imprison, starve, ruin and expatriate every person who wrote or acted or thought or might be suspected to think against them; misery and extermination would fill the country from one end to another [. . .]

This question I would answer by another.

Will you endure to pay the half of your earnings to maintain in luxury and idleness the confederation of your tyrants as the reward of a successful conspiracy to defraud and oppress you? Will you make your tame cowardice and the branding record of it the everlasting inheritance of your posterity? Not only this: will you render by your torpid endurance this condition of things as permanent as the system of castes in India, by which the same horrible injustice is perpetrated under another form?

Assuredly no Englishmen by whom these propositions are understood will answer in the affirmative; and the opposite side of the alternative remains.

When the majority in any nation arrive at a conviction that it is their duty and their interest to divest the minority of a power employed to their disadvantage, and the minority are sufficiently mistaken as to believe that their superiority is tenable, a struggle must ensue.

If the majority are enlightened, united, impelled by a uniform enthusiasm and animated by a distinct and powerful apprehension of their object – and full confidence in their undoubted power – the struggle is merely nominal. The minority perceive the approaches of the development of an irresistible force. By the influence of the public opinion of their weakness on those political forms of which no government but an absolute despotism is devoid, they divest themselves of their usurped distinctions; the public tranquillity is not disturbed by the revolution.

But these conditions may only be imperfectly fulfilled by the state of a people grossly oppressed and impotent to cast off the load. Their enthusiasm may have been subdued by the killing weight of toil and suffering; they may be panic-stricken and disunited by their oppressors and the demagogues; the influence of fraud may have been sufficient to weaken the union of classes which compose them by suggesting jealousies; and the position of the conspirators, although it is to be forced by repeated assaults, may be tenable until the siege can be vigorously urged. The true patriot will endeavour to enlighten and to unite the nation and animate it with enthusiasm and confidence. For this purpose he will be indefatigable in promulgating political truth. He will endeavour to rally round one standard the divided friends of liberty and make them forget the subordinate objects with regard to which they differ by appealing to that respecting which they are all agreed. He will promote such open confederations among men of principle and spirit as may tend to make their intentions and their efforts converge to a common centre. He will discourage all secret associations which have a tendency, by making national will develop itself in a partial and premature manner, to cause tumult and confusion. He will urge the necessity of exciting the people frequently to exercise their right of assembling in such limited numbers as that all present may be actual parties to the proceedings of the day. Lastly, if circumstances had collected a more considerable number as at Manchester on the memorable 16th of August [1819], if the tyrants command their troops to fire upon them or cut them down unless they disperse, he will exhort them peaceably to risk the danger, and to expect without resistance the onset of the cavalry, and wait with folded arms the event of the fire of the artillery, and receive with unshrinking bosoms the bayonets of the charging battalions. Men are every day persuaded to incur greater perils for a less manifest advantage. And this, not because active resistance is not justifiable when all other means shall have failed, but because in this instance temperance and courage would produce greater advantages than the most decisive victory. In the first place the soldiers are men and Englishmen, and it is not to be believed that they would massacre an unresisting multitude of their countrymen drawn up in unarmed array before them and bearing in their looks the calm, deliberate resolution to perish rather than abandon the assertion of their rights. In the confusion of flight the ideas of the soldier become confused and he massacres those who fly from him by the instinct of his trade. In the struggle of conflict and resistance he is irritated by a sense of his own danger; he is flattered by an apprehension of his magnanimity in incurring it; he considers the blood of his countrymen at once the price of his valour, the pledge of his security. He applauds himself by reflecting that these base and dishonourable motives will gain him credit among his comrades and his officers, who are animated by the same as if they were something the same. But if he should observe neither resistance nor flight he would be reduced to impotence and indecision. Thus far, his ideas were governed by the same law as those of a dog who chases a flock of sheep to the corner of the field and keeps aloof when they make the firm parade of resistance. But the soldier is a man and an Englishman. This unexpected reception would probably throw him back upon a recollection of the true nature of the measures of which he was made an instrument, and the enemy might be converted into the ally.

The patriot will be foremost to publish the boldest truths in the most fearless manner, yet without the slightest tincture of personal malignity. He would encourage all others to the same efforts and assist them to the utmost of his power with the resources both of his intellect and fortune. He would call upon them to despise imprisonment and persecution and lose no opportunity of bringing public opinion and the power of the tyrants into circumstances of perpetual contest and opposition.

All might, however, be ineffectual to produce so uniform an impulse of the national will as to preclude a further struggle. The strongest argument, perhaps, for the necessity of reform is the inoperative and unconscious abjectness to which the purposes of a considerable mass of the people are reduced. They neither know nor care. They are sinking into a resemblance with the Hindus and the Chinese, who were once men as they are. Unless the cause which renders them passive subjects instead of active citizens be removed, they will sink with accelerated gradations into that barbaric and unnatural civilisation which destroys all the differences among men. It is in vain to exhort us to wait until all men shall desire freedom whose real interest will consist in its establishment. It is in vain to hope to enlighten them while their tyrants employ the utmost artifices of all their complicated engine to perpetuate the infection of every species of fanaticism and error from generation to generation. The advocates of reform ought indeed to leave no effort unexerted, and they ought to be indefatigable in exciting all men to examine [. . .]

But if they wait until those neutral politicians, a class whose opinions represent the actions of this class, are persuaded that so soon [as] effectual reform is necessary, the occasion will have passed or will never arrive, and the people will have exhausted their strength in ineffectual expectation and will have sunk into incurable supineness. It was principally as the [effect of] a similar quietism that the populous and extensive nations of Asia have fallen into their existing decrepitude; and that anarchy, insecurity, ignorance, and barbarism, the symptoms of the confirmed disease of monarchy, have reduced nations of the most delicate physical and intellectual organisation and under the most fortunate climates of the globe to a blank in the history of man. The manufacturers to a man are persuaded of the necessity of reform; an immense majority of the inhabitants of London [. . .]

The reasoners who incline to the opinion that it is not sufficient that the innovators should produce a majority in the nation, but that we ought to expect such an unanimity as would preclude anything amounting to a serious dispute, are prompted to this view of the question by the dread of anarchy and massacre. Infinite and inestimable calamities belong to oppression, but the most fatal of them all is that mine of unexploded mischief which it has practised beneath the foundations of society, and with which, 'pernicious to one touch', it threatens to involve the ruin of the entire building together with its own. But delay merely renders these mischiefs more tremendous, not the less inevitable. For the utmost may now be the crisis of the social disease [which] is rendered thus periodical, chronic, and incurable.

The savage brutality of the populace is proportioned to the arbitrary character of their government, and tumults and insurrections soon, as in Constantinople, become consistent with the permanence of the causing evil, of which they might have been the critical determination.

The public opinion in England ought first to [be] excited to action, and the durability of those forms within which the oppressors entrench themselves brought perpetually to the test of its operation. No law or institution can last if this opinion be distinctly pronounced against it. For this purpose government ought to be defied, in cases of questionable result, to prosecute for political libel. All questions relating to the jurisdiction of magistrates and courts of law respecting which any doubt could be raised ought to be agitated with indefatigable pertinacity. Some two or three of the popular leaders have shown the best spirit in this respect; they only want system and co-operation. The tax-gatherer ought to be compelled in every practicable instance to distrain while the right to impose taxes, as was the case in the beginning of the resistance to the tyranny of Charles I, is formally contested by an overwhelming multitude of defendants before the courts of common law. Confound the subtlety of lawyers with the subtlety of the law. All of the nation would thus be excited to develop itself and to declare whether it acquiesced in the existing forms of government. The manner in which all questions of this nature might be decided would develop the occasions and afford a prognostic as to the success of more decisive measures. Simultaneously with this active and vigilant system of opposition, means ought to be taken of solemnly conveying the sense of large bodies and various denominations of the people in a manner the most explicit to the existing depositories of power. Petitions couched in the actual language of the petitioners, and emanating from distinct assemblies, ought to load the tables of the House of Commons. The poets, philosophers and artists ought to remonstrate, and the memorials entitled their petitions might show the diversity [of] convictions they entertain of the inevitable connection between national prosperity and freedom, and the cultivation of the imagination, and the cultivation of scientific truth, and the profound development of moral and metaphysical enquiry. Suppose these memorials to be severally written by Godwin, Hazlitt, Bentham and Hunt, they would be worthy of the age and of the cause; these, radiant and irresistible like the meridian sun, would strike all but the eagles who dared to gaze upon its beams, with blindness and confusion. These appeals of solemn and emphatic argument from those who have already a predestined existence among posterity would appal the enemies of mankind by their echoes from every corner of the world in which the majestic literature of England is cultivated; it would be like a voice from beyond the dead of those who will live in the memories of men, when they must be forgotten; it would be Eternity warning Time.

Let us hope that at this stage of the progress of reform, the oppressors would feel their impotence and reluctantly and imperfectly concede some limited portion of the rights of the people and disgorge some morsels of their undigested prey. In this case the people ought to be exhorted by everything ultimately dear to them to pause until by the exercise of those rights which they have regained they become fitted to demand more. It is better that we gain what we demand by a process of negotiation which would occupy twenty years than that by communicating a sudden shock to the interests of those who are the depositories and dependants of power we should incur the calamity which their revenge might inflict upon us by giving the signal of civil war. If, after all, they consider the chance of personal ruin and the infamy of figuring on the page of history as the promoters of civil war preferable to resigning any portion how small soever of their usurped authority, we are to recollect that we possess a right beyond remonstrance. It has been acknowledged by the most approved writers on the English constitution, which is in this instance merely [a] declaration of the superior decisions of eternal justice, that we possess a right of resistance. The claim of the [reigning] family is founded upon a memorable exertion of this solemnly recorded right.

The last resort of resistance is undoubtedly insurrection. The right of insurrection is derived from the employment of armed force to counteract the will of the nation. Let the government disband the standing army, and the purpose of resistance would be sufficiently fulfilled by the incessant agitation of the points of dispute before the courts of common law and by an unwarlike display of the irresistible number and union of the people.

Before we enter into a consideration of the measures which might terminate in civil war, let us for a moment consider the nature and the consequences of war. This is the alternative which the unprincipled cunning of the tyrants has presented to us, from which we must not sh[rink]. There is secret sympathy between destruction and power, between monarchy and war; and the long experience of the history of all recorded time teaches us with what success they have played into each other's hands. War is a kind of superstition; the pageantry of arms and badges corrupts the imagination of men. How far more appropriate would be the symbols of an inconsolable grief – muffled drums, and melancholy music, and arms reversed, and the livery of sorrow rather than of blood. When men mourn at funerals, for what do they mourn in comparison with the calamities which they hasten with all circumstance of festivity to suffer and to inflict! Visit in imagination the scene of a field of battle or a city taken by assault, collect into one group the groans and the distortions of the innumerable dying, the inconsolable grief and horror of their surviving friends, the hellish exultation, and unnatural drunkenness of destruction of the conquerors, the burning of the harvests and the obliteration of the traces of cultivation. To this, in civil war is to be added the sudden disruption of the bonds of social life, and 'father against son'.

If there had never been war, there could never have been tyranny in the world; tyrants take advantage of the mechanical organisation of armies to establish and defend their encroachments. It is thus that the mighty advantages of the French Revolution have been almost compensated by a succession of tyrants (for demagogues, oligarchies, usurpers, and legitimate kings are merely varieties of the same class) from Robespierre to Louis XVIII. War, waged from whatever motive, extinguishes the sentiment of reason and justice in the mind. The motive is forgotten, or only adverted to in a mechanical and habitual manner. A sentiment of confidence in brute force and in a contempt of death and danger is considered as the highest virtue, when, in truth and however indispensable, they are merely the means and the instruments, highly capable of being perverted to destroy the cause they were assumed to promote. It is a foppery the most intolerable to an amiable and philosophical mind. It is like what some reasoners have observed of religious faith: no false and indirect motive to action can subsist in the mind without weakening the effect of those which are genuine and true. The person who thinks it virtuous to believe will think a less degree of virtue attaches to good actions than if he had considered it as indifferent. The person who has been accustomed to subdue men by force will be less inclined to the trouble of convincing or persuading them.

These brief considerations suffice to show that the true friend of mankind and of his country would hesitate before he recommended measures which tend to bring down so heavy a calamity as war.

I imagine, however, that before the English nation shall arrive at that point of moral and political degradation now occupied by the Chinese, it will be necessary to appeal to an exertion of physical strength. If the madness of parties admits no other mode of determining the question at issue [. . .]

When the people shall have obtained, by whatever means, the victory over their oppressors and when persons appointed by them shall have taken their seats in the Representative Assembly of the nation and assumed the control of public affairs according to constitutional rules, there will remain the great task of accommodating all that can be preserved of ancient forms with the improvements of the knowledge of a more enlightened age in legislation, jurisprudence, government, and religious and academical institutions. The settlement of the national debt is on the principles before elucidated merely circumstance of form, and however necessary and important is an affair of mere arithmetical proportions readily determined; nor can I see how those, who, being deprived of their unjust advantages, will probably inwardly murmur, can oppose one word of open expostulation to a measure of such inescapable justice.

There is one thing which certain vulgar agitators endeavour to flatter the most uneducated part of the people by assiduously proposing, which they ought not to do nor to require: and that is, Retribution. Men having been injured desire to injure in return. This is falsely called a universal law of human nature; it is a law from which many are exempt, and all in proportion to their virtue and cultivation. The savage is more revengeful than the civilised man; the ignorant and uneducated than the person of a refined and cultivated intellect; the generous and [. . .]

[*The work was left incomplete.*]

A Defence of Poetry

According to one mode of regarding those two classes of mental action which are called reason and imagination, the former may be considered as mind contemplating the relations borne by one thought to another, however produced; and the latter, as mind acting upon those thoughts so as to colour them with its own light, and composing from them as from elements, other thoughts, each containing within itself the principle of its own integrity. The one is the τὸ ποιεῖν, or the principle of synthesis, and has for its object those forms which are common to universal nature and existence itself; the other is the τὸ λογιζειν,[319] or principle of analysis, and its action regards the relations of things, simply as relations; considering thoughts, not in their integral unity, but as the algebraical representations which conduct to certain general results. Reason is the enumeration of quantities already known; imagination is the perception of the value of those quantities, both separately and as a whole. Reason respects the differences and imagination the similitudes of things. Reason is to the imagination as the instrument to the agent, as the body to the spirit, as the shadow to the substance.

Poetry, in a general sense, may be defined to be 'the expression of the imagination': and poetry is connate with the origin of man. Man is an instrument over which a series of external and internal impressions are driven, like the alternations of an ever-changing wind over an Aeolian lyre, which move it by their motion to ever-changing melody. But there is a principle within the human being, and perhaps within all sentient beings, which acts otherwise than in a lyre, and produces not melody alone, but harmony, by an internal adjustment of the sounds and motions thus excited to the impressions which excite them. It is as if the lyre could accommodate its chords to the motions of that which strikes them, in a determined proportion of sound; even as the musician can accommodate his voice to the sound of the lyre. A child at play by itself will express its delight by its voice and motions; and every inflexion of tone and gesture will bear exact relation to a corresponding antitype in the pleasurable impressions which awakened it; it will be the reflected image of that impression; and as the lyre trembles and sounds after the wind has died away, so the child seeks, by prolonging in its voice and motions the duration of the effect, to prolong also a consciousness of the cause. In relation to the objects which delight a child, these expressions are what poetry is to higher objects. The savage (for the savage is to ages what the child is to years) expresses the emotions produced in him by surrounding objects in a similar manner; and language and gesture, together with plastic or pictorial imitation, become the image of the combined effect of those objects and his apprehension of them. Man in society, with all his passions and his pleasures, next becomes the object of the passions and pleasures of man; an additional class of emotions produces an augmented treasure of expression; and language, gesture and the imitative arts become at once the representation and the medium, the pencil and the picture, the chisel and the statue, the chord and the harmony. The social sympathies, or those laws from which as from its elements society results, begin to develop themselves from the moment that two human beings coexist; the future is contained within the present as the plant within the seed; and equality, diversity, unity, contrast, mutual dependence, become the principles alone capable of affording the motives according to which the will of a social being is determined to action, inasmuch as he is social; and constitute pleasure in sensation, virtue in sentiment, beauty in art, truth in reasoning, and love in the intercourse of kind. Hence men, even in the infancy of society, observe a certain order in their words and actions, distinct from that of the objects and the impressions represented by them, all expression being subject to the laws of that from which it proceeds. But let us dismiss those more general considerations which might involve an enquiry into the principles of society itself, and restrict our view to the manner in which the imagination is expressed upon its forms.

In the youth of the world, men dance and sing and imitate natural objects, observing in these actions, as in all others, a certain rhythm or order. And, although all men observe a similar, they observe not the same order, in the motions of the dance, in the melody of the song, in the combinations of language, in the series of their imitations of natural objects. For there is a certain order or rhythm belonging to each of these classes of mimetic representation from which the hearer and the spectator receive an intenser and purer pleasure than from any other: the sense of an approximation to this order has been called taste by modern writers. Every man in the infancy of art, observes an order which approximates more or less closely to that from which this highest delight results: but the diversity is not sufficiently marked, as that its gradations should be sensible, except in those instances where the predominance of this faculty of approximation to the beautiful (for so we may be permitted to name the relation between this highest pleasure and its cause) is very great. Those in whom it exists to excess are poets, in the most universal sense of the word; and the pleasure resulting from the manner in which they express the influence of society or nature upon their own minds, communicates itself to others, and gathers a sort of reduplication from the community. Their language is vitally metaphorical; that is, it marks the before unapprehended relations of things and perpetuates their apprehension, until words, which represent them, become, through time, signs for portions or classes of thought, instead of pictures of integral thoughts; and then, if no new poets should arise to create afresh the associations which have been thus disorganised, language will be dead to all the nobler purposes of human intercourse. These similitudes or relations are finely said by Lord Bacon[320] to be 'the same footsteps of nature impressed upon the various subjects of the world'* – and he considers the faculty which perceives them as the storehouse of axioms common to all knowledge. In the infancy of society every author is necessarily a poet, because language itself is poetry; and to be a poet is to apprehend the true and the beautiful, in a word, the good which exists in the relation subsisting first between existence and perception, and secondly between perception and expression. Every original language near to its source is in itself the chaos of a cyclic poem: the copiousness of lexicography and the distinctions of grammar are the works of a later age, and are merely the catalogue and the form of the creations of poetry.

But poets, or those who imagine and express this indestructible order, are not only the authors of language and of music, of the dance, and architecture, and statuary, and painting; they are the institutors of laws and the founders of civil society, and the inventors of the arts of life, and the teachers who draw into a certain propinquity with the beautiful and the true that partial apprehension of the agencies of the invisible world which is called religion. Hence all original religions are allegorical or susceptible of allegory, and, like Janus,[321] have a double face of false and true. Poets, according to the circumstances of the age and nation in which they appeared, were called, in the earlier epochs of the world, legislators or prophets:[322] a poet essentially comprises and unites both these characters. For he not only beholds intensely the present as it is, and discovers those laws according to which present things ought to be ordered, but he beholds the future in the present, and his thoughts are the germs of the flower and the fruit of latest time. Not that I assert poets to be prophets in the gross sense of the word, or that they can foretell the form as surely as they foreknow the spirit of events: such is the pretence of superstition, which

* *De Augment. Scient.*, Ch. I, lib. iii

would make poetry an attribute of prophecy, rather than prophecy an attribute of poetry. A poet participates in the eternal, the infinite, and the one; as far as relates to his conceptions, time and place and number are not. The grammatical forms which express the moods of time, and the difference of persons, and the distinction of place, are convertible with respect to the highest poetry without injuring it as poetry; and the choruses of Aeschylus,[323] and the book of Job, and Dante's *Paradise*,[324] would afford, more than any other writings, examples of this fact, if the limits of this essay did not forbid citation. The creations of sculpture, painting, and music, are illustrations still more decisive.

Language, colour, form, and religious and civil habits of action, are all the instruments and materials of poetry; they may be called poetry by that figure of speech which considers the effect as a synonyme of the cause. But poetry in a more restricted sense expresses those arrangements of language, and especially metrical language, which are created by that imperial faculty, whose throne is curtained within the invisible nature of man. And this springs from the nature itself of language, which is a more direct representation of the actions and passions of our internal being, and is susceptible of more various and delicate combinations, than colour, form, or motion, and is more plastic and obedient to the control of that faculty of which it is the creation. For language is arbitrarily produced by the imagination, and has relation to thoughts alone; but all other materials, instruments, and conditions of art, have relations among each other, which limit and interpose between conception and expression. The former is as a mirror which reflects, the latter as a cloud which enfeebles, the light of which both are mediums of communication. Hence the fame of sculptors, painters, and musicians, although the intrinsic powers of the great masters of these arts may yield in no degree to that of those who have employed language as the hieroglyphic of their thoughts, has never equalled that of poets in the restricted sense of the term; as two performers of equal skill will produce unequal effects from a guitar and a harp. The fame of legislators and founders of religion, so long as their institutions last, alone seems to exceed that of poets in the restricted sense; but it can scarcely be a question, whether, if we deduct the celebrity which their flattery of the gross opinions of the vulgar usually conciliates, together with that which belonged to them in their higher character of poets, any excess will remain.

We have thus circumscribed the word poetry within the limits of that art which is the most familiar and the most perfect expression of the faculty itself. It is necessary, however, to make the circle still narrower, and to determine the distinction between measured and unmeasured language; for the popular division into prose and verse is inadmissible in accurate philosophy.

Sounds as well as thoughts have relation both between each other and towards that which they represent, and a perception of the order of those relations has always been found connected with a perception of the order of the relations of thought. Hence the language of poets has ever affected a certain uniform and harmonious recurrence of sound, without which it were not poetry, and which is scarcely less indispensable to the communication of its influence than the words themselves, without reference to that peculiar order. Hence the vanity of translation; it were as wise to cast a violet into a crucible that you might discover the formal principle of its colour and odour, as seek to transfuse from one language into another the creations of a poet. The plant must spring again from its seed, or it will bear no flower – and this is the burthen of the curse of Babel.

An observation of the regular mode of the recurrence of harmony in the language of poetical minds, together with its relation to music, produced metre, or a certain system of traditional forms of harmony and language. Yet it is by no means essential that a poet should accommodate his language to this traditional form, so that the harmony, which is its spirit, be observed. The practice is indeed convenient and popular, and to be preferred, especially in such composition as includes much action: but every great poet must inevitably innovate upon the example of his predecessors in the exact structure of his peculiar versification. The distinction between poets and prose writers is a vulgar error. The distinction between philosophers and poets has been anticipated. Plato[325] was essentially a poet – the truth and splendour of his imagery, and the melody of his language, are the most intense that it is possible to conceive. He rejected the measure of the epic, dramatic and lyrical forms because he sought to kindle a harmony in thoughts divested of shape and action, and he forbore to invent any regular plan of rhythm which would include, under determinate forms, the varied pauses of his style. Cicero[326] sought to imitate the cadence of his periods, but with little success. Lord Bacon was a poet.* His language has a sweet and majestic rhythm, which satisfies the sense, no less than the almost superhuman wisdom of his philosophy satisfies the intellect; it is a strain which distends, and then bursts the circumference of the reader's mind, and pours itself forth together with it into the universal element with which it has perpetual sympathy. All the authors of revolutions in opinion are not only necessarily poets as they are inventors, nor even as their words

---

* See the *Filum Labyrinthi* and the 'Essay on Death' particularly.

unveil the permanent analogy of things by images which participate in the life of truth; but as their periods are harmonious and rhythmical, and contain in themselves the elements of verse; being the echo of the eternal music. Nor are those supreme poets, who have employed traditional forms of rhythm on account of the form and action of their subjects, less capable of perceiving and teaching the truth of things than those who have omitted that form. Shakespeare, Dante and Milton (to confine ourselves to modern writers) are philosophers of the very loftiest power.

A poem is the very image of life expressed in its eternal truth. There is this difference between a story and a poem, that a story is a catalogue of detached facts, which have no other connection than time, place, circumstance, cause, and effect; the other is the creation of actions according to the unchangeable forms of human nature, as existing in the mind of the Creator, which is itself the image of all other minds. The one is partial, and applies only to a definite period of time and a certain combination of events which can never again recur; the other is universal, and contains within itself the germ of a relation to whatever motives or actions have place in the possible varieties of human nature. Time, which destroys the beauty and the use of the story of particular facts, stripped of the poetry which should invest them, augments that of poetry, and for ever develops new and wonderful applications of the eternal truth which it contains. Hence epitomes have been called the moths of just history; they eat out the poetry of it. A story of particular facts is as a mirror which obscures and distorts that which should be beautiful: poetry is a mirror which makes beautiful that which is distorted.

The parts of a composition may be poetical, without the composition as a whole being a poem A single sentence may be considered as a whole, though it may be found in the midst of a series of unassimilated portions; a single word even may be a spark of inextinguishable thought. And thus all the great historians, Herodotus, Plutarch, Livy,[327] were poets; and although the plan of these writers, especially that of Livy, restrained them from developing this faculty in its highest degree, they made copious and ample amends for their subjection by filling all the interstices of their subjects with living images.

Having determined what is poetry, and who are poets, let us proceed to estimate its effects upon society.

Poetry is ever accompanied with pleasure: all spirits upon which it falls open themselves to receive the wisdom which is mingled with its delight. In the infancy of the world, neither poets themselves nor their auditors are fully aware of the excellence of poetry: for it acts in a divine and unapprehended manner, beyond and above consciousness; and it is reserved for future generations to contemplate and measure the mighty cause and effect in all the strength and splendour of their union. Even in modern times, no living poet ever arrived at the fullness of his fame; the jury which sits in judgement upon a poet, belonging as he does to all time, must be composed of his peers: it must be empanelled by time from the selectest of the wise of many generations. A poet is a nightingale, who sits in darkness and sings to cheer its own solitude with sweet sounds; his auditors are as men entranced by the melody of an unseen musician, who feel that they are moved and softened, yet know not whence or why. The poems of Homer[328] and his contemporaries were the delight of infant Greece; they were the elements of that social system which is the column upon which all succeeding civilisation has reposed. Homer embodied the ideal perfection of his age in human character; nor can we doubt that those who read his verses were awakened to an ambition of becoming like to Achilles, Hector, and Ulysses: the truth and beauty of friendship, patriotism, and persevering devotion to an object, were unveiled to their depths in these immortal creations: the sentiments of the auditors must have been refined and enlarged by a sympathy with such great and lovely impersonations, until from admiring they imitated, and from imitation they identified themselves with the objects of their admiration. Nor let it be objected that these characters are remote from moral perfection, and that they are by no means to be considered as edifying patterns for general imitation. Every epoch, under names more or less specious, has deified its peculiar errors; Revenge is the naked idol of the worship of a semi-barbarous age: and Self-deceit is the veiled image of unknown evil, before which luxury and satiety lie prostrate. But a poet considers the vices of his contemporaries as the temporary dress in which his creations must be arrayed, and which cover without concealing the eternal proportions of their beauty. An epic or dramatic personage is understood to wear them around his soul, as he may the ancient armour or modern uniform around his body; whilst it is easy to conceive a dress more graceful than either. The beauty of the internal nature cannot be so far concealed by its accidental vesture, but that the spirit of its form shall communicate itself to the very disguise, and indicate the shape it hides from the manner in which it is worn. A majestic form and graceful motions will express themselves through the most barbarous and tasteless costume. Few poets of the highest class have chosen to exhibit the beauty of their conceptions in its naked truth and splendour; and it is doubtful whether the alloy of costume, habit, &c., be not necessary to temper this planetary music for mortal ears.

The whole objection, however, of the immorality of poetry rests upon a misconception of the manner in which poetry acts to produce the moral improvement of man. Ethical science arranges the elements which poetry has created, and propounds schemes and proposes examples of civil and domestic life: nor is it for want of admirable doctrines that men hate, and despise, and censure, and deceive, and subjugate one another. But poetry acts in another and diviner manner. It awakens and enlarges the mind itself by rendering it the receptacle of a thousand unapprehended combinations of thought. Poetry lifts the veil from the hidden beauty of the world, and makes familiar objects be as if they were not familiar; it reproduces all that it represents, and the impersonations clothed in its Elysian light stand thenceforward in the minds of those who have once contemplated them as memorials of that gentle and exalted content which extends itself over all thoughts and actions with which it coexists. The great secret of morals is love; or a going out of our own nature, and an identification of ourselves with the beautiful which exists in thought, action, or person, not our own. A man, to be greatly good, must imagine intensely and comprehensively; he must put himself in the place of another and of many others; the pains and pleasures of his species must become his own. The great instrument of moral good is the imagination; and poetry administers to the effect by acting upon the cause. Poetry enlarges the circumference of the imagination by replenishing it with thoughts of ever new delight, which have the power of attracting and assimilating to their own nature all other thoughts, and which form new intervals and interstices whose void for ever craves fresh food. Poetry strengthens the faculty which is the organ of the moral nature of man, in the same manner as exercise strengthens a limb. A poet therefore would do ill to embody his own conceptions of right and wrong, which are usually those of his place and time, in his poetical creations, which participate in neither. By this assumption of the inferior office of interpreting the effect, in which perhaps after all he might acquit himself but imperfectly, he would resign a glory in the participation of the cause. There was little danger that Homer, or any of the eternal poets, should have so far misunderstood themselves as to have abdicated this throne of their widest dominion. Those in whom the poetical faculty, though great, is less intense, as Euripides, Lucan, Tasso, Spenser,[329] have frequently affected a moral aim, and the effect of their poetry is diminished in exact proportion to the degree in which they compel us to advert to this purpose.

Homer and the cyclic poets were followed at a certain interval by the dramatic and lyrical poets of Athens, who flourished contemporaneously with all that is most perfect in the kindred expressions of the poetical faculty: architecture, painting, music, the dance, sculpture, philosophy and, we may add, the forms of civil life. For although the scheme of Athenian society was deformed by many imperfections which the poetry existing in chivalry and Christianity has erased from the habits and institutions of modern Europe; yet never at any other period has so much energy, beauty and virtue been developed; never was blind strength and stubborn form so disciplined and rendered subject to the will of man, or that will less repugnant to the dictates of the beautiful and the true, as during the century which preceded the death of Socrates. Of no other epoch in the history of our species have we records and fragments stamped so visibly with the image of the divinity in man. But it is poetry alone, in form, in action, and in language, which has rendered this epoch memorable above all others, and the storehouse of examples to everlasting time. For written poetry existed at that epoch simultaneously with the other arts, and it is an idle enquiry to demand which gave and which received the light which all, as from a common focus, have scattered over the darkest periods of succeeding time. We know no more of cause and effect than a constant conjunction of events: poetry is ever found to coexist with whatever other arts contribute to the happiness and perfection of man. I appeal to what has already been established to distinguish between the cause and the effect.

It was at the period here adverted to, that the drama had its birth; and however a succeeding writer may have equalled or surpassed those few great specimens of the Athenian drama which have been preserved to us, it is indisputable that the art itself never was understood or practised according to the true philosophy of it, as at Athens. For the Athenians employed language, action, music, painting, the dance and religious institutions to produce a common effect in the representation of the highest idealisms of passion and of power; each division in the art was made perfect in its kind by artists of the most consummate skill, and was disciplined into a beautiful proportion and unity one towards the other. On the modern stage a few only of the elements capable of expressing the image of the poet's conception are employed at once. We have tragedy without music and dancing, and music and dancing without the highest impersonations of which they are the fit accompaniment, and both without religion and solemnity. Religious institution has indeed been usually banished from the stage. Our system of divesting the actor's face of a mask, on which the many expressions appropriated to his dramatic character might be moulded into one permanent and unchanging expression, is favourable only to a partial and inharmonious effect; it is fit for nothing but a monologue where all the attention may be directed to some great master of ideal mimicry. The modern practice of blending comedy with tragedy, though liable to great abuse in point of practice, is undoubtedly an extension of the dramatic circle, but the comedy should be as in *King Lear*, universal, ideal, and sublime. It is perhaps the intervention of this principle which determines the balance in favour of *King Lear* against the *Oedipus Tyrannus* or the *Agamemnon*,[330] or, if you will, the trilogies with which they are connected; unless the intense power of the choral poetry, especially that of the latter, should be considered as restoring the equilibrium. *King Lear*, if it can sustain this comparison, may be judged to be the most perfect specimen of the dramatic art existing in the world; in spite of the narrow conditions to which the poet was subjected by the ignorance of the philosophy of the drama which has prevailed in modern Europe. Calderon,[331] in his religious *Autos*, has attempted to fulfil some of the high conditions of dramatic representation neglected by Shakespeare; such as the establishing a relation between the drama and religion, and the accommodating them to music and dancing; but he omits the observation of conditions still more important, and more is lost than gained by the substitution of the rigidly defined and ever-repeated idealisms of a distorted superstition for the living impersonations of the truth of human passions.

But I digress. – The connection of scenic exhibitions with the improvement or corruption of the manners of men has been universally recognised: in other words, the presence or absence of poetry in its most perfect and universal form has been found to be connected with good and evil in conduct or habit. The corruption which has been imputed to the drama as an effect begins when the poetry employed in its constitution ends: I appeal to the history of manners whether the periods of the growth of the one and the decline of the other have not corresponded with an exactness equal to any example of moral cause and effect.

The drama at Athens, or wheresoever else it may have approached to its perfection, ever coexisted with the moral and intellectual greatness of the age. The tragedies of the Athenian poets are as mirrors in which the spectator beholds himself, under a thin disguise of circumstance, stripped of all but that ideal perfection and energy which everyone feels to be the internal type of all that he loves, admires, and would become. The imagination is enlarged by a sympathy with pains and passions so mighty that they distend in their conception the capacity of that by which they are conceived; the good affections are strengthened by pity, indignation, terror and sorrow; and an exalted calm is prolonged from the satiety of this high exercise of them into the tumult of familiar life; even crime is disarmed of half its horror and all its contagion by being represented as the fatal consequence of the unfathomable agencies of nature; error is thus divested of its wilfulness; men can no longer cherish it as the creation of their choice. In the drama of the highest order there is little food for censure or hatred; it teaches rather self-knowledge and self-respect. Neither the eye nor the mind can see itself, unless reflected upon that which it resembles. The drama, so long as it continues to express poetry, is a prismatic and many-sided mirror, which collects the brightest rays of human nature and divides and reproduces them from the simplicity of these elementary forms, and touches them with majesty and beauty, and multiplies all that it reflects, and endows it with the power of propagating its like wherever it may fall.

But in periods of the decay of social life, the drama sympathises with that decay. Tragedy becomes a cold imitation of the form of the great masterpieces of antiquity, divested of all harmonious accompaniment of the kindred arts; and often the very form misunderstood, or a weak attempt to teach certain doctrines, which the writer considers as moral truths; and which are usually no more than specious flatteries of some gross vice or weakness, with which the author, in common with his auditors, are infected. Hence what has been called the classical and domestic drama. Addison's[332] *Cato* is a specimen of the one; and would it were not superfluous to cite examples of the other! To such purposes poetry cannot be made subservient. Poetry is a sword of lightning, ever unsheathed, which consumes the scabbard that would contain it. And thus we observe that all dramatic writings of this nature are unimaginative in a singular degree; they affect sentiment and passion, which, divested of imagination, are other names for caprice and appetite. The period in our own history of the grossest degradation of the drama is the reign of Charles II, when all forms in which poetry had been accustomed to be expressed became hymns to the triumph of kingly power over liberty and virtue. Milton stood alone, illuminating an age unworthy of him. At such periods the calculating principle pervades all the forms of dramatic exhibition, and poetry ceases to be expressed upon them. Comedy loses its ideal universality: wit succeeds to humour; we laugh from self-complacency and triumphs instead of pleasure; malignity, sarcasm, and contempt, succeed to sympathetic merriment; we hardly laugh, but we smile. Obscenity, which is ever blasphemy against the divine beauty in life, becomes, from the very veil which it assumes, more active if less disgusting: it is a monster for which the corruption of society forever brings forth new food, which it devours in secret.

The drama being that form under which a greater number of modes of expression of poetry are susceptible of being combined than any other, the connection of poetry and social good is more observable in the drama than in whatever other form. And it is indisputable that the highest perfection of human society has ever corresponded with the highest dramatic excellence; and that the corruption or the extinction of the drama in a nation where it has once flourished, is a mark of a corruption of manners, and an extinction of the energies which sustain the soul of social life. But, as Machiavelli[333] says of political institutions, that life may be preserved and renewed, if men should arise capable of bringing back the drama to its principles. And this is true with respect to poetry in its most extended sense: all language, institution and form require not only to be produced but to be sustained: the office and character of a poet participates in the divine nature as regards providence, no less than as regards creation.

Civil war, the spoils of Asia, and the fatal predominance first of the Macedonian, and then of the Roman arms, were so many symbols of the extinction or suspension of the creative faculty in Greece. The bucolic writers,[334] who found patronage under the lettered tyrants of Sicily and Egypt, were the latest representatives of its most glorious reign. Their poetry is intensely melodious; like the odour of the tuberose, it overcomes and sickens the spirit with excess of sweetness: whilst the poetry of the preceding age was as a meadow-gale of June, which mingles the fragrance of all the flowers of the field, and adds a quickening and harmonising spirit of its own which endows the sense with a power of sustaining its extreme delight. The bucolic and erotic delicacy in written poetry is correlative with that softness in statuary, music, and the kindred arts, and even in manners and institutions, which distinguished the epoch to which I now refer. Nor is it the poetical faculty itself, or any misapplication of it, to which this want of harmony is to be imputed. An equal sensibility to the influence of the senses and the affections is to be found in the writings of Homer and Sophocles: the former, especially, has clothed sensual and pathetic images with irresistible attractions. The superiority in these to succeeding writers consists in the presence of those thoughts which belong to the inner faculties of our nature, not in the absence of those which are connected with the external: their incomparable perfection consists in a harmony of the union of all. It is not what the erotic poets have, but what they have not, in which their imperfection consists. It is not inasmuch as they were poets, but inasmuch as they were not poets, that they can be considered with any plausibility as connected with the corruption of their age. Had that corruption availed so as to extinguish in them the sensibility to pleasure, passion, and natural scenery, which is imputed to them as an imperfection, the last triumph of evil would have been achieved. For the end of social corruption is to destroy all sensibility to pleasure; and, therefore, it is corruption. It begins at the imagination and the intellect as at the core, and distributes itself thence as a paralysing venom, through the affections into the very appetites, until all become a torpid mass in which hardly sense survives. At the approach of such a period, poetry ever addresses itself to those faculties which are the last to be destroyed, and its voice is heard, like the footsteps of Astraea,[335] departing from the world. Poetry ever communicates all the pleasure which men are capable of receiving: it is ever still the light of life; the source of whatever of beautiful or generous or true can have place in an evil time. It will readily be confessed that those among the luxurious citizens of Syracuse and Alexandria, who were delighted with the poems of Theocritus, were less cold, cruel, and sensual than the remnant of their tribe. But corruption must utterly have destroyed the fabric of human society before poetry can ever cease. The sacred links of that chain have never been entirely disjoined, which descending through the minds of many men is attached to those great minds, whence as from a magnet the invisible effluence is sent forth, which at once connects, animates, and sustains the life of all. It is the faculty which contains within itself the seeds at once of its own and of social renovation. And let us not circumscribe the effects of the bucolic and erotic poetry within the limits of the sensibility of those to whom it was addressed. They may have perceived the beauty of those immortal compositions, simply as fragments and isolated portions: those who are more finely organised, or born in a happier age, may recognise them as episodes to that great poem, which all poets, like the co-operating thoughts of one great mind, have built up since the beginning of the world.

The same revolutions within a narrower sphere had place in ancient Rome; but the actions and forms of its social life never seem to have been perfectly saturated with the poetical element. The Romans appear to have considered the Greeks as the selectest treasuries of the selectest forms of manners and of nature, and to have abstained from creating in measured language, sculpture, music, or architecture, anything which might bear a particular relation to their own condition, whilst it should bear a general one to the universal constitution of the world. But we judge from partial evidence, and we judge perhaps partially. Ennius, Varro, Pacuvius, and Accius,[336] all great poets, have been lost. Lucretius[337] is in the highest, and Virgil[338] in a very high sense, a creator. The chosen delicacy of expressions of the latter are as a mist of light which conceal from us the intense and exceeding truth of his conceptions of nature. Livy is instinct with poetry.

Yet Horace, Catullus, Ovid,[339] and generally the other great writers of the Virgilian age, saw man and nature in the mirror of Greece. The institutions also, and the religion of Rome, were less poetical than those of Greece, as the shadow is less vivid than the substance. Hence poetry in Rome seemed to follow, rather than accompany, the perfection of political and domestic society. The true poetry of Rome lived in its institutions; for whatever of beautiful, true, and majestic, they contained, could have sprung only from the faculty which creates the order in which they consist. The life of Camillus, the death of Regulus; the expectation of the senators, in their godlike state, of the victorious Gauls; the refusal of the republic to make peace with Hannibal, after the battle of Cannae, were not the consequences of a refined calculation of the probable personal advantage to result from such a rhythm and order in the shows of life, to those who were at once the poets and the actors of these immortal dramas. The imagination beholding the beauty of this order, created it out of itself according to its own idea; the consequence was empire, and the reward everlasting fame. These things are not the less poetry, *quia carent vate sacro*.[340] They are the episodes of that cyclic poem written by Time upon the memories of men. The Past, like an inspired rhapsodist, fills the theatre of everlasting generations with their harmony.

At length the ancient system of religion and manners had fulfilled the circle of its evolutions. And the world would have fallen into utter anarchy and darkness, but that there were found poets among the authors of the Christian and chivalric systems of manners and religion, who created forms of opinion and action never before conceived; which, copied into the imaginations of men, became as generals to the bewildered armies of their thoughts. It is foreign to the present purpose to touch upon the evil produced by these systems: except that we protest, on the ground of the principles already established, that no portion of it can be attributed to the poetry they contain.

It is probable that the poetry of Moses, Job, David, Solomon and Isaiah had produced a great effect upon the mind of Jesus and his disciples. The scattered fragments preserved to us by the biographers of this extraordinary person are all instinct with the most vivid poetry. But his doctrines seem to have been quickly distorted. At a certain period after the prevalence of a system of opinions founded upon those promulgated by him, the three forms into which Plato had distributed the faculties of mind underwent a sort of apotheosis, and became the object of the worship of the civilised world. Here it is to be confessed that 'Light seems to thicken', and

> The crow makes wing to the rooky wood,
> Good things of day begin to droop and drowse,
> And night's black agents to their preys do rouse.[341]

But mark how beautiful an order has sprung from the dust and blood of this fierce chaos! how the world, as from a resurrection, balancing itself on the golden wings of knowledge and of hope, has reassumed its yet unwearied flight into the heaven of time. Listen to the music, unheard by outward ears, which is as a ceaseless and invisible wind, nourishing its everlasting course with strength and swiftness.

The poetry in the doctrines of Jesus Christ, and the mythology and institutions of the Celtic conquerors of the Roman empire, outlived the darkness and the convulsions connected with their growth and victory, and blended themselves in a new fabric of manners and opinion. It is an error to impute the ignorance of the dark ages to the Christian doctrines or the predominance of the Celtic nations. Whatever of evil their agencies may have contained sprang from the extinction of the poetical principle, connected with the progress of despotism and superstition. Men, from causes too intricate to be here discussed, had become insensible and selfish: their own will had become feeble, and yet they were its slaves, and thence the slaves of the will of others: but fear, avarice, cruelty, and fraud, characterised a race amongst whom no one was to be found capable of *creating* in form, language, or institution. The moral anomalies of such a state of society are not justly to be charged upon any class of events immediately connected with them, and those events are most entitled to our approbation which could dissolve it most expeditiously. It is unfortunate for those who cannot distinguish words from thoughts, that many of these anomalies have been incorporated into our popular religion.

It was not until the eleventh century that the effects of the poetry of the Christian and chivalric systems began to manifest themselves. The principle of equality had been discovered and applied by Plato in his *Republic*, as the theoretical rule of the mode in which the materials of pleasure and of power produced by the common skill and labour of human beings ought to be distributed among them. The limitations of this rule were asserted by him to be determined only by the sensibility of each, or the utility to result to all. Plato, following the doctrines of Timaeus and Pythagoras,[342] taught also a moral and intellectual system of doctrine, comprehending at once the past, the present, and the future condition of man. Jesus Christ divulged the sacred and eternal truths contained in these views to mankind, and Christianity, in its abstract purity, became the exoteric expression of the esoteric doctrines of the poetry and wisdom of antiquity. The incorporation of the Celtic nations with the exhausted population of the south, impressed upon it the figure of the poetry existing in their mythology and institutions. The result was a sum of the action and reaction of all the causes included in it; for it may be assumed as a maxim that no nation or religion can supersede any other without incorporating into itself a portion of that which it supersedes. The abolition of personal and domestic slavery, and the emancipation of women from a great part of the degrading restraints of antiquity, were among the consequences of these events.

The abolition of personal slavery is the basis of the highest political hope that it can enter into the mind of man to conceive. The freedom of women produced the poetry of sexual love. Love became a religion, the idols of whose worship were ever present. It was as if the statues of Apollo and the Muses had been endowed with life and motion, and had walked forth among their worshippers; so that earth became peopled by the inhabitants of a diviner world. The familiar appearance and proceedings of life became wonderful and heavenly, and a paradise was created as out of the wrecks of Eden. And as this creation itself is poetry, so its creators were poets; and language was the instrument of their art: 'Galeotto fù il libro, e chi lo scrisse.'[343] The Provençal Trouveurs,[344] or inventors, preceded Petrarch,[345] whose verses are as spells which unseal the inmost enchanted fountains of the delight which is in the grief of love. It is impossible to feel them without becoming a portion of that beauty which we contemplate: it were superfluous to explain how the gentleness and elevation of mind connected with these sacred emotions can render men more amiable, more generous and wise, and lift them out of the dull vapours of the little world of self. Dante understood the secret things of love even more than Petrarch. His Vita Nuova[346] is an inexhaustible fountain of purity of sentiment and language: it is the idealised history of that period, and those intervals of his life which were dedicated to love. His apotheosis of Beatrice in Paradise, and the gradations of his own love and her loveliness, by which as by steps he feigns himself to have ascended to the throne of the Supreme Cause, is the most glorious imagination of modern poetry. The acutest critics have justly reversed the judgement of the vulgar, and the order of the great acts of the 'Divine Drama', in the measure of the admiration which they accord to the Hell, Purgatory and Paradise. The latter is a perpetual hymn of everlasting love. Love, which found a worthy poet in Plato alone of all the ancients, has been celebrated by a chorus of the greatest writers of the renovated world; and the music has penetrated the caverns of society, and its echoes still drown the dissonance of arms and superstition. At successive intervals,

Ariosto. Tasso, Shakespeare, Spenser, Calderon, Rousseau[347] and the great writers of our own age, have celebrated the dominion of love, planting as it were trophies in the human mind of that sublimest victory over sensuality and force. The true relation borne to each other by the sexes into which human kind is distributed, has become less misunderstood; and if the error which confounded diversity with inequality of the powers of the two sexes has been partially recognised in the opinions and institutions of modern Europe, we owe this great benefit to the worship of which chivalry was the law, and poets the prophets.

The poetry of Dante may be considered as the bridge thrown over the stream of time, which unites the modern and ancient world. The distorted notions of invisible things which Dante and his rival Milton have idealised are merely the mask and the mantle in which these great poets walk through eternity enveloped and disguised. It is a difficult question to determine how far they were conscious of the distinction which must have subsisted in their minds between their own creeds and that of the people. Dante at least appears to wish to mark the full extent of it by placing Riphaeus,[348] whom Virgil calls *justissimus unus,* in *Paradise*, and observing a most heretical caprice in his distribution of rewards and punishments. And Milton's poem contains within itself a philosophical refutation of that system of which, by a strange and natural antithesis, it has been a chief popular support. Nothing can exceed the energy and magnificence of the character of Satan as expressed in *Paradise Lost*. It is a mistake to suppose that he could ever have been intended for the popular personification of evil. Implacable hate, patient cunning, and a sleepless refinement of device to inflict the extremest anguish on an enemy, these things are evil; and, although venial in a slave, are not to be forgiven in a tyrant; although redeemed by much that ennobles his defeat in one subdued, they are marked by all that dishonours his conquest in the victor. Milton's Devil[349] as a moral being is as far superior to his God as one who perseveres in some purpose, which he has conceived to be excellent in spite of adversity and torture, is to one who in the cold security of undoubted triumph inflicts the most horrible revenge upon his enemy, not from any mistaken notion of inducing him to repent of a perseverance in enmity, but with the alleged design of exasperating him to deserve new torments. Milton has so far violated the popular creed (if this shall be judged to be a violation) as to have alleged no superiority of moral virtue to his god over his devil. And this bold neglect of a direct moral purpose is the most decisive proof of the supremacy of Milton's genius. He mingled as it were the elements of human nature as colours upon a single pallet, and arranged them in the composition of his great picture according to the laws of epic truth, that is, according to the laws of that principle by which a series of actions of the external universe and of intelligent and ethical beings is calculated to excite the sympathy of succeeding generations of mankind. The *Divina Commedia* and *Paradise Lost* have conferred upon modern mythology a systematic form; and when change and time shall have added one more superstition to the mass of those which have arisen and decayed upon the earth, commentators will be learnedly employed in elucidating the religion of ancestral Europe, only not utterly forgotten because it will have been stamped with the eternity of genius.

Homer was the first and Dante the second epic poet: that is, the second poet, the series of whose creations bore a defined and intelligible relation to the knowledge and sentiment and religion of the age in which he lived, and of the ages which followed it: developing itself in correspondence with their development. For Lucretius had limed the wings of his swift spirit in the dregs of the sensible world; and Virgil, with a modesty that ill became his genius, had affected the fame of an imitator, even whilst he created anew all that he copied; and none among the flock of mock-birds, though their notes are sweet, Apollonius Rhodius, Quintus Calaber Smyrnaeus, Nonnus, Lucan, Statius or Claudian,[350] have sought even to fulfil a single condition of epic truth. Milton was the third epic poet. For if the title of epic in its highest sense be refused to the *Aeneid*, still less can it be conceded to the *Orlando Furioso*, the *Gerusalemme Liberata*, the *Lusiad*, or the *Fairy Queen*.[351]

Dante and Milton were both deeply penetrated with the ancient religion of the civilised world; and its spirit exists in their poetry probably in the same proportion as its forms survived in the unreformed worship of modern Europe. The one preceded and the other followed the Reformation at almost equal intervals. Dante was the first religious performer, and Luther surpassed him rather in the rudeness and acrimony than in the boldness of his censures of papal usurpation. Dante was the first awakener of entranced Europe; he created a language, in itself music and persuasion, out of a chaos of inharmonious barbarisms. He was the congregator of those great spirits who presided over the resurrection of learning: the Lucifer of that starry flock which in the thirteenth century shone forth from republican Italy, as from a heaven, into the darkness of the benighted world. His very words are instinct with spirit; each is as a spark, a burning atom of inextinguishable thought; and many yet lie covered in the ashes of their birth, and pregnant with a lightning which has yet found no conductor. All high poetry is infinite; it is as the first acorn, which contained all oaks potentially. Veil after veil may be undrawn, and the inmost naked beauty of the meaning never exposed. A great poem is a fountain forever overflowing with the waters of wisdom and delight; and after one person and one age has exhausted all its divine effluence, which their peculiar relations enable them to share, another and yet another succeeds, and new relations are ever developed, the source of an unforeseen and an unconceived delight.

The age immediately succeeding to that of Dante, Petrarch, and Boccaccio,[352] was characterised by a revival of painting, sculpture, and architecture. Chaucer caught the sacred inspiration, and the superstructure of English literature is based upon the materials of Italian invention.

But let us not be betrayed from a defence into a critical history of poetry and its influence on society. Be it enough to have pointed out the effects of poets, in the large and true sense of the word, upon their own and all succeeding times.

But poets have been challenged to resign the civic crown to reasoners and mechanists, on another plea. It is admitted that the exercise of the imagination is most delightful, but it is alleged that that of reason is more useful. Let us examine, as the grounds of this distinction, what is here meant by utility. Pleasure or good, in a general sense, is that which the consciousness of a sensitive and intelligent being seeks, and in which, when found, it acquiesces. There are two kinds of pleasure, one durable, universal and permanent; the other transitory and particular. Utility may either express the means of producing the former or the latter. In the former sense, whatever strengthens and purifies the affections, enlarges the imagination and adds spirit to sense, is useful. But a narrower meaning may be assigned to the word utility, confining it to express that which banishes the importunity of the wants of our animal nature, the surrounding men with security of life, the dispersing the grosser delusions of superstition, and the conciliating such a degree of mutual forbearance among men as may consist with the motives of personal advantage.

Undoubtedly the promoters of utility, in this limited sense, have their appointed office in society. They follow the footsteps of poets, and copy the sketches of their creations into the book of common life. They make space, and give time. Their exertions are of the highest value, so long as they confine their administration of the concerns of the inferior powers of our nature within the limits due to the superior ones. But while the sceptic destroys gross superstitions, let him spare to deface, as some of the French writers have defaced, the eternal truths charactered upon the imaginations of men. Whilst the mechanist abridges, and the political economist combines, labour, let them beware that their speculations, for want of correspondence with those first principles which belong to the imagination, do not tend, as they have in modern England, to exasperate at once the extremes of luxury and want. They have exemplified the saying, 'To him that hath, more shall be given; and from him that hath not, the little that he hath shall be taken away.' The rich have become richer, and the poor have become poorer; and the vessel of the state is driven between the Scylla and Charybdis[353] of anarchy and despotism. Such are the effects which must ever flow from an unmitigated exercise of the calculating faculty.

It is difficult to define pleasure in its highest sense: the definition involving a number of apparent paradoxes. For, from an inexplicable defect of harmony in the constitution of human nature, the pain of the inferior is frequently connected with the pleasures of the superior portions of our being. Sorrow, terror, anguish, despair itself, are often the chosen expressions of an approximation to the highest good. Our sympathy in tragic fiction depends on this principle; tragedy delights by affording a shadow of that pleasure which exists in pain. This is the source also of the melancholy which is inseparable from the sweetest melody. The pleasure that is in sorrow is sweeter than the pleasure of pleasure itself. And hence the saying, 'It is better to go to the house of mourning than to the house of mirth.' Not that this highest species of pleasure is necessarily linked with pain. The delight of love and friendship, the ecstasy of the admiration of nature, the joy of the perception and still more of the creation of poetry, is often wholly unalloyed.

The production and assurance of pleasure in this highest sense is true utility. Those who produce and preserve this pleasure are poets or poetical philosophers.

The exertions of Locke, Hume, Gibbon, Voltaire,[354] Rousseau,* and their disciples, in favour of oppressed and deluded humanity, are entitled to the gratitude of mankind. Yet it is easy to calculate the degree of moral and intellectual improvement which the world would have exhibited, had they never lived. A little more nonsense would have been talked for a century or two; and perhaps a few more men, women, and children, burnt as heretics. We might not at this moment have been congratulating each other on the abolition of the Inquisition in Spain.[355] But it exceeds all imagination to conceive what would have been the moral condition of the world if neither Dante, Petrarch, Boccaccio, Chaucer, Shakespeare, Calderon, Lord Bacon,

---

* Although Rousseau has been thus classed, he was essentially a poet. The others, even Voltaire, were mere reasoners.

nor Milton, had ever existed; if Raphael and Michael Angelo had never been born; if the Hebrew poetry had never been translated; if a revival of the study of Greek literature had never taken place; if no monuments of ancient sculpture had been handed down to us; and if the poetry of the religion of the ancient world had been extinguished together with its belief. The human mind could never, except by the intervention of these excitements, have been awakened to the invention of the grosser sciences, and that application of analytical reasoning to the aberrations of society, which it is now attempted to exalt over the direct expression of the inventive and creative faculty itself.

We have more moral, political and historical wisdom than we know how to reduce into practice; we have more scientific and economical knowledge than can be accommodated to the just distribution of the produce which it multiplies. The poetry, in these systems of thought, is concealed by the accumulation of facts and calculating processes. There is no want of knowledge respecting what is wisest and best in morals, government, and political economy, or at least what is wiser and better than what men now practise and endure. But we let *I dare not* wait upon *I would*, like the poor cat in the adage.[356] We want the creative faculty to imagine that which we know; we want the generous impulse to act that which we imagine; we want the poetry of life: our calculations have outrun conception; we have eaten more than we can digest. The cultivation of those sciences which have enlarged the limits of the empire of man over the external world, has, for want of the poetical faculty, proportionally circumscribed those of the internal world; and man, having enslaved the elements, remains himself a slave. To what but a cultivation of the mechanical arts in a degree disproportioned to the presence of the creative faculty, which is the basis of all knowledge, is to be attributed the abuse of all invention for abridging and combining labour, to the exasperation of the inequality of mankind? From what other cause has it arisen that the discoveries which should have lightened, have added a weight to the curse imposed on Adam? Poetry, and the principle of Self, of which money is the visible incarnation, are the God and Mammon of the world.

The functions of the poetical faculty are twofold; by one it creates new materials of knowledge, and power, and pleasure; by the other it engenders in the mind a desire to reproduce and arrange them according to a certain rhythm and order, which may be called the beautiful and the good. The cultivation of poetry is never more to be desired than at periods when, from an excess of the selfish and calculating principle, the accumulation of the materials of external life exceed the quantity of the power of assimilating them to the internal laws of human nature. The body has then become too unwieldy for that which animates it.

Poetry is indeed something divine. It is at once the centre and circumference of knowledge; it is that which comprehends all science, and that to which all science must be referred. It is at the same time the root and blossom of all other systems of thought; it is that from which all spring, and that which adorns all; and that which, if blighted, denies the fruit and the seed, and withholds from the barren world the nourishment and the succession of the scions of the tree of life. It is the perfect and consummate surface and bloom of all things; it is as the odour and the colour of the rose to the texture of the elements which compose it, as the form and splendour of unfaded beauty to the secrets of anatomy and corruption. What were virtue, love, patriotism, friendship, – what were the scenery of this beautiful universe which we inhabit; what were our consolations on this side of the grave – and what were our aspirations beyond it, if poetry did not ascend to bring light and fire from those eternal regions where the owl-winged faculty of calculation dare not ever soar? Poetry is not like reasoning, a power to be exerted according to the determination of the will. A man cannot say, 'I will compose poetry.' The greatest poet even cannot say it; for the mind in creation is as a fading coal, which some invisible influence, like an inconstant wind, awakens to transitory brightness; this power arises from within, like the colour of a flower which fades and changes as it is developed, and the conscious portions of our nature are unprophetic either of its approach or its departure. Could this influence be durable in its original purity and force, it is impossible to predict the greatness of the results; but when composition begins, inspiration is already on the decline, and the most glorious poetry that has ever been communicated to the world is probably a feeble shadow of the original conceptions of the poet. I appeal to the greatest poets of the present day, whether it is not an error to assert that the finest passages of poetry are produced by labour and study. The toil and the delay recommended by critics, can be justly interpreted to mean no more than a careful observation of the inspired moments, and an artificial connection of the spaces between their suggestions, by the intertexture of conventional expressions; a necessity only imposed by the limitedness of the poetical faculty itself: for Milton conceived the *Paradise Lost* as a whole before he executed it in portions. We have his own authority also for the muse having 'dictated' to him the 'unpremeditated song'[357]. And let this be an answer to those who would allege the fifty-six various readings of the first line of the *Orlando Furioso*. Compositions so produced are to poetry what mosaic is to painting. The instinct and intuition of the poetical faculty is still more observable in the plastic and pictorial arts: a great statue or picture grows under the power of the artist as a child in the mother's womb; and the very mind which directs the hands in formation, is incapable of accounting to itself for the origin, the gradations, or the media of the process.

Poetry is the record of the happiest and best moments of the happiest and best minds. We are aware of evanescent visitations of thought and feeling, sometimes associated with place or person, sometimes regarding our own mind alone, and always arising unforeseen and departing unbidden, but elevating and delightful beyond all expression: so that even in the desire and the regret they leave, there cannot but be pleasure, participating as it does in the nature of its object. It is as it were the interpenetration of a diviner nature through our own; but its footsteps are like those of a wind over the sea, which the coming calm erases, and whose traces remain only, as on the wrinkled sand which paves it. These and corresponding conditions of being are experienced principally by those of the most delicate sensibility and the most enlarged imagination; and the state of mind produced by them is at war with every base desire. The enthusiasm of virtue, love, patriotism, and friendship, is essentially linked with such emotions; and whilst they last, self appears as what it is, an atom to a universe. Poets are not only subject to these experiences as spirits of the most refined organisation, but they can colour all that they combine with the evanescent hues of this ethereal world; a word, a trait in the representation of a scene or a passion, will touch the enchanted chord, and reanimate, in those who have ever experienced those emotions, the sleeping, the cold, the buried image of the past. Poetry thus makes immortal all that is best and most beautiful in the world; it arrests the vanishing apparitions which haunt the interlunations of life, and veiling them, or in language or in form, sends them forth among mankind bearing sweet news of kindred joy to those with whom their sisters abide – abide, because there is no portal of expression from the caverns of the spirit which they inhabit into the universe of things. Poetry redeems from decay the visitations of the divinity in man.

Poetry turns all things to loveliness; it exalts the beauty of that which is most beautiful, and it adds beauty to that which is most deformed; it marries exultation and horror, grief and pleasure, eternity and change; it subdues to union, under its light yoke, all irreconcilable things. It transmutes all that it touches, and every form moving within the radiance of its presence is changed by wondrous sympathy to an incarnation of the spirit which it breathes: its secret alchemy turns to potable gold the poisonous waters which flow from death through life; it strips the veil of familiarity from the world, and lays bare the naked and sleeping beauty, which is the spirit of its forms.

All things exist as they are perceived; at least in relation to the percipient. 'The mind is its own place, and of itself can make a heaven of hell, a hell of heaven.'[358] But poetry defeats the curse which binds us to be subjected to the accident of surrounding impressions And whether it spreads its own figured curtain, or withdraws life's dark veil from before the scene of things, it equally creates for us a being within our being. It makes us the inhabitant of a world to which the familiar world is a chaos. It reproduces the common universe of which we are portions and percipients, and it purges from our inward sight the film of familiarity which obscures from us the wonder of our being. It compels us to feel that which we perceive, and to imagine that which we know. It creates anew the universe, after it has been annihilated in our minds by the recurrence of impressions blunted by reiteration. It justifies the bold and true word of Tasso: *Non merita nome di creatore, se non Iddio ed il Poeta.*[359]

A poet, as he is the author to others of the highest wisdom, pleasure, virtue and glory, so he ought personally to be the happiest, the best, the wisest, and the most illustrious of men. As to his glory, let time be challenged to declare whether the fame of any other institutor of human life be comparable to that of a poet. That he is the wisest, the happiest, and the best, inasmuch as he is a poet, is equally incontrovertible: the greatest poets have been men of the most spotless virtue, of the most consummate prudence, and, if we would look into the interior of their lives, the most fortunate of men: and the exceptions, as they regard those who possessed the poetic faculty in a high yet inferior degree, will be found on consideration to confine rather than destroy the rule. Let us for a moment stoop to the arbitration of popular breath, and usurping and uniting in our own persons the incompatible characters of accuser, witness, judge and executioner, let us decide without trial, testimony, or form, that certain motives of those who are 'there sitting where we dare not soar',[360] are reprehensible. Let us assume that Homer was a drunkard, that Virgil was a flatterer, that Horace was a coward, that Tasso was a madman, that Lord Bacon was a peculator, that Raphael was a libertine, that Spenser was a poet laureate. It is inconsistent with this division of our subject to cite living poets, but posterity has done ample justice to the great names now referred to. Their errors have been weighed and found to have been dust in the balance; if their sins 'were as scarlet, they are now white as snow': they have been washed in the blood of the mediator and redeemer, time. Observe in what a ludicrous chaos the imputations of real or fictitious crime have been confused in the contemporary calumnies against poetry and poets: consider how little is as it appears – or appears as it is; look to your own motives, and judge not, lest ye be judged.

Poetry, as has been said, differs in this respect from logic, that it is not subject to the control of the active powers of the mind, and that its birth and recurrence have no necessary connection with the consciousness or will. It is presumptuous to determine that these are the necessary conditions of all mental causation, when mental effects are experienced insusceptible of being referred to them. The frequent recurrence of the poetical power, it is obvious to suppose, may produce in the mind a habit of order and harmony correlative with its own nature and with its effects upon other minds. But in the intervals of inspiration, and they may be frequent without being durable, a poet becomes a man, and is abandoned to the sudden reflux of the influences under which others habitually live. But as he is more delicately organised than other men, and sensible to pain and pleasure, both his own and that of others, in a degree unknown to them, he will avoid the one and pursue the other with an ardour proportioned to this difference. And he renders himself obnoxious to calumny when he neglects to observe the circumstances under which these objects of universal pursuit and flight have disguised themselves in one another's garments.

But there is nothing necessarily evil in this error, and thus cruelty, envy, revenge, avarice, and the passions purely evil, have never formed any portion of the popular imputations on the lives of poets.

I have thought it most favourable to the cause of truth to set down these remarks according to the order in which they were suggested to my mind, by a consideration of the subject itself, instead of observing the formality of a polemical reply; but if the view which they contain be just, they will be found to involve a refutation of the arguers against poetry, so far at least as regards the first division of the subject. I can readily conjecture what should have moved the gall of some learned and intelligent writers who quarrel with certain versifiers; I, like them, confess myself unwilling to be stunned by the Theseids of the hoarse Codri of the day. Bavius and Maevius[361] undoubtedly are, as they ever were, insufferable persons. But it belongs to a philosophical critic to distinguish rather than confound.

The first part of these remarks has related to poetry in its elements and principles: and it has been shown, as well as the narrow limits assigned them would permit, that what is called poetry in a restricted sense, has a common source with all other forms of order and of beauty, according to which the materials of human life are susceptible of being arranged, and which is poetry in an universal sense.

The second part will have for its object an application of these principles to the present state of the cultivation of poetry, and a defence of the attempt to idealise the modern forms of manners and opinions, and compel them into a subordination to the imaginative and creative faculty. For the literature of England, an energetic development of which has ever preceded or accompanied a great and free development of the national will, has arisen as it were from a new birth. In spite of the low-thoughted envy which would undervalue contemporary merit, our own will be a memorable age in intellectual achievements, and we live among such philosophers and poets as surpass beyond comparison any who have appeared since the last national struggle for civil and religious liberty. The most unfailing herald, companion, and follower of the awakening of a great people to work a beneficial change in opinion or institution, is poetry. At such periods there is an accumulation of the power of communicating and receiving intense and impassioned conceptions respecting man and nature. The persons in whom this power resides, may often, as far as regards many portions of their nature, have little apparent correspondence with that spirit of good of which they are the ministers. But even whilst they deny and abjure, they are yet compelled to serve, the power which is seated on the throne of their own soul. It is impossible to read the compositions of the most celebrated writers of the present day without being startled with the electric life which burns within their words. They measure the circumference and sound the depths of human nature with a comprehensive and all penetrating spirit, and they are themselves perhaps the most sincerely astonished at its manifestations: for it is less their spirit than the spirit of the age. Poets are the hierophants of an unapprehended inspiration; the mirrors of the gigantic shadows which futurity casts upon the present; the words which express what they understand not; the trumpets which sing to battle and feel not what they inspire; the influence which is moved not, but moves. Poets are the unacknowledged legislators of the world.

Notes

I am immensely indebted to previous editions of Shelley's work in the preparation of these notes, in particular: Geoffrey Matthews and Kelvin Everest (eds), *The Poems of Shelley, Volume 1 1804–1817*, Longman, London 1989; Kelvin Everest and Geoffrey Matthews (eds), *The Poems of Shelley, Volume 2 1817–1819*, Longman, London 2000; Donald H. Reiman and Sharon B. Powers (eds), *Shelley's Poetry and Prose*, Norton, New York 1977; and David Lee Clark (ed.), *Shelley's Prose or The Trumpet of a Prophecy*, University of New Mexico, Albuquerque 1954. The annotations in all these editions are invaluable. Unless otherwise indicated, all translations are taken from the Matthews and Everest editions, which also annotate the references to Shelley's scientific interests in fascinating detail.

Poems from 1812–13

Queen Mab

1 (p. 3) *Epigraphs*   The first epigraph is from Voltaire (1694–1778), the French epitome of the Enlightenment: 'Crush the infamous thing!' was his motto. It was adopted by the international revolutionary Jacobins, the Illuminists, in the 1790s. The second epigraph is from Lucretius, Roman poet (*c.*99–55BC): 'I wander through a pathless region of poetry, trodden by no other foot before; it delights me to approach untainted springs, and to drink: and it delights me to pick unfamiliar flowers . . . whence the Muses have hitherto adorned no one's brows. First, because I teach great matters; and I go on to set minds free from the hard knots of superstition' (*De Rerum Naturae*, iv, 1–7). The third epigraph is from Archimedes, Greek scientist (*c.*287–212BC): Reiman and Powers translate it as, 'Give me somewhere to stand and I will move the earth.' This motto was used by Tom Paine to open the second part of *The Rights of Man* (1792), a work which deeply influenced Shelley.

2 (p. 3) *To Harriet* —   This dedicatory poem is addressed to Shelley's first wife.

3 (p. 5) *strange lyre*   a wind or aeolian harp, which was activated by the movement of a breeze across loose strings

4 (p. 10) *belt*   the Milky Way

5 (p. 11) *Hesperus*   Venus as the Evening Star

6 (p. 14) *Palmyra*   ancient city which rivalled Rome, destroyed in 273 AD by Emperor Aurelian leaving astonishing ruins frequently referred to as epitomising the transitoriness of empires

7 (p. 15) *Salem's haughty fane*   Solomon's temple at Jerusalem, built in the ninth century BC, was destroyed by Emperor Vespasian in 70 AD. Solomon is the 'dotard' referred to in line 148.

8 (p. 16) *Cicero and Antoninus*   Cicero (106–43BC), famous Roman orator; Antoninus (AD 86–161), philosopher and Emperor; both cited as virtuous men

9 (p. 35) *Milton . . . Cato . . . Newton*   John Milton (1608–74), English republican poet; Cato (95–46BC), Roman statesman opposed to Caesar; Sir Isaac Newton (1642–1727), English scientist; cited as embodying cultural achievements

10 (p. 36) *light of heaven*   refers to the window tax used by the government to raise money for the war against France

11 (p. 37) *hydra-headed*   The hydra was a mythical monster with multiple heads which rejuvenated when cut off.

12 (p. 46) *Seeva, Buddh, Foh, Jehovah*   Shiva, the Hindu god of destruction; Buddha, the founder of Buddhism; Foh, the contemporary name for the king who established the Chinese empire; Jehovah, the Old Testament God

13 (p. 46) *Brahmins*   the highest caste of Hinduism

14 (p. 47) *Ahasuerus*   the legendary Wandering Jew

15 (p. 68) *Godwin's Enquirer*   Shelley quotes this note from the essays of 1797 by the influential radical William Godwin (1756–1836), father of Shelley's wife Mary.

16 (p. 68) *Falsehood and Vice*   revised version of a poem Shelley probably wrote earlier in 1812

17 (p. 72) *jam pauca . . . relinquunt*   an adaptation of Horace, Latin poet (65–8BC) at the time of Emperor Augustus: 'Now splendid mansions leave few acres for the plough.' *Odes* 2, 15, 1–2

18 (p. 72) *caeteris paribus*   Latin, 'all things being equal'

19 (p. 74) *Lucretius*   first century BC Latin poet and philosopher: 'For often before now men have betrayed their country and their beloved parents, in seeking to avoid the dominions of hell.' *De Rerum Natura*, ii, 85–6

20 (p. 80) *il quod potest*   'that which is effective/empowers'

21 (p. 82) *Sale's Prelim. Disc. . . . to the Koran*   taken from George Sale's 1801 translation of *The Koran*

22 (p. 85) *onus probandi*   the burden of proof

23 (p. 85) *Newton*   Sir Isaac Newton (1642–1727), English scientist: 'I do not make hypotheses, for whatever is not deduced from the phenomena must be called a hypothesis, and hypotheses, whether in metaphysics, physics, or occult qualities, or mechanics, have no place in philosophy.' *Principia*, 1687

24 (p. 85) *peripatetics . . . Boyle . . . Herschel*   The peripatetics were a school of Greek philosophers founded by Aristotle and called after his habit of walking while teaching. Robert Boyle (1626–1691) was an Irish scientist; Frederick Herschel (1738–1822) was a British astronomer.

25 (p. 85) *Pour dire . . . lui même*   an unattributed quotation taken from Paul Holbach (1723–89), French Enlightenment writer: it translates as, 'To say what God is, you would have to be God.' *Systeme de la Nature*, 2, 275

26 (p. 86) *Lord Bacon*   Sir Francis Bacon (1561–1626), English philosopher whose stress on rational inductive methods inspired the scientific revolution

27 (p. 86) *Pliny*   Pliny the Elder (AD 23–79), Roman scholar: 'For this reason I think it is a mark of human folly to seek the appearance and shape of God. Whoever God is (if indeed he is a separate being) and in whatever place, he is all sense, he is all seeing, he is all hearing, all spirit, all mind, all himself . . . But the main consolations for nature's shortcomings in man are that not even God can do everything. For he cannot kill himself if he wants to, which he gave to man as the supreme blessing of life amid great sufferings; nor can he confer immortality on mortals, or call back the dead; nor can he make a man who has lived not to have lived, or one who has held honours not to have held them, nor has he any power over the past, except of forgetting it, nor (to make common case with God by a joking argument) of making twice ten not to be twenty, nor can he do many things of the same kind. By these facts the power of nature is proclaimed to be that which we call God.' *Naturalis Historia* (AD 77)

28 (p. 86) *Spinoza* Benedict Spinoza (1632–77), Dutch philosopher: 'For everything has happened through the power of God: indeed, since the power of nature is nothing but that very power of God, it is certain that we fail to understand the power of God in so far as we are ignorant of natural causes; so it is very silly to refer something to the power of God when we are ignorant of its natural cause – if that is itself the power of God.' *Tractatus Theologico-Politico* (1670)

29 (p. 87) *Ahasuerus, rise!* a translation of a German poem of 1783 which Shelley probably found in a magazine. Ahasuerus is a figure from superstition and legend.

30 (p. 91) *If God has spoken . . . convinced?* translated from *Système de la Nature* by Paul Holbach, French Enlightenment writer

31 (p. 94) *Lord Chesterfield* Shelley misremembers and exaggerates a famous letter of 1753 by Philip Dormer Stanhope, 4th Earl of Chesterfield.

32 (p. 96) *Mox numine viso . . . orbem* Claudianus (340–410), last of the great Latin poets and a pagan, so that the passage is probably ironical: 'Soon after the deity's visit, the virgin's breasts swelled, and the unmarried mother was secretly astonished that, about to experience her own maker, her vitals were filling with child. A mortal womb hid the author of the sky, and under one bosom lay he who encircles the whole wide globe.' ('Easter Hymn')

33 (p. 97) *Dark flood of time . . . unredeemed* an extract from Shelley's own poem 'To Harriet' ('It is not blasphemous to hope')

Poems from 1815

Alastor

34 (p. 100) *Alastor* The title should not be taken as the name of the central character, the Poet. In Greek 'Alastor' means 'an evil genius' or 'an avenging spirit'.

35 (p. 101) *'The good die first . . . the socket!'* slightly misquoted from Wordsworth's *Excursion*, Book 1, 500–2

36 (p. 101) *Nondum amabam . . . [a]mare* quotation from St Augustine: 'I was not yet in love, and I loved to be in love, I sought what I might love, loving to be in love.' *Confessions*

37 (p. 102) *lyre* a wind or aeolian harp, which was activated by the movement of a breeze across loose strings

38 (p. 102) *fane* sanctuary or temple

39 (p. 104) *His wandering step*   The journey here moves backwards in time through great civilisations which might offer wisdom, Greeks and Phoenicians (Athens, Tyre, Balbec), Jews and Babylonians, Egyptians (Memphis, Thebes), Ethiopians.

40 (p. 105) *The Poet wandering on*   The journey continues east to Arabia, Persia, the Karmin Desert in south-east Iran, over the Hindu Kush mountains to the valley of Kashmir in north-west India, the Indian Caucasus being considered at the time to be the area where the human race originated.

41 (p. 107) *He wandered on*   The Poet journeys through central Asia and Shelley uses the geographical terms familiar in classical times for these areas. Aornos was a mountain fortress in the upper Indus valley which Alexander the Great captured.

42 (p. 112) *yellow flowers*   narcissi, invoking the legend of Narcissus who pined away for love of his own reflection in a pond (from Ovid's *Metamorphoses*)

43 (p. 115) *windlestrae*   the remnant stalks of plants whose flowers have died

44 (p. 118) *Medea*   mythical sorceress who spilled a magic potion on the ground which caused grass and flowers to grow

45 (p. 119) *'deep for tears'*   quote from the last line of Wordsworth's 'Ode: Intimations of Immortality': 'To me the meanest flower that blows can give / Thoughts that do often lie too deep for tears.'

To —

46 (p. 121) *epigraph*   from Greek dramatist Euripides' play *Hippolytus*: 'I shall endure with tears an unfortunate fortune.'

Mutability

47 (p. 122) *forgotten lyres*   describes aeolian or wind harps, a favourite image for Shelley and other Romantics

Poems from 1816

Mont Blanc

48 (p. 127) *daedal*   intricately, cleverly fashioned; from Daedalus, the mythic craftsman who fashioned wings for his son Icarus

Hymn to Intellectual Beauty

49 (p. 129) *Title* 'Intellectual Beauty' for Shelley epitomised aspirations, material and non material, and so encompassed social ideals (lines 64–70), as well as embodying a more abstract, cosmic sense. Shelley reasserts his vision in defiance of Wordsworth's defeatist self-consolation in his 'Ode: Intimations of Immortality' which this poem echoes.

Poems from 1817

Laon and Cythna

50 (p. 132) *Epigraphs*   The opening epigraph is the same quotation from Archimedes which Shelley used for *Queen Mab* (see above): 'Give me a place to stand and I will move the earth'. Shelley transforms Archimedes' lever for this movement into the power of ideas and poetry. The second epigraph is from Greek lyric poet Pindar (*c.*522–*c.*440BC), lamenting the incapacity of modern mortals to attain the past achievements of heroes such as Perseus, who dined with the legendary Hyperboreans; the quotation may be rendered: 'Whatever splendour we mortals can attain, he reaches the limit of that voyage. Neither by ship nor on foot could you find the marvellous road to the meeting-place of the Hyperboreans.' *Pythian Odes*, 10

51 (p. 135) *Mr Malthus*   Thomas Malthus (1766–1834), economist whose *Essay on the Principles of Population* (1798) was a response to William Godwin's *Political Justice* (1793), and angered Godwin, Shelley and other radicals

52 (p. 136) *Pericles*   (*c.*495–429BC) main statesman of Athens, presiding over the great age of Greek drama

53 (p. 136) *Lord Bacon*   Sir Francis Bacon (1561–1626), English philosopher and rationalist renowned for his stylistically distinctive *Essays*

54 (p. 136) *Ford*   John Ford (*c.*1586–*c.*1639), dramatist whose eighteen plays include *'Tis Pity She's a Whore*

55 (p. 137) *the stanza of Spenser* Edmund Spenser (c.1552–1599), whose *The Faerie Queene* is written in a distinctive nine-line stanza

56 (p. 137) *Longinus . . . Boileau . . . Horace* Longinus: assumed author of *On the Sublime* (AD1); Boileau: Nicholas Despreaux (1636–1711), French critic and poet who translated Longinus's treatise into French; Horace: Latin poet (65–8BC) at the time of Emperor Augustus

57 (p. 138) *Lucretius* first-century-BC Latin poet and philosopher

58 (p. 138) *Ashtaroth* another name for Astarte, the Syrian moon goddess

59 (p. 138) *Socrates and Zeno* Socrates (469–399BC), Greek philosopher and master of Plato; Zeno (333–262BC), founder of the Stoic school of philosophy

60 (p. 140) *Dedication* The opening verses are addressed to Shelley's wife Mary and partly describe Shelley's own awakening to revolutionary sympathies. The epigram is from George Chapman's play *The Conspiracy of Charles, Duke of Byron* (1608).

61 (p. 169) *Propontis* ancient Greek name for the Sea of Marmara which connects Constantinople with the Aegean Sea

62 (p. 184) *Amphisbaena* a mythical serpent with a head at both ends

Ozymandias

63 (p. 194) *Title* The name is the Greek for the Egyptian pharaoh Rameses II (1304–1237BC), whose statue stood on the opposite bank of the Nile to Luxor, near Thebes.

Poems from 1818

Lines written among the Euganean Hills

64 (p. 195) *Title* the Euganean Hills near Padua in Italy

65 (p. 197) *Amphitrite* daughter of Oceanus ('her hoary sire', line 98) and wife of Poseidon, god of the sea in Greek mythology. She was destined to inherit Venice once the sea engulfed it.

66 (p. 198) *conquest-branded brow* Venice had been a conqueror in the past but had also more recently been conquered by Napoleon and by Austria, the 'Celtic Anarch' referred to in line 152; 'Celtic' at the time meaning northern or Teutonic, as opposed to Mediterranean.

67 (p. 199) *Swan* Lord Byron

68 (p. 199) *Albion* England

69 (p. 200) *Scamander* a river near Troy in Homer

70 (p. 200) *Petrarch's urn* the village of Arqua, in the Euganean Hills, burial place of the famous Italian poet

71 (p. 201) *Ezzelin* tyrant of Padua in the thirteenth century. Sin's compensation for losing the dice game is to become vice-emperor of Austria.

72 (p. 201) *lamp of learning* Padua had been one of Europe's most famous and long established universities since medieval times.

Sonnet: 'Lift not the painted veil'

73 (p. 224) *the Preacher* refers to Ecclesiastes (8:17) and the assertion that searching for truth was vanity

Poems from 1819

Prometheus Unbound

74 (p. 225) *Epigraph* 'Do you hear this, Amphiarus, in your home beneath the earth?', a line from a lost play by Greek dramatist Aeschylus (*c.*525–*c.*456BC), author of *Prometheus Bound*, which Shelley turns ironically against him to indicate his own disagreement with the classical dramatist's view of the Prometheus story

75 (p. 225) *Agamemnonian* Agamemnon was King of Argos and commander of the Greek army in the Trojan Wars; his murder by his wife Clytemnestra forms the story for the play named after him by Aeschylus.

76 (p. 225) *Jupiter* Roman version of Zeus, leader of the gods. Thetis, the sea goddess, was destined to bear a son greater than his father.

77 (p. 228) *Paley and Malthus* William Paley, a popular theologian, author of *Evidences of Christianity* (1794), whom Shelley attacks in letters and essays; Thomas Malthus (1766–1834), economist whose *Essay on the Principles of Population* (1798) was a response to William Godwin's *Political Justice* (1793), and angered Godwin, Shelley and other radicals

78 (p. 231) *Thou serenest Air . . . without beams* an example of the scientific accuracy of Shelley's imagery. Sunlight in the upper atmosphere is not refracted since there is no moisture. The whole of *Prometheus Unbound* is saturated with such scientifically inspired imagery, particularly from geology and vulcanicity, favourite subjects for Shelley, and often expressive of the theme of revolutionary uprising.

79 (p. 235) *Zoroaster* Persian king and religious prophet

80 (p. 235) *Hades or Typhon* Hades, king of the Underworld, and Typhon, a monster with a hundred heads, were Titans overthrown by Zeus/Jupiter.

81 (p. 239) *Maia* daughter of Atlas, mother of Mercury, Jupiter's messenger and son

82 (p. 239) *streams of fire and wail* two rivers of Hades, the Underworld, Phlegethon of fire and Cocytus of tears

83 (p. 239) *Geryon . . . Gorgon . . . Chimaera . . . Sphinx* various monsters from classical myth

84 (p. 241) *Sicilian* Damocles who was punished by having a sword suspended above him by a hair

85 (p. 257) *Hyacinth* killed by Zephyrus and transformed into a flower when mourned by his lover Apollo

86 (p. 262) *I have heard . . .* What follows is a description of the contemporary view of the cycle of hydrogen production.

87 (p. 262) *Silenus* tutor and helper to Dionysus/Bacchus, god of wine, and usually himself drunk, hence the 'undrawn' (unmilked) goats

88 (p. 263) *Maenads* female worshippers of Dionysus. Their cry accompanied their manic ecstasies in which they frenziedly killed anyone they came across.

89 (p. 267) *Elysian . . . Nepenthe, Moly, Amaranth* flowers associated with drugs or charms, and Elysium was the Greek version of paradise

90 (p. 270) *My coursers . . .* In this speech, Shelley anticipates solar powered transportation.

91 (p. 271) *Nereids* sea nymphs. The hyaline is the surface of the sea.

92 (p. 275) *Ganymede* cupbearer to the gods; abducted by Zeus

93 (p. 275) *Daedal* elaborately worked, from Daedalus the famous craftsman

94 (p. 276) *Thetis* a sea nymph

95 (p. 276) *Numidian seps* a poisonous snake from the Numidian desert

96 (p. 280) *Enna* Sicilian meadow near town of Himera

97 (p. 280) *Proteus* a sea god capable of changing his shape

98 (p. 283) *Bacchic Nysa* Dionysus/Bacchus, god of wine, inspirer of the frenzied female Maenads

99 (p. 283) *Praxitelean* from the Athenean sculptor Praxiteles

100 (p. 284) *dipsas* a snake in classical myth which caused raging thirsts in those it bit

101 (p. 287) *amphisbaenic snake*   one with a head at each end

102 (p. 288) *nepenthe*   a charmed drink which overcame anguish

103 (p. 295) *Our spoil is won* . . .   a passage owing much to Shelley's interest in astronomy.

The Cenci

104 (p. 309) *Dedication*   Leigh Hunt (1784–1859), the much admired radical journalist, poet and editor

105 (p. 315) *fief*   an estate; the Pincian gate is an entrance to Rome

106 (p. 317) *Aldobrandino*   the family name of Pope Clement VIII

107 (p. 334) *Galeaz Visconti, Borgia, Ezzelin*   the names of notable Italian tyrants

108 (p. 345) *Apulian Apennines*   a mountainous region of south-east Italy

109 (p. 354) *Campagna*   the flat valley of the River Tiber which surrounds Rome

110 (p. 356) *the Maremma*   a coastal swampy plain near Pisa reputed to be unhealthy

The Mask of Anarchy

111 (p. 387) *Castlereagh*   Robert Stewart, Viscount Castlereagh (1769–1822), infamous for his savage repression of dissent in Ireland, was Foreign Secretary and leader of the Tory-dominated House of Commons from 1812 until 1822, when he committed suicide by cutting his throat.

112 (p. 387) *bloodhounds*   Supporters of war under William Pitt's government had been known as bloodhounds, while in 1816 seven European nations similarly described collectively decided to postpone the abolition of the slave trade.

113 (p. 387) *Eldon*   John Scott, Baron Eldon was Lord High Chancellor from 1802–27 and the person who had denied Shelley custody of his children by his first wife on the grounds of his atheism.

114 (p. 388) *Sidmouth*   Henry Addington, Viscount Sidmouth was Home Secretary from 1812–21 and responsible for intensifying the network of spies and surveillance which Shelley himself was subjected to in 1812.

115 (p. 390) *Bank and Tower*   the Bank of England; the Tower of London

116 (p. 390) *pensioned Parliament*   Pensioning was a form of bribery in the corrupt unreformed Parliament against which the Peterloo radicals protested.

117 (p. 391) *Morning's* Venus's

118 (p. 396) *Gaul* France. The line refers to the anti-revolutionary alliance which fought against France.

Ode to the West Wind

119 (p. 401) *Destroyer and preserver* invoking the Hindu gods Shiva and Vishnu

120 (p. 402) *Maenad* Maenads were female worshippers of Dionysus renowned for their sexual passion and destructive fanaticism

121 (p. 402) *pumice isle in Baiae's bay* Pumice is a volcanic lava; Shelley vividly describes the origins of this verse in his letter to Peacock of 22 December 1818.

Lines Written during the Castlereagh Administration

122 (p. 404) *Title* Castlereagh: Robert Stewart, Viscount Castlereagh (1769–1822), infamous for his savage repression of dissent in Ireland, was Foreign Secretary and leader of the Tory-dominated House of Commons from 1812 until 1822, when he committed suicide by cutting his throat.

123 (p. 404) *Albion* an old name for England

Similes for Two Political Characters of 1819

124 (p. 406) *Title* The two characters referred to are Castlereagh and Sidmouth: Robert Stewart, Viscount Castlereagh (1769–1822), infamous for his savage repression of dissent in Ireland, was Foreign Secretary and leader of the Tory-dominated House of Commons from 1812 until 1822, when he committed suicide by cutting his throat; Henry Addington, Viscount Sidmouth was Home Secretary from 1812–21 and responsible for intensifying the network of spies and surveillance which Shelley himself was subjected to in 1812.

England in 1819

125 (p. 407) *king* King George III (1738–1820) reigned from 1760; he suffered a recurrence of a mental derangement in 1810, as a result of which the Prince of Wales was made Prince Regent and conducted a dissolute reign.

On the Medusa of Leonardo da Vinci in the Florentine Gallery

126 (p. 408) *Title* The picture referred to is attributed to Leonardo da Vinci. This poem was used as a departure point for Mario Praz's classic study *The Romantic Agony*.

Peter Bell the Third (extracts)

127 (p. 410) *Castles . . . Canning . . . Cobbett . . . Castlereagh* John Castles, a government spy and *agent provocateur* who incited conspiracies and then informed the authorities; George Canning (1770–1827), a Tory who became prime minister; William Cobbett (1763–1835), a popular journalist and leading radical; Robert Stewart, Viscount Castlereagh (1769–1822), infamous for his savage repression of dissent in Ireland, Foreign Secretary and leader of the Tory-dominated House of Commons from 1812 until 1822, when he committed suicide by cutting his throat

128 (p. 412) *Cretan-tongued* Cretans were popularly seen as liars.

129 (p. 412) *Alemannic* German

130 (p. 415) *Diogenes* Diogenes of Sinope (412–323BC), the Cynic philosopher of Athens renowned for his unconventional behaviour and austerity

131 (p. 417) *A man there came* a satirical portrait of the poet Samuel Taylor Coleridge (1772–1834)

132 (p. 419) *Mr —* Joseph Cottle bought Wordsworth and Coleridge's *Lyrical Ballads* for thirty guineas.

The Indian Girl's Song

133 (p. 420) *Title* This poem is often known as 'The Indian Serenade' but, as Reiman and Powers point out, Shelley's own fair-copy title indicates that the poem is a dramatic lyric spoken by the Indian girl.

Ode to Heaven

134 (p. 421) *Title* This poem relates strongly in style to the fourth act of *Prometheus Unbound*. It presents three different views of life in the universe.

Poems from 1820

The Sensitive Plant

135 (p. 423) *Title* A sensitive plant is a kind of mimosa (*mimosa pudica*), renowned for its capacity to close up its leaves and droop when touched.

136 (p. 423) *companionless* Sensitive plants are hermaphrodite and therefore do not need a companion.

137 (p. 423) *Naiad-like* Naiads were nymphs who inhabited natural locations.

138 (p. 424) *Maenad* Maenads were female worshippers of Dionysus renowned for their sexual passion and destructive fanaticism.

139 (p. 426) *Elysian* Elysium was the Greek version of paradise.

140 (p. 428) *ephemeris* a thin, transparent-bodied insect called the mayfly

141 (p. 428) *Baiae* a small bay near Naples and Mount Vesuvius

142 (p. 430) *darnels . . . henbane . . . hemlock* all poisonous plants

143 (p. 430) *agarics* poisonous mushrooms

144 (p. 432) *Exceeds our organs* This conclusion has a wry quality, in keeping with the way the rest of the story is told and reinforced by the seemingly convoluted nature of the ending: it suggests that, if there was a fault, it lies not with ideals themselves but with the human perception of them through limited capabilities, and with deficient attempts at implementing them.

Letter to Maria Gisborne

145 (p. 433) *Archimedean art* from Archimedes (*c*.287–212BC), Greek mathematician and scientific experimenter

146 (p. 433) *Vulcan* the mythological blacksmith who made a torture wheel for Ixion in Hell and the manacles to chain the Titan Prometheus

147 (p. 433) *St Dominic* (*c*.1170–1221), founder of the Dominican order, which became the leading force in the Spanish Inquisition. The relevance of the references to the Inquisition becomes clearer later – see Note 156.

148 (p. 433) *philanthropic council* an ironic reference to the ecumenical councils of the Catholic Church in the sixteenth century which drove the Counter-Reformation

149 (p. 434) *storm-encompassed isles* the Hebrides in Scotland where, as in Cornwall, wreckage from the ships of the Spanish Armada of 1588 was washed up, including implements of torture from the Inquisition

150 (p. 434) *Proteus* mythological god of the sea who could transform himself at will

151 (p. 434) *Tubal Cain* the first metal-worker in the Bible

152 (p. 435) *Laplace* (1749–1827), a French mathematician and astronomer. Saunderson and Sims were also mathematicians.

153 (p. 435) *Tott's Memoirs* of the Turks and Tartars translated 1786

154 (p. 435) *Archimage* Archimago is an evil magician in Spenser's *The Faerie Queene*.

155 (p. 435) *Libeccio* the south-west wind

156 (p. 437) *a land which now is free*   The revolution in Spain of January 1820 abolished the Inquisition and established a constitutional monarchy. This passage celebrates the spirit of liberation by quoting the New Testament (Mark 5:9) and the Spanish dramatist Calderon (1600–81). Shelley learned Spanish in order to read his works.

157 (p. 438) *Godwin*   William Godwin (1756–1826) was a renowned radical writer and Shelley's father-in-law. Like Coleridge, he had suffered an eclipse of his reputation.

158 (p. 438) *Hunt*   Leigh Hunt (1784–1859), the much admired radical journalist, poet and editor

159 (p. 438) *Shout*   Robert Shout, a maker of plaster copies of famous statues

160 (p. 438) *Hogg*   Thomas Jefferson Hogg (1792–1862), Shelley's friend at Oxford with whom he would discuss abstruse subjects such as metempsychosis

161 (p. 439) *Peacock*   Thomas Love Peacock (1785–1866), satirical novelist who had a job with the East India Company, hence the references to India, and had married a woman from the Welsh mountains

162 (p. 439) *Horace Smith*   (1779–1849), parodist and writer

163 (p. 440) *Pollonia*   Apollonia Ricci had a romantic infatuation for Henry

164 (p. 441) *Helicon or Himeros*   Helicon was the mountain home of the poetic muses; Himeros Shelley described as a 'synonym of Love' in a note.

165 (p. 441) *'Tomorrow to fresh woods and pastures new'*   quotation from the end of Milton's *Lycidas*

The Witch of Atlas

166 (p. 442) *Peter Bell*   poem by Wordsworth which Shelley parodies in 'Peter Bell the Third'

167 (p. 443) *Ruth or Lucy*   female characters in Wordsworth poems

168 (p. 443) *Scaramouch*   a puppet from Italy

169 (p. 443) *Atlas' mountain*   a range of mountains in North Africa, abode of a mythical giant, brother of Prometheus, fated to hold up the heavens as a punishment for revolt against the gods

170 (p. 444) *Atlantides*   nymphs who were the offspring of Atlas and Hesperus

171 (p. 444) *folding-star*   Venus rising in the evening was a signal for sheep to be put in their folds.

172 (p. 445) *Silenus*   tutor and helper to Dionysus / Bacchus, god of wine

173 (p. 445) *Dryope and Faunus*   Dryope was a nymph and mother of Pan; Faunus, a legendary king, was her consort in Italian myth.

174 (p. 445) *Pan*   the rural goat-god of nature famous for his pipes

175 (p. 445) *a want*   a mole

176 (p. 446) *Priapus*   god of sexuality, depicted with an erect phallus

177 (p. 446) *Garamant*   an African region noted for its people not needing clothing

178 (p. 446) *Polyphemes*   after the cyclops giant in *The Odyssey*, Book 9

179 (p. 446) *Centaurs and Satyrs*   Centaurs were mythological creatures, half horse and half man, while satyrs were half goat, half man. Both were associated with sexual passion.

180 (p. 448) *Saturnian Archimage*   The age of Saturn was associated with the Golden Age; Archimago was an evil magician in Spenser's *The Faerie Queene*.

181 (p. 449) *Ocean-nymphs . . . Naiads*   The various nymphs named inhabit different regions, oceans, forests, mountains, streams.

182 (p. 451) *Vulcan*   the mythological blacksmith who made manacles to chain the Titan Prometheus and was the husband of Venus, goddess of love

183 (p. 451) *Apollo*   god of the sun

184 (p. 452) *Evan*   Bacchus, the name coming from his cry 'Evve'

185 (p. 452) *Vesta*   goddess of the hearth of sacred fire tended by vestal virgins

186 (p. 452) *Pygmalion*   a king of Cyprus in Greek myth who made a statue of a beautiful woman which Aphrodite (Venus) brought to life for him

187 (p. 452) *A sexless thing*   a hermaphrodite which in myth was a perfect unity of the two sexes

188 (p. 454) *Elysian*   Elysium was the Greek version of paradise.

189 (p. 455) *Austral*   the southern hemisphere

190 (p. 455) *Thamondocana*   Timbuktoo in Mali, renowned for Muslim culture

191 (p. 455) *Canopus*   second brightest star in the sky

192 (p. 456) *Hydaspes*   river in Pakistan

193 (p. 457) *Arion*   a poet and musician from the seventh century BC; rescued from death by dolphins who were drawn by his music

194 (p. 457) *Nilus*   the River Nile

195 (p. 457) *Axumè*   region of Ethiopia

196 (p. 458) *Moeris and Mareotid*   lakes of the Nile in the region of Cairo

197 (p. 458) *Osirian*   Osiris was an Egyptian god who was killed and then resurrected, becoming an emblem of the yearly revival of the seasons.

198 (p. 460) *Aurora*   goddess of dawn. Her love for Tithonus led her to ask the gods to make him immortal, but she forgot to ask for him to have eternal youth.

199 (p. 460) *Proserpina*   Proserpine was the wife of the god of the Underworld and restored the beautiful youth Adonis to life on condition that he would spend half of the year with her and half with his consort Venus.

200 (p. 460) *Heliad*   child of the sun, referring to the Witch

201 (p. 460) *Dian*   Diana, goddess of hunting and the moon, who fell in love with Endymion and came down from the heavens each night to make love to him as he slept

202 (p. 461) *Apis*   Egyptian god

203 (p. 462) *Cyclopses . . . Vulcan*   Vulcan, the mythical blacksmith, forged weapons for the gods, and was aided in his work by the Cyclopses.

204 (p. 462) *Amasis*   a king of Egypt

Hymn of Apollo

205 (p. 463) *Title*   Apollo was initially the Greek god of poetry and musical inspiration, as well as an archer with destructive arrows of disease and an ideal of male beauty. He spoke through the oracle at Delphi, prophesying future events, and was later taken up as the god of the sun. Like the 'Hymn of Pan' below, this piece was composed for Mary Shelley's play *Midas*, and is a translation of a Homeric poem.

Hymn of Pan

206 (p. 464) *Title*   Pan was the rural goat-god of nature, famous for his pipes which were capable of causing pan-ic.

207 (p. 465) *Tmolus*   a character in Mary's Shelley's play *Midas*. He was silent through age.

208 (p. 465) *Peneus . . . Tempe . . . Pelion*   Peneus was a river in Thessaly which ran through the idyllic region of Tempe near Mount Olympus (Pelion), home of the gods.

209 (p. 465) *Sileni . . . Sylvans . . . Fauns*   different categories of minor nature gods, the male counterparts to nymphs

210 (p. 465) *daedal*   intricately, cleverly fashioned; from Daedalus, the mythic craftsman who fashioned wings for his son Icarus

211 (p. 465) *giant wars*   the conflict between the Titans and the Olympians, led by Zeus

212 (p. 465) *Maenalus . . . reed*   Maenalus is a mountain associated with Pan in the mythical ideal region of Arcadia. When Pan pursued the nymph Syrinx, she prayed for help and the Earth transformed her into reeds which Pan cut to make his pipes.

213 (p. 465) *both ye*   addressed to Apollo and Tmolus

To a Skylark

214 (p. 469) *star of heaven*   Venus in the evening

215 (p. 469) *silver sphere*   Venus in the morning

216 (p. 471) *Hymenaeal*   Hymen was the Greek god of marriage, hence wedding song.

Ode to Liberty

217 (p. 473) *Title*   written to celebrate the Spanish revolution of 1820

218 (p. 473) *Epigraph*   from Byron's *Childe Harold's Pilgrimage*, Book 4, verse 48, lines 1–2

219 (p. 473) *daedal*   intricately, cleverly fashioned; from Daedalus, the mythic craftsman who fashioned wings for his son Icarus

220 (p. 474) *Parian stone*   made from the marble associated with the Greek island of Paros

221 (p. 475) *For thou*   addressed to Athens as an ideal of human civilisation achieved through liberty

222 (p. 475) *that hill*   the Acropolis, citadel of ancient Athens and full of sacred shrines and temples

223 (p. 476) *Cadmaean Maenad*   Cadmus was founder of Thebes whose daughter Agave led the Maenads, female worshippers of Dionysus, renowned for their sexual passion and destructive fanaticism.

224 (p. 476) *Elysian*   Elysium was the Greek version of paradise; the food is liberty.

225 (p. 476) *Cadmillus . . . Atilius*   Cadmillus was a Roman general who was renowned for his integrity; Atilius Regulus (third century BC) determined to promote the war against Carthage even though it meant he would die.

226 (p. 476) *Capitolian*   The Capitoline Hill is one of the seven hills of Rome, embodying republicanism.

227 (p. 476) *Palatinus*   The Palatine is another hill, embodying imperialism.

228 (p. 476) *Hyrcanian*   a province of Persia near the Caspian Sea

229 (p. 476) *Naiad*   Naiads were nymphs associated with streams and fountains.

230 (p. 476) *Scald . . . Druid*   'skald' is Old Norse for 'poet' and scalds were poets of Iceland and Scandinavia between 800–1100; Druids were Celtic priests who preached reincarnation, and were also often associated with poetry and vision by Romantic writers.

231 (p. 476) *Galiliean serpent*   the Christian religion

232 (p. 477) *Saxon Alfred*   Alfred the Great (849–99), West Saxon king who fostered the emergence of the English nation. An olive garland represents a tribute of honour.

233 (p. 477) *Moon*   The moon was represented as Diana the huntress.

234 (p. 478) *Bacchanal*   a drunken orgy named after Bacchus, god of wine. The frenzied female followers of Bacchus/Dionysus were known as the Maenads and performed ceremonies involving rending flesh. They tore to pieces both Pentheus, King of Thebes, and Orpheus.

235 (p. 478) *France*   describes the excesses of the French revolution

236 (p. 478) *The Anarch*   Napoleon Bonaparte (1769–1821) emerged as the saviour of the French Revolution only to make himself dictator and finally emperor (1804–15). Shelley regarded his career as a betrayal of the revolutionary principles of liberty and equality.

237 (p. 479) *Vesuvius . . . Etna*   Italian volcanoes

238 (p. 479) *Aeolian isles*   islands north of Sicily

239 (p. 479) *Pithecusa . . . Pelorus*   coastal sites in the region

240 (p. 479) *Arminius*   a German tribal leader (18BC–AD19) who liberated Germany from Rome and foreign invasion

241 (p. 481) *Eoan*   Eos was goddess of the dawn

To the Lord Chancellor

242 (p. 482) *Title*   Eldon, the Lord Chancellor, had denied Shelley custody of his children by his first wife on the grounds of his atheism in 1817.

243 (p. 484) *crocodile*   The crocodile was associated with false tears in legend; Eldon was known for weeping in court.

Poems from 1821

Epipsychidion

244 (p. 488) *Title*   The title is Shelley's own derivation from the Greek *epi* (on) and *psychidion* (the little soul).

245 (p. 488) *Epigram*   from Teresea Viviani; Reiman and Powers translate it as: 'The loving soul launches beyond creation, and creates for itself in the infinite a world all its own, far different from this dark and terrifying gulf.'

246 (p. 488) *Advertisement*   Shelley seems both to declare the poem a fiction in denying it 'a matter-of-fact history' and claim its validity in the Italian quotation which Reiman and Powers translate as: 'Great would be his shame who should rhyme anything under the garb of metaphor or rhetorical figure; and being requested, could not strip his words of this dress, so that they might have a true meaning.' The stanza referred to was a version of the last nine lines of the first *canzone* from Dante's *Convito*, and the opening line quoted means, 'You who with intelligence move the third sphere.'

247 (p. 491) *Stranger*   usually taken to be an address to the reader of the poem

248 (p. 495) *Hesper*   the planet Venus as the evening star

249 (p. 496) *Endymion*   Endymion was granted immortality but also made to sleep forever, and as he slept the goddess of the moon, Diana, made love to him each night.

250 (p. 502) *Parian*   made from the marble associated with the Greek island of Paros

251 (p. 504) *Sovereign's*   i.e. Emily's

252 (p. 504) *Marina, Vanna, Primus*   'Marina' is Mary (Shelley's wife), 'Vanna' Jane Williams (from Giovanna) to whom Shelley also wrote love lyrics, and 'Primus' her partner Edward Williams.

Adonais

253 (p. 505) *Title*   The name has been taken as a conflation of the Greek 'Adonis', a beautiful heroic figure, and the Hebrew word 'Adonai' meaning 'Lord'.

254 (p. 505) *Epigraphs*   The first epigraph, attributed to Plato, Shelley himself translated, under the title 'To Stella', as follows:

> Thou wert the morning star among the living,
>   Ere thy fair light had fled; –
> Now, having died, thou art as Hesperus, giving
>   New splendour to the dead.

The epigraph to the 'Preface' comes from one of the central examples of the classical tradition of pastoral elegy, the 'Elegy for Bion', attributed to Moschus, and can be rendered: 'Poison came, Bion, to thy mouth – thou didst know poison. Did it come to such lips as thine and was not sweetened? What mortal was so cruel as to mix poison for thee, or could give it having heard thy voice? He will not be named in my song.'

255 (p. 507) *Urania*   muse of astronomy

256 (p. 508) *He died*   Milton

257 (p. 508) *the third among the sons of light*   The other two sons of light were Homer and Dante.

258 (p. 508) *Capital*   Rome

259 (p. 510) *anadem*   a garland

260 (p. 511) *Phoebus . . . Hyacinth . . . Narcissus*   Hyacinthus was loved by Phoebus, god of the sun, who turned him into a flower when he was killed; Narcissus pined away for love of his own reflection in a pond (from Ovid's *Metamorphoses*).

261 (p. 515) *Pythian of the age*   taken to refer to Byron's (Apollo) counter-attack on hostile reviewers (pythons) in his *English Bards and Scotch Reviewers* (1809)

262 (p. 515) *Pilgrim of Eternity*   Byron

263 (p. 515) *sweetest lyrist*   Thomas Moore (1779–1852), Irish poet (Irene being Ireland)

264 (p. 515) *one frail Form*   Shelley

265 (p. 515) *Actaeon-like*   Actaeon was killed by his own hunting dogs after having seen Diana, the goddess of hunting, naked.

266 (p. 516) *He*   Leigh Hunt who supported Keats in many ways, literary and personal

267 (p. 517) *murderer*   the reviewer whom Shelley's 'Preface' accuses of killing Keats through his harsh criticism

268 (p. 519) *Chatterton*   Thomas Chatterton (1752–70), poet who committed suicide aged seventeen

269 (p. 519) *Sidney*   Sir Philip Sidney (1554–86), poet and courtier

270 (p. 519) *Lucan*   Marcus Annaeus Lucanus (AD39–65), celebrated defender of republicanism who committed suicide

271 (p. 521) *grey walls*   the walls of Rome, built by Aurelian in the third centry AD near the cemetery where Keats was buried. The simile is a good example of how Shelley's imagery demands the reader's alert attention: the 'hoary brand' (describing the 'grey walls') is a burning log which has become covered in ash and is therefore being consumed (by Time) more slowly and with a dulled flame.

272 (p. 521) *pyramid*   referring to the tomb of Caius Cestius built in 1BC and made part of the walls

Written on Hearing the News of the Death of Napoleon

273 (p. 523) Title   Napoleon Bonaparte (1769–1821) emerged as the saviour of the French revolution only to make himself dictator and finally emperor (1804–15). Shelley regarded his career as a betrayal of the revolutionary principles of liberty and equality.

Political Greatness

274 (p. 526) *Title*   The poem describes a brief republic which was established by popular uprising in the town of Benvento, near Naples, only to be suppressed along with the revolution by the Austrian army in 1821.

Poems from 1822

With a Guitar, to Jane

275 (p. 533) Title   Shelley met Edward and Jane Williams in 1820 and they visited Pisa and the Shelleys in 1821 where they became friends. Shelley bought Jane Williams an Italian guitar and this poem accompanied it.

276 (p. 533) *Ariel to Miranda*   Ariel is the sprite who helps Prospero in Shakespeare's *The Tempest*. Miranda is Prospero's daughter, and Ferdinand who is mentioned later is the young prince Miranda falls in love with. Here they represent Shelley, Jane Williams and Edward Williams respectively.

Lines Written in the Bay of Lerici

277 (p. 537) Title   This was probably Shelley's last lyric and was unfinished. It takes Jane Williams as its subject.

The Triumph of Life

278 (p. 539) *The cone of night* the cone-shaped shadow or umbra cast behind the earth as the sun shines on its surface

279 (p. 539) *Apennine* The Apennines are a mountain range in Italy.

280 (p. 541) *Janus-visaged* Janus was the Roman god who guarded the gate or door, and so became the god of beginnings. He was depicted with two faces and gave his name to January.

281 (p. 542) *Imperial Rome* These lines describe the late-Roman practice of publicly displaying dominance over a conquered people by parading them through the streets in a processional 'triumph'.

282 (p. 542) *Athens or Jerusalem* The 'sacred few' exempt from Life's triumph include Socrates and Jesus.

283 (p. 544) *the grim Feature* Line 204 reveals this ghost to be that of French philosopher Jean Jacques Rousseau (1712–78), whose works were an inspiration to the French Revolution and the Romantic movement.

284 (p. 545) *The Child of a fierce hour* Line 224 reveals this to be Napoleon.

285 (p. 546) *Voltaire . . . Frederick . . . Catherine . . . Leopold* Voltaire (1694–1778) was a leading figure in the French Enlightenment; Frederick the great of Prussia (1712–86), Catherine the Great of Russia (1729–96) and Leopold II of Tuscany (1747–92) were influenced by the Enlightenment and became known as 'enlightened despots'.

286 (p. 546) *Plato* Plato (c.427–347BC), the Athenian philosopher who became the pupil of Socrates ('his master') and fell in love with a young boy, whereas Socrates had avoided love affairs with boys

287 (p. 547) *Bacon's eagle spirit* Sir Francis Bacon (1561–1626), English philosopher whose stress on rational inductive methods inspired the scientific revolution

288 (p. 547) *Proteus* a sea god capable of changing his shape

289 (p. 547) *Caesar . . . Constantine* Julius Caesar (c.100–44BC) established the status of the Roman emperor; Constantine the Great (c.AD274–337) became the first Roman emperor to promote Christianity.

290 (p. 548) *Gregory and John* names of Roman Popes

291 (p. 550) *Iris* the rainbow

292 (p. 550) *Nepanthe* a liquid drug

293 (p. 552) *Lucifer* a name for the morning star, Venus

294 (p. 552) *Brescian shepherd* Brescia is a city in Italy.

295 (p. 553) *Lethean*   Lethe was the river of forgetfulness in the Underworld.

296 (p. 554) *him who from the lowest depths of hell*   Dante (1265–1321), the greatest Italian poet, part of whose *Divine Comedy* charts his own journey led by Roman poet Virgil through Hell

Prose

A Declaration of Rights

297 (p. 560) *Awake! – arise!*   from Milton, *Paradise Lost*, 1, 330

A Letter to Lord Ellenborough

298 (p. 563) *de heretico comburendo*   'on the burning of heretics'

299 (p. 563) *Descartes . . . Voltaire . . . Galileo . . . Vanini*   René Descartes (1596–1650), French philosopher; Voltaire (1694–1778), leading figure in the French Enlightenment; Galileo (1564–1642), Italian astronomer condemned by the church for his work; Lucilio Vanini (1585–1619), Italian sceptic who was burned at the stake as an atheist

300 (p. 569) *If God has spoken . . . convinced?*   translated from *Système de la Nature* by Paul Holbach (1723–89), French Enlightenment writer

A Vindication of Natural Diet

301 (p. 571) *Immediately a place . . . rheums*   from Milton, *Paradise Lost*, 11, 477–88

302 (pp. 571–2) *Hesiod . . . Horace*   Hesiod was a Greek poet of the eighth century BC, known for his *Theogony*, a work on the origins of the universe and the gods; Horace was a Latin poet (65–8BC) at the time of Emperor Augustus. The passage from Horace may be rendered as: 'Daring to endure everything, the race of man is driven from crime to crime. Thus Prometheus, with evil-fated cunning, did lure fire from heaven for men. Once fire was stolen from its proper home on high, a slow corrosion and dismal collection of illnesses entered into the world, and death, though never far away, came nearer at hand.' (*Odes*, Book 1, Ode 3)

303 (p. 573) *But just disease . . . Man*   from Alexander Pope's *Essay on Man*, 150–3

304 (p. 576) *auto-da-fé*   used during the Spanish Inquisition to describe an execution by burning of a heretic

305 (p. 576) *Muley Ismael*   (1672–1727) was a tyrannical and bloodthirsty Sultan of Morocco

An Address to the People on the Death of the Princess Charlotte

306 (p. 584) *Title and Epigraph* Shelley adopted the prophetic-sounding pseudonym of 'The Hermit of Marlow' earlier in 1817 for the political pamphlet *A Proposal for Putting Reform to the Vote throughout the Kingdom*. The epigraph comes from Tom Paine's attack in *The Rights of Man* on Edmund Burke's maudlin homage to Marie Antoinette's execution in 1793.

307 (p. 585) *that bourne . . . returns* a misquotation from Shakespeare's *Hamlet*, 3, 1, 79–80

308 (p. 585) *Horne Took and Hardy* John Horne Tooke (1736–1812), English philologist and radical reformer; Thomas Hardy (1752–1832), a radical English reformer

309 (p. 588) *sans peur . . . tache* 'without fear and without stain'

A Philosophical View of Reform

Square brackets denote gaps in the manuscript and have where possible been filled in.

310 (p. 594) *one of those chiefs of a conspiracy . . . crime* Shelley refers here to Charles I, who was executed in 1649 by the revolutionary forces of the English Parliamentary Movement led by Oliver Cromwell.

311 (p. 595) *the Revolution* the 'Glorious Revolution' of 1688 by which the English Parliament established William II and Mary II as joint monarchs

312 (p. 602) *Nero, Christiern, Muley Ismael, or Ezzelin* Nero (AD 37–68) was a corrupt and tyrannical emperor of Rome who was blamed for the fire of Rome; Christiern was Christian II of Sweden who ordered the Massacre of Stockholm in 1520; Muley Ismael (1673–1727), Sultan of Morocco, killed his own son; Ezzelin was tyrannical Lord of Padua in the thirteenth century.

313 (p. 603) *our republican poet* Milton

314 (p. 604) *Wahabees* a liberal reforming sect in Arabia

315 (p. 604) *Ottoman Bey* a model of liberal intellectual attitudes who encouraged his nephew to study European knowledge which contradicted Islam

316 (p. 604) *free negroes* Shelley refers to the Haitian revolution against French colonial tyranny led by Toussaint L'Ouverture (1743–1803) – see C. L. R. James's famous account in *The Black Jacobins*.

317 (p. 605) *unacknowledged legislators* Shelley's more famous essay *A Defence of Poetry* reuses this passage.

318 (p. 616) *A writer of the present day*   Thomas Malthus (1766–1834), economist whose *Essay on the Principles of Population* (1798) was a response to William Godwin's *Political Justice* (1793), and angered Godwin, Shelley and other radicals

A Defence of Poetry

319 (p. 635) τὸ ποιειν ... τὸ λογιζειν   The Greek phrases are from the verbs *poiein*, to make, and *logizein*, to reason.

320 (p. 637) *Lord Bacon*   Sir Francis Bacon (1561–1626), English philosopher whose stress on rational inductive methods inspired the scientific revolution.   He died of a cold while stuffing a chicken with snow in an early experiment in refrigeration.

321 (p. 637) *Janus*   Janus was the Roman god who guarded the gate or door, and so became the god of beginnings. He was depicted with two faces and gave his name to January.

322 (p. 637) *legislators or prophets*   The Roman term for poet was *vates*, meaning 'a diviner, fore-seer or prophet', as Sir Philip Sidney states in *Apologie for Poetry* (1505)

323 (p. 638) *Aeschylus*   Athenian dramatist (*c.*525–*c.*456BC) whose tragedies used the chorus to articulate a general commentary on the nature of existence

324 (p. 638) *Dante's Paradise*   Dante (1265–1321), the greatest Italian poet, whose *Divine Comedy* charts his own journey led by Roman poet Virgil through Hell and up to Paradise

325 (p. 639) *Plato*   (*c.*427–347BC), the Athenian philosopher whose *The Symposium* Shelley translated in 1818 in an admirable version

326 (p. 639) *Cicero*   (106–43BC), a famous Roman orator

327 (p. 640) *Herodotus, Plutarch, Livy*   Herodotus (*c.*485–425BC), historian of the Greek wars; Plutarch (*c.* AD46–*c.*120), Greek historian, biographer and philosopher; Livy (*c.*59BC–AD17), Roman historian who produced a hundred and forty-two books

328 (p. 641) *Homer*   (*circa* ninth century BC), Greek poet to whom are attributed the earliest works of literature in Western culture, the epic poems the *Iliad* and the *Odyssey*. Achilles, Hector and Ulysses are characters from these poems

329 (p. 642) *Euripedes, Lucan, Tasso, Spenser*   Euripedes (*c.*480–406BC), Greek tragic dramatist; Lucan (39–65), Latin republican poet who committed suicide; Tasso (1544–95), Italian poet and subject of a projected drama by Shelley; Spenser (1552–99), Elizabethan poet

whose long poem *The Faerie Queene* formed a model for Shelley's *Laon and Cythna*

330 (p. 644) *Oedipus Tyrannus or the Agamemnon* plays by Greek tragedians Sophocles and Aeschylus

331 (p. 644) *Calderon* (1600–81), Spanish dramatist who wrote numerous religious plays (*autos sacramentales*), many of them for outdoor festivals. Shelley learned Spanish in order to read his works.

332 (p. 645) *Addison* Joseph Addison (1672–1719), English essayist and poet

333 (p. 646) *Machiavelli* (1469–1527), Italian statesman and political theorist best known for his *The Prince* (1532)

334 (p. 646) *The bucolic writers* Greek pastoral poets such as Theocritus (*c.*310–250BC)

335 (p. 647) *Astraea* goddess of justice. When driven from the earth by human evil, she became the constellation Virgo, with the scales in one hand and a sword in the other.

336 (p. 647) *Ennius, Varro, Pacuvius, Accius* Ennius (*c.*239–169BC), Latin poet and dramatist of whose epic *Annales* only six hundred lines survive; Varro (116–27BC), Roman scholar and author who wrote over six hundred books of which only one survives; Pacuvius (200–130BC), tragic dramatist who wrote thirteen plays of which only four hundred lines survive; Accius (170–85BC), Latin tragic poet of whose forty plays only seven hundred lines survive

337 (p. 647) *Lucretius* first-century-BC Latin poet and philosopher

338 (p. 647) *Virgil* (70–19BC), greatest of the Latin poets; wrote the epic *Aeniad* as well as the pastoral *Eclogues* and *Georgics*

339 (pp. 647–8) *Livy . . . Horace, Catullus, Ovid* Livy (59BC–AD17), Roman historian who produced a hundred and forty-two books; Horace (65–8BC), a Latin poet and satirist at the time of Emperor Augustus (63BC–AD14); Catullus (*c.*84–*c.*54BC), Latin lyric poet; Ovid (43BC–AD17), Latin poet famous for his *Metamorphoses* which collected the myths of transformation

340 (p. 648) *quia carent vate sacro* 'because they lack a sacred poet' (from Horace, *Odes*, 9, 28)

341 (p. 649) *The crow makes wing . . . do rouse.* Shakespeare, *Macbeth*, 3, 2, 50–3, quoted inaccurately

342 (p. 649) *Plato . . .Timaeus . . . Pythagoras* Plato (*c.*427–347BC), the Athenian philosopher who became the pupil of Socrates. Pythagoras

was a sixth-century-BC Greek philosopher and mathematician whose philosophy included the transmigration of souls, and Timaeus was probably his pupil

343 (p. 650) *Galeotto . . . scrisse* 'Galeotto [Galahad] was the book, and he who wrote it' (Dante, *Inferno*, 5, 137). Galahad was used to describe a go-between who arranged romantic encounters such as the one between Lancelot and Guinevere in Arthurian legend.

344 (p. 650) *Provençal Trouveurs* medieval court poet-musicians, also known as troubadours

345 (p. 650) *Petrarch* (1304–74), Italian poet whose poems to Laura provided a model for courtly love poetry

346 (p. 650) *Dante . . . Vita Nuova* Dante (1265–1321), the greatest Italian poet; his *La Vita Nuova* ('The New Life') was a series of courtly love poems addressed to his divine beloved Beatrice, who was also his inspiration for the *Divine Comedy*, which charts his journey led by Roman poet Virgil through Hell and by Beatrice up to Paradise

347 (p. 651) *Ariosto . . . Rousseau* Ludovico Ariosto (1474–1533), Italian poet famous for his *Orlando Furioso*; Jean Jacques Rousseau (1712–78), whose works were an inspiration to the French Revolution and the Romantic movement

348 (p. 651) *Riphaeus* in Virgil's *Aeneid* (2, 424–7) Aeneas calls him 'one man who was most just' and one whose death was meaningless; also appears in Dante's *Paradiso*

349 (p. 651) *Milton's Devil* Shelley asserts like Blake that 'Milton was of the Devil's party without knowing it' (Blake, *Marriage of Heaven and Hell*).

350 (p. 652) *Apollonius . . . Claudian* Apollonius of Rhodes (b.295BC), author of a romance epic; Quintus Smyrnaeus, author in *c.*375 AD of a fourteen-book sequel to Homer; Nonnus (*c.*AD425–50), author of a forty-eight-book epic on Dionysus and a favourite poet of Peacock; Statius (*c.*45–96 AD), Roman court poet; Claudian (AD370–404), author of an epic on Proserpine's rape

351 (p. 652) *Orlando Furioso . . . Fairy Queen* Romance epics

352 (p. 653) *Boccaccio* (1313–75), Italian writer of *The Decameron*

353 (p. 654) *Scylla and Charybdis* the opposing rocks and whirlpool which Odysseus had to negotiate (*Odyssey*, 9)

354 (p. 654) *Locke . . . Voltaire* John Locke (1632–1704), English empirical rationalist philosopher whose *On Government* (1698) inspired the

American and French revolutionaries; David Hume (1711–76), Scottish philosopher and historian known for his atheism; Edward Gibbon (1737–94), British historian famous for his history of the Roman empire; Voltaire (1694–1778), a leading figure in the French Enlightenment

355 (p. 654) *Inquisition in Spain*   suppressed by the Spanish revolution of 1820; reinstated 1823; abolished 1834

356 (p. 655) *I dare not . . . the adage*   Shakespeare, *Macbeth*, 1, 7, 44–5

357 (p. 656) *unpremeditated song*   Milton, *Paradise Lost*, 9, 21–4

358 (p. 658) *The mind is . . . of heaven*   Milton, *Paradise Lost*, 1, 254–5

359 (p. 658) *Non merita . . . il Poeta*   'No one deserves the name of Creator but God and the poet', attributed to Tasso

360 (p. 658) *there sitting . . . not soar*   Milton, *Paradise Lost*, 4, 829

361 (p. 659) *Theseids . . . Maevius*   Codrus, the author of the *Theseid*, and the others named were attacked by Roman authors Juvenal, Virgil and Horace for their poor poetry.

Index of First Lines to the Poems

Index to the Titles of the Poems and Prose